ST. PETER'S IN THE VATICAN

Wherein lies the significance of St. Peter's in the Vatican? – in its role as first church of Roman Catholicism? as preeminent symbol of an ancient city? as major monument of Western civilization? This book posits an answer to the question (while recognizing that it is only one among many): the significance of the edifice lies in its extraordinary and extraordinarily tormented history. Founded in the fourth century to honor the tomb of Saint Peter, the church gained enormous prestige in the Middle Ages as a repository of holy relics and objects, and as the site of epoch-making events. But with the return of the papacy from Avignon and the shift in papal residence from the Lateran to the Vatican, the building needed to be renovated. Beginning in the fifteenth century and over the course of the next three hundred years, Old St. Peter's was gradually torn down, and in its midst arose the new structure now in place. The transmutation was far from easy. It involved many changes in design and concept, and interwove the careers of some of the most brilliant – and contentious – architects and artists of the day, including Bramante, Michelangelo, and Bernini. This volume, focusing on selected and key moments in the history of the church from the late antique period to the twentieth century, offers an expertly researched and thoughtful overview of St. Peter's, full of new insights and appreciation.

William Tronzo teaches in the Department of Visual Arts at the University of California, San Diego. A scholar of medieval Italy, he is the author of *The Cultures of His Kingdom: Roger II and the Cappella Palatina in Palermo*.

ST. PETER'S IN THE VATICAN

Edited by

WILLIAM TRONZO

CAMBRIDGE
UNIVERSITY PRESS

CAMBRIDGE UNIVERSITY PRESS
Cambridge, New York, Melbourne, Madrid, Cape Town, Singapore, São Paulo, Delhi

Cambridge University Press
32 Avenue of the Americas, New York, NY 10013-2473, USA

www.cambridge.org
Information on this title: www.cambridge.org/9780521732109

First published 2005
First paperback edition 2008

Printed in the United States of America

A catalog record for this publication is available from the British Library.

Library of Congress Cataloging in Publication Data

St. Peter's in the Vatican / [edited by] William Tronzo.
p. cm.
Includes bibliographical references and index.
ISBN 0-521-64096-2 (HB)
1. Basilica di San Pietro in Vaticano – History. 2. Vatican City – Buildings,
structures, etc. I. Title: St. Peter's in the Vatican. II. Tronzo, William.
NA5624.S7   2003
726.5'09456'34–dc21   2002074068

ISBN 978-0-521-64096-1 hardback
ISBN 978-0-521-73210-9 paperback

CONTENTS

ILLUSTRATIONS

CONTRIBUTORS

ALESSANDRA ANSELMI is Professor of Iconography and Iconology at Università degli Studi della Calabria. She received her degree in art history from the Università degli Studi di Roma, "La Sapienza," and her doctorate from the Universität Autònoma de Barcelona. She has been a Fellow at the Warburg Institute in London and the Casa de Velásquez in Madrid. Her research concerns principally seventeenth-century Rome and, specifically, relations between the pontifical court and Spain. Her publications include "The High Altar of S. Carlo ai Catinari, Rome," in *The Burlington Magazine*, 1996; "Arte, politica e diplomazia: Tiziano, Correggio, Raffaello. L'investitura di Piombino e notizie su agenti spagnoli a Roma," in *The Diplomacy of Art* (Milan, 2000); "I progetti di Bernini e Rainaldi per l'abside di Santa Maria Maggiore," in *Bollettino d'Arte*, 2001; and *Il Palazzo dell'Ambasciata di Spagna* (Rome, 2001). She is currently preparing a critical edition of the travel diary of Cassiano dal Pozzo in Spain.

GLEN W. BOWERSOCK received his A.B. from Harvard in 1957 and his B.A., M.A., and D.Phil. from Oxford in 1962. He holds honorary degrees from the University of Strasbourg and the École Pratique des Hautes Études. He was Professor of Classics and History at Harvard University from 1962 to 1980 and then Professor of Ancient History at the Institute for Advanced Study, Princeton, NJ. He is now Professor Emeritus of Ancient History at the Institute. He is the author of more than a dozen books on such subjects as the Roman East, the Second Sophistic, Julian the Apostate, Roman Arabia, late Hellenism, early martyrdom, and ancient fiction. He is a Fellow of the American Academy of Arts and Sciences and the American Philosophical Society, and Membre de l'Institut de France.

RICHARD A. ETLIN is Distinguished University Professor at the School of Architecture, University of Maryland. His most recent books include *In Defense of Humanism: Value in the Arts and Letters* and the edited volume *Art,*

Culture, and Media under the Third Reich. Richard Etlin is a Fellow of the American Academy in Rome and a Senior Fellow in Landscape Architecture, Dumbarton Oaks, Harvard University. He also serves as editor for the Cambridge University Press book series "Modern Architecture and Cultural Identity."

ANTONIO IACOBINI is Professor of Byzantine Art History and of the History of Manuscript Illumination at the University of Rome, "La Sapienza," as well as editor of the journal *Arte medievale* and of the *Enciclopedia dell'arte medievale*. His publications include *L'albero della vita nell'immaginario medievale* (1994), *Il Vangelo di Dionisio* (1998), and *Visioni dipinte. Immagini della contemplazione negli affreschi di Bawit* (2000). He has also collaborated on the exhibitions "Fragmenta picta" (Rome, 1990) and "Il primo giubileo: Bonifacio VIII e il suo tempo" (Rome, 2000).

DALE KINNEY is Professor of History of Art and Dean of the Graduate School of Arts and Sciences at Bryn Mawr College, where she has taught since 1972. Her interest in spolia originated with her dissertation on S. Maria in Trastevere and has resulted in articles in the *Art Bulletin* (1986), the *Memoirs of the American Academy in Rome* (1997), and other venues, as well as a National Endowment for the Humanities Summer Seminar in 1993. Her current research is focused on twelfth-century Rome and the milieu of the *Mirabilia urbis Romae*. She is a Fellow of the American Academy in Rome and past editor of *Gesta* (1997–2000).

IRVING LAVIN is Professor Emeritus of the History of Art at the Institute for Advanced Study, Princeton, NJ. For many years previously he taught at the Institute of Fine Arts, New York University. Best known for his work on Gian Lorenzo Bernini (1598–1680), his research and publications cover a wide range of subjects from Late Antiquity to Jackson Pollock. Among his distinguished lectureships and guest professorships: Charles T.

Mathews Lectures, Columbia University, 1957; Franklin Jasper Walls Lectures, Pierpont Morgan Library, New York, 1975; Collège de France, 1984, 1990; Slade Lectures, Oxford University, 1985; Jerome Lectures, University of Michigan and American Academy in Rome, 1985–6; Una's Lectures in the Humanities, University of California, Berkeley, 1987. Lavin is a Fellow of the American Academy of Arts and Sciences; member and past-President of the U.S. National Committee for the History of Art; past-President of the International Committee for the History of Art; Foreign Member of the Accademia Nazionale dei Lincei, Rome; and Foreign Member of the Accademia Clementina, Bologna. Among his books are: *Bernini and the Unity of the Visual Arts* (New York and London, 1980); *Past-Present. Essays on Historicism in Art from Donatello to Picasso* (Berkeley, 1993); *Erwin Panofsky. Three Essays on Style* (Cambridge, MA, and London, 1995); (with Marilyn Aronberg Lavin) *The Liturgy of Love. Imagery from the Song of Songs in the Art of Cimabue, Michelangelo, and Rembrandt* (Lawrence, KS, 2001).

HENRY A. MILLON is Dean Emeritus of the Center for Advanced Study in the Visual Arts, National Gallery of Art. Educated at Tulane University and Harvard University in architecture and history of art, he has served as Visiting Professor at Massachusetts Institute of Technology since 1980 and was Professor of History of Architecture and Architectural Design at MIT from 1960 to 1980. He was Resident Art Historian at the American Academy in Rome in 1966, where he served as director from 1974 to 1977. He was a Fulbright Fellow and Fellow of the American Academy in Rome from 1957 to 1960 and was a member of the Institute for Advanced Study in 1978. Professor Millon has also received fellowships from the National Endowment for the Humanities and the American Council of Learned Societies. He is a delegate of the International Committee for the History of Art, a member of the U.S. National Committee for the History of Art, and a convener of the Architectural Drawings Advisory Group, and he served on the editorial board of the Architectural History Foundation. He is a member of the American Philosophical Society; American Academy of Arts and Sciences; Deputazione Subalpina di Storia Patria; Accademia di San Luca, Rome; and the Accademia delle Scienze di Torino. His selected publications include *The Triumph of the Baroque: Architecture in Europe 1600–1750* (editor), 1999; *The Renaissance from Brunelleschi to Michelangelo: The Representation of Architecture* (with Vittorio Lampugnani), 1994; *Michelangelo Architect* (with Craig H. Smyth), 1988; *Filippo Juvarra: Drawings from the Roman Period. 1704–1714*, 1984; *Key Monuments of the History of Architecture*, 1964; and *Baroque and Rococo Architecture*, 1961.

CHRISTOF THOENES lives in Rome where he is a Wissenschaftlicher Mitarbeiter der Bibliotheca Hertziana (Max-Planck-Institut). He has studied art history, German language and literature, and philosophy in Berlin and Pavia. His field is Italian art history with a special focus on Renaissance architecture, on which he has written numerous books and articles. He has taught in Berlin, Hamburg, and Venice, and he is a member of the Consiglio Scientifico of the C.I.S.A. Andrea Palladio in Vicenza, the Accademia Nazionale di San Luca in Rome, and the Accademia Raffaello in Urbino.

WILLIAM TRONZO teaches in the Department of Visual Arts at the University of California, San Diego. His main field of interest is medieval Italy, on which he has written extensively beginning with his dissertation on the Via Latina Catacomb in Rome (College Art Association Monograph, 1986). Recent publications include studies of narrative art (Spoleto, 2000) and gardens (Parma, 2000), and a monograph on the palatine chapel of the Norman kings of Sicily, *The Cultures of His Kingdom: Roger II and the Cappella Palatina in Palermo* (Princeton, 1997). In addition to numerous fellowships and awards he has held research appointments at Dumbarton Oaks Center for Byzantine Studies, the Bibliotheca Hertziana (Max-Planck-Institut), and the École des Hautes Études en Sciences Sociales. He is a Fellow of the American Academy in Rome.

I

INTRODUCTION

WILLIAM TRONZO

The point of this book could not be made in terms any more concrete than its illustrations: their greatest power lies, perhaps, in their capacity as a sequence to reveal at a glance the life of a building from beginning to end. As a sequence they make this life a reality on an almost cinematographic scale. It seems right. The story of St. Peter's in the Vatican is like a grand drama on the big screen: large and yet intricate and convoluted, full of brilliance and darkness, idealism and compromise. And almost immediately, too, our sequence of images reveals a salient dimension of the plot. Having been built, destroyed, and built again from the ground up, St. Peter's in the Vatican has had, not one but two lives, both richly detailed and full of incident. The building thus embraces one of the most resonant archetypes of our historical consciousness, the duality of ancient and modern, as it provides a case for exploring the multifariousness of relationships that could be enacted between them. It would be unfortunate, especially in these few introductory words, to deny this dimension to the building by making it adhere to the framework of a linear chronicle. I shall begin, therefore, not at the absolute chronological beginning, but in medias res, and with a moment of impending doom: Old St. Peter's on the verge of its destruction. Such a position will allow us to look both backward and forward, which is one of the eternal themes of this compelling narrative.

It was customary in the fifteenth century to come to Old St. Peter's from the *Urbs leonina*, now called the Borgo, a walled town whose tangle of streets was rich with the sights and sounds of activities in service of churchman and pilgrim. Only a few of the streets were straight enough and wide enough to permit a view of the church from a distance – the pitched roof of the nave rising above the facade of the old atrium (part of which was now covered by a luminous Benediction Loggia) and the flight of steps that led up to it. These steps were as much a physical form as a sign of the journey of the spirit: to enter the church one had to ascend.

Passing through the doors of the facade one would have reached the atrium. Perhaps it was the fountain of the bronze pinecone, the *Pigna*, that would have captured one's attention first. Its construction was deliberately magical, an amalgam of past (fragments from Antiquity) and future (imagery of paradise). Or perhaps it was the great medieval image of Christ Enthroned with the evangelists and their symbols and the twenty-four elders (drawn from the Book of Revelations) poised on the eastern facade of the nave. The image, following the line of the building, curved outward at the top as if, then and there, it were being unfurled. If one turned and faced east, one would also have seen the other great image in the atrium, the mosaic of the "Navicella" attributed to Giotto (it was probably based on the painter's design), which represented the scene of Peter's attempt to walk on water as narrated in the Gospel of Matthew. This image was apparently created in the early fourteenth century in order to assure visitors to the basilica that, whatever the vicissitudes of the moment, the church was in the good hands of Christ. These images – magniloquent, hyperbolic – were signs too of the rhetoric and power that cast its spell on this place.

Entering the narthex, one's attention might then have been drawn to the middle portal, the Porta Argentea, which had been embellished by Eugene IV (1431–47) with a set of great bronze doors designed by Antonio di Pietro Averlino (Filarete). Into the nave immediately thereafter one's sensory field would have changed. Was the light dimmed and diffused by the thick glass in the windows of the clerestory, or gathered up in the hundreds of lamps that hung beside the altars and shrines that lined the walls of the aisles and the colonnades? Was the air heavy with dampness, or was it the residue of incense from an inheritance of ceremonies now centuries-old? There is a report in the fifteenth century that the upper wall of the nave on the south side listed outward alarmingly, which may well have created the impression of a world gone slightly askew. It was certainly a world that was fading. Many of the large figures enacting stories from the Old and New Testaments lining the walls had long since disappeared from the nave.

The compensation was in the dozens of altars, shrines, tombs, and other churchly furnishings that grew up beneath them. For the knowledge of these features we must credit, above all, the sixteenth-century canon who wrote an exhaustive description of the old basilica, Tiberio Alfarano. Drawings from the early seventeenth century that accompany an account by Giacomo Grimaldi, another canon of St. Peter's, of the part of the old basilica then still standing give some of the details. Many of these places were like the great church in miniature, with elaborate architecture, painting, and sculpture, but unique. Taken together they must have given the impression that St. Peter's was a vast gallery of the most precious artifacts of Christian devotion and memory – with one accent. The high altar, raised up above the floor of the nave and set beneath a majestic image of the enthroned Christ flanked by Peter and Paul, marked the place of the tomb of the founder of the Roman church, Peter. Nonetheless, it would have been difficult to know where to begin.

Most of these holy sites in St. Peter's, with the exception of the high altar (albeit in a different form), were the patrimony of the Middle Ages. The church as originally conceived in the fourth century would have been quite different. For one thing it would have seemed emptier. Fourth-century St. Peter's was above all an orchestrated ensemble of materials, forms, and colors, from the differently hued and patterned columns of the colonnades, to the intricately worked revetments of the walls, to the brilliant gold mosaic in the apse. No figures or figural decoration, however, except for rare passages on unusual forms such as the twisted columns that screened apse from transept and defined the functional-liturgical focus of the edifice. Vast, clean, and resplendent in painting, marble, and mosaic, the St. Peter's of the fourth century was a magnificent basilica in the Roman imperial mode. It betokened the entry of a mystery religion from Palestine into the public life of a great civilization that conceived of itself in terms of reason and magnificence. Only in hindsight could one see the early church as an almost empty vessel.

Medieval Christianity shattered the delicate metaphor of the fourth century by filling St. Peter's with the burgeoning material apparatus of the religion, the holy objects and bodies that were the focus of devotion and cult. It did so, moreover, haphazardly. The process was one of accumulation over centuries, and there is little indication in the final result as recorded by Tiberio Alfarano of a master plan for the church as a functioning environment. This apparatus, of course, enriched the church and added enormously to its prestige. At the same time, it diffused its singular focus on the altar in the apse and the tomb of Peter.

It was precisely this focus which the project of the Renaissance sought, implicitly or explicitly, to regain, and in fact finally did in the seventeenth century after the completion of the dome, with the decoration of Bramante's piers, and the addition of Bernini's baldachino and throne to altar and apse. This was a return, at least in spirit (the spirit of a unifying endeavor), to the edifice of the fourth century. But New St. Peter's did not turn its back on the medieval customs and uses that had inscribed themselves in the church.

In Bramante's famous parchment plan, Uffizi 1A, the walls of St. Peter's are filled with niches that could have served to accommodate the altars and relics, tombs and shrines moved there from the old basilica. Eventually this intention would be worked out in the very different arrangement now in place. But the idea that this mass of material had to be given order persisted. The variety, or perhaps more accurately, the cacophony that was the medieval church was rationalized and re-presented to the viewer as a totally coherent system, as the religion of Christianity itself was rationalized and re-presented to adherents by the Counter-Reform church. The linchpin in all of this was the installation of the four great relics of the church in the crossing around the tomb of Peter, as a wreath of victory, a crown, a frame. The composition was the brilliant exploitation of Bramante's architecture on the part of the seventeenth century, unforeseen and unintended in the original design, but in a sense its fulfillment in an age with an entirely different frame of reference. New St. Peter's had what the old basilica had come increasingly to lack: the order of hierarchy.

It is difficult to imagine treating any part of the long history of St. Peter's without invoking a manner of remembering. Memory is embodied above all in the saint for whom the church is named, and whose mortal remains are believed to be contained deep in the ground beneath it: the memory of an individual. There is the memory of response to this saint in the form of devotion and cult going back to the second century in the inscriptions on the red wall, and continuing up to the present day: the memory of a collectivity. There is the memory of the papacy, whose role as custodian gave and continues to give the site shape: the memory of an institution. There is the memory of the princes who envisioned and exploited the political implications of this place: the memory of the state. There is the memory of the architects, sculptors, and painters who gave St. Peter's form, and finally, and perhaps most important, there is the memory of the building itself and all that is contained within it: the memory of art. All of these memories are intertwined and interpenetrating, insupportable outside of the context in which they all came into being, so that to invoke one inevitably means calling to mind the others.

The subject of St. Peter's is thus a large one, and the following essays will treat it only in a partial way.

Although this book touches on almost every important phase in the history of the basilica, it should not be construed as a descriptive narrative, nor should the illustrations and references accompanying the text, ample as they are in number, be understood as a visual or bibliographical survey. The intention here was never to create a uniform narrative or to provide coverage of all periods in the history of St. Peter's, but to attempt to give insight into specific moments in the life of the basilica, however differently the duration of these moments may be defined. The reader, attentive to the form or history of the church, will inevitably make note of something important missing in the various discussions of the text or in the scholarly apparatus. Everything here, in fact, has taken shape under the direction of the authors who have assumed the task, within their given fields and topics, of the particularity of research and the discipline of generalization, of scholarship and synthesis at the same time.

It would be best to think of this book as a concatenation of individual views that embrace discrete, exemplary moments in the history of the church, each carefully constructed in itself, but forming a set, part of whose efficacy as a narrative device derives from the fact that it moves from one side of the story to the other, from the beginning of the basilica to the twentieth century. It would be impossible to encompass the complexity that is St. Peter's within the covers of a book unless one were selective. But there is something important to be gained, I believe, by having in one's hand and before one's eyes in a convenient and graspable format an image of the whole, even if, in the end, it is only a shadow outline. Only rarely has the European tradition bequeathed to us a monument of this magnitude, whose realization was one to which so many different eras and points of view contributed, and it is compelling in some sense, in the contemplation of the whole, that the discrete and momentary achievements of individuals and groups emerge more clearly. But it is this context, too, that gives the historical imagination scope to contemplate themes that bind the parts together.

The focus of contributions ranges from the specific (Bowersock, Iacobini, Lavin, Anselmi) to the general (Kinney, Thoenes, Millon, Etlin). The volume opens with the essay of Glen W. Bowersock, where the origins of the basilica are probed in the conjunction of two figures whose names have come to be inextricably bound up with the site: the patron saint and the emperor-patron, Peter and Constantine. This chapter is devoted to a detailed examination of the literary and material evidence regarding the connection of the two with the Vatican, and what emerges is an interesting dichotomy. Whereas the tradition associating Peter with the site may be deemed plausible, the assertion of Constantine's role in the cult of Peter is problematic and (to quote

the author) "probably came only when both of them [that is to say, Peter and Constantine] were dead." What appears here is an important new frame of reference – chronological and cultural (and the author interestingly points to Constantinople) – for understanding the foundation and architecture of St. Peter's, as well as the installation of the memory of its patrons.

Dale Kinney's chapter presents us with a survey of the old basilica in Late Antiquity in its most material form – the many bits and pieces of ancient architecture and sculpture, especially the columns and capitals, that constituted its distinctive building blocks. This material is of interest both backward and forward. Through it the building is embedded in Antiquity (and precisely in the ancient Roman tradition that the edifice itself reshapes). But it is also by means of this material that the old basilica embeds itself in the new. These often highly prized ancient fragments reused in the old church are omnipresent in New St. Peter's, though sometimes difficult to identify with precision, as Kinney observes.

The Middle Ages added much to the edifice of Old St. Peter's, to which a book in itself could easily be devoted. Antonio Iacobini's study of the patronage of Innocent III and Gregory IX provides us with a case of medieval intervention that is exemplary in two respects. It treats of important areas of the western and eastern ends of the church (apse and facade) – places where venerable images stood, critical to the meaning of the edifice. It also concerns a situation where a program of decoration and a patron's intentions can be reconstructed or, perhaps more accurately, argued with unusual conviction and clarity for the Middle Ages on the basis, not only of material remains, but also of texts (some of which may be attributed to the popes themselves).

Convulsive change marked the fifteenth and sixteenth centuries in St. Peter's. Christof Thoenes's streaming narrative provides insight into the real structure and purpose of this tumult: a means of giving expression to the desire – at times overwhelmingly intense and all-embracing – of patrons endowed with new powers of personal fulfillment, and the vision – at times fervent and radical – of architects whose status and prestige had changed fundamentally from that of the Middle Ages. In reading Thoenes's essay, I was especially struck by the characterization of the Renaissance planning process as stemming from the forceful dismissal of reality. How inappropriate by contrast, it seemed to me, would it be to make such a statement about the building of the fourth-century church: the tone and nature of its ambition were completely different.

The thread that Henry A. Millon then follows is one of perfecting and refinement. This is the age that witnessed the decisive influence of Michelangelo on plans, elevations, and vaults, as well as the decision to extend the nave that sealed the fate of the eastern portion of the old basilica then still standing. It is also the age in which the entire public presentation of the basilica to the viewer from the outside was determined, including the eastern facade and the profile of the dome that now serves to define for many the city of Rome.

In his complementary study, Irving Lavin explores the extraordinarily complicated and thoughtful role the great seventeenth-century sculptor and architect, Gian Lorenzo Bernini, played in visualizing and orchestrating the holy objects and holy sites in St. Peter's in order to create an image of the Counter-Reform Church. The throne, the Baldacchino, the colonnade, and the piazza: these quintessential achievements of seventeenth-century Rome have often been studied by scholars in isolation. Lavin makes the case that they are best understood as a vast, symphonic composition spanning Bernini's life and many pontificates, rising in crescendo at the site from east to west, and whose content and extent were prefigured in a statement imputed to the artist at the very beginning of his career.

That the ceremonies and activities of St. Peter's, both customary and unique, were molded and shaped in the space of the church by an ephemeral architecture within an architecture, an array of draperies and platforms, portable images and canopies, is abundantly attested in the sources. Alessandra Anselmi's chapter gives us a view of a linked sequence of situations, gathered together under the functional rationale of the canonization of saints, in which this was the case. Among the many vantage points offered by this material is one into the processes of social signification and the exercise of power in the papal court, whose leader in this arena, the pope, clearly played a critical role.

In the chapter by Richard A. Etlin, our view expands to embrace Europe as a whole from England to Russia, and even extends to America. This is the stage in which the account of St. Peter's is played out in the modern era. Major interventions in the building itself have now abated, and at the site as well, with the exception of Benito Mussolini's project of the Via della Conciliazione. The edifice, however, becomes a potent model to emulate, albeit in a highly sublimated form, even in secular and commercial contexts.

In the end it is difficult to avoid the notion of "larger than life" when speaking of St. Peter's. But such a notion would seem to be inimical now to prevailing views of human achievement in history. Ours, after all, is a post-heroic age. But perhaps the "exception that proves the rule" is the enormous impact St. Peter's has had worldwide as an image in the media (especially television). The papacy continues to use St. Peter's, including the piazza in front of the basilica, as the setting for important events, ceremonies, and speeches, to the extent that it has become the most vivid and well-known image of the Catholic Church, and one of the most well-known buildings of all time. Anything less "photogenic," of course, could not possibly sustain such extraordinary inflation and diffusion. As the essays in the present volume make clear, and scholarship, criticism, and appreciation elsewhere has continuously shown, this supremely contemporary value has come about, not in an instant, but over the course of many hundreds of years marked by both failure and success.

I would like to express my gratitude to Beatrice Rehl, who invited me to create a book on St. Peter's; to the Kress and Graham Foundations, for their generous provision of the necessary financial support; and to the authors, for their contributions.

PETER AND CONSTANTINE

G. W. BOWERSOCK

Accounts of the great edifice of St. Peter's on the Vatican regularly give pride of place to the emperor Constantine's veneration of the apostle as expressed in his foundation of the first basilica on the site. Even modern works on quite different subjects that have occasion to allude to the present basilica normally make an obligatory reference to Constantine's patronage of Peter. In a recent volume on Bernini as architect, Tod Marder leads off his chapter on the Baldacchino with a reference to Constantine's defeat of Maxentius at the Milvian Bridge and goes on to state, "He attributed his victory to Christ, and, in thanksgiving, founded the basilica at the shrine over the burial site of Saint Peter, the first apostle."[1]

But it is a fact, rarely observed, that most accounts of the reign of Constantine usually fail to mention either Peter or the Vatican at all. Historians of the first Christian emperor of antiquity seem to find no occasion whatever to comment upon Constantine's interest in Peter or his supposed foundation of the original basilica on the slope of the Vatican hill. That is a strange omission, if historians of the Vatican are right. Nor is it an omission that can readily be explained by the traditional lack of communication between ecclesiastical scholars and classical scholars. Jacob Burckhardt, who was deeply interested not only in religion but in monumental art, found no space in his influential work, *Die Zeit Constantins des Grossen* (1853), for even a passing reference to the basilica of Peter. He maintained that Constantine's relations with the Christians in Rome were very much in doubt.[2] In more recent times, A. H. M. Jones, who, among his many distinctions, held a doctorate of divinity, said nothing in his widely read *Constantine and the Conversion of Europe* (1949) about any devotion to Peter on the part of the emperor. Exceptionally, T. D. Barnes, in the alert and thorough manner in which he conducts all his research, recorded the tradition of Constantine's foundation of St. Peter's in one brief line of his important book *Eusebius and Constantine*, but his trenchant notes exposed several disturbing problems in the evidence.[3]

Particularly striking is the absence of the whole subject in Edward Gibbon's *Decline and Fall of the Roman Empire*. Gibbon, after all, wrote at great length about the character and reign of Constantine, and at even greater length about the early Christian church. Under neither rubric did he present Constantine as the founder of the church of St. Peter's on the Vatican, although he was well aware of the existence of the late antique basilica. He mentioned it with delicious irony immediately after an allusion to the site of Nero's notorious crucifixion of Christians in A.D. 64: "On the same spot, a temple, which far surpasses the ancient glories of the Capitol, has been erected by the Christian Pontiffs, who, deriving their claim of universal dominion from an humble fisherman of Galilee, have succeeded to the throne of the Caesars, given laws to the barbarian conquerors of Rome, and extended their spiritual jurisdiction from the coast of the Baltic to the shores of the Pacific Ocean."[4] The popes, not Constantine, are held responsible for the basilica of Peter on the Vatican.

Is the Constantinian connection a mirage? Textual evidence for Constantine's initiative comes from the *Liber Pontificalis* of no earlier than approximately two hundred years after his reign. Even allowing for an early version of a source such as the legendary life of Pope Silvester, from which the *liber* may have drawn, we cannot trace the story of Constantine's involvement with the Vatican before the end of the fifth century.[5] It was clearly in the interest of the papacy to strengthen its links with the first apostle and the first Christian emperor. The figure of Constantine, like so many historical figures who have arguably altered the course of history, tends to attract over time a series of unhistorical documents, deeds, and stories that serve the purposes of later generations. The *Donation of Constantine*, so mercilessly exposed as a forgery by Lorenzo Valla in the fifteenth century, is undoubtedly the most famous of these Constantinian accretions.[6] Others, such as Silvester's fictitious baptism of Constantine, can already be found in the *Liber Pontificalis*.[7] Another item in the *liber* has now been decisively relegated to the category of fiction by the dramatic excavations conducted directly beneath the Vatican basilica in the forties and fifties of the twentieth century. The basilica was raised over a necropolis, not, as the *liber* asserts, over a temple of Apollo.[8]

The Vatican excavations have undoubtedly provided the most exciting new documentation for the original basilica of Peter since the construction of the present one in the sixteenth century. The old basilica was still standing at that time, and its remains lingered as the new work went on. The careful drawings of one Tiberio Alfarano have long provided historians of Late Antique monuments with precious glimpses into standing parts of the old structure.[9] The excavations under the Vatican in the century just ended have fully confirmed the Late Antique – and probably fourth-century – construction of the first basilica over the graves of pagans and Christians.[10] The excavations have also sensationally confirmed that the construction was carried out over a preexisting shrine that was meticulously incorporated within the new church in a highly prominent position on the chord of the apse (Fig. 1). No one can reasonably doubt that this shrine was believed to commemorate the apostle Peter, either because it stood over his tomb or because it marked the place of his crucifixion. So the latest round of excavations has revealed much about the veneration of Peter in Rome, but they too are utterly silent on any role played by the emperor Constantine.

It would be prudent, therefore, to examine these two topics independently and then to determine whether there is any substantial basis for bringing them together. Even before the excavations hardly any historian, ecclesiastical or secular, would have denied that Peter died in Rome. After the excavations it became obvious that the shrine around which the basilica had been carefully, and inconveniently, located could only have commemorated the eponym of the building. Pertinent texts, if not so specific as one might like, were nonetheless compelling: Peter's own letter written, as he says, from Babylon, which has to be Rome (it would be absurd to put the apostle in Mesopotamia), and an oblique allusion in the letters of Ignatius to the martyrdom suffered by Peter and Paul in Rome.[11] The scene of the martyrdom is unforgettably described by Tacitus in the *Annals*, when he reports the terrible deaths that Nero inflicted upon the Christians, whom he held collectively responsible for the great fire in the city. The crucifixions took place across the Tiber in the area of Nero's gardens (the former *horti Agrippinae*) and the circus of Gaius and Nero, in other words, in the region just south and east of the Vatican basilica.[12] Paul, as a Roman citizen, would have suffered decapitation rather than the more ignominious crucifixion, and he may therefore have died in another part of Rome.

No one tells us whether or how the bodies of the two martyrs were recovered or, if so, what was done with them. It is highly likely that both corpses disappeared into the welter of the dead after the persecution. The crucified Christians might well have been thrown into the Tiber, and it is hard to credit that any Christians would have been able to step forward in the frenzy of the occasion and securely remove the remains of Peter or Paul. But the one explicit testimony that survives, to the veneration of these two, before the fourth century leaves no doubt that the memory of them, and possibly what were thought to be their bones, held a special place in the regard of Christians at Rome. Eusebius, in his church history, incorporated a precious citation from Gaius, an early-third-century Christian Roman, who reported the existence of what he called *tropaia* of Peter and Paul on the Vatican hill and on the Ostian road, respectively.[13] So here, without any doubt, we have textual proof of the veneration of Peter on the Vatican in the early third century. What Gaius does not make plain, nor have centuries of learned exegesis succeeded in clarifying, is the sense of *tropaia*. A "trophy" was a Roman victory monument and not a tomb, although there is no reason why such a monument should not have been erected above or around a tomb. Gaius may simply have been exercising prudence in choosing a word that would not presuppose the presence of the bones of the martyrs. It is entirely possible that many of the faithful believed that the bones were there, even if they were not. But either a shrine or a tomb for both Peter and Paul can be guaranteed.

Another place of veneration for both martyrs turns up in a problematic text of the mid-fourth century with reference to the mid-third. A fifth-century chronographer reports that on 29 June 258 both Peter and Paul were celebrated in the catacombs along the Appian Way, and this tradition is reinforced by the old name of the church of S. Sebastiano on the spot as the church of the apostles (*ecclesia apostolorum*).[14] The chronographer of 354 mentions the cult on the Appian Way but names only Peter,[15] but an inscribed epigram by Pope Damasus from the very place alludes also to a joint cult. The lines of Damasus even declare that the two saints formerly dwelt there (*hic habitasse prius sanctos cognoscere debes / nomina quisque Petri pariter Paulique requiris*, "You should know that in former time the saints dwelt here, you who look for the names of both Peter and Paul").[16] These three texts, the earliest of them coming about a half-century after that of Gaius, have led to the most extravagant speculation about the possibility of moving bones from one place to another under the pressures of the Valerian persecution in 258. Such speculation has often entailed moving the bones back again later to the places mentioned by Gaius.[17] But the simple fact is that nowhere is there any explicit mention of the translation of the bones of either of these martyrs, although Damasus's *habitasse* could be taken to imply that bones had once been present, but for whatever reason, were there no longer. The fourth-century chronographer is aware of Paul's shrine on the Ostian Way, but embarrassingly not of Peter's on the Vatican. Although his text has often been emended to incorporate the Vatican, others (notably the excellent Charles Pietri) have preferred to believe that a Vatican shrine was not yet finished or functioning in 354.[18]

Since we do not know whether there were any bones in the shrines mentioned by Gaius, it seems pointless to speculate whether bones were translated to the Appian Way and back again later. What is clear is that there was a joint cult of Peter and Paul, and there were also separate shrines for each, one on the Vatican and one on the Ostian Way. For the shrine of Peter the excavations in the 1940s provided a marvelous confirmation.[19] Within the necropolis directly beneath the papal altar of the present basilica the excavators discovered the remains of a small but impressive monument, conventionally called the *aedicula* ("little building"), which was constructed at the same time as a drain running alongside the wall into which the *aedicula* was built (Fig. 1). The drain is dated by tiles to about A.D. 160, and that is therefore the date of the monument. The structure had two distinct levels, with two niches separated by a projecting travertine slab supported by columns standing in front of the lower niche. (A mysterious third niche was cut into the subterranean part of the wall.) The *aedicula* was designed to look out upon a piazza that might have held thirty or forty people. The odd placement of the whole complex in the middle of a cemetery would imply not only that this was a shrine, but was one that had to be fitted into that place and no other. In other words, this must have been considered the precise location of a very special tomb. As the first basilica of Peter was awkwardly but deliberately positioned to incorporate this shrine in the most prominent spot in the church, we must assume that already in the second century Christians believed, rightly or wrongly, that this was the tomb of Peter. We can be confident that the *aedicula* is none other than the *tropaion* of Peter mentioned by Gaius.

Gibbon was well acquainted with the important quotation from Gaius in Eusebius. He alluded to it in chapter 28 of *The Decline and Fall* when he commented on the emerging cult of martyrs:

> One hundred and fifty years after the glorious deaths of St. Peter and St. Paul, the Vatican and the Ostian road were distinguished by the tombs, or rather by the trophies, of those spiritual heroes. In the age which followed the conversion of Constantine, the emperors, the consuls, and the generals of armies devoutly visited the sepulchres of a tentmaker and a fisherman; and their venerable bones were deposited under the altars of Christ, on which the bishops of the royal city continually offered the unbloody sacrifice.[20]

1. Rome, Vatican Necropolis, second-century shrine (the *aedicula*), drawing by G. U. S. Corbett. Photo: after Jocelyn Toynbee and John Ward Perkins, *The Shrine of St. Peter and the Vatican Excavations* (London, 1956), fig. 17

Here Gibbon moved directly from the pre-Constantinian trophies to the churches that replaced them, one on the road to Ostia (the Church of St. Paul) and one on the Vatican Hill (the Church of St. Peter). These buildings are placed vaguely after the conversion of Constantine and conspicuously without reference to any intervention from that emperor. Gibbon's earlier comment that the popes were responsible for what he called the temple on the Vatican is wholly consistent with his observation in chapter 28.

It would now be appropriate to address the plausibility of Constantine's direct personal intervention in the founding of the original basilica on the Vatican. The usefulness of this association in establishing papal authority is beyond question. Hence there would have been every reason to advertise Constantine's role, if he had one, and to fabricate it, if not. We have seen already that the first recorded notice of Constantine's foundation of the Vatican basilica occurs in the *Liber Pontificalis*, a document that contains some incontrovertibly erroneous information such as Silvester's baptism of the emperor and the Vatican temple of Apollo. But the presence of such material obviously does not preclude the inclusion of authentic testimony. The endowment of the church, consisting of properties in the eastern portion of the empire, evidently presupposes Constantine's defeat of Licinius in 324 and his consequent assumption of control over the East.[21] The properties would not have been his to provide before that date. But this can serve, at best, only as an ultimate terminus post quem.

The archaeological evidence for the original basilica and its incorporation of the old *aedicula* on the line between transept and apse provides no evidence at all that Constantine was responsible for this work. There is a graffito on an adjacent wall that evokes the miracle at the Milvian Bridge (*ho[c] vin[ce]*),[22] but since this was the defining moment in the Christianization of the Roman state, as shown by Lactantius, Eusebius, and others later, it could have been recalled at almost any time. There is no inscription or tile that provides the kind of dating we have for the *aedicula*. The shrine itself was actually encased in marble with porphyry pilasters at the corners, much as the *Liber Pontificalis* describes it, but of the solid bronze coffin that Constantine reportedly made for Peter's corpse there is not a trace.[23] The *aedicula* was presented to the faithful in the basilica within a pergola with four columns decorated with an ivy motif, and the back of the pergola was aligned with two columns at either side of the opening of the apse, thus forming a screen separating the transept from the apse. The reconstruction of all this on the basis of the archaeological finds appears to be confirmed by a representation of the scene on a casket from Pola, in which both shrine, pergola, and the two columns on either side of the entrance to the apse can be clearly distinguished (Fig. 2).[24] Accordingly, we can form a fairly precise notion of the way in which the second-century shrine was incorporated into the fourth-century basilica. But again nothing speaks of Constantine.

Other oblique testimony has been invoked in support of a Constantinian church. The Vatican Phrygianum, a pagan shrine dedicated to the Phrygian goddess Cybele (the Great Mother), is thought to have halted for twenty-eight years its grim rites of the *taurobolium*, in which votaries received the blood of bulls slaughtered over their heads. Some have seen the interruption of this ceremony as having been caused by the building of the Vatican close by. The inscription mentioning the interruption was found in 1919 near St. Peter's and presumably belonged to the Phrygianum, but unfortunately it has no date. When originally published it was assumed to come from the later fourth century, like most of the other surviving inscriptions from that shrine. Before A.D. 370 there are no dated inscriptions from the Phrygianum apart from one in 305 and one in 350. This clearly leaves too capacious a period to locate a twenty-eight-year cessation within it. Although a dedication to the Great Mother from A.D. 319 has been brought in to create a somewhat narrower time frame, unfortunately that inscription is not connected with the Vatican Phrygianum.[25] So proponents of this hypothesis have simply calculated back twenty-eight years from the attested rites of A.D. 350 and come up with A.D. 322 for the start of the construction of the basilica. So tortured and unsupported an argument cannot be allowed to stand.

Similarly, an imperial decree in the Theodosian Code[26] with a severe penalty for tomb violation has been seen as a reflection of violations that must inevitably have taken place during the construction of the Vatican basilica. The text curiously includes punishment retrospectively for any violations committed over the previous sixteen years. If the document was issued by Constans in 349, which is the date it bears, this ought to mean that serious invasions of tombs had been building up alarmingly from 333 onward. It is a far less plausible assumption that there had been open season on breaking into tombs before that year. In their edition of the code, Mommsen and Krüger actually ascribe the law to Constantius, Augustus for the Eastern empire.[27] If he is the author of this decree, it can obviously have no bearing at all on the desecration of the Vatican cemetery. But whoever the author may have been, the document has no probative value.

Oddly, the only explicit evidence, apart from the *Liber Pontificalis*, for Constantine's role in founding the first basilica of St. Peter's is considerably later in date than the *liber*. This is a mosaic text that was seen sometime before the ninth century and was recorded in a collection of inscriptions kept in the monastery of Einsiedeln. The mosaic, which was placed on the triumphal arch between the nave and the transept of the old St. Peter's, depicted Constantine presenting the church to Christ in the company of Peter himself. The mosaic inscription contained two hexameters: *quod duce te mundus surrexit in astra triumphans / hanc Constantinus victor tibi condidit aulam* ("Because under your leadership the world in triumph has risen to the stars, victorious Constantine has founded this hall for you").[28] The text undoubtedly confirms the assertion of the *liber*, but unfortunately we have no way of telling when the mosaic with these lines was installed on the arch. Since there were extensive renovations and changes made in the basilica between the fourth century and the ninth, including, in the time of Gregory the Great, a new altar over the supposed tomb, a mosaic such as this could easily have been put up under the influence of the tradition recorded in the *Liber Pontificalis*.

The great church of Hagia Sophia in Constantinople provides an interesting comparison here. Still today the visitor can see in the southwest vestibule a tenth-century mosaic showing Constantine and Justinian flanking the

2. Capsella of Samagher (Pola casket) with image of St. Peter's, Museo Archeologico, Venice, inv. 1952, n. 279. (Photo: Ministero per i Beni culturali e ambientali, Soprintendenza Archeologico per il Veneto)

Virgin and Child. The implication is obviously that the Justinianic building we now see represented an original foundation by Constantine, and this has long been the common assumption. But, as Cyril Mango and others have emphasized, the original church was built later than Constantine – under the Arian Constantius II – although it was, like so much else, subsequently attached to the first Christian emperor.[29] The mosaic proves only what was promulgated and doubtless believed in later centuries. It tells nothing about the founder of the first church, and something similar may underlie the lost mosaic seen by the Einsiedeln pilgrim.

An inscription, seen much later still and after additional renovations and changes in the church, provides even more tenuous documentation for Constantine's involvement. This is another mosaic inscription, which was seen in the fifteenth century on an arch over the altar in the apse of the dilapidated old building. It was read fragmentarily as follows: *Constantini . . . expiata . . . hostili incursione* ("Of Constantine . . . a hostile incursion . . . expiated").[30] Although this text has recently been associated with Constantine's repulse of the Sarmatians in 323,[31] it obviously could refer to any number of conflicts. It is likely, in fact, that this text adds to the program of the Einsiedeln mosaic text in providing emphatic and deliberate documentation of the received view that Constantine founded the church.

The legendary life of Silvester, mirrored in the *Liber Pontificalis*, preserves another text that may have been seen at some stage in St. Peter's. It is in some ways the most attractive inscription in support of a Constantinian date. Said to have been inscribed upon a golden cross above the *aedicula*, it is supposed to have displayed the following words: *Constantinus Augustus et Helena Augusta. hanc domum regalem simili fulgore coruscans aula circumdat.*[32] In 1899 a perplexed scholar proposed inserting the words *auro decorant quam* after *regalem*, although the transmitted text can be construed perfectly well.[33] With the supplement included (as it normally is), the text after the two names would read: "They adorn with gold this royal house, which the hall surrounds, gleaming with a comparable radiance." The titulature of Helena looks authentic and seems to imply a date between her taking the title Augusta in late 324 or in 325 and her death in the winter of 327/8. As Constantine and Helena visited Rome in 326, this visit could have been the occasion of the donation of the golden cross. But if this text is authentic, as it might be, there is the problem with *domus regalis*, which Krautheimer thought to refer to the *aedicula* itself or the ciborium above it.[34] The idea of an encompassing *aula*, as introduced by the modern supplement to the inscription, may have been in the back of his mind, but it is not in the transmitted text that we have. The Latin phrase *domus regalis* would naturally

3. Giacomo Grimaldi, *Descrizione della basilica antica di S. Pietro in Vaticano*, Biblioteca Apostolica Vaticana, Vatican City, cod. barb. lat. 2733, fol. 165ᵛ (Photo: Biblioteca Apostolica Vaticana)

mean a royal palace. It is far more probable that this cross had originally adorned a palace chamber, perhaps a chapel, and was subsequently moved to St. Peter's. It is exceedingly hard to imagine that the *aedicula* could be called a *domus*, and certainly not a royal one. As it happens, we know that Helena had a church built for herself in the Sessorium palace – a church that at one time was known as the Heleniana.[35]

Where does all this discussion leave us? A great basilica of St. Peter's was erected on the Vatican after the conversion of Constantine and almost certainly within the fourth century. The foundations that have been discovered, the shape of the church as it has been reconstructed (with steps and a broad esplanade leading up to a grand church with a five-aisle nave), and the style of the graffiti and inscriptions found in the context of the building all point to a date in this period. But of Constantine's veneration of Peter and his foundation of this church there is no evidence for nearly two centuries. Although Constantine's biographer Eusebius was far more interested in the Eastern realm, he does occasionally take note of the Christian community in Rome, but neither his vast biography of the emperor nor any of his other writings show that Constantine had any particular attachment to Peter. It was, of course, very much in the interest of the popes to trace their authority to Constantine.[36] In the course of time the Constantinian connection may have helped in any rivalry with the Lateran church at Rome, which is generally agreed to have preceded St. Peter's. In the end it would seem that Gibbon took the most prudent course when he attributed the basilica to the "Christian Pontiffs." In the view of the *Liber Pontificalis*, Constantine's generosity was ultimately due to healing, conversion, and baptism at the hands of Pope Silvester. Although this legend, for such it must be, may conceivably point to the truth – that Constantine founded the first St. Peter's – the reality is far more likely to have been construction under one of his successors.[37]

Constantine's son Constans, who assumed the rule in Italy in A.D. 337 and held it until his death in 350, most probably deserves the credit for building the first basilica on the Vatican. An early-seventeenth-century description of brick stamps found in the apse of the old structure at the time of its demolition gives the abbreviation D N CONSTANT AVG. This is not to be expanded into a nominative form of the name of Constantine. A genitive here would be normal. The correct reading has to be *D(omini) N(ostri) Constant(is) Aug(usti)*, exactly as it appears on a brick stamp with the emperor's name written in full (Fig. 3).[38]

Furthermore, another Einsiedeln text, recorded in the apse of the old St. Peter's sometime before the ninth century, seems to proclaim the generosity of one of the sons of Constantine. The four hexameter lines appear to have accompanied a representation, as Krautheimer suggests,

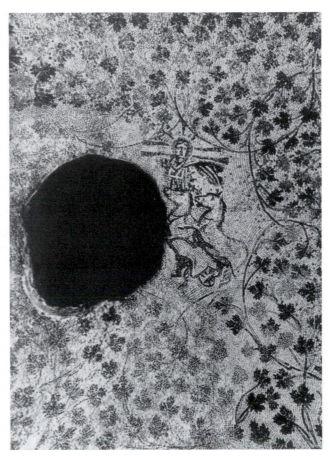

4. Rome, Vatican Necropolis, Tomb M, mosaic of Christ as Helios the Charioteer (Photo: after John Beckwith, *Early Christian and Byzantine Art*, 2d ed., New York; Penguin [1979], pl. 1)

of the *traditio legis: Iustitiae sedes fidei domus aula pudoris / haec est quam cernis pietas quam possidet omnis, / quae patris et filii virtutibus inclyta gaudet / auctoremque suum genitoris laudibus aequat* ("This that you see is a seat of justice, a house of faith, a hall of modesty which is entirely possessed of piety, which famously rejoices in the virtues of the Father and the Son and renders the one who made it equal in glory to his parent").[39] Although some interpreters have understood the father and the son in line three to be Constantine and Constans (or even Constantine and Constantius), the context of *pietas* would appear to require that the reference here be to God the Father and to Christ. Furthermore, the first two words of the fourth line (*auctoremque suum*) deserve close scrutiny. They can only denote the maker of the church (*suum*, like *haec*, referring to the *sedes/domus/aula*).[40] The final line asserts that the *auctor*, through the piety represented by his building, is now equal to his parent in glory. This could, of course, mean that he has completed a church started before him, but such an interpretation would be difficult to sustain in view of the unambiguous word *auctor*.[41] The son would now be represented as having achieved a glory comparable to his father's through the pious foundation of his building.

The endowment of St. Peter's, as recorded in the *Liber Pontificalis*,[42] might be thought to present a difficulty if placed in the reign of Constans. The properties are all in the East (in Syria, Egypt, and Euphratensis), as has often been observed. In the reign of Constantine himself, this would impose a date after the defeat of Licinius in A.D. 324, but in the reign of Constans the territories would have been under the jurisdiction of Constantius and unlikely to have been available for a gift to Peter. But once again we have to confront the unreliability of the text. As Glanville Downey observed with reference to the properties at Antioch, "We have no way of being sure how and when these properties passed into the possession of St. Peter's, and how long they were owned by the Roman church."[43] Worse still, the received listing of the properties makes reference to revenue in *tremisses,* which were not minted before A.D. 383.[44] On the other hand, the territories are all said to be comprised in the *dioecesis Oriens*, from which Egypt was broken off in about A.D. 370 to become an independent *dioecesis* (as it appears in the *Notitia Dignitatum*).[45] This proves that the endowment listings in the *Liber Pontificalis* are a confection of items from mutually incompatible periods. Some parts presumably derive from a text composed before A.D. 370, but, as Downey recognized, there is simply no way of telling which parts belong to which epoch. The endowments, as handed down in the *liber,* could have been attributed to St. Peter's at almost any time in its first two centuries, and they certainly need not all have been conveyed at once. It could readily be imagined that initially St. Peter's received revenues from Italy and Sicily, much as the Lateran church appears to have done.

Finally, one text remains to be considered with reference to the personal involvement of Constantine in the foundation of the Vatican basilica. It is sometimes invoked as proof that Eusebius knew about the existence of the church even though he said nothing about Constantine's role in building it. The text occurs in Eusebius's *Theophany,* a work known only through a Syriac translation and some scraps of the Greek original. Barnes has convincingly assigned it to A.D. 325.[46] Writing of Peter, Eusebius evoked the special devotion of Roman Christians as shown by the fine tomb they built for him: they revered him to such an extent "that they honored him with a splendid tomb in front of the city, to which, as to a great sanctuary and temple of God, crowds of people came from the Roman Empire."[47] If these lines were taken to allude to an already existing basilica, as Margherita Guarducci thought,[48] the edifice would have risen with unexampled celerity. Guarducci herself published a coin of A.D. 317/8 from an undisturbed level in

the cemetery beneath the church and, allowing a decent interval for the burial in which it was found, argued that 319 was an absolute terminus post quem for work on the basilica. Reverting to the idea that the nearby *taurobolia* ceased in 322, she postulated that the actual work began in that year. She could do this only by ignoring the implications of the Eastern church properties that could not have been acquired before the defeat of Licinius in 324.[49] Even on her own terms, three years for the building of St. Peter's is unthinkable. Pietri, as we have seen, believed that the basilica was still unfinished in the middle of the century.

Eusebius's text has been manifestly misunderstood. His words in no way document the existence of the Vatican basilica. On the contrary, they describe veneration at the tomb of Peter, which we know from the archaeological discoveries had been prominent since the second century. What Eusebius does not say is that the tomb was also "a great temple and sanctuary of God." He is saying that crowds went to the tomb just as if they were going to a major church: being a holy place, the tomb and the piazza in front of it attracted pilgrims just as great churches and sanctuaries did.[50] This text is proof, not of the existence of the Vatican basilica in A.D. 325, but rather of its absence. The *aedicula* and the space in front of it were still functioning north of the Tiber ("in front of the city") as the holy place of Peter.

At some date, therefore, after A.D. 325 and very probably after the death of Constantine the first church dedicated to Peter on the Vatican was built. It seems apparent that the Western emperor Constans was responsible for this work. No literary source tells us about him in this role, but this is by no means so surprising as the silence of the Constantinian sources. Evidence for his reign, unlike Constantine's, is relatively exiguous and overshadowed by the record of Constantius, who assumed control of the entire Roman world at the death of Magnentius. But since Constantius, who was an Arian, undertook to build both the Church of Holy Wisdom and the Church of the Holy Apostles in Constantinople, it would be understandable if the Catholic Constans chose to respond to such initiatives, perhaps at the prompting of the papacy, with a magnificent basilica over the presumed tomb of Peter. Or, inasmuch as the dedication of Hagia Sophia came ten years after Constans's death and the dedication of the Holy Apostles a decade later, Constantius may perhaps have been responding to an initiative from Constans. The Church of the Holy Apostles incorporated into its design the preexisting rotunda of Constantine's mausoleum, and the preexisting rotunda adjacent to St. Peter's on the southwestern side provides a partial parallel. The Vatican rotunda could have served for imperial burials, as we know the rotunda in Constantinople did. An architectural rivalry between these two Augusti, who proclaimed their Constantinian descent while dividing between themselves the eastern and western parts of the Mediterranean world, might make sense.[51]

The shifting of the construction of St. Peter's into the reign of Constans has an unexpected and welcome confirmation from one of the most celebrated of all the images to have emerged from the Vatican tombs that lay underneath the first basilica. Tomb M, which was the burial place for a Christian family, displays a stunning representation of Christ as Helios the Charioteer rising splendidly heavenward (Fig. 4). The solar imagery here ought to be yet another manifestation of Constantinian devotion to *Sol Invictus*,[52] but on the conventional dating of the first St. Peter's there would be very little time available for this Constantinian motif to find its reflection in Tomb M. A post-Constantinian date for the basilica provides a much more comfortable chronology.

We shall never know with absolute certainty who founded St. Peter's, but it was very probably Constans, not Constantine. What can confidently be affirmed is that Peter was and remains a central figure in the history of Christian Rome. As for Constantine, he proved no less central than Peter to the papacy's image of itself, as it was put together over the two centuries following his death in A.D. 337. Regrettably, there is really nothing to join these two great icons of early Christianity to one another within Constantine's lifetime. There is no reliable witness to the emperor's special regard for the fisherman of Galilee. The inextricable union of Peter and Constantine probably came only when both of them were dead.

Notes

1   T. A. Marder, *Bernini and the Art of Architecture* (New York, 1998), 27. I am grateful to William Tronzo for urging me to take up this subject in the first place and for his helpful comments on the essay as it evolved. I have also profited from the valuable observations of Slobodan Ćurčić, Christopher Jones, and Irving Lavin. I am much indebted to the late John Shearman for his support and for providing the precious reference to Grimaldi's account of early brick stamps from the apse of the first basilica on the Vatican. An earlier and unillustrated version of this paper appeared in *Humana sapit: Mélanges . . . Ruggini* (Paris, 2002), 209–17.

2   J. Burckhardt, *Die Zeit Constantins des Grossen*, chap. 10, p. 303, in the handsome Phaidon edition from the 1930s (no date given): *die ungeheure Pracht seiner Kirchenbauten und Weihgeschenke . . . beschränkt sich in der Wirklichkeit auf ein vehältnismässig Weniges.* The Phaidon edition was enlarged with many illustrations, which were selected and captioned by Ludwig Goldscheider. It is amusing to see that no. 32 is a sixteenth-century engraving of the original St. Peter's with a caption stating, *Bau begonnen unter Constantin dem Grossen.*

3   T. D. Barnes, *Constantine and Eusebius* (Cambridge, Mass., 1981), 49 with n. 57 and 61 on 310.

4   Edward Gibbon, *The Decline and Fall of the Roman Empire*, chap. 16 (Everyman ed., 2: 16; Bury ed. [1909], 2: 92).

5   For the *Liber Pontificalis*, the great edition of L. Duchesne (Paris, 1883; republished 1955) remains fundamental. Hereafter cited as *LP*.

6   The Latin text of this extraordinary work, entitled *De falso credita et ementita Constantini donatione*, may be found, edited by Wolfram Setz, in the series *Monumenta Germaniae Historica*, vol. 10 (Weimar, 1976). A French translation by Jean-Baptiste Giard, with an introduction and notes by him and a preface by Carlo Ginzburg, appeared in the series *La roue à livres* (Paris, 1993) under the title *Lorenzo Valla: La Donation de Constantin*. It is important to recall that Cardinal Baronius stoutly defended the Donation as late as the end of the sixteenth century as a part of his effort, in his *Annales Ecclesiastici*, to shore up the dignity of the Church and the derivation of papal authority from Constantine. Cf. C. K. Pullapilly, *Caesar Baronius* (Notre Dame, Ind., 1975), 146–7 and 167–8.

7   On the baptism, see Vincenzo Aiello, "Costantino, la lebbra e il battesimo di Silvestro," in *Costantino il Grande, dall'antichità all'umanesimo*, ed. G. Bonamente and F. Fusco (Macerata, 1992), 1:17–58. Once again Baronius, for all his erudition and diligence, vigorously defended the story of Silvester's baptism of Constantine. Cf. Pullapilly, *Caesar Baronius*, 168–9.

8   *LP*, 176, 1: "Eodem tempore Augustus Constantinus fecit basilicam beato Petro apostolo in templum Apollinis."

9   T. Alfarano, *De Basilicae Vaticanae antiquissima et nova structura*, ed. M. Cerrati (Rome, 1914). For an exhaustive treatment of the architecture of the old St. Peter's with full bibliography, see now Alberto Carlo Carpiceci and Richard Krautheimer, "Nuovi dati sull'antica basilica di San Pietro in Vaticano," *Bollettino d'Arte* 93–4 (1995): 1–70, and 95 (1996): 1–84.

10   The literature on the Vatican excavations is enormous. The work by Carpiceci and Krautheimer (n. 9) contains a substantial bibliography. Essential is B. M. Apolloni Ghetti, A. Ferrua, E. Josi, and E. Kirschbaum, *Esplorazioni sotto la Confessione di San Pietro in Vaticano*, vols. 1–2 (Vatican, 1951). See also J. Toynbee and J. Ward Perkins, *The Shrine of St. Peter and the Vatican Excavations* (London, 1956); Th. Klauser, *Die römische Petrustradition im Lichte der neuen Ausgrabungen unter der Peterskirche*, Arbeitsgemeinschaft für Forschung des Landes Nordrhein-Westfalen-Geisteswissenschaften, Heft 24 (Cologne, 1956); A. Prandi, *La zona archeologica della Confessio Vaticana. I monumenti di II secolo* (Vatican, 1957); E. Kirschbaum, *Die Gräber der Apostelfürsten*, 2d ed. (Frankfurt, 1959); M. Guarducci, *The Tradition of Peter in the Vatican in the Light of History and Archaeology* (Vatican, 1963).

11   I Peter 5. 13: ἀσπάζεται ὑμᾶς ἡ ἐν Βαβυλῶνι συνεκλεκτή. Ignatius, *epist. ad Romanos* 4. 3: οὐχ ὡς Πέτρος καὶ Παῦλος διατάσσομαι ὑμῖν. I Clement 5. 1 and 6.1, which mention the martyrdoms of Peter and Paul, have also been invoked in support of their dying in Rome. Although Clement does not explicitly locate the place of their deaths, he was writing from the city and about the Neronian persecution.

12   Tacitus, *Ann.* 15.44.2–5: "ergo abolendo rumori Nero subdidit reos et quaesitissimis poenis affecit, quos per flagitia invisos vulgus Christianos appellabat . . . hortos suos ei spectaculo Nero obtulerat et circense ludicrum edebat."

13   Eusebius, *Hist. Eccles.* 2.25.5–7, reports the beheading of Paul and the crucifixion of Peter in Rome and confirms this report by reference to cemeteries in the city named for Peter and Paul. For further confirmation he cites Gaius's polemic against the Montanist Proclus, in which Gaius speaks of the places where the σκηνώματα of the two apostles were buried in Rome: ἐγὼ δὲ τρόπαια τῶν ἀποστόλων ἔχω δεῖξαι. Gaius then specifies the Vatican and the road to Ostia.

14 *Martyrologium Hieronymianum* (Acta Sanctorum, November ii. 1, 1894, p. 84): "III kal. Iul. Petri et Pauli. Petri in Vaticano, Pauli vero in Via Ostensi, utrumque in Catacumbas, Basso et Tusco cons." On San Sebastiano, see Klauser (n. 10), 23.

15 Chronogr. 354, *Monumenta Germaniae Historica*, Auct. ant. 9. 71: "III kal. Iul. Petri in Catacumbas et Pauli Ostense Tusco et Basso cons." On this text, see M. R. Salzman, *On Roman Time: The Codex-Calendar of 354 and the Rhythms of Urban Life in Late Antiquity* (Berkeley, 1990), 46–7.

16 G. B. De Rossi, *Inscriptiones Christianae Urbis Romae*, n.s. 5, ed. A. Ferrua (1971), no. 13273.

17 Reviewing the problem of moving the bones, Toynbee and Ward Perkins (n. 10), 179–82. Cf. Cyril Mango, "Constantine's Mausoleum and the Translation of Relics," *Byzantinische Zeitschrift* 83 (1990): 51–62 and 434, emphasizing that the movement of bones is unattested before A.D. 350 (or conceivably, but improbably 336, if that was the year in which the remains of three apostles were brought to Constantinople). The translation of bones, and the tomb violations it entails, would be inconceivable for the third century.

18 C. Pietri, *Roma Christiana. Recherches sur l'église de Rome, son organisation, sa politique et son idéologie de Miltiade à Sixte III* (Rome, 1976), 366–80.

19 See the basic bibliography provided above in n. 10.

20 Edward Gibbon, *The Decline and Fall of the Roman Empire*, chap. 28 (Everyman ed., 3: 140; Bury ed. [1909], 3: 219–20).

21 *LP*, 177–8.

22 Cf. Guarducci (n. 10), 55. It would be wise not to give much attention to another graffito, which she invokes on page 57: Πέτ[ρος] ἔνι. The scratching is too lacunose to deliver a certifiable reading, and even were it to indicate that the writer thought Peter's body was there, we hardly need confirmation that the faithful in late antiquity believed that it was. For the graffiti generally, see M. Guarducci, *I graffiti sotto la Confessione di San Pietro in Vaticano*, 3 vols. (Vatican, 1958).

23 *LP*, 176: "ipsum loculum undique ex aere cypro conclusit, quod est immobile."

24 The best photograph of this casket that I know may be seen in the catalogue volume *Age of Spirituality: Late Antique and Early Christian Art, Third to Seventh Century*, ed. K. Weitzmann (New York, 1979), 595. The object is in the Museo Archeologico of Venice.

25 The argument was first hinted at in two brief reports of communications before learned bodies by E. Josi: *Rendiconti della Pontificia Accademia Romana di Archeologia* 26(6) (1949–51), 4 (one page only), and *Comptes Rendus de l'Académie des Inscriptions et Belles-Lettres* 1950, 434–5 (containing only a summary of discussion after the communication). The idea was taken up by M. Guarducci *in Cristo e San Pietro in un documento precostantiniano della Necropoli Vaticana* (Rome, 1953), 65, and again in the article cited below in no. 49. The inscription alluding to a twenty-eight-year interruption consists of three Greek distichs and a fourth: *Supplementum Epigraphicum Graecum* 2. 518. Of the Vatican texts from the Phrygianum (*Corpus Inscriptionum Latinarum* VI. 1. 497–504), the two dating from before A.D. 370 are nos. 497 (A.D. 305) and 498 (A.D. 350). Text no. 508, providing the date of A.D. 319, is explicitly stated to be of unknown provenance.

26 *Cod. Theod.* IX. 17. 2, ed. Th. Mommsen and P. Krüger, 464.

27 There is an apparent mistake in Toynbee-Ward Perkins (n. 10), 197: "Mommsen and P. Krüger...ascribe the law to Constantius, Caesar in 324." They did indeed ascribe the law to Constantius but accepted the consular date it contains, namely 349. That should mean that they believed it to have been issued by Constantius as Augustus. Since the document was addressed to Ulpius Limenius as *praefectus praetorio*, it is possible that Mommsen and Krüger simply erred. Limenius was simultaneously *praefectus praetorio* of Italy and *praefectus urbis Romae* in 349 (A. H. M. Jones, J. R. Martindale, and J. Morris, *Prosopography of the Later Roman Empire* [Cambridge, 1971], 510). But it should be noted that Limenius was also consul in 349.

28 *Corpus Inscriptionum Latinarum* VI. 1, no. 6 = G. B. De Rossi, *Inscriptiones Christianae Urbis Romae*, n.s. 2, ed. A. Silvagni (1935), no. 4092, with useful bibliography.

29 C. Mango, in the article "Hagia Sophia," *Oxford Dictionary of Byzantium*, ed. A. Kazhdan (Oxford, 1991), 2: 892. Similarly T. E. Gregory, in the article "Constantius II" for the same dictionary, 1:524. The *Chronicon Paschale* records the emperor's donations at the consecration of the church in 360. Richard Krautheimer remained outside the consensus and offered an unconvincing, if moving, defense of what he acknowledged to be his "imprudence," in his article "The Ecclesiastical Building Policy of Constantine," in *Costantino il Grande, dall'Antichità all'Umanesimo*, a colloquium held at Macerata in 1990, ed. G. Bonamente and F. Fusco (Macerata, 1993), 2:509–51, with a long presentation of his belief in a Constantinian date for the first Hagia Sophia in n. 88 on 548–9.

30 G. B. De Rossi, *Inscriptiones Christianae Urbis Romae*, n.s. 2, ed. A. Silvagni (1935), no. 4095.

31 By Richard Krautheimer, in the collection of historical sources provided for the articles in the *Bollettino d'Arte* cited above in note 9. The proposed reference to Sarmatians occurs in the first article on page 5.

32 *LP*, 176, 8. C. P. Jones has acutely pointed out to me that the lines contain an embedded fragment of hexameter verse in *simili fulgore coruscans*. This appears to be the second half of a line, immediately following a strong caesura.

33 H. Grisar, *Analecta Romana* 1 (1899): 294–5. Grisar's supplement was incorporated between square brackets in the text that now stands in G. B. De Rossi, *Inscriptiones Christianae Urbis Romae*, n.s. 2, ed. A. Silvagni (1935), no. 4093. Silvagni also converted *Augustus* and *Augusta* both into *Aug.* to make the text look more epigraphic.

34 In the first of the two articles cited above in n. 9, p. 6.

35 See Duchesne in *LP*, 196. As the inscription is said to have been on a golden cross, it is perhaps pertinent to recall, as S. Ćurčić has reminded me, that the church is known today as S. Croce in Gerusalemme.

36 Baronius stubbornly maintained that they did: see notes 6 and 7 above on his defense of the Donation of Constantine and Pope Silvester's baptism of the emperor. His testimony was never disinterested, perhaps least of all when he chose to insert an addition to his account of the year 324, under which he had defended the Donation. This addition was placed as a "stop-press" item following the index at the very back of the 1594 edition of volume 3 of the *Annales Ecclesiastici*. There Baronius announced that during the demolition of the apse of the original basilica the workmen had found many bricks (*quamplurimos quadratos lateres*) with stamps bearing Constantine's name in the nominative case (D N CONSTANTINVS AVG). No such bricks now exist (cf. *Corpus Inscriptionum Latinarum* XV. 1. 1656).

37 Burckhardt (n. 2) called the story of Silvester's baptism of Constantine *eine blosse Sage*, which he believed arose from a desire to remove the Arian Eusebius from this important role. In his note 839 Burckhardt observed, with evident approval, that B. G. Niebuhr had admitted only the Lateran as a Constantinian building in Rome.

38 Baronius (n. 36 above) has willfully mispresented the text of the brick stamps that were found in the apse as D N CONSTANTINVS AVG. I am most grateful to the late John Shearman for drawing

my attention to the publication in 1972 of Grimaldi's description and drawing of the brick stamps discovered in the apse of the first basilica: Giacomo Grimaldi, *Descrizione della basilica antica di S. Pietro in Vaticano, Codice Barberini Latino 2733*, ed. R. Niggl (Vatican, 1972), 205. The brick stamps are mentioned with drawings on p. 205. *Corpus Inscriptionum Latinarum* XV. 1. 1658: D N CONSTANTIS AVG provides the necessary parallel.

39 G. B. De Rossi, *Inscriptiones Christianae Urbis Romae*, n.s. 2, ed. A. Silvagni (1935), no. 4094. For Krautheimer's suggestion of the *traditio legis*, see p. 6 of the first of the two articles cited above in n. 9.

40 Cf. the inscription from the original S. Maria in Trastevere, a building securely ascribed to Constans: "Haec domus est Christi semper mansura pudori / Iustitiae cultrix plebi servavit honorem" (G. B. De Rossi, *Inscriptiones Christianae Urbis Romae* 2 [1888], 151). This text, which John Shearman brought to my attention, incorporates the same triad of *iustitia, domus*, and *pudor*. The expression *aula pudoris* reappears in the original basilica of S. Agapitus, near Praeneste: *Corpus Inscriptionum Latinarum* XIV. 3415.

41 Silvagni (previous note), believing that the father and son must be Constantine and Constans, and that the father had begun the basilica, was awkwardly obliged to understand *auctor* as meaning *perfector*, "the one who finished the work." This is pure *contresens*. An *auctor* initiates a project.

42 *LP*, 177–8.

43 G. Downey, *A History of Antioch in Syria from Seleucus to the Arab Conquest* (Princeton, N.J., 1961), 516, n. 58.

44 As acutely noted by T. D. Barnes, *Constantine and Eusebius* (Cambridge, Mass., 1981), 310, n. 57, with citation of F. Vittinghoff, Pauly-Wissowa, *RE* VII.A (1948), col. 105.

45 A. H. M. Jones, *The Later Roman Empire 284–602* (Oxford, 1964), 1:141 and idem, *Journal of Theological Studies* 5 (1954): 224–7.

46 Barnes (n. 39), 186–8.

47 Eusebius, *Theophania* 4. 7, in *Die griechischen christlichen Schriftsteller: Eusebius*, 3.2, ed. H. Gressmann (1904), p. 175.

(German translation). A corrected reprint of this volume appeared in 1992 with the help of Adolf Laminski. The Syriac text was originally published by Samuel Lee, Eusebius: *On the Theophania…a Syrian version edited from an ancient manuscript recently discovered* (London, 1842). In the next year Lee published an English translation with the Cambridge University Press.

48 Guarducci (n. 10), 72.

49 M. Guarducci, "Una moneta della Necropoli Vaticana," *Rendiconti della Pontificia Accademia Romana di Archeologia* 39 (1966–7): 135–43.

50 Gressmann's German version, cited above in n. 47, reads: "…sodass er [d.h. Petrus] sogar einer herrlichen **Grabstätte** vor der Stadt gewürdigt wurde, **zu dem wie zu einem grossen Heiligtum und Tempel Gottes** Myriaden Scharen des römischen Reiches eilten." There is no room for ambiguity here. The Syriac text, as published by Lee (n. 47 above), is *wnrhtwn lh 'yk dlnws' rb' whykl' d'lh'*. The people were going to the *byt qbwr'* ("the tomb"). This is the antecedent noun for the "it" in *lh*, meaning "to it."

51 I am grateful to S. Ćurčić for drawing my attention to the rotundas, and to W. Tronzo for informing me that the preexisting Vatican rotunda remained separate from the church until a second one was built off the southern transept arm under Honorius. For the rotunda in Constantinople (Constantine's mausoleum), see the papers by Mango cited above in note 17. The westward orientation of St. Peter's and its construction technique (*opus listatum*) have been particularly associated with the Constantinian period, as Professor Ćurčić tells me, but obviously such projects do not cease overnight when an emperor dies, and we are considering here only the thirteen-year span immediately after Constantine's death.

52 R. Krautheimer, *Three Christian Capitals: Topography and Politics* (Berkeley, 1983), 62–3. Cf. recently S. Ćurčić, "From the Temple of the Sun to the Temple of the Lord: Monotheistic Contribution to Architectural Iconography in Late Antiquity," *Architectural Studies in Memory of Richard Krautheimer*, ed. C. L. Striker (Mainz, 1996), 55–9.

3

SPOLIA

DALE KINNEY

PROLOGUE

"THE TEMPLE OF THE PRINCE OF THE APOSTLES in the Vatican was not rich except for the columns, bases, capitals, architraves, cornices, doors, and other revetments and ornaments, which had all been taken from . . . buildings erected earlier with great magnificence."[1] So Giorgio Vasari judged the Early Christian basilica of St. Peter, which he knew partly from hearsay and partly from the remnant of the nave that was still standing when he wrote around 1568. From an artistic standpoint the building could be appreciated only for its reused ornament, which had been made in better times. In its day this was a relatively generous assessment. In the fifteenth century Alberti had pronounced St. Peter's a structural abomination:

> I have noticed in the Basilica of St. Peter's in Rome a crass feature: an extremely long and high wall has been constructed over a continuous series of openings, with no curves to give it strength, and no buttresses to lend it support. . . . The whole stretch of wall has been pierced by too many openings and built too high. . . . As a result, the continual force of the wind has already displaced the wall more than six feet from the vertical; I have no doubt that eventually some . . . slight movement will make it collapse. . . .[2]

The basilica's poor design was attributed by a later writer to the condition of the culture that produced it, "a crude age ignorant of finer architecture."[3] But Vasari knew that there was something worse than Early Christian design: Gothic. He preferred Early Christian buildings, claiming that the memory of ancient excellence was kept alive in them precisely by their reused columns and capitals, that is, by spolia. "Architecture . . . maintained itself, if not in as perfect a state [as in antiquity], at least better [than sculpture and painting] . . . and this was because since nearly all large [Early Christian] buildings were made of spolia, it was easy for architects in making new buildings to imitate in large part the old ones which they had always before their eyes."[4]

In the rebuilding that was begun in 1506, some of St. Peter's spolia were destroyed. This was quickly recognized as a mistake, since, as Michelangelo observed later, "it was easy to put one brick on top of another, but . . . to make such a column was extremely difficult. . . ."[5] When Antonio da Sangallo the Younger became head architect of the new construction in 1520, the surviving column shafts in the nave and aisles were carefully inventoried in drawings by his assistants, apparently with a view to reusing them (Figs. 13, 20). Following the erection of the "dividing wall" in 1538, everything that survived of the old basilica – the eastern half of the nave and aisles, the main altar and the apse, and the atrium – became objects of the sentimental and ideological attachment of a large faction, not only clergy, who lobbied to have them preserved.[6] Thanks to these attitudinal changes, Old St. Peter's is extremely well recorded. The astonishingly detailed ground plan by Tiberio Alfarano (Fig. 5) was a labor of love by a cleric who had lived at St. Peter's for twenty-six years by the time he completed the first version of it in 1571.[7] Alfarano's written description, finished in 1582, was informed by the recollections of his mentor, the *altarista* Giacomo Hercolano, "who taught me about all of the memorable antiquities before they were dismantled in order to make the church one sees today."[8] The other most extensive record of this period is the compilation of *Instrumenta autentica* by Giacomo Grimaldi, notary and archivist of St. Peter's, which documents day by day the destruction of altars, tombs, reliquaries, and eventually of roofs and walls following the papal decree of 3 October 1605 that the remaining parts of the old basilica should be demolished. Drawings of some of the condemned monuments were copied into the manuscript of the *Instrumenta* that was presented to Pope Paul V in 1620, and larger versions of them, two of which are signed by Domenico Tasselli, survive separately in an album in the archive

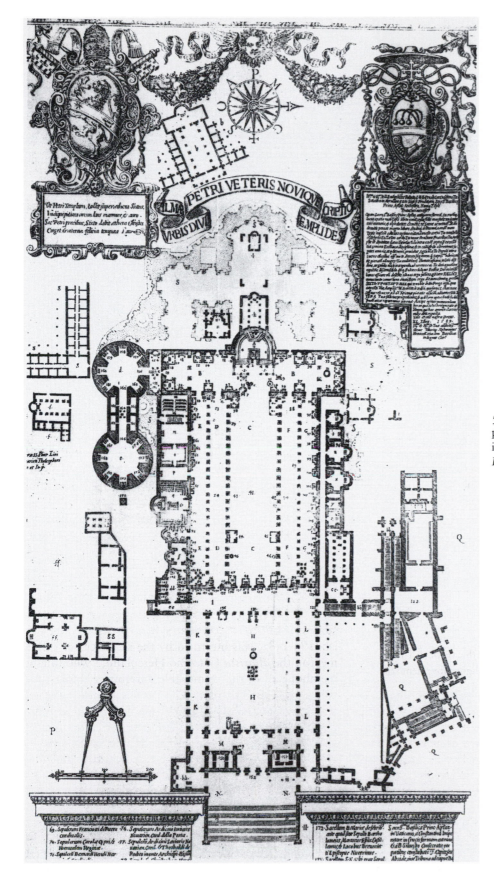

5. Ground plan of Old St. Peter's published by Tiberio Alfarano in 1590 (*Tiberii Alpharani De Basilicae . . . structura*)

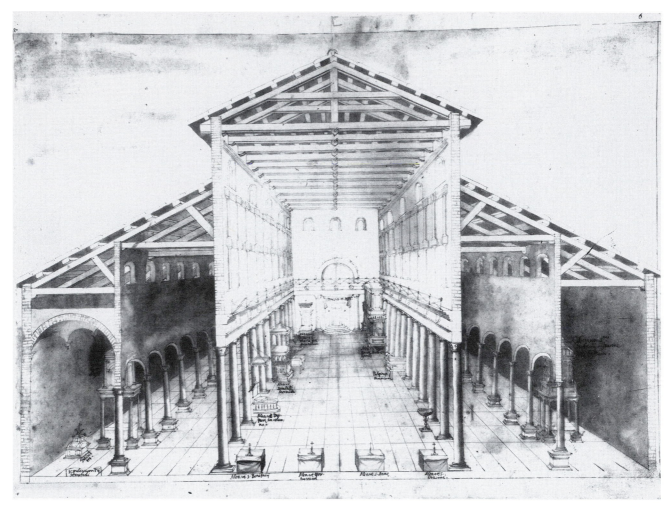

6. Old St. Peter's, transverse section through the nave and aisles by Domenico Tasselli, before 1620. Biblioteca Apostolica Vaticana, Vatican City, Archivio del Capitolo di San Pietro, A 64 ter, fol. 12ʳ. (Photo: © Biblioteca Apostolica Vaticana [Vatican])

of the chapter of St. Peter's in the Biblioteca Vaticana (Figs. 6, 7).[9]

Drawings of a different sort record St. Peter's as it stood after the sack of Rome in 1527, when the old building was semi-destroyed and the new one an abandoned fragment. Evidently intrigued by the spectacle of modern ruins, the draftsman rendered the site from every direction, with an accuracy that has seemed almost photographic to modern architectural historians. The well-known image of the nave drawn from a point near the entrance (Fig. 8) must have been made before the *muro divisorio* blocked this view in 1538.[10] Another drawing shows the crossing from inside the annex at the end of the north transept, with a column of the south annex visible in the distance and, in the middle ground, the early sixteenth-century "tegurium" that enclosed the main altar and what remained of its medieval surroundings (Fig. 9).[11] Information about the original disposition of this focal area was garnered by excavations conducted after 1939 underneath the

present basilica.[12] The finds confirmed that the shrine in front of the apse initially looked much like the image of it on the ivory box from Samagher now in Venice (Figs. 2, 10).[13]

The different, complementary sorts of evidence yield a fine-grained picture of the old basilica.[14] It was constructed on a platform made by leveling much of the cemetery where the tomb of St. Peter was thought to be, leaving only his marker – the "trophy" – rising above the ground. The apse was at the west, creating a monumental shell around the tomb, which stood under its front arch. The rest of the building formed a cross, with a long and relatively narrow transept (about 57 ft. deep) intervening between the apse and the longitudinal block of nave and four aisles (Fig. 11).[15] The transept was clearly a separate space, visible to the nave through a grand triumphal arch but screened from the aisles by pairs of columns carrying walls. The nave was long, wide, and high: nearly 298 feet by circa 77 1/2 feet by almost 125 feet to the ridge of the roof. It was defined by monumental

7. Facade of Old St. Peter's, drawing by Domenico Tasselli, before 1620. BAV, Archivio del Capitolo di San Pietro, A 64 ter, fol. 10^r. (Photo: © Biblioteca Apostolica Vaticana [Vatican])

colonnades (45 1/4 feet to the top of the architrave) that carried brick-faced walls soaring another 60 feet. The colonnades dividing the aisles were lower (ca. 25 1/2 ft. including their pedestals) and they carried walls only 29 ft. high. Light must have been brightest in the nave, where there were eleven large windows over 16 feet tall in each longitudinal wall, and six windows of the same size in the facade. Eleven smaller windows pierced each aisle wall. There is some evidence that the nave and transept had coffered ceilings.

The drawings by Tasselli (Fig. 6), though not to scale, give some sense of the audacity of the structure, which was both colossal and delicate, even fragile, although when Alberti disparaged the latter quality the basilica had already withstood 1,100 years. The nave alone was nearly as long as an American football field and taller than a ten-story building. It rose as high as the main vessel of Bourges cathedral, higher than the nave of Chartres, and it was considerably wider than both.[16] Yet the walls that extended to this elevation were sheer

verticals less than one meter thick, held in place by inertia and the roof beams.

The basilica was preceded by an atrium – the "paradise" of later documents – as long and wide as the nave and aisles (298 ft. × 216 1/2 ft.; Figs. 7, 12).[17] The atrium was paved with marble and featured a monumental fountain in the center. A portico on its west side doubled as the porch of the basilica, and there probably were porticoes on the other three sides as well.[18] The outer face of the east portico overlooked a flight of steps. Visitors coming to St. Peter's from this side – that is, from the city and the river – would have been unable to grasp the full extent of the complex until they had climbed the hill and passed through this facade and spaces began to open up to them: the huge atrium, the unimaginably long nave, and finally the transept. Coming from the south, it was possible to see remnants of the circus of Caligula and Nero, which stood on the site before the cemetery.[19] The obelisk that marked the *spina* of the circus and a rotunda which had been built next to the obelisk in the early third

8. Nave of Old St. Peter's and crossing piers of New St. Peter's in 1538, drawing in the style of Marten van Heemskerck. Berlin, Kupferstichkabinett 79 D 2a, fol. 52ʳ. (Photo: Staatliche Museen zu Berlin – Preussischer Kulturbesitz, Kupferstichkabinett/bpk, 2002)

9. View from the annex of the north transept with the *Colonna santa* in the middle ground at left, drawing in the style of Marten van Heemskerck, 1538. Statens Konstmuseer, Nationalmuseum, Stockholm, Coll. Ankersvärd 637. (Photo: Nationalmuseum)

century survived on the boundary of the new Christian complex, but visually and functionally they belonged to a zone outside St. Peter's, at least initially (Fig. 12).

Vasari was right that the principal adornments of the fourth-century basilica were its reused columns and their appurtenances. They were especially impressive in the nave. According to the sketches made by Peruzzi in the 1520s (Fig. 13), the monolithic nave shafts were of several different materials: "white granite," red granite, *cipollino*, and "mixed."[20] *Granito rosso*, Syenite or Assouan granite, was the stone of obelisks, called by the Romans *pyrrhopoecilos:* "mottled red." It can resemble

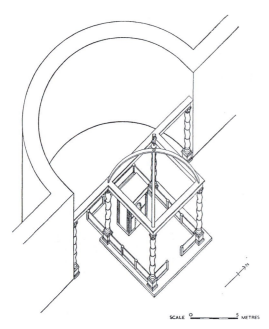

SCALE 0 ———————— 5 METRES

10. Shrine of St. Peter, reconstruction by Jocelyn Toynbee and John Ward Perkins, *The Shrine of St. Peter and the Vatican Excavations* (London, 1956), fig. 20

fire in the ember stage, glowing red with zones of black.[21] *Granito bianco* could designate a number of white-flecked granites, now usually vernacularly called "gray," from Asia Minor, Egypt, and Elba.[22] *Cipollino* is a pale-greenish Greek marble with darker gray-green veins, which when it is *undosa* billow and eddy like the sea.[23] By "mistio" Peruzzi apparently designated breccias, stones comprising varicolored fragments in a matrix. The six shafts so identified all stood near the entrance, at the first, third, and fourth spots from the door. Four were of *portasanta*, a mottled or striated, predominantly reddish marble from the imperial quarries on Chios. The other two were of Lucullan marble, popularly called "africano" (though it was quarried in Asia Minor) because the matrix is dark, and the red, white, and other colored particles glow against it.[24] The *africano* columns stood closest to the central doorway. The white marble columns that followed them probably were medieval replacements for two more shafts of *africano*, which, so Grimaldi opined, must have been "given away as a gift to some great prince."[25] Four pairs of richly colorful breccia columns would have made a magnificent opening of the nave. As it was, the two surviving shafts of *africano* were said by Alfarano to be "priceless...none similar are found anywhere in

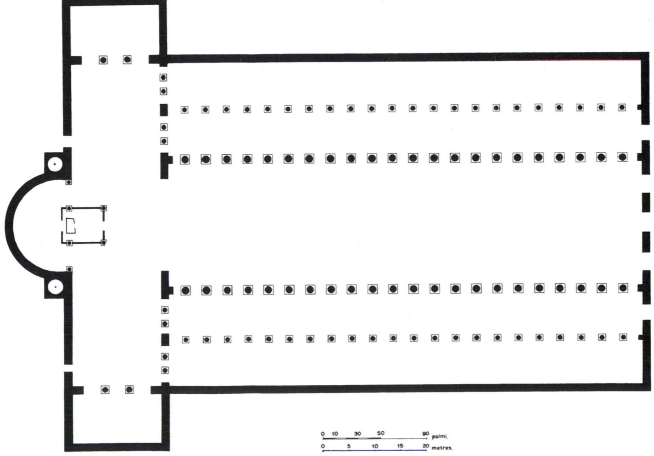

0 10   30   50   90 palmi.

0   5   10   15   20 metres.

11. Ground plan of Old St. Peter's by H. A. van Dijk, Jr. From J. H. Jongkees, *Studies on Old St. Peter's* (Groningen: 1966), pl. I

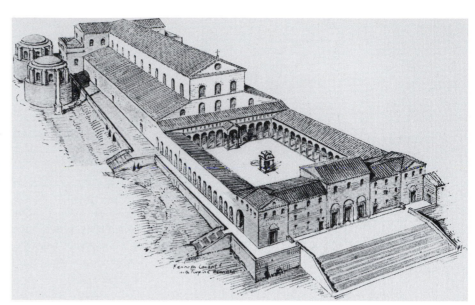

12. Reconstruction of Old St. Peter's in the fourth century by Kenneth John Conant and Turpin C. Bannister, *Carolingian and Romanesque Architecture 800 to 1200* (Harmondsworth, 1973), pl. IA

the city nor in the world"; they may also have been the columns that Pope Paul II (1464–71) is said to have valued "more than the whole city of Venice."[26] Although Lucullan marble was much more commonly encountered in the fourth century than in the fifteenth (all of the columns surrounding the central space of the Basilica Aemilia were of *africano*, for example), it was still very expensive, according to the Edict on Prices of 301.[27]

The columns dividing the aisles were smaller and presented a different combination of materials: "white" granite, red granite, "mixed," "striated" or "channeled" marble (i.e., fluted shafts, probably of a light-colored marble), and *saligno (salignia),* which seems to have been a veined marble similar to *cipollino*.[28] The capitals and bases of all four colonnades were heterogeneous, and some probably were fourth-century products rather than spolia. Five bases were discovered in the excavations of the 1940s: one in the line of the north nave colonnade, three from the aisle colonnades, and one on the site of the two-column screen that separated the north transept annex from the transept proper (Fig. 9). The base of the nave colonnade has a peculiarly flaccid profile, which Richard Krautheimer judged "barbarous" and therefore Constantinian. Two of the aisle bases are of limestone or travertine rather than marble, and may also have been made in the fourth century. The remaining two bases are older marble ones that were reused.[29]

The columns between the aisles carried arches, while those framing the nave supported a massive entablature, which projected so far from the plane of the wall that its upper surface formed a walkway, with an outer railing to prevent those who walked on it from falling into the nave (Fig. 6).[30] The walls above the entablature eventually were covered with paintings depicting scenes from the Old and New Testaments; these

usually are considered to be additions of the fifth century, when the eastern facade also was decorated with figural mosaic.[31] It cannot be determined whether any figural representation existed earlier in the basilica's decoration. In the sixteenth century Cardinal Domenico Jacobacci claimed to have seen on the triumphal arch a mosaic image of Constantine presenting a model of the basilica to Christ and St. Peter; this could have been a contemporary donor portrait, but equally well a later embellishment.[32]

Competing with the spolia for the viewer's admiration were the even more precious materials that set off the shrine and the upper reaches of the building. According to the sixth-century compilers of the *Liber pontificalis*, one of the founder's dedicatory inscriptions described his building as *coruscans*, flashing or glittering: "Constantine Augustus and Helena Augusta. A hall [the basilica] surrounds this royal house [the tomb], glittering with similar brightness."[33] In a letter written from Campania in 396, Bishop Paulinus of Nola remembered the basilica "gleaming from afar with the tomb of the apostle, strik[ing] the eyes of those who enter and rejoic[ing] their hearts."[34] "Gleaming" and "glittering" were topoi of contemporary architectural *ekphrasis*, but topoi are not necessarily unreal. The *Liber pontificalis* records that the conch of the apse over the tomb actually was covered with "sheets of gold."

Under the glittering apse, the shrine of Peter's tomb was cased in bronze and adorned with "columns of porphyry and other vined columns."[35] The latter must be the famous twisted columns that immediately became St. Peter's hallmark (Figs. 14, 15, 16). Probably made in the second or third century, they are the only spolia among Constantine's recorded donations. The notice that the emperor "brought them from Greece"

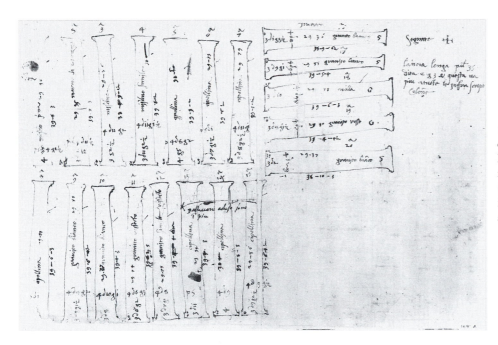

13. Shafts of the south nave colonnade, sketch by Baldassare Peruzzi. Uffizi, Florence, Gabinetto dei Disegni, Arch. 108ᵛ (Photo: by permission of the Ministero dei Beni e le Attività Culturali, 113979)

may be an allusion to their reuse, though it may also account for their exotic shape and decoration. The shrine underwent several rearrangements before it was finally dismantled in the sixteenth century.³⁶ At the end of the sixth century a higher floor was installed in the apse, covering the shrine so that an altar could be placed above it. A corridor was inserted under the floor to give access to the now buried tomb. The porphyry columns probably were removed from the tomb casing and reused to support a ciborium over the altar. The ciborium would later be remade many times: by Popes Leo III (795–814), Callistus II (1123), Honorius III (1216–17), and Sixtus IV (1471–84), always with porphyry columns.³⁷ When the altar was finally demolished in 1594, the porphyry columns were transferred to places of honor on the two major altars in the new transept, evidently in the belief that they came from the shrine of Constantine.³⁸ The Constantinian porphyry columns, however, seem to have been sent to S. Maria Maggiore by Pope Leo III, who replaced them with larger ones; it is the Carolingian replacements that survive in the present basilica.³⁹

In the first major rearrangement of the late sixth century, the "Greek" twisted columns were repositioned in a straight line before the new sanctuary. Much later, Pope Gregory III (731–41) obtained six more twisted columns from the Byzantine exarch. Engaged in a struggle to oppose the newly declared iconoclasm of Byzantium, Gregory III used his spolia, aligned in front of the original six, to support a silver-plated beam decorated with holy images.⁴⁰ The images were relatively short-lived, as the silver was replaced by Leo III and again after Arab raiders made off with it in 846.⁴¹ The twisted columns

remained in place, however, until Bramante dispersed the outer row in 1506–7.

The structure of the fourth-century basilica was almost unchanged in the millennium-plus of its existence, but many additions and rebuildings occurred outside it.⁴² Around 400, a second rotunda was erected on the south, between the third-century rotunda and the transept (Fig. 12). From this point forward, the monuments on the old circus *spina* were drawn into the functional sphere of St. Peter's, and after a century the older rotunda was dedicated to Saint Andrew by Pope Symmachus (498–514). The younger one (originally a mausoleum for the imperial family of Honorius and Galla Placidia) eventually was dedicated to Saint Petronilla by Pope Paul I (757–67).⁴³ Somewhat later Pope Leo III built a reception room "in Acoli," that is, near the obelisk, which had come to be called *agulia* (*acula*, from *acus*, needle). Pope Gregory IV (827–44) added an apartment "where the pope . . . could rest his limbs after matinal prayers or mass." In the twelfth century these rooms were still in use, under the name *domus Aguliae*.⁴⁴

The east end of the complex, outside the atrium, was improved and developed by Pope Symmachus, who also embellished the atrium itself and its fountain. The fountain went back to the fourth century, when Paulinus of Nola could recall "a dome of solid bronze [that] adorns and shades a *cantharus* serving flowing streams to our hands and faces, not without a mystic aspect surrounding the streams of water with four columns."⁴⁵ The facade of the atrium eventually acquired a blocky Carolingian aspect, with a central chapel called S. Maria in Turri. Pope Paul I covered the upper part of it with mosaic, and his near successor Hadrian (772–95), evidently exploiting

14. Twisted columns of the fourth-century donation, reused on the pier of St. Veronica. (Photo: Deutsches Archäologisches Institut, Rome, 79.3491)

15. Twisted columns of the eighth-century donation, reused on the pier of St. Longinus. (Photo: Deutsches Archäologisches Institut, Rome, 79.3498)

the concession of previously imperial and Lombard territories to the papacy, removed some bronze doors "of wondrous size" from Perugia and installed them in the doorway below.[46]

There were other post-Constantinian spolia in St. Peter's. Pope Honorius I (625–38) covered the roof with bronze tiles that he petitioned the emperor Heraclius to allow him to remove from the Temple of Rome in the Forum.[47] Had the pope not gotten to them first, the tiles might have been seized by the emperor Constans II, who notoriously "took down everything of bronze that adorned the city," including the bronze tiles of the Pantheon, for shipment to Constantinople in 667.[48] This may be cause to suspect that the giant bronze pinecone (Fig. 17) that eventually formed part of the atrium fountain was already in this privileged location by the seventh century, else the emperor might have made off with it as well. This is conjecture, because there is no written mention of the pinecone until the twelfth century, when it was the object of intensive antiquarian speculation.

The pinecone is typical of St. Peter's spolia in lacking its own history. Devoted to the memory of Peter and Constantine, the basilica subsumed its ornaments and likewise their pre-Christian histories. But Peter himself lacked history; there was no unambiguous record of when, where, why, and how he died and was buried.[49]

16. Twisted columns of the eighth-century donation (?), reused on the altar of St. Francis in the Cappella del SS. Sacramento. (Photo: Deutsches Archäologisches Institut, Rome, 79.3468)

Popular traditions proliferated and collided, and the construction of the basilica intervened in an ongoing production of memory. "The memory of [Peter] now is greater among the Romans than it was earlier so that he is deemed worthy of a glorious sepulture by the State..." – so wrote Eusebius in the 330s.[50] At the end of the fourth century, Jerome wrote more fully that Peter was buried "in Rome, in the Vatican, near the via Triumphalis."[51] The via Triumphalis did not pass the site of the circus of Nero where the Christian basilica was then standing. It ran closer to the "Gaianum," which may have been another circus, and to the Naumachia, both in an area northwest of the Mausoleum of Hadrian.[52] Jerome's toponymy may have reflected alternative traditions about Peter's death, or it may have been a mistake that spawned them later. In any case, by the sixth century different versions of the passion of Saint Peter buried him variously "under the Terebinth near the Naumachia" and "in a place called Naumachia next to the obelisk."[53] The first editions of the *Liber pontificalis* show a desperate effort to absorb or reconcile all conflicting possibilities: "He was buried on the via Aurelia, in the temple of Apollo, near the place where he was crucified, near the palace of Nero, in the Vatican, in the *territurium Triumphale....*"[54] The "temple of Apollo," found for the first time in this passage, entered St. Peter's history, like the spolia, from an unknown source.

SPOLIAVERUNT AEGYPTIOS

The obelisk is no longer a landmark of the circus. Moved over 800 feet from its previous location on the *spina*, it now stands in front of the basilica and serves as an enormous holder for a large bronze cross (Fig. 18).[55] The meaning of the ensemble is unambiguously explained by Latin inscriptions on the four sides of its base:

> Behold the cross of the Lord. Adversaries, flee. The lion of the tribe of Judah has conquered.

> Sixtus V Pontifex Maximus with great effort moved the Vatican obelisk, once dedicated to the impious cult of the gods of the pagans, to the threshold of the Apostles in the second year of his pontificate, 1586.

> Christ conquers, Christ reigns, Christ commands, Christ defends his people from all evil.

> Sixtus V Pontifex Maximus consecrated the Vatican obelisk, purged of filthy superstition, more justly and auspiciously to the invincible cross in the second year of his pontificate, 1586.[56]

The inscriptions resurrect the obelisk's religious significance in order to celebrate the triumph of Christianity over a generically pagan past. In a guidebook for pilgrims

17. Bronze pinecone and peacocks from the atrium fountain, now in the Musei Vaticani, Vatican City, Cortile della Pigna (Photo: Deutsches Archäologisches Institut, Rome, 83.308)

published two years later, Pompeo Ugonio took a somewhat different tack, re-creating the obelisk's specific history in order to sustain a metaphorical description of the present:

> Previously it was placed by Gaius Caligula in the circus that he built, and consecrated to the two emperors who preceded him, Augustus and Tiberius. At first one saw at the top of the obelisk a gilded metal ball, which was placed there to signify the globe of the world subject to the Roman empire; or to denote the globe of the sun, to which obelisks like this were particularly dedicated; or because, as rumor has it, the ashes of one of the Caesars were inside it. However it was, it was all profane and despicable. But now, just as Moses used the vessels of gold and silver taken from the Egyptians for the cult of the true God – just so, I say, this new Moses has despoiled the Egyptians of this towering mass, and appropriating it from the pagan emperors, he transferred it to the honor of him who is king of kings, and emperor of emperors....[57]

The Old Testament metaphor of the "spoils of the Egyptians," famously allegorized by Saint Augustine in the treatise *De doctrina christiana*, is often invoked by modern interpreters to explain the practice of using spolia in architecture and works of art.[58] Defined as artifacts made for one physical and cultural context, and reused in another, spolia seem to be natural symbols of succession or supersession, especially when the reused object is a classical antiquity and the new setting is Christian. The obelisk, of course, is more than classical; it is an

18. The Obelisk in Piazza S. Pietro. (Photo: Alinari 1933)

Ur-antiquity, literally a spoil of Egypt, and this makes the association with the biblical metaphor more insistent. The crowning cross seems to echo the Augustinian exegesis. According to Augustine, the precious goods of the Egyptians signified the treasures of pagan learning which Christians might appropriate for use in their study of the Bible; but he went on to warn that these riches would bring no good to those who had not immersed themselves in Christ's love, as measured by the cross. "In the Sign of the Cross the whole action of the Christian is described...."[59] Only the cross made Egyptian spoils worth taking. While such an obvious parallel to a seminal text by Saint Augustine is not surprising in a monument created in the 1580s, during the Counter-Reformation, historians must bear in mind that in the early fourth century, when St. Peter's was erected near the obelisk's domain, even Augustine had not yet been born. Then the obelisk's pagan significance was still vital, and the intrusion of the basilica could not have instantly suppressed it.

Pliny noted that the Vatican obelisk was the latest of three which had been taken to Rome by his time, after one erected by Augustus on the *spina* of the Circus Maximus and a second placed by the same emperor on a pavement in the Campus Martius, where it served as a giant sundial.[60] These trophy obelisks were more than exotic urban ornaments. Unlike Christians, traditional Romans did not attempt to dispossess them of their original religious meaning; on the contrary. The Roman mode of spoliation was just the opposite of what Saint Augustine would later prescribe. The obelisk in the Circus Maximus, removed from Heliopolis, was formally rededicated to the sun by Augustus in 10 B.C.E.[61] The connection of circuses with the sun was intimate and

perduring. Around 200 Tertullian figured it etymologically, tracing "circus" to Circe, the sun's daughter. He forbade Christians to go there.[62]

Tarred by association with two bad emperors, the Vatican circus fell early into disuse, and by the second century tombs had been built against its enclosing walls and over the track. Fourth-century biographies claim that Lucius Verus (d. 169) buried a favorite racehorse in a tomb "in Vaticano" and that Elagabalus (d. 222) drove an elephant quadriga "in Vaticano," "destroying the tombs which obstructed the way."[63] The last text has been read by at least one scholar as a satire on the reign of Constantine, and the quoted passage in particular as a parody of the razing of the Vatican cemetery in order to build St. Peter's.[64] Whether or not this interpretation is correct, the Christian erasure was remarkable: over one million cubic feet of earth were moved, obliterating the north side of the circus along with the tombs.[65] But the obelisk and the rotunda next to it were spared, and so was the Phrygianum, a famous shrine to Magna Mater (Cybele) where high-born pagans continued to perform and commemorate taurobolia long after St. Peter's was in use, until 390. Some of their altars were discovered in 1609 during the excavation for the new facade, "hammered to pieces by the Christians...and buried 30 *palmi* under the earth...."[66] The obelisk stood very near where the Phrygianum must have been. Any association with this mystery religion would have perpetuated its emblematic, if not its functional, relation to the sun cult.[67]

The sun was ubiquitous in the official religious culture of late antiquity. The "Unconquered Sun" was a particular patron of the emperor, especially of Constantine, whose early coins presented him as the companion

19. Drawing of the obelisk by Antonio Dosio, ca. 1548–69. Uffizi, Florence, Gabinetto dei Disegni, Arch. 2536 (Photo: by permission of the Ministero dei Beni e le Attività Culturali, 227473)

(Soli Invicto Comiti) and even the equivalent of Sol Invictus (Soli Invicti Aeterno Augusto).[68] Licinius, Constantine's equal in the eastern half of the empire, also acted in the name of Sol Invictus. After Constantine became sole ruler by defeating him in 324, his coins began to advertise another Sol, the Sun of Justice (Sol Iustitiae). The Sun of Justice was Christ.[69] The basilica on the Vatican was "Iustitiae sedis," according to an inscription read later in its apse.[70] It faced east, so that the rays of the rising sun were captured by the atrium and entered through the great doors of the nave.[71] In the fifth century Pope Leo I was aggrieved that "some Christians [still] think that they behave devoutly when, before arriving at the basilica of . . . Peter . . . , they climb the steps which go up to the platform . . . , turn themselves around towards the rising sun, and bow down to honor its shining disk."[72] The solar orientation of the new basilica evidently was redundant with the symbolism of the obelisk. With the definitive suppression of non-Christian cults in 391, however, this redundancy began to disappear. Eventually, its pagan meaning suppressed and then forgotten, the obelisk was subsumed into St. Peter's expanding chorography. It became the "needle," a familiar but enigmatic feature of the thoroughly Christianized terrain (Fig. 19).

COLUMNAE VALDE ADMIRABILES

The thresholds of St. Peter's basilica opened into grand avenues of columns, four rows of twenty-two each, eighty-eight shafts in all. Unlike the neoclassical suites of uniform color seen in S. Maria Maggiore or the rebuilt St. Paul's outside-the-walls, the colonnades of St. Peter's presented a spectrum of strongly differentiated hues: red, gray, green-striped, "mixed." Another pattern of difference appeared in their size, as the shafts in the nave varied by over a foot in height and diameter (from 28 ft. 5 in. to 29 ft. 5 in., and from slightly over 3 ft. to nearly 4 ft.), and those in the aisles even more (from 18 1/2 ft. to 20 1/4 ft., and from ca. 1 ft. 11 in. to ca. 2 ft. 8 in.).[73] Some of the architects' drawings of the sixteenth century align the shafts at their tops or bottoms (Fig. 20), which emphasizes the effect of their inequalities.[74] Builders of spoliate colonnades had to compensate for such vertical discrepancies among their shafts with differently sized capitals and bases, chosen or adapted to bring each complete column to the designated height of the architrave. Given the range of shaft

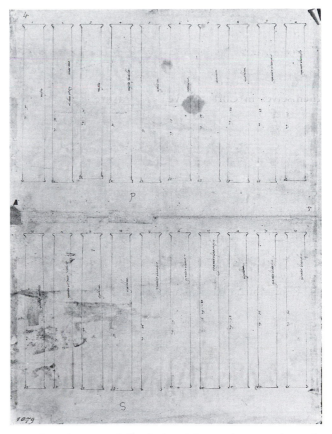

20. Clean drawing of the shafts of the south nave colonnade with tops horizontally aligned, after Arch. 108ᵛ, by the workshop of Antonio da Sangallo. Uffizi, Florence. Gabinetto dei Disegni, Arch. 1079ʳ (Photo: by permission of the Ministero dei Beni e le Attività Culturali, 310987)

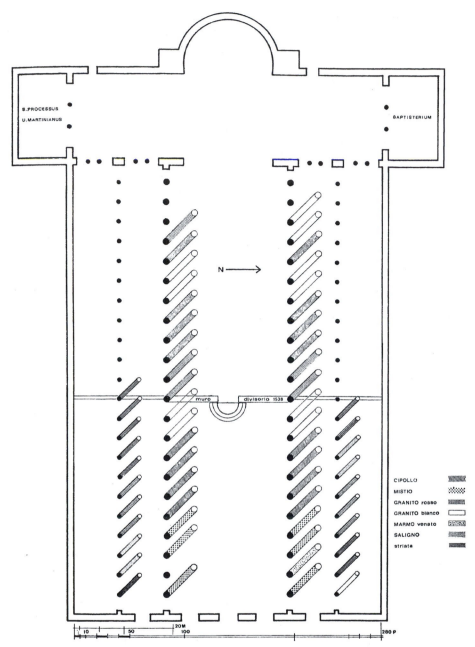

21. Distribution of materials in the nave shafts, analysis by Jürgen Christern, *Römische Quartalschrift* 62 (1967)

heights at St. Peter's, the colonnades could not have had the uniformly sized capitals and bases shown in the drawing of 1538 (Fig. 8), even if they had been all of one type. And they were not of one type; on the contrary, there is plenty of verbal evidence that the compensatory elements were even more miscellaneous than the shafts.

> One could see that … the basilica was built hastily by Constantine in a brief period of time. The capitals were partly complete, partly unfinished. Many bases were unlike the columns. … The lintels were of large marble blocks which were taken from the circus,

or from the ruins of another building, as the lower part gave evidence of having been buried, and under one of the slightly curved blocks could be seen carved roses; under another one could read these letters: CVM. SPECVLATOR. … [75]

The colonnades seemed to have been composed of refuse, dislocated pieces brought together as if in a parody of Vitruvian decorum. Most if not all of this material would have come from dilapidated public buildings or from official stockpiles of recyclable materials; witness the inscribed blocks of a long dedication by the emperor Trajan to Titus, which Grimaldi read when the frieze over the nave colonnade was dismantled: DIVO TITO DIVI . . . SIANO AVGVSTO IMP CAESAR DIVI NERVAE F, and so on.[76] Although this particular evidence of spoliation was not visible when the building was intact, it must have been obvious even in the fourth century that the marble ornaments came from multiple prior locations. To Grimaldi and his contemporaries, eclectic reuse was an index of hasty and opportunistic construction, and some viewers in late antiquity might have drawn the same conclusion.[77] Others, however, might have been disposed to see the heterogeneous assemblage as a museum of grandeur, a repository of heirlooms made more precious by their fortuitous, nonsystematic preservation.

F. W. Deichmann was the first to ask whether spoliate colonnades showed any principle of order. He found that in many fourth- and fifth-century examples, columnar elements (spoliate or not) were organized in pairs. Focusing on capitals, he did not find his "pair principle" at St. Peter's, but Jürgen Christern discovered it later in the shafts.[78] If the shafts stood in the order in which Peruzzi drew and numbered them, the same stones occurred in the same positions on both sides of the nave (Fig. 21).[79] And if this was so, the shafts must have been the organizing element optically as well as structurally. Distributed in clusters along the longitudinal axes, they formed easily visible blocks of color, three or four pairs of breccia at the entrance end, followed by four pairs of *cipollino*, two of gray granite, two of red granite, and so forth.[80] Clustering strengthened coloristic oppositions, thereby pointing to color and its variety as dominant aesthetic characteristics.

Variety has been isolated by the most recent interpreters as the driving aesthetic motive for the revolutionary use of spolia in late antiquity. Beat Brenk speaks of an "aesthetic of *varietas,*" grounding the term in ancient theories of rhetoric.[81] But *varietas* is also biblical. The bride of Psalm 44, an easy allegory of the Christian Church according to Saint Augustine, is *circumamicta varietate*, "enveloped in many colors."[82] The walls of the heavenly Jerusalem are described as green, standing on foundations adorned with green, blue, red, and purple gemstones.[83] It is not impossible that such passages encouraged the builders of St. Peter's to seek variety in their spolia, but even if it was unsought, the colonnades' diversity could have been perceived as meaningful. The colonnades are probably best understood as part of a larger semantic system comprehensively described by Michael Roberts, who observed it in many forms of art and literature of late antiquity. This "jeweled style" prized *variatio* as well as its attendant features, discontinuity and contrast.[84]

The *variatio* of spolia in St. Peter's and other contemporary buildings was a default virtue, as the breakdown of production in the imperial quarries impeded or precluded the provision – at least to the western provinces – of newly manufactured ornaments in non-Italian stones. In a context of industrial failure, the colonnades of St. Peter's were *bricolage*, an inspired improvisation in which the trophies of the old quarry system were recuperated and combined paradigmatically, rather than subordinated to the classical syntagma of the colonnade.

> [St. Peter] was buried in the church that for a long time has been called the Vatican. This church has four rows of truly spectacular columns [*columnarum valde admirabilium*], ninety-six in all. There are four more columns at the altar, which make a total of one hundred, excepting those that support the ciborium over the tomb.[85]

In Gregory of Tours's description of around 590, the columns are synecdochical; their number and quality represent the size and splendor of the basilica as a whole. This must have been how many visitors actually experienced the building, through the columns, counting them (or perhaps miscounting them, like Gregory's informant) as a way to mark their progress toward the shrine. Counting quantified the otherwise immeasurable space, and also provided an occasion to observe the columns individually, to enjoy their singular beauties and the *variatio* that many singularities produced.

COLUMNAE DEI RES SUNT

Tertullian scornfully dismissed the arguments of fellow Christians who claimed that the buildings in which pagan spectacles were staged were morally neutral because materially they were works of God: "the stones, cement, marbles, columns, are all God's own, who gave all those things to furnish the earth...."[86] He would have been aghast at St. Peter's, which was full of ornament from profane sources and even displaying pagan imagery. The most privileged spolia of the original basilica, the six large (15 1/2 ft. high) twisted columns of Greek marble that surrounded the apostle's tomb, were decorated with naked *amores* frolicking in the ancient Dionysiac motif of twining grapevines (Figs. 14–15). Much of this relief has been picked off, probably by pious souvenir seekers rather than irate iconoclasts. Urbane Christians of the fourth century would not have been offended by such imagery, although, strictly speaking, celebration of the orgiastic grape was considered quite objectionable.[87] The *Liber pontificalis* blandly describes the twisted columns as "vined columns brought from

Greece," and Gregory of Tours mentioned only their color ("shin[ing] like snow") and craftsmanship ("wonderfully elegant"), even though his informant must have been able to look closely at the iconography when he approached the shrine to thrust his head into the *confessio*.[88] The six similar columns added to the reconfigured precinct under Pope Gregory III (731–41) are described in his biography only as "twisted onyx columns," although they too are carved with vines (Fig. 16). Denoting a yellowish marble that was most prized, according to Pliny, when "honey-coloured, marked with spirals, and opaque," onyx is a misnomer that betrays a continuing tendency to categorize columnar ornament principally as wrought material, that is, as specimens of marvelous stones.[89]

Twisted columns – columns with torqued shafts, as opposed to cylindrical shafts with spiraled fluting – on an architectural scale are exceptionally rare.[90] It is remarkable that nearly all of the surviving examples are in St. Peter's, and more so that they came there in donations made more than four hundred years apart. The columns of the eighth-century donation, though virtually identical in type and size to those presented to the shrine in the fourth century, differ from them as well as among themselves in ornament and style; the differences are rendered clearly in a drawing by Étienne Dupérac of around 1575 (Fig. 22).[91] According to John Ward Perkins, three of these columns are datable to the third century and two to the first century (the sixth has disappeared). The six columns of the fourth-century gift are homogeneous and were ascribed to the late second or third century. These distinctions notwithstanding, archaeologists agree that all twelve columns were indeed "from Greece," perhaps from Ephesos where pieces of twisted columns with very similar relief decoration were excavated in 1957.[92]

These twelve were not the only twisted columns in St. Peter's in the Middle Ages. In 1452 the Nürnberger Nikolaus Muffel counted fourteen: "... there are also fourteen columns which once stood in the Temple of Solomon, which are all of the same manufacture, and two stand near the Veronica altar ... and the other twelve are in the choir...."[93] Grimaldi's illustrations show these two additional columns decorating the oratory of the Mother of God founded by Pope John VII (705–7) at the east end of the outer north aisle, where the altar of the Veronica was established later (Fig. 23).[94] Originally an enclosure abutting the basilica's inner facade, the oratory was partially dismantled in 1499 when the *porta santa* was broken through the facade where its altar had been, and the enclosing walls were demolished to facilitate the movement of pilgrims.[95] This is only one reason to suspect that the seventeenth-century documentation may not record the chapel's ornament as it was originally

installed, yet most scholars assume that the drawings show the twisted columns in their eighth-century position, framing the site of the altar and carrying a shallow barrel vault inscribed "The House of Mary Holy Mother of God."[96]

The six strips with vine scrolls that also appear in Grimaldi's drawings were unequivocally identified by him and others with a set of five pilasters carved with foliage and figures, which survive in the grottoes underneath the modern basilica (Fig. 24).[97] They are datable by style to around the turn of the third century.[98] The principal pilaster, about one-and-a-half times wider than the others, is devoted to Apollo, who appears in two forms: at the bottom as oracle, leaning on the Delphic tripod; and at the top as patron of the arts, with his lyre, the defeated Marsyas, and the muses of tragedy and comedy. In the center of this shaft is the personification of Tellus, the fruitful earth, surrounded by busts of the four seasons. The remaining four pilasters are decorated with animals and armed *amorini* who seem to be hunting them, while pairs of *amores* hold wreaths at the top.

The profuse, unmistakably pagan imagery of the spolia in Pope John VII's chapel seems hard to reconcile with the ostentatious Christian piety of this self-styled "servant of the Mother of God." The pope's epitaph aggressively dissembled the contradiction:

> Ancient squalor cleared away, ornament from everywhere
> He collected here, so that posterity would marvel at its abundance.
> Not from desire for show, which under him fled the world,
> But from pious passion for the Mother of God.[99]

The epitaph represents the spolia as precious residues of urban renewal, and the reference to "ancient squalor" (*prisco squalore*) seems to echo late antique inscriptions praising prefects and other officials for rescuing marble statues from "filthy places."[100] The ornament came from "everywhere" (*omne loco*), not necessarily the Vatican. The coincidence between the Apolline iconography of the principal pilaster and the assertion in the *Liber pontificalis* that St. Peter's was built in a temple of Apollo is striking but equivocal.[101] It is impossible to know whether the pilaster inspired the story or, vice versa, the story justified the eighth-century acquisition of the pilaster. Of the twisted columns one can at least say that they must have come from the same site as some of the columns in the transept. In the seventeenth-century drawings they look much like some of the shafts sketched by Dupérac (Fig. 22), with a zone of spiral fluting below an area about twice as high, carved with foliage.[102] These are the columns dated to

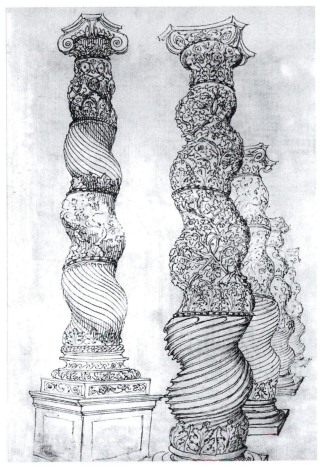

22. Drawing of five twisted columns by Étienne Dupérac, ca. 1575. Kupferstichkabinett, Berlin. KdZ 16792 (Photo: Staatliche Museen Zu Berlin – Preussischer Kulturbesitz, Kupferstichkabinett/bpk, 2002)

the Flavian period by Ward Perkins. The building whence they were despoiled must have been imperial property (as indicated by the involvement of the exarch in 731–41); and the father of Pope John VII, notoriously, was the *cura palatii* (curator of the palace) in Rome.[103] He died before John became pope, however, so this is another coincidence that titillates without resolving the question of where the columns were procured.

Of equally obscure origin is the colossal pinecone (*pigna*), over 11 feet tall, which dominated the immediate approach to the basilica as the centerpiece of the fountain in the atrium (Figs. 17, 25). Signed by its maker, the freedman Publius Cincius Salvius, the *pigna* has been dated on the basis of the letter forms to the first century C.E.[104] It may have been made as a fountain. As icons of fecundity and regeneration, pinecones appeared from time immemorial on the tip of the Bacchic thyrsus. The Romans placed them in fountains, and monumental cones were also placed as finials on funerary buildings, with the same symbolic connotations.[105] In late antiquity, the most conspicuous use of the ancient regenerative symbolism was made by the cultists of Cybele, whose rites, as noted earlier, were practiced on St. Peter's doorstep until the very end of the fourth century. The pine tree signified Cybele's fickle lover, Attis, and the ritual felling of a pine on the spring equinox, during the public festival called Hilaria, baldly symbolized Attis's castration, thanks to which he was able to rise to a higher order of being.[106] Pine trees with prominent cones appear on most of the taurobolium altars that have survived, including those attributable to the Vatican Phrygianum.[107]

In its most complete form, recorded in several

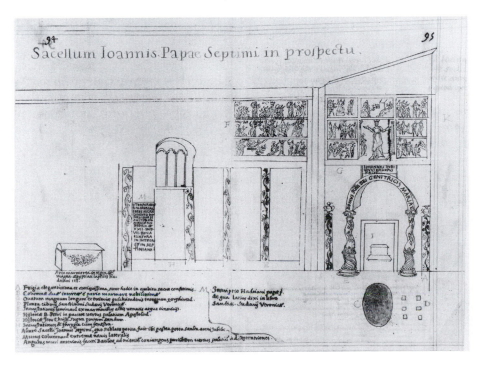

23. Drawing of the oratory of Pope John VII in the presentation copy of Grimaldi's *Descrizione*. Biblioteca Apostolica Vaticana, Vat. Barb. Lat. 2733, fols. 94[v]–95[r]. (Photo: © Biblioteca Apostolica Vaticana [Vatican])

24. Ornamental pilasters from the oratory of Pope John VII, now in the Vatican Grottoes. (Photo: Musei Vaticani XV.2.27)

drawings of the fifteenth and sixteenth centuries (Figs. 7, 25), St. Peter's fountain was a fabulous concoction enclosed by eight porphyry columns forming a kind of cage around the *pigna*.[108] At least two of the porphyry shafts bore the projecting bust of a deified emperor (Fig. 26).[109] The columns were joined by marble parapets carved with confronted griffins, and they supported architraves, which in turn carried bronze lunettes filled with grilles. In front of one of the lunettes was a pair of gilded bronze peacocks, and a bronze dolphin shot out at each corner. Crowning each lunette was a wreathed *chrismon*, the monogram often identified as the sign given to Constantine at the Milvian Bridge. It was a triumphal sign par excellence, and with the pagan *pigna* in the center, the whole assemblage seems like an image of religious conquest, not unlike the cross-bearing obelisk that eventually replaced it in front of the basilica's facade

(Fig. 18). In the Middle Ages, however, the triumphalist connotations would not have been construed as they were in the Counter-Reformation, not least because the *pigna* probably did not stand for paganism then as the obelisk was made to do later.

The *pigna* fountain was a cumulative work of art. In the fourth century, Paulinus of Nola saw four columns carrying a bronze canopy. The "Life" of Pope Stephen II (752–7) describes a remaking: "he renewed eight marble sculpted columns of wondrous beauty; he linked them on top by stone blocks, and over the top he placed a bronze roof."[110] There is no mention in this passage of the *pigna*, or of the peacocks or the dolphins. All of these elements could have been already present in the preexisting fountain, or they could have been added later, after the mid-eighth century.[111] A *terminus ante quem* may be inferred from the bronze pinecone fountain

25. Drawing of the fountain of the *pigna* by an anonymous draftsman, after 1489. Uffizi, Florence, Gabinetto dei Disegni, Santarelli 157ᵛ. (Photo: by permission of the Ministero dei Beni e le Attività Culturali, 333339)

26. Porphyry columns with bust of Trajan possibly from the fountain of the *pigna*, now in the Louvre, Paris. (Photo: Réunion des Musées Nationaux)

that was erected – evidently in some relation to St. Peter's – in the courtyard of the palace chapel at Aachen, but the date of the Aachen pinecone is uncertain, and may be as late as circa 1000.[112]

In the twelfth century it was said that the *pigna* had once crowned the Pantheon. Moved by this suggestion, topographers since the fourteenth century have supposed that it was taken from the city district still called Pinea, which does not include the Pantheon but is nearby.[113] Despite the etymological parallel, however, there is no archaeological basis for tracing the *pigna* to the Campus Martius.[114] Other possible points of origin include the Vatican Phrygianum, whose ornaments – perhaps including the obelisk – would have become available after the 390s, and the Mausoleum of Hadrian, which is commonly believed to have been the source of other components of the fountain, notably the bronze peacocks and the porphyry column shafts.[115]

On the base of the pinecone at Aachen are four figures personifying the rivers of paradise. This implies that the pinecone's Roman model was also understood as paradisiac, a symbolic fountain of life.[116] The peacocks and the *chrismon* would have been consonant with such a message. If this was the intended meaning of the ensemble, the pinecone's medieval reception was unusual. Unlike the obelisk, whose solar symbolism had to be forgotten, or the twisted columns, whose Dionysiac references were tactfully ignored, the pinecone passed into the semantic domain of St. Peter because of its ancient symbolism rather than in spite of it. It continued to be an emblem of renewal, synecdochically representing the tree which, though dead in one instantiation, returns more vigorous than ever in another. Only history had to be forgotten: the pre-Christian times and places in which the very same meaning of the pinecone had been celebrated by adepts of other religions, in homage to other gods.

PEREGRINORUM ET ROMANORUM VANAE FABULAE

> Within the palace of Nero is the temple of Apollo, which is called St. Petronilla, in front of which is the basilica which is called Vatican.... And there is another temple which was Nero's wardrobe, which is now called St. Andrew. Next to it is the memorial of Caesar, that is the *agulia*, where his ashes rest honorably; and just as while he was alive the whole world was subjected to him, so now that he is dead it will lie beneath him til the end of time.... The upper part at the apple, where he lies, is decorated with gold and precious stones. There it is written: "Caesar, you were once as great as the world / But now you are closed inside a little space."[117]

Around the middle of the twelfth century, an anonymous Roman composed the text now called *Mirabilia urbis Romae*.[118] Acknowledged by historians to be a key text of the so-called *renovatio* of the twelfth century, the *Mirabilia* is remarkable for its attempt to recover the history of the landmarks and topography of pre-papal Rome. Its author – probably a cleric – worked from basic administrative sources like the *Liber pontificalis*; from a few classical works, including Ovid's *Fasti*; and from decades or centuries of local tradition. In the excerpt quoted, the "palace of Nero" and the "temple of Apollo" follow the *Liber pontificalis*, and "Nero's wardrobe" (*vestarium Neronis*) is an extrapolation from the same source.

The interpretation of the obelisk is more original and dynamic, constructed by a process that has been called "novelistic etiology."[119] Interpretations in this mode depart from conspicuous or puzzling details of the object in question and explain them by incorporation into a coherent story developed by inference, association, and the logic of narrative itself. In the case of the obelisk, the salient details were two identical inscriptions at the bottom and the bronze globe at the top. The inscriptions had been incised into opposing faces of the monument in the reign of Tiberius (14–37 C.E.):

> DIVO CAESARI DIVI IVLII F(ilio) AVGVSTO / TI(berio) CAESARI DIVI AVGVSTI F(ilio) AVGVSTO / SACRVM.

Later the letters were partially erased, and the crux TI(berio) can now be read on only one side.[120] Medieval readers failed to make it out.[121] DIVO CAESARI DIVI IVLII does not mean "to the divine Julius Caesar," but it was

close enough. Caesar was dead. The shaft inscribed with his name must be his monument; if so, his ashes would be in the globe on its tip. Good stories have morals, and the moral of this one was obvious: earthly greatness is always reduced to dust. There was a verse about that; it must be inscribed under the globe, even if one could not see it.[122]

About fifty years later, another text called "Marvels of Rome" was produced by a visiting Englishman known only as "Master Gregory."[123] This author had much more classical learning than his twelfth-century predecessor, and he professed to despise the "frivolous tales (*vanae fabulae*) of pilgrims and the Romans," yet his own explication of the obelisk is not fundamentally different from theirs:

> There are many pyramids in Rome, but of all of them the one which deserves the greatest admiration is the pyramid of Julius Caesar, made of a single porphyry block.... They say that its height is 250 feet. At the top there is a bronze sphere, in which Julius Caesar's ashes and bones are deposited. Someone marvelling at it has commented: "If it be one stone, tell me how it was raised. / If there be many stones, tell me where they join." They say that it stands on the spot where a certain person encountered Julius, who was on his way to an assembly [there follows what Gregory remembered of Suetonius, 1.81–2, and a quotation of three lines from Vergil's fifth *Eclogue*].... And so Caesar, lord and master of the world...now reposes in this bronze sphere, his body reduced to ashes. The pilgrims call this pyramid "St. Peter's Needle," and they make great efforts to crawl underneath it, where the stone rests on four bronze lions, claiming falsely that those who manage to do so are cleansed from their sins....[124]

Master Gregory was able to improve the basic tale with erudite quotations, moving by literary association from the name of Caesar to Suetonius's account of Caesar's death to Vergil's epitaph for Daphnis, which was explained by Servius as an allegorical reference to Caesar.[125] The result was unquestionably much more scholarly, but no closer to modern standards of history than the *Mirabilia urbis Romae*.[126]

The *pigna* did not offer narratable details, and its story was constructed in another way:

> In the paradise of St. Peter is the cantharus which was made by Pope Symmachus, adorned with porphyry columns connected by marble plaques with griffins.... In the middle of the cantharus is the bronze pinecone, which with a gilded bronze grate was the cover above the statue of Cybele, mother of the gods, in the hole of the Pantheon....[127]

In this case the author of the *Mirabilia* seems to have created a history of the artifact by importing knowledge of another site. A previous chapter relates that Agrippa, who founded the Pantheon in fulfillment of a vow to Cybele, "in honor of this same Cybele...made a gilded statue, which he placed on the top of the temple over the hole, and he put over it a wonderful cover of gilded bronze." In the Christian era Pope Boniface [IV] asked the emperor Phocas to cede the temple to him, "so that just as on the kalends of November it had been dedicated in honor of Cybele, mother of the gods, so he would dedicate it on the kalends of November to the blessed ever-virgin Mary, who is the mother of all saints."[128] A purposeful parallelism of the pagan and Christian dedications – all gods, all saints – was remarked by Bede in the eighth century, but Cybele seems to have been a twelfth-century innovation.[129] The attribution of the pinecone to the Pantheon is also a twelfth-century invention, evidently connected to the fictive statue. If the association of the pinecone with Cybele rested on a vestigial knowledge of the ancient symbolism of her cult, this would be an exceptional instance in a text that normally feigns antiquity with "fables," as they would be disparaged by Master Gregory and, more justifiably, by Boccaccio.[130] Even in the time of Boccaccio, however, the *pigna* continued to inspire fabulous improvisation. Around 1350, Hermann of Fritzlar wrote that when the pope converted the Pantheon to Christ, "the devil took the pinecone away from the top...carried it in front of St. Peter's...and the hole in the church where the pinecone was...remains open and nobody wants to close it."[131]

Pilgrims produced fables of another sort, like the one dismissively reported by Master Gregory, of sinners being cleansed by crawling under the *agulia*. Pilgrim fables satisfied the desire for healing or theophany that drew pious travelers to Rome. Some such fables must have been the pilgrims' own productions; others were invented for them, more or less cynically, by the custodians of shrines seeking to attract their business. The tale of the twisted columns is a case in point:

> This is the column on which leaned our Lord JESUS CHRIST. He stood against it while he preached to the people and prayed to God the Father in the Temple. Brought in triumph with the other eleven columns here surrounding it from the Temple of Solomon, it was placed in this basilica. It expels demons and restores those afflicted by unclean spirits to freedom, and it performs many miracles daily. Adorned by the most reverend father and lord Cardinal Orsini in the year of our Lord 1438.[132]

The Orsini cardinal in question must have been Giordano, who died on 29 May in the year of this inscrip-

tion, which was incised in a marble parapet surrounding one of the twisted columns of the outer (eighth-century) screen in the transept (Fig. 22). It is unsettling to find a very notable humanist, owner of the best classical and patristic library in Rome, sponsoring this patent fabrication, but by the time of Giordano Orsini the story was guaranteed by decades of pious repetition.[133] The "Colonna Santa" was already healing demoniacs in 1382, when it was described as "white, sculpted, surrounded by wooden gates;...carried long ago from Jerusalem from the Temple of Solomon, [where] Christ had leaned against it while he was preaching."[134] The picture of Jesus reclining against the column may have been justified by a passage in St. John's Gospel that describes the lord disputing with some Jews while "he was walking in the Temple, in the portico of Solomon."[135] But in every other respect, the association of the Dionysian twisted marble shafts in St. Peter's with any of the buildings in Solomon's precinct seems almost perverse. If nothing else, everyone should have known that the distinctive columns of the Temple, Iachin and Booz, were of bronze.[136]

Two texts from the reign of Pope Alexander III (1159–81) offer evidence that the Solomonic origins of St. Peter's twisted columns was not yet common belief. On the one hand, Petrus Mallius's *Descriptio Basilicae Vaticanae*, a detailed guide to St. Peter's devotional attractions, repeats the tradition of the *Liber pontificalis* that the twisted vined columns were gifts of Constantine "from Greece," only specifying that "Greece" meant "the temple of Apollo at Troy."[137] On the other hand, the account of his travels by the Spanish Jew Benjamin of Tudela, who passed through Rome around 1160, records an encounter with columns from the Temple, not in St. Peter's but in the Lateran cathedral: "In the church of St. John in the Lateran there are two bronze columns taken from the Temple, the handiwork of King Solomon, each column being engraved 'Solomon the son of David.' The Jews of Rome told me that every year on the ninth of Ab they found the columns exuding moisture like water."[138] The columns that wept each year on Tisha be-Av, the day when the Temple was destroyed, were probably among the four colossal bronze shafts still in the cathedral today, on the altar of the SS. Sacramento. In the Middle Ages they stood in a row across the nave, a vestige of the *fastigium*, one of Constantine's foundation gifts to the cathedral.[139] The *Descriptio Lateranensis Ecclesiae*, written originally in the eleventh century and revised in the time of Benjamin of Tudela, refers to these "four marvelous columns of copper" but says nothing of a Solomonic provenance, which may then have been only secret lore among the Jews.[140] Other Roman texts of the twelfth century trace the Lateran's columns to diverse origins, including the Capitol and the temple of Jupiter, where – according to an embellishment by

Master Gregory – they had supported the bronze equestrian statue known today as Marcus Aurelius.[141] There was a long-standing tradition that other relics from the Jerusalem Temple were kept in the Lateran, however, and by the end of the thirteenth century the bronze columns had been officially assimilated to them. A mosaic inscription on the wall of the cathedral's new apse, dated 1291, advertised that:

> . . . Titus and Vespasian had this ark and the candelabrum and . . . the four columns here present taken from the Jews in Jerusalem and brought to Rome. . . .[142]

St. Peter's claim to have Solomonic columns may go back to the twelfth or thirteenth century, when Roman marble workers produced the half-sized imitations of the twisted shafts that are preserved in SS. Trinità dei Monti in Rome and in a church at Cave, near Palestrina. The plinths of the columns in Cave are inscribed "marble columns of the Temple of Solomon," but probably by a post-medieval hand.[143] The origin of the legend probably had something to do with a widespread interest in supposedly Solomonic structures awakened by the Crusades, and with the related vogue for knotted columns. Traceable to the tenth or eleventh century in Byzantine art, knotted or braided columns could be seen in Crusader additions to the buildings in Jerusalem, and there were monumental examples in Italy by 1135, the date of Ferrara cathedral. Some of these knotted columns – though not those at Ferrara – are explicitly labeled Iachin and Booz.[144] Pilgrims with knowledge of such columns might have urged one another to recognize the twisted shafts of St. Peter's as somehow like them, and faced with a growing demand for more visible and tangible relics, the canons might have been happy to indulge their speculations.[145] However it came about, the transformation of the twisted columns from Grecian gifts of Constantine to Jewish spolia marked a victory for St. Peter's in a hot, almost vicious battle with the Lateran for prestige.[146] To this day, the phrase "Solomonic columns" denotes, however implausibly, torqued shafts and, often, viny ornament.[147]

"[LA] MATERIA CH'HÀ DELL'ETERNO"

Solomonic columns were among the first casualties of what would ultimately be a devastating campaign to build the new basilica. In the second edition of his life of Bramante, Vasari wrote that the architect "demolished half of [the old building]" to erect the four great piers and their arches, which would eventually support the dome. In his zeal for the project, "they say," Bramante destroyed many tombs, paintings and mosaics; "he saved only the altar of St. Peter and the old apse, and around it

27. Twisted columns from the eighth-century donation (?) reused on the altar of the Corpus Christi, drawing by Domenico Tasselli. Biblioteca Apostolica Vaticana, Archivio del Capitolo di San Pietro, A 64 ter, fol. 22ʳ. (Photo: © Biblioteca Apostolica Vaticana [Vatican])

he made an ornament of a beautiful Doric order. . . ."[148] The "detestable and lachrymatory ruin of the Basilica" made life miserable for the papal master of ceremonies, whose diary recounts the indignities that turned many a mass at the papal altar into farce. The situation was mitigated, but not resolved, by the construction of the tegurium (the Doric "ornament") in 1514.[149] The tegurium abutted the apse, enclosing the altar and the inner row of twisted vined columns. The outer row of columns was taken away except for the Colonna Santa, which remained with a protective grille amid the debris of the transept (Fig. 9). The Colonna Santa continued to stand there until 1544, when it was moved to a spot in front of the northeast pier. When Bernini's program for the crossing found no place for it, it was moved again, more than once. It now stands outside the basilica entirely, among other once auratic objects in the Museo Storico-Artistico.[150]

28. Raphael's cartoon for The Healing of the Lame Man, showing the Portico of Solomon with twenty twisted columns. Victoria and Albert Museum, London. (Photo: Courtesy of the Trustees of the V&A Picture Library)

The odysseys of the five demounted columns of the outer screen are hard to trace. Two were identified by John Ward Perkins as framing the relic niche on the pier of St. Longinus (Fig. 15).[151] It is not known where they spent the years between 1507–14 and 1606, when they would have been among the ten twisted columns deployed around the new papal altar in the apse.[152] Six of these ten columns came from the inner screen of the old shrine, liberated from the *tegurium* in 1592.[153] They too wound up decorating the relic niches made in the 1620s by Bernini.

"Two large twisted vined columns" were among the donations made by Pope Paul III before 1548 to the chapel of the Corpus Christi (Fig. 27) on the south side of the old nave.[154] When this chapel was demolished in 1605, parts of it were given to "Cardinal Farnese" (Odoardo Farnese, 1591–1626), but the source does not say that the twisted columns were part of the gift.[155] Probably, they are the columns now framing an altar in the chapel of the Holy Sacrament on the north side of the basilica (Fig. 16), which have been identified as the Corpus Christi columns by Irving Lavin and as the supernumerary columns from the chapel of Pope John VII by John Ward Perkins.[156] Either way, since only eleven columns, including the Colonna Santa, still exist, three twisted columns are missing: three from the donation of the eighth century, or one from that donation and two from the oratory of Pope John VII.

It is hard to imagine that even a single column from the Temple of Solomon was allowed to simply disappear in the sixteenth century, but it seems to have happened. Only three of the six outer shafts came through the period intact (the Colonna Santa and the two on the pier of St. Longinus); two (if they are the shafts in the Holy Sacrament chapel) are pieced together.[157] It

may be that these were the columns "broken in many parts" in Bramante's clumsy demolition.[158] If the architect was careless, it was not because the legend of the spoils of Jerusalem had ceased to be credible with the dawn of the Renaissance. On the contrary, the myth was treated more seriously than ever in the sixteenth century, achieving pictorial apotheosis in Raphael's tapestry of St. Peter Healing the Lame Man of 1515–21 (Fig. 28). Raphael's careful preparatory studies of the columns circulated among his followers for years afterward.[159] The final image shows the miracle taking place in the portico of Solomon, which is reconstructed with no fewer than twenty twisted columns almost exactly like those of the then still extant inner screen, although their material has been upgraded to silver.[160]

Some of the anonymous shafts of the nave and aisle colonnades may also have gone missing under Bramante, but on the whole they were treated with respect. The drawings of 1538 show that, although the western half of the nave and the transept had been unroofed, so much of the colonnades and walls was still standing that it is difficult to imagine how the colossal piers could have been built without disturbing them.[161] According to the analysis of Alberto Carlo Carpiceci, the piers had replaced five columns on each side of the nave; counting from the entrance, columns 1–12, 15–17, and 21–22 were still erect (Fig. 8).[162] In the transept, the two-column screens of the annexes were completely preserved with much of the walls above them, and four of the eight columns at the ends of the aisles also were still in situ (Fig. 9). These results accord approximately with the sketches of the nave shafts by Peruzzi (Fig. 13), which indicate that five columns on each side had been demounted ("intera" = *in terra*), fifteen on each side were standing, and two on each side were missing.

29. Composite capital in Old St. Peter's drawn by Bernardo della Volpaia. Sir John Soane's Museum, London, Codex Coner no. 151. (Photo: The Conway Library, Courtauld Institute of Art, B84/887)

Plans to reuse these ancient columns have been discerned by scholars of the new basilica in projects ranging from Bramante's of 1506 through those of Antonio da Sangallo the Younger after the sack of Rome.[163] Such speculations should be controlled by what is known about the quantity and quality of the spolia. The brilliant fluted shafts that presently frame the central niches in the north and south cross arms – focal points of the cruciform space – are almost exactly the size of the old nave shafts, but because they are of *giallo antico*, a material not recorded by Peruzzi et al. among those columns, they must have been acquired elsewhere. Archaeologists are convinced that they came from the Forum of Trajan.[164] These specimen marbles are set off in the lateral niches by couples of red granite, gray granite, and *cipollino*, all stones that were present in the old nave. But under scrutiny some of the granite shafts here and in the northeast corner chapel of S. Michele appear to be amalgams of disparate pieces, even of different stones. Sandro Lorenzatti has argued that they are columns from the Temple of Venus and Rome, which were purchased, whole and in pieces, from S. Maria Nova between 1545 and 1547.[165]

> Whereas for the building of the fane of the Prince of the Apostles it is of greatest importance that it be provided with an abundance of stones and marbles...[and] it seems that the ruins of the City can most easily supply them...I authorize you, as master of the construction, to buy for me all of such marbles and stones which might be dug up here in Rome, or outside Rome for the distance of 10,000 paces, as might be suited for the construction of the temple....[166]

30. Composite capital in Old St. Peter's, drawing attributed to Giovanni Francesco da Sangallo. Uffizi, Florence, Gabinetto dei Disegni, Arch. 1804ᵛ. (Photo: by permission of the Ministero dei Beni e le Attività Culturali, 113991)

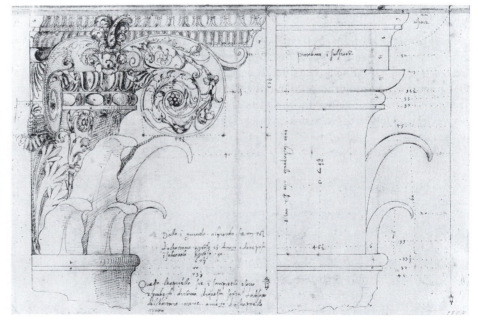

31. Corinthian order in Old St. Peter's, drawing attributed to Alberto Alberti. Istituto Nazionale per la Grafica, Rome, FN 8066. (Photo: by permission of the Ministero per i Beni e le Attività Culturali)

The brief of Pope Leo X on behalf of Raphael is dated 27 August 1515, but it must have been evident from the very beginning that a building on the supercolossal scale envisioned by Bramante could not have been outfitted using only what was available in situ. Stones were being prospected before the brief. A drawing attributed to Fra Giocondo is captioned: "this cornice was found at the Arco di Camigliano and I measured it at St. Peter's."[167] Documents concerning the bringing of columns go back at least to 1521, but many more shafts were imported in the 1540s, when the construction site of St. Peter's became like an enormous maw into which tons and tons of stones from Rome's most venerable monuments were tossed to be chewed into dust.[168]

This is not to say that the old columns were not valued by the multiple architects of the new basilica; but it seems important to distinguish the accidents of the spolia from the ideal they were made to represent. The nave shafts live on in the present building as a module, regulating the scale of the ground-level niches that organize the undulating perimeter around the three cross arms and their corner chapels. This idea goes back to Antonio da Sangallo the Younger, and Michelangelo

followed through with it.[169] It may have been executed initially with some or all of the ten shafts that were gone from the nave by the time of the drawing of 1538. When Michelangelo took over in the 1540s, more shafts had just been made available by the construction of the *muro divisorio*, which enabled the dismantling of everything west of a line through the eleventh columns.[170] Some of these newly available shafts probably were reused as well, but the influx of columns from other sites makes identifying them difficult, if not hopeless.

The new antiquarian scholarship that sprung up around 1500, and flourished in a peculiar symbiosis with a ferocious consumption of antique remains, traced St. Peter's monolithic column shafts to the Mausoleum of Hadrian.[171] This pedigree did little more than the Temple of Solomon to preserve individual shafts. The ideal of the old columns could be embodied in any material, their own or others.[172] Once the idea of their size had been abstracted, the shafts themselves were just a residue, a capital that could be invested in the new structure or exchanged.[173] Columns were exported from St. Peter's as well as imported there, like the four shafts from the transept which were sent off to ornament the Porta del Popolo in 1562.[174] The shafts that remained for reuse in the new building were "adjusted," "molded," "polished," and otherwise improved.[175] Vasari wrote of the superior quality of the ancient stones, but he celebrated even more the ability of contemporary *scarpellini* to rework them, "bring[ing] the [gray granite] columns . . . to the desired thinness, and . . . giv[ing] them a beautiful polish like that of porphyry."[176]

What was true of the column shafts was even more true of their appurtenances: bases, capitals, and architraves. These spolia were too miscellaneous to be readily reused as such. Many probably were considered so much raw material, but a few were admired for their form.[177] One composite capital was drawn repeatedly, by Bernardo della Volpaia (Fig. 29), by Antonio da Sangallo the Younger, and again by his cousin Giovanni Francesco (Fig. 30), with the note "This capital is in St. Peter's, and it is the most beautiful in Rome of this type."[178] When he succeeded Raphael as chief architect, Sangallo the Younger selected some capitals at the entrance end of the north aisle as models for the *scarpellini*, who contracted to imitate them.[179] Bases were likewise singled out for study and emulation.[180] By exercising selectivity it was possible to compose an entire order of Old St. Peter's, as in a remarkable drawing attributed to Alberto Alberti (Fig. 31), but there is no evidence that it was ever the architects' intention to translate such an order to the new basilica.[181] Bramante's eclecticism was more ambitious; as is well known, he had his stonecutters copy Corinthian capitals in the porch of the Pantheon for the internal giant order of his choir.[182]

Thanks to Grimaldi, it is possible to be much more specific about what happened to the architectural spolia that were preserved in situ east of the *muro divisorio* until 1606. Leaving aside two that were undistinguished fourteenth-century replacements, twenty shafts of the nave colonnades were immediately reused in Carlo Maderno's new building.[183] The celebrated *africano* columns were given pride of place in the central doorway of the new facade (Fig. 18); eight shafts of *cipollino* were also reerected in the porch; and two pairs of *portasanta* flank the present altars of St. Sebastian and the Presentation in the north and south aisles.[184] Peruzzi also recorded four shafts of gray granite at this end of the nave. There are four columns of *granito del foro* currently in Maderno's porch, and he is said to have used gray granite in the niches of the aisles as well.[185] As before, more shafts were needed than the old basilica could provide, and columns were brought in from elsewhere. Also as before, the shafts were given new capitals and bases, while the old capitals and much of the other spolia were consumed as raw material or dispersed.[186] Four columns from the atrium and two from the aisles were assigned to Pope Paul V's new fountain on the Janiculum; four red granite columns were sold to Cardinal Borghese for the family's palace; and many columns went to S. Maria Maggiore for the pope's new mortuary chapel.[187]

> In the pontificate of Innocent X [1644–55] they began to remove the ancient columns of different granites, which in their strength and hardness had no fear of fire or steel, and time itself, which drives everything into the ground, not only failed to destroy them, but did not even change their color; and they had been placed there by Constantine the Great, and sanctified by the consecration of the church by Pope Sylvester; and for the memory of that and for veneration of a material that has something eternal (*ch'hà dell'eterno*) . . . they had been adapted in the new church by Buonarroti and by popes up to Paul V. . . .[188]

Bernini's move to replace some of the spoliate shafts inside the basilica with assemblages of *cottanello*, a colorful and vulgar stone from Italy, was a decisive break with a more than millennial tradition of reuse. The diatribe against his innovation by Borromini's friend Fioravante Martinelli goes to the opposite extreme, invoking an unconditional reverence for the materials that is contradicted by the way spolia actually were handled in the sixteenth century. Spolia were a resource, and as such they were treated pretty much as the twentieth century treated forests and rivers, piously preserving some and unsentimentally consuming others.[189] This was as true of Roman spolia in the fourth century as in the sixteenth. By the sixteenth century, however, spolia were much older and very much scarcer than they had been in the early Middle Ages; they had become antiques.[190] Martinelli's appeal to the changelessness of the material recalls the old view that they were "things of God"; but antiquities were things of men. When this category shift from timeless material to ancient artifact began in the twelfth century, the charisma of spolia was intensified because they so outshone the works of contemporary craftsmen. By the sixteenth century this was no longer true. Spolia could serve as admirable exemplars, but the products of living *scarpellini* were more refined. The aura of the old stones was tarnished. Bernini's attempt to banish them was the inevitable next step.

NOTES

1   Giorgio Vasari, *Le Vite de' più eccellenti pittori scultori e architettori nelle redazioni del 1550 e 1568*, ed. Rosanna Bettarini, commentary by Paola Barocchi, *Testo*, vol. 2 (Florence, 1967), 15.

2   Leon Battista Alberti, *On the Art of Building in Ten Books*, trans. Joseph Rykwert, Neil Leach, and Robert Tavernor (Cambridge, 1988), 26.

3   Sigismondo dei Conti da Foligno, cited by Christoph Liutpold Frommel, "Die Peterskirche unter Papst Julius II. im Licht neuer Dokumente," *Römisches Jahrbuch für Kunstgeschichte* 16 (1976): 124, no. 373.

4   Vasari, *Le Vite*, ed. Bettarini, *Testo*, 2:15.

5   *The Life of Michelangelo by Ascanio Condivi*, trans. Alice Sedgwick Wohl (Oxford, 1976), 57. Cf. n. 85 below.

6   Christoph Thoenes, "S. Pietro: Storia e ricerca," in Gianfranco Spagnesi, ed., *L'Architettura della Basilica di San Pietro. Storia e costruzione. Atti del convegno internazionale di studi, Roma, Castel S. Angelo, 7–10 novembre 1995* (Quaderni dell'Istituto di Storia dell'Architettura, n.s. fasc. 25–30, 1995–7) (Rome, 1997), 23–4; Hubertus Günther, "I Progetti di ricostruzione della Basilica di S. Pietro negli scritti contemporanei: giustificazioni e scrupoli," ibid., 143–7; Gaetano Miarelli Mariani, "L'antico San Pietro. Demolirlo o conservarlo?" ibid., 231–9; Louise Rice, "La coesistenza delle due basiliche," ibid., 255–60.

7   *Tiberii Alpharani De Basilicae Vaticanae antiquissima et nova structura*, ed. D. Michele Cerrati (Studi e testi, 26) (Rome, 1914), xxvii–xxviii; Christoph Luitpold Frommel, in *The Renaissance from Brunelleschi to Michelangelo. The Representation of Architecture*, ed. Henry A. Millon and Vittorio Magnago Lampugnani (New York, 1994), 598, no. 277. The original plan is preserved in a side room of the basilica: Enzo Bentivoglio, "Tiberio Alfarano: Le piante del vecchio S. Pietro sulla pianta del nuovo edita dal Dupérac," in *L'Architettura della Basilica di San Pietro*, 253, n. 19. A revised version made by Alfarano in 1576 is lost: Cerrati, xxviii. A second revision was engraved at Alfarano's expense and published in 1590: Cerrati, xli–xlii.

8   *Tiberii Alpharani De Basilicae . . . structura*, ed. Cerrati, xxiv.

9   Giacomo Grimaldi, *Descrizione della Basilica antica di S. Pietro in Vaticano. Codice Barberiniano latino 2733*, ed. Reto Niggl (Vatican City, 1972); Biblioteca Apostolica Vaticana, Archivio del Capitolo di San Pietro, A 64 ter.

10   Berlin, Kupferstichkabinett, Römische Skizzenbücher, vol. 2, fol. 52[r]. Christof Thoenes, "St. Peter als Ruine. Zu einigen Veduten Heemskercks," *Zeitschrift für Kunstgeschichte* 49

(1986): 481–501, esp. 499–501; Alberto Carlo Carpiceci, "La Basilica Vaticana vista da Martin van Heemsckerck," *Bollettino d'arte* 72, fasc. 44–5 (1987): 74–6; Franz Graf Wolff Metternich, *Die frühen St.-Peter-Entwürfe 1505–1514*, ed. Christof Thoenes (Römische Forschungen der Bibliotheca Hertziana, 25) (Tübingen, 1987), 199; Ilja M. Veldman, "Heemskercks Romeinse tekeningen en 'Anonymous B,'" *Nederlands Kunsthistorisch Jaarboek* 38 (1987): 369–82; Frommel, in *The Renaissance from Brunelleschi to Michelangelo*, 629, no. 341. Thoenes estimates the viewpoint at the second or third pair of columns from the entrance; Carpiceci places it at the fourth pair. The familiar attribution of this view to Marten van Heemskerck has been disproved. The drawing, which has a watermark of around 1576 (Veldman, 372), must be a copy of an original made in 1538 exactly, as it shows part of the *muro divisorio* under construction in the right aisle (Carpiceci). Van Heemskerck left Rome in 1537 at the latest.

11 Stockholm, Statens Konstmuseer, Nationalmuseum, Coll. Ankersvärd 637; Carpiceci, "La Basilica Vaticana," 76–80; Metternich, *Die frühen St.-Peter-Entwürfe*, 199–201; Frommel, in *The Renaissance from Brunelleschi to Michelangelo*, 631, no. 345.

12 B. M. Apollonj Ghetti, A. Ferrua, E. Josi, and E. Kirschbaum, *Esplorazioni sotto la confessione di San Pietro in Vaticano eseguite negli anni 1940–1949*, 2 vols. (Vatican City, 1951). On the reception of this work, see Achim Arbeiter, *Alt-St. Peter in Geschichte und Wissenschaft. Abfolge der Bauten. Rekonstruktion. Architekturprogramm* (Berlin, 1988), 22.

13 J. B. Ward Perkins, "The Shrine of St. Peter and Its Twelve Spiral Columns," *Journal of Roman Studies* 42 (1952): 21–33; Sible De Blaauw, *Cultus et decor. Liturgia e architettura nella Roma tardoantica e medievale*, II (Studi e testi, 356) (Rome, 1994) 470–84.

14 For the fullest authoritative account, see Richard Krautheimer, Alfred K. Frazer, and Spencer Corbett, *Corpus Basilicarum Christianarum Romae*, vol. 5 (Vatican City, 1977), 165–285.

15 The dimensions in this description are rough translations into feet of the metric figures in Arbeiter, *Alt-St. Peter*, 90–166. They are all approximate.

16 Corrado Bozzoni, "L'immagine dell'antico S. Pietro nelle rappresentazioni figurate e nella architettura costruita," in *L'Architettura della Basilica di San Pietro*, 64. We must admit that the vertical measurement is to the presumed height of the roof ridge, not to the ceiling.

17 Jean-Charles Picard, "Le Quadriportique de Saint-Pierre-du-Vatican," *Mélanges de l'École Française de Rome. Antiquité* 86 (1974): 851–90.

18 The lateral porticoes may have been built only around 500: Arbeiter, *Alt-St. Peter*, 190.

19 On the Vatican circus, see John Humphrey, *Roman Circuses. Arenas for Chariot Racing* (London, 1986), 545–52.

20 Florence, Uffizi, Gabinetto dei Disegni, Dis. Arch. 108^{r–v} (Heinrich Wurm, *Baldassare Peruzzi. Architekturzeichnungen. Tafelband* [Tübingen, 1984], 117–18); Dis. Arch. 1079^{r–v}, 1851; Vienna, Österreichische Nationalbibliothek, Cod. 10935, fol. 33^{r}. Arbeiter, *Alt-St. Peter*, 74, 124–7; Paola Zampa, in *The Architectural Drawings of Antonio da Sangallo the Younger and His Circle*, vol. 2: *Churches, Villas, the Pantheon, Tombs, and Ancient Inscriptions*, ed. Nicholas Adams (New York, 2000), 203–5.

21 Pliny, *Natural History* 36.63, trans. D. E. Eichholz (Loeb Classical Library, *Pliny, Natural History* 10), 50, note a; Raniero Gnoli, *Marmora romana*, 2d ed. (Rome, 1988), 145–7, figs. 111, 113–14.

22 Gnoli, *Marmora*, figs. 102, 103, 112. Pensabene has proposed to identify *granito bianco* as Troadense, which was not highly prized: Patrizio Pensabene, "Il reimpiego nell'età costantiniana a Roma," in *Costantino il Grande dall'antichità all'umanesimo. Colloquio sul Cristianesimo nel mondo antico*, ed. Giorgio Bonamente and Franca Fusco (Macerata, 1993), 2:755; cf. Gnoli, 153. Given the quality of the other stones employed, I think it might rather have been from Mons Claudianus, *granito del foro* (Gnoli, 148–50).

23 Gnoli, *Marmora*, 181–3, figs. 204–5.

24 Ibid., 172–3, figs. 128–30 (*portasanta*); 174–8, figs. 132–3 (*africano*).

25 Grimaldi, *Descrizione*, ed. Niggl, 213. A coin with the legend LODOVICVS.ROMANORVM.SECVNDVS.REX was found underneath the northern white marble column when it was removed in 1607. Grimaldi seems to have identified Lodovicus II as the son of Charlemagne; Niggl suggests that the coin was an issue of King Louis I of Anjou (1382–4).

26 *Tiberii Alpharani De Basilicae…structura*, ed. Cerrati, 9; Francesco Albertini, *Opusculum de Mirabilibus Novae & veteris Vrbis Romae*, in Peter Murray, *Five Early Guides to Rome and Florence* (1972), p. Oiv^{v}.

27 *Edictum Diocletiani et Collegarum de pretiis rerum venalium*, ed. Marta Giacchero, vol. 1 (Genoa, 1974), 210–11; Gnoli, *Marmora*, 151. *Marmor luculleum* was the third most expensive stone at 150 *denarii*, after porphyry and serpentine (green porphyry) at 250 *den.*, and *giallo antico* and Docimian marble at 200 *den.* Assouan granite, *granito del foro*, and *cipollino* were one step lower in price at 100 *den.* The set price probably was for veneer; the cost of columns is much more difficult to calculate: Simon Corcoran and Janet DeLaine, "The unit measurement of marble in Diocletian's Prices Edict," *Journal of Roman Archaeology* 7 (1994): 263–73.

28 Arbeiter, *Alt-St. Peter*, 123–31; Zampa, in *The Architectural Drawings*, 205–6. On the identification of *saligno*: Vasari, *Le Vite*, ed. Bettarini, *Testo*, 1:46; Pensabene, "Il reimpiego," 755, proposes Proconnesian marble.

29 Krautheimer et al., *Corpus Basilicarum*, 5: 201–5.

30 *Tiberii Alpharani De Basilicae…structura*, ed. Cerrati, 9.

31 Herbert L. Kessler, "'Caput et speculum omnium ecclesiarum': Old St. Peter's and Church Decoration in Medieval Latium," in *Italian Church Decoration of the Middle Ages and Early Renaissance: Functions, Forms and Regional Traditions*, ed. William Tronzo (Bologna, 1989), 119–24, argues that the nave was painted in the fourth century. For the facade mosaic, see Dale Kinney, "The Apocalypse in Early Christian Monumental Decoration," in *The Apocalypse in the Middle Ages*, ed. Richard K. Emmerson and Bernard McGinn (Ithaca, N.Y., 1992), 203–5.

32 Arthur L. Frotheringham, Jr., "Une mosaïque constantinienne inconnue à Saint-Pierre de Rome," *Revue archéologique* ser. 3, no. 1 (1883): 68–72. Some think it was Carolingian: Krautheimer et al., *Corpus Basilicarum*, 5:272, followed by De Blaauw, *Cultus et decor*, 2:461–2.

33 *Le Liber pontificalis. Texte, introduction et commentaire*, ed. L. Duchesne, vol. 1 (repr. Paris, 1981), 79, 176.

34 *Epistula* XIII, to Pammachius, in *Paolino di Nola, Le lettere*, ed. and trans. Giovanni Santaniello, vol. 1 (Naples, 1992), 416. Similarly Prudentius, *Peristephanon* XII, 31–42, in *Prudentius*, trans. H. J. Thomson (Loeb Classical Library), vol. 2 (London, 1953), 324–5.

35 *Liber pontificalis*, ed. Duchesne, 1:79, 176.

36 De Blaauw, *Cultus et decor*, 2:530–66, 647–61.

37 De Blaauw notes that while the fifteenth-century ciborium is generally ascribed to Pope Sixtus IV, payments for it were made under Paul II in 1467 (ibid., 648).

38   Grimaldi, *Descrizione*, ed. Niggl, 198.

39   *Liber pontificalis*, ed. Duchesne, 2:27; Sible De Blaauw, "Papst
     und Purpur. Porphyr in frühen Kirchenausstattungen in Rom,"
     in *Tesserae. Festschrift für Josef Engemann* (Jahrbuch für Antike
     und Christentum, Ergänzungsband 18) (Münster, 1991), 41–2.

40   *Liber pontificalis*, ed. Duchesne, 1:417; De Blaauw, *Cultus et
     decor*, 2:555.

41   Prudentius of Troyes, *Annales*, quoted in *Liber pontificalis*, ed.
     Duchesne, 2:104, n. 38; De Blaauw, *Cultus et decor*, 2:557–9.

42   For the architectural changes, see Krautheimer et al., *Corpus
     Basilicarum*, 5:277–8.

43   *Liber pontificalis*, ed. Duchesne, 1:464; the saint's marble sar-
     cophagus, with an inscription "carved by the hand of Peter him-
     self," was translated from the catacomb of Domitilla. Though
     an authentic Roman martyr, Petronilla was not, as legend had
     it, Peter's daughter; Agostino Amore, in *Bibliotheca sanctorum*,
     10 (Rome, 1968): 514–17.

44   *Liber pontificalis*, ed. Duchesne, 2:8, 81; L. Duchesne, "Notes
     sur la topographie de Rome au moyen-âge. XII. Vaticana
     (suite)," *Mélanges d'archéologie et d'histoire* 34 (1914):
     346–7.

45   Paulinus, *Epistula XIII*, ed. Santaniello, 416; for the transla-
     tion see Hermann Tränkle, "Das Brunnen im Atrium der Pe-
     tersbasilikd und der Zeitpunkt van Prudentius' Romaufenhalt,"
     Zeitschrift für antikes Christentum 3 (1999): 101–2. Tränkle
     argues that the fountain was built by Pope Damasus (366–84)
     and was also described by Prudentius, *Peristephanon* 12.33–44.
     On the Roman type of fountain called *cantharus*, see Wolfram
     Letzner, *Römische Brunnen und Nymphaea in der westlichen
     Reichshälfte* (Münster, 1990), 89–92; on its Christian history
     and symbolism, see Ulrich Schulze, *Brunnen im Mittelalter.
     Politische Ikonographie der Kommunen in Italien* (Europäische
     Hochschulschriften, ser. 28, Kunstgeschichte, 209) (Frankfurt
     am Main, 1994), 43–9. Thanks to Christine Verzár for refer-
     ring me to this last book.

46   *Liber pontificalis*, ed. Duchesne, 1:514.

47   Ibid., 323.

48   Ibid., 343.

49   See the review of the written sources by Daniel William
     O'Connor, *Peter in Rome: The Literary, Liturgical, and Arche-
     ological Evidence* (New York, 1969), 53–134.

50   Eusebius, *De theophania*, trans. Daniel William O'Connor, in
     Peter in Rome, 103.

51   Jerome, *De viris inlustribus*, ed. Guilelmus Herding (Leipzig,
     1879), 7.

52   Filippo Coarelli, *Guida archeologica di Roma* (Verona, 1974),
     319.

53   O'Connor, *Peter in Rome*, 102.

54   *Liber pontificalis*, ed. Duchesne, 1:53, 118. Duchesne took the
     "palace of Nero" to be a garbled reference to the circus. Bianchi
     refers it to a villa-like building overlooking the circus, argu-
     ing that the circus itself was too ruined to be recognizable in
     the fourth century: Lorenzo Bianchi, "*Palatiolum* e *palatium
     Neronis*: topografia antica del Monte di Santo Spirito in Roma,"
     Bollettino della Commissione Archeologica Comunale di Roma
     95 (1993): 25–46.

55   On the obelisk: Cesare D'Onofrio, *Gli obelischi di Roma*,
     2d ed. (Rome, 1967), 13–103; Erik Iversen, *Obelisks in
     Exile*, vol. 1: *The Obelisks of Rome* (Copenhagen, 1968),
     19–46; Géza Alföldy, *Der Obelisk auf dem Petersplatz in
     Rom. Ein historisches Monument der Antike* (Heidelberg,
     1990).

56   Iversen, *Obelisks in Exile*, 1:38–40.

57   Pompeo Ugonio, *Historia delle Stationi di Roma che si celebrano
     la Quadragesima* (Rome, 1588), 90^v–91^r.

58   Exodus 12:36: "spoliaverunt Aegyptios"; Augustine, *De doc-
     trina christiana* 2.40.

59   Augustine, *De doctrina christiana* 2.41; trans. D. W. Robertson,
     Jr., as *On Christian Doctrine* (Indianapolis, 1958), 77.

60   Pliny, *Natural History* 36.74; trans. Eichholz, 59.

61   Iversen, *Obelisks in Exile*, 1:65; Humphrey, *Roman Circuses*,
     269–70.

62   Tertullian, *De spectaculis* 8.3; Emanuele Castorina, *Quinti Sep-
     timi Florentis Tertulliani De spectaculis. Introduzione, testo
     critico, commento e traduzione* (Florence, 1961), 164–8. Cf.
     Bente Kiilerich, *The Obelisk Base in Constantinople: Court
     Art and Imperial Ideology* (Acta ad Archaeologiam et artium
     historiam pertinentia, series altera in 8°, X) (Rome, 1998),
     153–6.

63   Julius Capitolinus, *Verus* 6.4; Aelius Lampridius, *Antoninus
     Elagabalus* 23.1, trans. David Magie, *Scriptores Historiae Au-
     gustae* Loeb Classical Library, 2:151.

64   Robert Turcan, "Héliogabale précurseur de Constantin?" *Bul-
     letin de l'Association Guillaume Budé* (1988), 38–52, esp.
     45–6; idem, *Histoire auguste*, vol. 3, 1: pt. *Vies de Macrin,
     Diaduménien, Héliogabale* (Paris, 1993), 71.

65   Jocelyn Toynbee and John Ward Perkins, *The Shrine of St. Peter
     and the Vatican Excavations* (London, 1956), 12–13.

66   Grimaldi, *Descrizione*, ed. Niggl, 89, 309; M. J. Vermaseren,
     Corpus Cultus Cybelae Attidisque (CCCA), vol. 3: *Italia-
     Latium* (Leiden, 1977), 49. Ralf Biering and Henner von Hes-
     berg have argued that the Phrygianum was in the third-century
     rotunda: "Zur Bau- und Kultgeschichte von St. Andreas apud S.
     Petrum. Vom Phrygianum zum Kenotaph Theodosius der Gr.?"
     Römische Quartalschrift 82 (1987): 163; Richardson, *New To-
     pographical Dictionary*, 290.

67   Garth Fowden, "Nicagorus of Athens and the Lateran Obelisk,"
     Journal of Hellenic Studies 107 (1987): 51–7; Caroline and
     Oliver Nicholson, "Lactantius, Hermes Trismegistus and Con-
     stantinian Obelisks," *Journal of Hellenic Studies* 109 (1989):
     198–200.

68   Gaston H. Halsberghe, *The Cult of Sol Invictus* (Leiden, 1972),
     esp. 167–71; cf. Richard Krautheimer, *Three Christian Capitals:
     Topography and Politics* (Berkeley, 1983), 31–6, 62–7; Kiilerich,
     The Obelisk Base, 145. A recent, revisionist review of the evi-
     dence for the cult of Sol Invictus is made by Steven E. Hijmans,
     "The Sun which Did Not Rise in the East: The Cult of Sol Invic-
     tus in the Light of Non-Literary Evidence," BABESCH: *Bulletin
     Antieke Beschaving* 71 (1996): 115–50.

69   Malachi 4:2: "Et orietur vobis timentibus nomen meum Sol
     iustitiae.…"

70   Richard Krautheimer, "A Note on the Inscription in the Apse of
     Old St. Peter's," *Dumbarton Oaks Papers* 41 (1987): 317–20.

71   Alfarano claimed that on the equinox, the rays of the rising sun
     struck the main altar over the body of the apostle: *Tiberii Alpha-
     rani De Basilicae…structura*, ed. Cerrati, 19. A similar claim
     has been made for S. Maria Maggiore on the winter solstice:
     Carlo Bertelli, "Richard Krautheimer e la Basilica Liberiana,"
     in *In Memoriam Richard Krautheimer. Relazioni della giornata
     di studi Roma, 20 febbraio 1995, Palazzo dei Conservatori, Sala
     dell'Ercole* (Rome, 1997), 54.

72   Leo the Great, *Sermon* 27, 4, trans. Jane Patricia Freeland
     and Agnes Josephine Conway (The Fathers of the Church, 93)
     (Washington, D.C., 1996), 113. Christian solar syncretism may
     be seen in the Vatican as early as the third century in the mosaic
     of Sol in the vault of the Christian tomb "M," only 30 feet or
     so from St. Peter's shrine; Sister Charles Murray, *Rebirth and
     Afterlife. A Study of the Transmutation of Some Pagan Imagery
     in Early Christian Funerary Art* (BAR International Series, 100)
     (Oxford, 1981), 64–97.

73 In metric units: height of nave shafts, 8.65–8.97 m, diameters, .96–1.21 m; height of aisle shafts: 5.68–6.19 m, diameters, .577–.819 m. Zampa, in *The Architectural Drawings*, 204, slightly revising Arbeiter, *Alt-St. Peter*, 117, 131.

74 Florence, Uffizi, Gabinetto dei Disegni, Dis. Arch. 1080ʳ (Francesco Bartolomeo da Sangallo[?]); see above, n. 20.

75 Grimaldi, *Descrizione*, ed. Niggl, 242 (fol. 207ᵛ); similarly Cesare Baronio, *Annales ecclesiastici*, vol. 3 (Rome, 1592), ad ann. 324, p. 240. Some blocks of the entablature had Antonine profiles: Jürgen Christern and Katharina Thiersch, "Der Aufriss von Alt-St.-Peter. 2. Teil," *Römische Quartalschrift* 64 (1969): 2.

76 *Corpus inscriptionum latinarum* VI, pt. 1, no. 946; Grimaldi, *Descrizione*, ed. Niggl, 242–3 (fols. 207ʳ⁻ᵛ). Magi's assertion that the Trajanic inscription was removed from the Arch of Titus for reuse at St. Peter's has been refuted: Filippo Magi, "L'iscrizione perduta dell'arco di Tito. Una ipotesi," *Römische Mitteilungen* 82, no. 1 (1975): 99–116; Martin Spannagel, "Wiedergefundene Antiken: Zu vier Dal-Pozzo-Zeichnungen in Windsor Castle," *Archäologischer Anzeiger* (1979) (Deutsches Archäologisches Institut, Jahrbuch 94, pt. 2), 376–7. Pensabene has pointed to the existence of a ruined or unbuilt Trajanic structure of which blocks were reused elsewhere in the third and fourth centuries: Patrizio Pensabene and Clementina Panella, "Reimpiego e progettazione architettonica nei monumenti tardo-antichi di Roma," *Rendiconti della Pontificia Accademia Romana di Archeologia* 66 (1993–4): 122, 131. On the existence of stockpiles, see Pensabene and Panella, ibid., 128–37; Dale Kinney, "*Spolia: Damnatio* and *Renovatio Memoriae*," *Memoirs of the American Academy in Rome* 42 (1997): 122–9.

77 Kinney, "*Spolia*," 145–6; cf. Zosimus, *Nea Historia* 2.32.

78 Friedrich Wilhelm Deichmann, "Säule und Ordnung in der frühchristlichen Architektur," *Römische Mitteilungen* 55 (1940): 121–9; Jürgen Christern, "Der Aufriss von Alt-St.-Peter," *Römische Quartalschrift* 62 (1967): 172–5.

79 On Uffizi, Dis. Arch. 108ʳ⁻ᵛ (above, n. 20) the shafts on each side are numbered 1–20, and numbers 21–24 are missing. The numbers through 12 probably correspond to the columns' actual position; above that, one has to allow for gaps created by the insertion of Bramante's piers. See below, n. 162.

80 Arbeiter, *Alt-St. Peter*, 122. The twelve shafts in the transept – of *pavonazzetto* (Phrygian marble) and red and gray granite – were also grouped by color: Christern and Thiersch, "Der Aufriss von Alt-St.-Peter. 2," 12–14.

81 Beat Brenk, "Spolien und ihre Wirkung auf die Ästhetik der *varietas*. Zum Problem alternierender Kapitelltypen," in *Antike Spolien in der Architektur des Mittelalters und der Renaissance*, ed. Joachim Poeschke (Munich, 1996), 49–80.

82 Psalm 44:15 (Vulgate): "In vestitu deaurato, circumamicta varietate." Augustine, *De civitate Dei* 17.xvi.

83 Revelation 21:18–20.

84 Michael Roberts, *The Jeweled Style: Poetry and Poetics in Late Antiquity* (Ithaca, N.Y., 1989).

85 Gregory of Tours, *Glory of the Martyrs*, 27, trans. Raymond van Dam (Liverpool, 1988), 45; Krautheimer et al., *Corpus Basilicarum*, 5:174. Cf. Onuphrius Panvinius, *De praecipuis Vrbis Romae sanctioribusque Basilicis, quas septem Ecclesias uulgo uocant liber* (Rome, 1570), 35: "...basilica[m] uaticana[m] centu[m] marmoreis nobilibusq[ue] sublime[n] colu[m]nis B. Petro erexit...." Modern descriptions still give the number of 100 columns, counting 22 in each colonnade, 2 at the end of each aisle, and 2 at each end of the transept (88 + 8 + 4), but omitting the two columns under the triumphal arch, which, though mentioned by Alfarano (*De Basilicae...structura*, ed. Cerrati, 10), are not shown on his ground plan; Krautheimer

et al., *Corpus Basilicarum*, 5:211–12. Georg Satzinger, "Nikolaus V., Nikolaus Muffel und Bramante: Monumentale Triumphbogensäulen in Alt-St.-Peter," *Römisches Jahrbuch der Bibliotheca Hertziana* 31 (1996): 91–105, argues that two enormous columns brought across the Tiber to St. Peter's under Pope Nicholas V (1447–55) were erected under a new triumphal arch that was demolished by Bramante; in other words, if it existed, Alfarano could not have seen this arch but might have heard of it. Satzinger identifies the broken columns regretted by Michelangelo (see above, n. 5) as well as the "ingentes columnas" admired by Pope Paul II (see above, n. 26) as these two.

86 Tertullian, *De spectaculis*, II: "...extructiones locorum, quod saxa, quod caementa, quod marmora, quod columnae dei res sunt...."; trans. T. R. Glover (Loeb Classical Library), 233.

87 Murray, *Rebirth and Afterlife*, 88–9, points out that the vine depicted in the third-century vault mosaic of Tomb M in the Vatican cemetery bears no grapes, in accordance with the opposition of Christianity to Dionysiac ecstasy taught by Clement of Alexandria.

88 *Liber pontificalis*, ed. Duchesne, 1:176; Gregory of Tours, *Glory of the Martyrs*, 27, trans. van Dam, 46; Ward Perkins, "The Shrine," 22.

89 *Liber pontificalis*, ed. Duchesne, 1:417; trans. Raymond Davis, *The Lives of the Eighth-Century Popes (Liber pontificalis)* (Liverpool, 1992), 22. Pliny, *Natural History* 36.61, Eichholz trans., 49.

90 Max Wegner, "Gewundene Säulen von Ephesos," *Jahreshefte des Österreichischen Archäologischen Institutes in Wien* 51 (1976–7), *Beiblatt* 49–64. Smaller, ornamental twisted shafts were more common, e.g., Pierre Gusman, *L'art décoratif de Rome de la fin de la république au IVᵉ siècle* (Paris, 1912), 2:18 and pl. 104; Beatrice Palma and Lucilla De Lachenal, *I Marmi Ludovisi nel Museo Nazionale Romano* (Museo Nazionale Romano, Le Sculture, I, 5) (Rome, 1983), 121–3, no. 53.

91 Berlin, Staatliche Museen Preussischer Kulturbesitz, Kupferstichkabinett, KdZ 16792; *Zeichner sehen die Antike. Europäische Handzeichnungen 1450–1800* (Berlin, 1967), 129–30, no. 80. The drawing is fantastic in several respects; not least, the outer row of columns had been dispersed by the time it was made. See the section titled "[la] materid ch'hà dell'eterno" below.

92 Ward Perkins, "The Shrine," 30–1; Wegner, "Gewundene Säulen." Barbara Nobiloni, "Le colonne vitinee della basilica di San Pietro a Roma," *Xenia* 6 (1997): 91–116, redates the earliest columns to the second century but otherwise follows Ward Perkins on the dating and on the columns' Eastern provenance (via Constantinople).

93 *Nikolaus Muffels Beschreibung der Stadt Rom*, ed. Wilhelm Vogt (Stuttgart, 1876), 21. This passage seems to have been overlooked until the Ph.D. dissertation by Ann Karin van Dijk, "The Oratory of Pope John VII (705–707) in Old St. Peter's" (Johns Hopkins University, 1995), 108–9. I am grateful to Dr. van Dijk for giving me a copy of this part of her text. Nobiloni, "Le colonne vitinee," 85–87, also noticed the extra columns and quotes additional testimonies. For the legend that the twisted columns came from the Temple of Solomon, see below, "*Peregrinorum et Romanorum vanae fabulae*."

94 Grimaldi, *Descrizione*, ed. Niggl, 106. The altar of the *sudarium* (popularly called the Veronica) seems to have been made in the twelfth century; see William Tronzo, "Setting and Structure in Two Roman Wall Decorations of the Early Middle Ages," *Dumbarton Oaks Papers* 41 (1987): 491.

95 For the original form of the oratory with two lateral walls, see *Liber pontificalis*, ed. Duchesne, 1:385 ("...cuius parietes musibo depinxit...venerabilium Patrum dextra levaque vultus

erexit"). For the construction of the *porta santa*, see *Johannis Burckardi Liber Notarum ab anno* MCCCCLXXXIII *usque ad annum,* MDVI ed. Enrico Celani, vol. 2 (Città di Castello, 1943), 179 ("mandavit…muros ante et a latere predictam capellam claudentes omnino amoveri, ut populus liberius posset pertransire"); Eva-Maria Jung-Inglessis, "La Porta Santa," *Studi romani* 23 (1975): 473–80. Before the *porta santa* existed, Muffel recounted the legend of a sealed "golden door" in the same location, "hinder der altar"; *Nikolaus Muffels Beschreibung,* 19–20.

96 There are many discrepancies between the drawings and the form of the extant ornament; see next note and Tronzo, "Setting and Structure," 490–2.

97 Grimaldi, *Descrizione,* ed. Niggl, 106, note a; Francesco Maria Torrigio, *Le Sacre Grotte Vaticane* (Viterbo, 1618), 61. The strips with vine scrolls do not appear in all of Grimaldi's illustrations, and when they do they differ from the extant pilasters. The pilasters are uniform in height but not in width, while the drawings show the opposite; the two strips flanking the twisted columns in the drawings support vases and seem to be like small piers rather than pilasters; there are six strips but five pilasters. Nordhagen turned this last discrepancy into positive evidence that the pilasters were reused under John VII: Per Jonas Nordhagen, "A carved marble pilaster in the Vatican Grottoes. Some remarks on the sculptural techniques of the Early Middle Ages," *Acta ad Archaeologiam et Artium Historiam pertinentia* 4 (1969): 113–19.

98 J. M. C. Toynbee and J. B. Ward Perkins, "Peopled Scrolls: A Hellenistic Motif in Imperial Art," *Papers of the British School at Rome* 18 (1950): 20–1; Friederike Sinn, *Die Grabdenkmäler,* vol. 1: *Reliefs Altäre Urnen* (Vatikanische Museen, Museo Gregoriano Profano ex Lateranense, Katalog der Skulpturen, I, 1) (Mainz, 1991), 61–2.

99 Wilhelm Levison, "Aus Englischen Bibliotheken. II," *Neues Archiv für ältere deutsche Geschichtskunde* 35 (1910): 363–4; cf. Ann van Dijk, "The Angelic Salutation in Early Byzantine and Medieval Annunciation Imagery," *Art Bulletin* 81 (1999): 432.

100 Hugo Brandenburg, "Die Umsetzung von Statuen in der Spätantike," in *Migratio et Commutatio. Studien zur alten Geschichte und deren Nachleben. Thomas Pekáry zum 60. Geburtstag am 13. September 1989 dargebracht von Freunden, Kollegen und Schülern,* ed. Hans-Joachim Drexhage and Julia Sünskes (St. Katharinen, 1989), 235–46.

101 Margaret Finch, "The Cantharus and Pigna at Old St. Peter's," *Gesta* 30 (1991): 20.

102 They also resemble two columns preserved in the chapel of the SS. Sacramento (Fig. 16). Ward Perkins, "The Shrine," 24, followed by van Dijk, "The Oratory," 113–15, holds that these columns and those once in John VII's oratory are the same, but this is debatable; see below, "[la] materia ch'hà dell'eterno."

103 *Liber pontificalis,* ed. Duchesne, 1:386, n. 1.

104 E. Simon, in Wolfgang Helbig, *Führer durch die öffentlichen Sammlungen klassischer Altertümer in Rom,* ed. Hermine Speier, vol. 1: *Die Päpstlichen Sammlungen im Vatikan und Lateran* (Tübingen, 1963), 375–7, no. 478.

105 Eugene J. Dwyer, *Pompeian Domestic Sculpture: A Study of Five Pompeian Houses and Their Contents* (Rome, 1982), 60, no. iii, fig. 72. Dwyer suggests that the relatively small cone (.17 m tall) in Pompeii might have been a copy of the *pigna* in Rome, evidence that the latter was famous in its own day (personal communication).

106 Julian, *Oration V. Hymn to the Mother of the Gods* 167–9; Michele Renée Salzman, *On Roman Time: The Codex Calendar of 354 and the Rhythms of Urban Life in Late Antiquity* (Berkeley, 1990), 164–9.

107 Grimaldi, *Descrizione,* ed. Niggl, 312, fig. 170b; Vermaseren, *CCCA,* nos. 226, 233, 236, 237, 241a, 241b, pls. CXIX, CXXI–CXXIII, CXXVII, CXXIX–CXXX; Finch, "The Cantharus and Pigna," 20, fig. 5.

108 Ch. Huelsen, "Der Cantharus von Alt-St.-Peter und die antiken Pignen-Brunnen," *Römische Mitteilungen* 19 (1904): 88–102. On the authorship of the drawing shown here in Figure 25, which was long attributed to Il Cronaca, see Hubertus Günther, *Das Studium der antiken Architektur in den Zeichnungen der Hochrenaissance* (Römische Forschungen der Bibliotheca Hertziana, 24) (Tübingen, 1988), 69–70.

109 These shafts may be the same as two now in the Louvre: Kate de Kersauson, *Catalogue des portraits romains,* II, *De l'année de la guerre civile (68–69 après J.-C.) à la fin de l'Empire* (Paris, 1996), 60–1, no. 21, and 68–9, no. 24; but de Kersauson points out that there is a discrepancy between Grimaldi's mention that one of the busts on St. Peter's columns was destroyed in the seventeenth century and the presence of two intact busts (identified as Nerva and Trajan) on the shafts in Paris.

110 *Liber pontificalis,* ed. Duchesne, 1:455; trans. Davis, *The Lives,* 76. The passage is an eighth-century interpolation that could have been made as late as 791–2: Duchesne, 1:ccxxvii.

111 Krautheimer et al., *Corpus basilicarum,* 5:267, 271, is noncommittal about when the *pigna* was added to the fountain; Paolo Liverani, "La Pigna Vaticana. Note storiche," *Bollettino. Monumenti, Musei e Gallerie Pontificie* 6 (1986): 62, argues for the eighth century, as do Finch, "The Cantharus and Pigna," 17–18, and Schulze, *Brunnen im Mittelalter,* 123–5.

112 Peter Lasko, *Ars sacra 800–1200,* 2d ed. (New Haven, Conn., 1994), 11, argues for a dating in the reign of Charlemagne, as does Schulze, *Brunnen im Mittelalter,* 193–204. However, a significant body of opinion holds that the Aachen pinecone is Ottonian; cf. Arne Effenberger and Hans Drescher, in *Bernward von Hildesheim und das Zeitalter der Ottonen, Katalog der Ausstellung Hildesheim 1993,* ed. Michael Brandt and Arne Eggebrecht (Hildesheim, 1993), 2:115–18, no. III-4. A comparable fountain in Constantinople was made by the emperor Basil I (867–86): Liverani, "La Pigna," 59.

113 Giovanni Cavallini, *Polistoria de virtutibus et dotibus Romanorum,* ed. Roberto Valentini and Giuseppe Zucchetti, *Codice topografico della città di Roma,* vol. 4 (Rome, 1953), 50–1; cf. Liverani, "La Pigna," 54–8; Finch, "The Cantharus and Pigna," 18; F. Coarelli, in *Lexicon topographicum urbis Romae,* ed. Eva Margareta Steinby, vol. 3 (Rome, 1996), 108. The epithet *de pinea* appears in a document of 962, but *Pigna* became the common name for the zone only in the fourteenth century: *Rione IX–Pigna* (Guide rionali di Roma), vol. 1, ed. Carlo Pietrangeli (Rome, 1977), 5.

114 The proposed site in the Campus Martius is in the area of the Serapeum. For an argument *ex silentio* against it see Michel Malaise, *Inventaire préliminaire des documents égyptiens découverts en Italie* (Leiden, 1972), esp. 211.

115 Grimaldi suggested that the *pigna* came from the Phrygianum: *Descrizione,* ed. Niggl, 89, n. c; similarly Cesare D'Onofrio, *Le Fontane di Roma con documenti e disegni inediti* (Rome, 1957), 143–4. Cf. E. Simon, in Helbig, *Führer,* 1:377–8, no. 479; Effenberger, in *Bernward von Hildesheim,* 2:113–15, no. III-3; de Kersauson, *Catalogue des portraits,* 2:68, no. 24.

116 Schulze, *Brunnen im Mittelalter,* 193n3, 113–22.

117 *Mirabilia urbis Romae,* ed. Valentini and Zucchetti, *Codice topografico,* vol. 3 (Rome, 1946), 43–4.

118 Ibid., 17–65. The commonly accepted attribution of the *Mirabilia* to Benedict, canon of St. Peter's, who authored the

so-called *Ordo romanus XI* at the behest of Cardinal Guido of Città di Castello before 1143, has been challenged by Bernhard Schimmelpfennig, *Die Zeremonienbücher der römischen Kurie im Mittelalter* (Tübingen, 1973), 6–15, and Cesare D'Onofrio, *Visitiamo Roma mille anni fa. La città dei Mirabilia* (Rome, 1988), 14–39.

119 Albin Lesky, "Ein verschollenes Aition zur Reiterstatue des Mark Aurel," *Wiener Studien*, 61–2 (1943–4): 191.

120 Bernardo Gamucci, *Libri Quattro delle Antichità della Città di Roma* (Venice, 1565), 195.

121 Cf. Giovanni Dondi, *Iter romanum*, ed. Valentini and Zucchetti, *Codice topografico*, 4:68.

122 The verse is actually the opening of a *planctus* for an anonymous emperor identified by William of Malmesbury as Henry III (d. 1056), but by modern editors as Lothar I (d. 855). It is found in at least five manuscripts of tenth- to twelfth-century date; *Monumenta Germaniae Historica, Poetae latini aevi carolini*, 4:2–3, ed. Karolus Strecker (Berlin, 1923), 1072–5. Alföldy, *Der Obelisk*, 90–4, argues that the verse actually appeared on the obelisk, incised on bronze plaques that would have been attached in the area of the Roman inscriptions.

123 *Master Gregorius. The Marvels of Rome*, trans. John Osborne (Toronto, 1987), 12–15.

124 *Narracio de mirabilibus urbis Romae*, ed. Valentini and Zucchetti, *Codice topografico*, 3:164–5; trans. Osborne, 34–5; on the sources: Osborne, 93–4. Cf. *Narracio*, ed. Valentini and Zucchetti, 146: "peregrinorum et Romanorum . . . vanas fabulas penitus declinabo. . . ."

125 Vergil, *Eclogues* 5.56 and 43–4; *Servii Grammatici qui feruntur in Vergilii Bucolica et Georgica Commentarii*, ed. Georg Thilo (Leipzig, 1887, repr. Hildesheim, 1961), 59; *Master Gregory*, trans. Osborne, 94.

126 The legend that the obelisk was Caesar's tomb was still repeated by Petrarch and even by Bramante, who (as reported by Aegidius of Viterbo) tried to persuade Pope Julius II to allow him to rotate the axis of the new basilica 90 degrees, so that "the temple of Julius the pope would have at its entrance the venerable monument of Julius Caesar – as it is commonly identified. . . ." Hans Hubert, "Bramantes St.-Peter-Entwürfe und die Stellung des Apostelgrabes," *Zeitschrift für Kunstgeschichte* 51 (1988): 196; Hans-Christoph Dittscheid, "Form versus Materie. Zum Spoliengebrauch in den römischen Bauten und Projekten Donato Bramantes," in *Antike Spolien*, ed. Poeschke, 282–3, 294n35.

127 *Mirabilia urbis Romae*, ed. Valentini and Zucchetti, *Codice topografico*, 3:44–5.

128 Ibid., 35.

129 Bede, *The Ecclesiastical History of the English People*, 2:4; T. Buddensieg, "Criticism and Praise of the Pantheon in the Middle Ages and the Renaissance," in *Classical Influences on European Culture A.D. 500–1500*, ed. R. R. Bolgar (Cambridge, 1971), 259.

130 Boccaccio, letter to Francesco Nelli (1363), cited by Salvatore Settis, "Von *auctoritas* zu *vetustas*: Die antike Kunst im mittelalterlicher Sicht," *Zeitschrift für Kunstgeschichte* 51 (1988): 177–8.

131 Quoted and translated by Buddensieg, "Criticism and Praise," 260.

132 Grimaldi, *Descrizione*, ed. Niggl, 145.

133 W. A. Simpson, "Cardinal Giordano Orsini (d. 1438) as a Prince of the Church and a Patron of the Arts: A Contemporary Panegyric and Two Descriptions of the Lost Frescoes in Monte Giordano," *Journal of the Warburg and Courtauld Institutes* 29 (1966): 135–6; Charles L. Stinger, *The Renaissance in Rome* (Bloomington, Ind., 1985), 283.

134 *Memoriale de mirabilibus et indulgentiis quae in urbe Romana existunt*, ed. Valentini and Zucchetti, *Codice topografico*, 4:81; Walter Cahn, "Solomonic Elements in Romanesque Art," in *The Temple of Solomon. Archaeological Fact and Medieval Tradition in Christian, Islamic, and Jewish Art*, ed. Joseph Gutmann (Missoula, Mont., 1976), 67n29. Thanks again to Christine Verzár for this last reference.

135 John 10:23.

136 3 Regum 6–7; 2 Paralipomenon 3.

137 *Petri Mallii Descriptio Basilicae Vaticanae*, ed. Valentini and Zucchetti, *Codice topografico*, 3:384. Mallius conflates the separate entries of the *Liber pontificalis* to describe all twelve columns as gifts of Constantine.

138 *The Itinerary of Benjamin of Tudela: Travels in the Middle Ages*, introductions by Michael A. Signer, Marcus Nathan Adler, and A. Asher (Malibu, Calif., 1987), 64.

139 De Blaauw, *Cultus et decor*, 1:251–2; Jack Freiberg, *The Lateran in 1600. Christian Concord in Counter-Reformation Rome* (Cambridge, 1995), 131, 134–8. I am grateful to David Freedberg for alerting me to the significance of the ninth of Ab, and to my colleague David Rabeeya for bibliography. See Michael Strassfeld, *The Jewish Holidays: A Guide and Commentary* (New York, 1985), 85–9.

140 *Descriptio Lateranensis Ecclesiae*, ed. Valentini and Zucchetti, *Codice topografico*, 3:338–9.

141 *Master Gregory*, trans. Osborne, 19. For the medieval reception of the bronze columns, see Ursula Nilgen, "Das Fastigium in der Basilica Constantiniana und vier Bronzesäulen des Lateran," *Römische Quartalschrift* 72 (1977): 18–24.

142 Nilgen, "Das Fastigium," 21.

143 MARMOREAE COLVMNAE SALOMONICI TEMPLI. Enrico Mauceri, "Colonne tortili cosi dette del Tempio di Salomone," *L'Arte* 1 (1898): 381; Ward Perkins, "The Shrine," 32 and pl. VII, 3–4; Peter Cornelius Claussen, *Magistri doctissimi romani. Die römischen Marmorkünstler des Mittelalters* (Stuttgart, 1987), 14n63 and Fig. 33; Nobiloni, "Le colonne vitinee," Figs. 61–62. Claussen is coy about the columns' date, associating them with a "group of Roman reliefs of the twelfth century" (55), some of which he dates close to 1200 (118–19). He traces the medieval derivations to a hypothetical ciborium made for the new main altar of Pope Callixtus II in 1123 (14n63). The late date of the epigraphy on the plinths in Cave was noticed by Cahn, "Solomonic Elements," 67n28 bis, and is clear in the photos published by Nobiloni.

144 Cahn, "Solomonic Elements"; Ioli Kalavrezou-Maxeiner, "The Byzantine Knotted Column," in *Byzantine Studies in Honor of Milton V. Anastos*, ed. Speros Vryonis, Jr. (Byzantina kai Metabyzantina, IV) (Malibu, Calif., 1985), 95–103.

145 Debra J. Birch, *Pilgrimage to Rome in the Middle Ages: Continuity and Change* (Woodbridge, Suffolk, Eng., 1998), 110, 114–15.

146 *Codice topografico*, ed. Valentini and Zucchetti, 3:321–2, 379–80; Brenda M. Bolton, "Advertise the Message: Images at Rome at the Turn of the Twelfth Century," in *The Church and the Arts: Papers Read at the 1990 Summer Meeting and the 1991 Winter Meeting of the Ecclesiastical History Society*, ed. Diana Wood (Oxford, 1992), 117–130; Birch, *Pilgrimage to Rome*, 111–13.

147 Nobiloni, "Le colonne vitinee," 121–23. Although art historians often do it, twisted shafts should not be equated as a type with spirally grooved cylindrical shafts (e.g., Eric Fernie, "The Spiral Piers of Durham Cathedral," *Medieval Art and Architecture at Durham Cathedral* [British Archaeological Association Conference Transactions 3 (1977)] [Leeds, 1980], 49–58; and Robert Ousterhout, "The Temple, the Sepulchre, and the *Martyrion* of the Savior," *Gesta* 29 [1990]: 48]. On the distinction,

see Nobiloni and Alois Fuchs, "Die Spiralsäule in der Kunst-geschichte," *Westfalen* 29 (1951): 127–30.

148 Vasari, *Le Vite*, ed. Bettarini, *Testo*, vol. 4 (Florence 1976), 82–4.

149 John Shearman, *Raphael's Cartoons in the Collection of Her Majesty the Queen and the Tapestries for the Sistine Chapel* (London, 1972), 9; Ennio Francia, *1506–1606. Storia della costruzione del nuovo San Pietro* (Rome, 1977), 61; William Tronzo, "Il Tegurium di Bramante," in *L'Architettura della Basilica di San Pietro*, 161–6.

150 *Tiberii Alpharani De Basilicae... structura*, ed. Cerrati, 55, 158, doc. 13; Irving Lavin, *Bernini and the Crossing of St. Peter's* (New York, 1968), 3, 19–22. For some time the Colonna Santa shared the chapel nearest the northeast entrance with Michelangelo's Pietà; see the view in Louise Rice, *The Altars and Altarpieces of New St. Peter's. Outfitting the Basilica, 1621–1666* (Cambridge, 1997), fig. 82.

151 Ward Perkins, "The Shrine," 24.

152 Lavin, *Bernini and the Crossing*, 6–7n27; Howard Hibbard, *Carlo Maderno and Roman Architecture 1580–1630* (London, 1971), 73, 166; W. Chandler Kirwin, "Bernini's Baldacchino Reconsidered," *Römisches Jahrbuch für Kunstgeschichte* 19 (1981): 153–57; Nobiloni, "le colonne vitinee," 87–89.

153 On the date of the destruction of the *tegurium*, Kirwin, "Bernini's Baldacchino," 144.

154 Grimaldi, *Descrizione*, ed. Niggl, 70.

155 Biblioteca Apostolica Vaticana, Archivio del Capitolo di San Pietro, A 64 ter, fol. 22 (26): "quod in demolitione habuit Card. Farnesius"; "quod" seems to refer to the chapel's painted ceiling.

156 Lavin, *Bernini and the Crossing*, 15–16n70; Ward Perkins, "The Shrine," 24; Rice, *Altars and Altarpieces*, 213–16, no. 7.

157 Lavin's suggestion that one of the missing columns was sacrificed to repair the two now in the Holy Sacrament chapel nicely accounts for all of the columns from the outer row (*Bernini and the Crossing*, 15–16n70); but cf. Nobiloni, "le colonne vitinee," 89–91, 100.

158 "Pretiosas columnas a Constantino erectas temere prosterneret, et in plures partes diffractas..."; quoted by Rodolfo Lanciani, *Storia degli scavi di Roma e notizie intorno le collezioni romane di antichità*, vol. 1, ed. Leonello Malvezzi Campeggi (Rome, 1989), 187.

159 Arnold Nesselrath, *Das Fossombroner Skizzenbuch* (London, 1993), 144–8.

160 Shearman, *Raphael's Cartoons*, 55–7, argues at length that the structure shown is "a cross section of the *Porta speciosa*" (Acts 3:2), but to me it looks like a straightforward rendition of Acts 3:11: "...all the people ran together to them in the portico called Solomon's." The tapestry shows nineteen columns, but one must be cut off at the left edge. If the building shown is assumed to be symmetrical, it had many more columns than that. Before Raphael, Jean Fouquet made similar historicizing use of the twisted columns to illustrate the *Antiquities* of Flavius Josephus: Fuchs, "Die Spiralsäule," 136.

161 Carpiceci, "La Basilica Vaticana," 97.

162 Ibid., 75, 97. Since Carpiceci reconstructs a half-column at the east end of each colonnade, his plan (Tav. C) shows twenty-two and a half columns rather than the normal twenty-two. A defect of his analysis is the failure to consult the Peruzzi–Da Sangallo drawings, which led to errors concerning the dimensions of the column shafts, the supposed homogeneity of the colonnade, and others: ibid., 115n58, 118n62, etc.

163 Christoph Luitpold Frommel, in *Raffaello architetto*, ed. C. L. Frommel, S. Ray, M. Tafuri (Milan, 1984), esp. 287–8, Cat. 2.15.33; also 256, Cat. 2.15.1, 258, Cat. 2.15.3, 267, Cat. 2.15.11, 286, Cat. 2.15.32, 305–306, Cat. 2.15.46; Metternich,

Die frühen St.-Peter-Entwürfe, 120, 149; Arnaldo Bruschi, "L'idée del Peruzzi per il nuovo S. Pietro," in *Saggi in onore di Renato Bonelli*, vol. 1 (Quaderni dell'Istituto di Storia dell'Architettura, n.s. 15–20 [1990–2]): 459, 462–3, 467, 480nn64, 67; Hans-Christoph Dittscheid, "St. Peter in Rom als Mausoleum der Päpste. Bauprojekte der Renaissance und ihr Verhältnis zur Antike," in *Blick in die Wissenschaft. Forschungsmagazin der Universität Regensburg* 1 (1992): 64–8; idem, "Form versus Materie," 281, 286–90; Frommel, in *The Renaissance from Brunelleschi to Michelangelo*, 411, 412, 413, 418, 601 no. 283, 603–4 no. 287, 604 no. 288, 613 no. 305, 616 no. 311, 623 no. 327, 630 no. 344; Zampa, in *The Architectural Drawings*, 204–5; Arnaldo Bruschi, in ibid., 82–84; Bruschi and Fritz-Eugen Keller, in ibid., 145.

164 One of the *giallo antico* shafts has been measured recently: height 9.02 m (8.8 m below the collar), diameter 1.08 m above the lower apophyge; James E. Packer, *The Forum of Trajan in Rome: A Study of the Monuments* (Berkeley, 1997), vol. 1, 309 Cat. 46, vol. 2, pl. 78.1; cf. Rice, *Altars and Altarpieces*, 232n25. The forty shafts of the old nave measured by Peruzzi averaged 8.8 m in height and 1.07 m in diameter; cf. Krautheimer et al., *Corpus Basilicarum*, 5:234. The thirty-four recorded shafts of the aisle colonnades ranged in height from 5.65 m to 6.2 m, and in diameter from .577 m to .819 m; see above, n. 73. No measured sketches survive of the twelve columns bounding the transept.

165 Sandro Lorenzatti, "Vicende del Tempio di Venere e Roma nel Medioevo e nel Rinascimento," *Rivista dell'Istituto Nazionale d'Archeologia e Storia dell'Arte*, n.s. 3, no. 13 (1990): 134–8.

166 Vincenzo Golzio, *Raffaello nei documenti, nelle testimonianze dei contemporanei e nella letteratura del suo secolo* (Vatican City, 1936), 38–9; Karl Frey, "Zur Baugeschichte des St. Peter. Mitteilungen aus der Reverendissima Fabbrica di S. Pietro," vol. 1, *Jahrbuch der Königlich Preuszischen Kunstsammlungen*, 31. *Beiheft* (Berlin, 1911), 55. The importation of ancient columns and other stones to St. Peter's had begun long before Bramante, in the mid-fifteenth century: Satzinger, "Spolien," 254. In 1471 Pope Sixtus IV authorized the architects of the new Vatican library to dig everywhere for stones to build it: Lanciani, *Storia degli scavi*, 1:93.

167 Alfonso Bartoli, *I monumenti antichi di Roma nei disegni degli Uffizi di Firenze, Testo* (Rome, 1914), 12, 19; *Tavole*, I, XLVII fig. 75; Günther, *Das Studium der antiken Architektur*, 375, no. 17.

168 Frey, "Zur Baugeschichte des St. Peter", 1:70; vol. 2, *Jahrbuch*, 33. *Beiheft* (Berlin, 1913), 39, 43, 48, 50, 53, 54, 55, etc.; Francia, *1506–1606*, 62–3, 83, 105, 111, etc.

169 Frommel, in *Raffaello architetto*, 287–8, Cat. 2.15.33; Christof Thoenes, in *The Renaissance from Brunelleschi to Michelangelo*, 638 no. 350, 640 no. 357; Henry Millon et al., ibid., 666 no. 400, also 398.

170 The demolition would have freed fourteen shafts from the nave and an uncertain number from the aisles. For the aisle shafts, see Arbeiter, *Alt-St. Peter*, 123–32.

171 Albertini, *Opusculum*, p. Ri; Vasari, *Le Vite*, ed. Bettarini, *Testo*, 2:19; Dittscheid, "Form versus Materie," 285–9.

172 Bruschi, in *The Architectural Drawings*, 82. Dittscheid, "Form versus Materie," 289, cites Ovid: "opus superabat materiam."

173 Peruzzi calculated the price of a single column of this size as 390 ducats; Frommel, in *The Renaissance from Brunelleschi to Michelangelo*, 623, no. 326.

174 Enzo Bentivoglio, "Vestigie romane nella Porta del Popolo integrate nell'ornamentazione di Nanni di Baccio Bigio," in

Saggi in onore di Guglielmo De Angelis d'Ossat (Quaderni dell'Istituto di Storia dell'Architettura, n.s., 1–10 [1983–7]) (Rome, 1987) 269 Doc. 1 ("quattro colonne...doi di marmo e doi di granito"), 270 Doc. 4, 271 Doc. 5, 272 Doc. 7. The shafts are of Assouan granite and *pavonazzetto*. Some of St. Peter's shafts were just abandoned; three such were found in the 1940s in the area of the transept: Christern and Thiersch, "Der Aufriss von Alt-St.-Peter. 2," 12–14; Krautheimer et al., *Corpus Basilicarum*, 5:253.

175 There are many payments for "racconciare colonne" (1523/24), "mondandum collunnas" (1541/42), "expoliatione... colunnarum" (1542), "rifare una colonna" (1546); Frey, "Zur Baugeschichte des St. Peter," 1:73, 2: 38–9, 54, etc.

176 Vasari, *Le Vite*, ed. Bettarini, vol. 1, *Testo*, 40; cf. Frommel, in *Raffaello architetto*, 287, Cat. No. 2.15.33.

177 Christiane Denker Nesselrath speculated that Bramante reused ten bases for the Doric columns of his *tegurium*: *Die Säulenordnung bei Bramante* (Worms, 1990) 43–4. She also has found at least one antique base reused in the present basilica, but its profile does not match those of the bases excavated in Old St. Peter's in the 1940s: Krautheimer et al., *Corpus basilicarum*, 5:202–5, figs. 181–3, 186–92; Dittscheid, "Form versus Materie," 301, fig. 10. This may have been an exceptional specimen; cf. n. 181 below.

178 T. Ashby, Jr., *Sixteenth-Century Drawings of Roman Buildings Attributed to Andreas Coner* (Papers of the British School at Rome 2 [1904]), 72, pl. 151; the codex was recognized as Bernardo della Volpaia's by Tilmann Buddensieg, "Bernardo della Volpaia und Giovanni Francesco da Sangallo. Der Autor des Codex Coner und seine Stellung im Sangallo-Kreis," *Römisches Jahrbuch für Kunstgeschichte* 15 (1975): 89–108, esp. 89–95; see further Günther, *Das Studium der antiken Architektur*, 165–202. Uffizi, Gabinetto dei Disegni, Arch. 32ʳ: Bartoli, *Monumenti antichi, Testo*, 67, *Tavole*, III, CCX, fig. 351; Arch. 1804ᵛ: ibid., *Testo*, 102, *Tavole*, IV, CCCXXXIII, fig. 560. The attribution of 1804ᵛ to Giovanni Francesco da Sangallo is Buddensieg's: p. 108.

179 A. Bertolotti, "Nuovi documenti intorno all'architetto Antonio da Sangallo (il Giovane) ed alla sua famiglia (fine)," *Il Buonarroti* ser. 3, 4 (1892): 319; Denker Nesselrath, *Die Säulenordunung*, 86.

180 Dittscheid, "St. Peter," 67, citing a drawing in the Mellon Codex in the J. Pierpont Morgan Library.

181 Gabinetto Nazionale delle Stampe, Rome, FN 8066, Taccuini Alberti; Giovanna Maria Forni, *Monumenti antichi di Roma nei disegni di Alberto Alberti* (Atti dell'Accademia Nazionale dei Lincei 386 [1989], Memorie, ser. 8, 33) (Rome, 1991), *Testo*,

103. The profile of the smaller base matches that of an ancient spoil reused in the new basilica: Denker Nesselrath, *Die Säulenordnung*, 43. The drawing has been published repeatedly under the name of Cherubino Alberti, but with many others it has been reattributed by Forni to his father, who died in 1598 (9–14). Forni transcribes the inscription as: "la colona qui disegniata e dilla nauata grande di Sa[n]to pietro dille piu belle...." (103). For drawings of other spolia connected with St. Peter's, see pp. 35–36 (pl. XLI), 67 (pl. CI), 91 (pl. CLII), 105–6 (pl. CLXXXIV), 141 (pls. CCLVI–CCLVII), 143 (pls. CCLX–CCLXI), 170–1 (pl. CCCXXV), and 180 (pl. CCCLXXXIII).

182 Metternich, *Die frühen St.-Peter-Entwürfe*, 118; Denker Nesselrath, *Die Säulenordnung*, 79–86; Frommel, in *The Renaissance from Brunelleschi to Michelangelo*, 608, no. 295.

183 Grimaldi, *Descrizione*, ed. Niggl, 213.

184 Faustino Corsi, *Delle pietre antiche*, 3d ed. (Rome, 1845), 392, 394; Hibbard, *Carlo Maderno*, 172–3.

185 Corsi, *Delle pietre antiche*, 392, found a total of six shafts of *granito del foro* and two of Assouan granite in the porch; Lorenzatti, "Vicende del Tempio," 136, identified four columns of *granito del foro* and four of Assouan granite.

186 *Fonti per la storia artistica romana al tempo di Paolo V*, ed. Anna Maria Corbo and Massimo Pomponi (Pubblicazioni degli Archivi di Stato, Strumenti, 121) (Rome, 1995), 12: "è da tener presente...che la demolizione dell'antica basilica Vaticana costituiva un centro enorme di recupero di materiale antico che veniva smistato nelle fabbriche in corso nella città." Arnold Esch kindly referred me to this publication.

187 Maria Grazia Tolomeo, "La mostra dell'Acqua Paola," in *Il Trionfo dell'Acqua. Acque e acquedotti a Roma IV sec. a.C.– XX sec.* (Rome, 1986), 250–1; Howard Hibbard, *The Architecture of Palazzo Borghese* (Rome, 1962), 128, Doc. 33; *Fonti per la storia artistica*, 34 s.v. "Bellucci," 46 s.v. "Ticci," 52 s.v. "Bellini." The rumor that Palazzo Borghese contains eighty-eight columns from Old St. Peter's seems preposterous; Francia, *1505–1605*, 18n20.

188 Cesare D'Onofrio, *Roma nel Seicento* (Florence, 1969), 159; thanks to Patricia Waddy for this reference. In 1656 Bernini proposed installing shafts of *cottanello* in place of two granite ones flanking the central niche in the western apse, but the plan was abandoned in favor of the final design for the *cathedra Petri*: Rice, *Altars and Altarpieces*, 267.

189 Cf. Arnold Esch, "Spolien. Zur Wiederverwendung antiker Baustücke und Skulpturen im mittelalterlichen Italien," *Archiv für Kulturgeschichte* 51 (1969): 31–3.

190 Kinney, "Spolia," 120–2.

4

EST HAEC SACRA PRINCIPIS AEDES

The Vatican Basilica from Innocent III to Gregory IX (1198–1241)

ANTONIO IACOBINI

LIKE ALL OF CHRISTIANITY'S MOST IMPORTANT sites, though perhaps more so than others, St. Peter's basilica was a great organism devoted to self-preservation during the Middle Ages (Fig. 7). In fact, even though it underwent continuous enrichment and modification for centuries, the basilica retained, to a large extent, its original structure unaltered up to the time when the "subversive" Renaissance project took shape to replace the old and decrepit body of the Constantinian structure. The medieval history of the basilica saw architecture and furnishings, and architecture and monumental decoration, as intimately combined in a kind of symbiotic unity of the arts, forming a coalition to maintain the venerable sanctuary of the Prince of the Apostles alive and up-to-date, but always recognizable, ancient and modern at the same time.[1]

After the early medieval reorganization of the choir area, which perhaps dated to the time of Gregory the Great (590–604), and the raising of the north transept ordered by Adrian IV (1154–9),[2] the basilica again became the object of radical interventions in the first decades of the thirteenth century. These interventions were destined to redefine the image of the church in connection with the period of the greatest expansion of the theocratic politics of the papacy.[3] The work put in motion by Innocent III (1198–1216) in the area of the apse and that promoted by Gregory IX (1227–41) on the facade, notwithstanding the interval of the few decades separating them, can be interpreted as part of a unified progression which ideally unites the program of Innocent, first pope from the Conti family, with that of his younger relative and successor, Gregory.[4]

As inevitably happens with medieval St. Peter's, we are constrained, also in this case, to exert some measure of imagination in the attempt to recontextualize, in the interior of the lost monument, the few fragments – perhaps better referred to as relics – that escaped destruction during the Counter-Reformation. In this ideal "reassembly of spolia," the designs and notes of the first archaeologists and antiquarians of the Christian Middle Ages (Ciacconio, Panvinio, Grimaldi, and others), as well as information supplied by simple visual testimony, are quite helpful to us.[5] But it still remains true that at every step one has the feeling of seeing a possibility dissolve before one's eyes, that is to say, the possibility of gathering the connections or references that bound together, as on a palimpsest, the large and small works of art from various ages.

But so it is, and it is necessary – notwithstanding the power of the appeal – in a certain sense to surrender to a reconstructive operation that from the very beginning acknowledges itself to be only partial. In fact, it must not be forgotten that we have only fragments at our disposal: *disiecta membra* of architecture, sculpture, and, above all, mosaics, which (as we shall see) have often been transported far from Rome and rendered anonymous by the tortuous paths of an ancient hobby of collecting things, and later by those of the modern market.[6]

In the *Gesta Innocentii*, the ingratiating papal biography written by a Roman cleric between 1203 and 1208,[7] we find rather ample information concerning the architectural interventions carried out in the area of the Vatican by the first Conti pope (Fig. 32). This is enough to evoke, before our eyes, a varied sequence of building nuclei defended by towers and walls, conceived of as a new alternative permanent residence for the Lateran patriarchy:

> Since [Innocent] considered it not only convenient but useful for the Supreme Pontiff to have a worthy palace also near St. Peter's, he had the following buildings constructed from scratch: a chaplain's residence, with a room and a chapel; a bakery, a cellar, a kitchen, and a *marescalcia* [stables and premises for the official in charge of these]; residences and offices for the chancellor, *camerarius*, and almoner. On the other hand, he also had the audience hall restored and the loggia redone, and the whole palace surrounded by a wall with

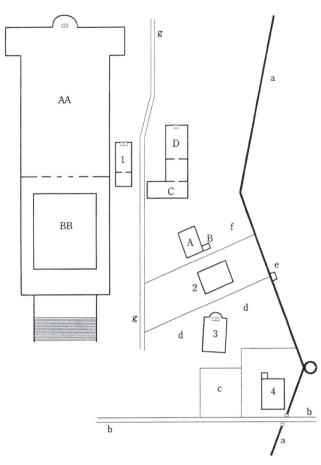

32. The topography to the north of the Vatican basilica at the beginning of the thirteenth century (from Amma Maria Voci, *Nord o Sud? Note per la storia del medioevale* Palatium apostolicum apud Sanctum Petrum *e delle sue cappelle*, Vatican City, 1992)

towers above the entrances. In addition, he acquired a house positioned within the palace walls, and assigned it as a dwelling to his doctor.[8]

Nothing remains of the "palazzi di assai buona maniera" that Vasari thought he saw here,[9] with the possible exception of the so-called *marescalcia* (Fig. 33), at one time annexed to the complex of the *palatium inferius* on the north side of the atrium. This concerns a vast area found at present beneath the Sala Regia of Bernini, with walls made of tufa blocks, divided into two aisles by columns with Ionic capitals and covered by ample cross vaults: a space whose conception undoubtedly involves Roman Cistercian precedents, such as the chapter house of the abbey of SS. Vincenzo e Anastasio alle Tre Fontane.[10]

More interested in architecture than in painting, the author of the *Gesta* mentions the works commissioned by the pope for the interior of the basilica only in passing.[11] If it is true that, due to the lack of mention, the date of the text (ca. 1208) might serve as a reference

point for the date of the mosaic, this nevertheless does not detract from the fact that the reconstruction of the apse is rather elusive; one must keep in mind, above all, that the apse was the greatest decorative undertaking commissioned by Innocent, and the one with which he intended to endow, in a place of the highest symbolic value, the official image of pontifical *auctoritas* and of the *Ecclesia Romana*.[12]

Before it was demolished in July 1592, the ancient composition, known by means of a rich series of drawings, was copied and attentively described (Fig. 34).[13] Pieces of the mosaic were also salvaged and sent as a papal gift to the family of the original patron of the work. This was the fate of the pontiff's portrait – reduced to a half-bust – as well as the roundel with the phoenix, both of which belonged to the central area of the lower register (Figs. 35, 36). Specifically, the pope was located to the left of the throne, while the phoenix rested on the palm tree behind him. These were given as the gift of Clement VIII in 1596 to Lothar Conti II. They remained in the chapel of the Poli palace for three and a half centuries (until 1953), embedded in the seventeenth-century stucco work of an altar. A precious third fragment of the *Ecclesia Romana*, the female figure previously located to the right of the throne, had rather a more obscure fate (Fig. 37). Spared not for reasons of family history but because (perhaps), once removed, it resembled an icon of

33. Vatican palaces, hall of the *marescalcia*, Rome

34. The destroyed apsidal mosaic of St. Peter's in a watercolor of ca. 1590. (Biblioteca Apostolica Vaticana, Vat. lat. 5408, fols. 29ᵛ–30ʳ)

the Maria Regina type, it immediately lost every link to its original context along with its true iconographic identity. If the public evidence of its former setting is considered, it seems almost a "contrappasso" to discover it, at the beginning of this century, in the bedroom of a collector, Baron Giovanni Barracco (Fig. 38).[14] Unfortunately, nothing is known of the whereabouts of this piece after its removal. The catalogue of the collection to which it pertains laconically states, "da casa Barberini,"[15] which is not enough to shed light on the matter for us. As I suggested a few years ago, this information could in fact carry us back as far as to the first decades of the seventeenth century, specifically to Cardinal Francesco Barberini, a passionate lover of Christian antiquities as well as a sponsor of the restoration, undertaken in 1625, of the Carolingian mosaic of the Lateran Triclinium – an ideal collector for a piece of this type.[16]

But let us examine more closely the ancient Vatican decoration (Fig. 34). It was divided into two levels: the vault itself and a register below, delimited at the bottom by a monumental *titulus*. Above, on the background of

a golden sky, Christ Enthroned was flanked by standing images of Peter and Paul, accompanied by two palm trees converging toward the semicircle of heaven with the hand of God. A landscape with little buildings, trees, animals, and shepherds unfolded at the figures' feet. The only pause, in the center, was provided by the little mountain of Paradise under Christ's throne, at which two stags gazed. With respect to the Early Christian apse, whose composition can probably be inferred from the ivory casket of Samagher,[17] Innocent's new edition of the mosaic already introduced some changes of plan at this level: the *Maiestas* came to supplant perhaps a *Traditio legis*;[18] the rustic landscape took the place of two lines of lambs. But the most relevant innovations involved, above all, the lower register, where the Twelve Apostles of the Early Christian image were expunged, though the middle group with the throne and the Lamb were preserved. The apostles were replaced by the lambs processing out of Jerusalem and Bethlehem, while at the center two new figures were introduced. These figures constitute a true iconographic *hapax*.[19] The figures in question

35. Head of Innocent III. Museo di Roma, Rome

Triclinium mosaic) and is crowned by a showy jeweled diadem that represents her unequivocally as *imperatrix*. Innocent, for his part, wears the *phrygium*, the headgear which, according to tradition, Constantine bequeathed to Sylvester with the Donation as emblem of the *translatio* of the temporal power over the West into the hands of the popes.

At root the important iconographic innovations of Innocent's register contain, I believe, a clear programmatic intention. The pope, as patron, thus entrusts to images in the most symbolic site of Christianity a quite precise concept of pontifical *auctoritas*, whose scope would not be fully comprehensible without a reading keyed to the background of historical events, based on the rapport between papacy and empire which, in the first decade of the thirteenth century, involved Innocent, Philip of Swabia, Otto of Brunswick, and the young Frederick II.

The dual concept pope/*Ecclesia* introduced in the mosaic represents one of the key points of Innocent's thought, and it is purposely employed in order to translate his doctrine of powers into an image. As it is specified in his third sermon, *In consecratione pontificis*, the pope, in his capacity as *Vicarius Christi*, is mystically united in marriage to *Ecclesia*, just as Christ – according to the tradition of allegorical exegesis – is the bridegroom of the virgin of the Song of Songs, and the virgin recognizable, in fact, as the Church itself.[20] This spiritual wedding procures for the pontiff, as dowry, the *plenitudo potestatis*, the exclusive power that establishes him as "citra Deum sed ultra hominem,"[21] in a space superior to the human, to which perhaps the register of the Vatican apse is able

are Innocent III (to the left) and *Ecclesia Romana* (to the right), emphasized in their roles as heads of the two lines of lambs and stationed in the strictest contiguity with the throne, in a vertically axial position in relationship to the Christ of the *Maiestas*.

With respect to the inveterate tradition of Roman apses (from SS. Cosma and Damiano to S. Maria in Trastevere), the presentation of the papal figure includes at least two major novelties. On the one hand, the pontiff assumes a totally new position of centrality, in a way that surpasses the basically ancillary role of donor usually attributed to him. On the other hand, thus freed from the individual dimension deriving from his function as patron, he acquires a highly paradigmatic significance, authenticated by his pairing with the erect and triumphal personification of *Ecclesia*. The political (as well as ecclesiastical) meaningfulness of the theme that takes form here is for the rest underscored by the evidence of the insignia. *Ecclesia* holds up a banner of imperial significance (analogous to Charlemagne's banner in the Lateran

36. Phoenix. Museo di Roma, Rome

37. *Ecclesia Romana.* Museo Barracco, Rome

to allude. Papal power, according to Innocent, does not in fact come from Peter alone, but by means of Peter *ab ipso Domino* (in the mosaic one notes the underlying vertical axiality of the middle area with the patron and *Ecclesia*). It is at once a universal, spiritual, and temporal power, which sums up in itself both the sacerdotal dignity and the royal dignity of Christ, and, because of this, is itself superior to the empire.

As a parallel to the images, the text of the new *titulus* also seems amply to reflect a triumphal concept of *Ecclesia*: "Summa Petri sedes est haec sacra principis aedes...."[22] Yet, within the universal context of the declaration perhaps an even more specifically Roman reference connected to the age-old rivalry for supremacy between the Vatican and the Lateran was intended. In fact, the continuation of the inscription, "Mater cunctarum decor et decus ecclesiarum," a title traditionally associated with St. John but here attributed to St. Peter, uses terms that (as Maccarrone has noted) bring to mind precisely those of a papal bull promulgated in 1205.[23]

The iconological value of the mosaic, however, cannot be completely understood without also clarifying the rapport between it and the new furnishings that Innocent had made for the choir of the basilica, both tied, it seems, to a unitary design, or at least understandable as such, even if only within successive stages of achievement.

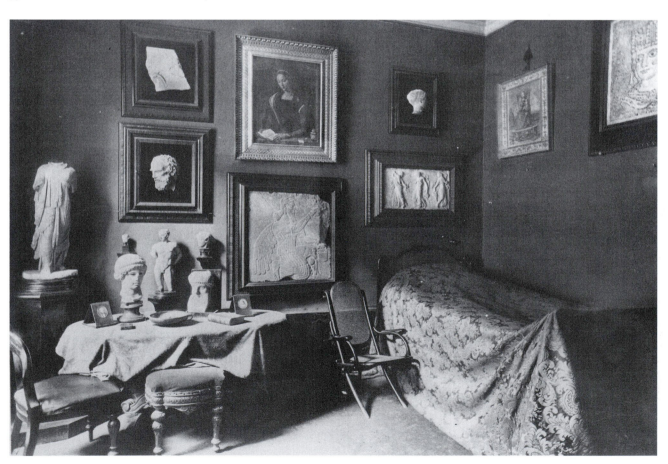

38. Baron G. Barracco's bedroom: hanging (*above right*) is the mosaic fragment of the *Ecclesia Romana*

39. Arrangement of St. Peter's choir in an engraving from 1581

The marble furnishings, which were lost during the demolitions carried out during the Renaissance, can be reconstructed with the help of a few written and iconographic testimonies. Among the latter, the oldest is an engraving of 1581 based on a drawing of a parish priest of Fribourg, Sebastian Werro (Fig. 39).[24] The papal cathedra was located in the middle of the apsidal cylinder (therefore at the base of the vertical axis descending from the spherical vaulted covering). Even though summarily sketched, two fundamental elements can be distinguished: the lions, placed on each side so that they form the armrests of the chair ("duobus leonibus ornata," Grimaldi says of the cathedra)[25] and, above all, a backrest topped by a triangular form. The latter element was the one that conferred on the "thronum marmoreum maximum auro vermiculatum ac caelatum," as described by Alfarano,[26] a connotation sui generis in the Roman panorama of the early thirteenth century. The type of cathedra current at this time was, rather, one with a backrest topped by a circular form, alluding to the pontifical *sanctitas*.[27] In fact, the choice of the new silhouette, as Gandolfo has shown, contains a direct reference

to the *cathedra Petri* (Fig. 40), the ancient wooden chair that acquired, precisely during Innocent's reign, the ever-increasing fame of being the real, true apostolic relic; it was even considered the most important possession of the basilica in terms of its primatial claims against the Lateran.[28] In my opinion, however, in order to understand better this characterization also conferred on the marble throne, another element must be considered. It is necessary, in fact, to recall that, after the election of January 1198, the episcopal consecration of Innocent III was carried out in St. Peter's on February 22, the feast day of the Cathedra, a liturgical commemoration of Peter's installation in the Roman *sedes*.[29] This was a co-incidence which the pontiff himself did not hesitate to emphasize by writing to the basilica's chapter,[30] an even more significant coincidence, because on that day – and the *Gesta* refer to it – he was seated, not on a marble cathedra, but on the throne believed to be the apostle's own.[31] The new chair commissioned by Innocent for the Vatican apse was therefore understood as *his* cathedra, and the special triangular form of the backrest ornamentation confirmed the elective bond that linked the pope to the Prince of the Apostles.

The sumptuous marble furnishings – from what is known – must have also included other pieces, such as a large ambo. The documentary trace of this ambo has

40. The *Cathedra Petri*. St. Peter's, Rome

been preserved in an inscription, transcribed by Pietro Sabino,[32] from which we learn that the authors were Lorenzo and Jacopo, father and son. These two marble masons were active on many occasions in the undertakings sponsored by Innocent, and their joint activity does not go beyond the first five years of the thirteenth century.[33] According to Alfarano, the ambo was located behind the southwest pillar at the place marked 7 on his plan, where a double stairway structure leading to a central platform is reproduced (Fig. 41). Claussen has been able to discern some of its fragments among the erratic materials of the Vatican Grottoes – four little columns and part of the semipolygonal platform, documented here in an old photograph (Fig. 42).[34] A relatively faithful representation of this monumental piece of furnishing is recognizable, in my opinion, in two historiated initials of *Exultet* B78 of St. Peter's Archive, a masterpiece of Roman miniature painting carried out at the end of the thirteenth century, perhaps specifically for the Vatican basilica (Fig. 43).[35]

Innocent's intervention was not limited to the upper zone of the basilica; it also touched the venerable Confessio containing Peter's tomb. This "descent" *inferioribus locis* serves to demonstrate the precise will of the pope to leave his seal, based on an organic design, on all three levels of the most sacred area of the building. As a matter of fact, he commissioned a large metallic frontal (now dismantled) in order to cover the niche of the pallium (Fig. 44). It was positioned above the original tomb at the intermediate level of the funerary apparatus, below the main altar that had been renovated by Callistus II in 1123 (Fig. 45).[36] The great decorative facade – the work of artists from Limoges – must have constituted, in its day, something completely new for Rome, with the scintillating effect of the piece, which was made of gilded copper and enamels. According to Gauthier's reconstruction based on the few surviving fragments (Fig. 46), the upper part of the antependium was made up of a wide fret-worked grille of gilded bronze, which is still visible in the present-day Confessio, crowned by a long inscription bearing the name of the patron (Fig. 44). Underneath, as seen also in the Limousin altar of St. Miguel in Excelsis (ca. 1190), there was a facade of two rows of small arches on little columns, in which the apostles would have been inserted at the sides of Christ in Majesty (Fig. 47). In contrast to what Gauthier has suggested, Sible de Blauuw recently pointed out a series of elements which would seem to indicate that this part of the work was not originally aligned with the altar above, but set a bit behind the protection offered by the grille.[37] However, the central part, on which the mandorla of God was positioned, must have constituted a sliding door that allowed access to the niche behind it, where the pallium that the pope granted to newly elected metropolitans was required to

be kept. The arched summit of this door was occupied by a lunette (today located in the Palazzo Venezia) decorated on two sides (Figs. 48, 49), without a doubt the most interesting part of the frontal, which Gauthier has brilliantly linked to the other pieces. The iconographic program developed here is completely centered on a theme particularly dear to Innocent's vision, that of episcopal power, directly connected to the intended purpose of the niche.[38] On the front side, framed by busts of prophets and apostles in relief, the middle medallion and the one placed at the apex of the arch in particular attest to this theme (Fig. 48). In the former, the cross-bearing lamb in between the symbols of the evangelists – "Ego sum ostium i(n) ovile ovium" reads the inscription – alludes precisely to the pastoral charisma of bishops, while the concept of Christ/door is established by the small relief above the Lamb, which constitutes in turn a reference to the very door of the niche. The symbols contained in the upper medallion are, in fact, precisely those of episcopal power: the mitre and the throne. The latter, depicted as a *sella curulis*, has two large armrests decorated with a lion's head and griffon's head, whose coupling perhaps implies a possible Christological connotation with reference to the pastoral teaching of the pontiff himself: "Christus," wrote Isidore of Seville, "est leo pro regno et fortitudine... aquila propter quod post resurrectionem ad astra remeavit."[39]

On the inner side, decorated only by engraved images, the theme of investiture becomes even more explicit, passing from divine simile to the more concrete sphere of an assize of bishops (Fig. 49). At the center, the pontiff appears on a throne adorned with episcopal insignia, but provided with Peter's keys and book as well and accompanied by the Holy Spirit, which gives him divine counsel. The prelates who surround him, even though endowed with mitres, chasubles, and books, are all, nevertheless, lacking the pallium, which only the pope is wearing. I do not believe that we are dealing here with a mere oversight, but rather a conscious iconographic device, intended to recall the rigorous and centralistic formalities of investiture maintained by Innocent. As a matter of fact, the metropolitans, canonically elected, always had to kneel to request the pallium in Rome as an indispensable seal of legality. Therefore, the fact that in our lunette the pope is the only one wearing the pallium signifies that he is the only one with the power to confer the *auctoritas* that such a symbol represents, in his capacity as vicar of Christ and successor of Peter. Moreover, the inscription refers to the idea of a power that proceeds from above: "I, the life-giving Spirit of the Council, cover you [that is, I invest you], so that you in turn may invest those who must be invested...."[40] And here, what is to be understood as the symbol of the attribution of power to the bishops is, in fact, the

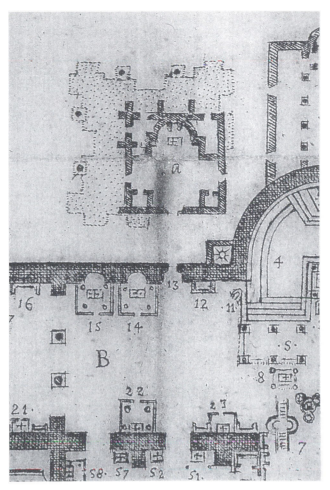

41. T. Alfarano, portion of the plan of Old St. Peter's

pallium – not the mitre, as Gauthier suggested. And the pallium would have been taken out from the very niche that stood behind the antependium.[41]

As it will be understood, we are dealing with a further aspect of the discourse on pontifical *auctoritas* to which Innocent III intended to give form in the new decorative order of the Vatican choir, a discourse that started at the apsidal mosaic, passed onto the cathedra below it, and descended to the level of Peter's tomb.

The last significant stage, in the fervor of renovation that swept through the basilica in the first three decades of the thirteenth century, is represented by the work on the facade, put in motion by Gregory IX, the second pope of the Conti family.[42]

In this case, too, as in the case of Innocent's apse, the possibility of reconstituting the original structure, demolished in 1606, and the mosaic decoration that covered it, is tied to the testimony of written sources and drawings.[43] These two watercolors (Figs. 7, 50) – which are best examined in tandem – show that the exterior was covered by a single large composition divided into three registers, the lower one being separated from the other two by means of a framing cornice. Below were arranged the twenty-four elders of the Apocalypse, between lambs processing out of Bethlehem and Jerusalem. On the second tier, in between the windows, were the four acclaiming figures of the evangelists, partially looking upward. The symbols of the evangelists appeared two by two in the upper register, while at the center was Christ Enthroned. The pope patron knelt at his feet, while at his sides were the Virgin and Saint Peter – a sort of Vatican

42. Vatican Grottoes, St. Peter's basilica, fragments of the basilica's medieval ambo

43. Biblioteca Apostolica Vaticana, *Archivio del Capitolo di S. Pietro*, Exultet B 78, fol. 15ᵛ

44. The pallium niche, St. Peter's, Rome

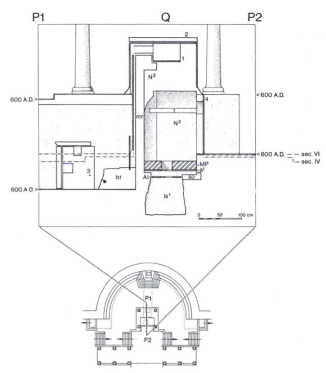

45. St. Peter's, sectional diagram and plan for the high altar after 1123. The frontal of the pallium niche is at no. 4 (from de Blaauw 1994)

46. St. Peter's, a reconstruction of the metal frontal of the pallium niche (from Antonio Iacobini, *La pittura e le arti Suntuarie da Innocenzo III a Innocenzo IV (1198–1254)*, in *Roma nel Duecento. L'arte nella città dei papi da Innocenzo III a Bonifacio VIII*, Turin, 1991)

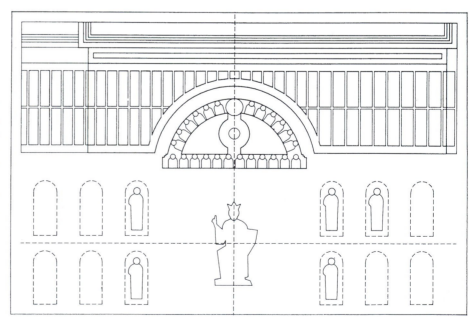

47. St. Peter's, statuettes from the frontal of the pallium niche. Museo Sacro Vaticano, Vatican

48. St. Peter's, the door to the pallium niche, front and back. Museo Nazionale di Palazzo Venezia, Rome

49. St. Peter's, the door to the pallium niche, front and back. Museo Nazionale di Palazzo Venezia, Rome

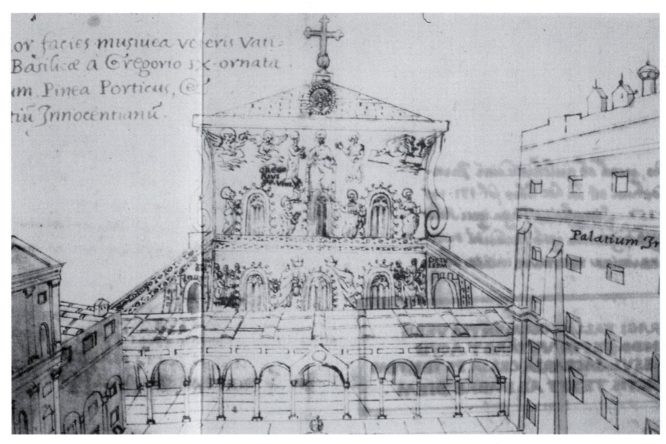

or facies musiuea ve ieris Vati:
Basilicæ à Gregorio ix-ornata.
in Pinea Porticus, e
iñ Innocentianu.

Palatium Jn

50. The facade of old St. Peter's. Biblioteca Apostolica Vaticana, Barb. Lat. 2733, fol. 133ʳ

edition of the *Deesis*.[44] The central nucleus of the up-per composition, whose iconography has been discussed many times, had already been reproduced faithfully by Cimabue before 1280 in the *Ytalia* fresco at Assisi. This fresco constitutes, in an abbreviated form, the oldest rep-resentation of the new facade of St. Peter's.[45]

Until a few years ago, by a twist of fate, out of the whole vast mosaic only the few square centimeters of a very compromised papal portrait were known – a por-trait which, like Innocent's, was removed and given to the Conti family (Fig. 51). But during the demolition two other fragments were saved, which nevertheless, in the almost four centuries since their removal had completely lost their identity. One – recognized by Andaloro and Etinhof – is a head of the Virgin preserved in the Pushkin Museum in Moscow (Fig. 52). It had been acquired in Rome in 1863, probably already with a restoration in the area of the veil.[46] The other piece – today well-restored – is the beautiful head of Luke in the Vatican Pinacoteca (Fig. 53). This piece, though never moved from Rome, was nevertheless reduced to an almost totally unrecog-nizable state. Since the beginning of the seventeenth cen-tury it had been embedded in a lunette of the Palazzo Altemps, mounted inside a badly made half-length por-trait painted *a secco* (Fig. 54).[47]

As with the apse mosaic, Gregory IX's new compo-sition replaced an Early Christian one that in this case dated back to the time of Leo the Great (440–61).[48] We are familiar with a "copy" of the older mosaic from the eleventh-century pen-and-ink drawing of a codex from Farfa at Eton College, Windsor (Cod. 124, fol. 122), a drawing that illustrates the funeral of Gregory the Great (Fig. 55). As one can see, the decorative theme was once again apocalyptic according to the classic scheme that was normally reserved for the triumphal arch in Roman churches. The twenty-four elders were placed between the windows and under the secondary roofs. Above the elders appeared the symbols of the evangelists, and above these, in the center, was a large tondo with the Lamb, made perhaps at the end of the seventh century to re-place a bust of Christ.[49]

As far as we know, the Early Christian mosaic was preserved like this until the beginning of the thirteenth century, when, as the *Gesta* record, Innocent III car-ried out a restoration in order to obviate his "grave consumption."[50] The fact that a few years later Gregory proceeded with its total reconstruction is therefore not explicable in terms of a restoration need; rather, it might be better to consider it as a result of the pope's intention to update its comprehensive program. Contextually, an

51. Head of Gregory IX. Museo di Roma, Rome

52. Head of the Virgin. Pushkin Museum, Moscow

53. Head of St. Luke. Pinacoteca Vaticana, Vatican

54. Head of St. Luke before its removal from Palazzo Altemps

architectural resystematization was also accomplished in which the facade was furnished with a cornice *a cavetto*. This change generated a more extensive surface to be covered with mosaic by pushing upward the symbols of the evangelists.

Even while maintaining the apocalyptic theme, the thirteenth-century mosaic presents a decidedly more ample and complex articulation involving the introduction of numerous new elements: the four large figures of the evangelists on the second level; and, above all, the upper central scene, toward which the entire composition converges – the *Deesis* with Christ Enthroned between Peter and Mary, in which the small figure of the pope patron is inserted, represented kneeling to the left of the divine throne but in direct contact with the *Maiestas*. Yet the written and graphic sources are not in agreement on the precise attitude conferred upon the pontiff. Grimaldi asserts that he was seen in the act of offering some gold, on a pillow, to Christ.[51] Such a gesture, in his opinion, referred to the rite that would have been enacted on the occasion of the coronation, when the emperor would have made a similar offering to the pope to signify his

56. Gregory IX, from the mosaic of the facade of St. Peter's, drawing by Alfonso Ciacconio. Biblioteca Apostolica Vaticana, Vat. Lat. 5407, p. 43

submission to Christ, according to a custom introduced near the end of the twelfth century. However, this reading contrasts with Ciacconio's graphic testimony,[52] which reproduces, in detail, the figure of Gregory VIII with joined hands raised toward Christ (Fig. 56). This leads one to suggest, as Ladner has observed,[53] an error of interpretation on the part of Grimaldi, who could have misunderstood the decoration of the pillow at the foot of the enthroned figure.

Still, on the level of representative logic, the gesture has essentially an equivalent meaning. As Ladner explained,[54] it derives from the repertoire of the feudal world, from the rite of the *commendatio*: the placing of the vassal's joined hands inside those of his own lord's was a sign of submission and loyalty. Therefore, the pontiff, with his head covered by the tiara and thus represented in the fullness of his power, intended to present himself, in a certain sense, as a vassal of Christ, in this way establishing a precise hierarchical scale, which placed him in direct contact with the divinity, the prime originator of his *auctoritas*, in an exquisitely theocratic perspective.[55] This is an iconographic choice, knowingly related therefore to the ideology transposed into images by Innocent in the apse of the basilica.

Even the *titulus*, which Grimaldi says was placed on the cornice that separated the two tiers of windows and which Tasselli, seeing its length, transcribed in a rather

55. The facade of St. Peter's before its remaking by Gregory IX. Eton College, Windsor, Cod. 124, fol. 122[r]

unorganized way in the remaining usable space on the finished drawing sheet, ultimately seems to refer to the same conceptual horizon. The translated text reads more or less as follows: "As when the heavenly orb of the sun burns, and shines on everything, and gleams like gold above every other metal, thus, this haven of peace built of stone is filled with fervor by doctrine and by faith and expands its power everywhere."[56]

St. Peter's basilica, that is, the *Ecclesia Romana*, shines, therefore, thanks to its primacy and its doctrine, like the sun. I do not believe that we are dealing with a generic image influenced by the metaphysics of light;[57] the comparison with the greatest of the luminaries – which here alludes to the universal power of the Church – seems rather to recall the successful metaphor already used some decades before by Innocent III to explain his doctrine of the powers: "God has placed in the firmament of the heavens two great heavenly bodies, the sun to preside over the day and the moon over the night; in the same way, in the firmament of the Universal Church . . . he has placed two supreme authorities: . . . the pontifical power and the royal. But just as the moon receives its light from the sun, . . . in like manner the imperial power receives the splendor of its dignity from the papal power."[58]

Whatever the precise reference intended by the inscription, its text proves to have several meanings, and also recalls (*ad evidentiam*) the dazzling spectacle of light that the golden backdrop of the mosaics offered to those who entered the atrium of the basilica (Fig. 1). After dressing it up in new vestments – approximately eight centuries after the great Early Christian decorative projects – the two "restorer" popes, Innocent and Gregory, handed over to their successors a see truly worthy, in an imperial sense, of the Prince of the Apostles ("Est haec sacra principis aedes," according to the *titulus* of the apse): a sumptuous complex of architecture and decoration destined to become the great theater of the first Jubilee of 1300.

NOTES

The text was first published in *L'architettura della Basilica di San Pietro. Storia e costruzione (Atti del Convegno internazionale di studi, Roma, Castel S. Angelo, 7–10 novembre 1995)*, ed. Gianfranco Spagnesi (Rome, 1997); it was translated from the Italian by Teri F. Chalmers.

1   R. Krautheimer and A. K. Frazer, "San Pietro," in R. Krautheimer, R. K. Spencer Corbett, and A. K. Frazer, *Corpus basilicarum christianarum Romae*, vol. 5 (Vatican City, 1980), 171–285; A. Arbeiter, *Alt-St. Peter in Geschichte und Wissenschaft: Abfolge der Bauten, Rekonstruktion, Architekturprogramm* (Berlin, 1988), esp. particularly 51–191; S. DeBlaauw, *Cultus et decor. Liturgie en architectur in laatantiek en middeleeuws Rome* (Delft, 1987), Ital. trans. *Cultus et decor. Liturgia e architettura nella Roma tardoantica e medievale*, vol. 2 (Vatican City, 1994), 2: 451–756.

The following is a list of the relevant works that have appeared since my study was published in 1997:
A. Iacobini, "Innocenzo III e l'architettura. Roma e il Nord del *Patrimonium Sancti Petri*," in *Innocenzo III. Urbs et Orbis* (Rome, 2002), 2:1261–91; E. Castelnuovo and A. Monciatti, "Préhistoire du Palais des Papes," in *Monument de l'histoire. Construire, reconstruire le Palais des Papes, XIVe–XXe siècle*, exh. cat., Avignon, Palais des Papes, 29 June–29 September 2002 (Avignon, 2002), 116–21. On the Basilica of St. Peter's at the time of Innocent III and Gregory VII: A. C. Carpiceci and R. Krautheimer, "Nuovi dati sull'antica basilica di San Pietro in Vaticano," part 1, *Bollettino d'arte* 93–4 (1995): 1–70, part 2, ibid. 95 (1996): 1–84; A. Paravicini Bagliani, *Le Chiavi e la Tiara. Immagini e simboli del papato medievale* (Rome, 1998), 17–26, 43–49; H. L. Kessler, "La decorazione della basilica medievale di San Pietro," in *Romei e Giubilei. II pellegrinaggio medievale a San Pietro (350–1350)*, exh. cat., Rome, Palazzo Venezia, 29 ottobre 1999–26 febbraio 2000, ed. M. D'Onofrio (Milan, 1999), 263–70; S. de Blaauw, "L'arredo liturgico e il culto in San Pietro," in ibid., 271–7; A Pinelli, "L'antica basilica," in *La Basilica di San Pietro in Vaticano*, ed. A. Pinelli (Modena, 2000), 9–51 and 913–16; M. Adaloro and S. Romano, "L'immagine nell'abside," in *Arte e iconografia a Roma da Costantino a Cola di Rienzo*, ed. M. Andaloro and S. Romano (Milan, 2000), 93–132; F. Gandolfo, "Il ritratto di committenzo," in ibid., 175–92. On the mosaic fragment of the head of Mary from the facade of St. Peter's, documented in the Giustiniani collection from 1621: S. Danesi Squarzina, "Frammenti dell'antico S. Pietro in una collezione del primo Seicento," in *Arte d'Occidente: Temi e metodi. Studi in ornore di Angiola Maria Romanini*, ed. A. Cadei, M. Righetti Tosti-Croce, A. Segagni Malacrat, and A. Tomei (Rome, 1999), 3:1187–97. On the gesta of Innocent III: G. Barone, "I *Gesti Innocentii III*: Politica e cultura a Roma all'inizio del Duecento," in *Studi sul Medioevo per Girolamo Arnaldi*, ed. G. Barone, L. Capo, and S. Gasparri (Rome, 2001), 1–23.

2   Concerning these two interventions, see, respectively: Krautheimer and Frazer, "San Pietro," 265–7, 182, 284; DeBlaauw, *Cultus et decor*, 2:530–4, 632–3.

3   M. Maccarrone, *Studi su Innocenzo III* (Padua, 1972); B. Bolton, *Innocent III: Studies on Papal Authority and Pastoral Care* (London, 1995); A. Paravicini Bagliani, *Il trono di Pietro: L'universalità del Papato da Alessandro III a Bonifacio VIII* (Rome, 1996).

4   As to the relationship between the two popes and the relevant historical discussion, see M. Dykmans, "D'Innocent III à Boniface VIII. Histoire des Conti et des Annibaldi," in *Bulletin de l'Institut historique belge de Rome* 45 (1975): 19–21.

5   B. Agosti, *Collezionismo e archeologia cristiana nel Seicento. Federico Borromeo e il Medioevo artistico tra Roma e Milano* (Milan, 1996), 9–51; DeBlaauw, *Cultus et decor*, vol. 2, passim.

6   For a methodically articulated approach to the study of the Vatican fragments, see the general considerations and analyses of specific cases contained in *Fragmenta picta. Affreschi e mosaici del Medioevo romano*, exh. cat. (Rome, Castel Sant'Angelo, 15 December 1989–18 February 1990), by M. Andaloro, A. Ghidoli, A. Iacobini, S. Romano, and A. Tomei (Rome, 1989).

7   B. Bolton, "Too Important to Neglect: The *Gesta Innocentii PP III*," in *Church and Chronicle in the Middle Ages: Essays Presented to John Taylor*, ed. G. A. Loud and I. N. Wood (London, 1991), 87–99, now in B. Bolton, *Innocent III*, Essay IV.

8   *Gesta Innocentii PP. III*, *P.L.*, CCXIV, col. CCXI: "Quia vero non tam honorabile, sed utile censuit, ut summus pontifex apud Sanctum Petrum palatium dignum haberet, fecit ibi fieri

domos istas de novo: capellaniam, cameram et capellam, panattariam, buccellariam, coquinam et marescaltiam; domos cancellarii, camerarii, et eleemosynarii; aulam autem confirmari praecepit, ac refici logiam, totumque palatium claudi muris, et super portas erigi turres; emit etiam domum inter clausuram palatii, quam ad habitationem medici deputavit."

9 "Fece poi fare Innocenzio Terzo in sul monte Vaticano due palazzi, per quel che si è potuto vedere di assai buona maniera; ma perché da altri Papi furono rovinati, e particolarmente da Nicola Quinto, che disfece e rifece la maggior parte del palazzo, non ne dirò altro se non che si vede una parte d'essi nel torrione tondo e parte nella sagrestia vecchia di S. Piero." G. Vasari, *Le vite de' più eccellenti pittori scultori e architettori*, vol. 2, ed. R. Bettarini and P. Barocchi (Florence, 1967), 49. Concerning the Vatican palaces during the Middle Ages: D. Redig de Campos, "Les constructions d'Innocent III et de Nicolas III sur la colline Vaticane," *Mélanges d'archéologie et d'histoire* 71 (1959): 359–64; K. B. Steinke, *Die mittelalterlichen Vatikanpaläste und ihre Kapellen* (Vatican City, 1984); A. M. Voci, *Nord o Sud? Note per la storia del medioevale* Palatium apostolicum apud Sanctum Petrum e *delle sue cappelle* (Vatican City, 1992), 45–104, with new documents and hypotheses on the topography of the area during Innocent's reign.

10 P. F. Pistilli, "L'architettura a Roma nella prima metà del Duecento (1198–1254)," in *Roma nel Duecento. L'arte nella città dei papi da Innocenzo III a Bonifacio VIII*, ed. A. M. Romanini (Turin, 1991), 19.

11 On Innocent III as an art patron more generally, see A. Iacobini, "s.v. Innocenzo III," *Enciclopedia dell'Arte Medievale*, vol. 7 (Rome, 1996), 386–92; to which it is necessary to add B. Bolton, "Advertise the Message: Images in Rome at the Turn of the Twelfth Century," in *Studies in Church History* 28 (1992): 117–30, now in idem, *Innocent III*, Essay XVII.

12 For information on the Vatican mosaic, the following are most helpful: G. B. Ladner, *Die Papstbildnisse des Altertums und des Mittelalters: II. Von Innozenz II. Zu Benedikt XI.* (Vatican City, 1970), 56–8; Antonio Iacobini, "Il mosaico absidale di San Pietro in Vaticano," *Fragmenta picta* (1991), 119–29; idem, "La pittura e le arti suntuarie da Innocenzo III a Innocenzo IV (1198–1254)," *Roma del Duecento*, 240–5.

13 S. Waetzoldt, *Die Kopien des 17. Jahrhunderts nach Mosaiken und Wandmalereien in Rom* (Vienna-Munich, 1964), 71–2, nos. 943–57.

14 Antonio Iacobini, "Il mosaico absidale," 121. The photograph of the bedroom is part of the album "Interno di una casa," found in M. Nota, "Una casa o un museo?" in an exhibition catalogue of the Museo Barracco in Rome, *La biblioteca di un collezionista* (June–September 1983), 21–33.

15 G. Barracco and W. Helbig, *Collezione Barracco* (Rome, 1907), 11.

16 Iacobini, "Il mosaico absidale," 121; and "Il mosaico del Triclinio Lateranense," *Fragmenta picta*, 189–96. On Francesco Barberini as a collector of medieval antiquities, see E. Bassan, "s.v. Barberini, Francesco," *Enciclopedia dell'Arte Medievale*, vol. 3 (Rome, 1992), 65–69; I. Herklotz, "Cassiano and the Christian Tradition," *Cassiano dal Pozzo's Paper Museum*, vol. 1 (*Quaderni Puteani*, vol. 2) (Milan, 1992), 31–48, esp. 32, 36–42.

17 J. Ruysschaert, "L'inscription absidale primitive de S. Pierre: Texte et contextes," *Atti della Pontificia Accademia Romana di Archeologia. Rendiconti* 40 (1967–8): 171–90.

18 G. Matthiae, *Mosaici medievali delle chiese di Roma* (Rome, 1967), 330–2; R. Krautheimer, "A Note on the Inscription in the Apse of Old St. Peter's," *Dumbarton Oaks Papers* 41 (1987): 317–20, esp. 318. For a different reconstruction of the Early

Christian prototype, considered to be already provided with a scene of *Maiestas*: G. Bovini, *Mosaici paleocristiani di Roma (secoli III–VI)* (Bologna, 1971), 67–72 (with bibliography); U. Nilgen, "Maria Regina – Eine politischer Kultbildtypus?," *Römisches Jahrbuch für Kunstgeschichte* 19 (1981): 28 n. 68; G. Wolf, *Salus Populi Romani. Die Geschichte römischer Kultbilder im Mittelalter* (Weinheim, 1990), 117–19, 200–3.

19 Iacobini, "Il mosaico absidale," 126–9.

20 "Innocentii III Papae Sermones de diversis. Sermo III. In consecratione pontificis," P.L., 217, cols. 662–5.

21 Ibid., col. 658.

22 The following is the complete text: "Summa Petri sedes est haec sacra principis aedes, Mater cunctarum, decor et decus ecclesiarum. Devotus Christo qui templo servit in isto, Flores virtutis capiet fructusque salutis." Cf. Ladner, *Papstbildnisse*, 2: 67.

23 M. Maccarrone, "L'indulgenza del Giubileo del 1300 e la basilica di San Pietro," *Roma anno 1300, Atti della IV Settimana di Studi di Storia dell'Arte Medievale dell'Università di Roma 'La Sapienza,' 19–24 maggio 1980*, ed. A. M. Romanini (Rome, 1983), 737; M. Maccarrone, "La 'Cathedra Sancti Petri' nel Medio Evo: da simbolo a reliquia," *Rivista di Storia della Chiesa in Italia* 39 (1985): 349–477, now in Maccarrone, *Romana Ecclesia, Cathedra Petri*, vol. 2, ed. P. Zerbi, R. Volpini, and A. Galuzzi (Rome, 1991), 1352–5; F. Gandolfo, "Assisi e il Laterano," *Archivio della Società Romana di Storia Patria* 106 (1983): 84, 113.

24 F. Wymann, "Die Aufzeichnungen des Stadtpfarres Sebastian Werro von Freiburg i. Ue. über seinem Aufenthalt in Rom von 10.–27. Mai 1581," *Römische Quartalschrift* 33 (1925): 39–71; Gandolfo, "Assisi e il Laterano," 111–13.

25 G. Grimaldi, *Descrizione della basilica antica di San Pietro in Vaticano. Codice Barberini latino 2733*, ed. R. Niggl (Vatican City, 1972), 416.

26 T. Alfarano, *De Basilicae Vaticanae antiquissima et nova structura*, ed. M. Cerrati (Rome, 1914), 32.

27 For example, this is the case of the cathedra of S. Saba (ca. 1205). On this theme, see: F. Gandolfo, "La cattedra papale in età federiciana," *Federico II e l'arte del Duecento italiano, Atti della III Settimana di Studi di Storia dell'Arte Medievale dell'Università di Roma, 15–20 maggio 1978*, vol. 1, ed. A. M. Romanini (Galatina, 1980), 339–66, esp. 339–43.

28 Gandolfo, "Assisi e il Laterano," 112–13.

29 Maccarrone, "Cathedra Sancti Petri," 1349–50.

30 Specifically, the letter of 13 March 1198, "Cathedra Sancti Petri," 1349.

31 *Gesta*, col. XX; Maccarrone, "Cathedra Sancti Petri," 1349–51.

32 P. C. Claussen, *Magistri doctissimi romani. Die römischen Marmorkünstler des Mittelalters* (Stuttgart, 1987), 64–5.

33 Ibid. In addition, see E. Bassan, "s.v. Jacopo di Lorenzo," *Enciclopedia dell'Arte Medievale*, vol. 7 (Rome, 1996), 246–9.

34 Claussen, *Magistri*, 64–5.

35 E. Condello, "I codici Stefaneschi: Uno scriptorium cardinalizio del Trecento tra Roma e Avignone?" *Archivio della Società Romana di Storia Patria* 110 (1987): 21–61, 44–8; A. Tomei, "Libri miniati tra Roma, Napoli e Avignone. Arte di curia, arte di corte, 1300–1377, ed. A. Tomei (Turin, 1996), 179–84.

36 M. M. Gauthier, "La clôture émaillée de la Confession de Saint-Pierre au Vatican, lors du Conceil Latran IV, 1215," *Synthronon. Art et Archéologie de la fin de l'Antiquité et du Moyen Age* (Paris, 1968), 237–46.

37 De Blaauw, *Cultus et decor*, 2: 654–6, 655.

38 Gauthier, "La clôture," 244–5; Iacobini, "La pittura e le arti suntuarie," 315–17.

39 *Isidori Hispalensis Episcopi Etymologiarum sive Originum libri*, bk. VII, chap. 2, ed. W. M. Lindsay (Oxford, 1911).

40 The complete text states: "Sp(iritus) C(onsilii) almus ego tegas ut tegenda te tego. Vir dico pasce greges quia nullis epulis eges."

41 Gauthier, "La clôture," 244; Iacobini, "La pittura e le arti suntuarie," 317.

42 Krautheimer and Frazer, "San Pietro," 235–6.

43 F. Gandolfo, "Il ritratto di Gregorio IX dal mosaico di facciata di San Pietro in Vaticano," *Fragmenta picta*, 131–4.

44 The definition is from M. Andaloro, "Ancora una volta sull'*Ytalia* di Cimabue," *Arte Medievale* 2 (1984): 143–77, esp. 156.

45 Ibid.

46 M. Andaloro, "'A dexteris eius beatissima deipara Virgo': Dal mosaico della facciata vaticana," *Fragmenta picta*, 139–40; O. Etinhof, "I mosaici di Roma nella raccolta di P. Sevastianov," *Bollettino d'arte* 76, no. 66 (1991): 29–38, esp. 30–4.

47 A. Ghidoli, "La testa di San Luca dal mosaico di facciata di S. Pietro in Vaticano," *Fragmenta picta*, 135–8.

48 Matthiae, *Mosaici medievali*, 126–9.

49 Ladner, *Papstbildnisse*, 2:98–105; Gandolfo, "Il ritratto," passim.

50 *Gesta*, col. CCV: "...et in fronte ipsius basilicae fecit restaurari musivum quod erat ex magna parte consumptum."

51 Grimaldi, *Descrizione*, 164.

52 Waetzoldt, *Die Kopien*, n. 890.

53 G. B. Ladner, "The Gestures of Prayer in Papal Iconography of the Thirteenth and Early Fourteenth Centuries," *Didascaliae. Studies in Honor of Anselm M. Albareda* (New York, 1961), now in Ladner, *Images and Ideas in the Middle Ages*, vol. 1 (Rome, 1983), 214.

54 Ibid., 220–5.

55 Gandolfo, "Il ritratto," 133–4.

56 "Ceu sol fervescit sidus super omne nitescit/Et velut est aurum rutilans super omne metallum / Doctrina atque fide calet et sic pollet ubique / Ista domus petram supra fabricata quietam." Cf. Grimaldi, *Descrizione*, 163; Ladner, *Papstbildnisse*, 2:104.

57 Maccarrone, "L'indulgenza," 737n39.

58 "Innocentii III Romani Pontificis Regestum sive Epistolarium, Epistula CCCCI," *P.L.*, 214, col. 337: "...Deus duo magna luminaria in firmamento coeli constituit, luminare majus ut praeesset diei, et luminare minus ut nocti praeesset; sic ad firmamentum universalis Ecclesiae...duas magnas instituit dignitates:... pontificalis auctoritas et regalis potestas. Porro sicut luna lumen suum a sole sortitur [...] sic regalis potestas ab auctoritate pontificali suae sortitur dignitatis splendorem" (cf. also *P.L.*, 216, cols. 997, 1184). More generally, for the literary tradition of "political metaphors" pertaining to the papacy and the empire, see Paravicini Bagliani, *Il trono di Pietro*, 165–8.

5

RENAISSANCE ST. PETER'S

CHRISTOF THOENES

NICHOLAS V

HISTORY

WITH THE RETURN OF THE PAPACY FROM Avignon, the Middle Ages in Rome came to an end. The most notable sign of this change in era was the turning away from the Lateran, which had served as the official residence of the bishops of Rome since the elevation of Christianity to a state religion by Constantine the Great. Now the second of the great Constantinian basilicas, the martyrium of St. Peter, became the primary church of the popes. St. Peter's had gained steadily in significance during the course of the Middle Ages as a destination for pilgrims as well as a location for papal ceremonial services. It was not merely the tomb of the apostle but also the basilica's wealth in relics that attracted the masses, the prime exhibit being Veronica's veil, whose ceremonial display provided the climax of the Jubilee years of the fourteenth and fifteenth centuries. Thus the basilica of St. Peter's, notwithstanding its eccentric location on the west bank of the Tiber, moved to the center of the religious life of the city. In the area between the church and the Castel Sant'Angelo, which had already been enclosed by a wall by Leo IV (847–55), a suburb developed, primarily on the basis of pilgrim traffic. The bridge of Sant'Angelo between the suburb and the "abitato" in the plain on the left bank of the Tiber became the vital line of the city, while the hilly regions of ancient Rome fell more and more into desolation.[1]

For the papacy this change of location coincided with a fundamental political reorientation.[2] Connected with the Lateran was a long-standing notion of papal-imperial universal monarchy, but also the memory of a century-long struggle between factions for power in the Eternal City. The issue that faced the papacy now was the conversion of the patrimony of St. Peter into a modern territorial principality. The pope had to enforce his primary position not only as Christ's representative on earth but also as sovereign of the church state in relation to the European powers, as well as in opposition to

the growing conciliar and schismatic tendencies within the Church. One aspect of these politics was the transformation of Rome into a papal residential city.[3] This transformation presupposed the subjugation of the Roman citizenry, whose ambitions toward autonomy had reached their height during the papal exile in Avignon. To that end the Vatican provided the suitable strategic basis. While the Lateran was in the open area inside the old city wall and was exposed without protection to warring factions, the Vatican and *Urbs leonina* formed a kind of citadel on the opposite side of the river, with its own walls and an entrance controlled by the Castel Sant'Angelo. This was the frame within which the question of rebuilding the basilica moved into the foreground.

After a century of papal absence the Vatican buildings were in a certain disrepair, as were nearly all the monumental buildings of the city. The first task for the returning popes, therefore, was to initiate the most urgent repairs. The palace located on the hill north of the basilica had to be made habitable. In the basilica the narthex especially was in dire need of rebuilding. For the holy year of 1425, Martin V (1417–31) had its roof renewed; his successor, Eugene IV (1431–47), commissioned Antonio Averlino, called Filarete, to make two bronze door wings for the middle portal. This was the type of activity attested in the *Liber Pontificalis* for the popes of the Middle Ages: it served the conservation of the venerable edifice and the enrichment of its possessions through the donation of precious appointments. Conservation work is also confirmed for Eugene's successor, Nicolas V (1447–55). But five years after his ascent to the chair, we find payments for work on a new "tribuna di S. Pietro":[4] they began in June 1452, increased during 1453, then decreased in 1454, and by the end of that year stopped entirely. Their result was the "fundamenta altissima" behind the apse of the old building, mentioned by the apostolic secretary Mattia Palmieri in his chronicle for the year 1452,[5] and whose existence was still attested to by Michelangelo, who visited it in 1505 with Pope Julius II.[6] This was no longer a conservation

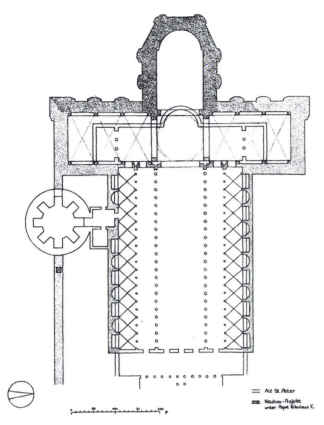

57. St. Peter's, Project of Pope Nicholas V (Urban 1963)

measure, but the beginning of a "novum et ingens aedificium," as Maffeo Vegio, canon of St. Peter's, formulated it in his treatise on the basilica.[7] It is with Nicholas that the story of the New St. Peter's begins.

THE PROJECT

Tommaso Parentucelli from Sarzana, who ascended the throne as Nicholas V in 1447, was a true "Renaissance pope"; in many respects he can be viewed as the founder of papal patronage in the modern age.[8] "All my money I want to spend on books and buildings," he was supposed to have exclaimed while still cardinal.[9] In that sense his election was understood by the Italian humanists as the beginning of a new era.[10] If he is less present in the memory of a later age than many of his great followers, it is because he cared little about the representation of his own person. His tomb was modest, and we do not have a representative portrait of him. But even in the many churches, city walls, roads, bridges, fortifications, fountains, and aqueducts that he restored in Rome, the personality of the patron hardly emerges. His merit as founder of the Vatican library was, only a short time later, overshadowed by Sixtus IV. Moreover, his early death at age fifty-five after many years of illness left him little time to realize his plans. Thus the main witness

to his art-related activities remains a kind of testament stylized by his biographer and confidant, the Florentine humanist Gianozzo Manetti, as an address to the cardinals gathered around the pope's deathbed.[11] It became something like a Magna Carta of papal building policy in the next three centuries.

In this text a central role is played by Nicholas's plan for the *Urbs leonina*, the Vatican palace, and the church of St. Peter's. If one reads the description in toto, one could easily receive the impression of a more or less "ideal plan," the realization of which would neither then nor later be taken seriously. But Nicholas began building in the palace as well as in the basilica, and with a longer life and better health he would have accomplished more. There remained, of course, a discrepancy between the magnitude of the undertaking and the life span of an individual, that is, the average period of the reign of a pope: a problem which left its imprint on the building history of New St. Peter's until its completion in the seventeenth century.

Manetti's description is fairly extensive, but it was written by a member of the literati, not an architect, and the Latin text is not always easy to understand. Another problem is the form in which the project was available to Manetti. Ground plans in those days were more like linear schemes than detailed drawings; elevations were customarily explained verbally until one progressed to the construction of a three-dimensional model. But no model is mentioned anywhere in the sources. Manetti's references to measurements are numerous, but not without contradiction; apparently the author was more concerned with the demonstration of

58. Maerten van Heemskerck, St. Peter's Square, detail, 1532/6. Albertina, Vienna

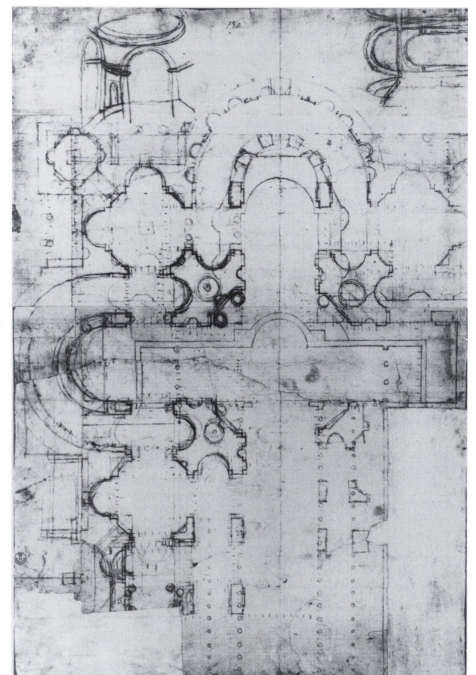

59. Donato Bramante, Project for
St. Peter's, 1505/6. Uffizi, Florence
Gabinetto dei Disegni, 20A

proportional relationships than exact information.[12] A particular problem is presented by the unit of measure used by Manetti. "Cubitus," the "yard" of antiquity, can stand in the Latin of the humanists also for the post-antique, considerably longer *braccio*, which however is translated correctly, as for example by Alberti, as "bracchium." In any case, one comes closest to the measurements of the old basilica, on which Nicolas's plans were based, if one understands Manetti's numbers as *braccia fiorentine*, which were familiar to the native Florentine author, possibly also to the architects of the

pope. On the other hand, Florentine and Roman measurements were not compatible with each other; thus the round numbers mentioned by Manetti can only represent approximations.

In view of these uncertainties the clean ground plan of the Nicolas building on which Bramante's later design Uff. 20 A is based is welcome (Fig. 59); a part of it reappears on sheet Uff. 7945.[13] Here one can read the dimensions in *palmi romani*, the customary Roman building measurement, and they should be reliable, since Bramante derived his own plans from them. However,

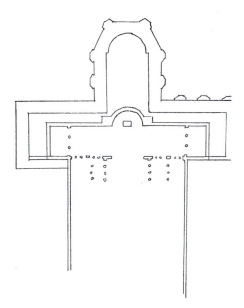

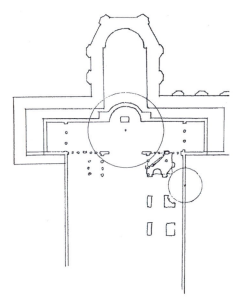

60. Uff. 20 A O (Thoenes 1994). Schematic drawings by Thoenes, Geymüller

61. Uff. 20 A I (Thoenes 1994). Schematic drawings by Thoenes, Geymüller

this sheet also presents new problems, as Bramante not only drew the arm of the choir but also the transept of the Nicholas project, whose existence is not attested anywhere else. Moreover, its erection would have required the destruction of the rotunda of S. Petronilla. Thus it is likely that Bramante also looked at a quattrocento plan which he either copied or combined with his own measurement. Be that as it may, the basic form of the Nicholas project is clear enough, and the different reconstructions presented by research provide roughly converging results (Fig. 57).[14] These can be summarized as follows.

The transept and apse of the old basilica were to be torn down and replaced by a square crossing with three arms of equal length. But because the width of the crossing had to correspond to the width of the central nave, the crossing necessarily extended a good deal beyond the old transept wall toward the west, and, as a result, the old tomb altar lost its dominant place in the center of the apse. It now came to be positioned under the dome, however, not in its middle but in the slightly eccentric placement that it still inhabits today. The internal length of the crossing arms was 200 *palmi* each; a quarter of the west arm was occupied by the apse. Side chapels or other side rooms were not planned for this area. The exterior walls were extraordinarily thick, due in part to reasons of fortification, but also because the western part of the building was intended to be vaulted. Above the crossing a semicircular dome was planned to rise. Groined cross vaulting resting on colossal columns placed in front of the walls, similar to that found in the imperial baths or the basilica of Maxentius, was designed for the cross arms. The basic disposition of a five-aisled columned basilica was

to remain in the nave, although structurally consolidated and accompanied by identically shaped rows of chapels. The side aisles were supposed to be vaulted, and large round windows were to be placed in the walls of the main nave. The narthex was intended to be flanked by campanili, and the atrium renewed in a symmetrical form.

TRADITION AND INNOVATION

The motives that occasioned the pope to engage in new construction were complex and it is not easy to evaluate them appropriately. No doubt in the forefront stood the dilapidated state of the old basilica. Nicholas himself stated in his bull of 1451 that the building was in danger of collapse ("ut ruinam minetur").[15] One could consider this the pretext of a patron desirous of building, or at least an exaggeration. Indeed, the old nave did not collapse, not then or later, but had to be torn down by Bramante, and its eastern half survived this certainly not very carefully executed operation; it remained standing for liturgical use into the seventeenth century. On the other hand, the poor condition of the building was notorious. Alberti was of the opinion that the upper walls of the nave, which were leaning outward on the southern side, were held in place only by the roof beams. The slightest pressure or push could topple the building.[16] The overhang, according to measurements taken by Antonio da Sangallo in 1538, amounted to approximately 80 centimeters.[17] If Grimaldi's notation from the beginning of the seventeenth century of 5 *palmi* (ca. 110 cm) is correct, then the building had further moved in the interim, despite the buttressing by Sangallo.[18] Thus the danger was real. Yet it was not sufficient to motivate

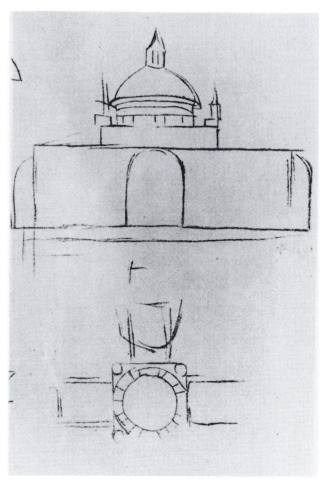

62. Uff. 20 A verso, detail. (Geymüller 1875/80)

the pope's undertaking, as making the building secure would have required measures other than the building of a new choir. That the choir was given priority is one clear indication that new construction took precedence over an interest in preservation.

The concentration of the project on the western part of the basilica can be explained by functional considerations. The transept and apse of the old building no longer provided sufficient room for the papal ceremonies as they had developed in the course of the Middle Ages. A choir arm had to be added. However, this argument, which seems so convincing in a comparison of ground plans, diminishes in persuasiveness if one brings to mind the actual spatial relationships. The distance from the tomb altar to the background of the new apse, where the papal throne would have been placed, was a good fifty meters – a vacuum that could never have been filled by any conceivable ceremony. Indeed, the problem of the new construction, as it was realized later, was more one of too much room: when the new western arm was about to be furnished for service at the beginning of the seventeenth century, it was not possible to localize the liturgically important elements (altar, papal throne, choir stalls) in harmony with the architecture. Narrowing additions were proposed; even a relocation of the tomb was considered.[19] Thus, the need for space may have played some role in Nicholas's motivation to engage in new construction, but it was not decisive for the design of the plan.

Far more important was another aspect of the old building: the lack of order engendered over the centuries

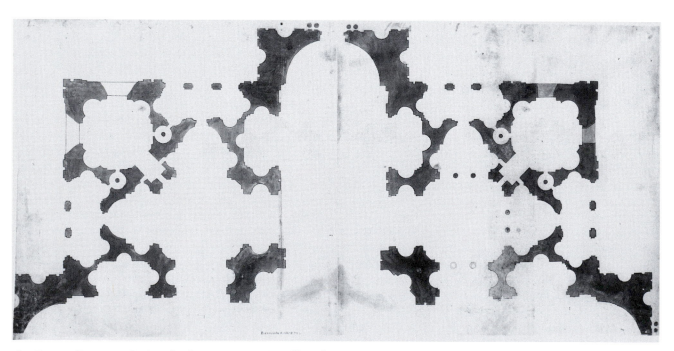

63. Donato Bramante, Project for St. Peter's. 1505/6. Uffizi, Florence, Gabinetto dei Disegni, 1A

64. Cristoforo Foppa Caradosso, foundation medal of St. Peter's, 1506. Bibliothèque Nationale, Cabinet des medailles, Paris

within its walls. The choir of the chapter, which had grown to ninety-two members by the end of the Quattrocento, had installed itself at the western end of the central nave, thus blocking a view of the presbytery;[20] opposite it and also in the central nave were the statue of the seated Saint Peter and the large organ; in the side aisles one encountered altars, tombs, and commemorative plaques of all sorts; chapels and side rooms of varying designations had attached themselves to the external walls. All these entities formed an immense repertoire of the histories of church and faith which later on was conjured nostalgically by historians of the basilica, but which actually must have had a confining and distressing effect. How much the pope must have disliked them becomes evident by his wish, reported by Manetti, to keep the new building entirely free of tombs.[21]

Here the central motif of Nicholas's building project becomes evident: the modernization of the basilica. This is a revolutionary motif and as such truly amazing in the history of the papacy. To understand it, one has to keep in mind two conditions that were contained in the person of this pope: his humanistic education and his ideas concerning the authority of the apostolic chair. A new relationship to history had developed in the philological practice of the humanists. Instead of reading the old texts as they were passed on, one sought to recapture their original form. Thus tradition became the subject

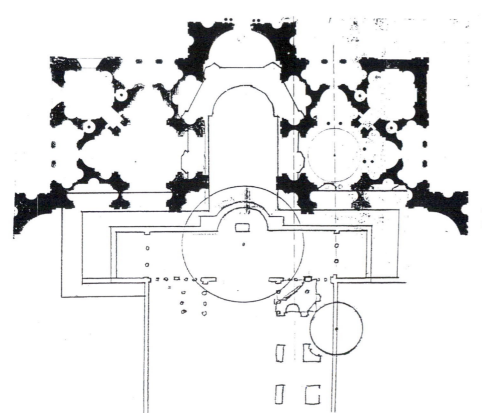

65. Uff. 1A and Uff. 20 A I (Thoenes 1994)

of criticism. Old truths which one had once thought to possess became paradigms to be constructed or reconstructed. In place of a culture of adherence and conservation emerged one of making and renewal; Jakob Burckhardt expressed this notion with his formula of "the state as a work of art." Nicholas was moving along these lines when he understood his role of patron of St. Peter's as a creative one. Not by caring for and securing the things that had become venerably old, but by building anew and on a monumental scale was he able to represent that which had been lost, or at least could not be found in the extensive disarray of the old building: the unity of the Church under the primacy of the bishop of Rome.[22]

Against the foil of the audacity of Nicholas's decision to build, the form of his plan appears rather traditional. As before, St. Peter's would have presented itself as a five-aisled columned basilica of the Early Christian type. Even the reshaping of the western part into a Greek cross structure only repeated what had become a central theme of Christian church architecture in the Middle Ages. Thus Manetti's comparison of the plan with a man lying on the ground – the image of the crucifix – represented nothing new, but only summarized a medieval tradition of interpretation;[23] moreover, Manetti had described the ground plan of the Florentine cathedral in 1436 in almost identical terms.[24] Finally, even the domed square was a traditional motif of medieval Italian cathedral architecture, and neither Manetti nor any other contemporary writer gives any indication that it would have been understood as a revival of an antique mausoleum relating to the tomb of St. Peter. If the plan of Nicholas contained any Renaissance elements, they would have been stylistic in nature, such as the *all'antica* treatment of walls and vaults (whose details remain difficult to comprehend from the description), or the homogeneity of the overall picture. Rational organization triumphed over the variety of accreted structures; from the square of the crossing, measures and proportions arranged themselves into a system. At the same time the connection to the historical content of the building loosens. The tomb of St. Peter no longer appears as the only focus of the church. Manetti does not mention the tomb at all; Bramante would see it as furnishing that could can be placed randomly in the new building.

THE QUESTION OF AUTHORSHIP

The current customary designation of the undertaking described by Manetti as the "Nicholas plan" masks a predicament: we do not know who actually designed the plan. In the older literature, the prevailing opinion is that a project of this rank had to go back to Leon Battista Alberti (1401–72), the brightest and most innovative of all spirits who at that time concerned themselves with architecture.[25] Alberti lived in Rome from 1443 to 1452; he belonged to the papal court and was a "familiaris" of Nicholas V, whom he knew from his student days in Bologna. In 1452, the year of the commencement of work on the new tribuna, he handed the pope the first draft of his great treatise, "De re aedificatoria." But neither Manetti nor other contemporary witnesses connect him with Nicholas's St. Peter's project, with the exception of the chronicle of Mattia Palmieri, whose statement is negative: Alberti, that ingenious man, trained in all the arts, advised the pope against the continuation of the construction.[26] This points to the position of an uninvolved advisor, not one of an originator, much less of a designing architect. As a matter of fact, the new building, as described by Manetti, shows no relationship to what Alberti later built. Furthermore, there are no significant agreements with Alberti's treatise on architecture, except for the above-mentioned aversion toward tombs in the interior of a church, which Nicholas shared with Alberti.[27]

The old basilica is repeatedly mentioned in Alberti's treatise, but exclusively with regard to the technical aspects of building. Alberti criticized the construction of the nave (the architraved colonnade was poorly suited to carry the high upper wall), described the resulting precarious condition of the building,[28] and made, toward the end of the work, recommendations regarding its consolidation;[29] elsewhere he analyzed the function of the side chapels in relation to the stability of the nave.[30] A positive attitude toward the Constantinian building cannot be inferred from the text, nor should it be expected: uninterested in the values of tradition, Alberti considered the basilica in general as a wrong track in the development of sacred architecture.[31] This fact could explain his reservations toward the pope's intention: the old building could not be improved by partial renovation. The result would never be a "templum" in accordance with his radical humanistic theories.

A second motif might be seen in Alberti's often stated rejection of monumental building that eluded the control of a single architect. In a passage in the second part of the treatise, as if aiming at Nicholas's plans, Alberti mocks those who hastily and without thought ("inconsiderati et praecipites") tear down old buildings and put up huge foundations.[32] In fact, no architect should undertake anything that he himself cannot complete;[33] nothing does more harm to the reputation of an architect than a building that remains unfinished because of lack of funds, or is deformed by his successors.[34] With this concept of architecture as an architect's personal creation[35] – which Alberti later tried to realize in his Mantuan buildings – the undertaking initiated by Nicolas could not be reconciled. It seems only logical that Alberti preferred

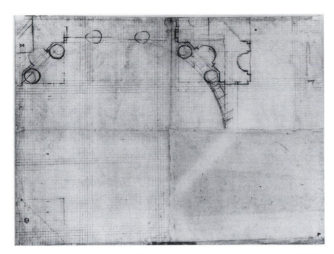

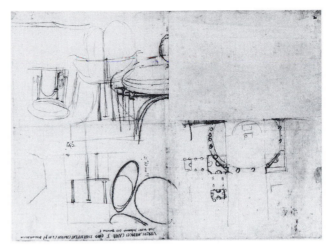

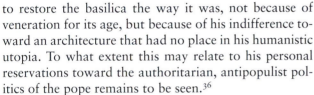

66. Donato Bramante, Projects for St. Peter's, 1505/6. Uffizi, Florence, Gabinetto dei Disegni, 7945Aʳ

67. Donato Bramante, Projects for St. Peter's, 1505/6. Uffizi, Florence, Gabinetto dei Disegni, 7945Aᵛ

to restore the basilica the way it was, not because of veneration for its age, but because of his indifference toward an architecture that had no place in his humanistic utopia. To what extent this may relate to his personal reservations toward the authoritarian, antipopulist politics of the pope remains to be seen.[36]

Among the other names that can be connected to Nicholas's St. Peter's project, that of the Florentine architect Bernardo Rossellino (1409–64) ranks first. Called to Rome by the pope in 1451, he appears to have functioned as a kind of head architect of the Vatican buildings. Vasari described the building plan of Nicholas V in his biography of Rossellino as one of the architect's personal creations.[37] But his remarks in reference to St. Peter's are particularly vague, if not cryptic: the designs were supposed to have been grandiose, but the model was a failure ("andato male"), and other "architettori" were called in to construct new ones. Their names are not mentioned by Vasari, and the question as to whether they are to be identified with the persons mentioned in the building documents (Beltrame di Martino, Amadei, Nello, Spinelli)[38] must be left open as long as the designation of responsibilities between the papal employer and his advisors, architects, builders, and contractors remains unclear to us. Each one of them could have influenced the plan in his own way. But the figure of the "architetto autore," as Alberti envisioned it and as Vasari retrospectively projected it back from his own era, seems not yet to have made its appearance in the entourage of Nicholas V.

LATER HISTORY

We do not know if Alberti's objections caused the significant slowdown in building activity on the choir noticeable in 1454. In any case, work did not continue after the death of the pope. His successor, Callistus III (1455–58) from the house of Borgia (Borja), forestalled any kind of building activity. The funds thus made available were designated for mobilization against the Turks who had been threatening Europe after Sultan Mohammed II's conquest of Constantinople in 1453. The next pope was the art-loving Pius II (1458–64), Enea Silvio Piccolomini. He again turned toward St. Peter's but set himself an entirely different goal: the entrance facade of the atrium of the basilica was to receive a new face.[39] Therefore he occasioned his court architect, Francesco del Borgo, to erect a three-story loggia front that would have stretched across the entire width of the building in eleven bays. But when Pius died, only the four northern bays bordering on the palace had been started; they were completed in the 1470s and served subsequent popes as a benediction loggia (Fig. 58) until Paul V, at the beginning of the seventeenth century, erected the new nave and had the old atrium facade torn down.

Pius's successor, Paul II (1464–71), Pietro Barbo from Venice, attempted to return to Nicholas's building project.[40] The impetus must have been provided by the Anno Santo of 1475, which Paul had proclaimed in 1470. In this year new payments for work on the "Tribuna Sancti Petri" commenced. Giuliano da Sangallo and Meo da Caprina are named as architects. The pope might have hoped to realize at least this part of the new building for the jubilee and to connect it somehow with the basilica. Here, for the first time, the separation of planning and reality, which was to become characteristic of the building history of New St. Peter's, becomes evident. The overall projects remained on paper; what was realized were fragments that, for now, had to coexist with the old building. Paul was sufficiently optimistic to strike a medal depicting the interior of the new choir

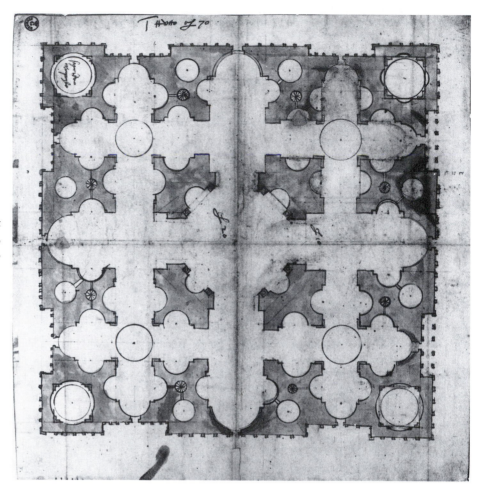

68. Giuliano da Sangallo, Project for St. Peter's, 1505/6. Uffizi, Florence, Gabinetto dei Disegni, 8A^r

arm. But already under his successor, the della Rovere Pope Sixtus IV (1471–84), work stopped again. The first personal building measure of the new pope consisted of the addition of a further side chapel to the southern aisle of the old nave, which was to contain the choir of the chapter and also to serve Sixtus as his final resting place.[41]

The first phase of the new construction of St. Peter's had thus failed. One might say that the time was not yet ripe for it, that the forces of change were as yet insufficient to begin this gigantic work. But, as we shall see, it was no different in the sixteenth century. What was added then was the suggestive power of Bramante's design, which was strong enough to keep the architects of the building spellbound for over a hundred years. In this respect the Nicholas plan shows the limits of what an employer alone can achieve without a congenial artistic partner. The foundation wall of the choir building remained as a concrete trace of his great idea. It played an ambivalent role in the subsequent building history. Bramante erected his "Julius choir" above it, but in its plan it remained a foreign body, a residue of the Quattrocento that was later to be rejected and replaced by a choir arm conforming with the overall design of the

church. On the other hand, the existence of these walls in 1505 provided the impetus for new construction; indeed, one could even go so far as to ask if the decision on the "Templi Petri Instauracio," announced by Julius one year later in his foundation medal, would have been made without it.

JULIUS II AND BRAMANTE

THE POPE

During the ten-year pontificate of Julius II, Giuliano della Rovere (1503–13), the Roman Renaissance reached its climax. Michelangelo's Julius tomb and his Sistine Chapel ceiling, Raphael's Stanze and his Sistine Madonna, Bramante's Cortile del Belvedere and the new building of St. Peter's all owe their existence to Julius. More goal-oriented and energetic than his predecessors, Julius fell back on Nicholas V's intention to solidify and secure the authority of the papal chair through monumental buildings. Contemporaries saw Julius mainly as a *homo politicus*; not coincidentally he appeared as role model in Machiavelli's *Il Principe*. In order to achieve his foreign-policy goals, the reconstruction of the church

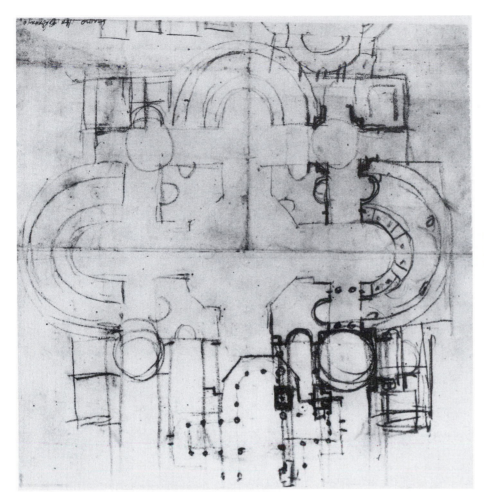

69. Donato Bramante, Project for St. Peter's, 1505/6. Uffizi, Florence, Gabinetto dei Disegni, 8A^v

state, and the liberation of Italy from the hands of foreign "barbarians," he relied on diplomatic as well as military means, with varying success. In terms of church politics, his struggle was directed against all conciliar ambitions that aimed to question the leadership of the pope. Through consistent expropriation of the powers of the old communal institutions Julius achieved the centralization of the church state.[42] In the same sense he reorganized the papal building environment: all forces were consolidated under the administrative apparatus of the papal palace, payments were only made by the Camera Apostolica and the Tesoreria segreta del papa, and all key positions were manned by trusted men of the pope.[43]

Julius's reign differs in two important respects from that of Nicholas. One is the emergence of the pope as an individual. Julius's physical appearance is familiar to us through the portraits by Raphael, and in the frescoes of the Heliodorus stanza we can see him in action. His character – conscious of power, impulsive, choleric, frightening, and magnanimous – confronts us in numerous accounts and serves us as a key to understanding his deeds. Church and state appeared in the consciousness

of his contemporaries as inseparably united in his person. A second difference between the two reigns is embodied in Julius's idea of a succession from the house of della Rovere on the papal throne. As the nephew of Sixtus IV, Julius not only felt obligated to his office but also to his family; the attempt to secure a princely rank for it in perpetuity was one of the determining factors in his political actions as well as his art-related activities. To that end, while still cardinal, he had endowed a tomb for his uncle Sixtus which evidenced dynastic ambitions. For himself he planned a far more demanding monument. With this project, the utopia of a new building for the basilica free of any personal reminiscences and devoted exclusively to the idea of the papacy, as Nicholas had envisioned it, was finally placed *ad acta*.[44]

In his bull of 1507 Julius explained that ever since he had been raised to the position of cardinal by Sixtus IV, he had hoped to resume the expansion and renovation of the basilica (which Sixtus himself had not continued).[45] In the same year the Augustinian general Egidio da Viterbo provided a theological explanation: Sixtus was the new David, ordered by God to leave the rebuilding of the temple to the first successor from his own tribe, Julius, the new Solomon.[46] Thus the new appeared in the form of the old; Julius was able to consider himself the executor of divine will and simultaneously fulfiller of family obligations. In his last bull concerning the building of St. Peter's, that of February 1513, he returned to this thought and elaborated on it further.[47] All of this looks like an a posteriori prophecy which in any case is not supported by older documents. Certainly the old basilica was a candidate for renewal and Julius did not close his eyes when faced with the task. But the priorities he established were different. His first concern was the completion of the papal residence, begun by Bramante in 1504; the second, his own tomb. For the latter he entered into a contract with Michelangelo in the beginning of 1505. Subsequent events are known through Michelangelo's later accounts. In the search for a suitable location, the choir begun by Nicholas came to mind, and Julius, acting quickly, approved the finances for continuation of its construction.[48] This undertaking, however, necessitated the building of a new transept and, thus, the question of the construction of a new basilica was actually raised.

THE ARCHITECT

Now was the hour of the architect. Donato Bramante from Fermignano near Urbino (1444–1514) was only a few months younger than Julius II. As the latter as pope, so Bramante as artist embodied the emancipation of the human personality at the moment of transition from feudal society to the culture of absolutism. Thus courtly art in the Roman Renaissance reached its climax: it came into existence as a result of the interactions between men of different ranks who respected and recognized each other as individuals. Between them the decision process took place; what resulted from it reflected the coincidences as well as the divergences of opinions and characters. Bramante had proven his professional qualifications as court architect of Lodovico il Moro in Milan. As Wolfgang Lotz recognized, the Piazza in Vigevano already shows the marks of Bramante's Roman works: "extraordinary dimensions, lavish and, at the same time, reckless planning, an adaptation of antique ideas free of any imitation."[49] Thus he was the appropriate man to attack a project that had to begin with an act of destruction.[50]

The demolition of the old building, or at least its western part, had already been intended by Nicholas. Nevertheless, construction work carried out under him took place behind the old apse. It required the removal of the Probus mausoleum located there, but the building of Constantine did not need to be touched. The concept, most likely, was that of a successive renovation of the building starting from the choir and continuing

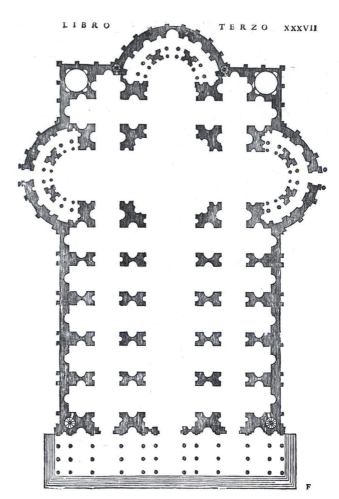

70. Raphael's first project for St. Peter's (Serlio 1540)

to the facade, as is known from the building histories of medieval cathedrals. Bramante, however, began his building in the center, with the erection of the four dome piers. The foundation stone was laid at the southwest pier, still outside the basilica, sacrificing in its wake the monastery of St. Martin founded in the ninth century.[51] But one year later the foundations for the eastern dome piers were begun, and in 1510 also that of the first piers of the nave. This necessitated the demolition of large parts of the transept and the western half of the old nave. The energy with which the destruction was tackled horrified contemporaries. It seemed as if the pope himself was in the process of eradicating the most important monumental testimony to the Roman tradition of Peter. The papal master of ceremonies, Paris de Grassis, baptized Bramante, sarcastically, "Ruinante" – a nickname that stuck, not least because it contributed to relieving Julius from the responsibility for these events.[52] Thus, Church historians of the Counter-Reformation from Panvinio to Buonanni describe how Bramante had persuaded the pope to sacrifice the old basilica to his new building.[53]

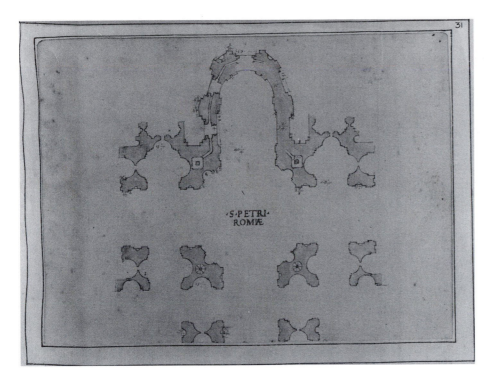

71. Bernardo della Volpaia, plan of St. Peter's, 1505/16. Sir John Soane's Museum, London, Codex Coner, n. 31

Even though we have no firsthand information to judge, it is plausible that Bramante recognized the consequences of the new choir building earlier and more clearly than the pope, and that, without qualms, he steered the process toward what he had envisioned: a temple structure of unprecedented size and beauty. That Julius appropriated this idea as his own is proven by his foundation medal (Fig. 64). But his attitude was necessarily split between the confidence of an innovator, who trusted himself to replace the old with an improved new, and the traditional thinking customary in the Church. His dilemma became apparent in the famous argument over the tomb of St. Peter to which Egidio da Viterbo refers in his "Historia viginti saeculorum" written under Leo X.[54] Bramante's plan to relocate the tomb to a more suitable site inside the new building was undone by the pope's veto; moreover, the latter insisted that nothing in the old building could be removed from its location ("nihil ex vetere templi situ inverti"), a decree to which Bramante neither could nor wished to adhere.

The problem of the Egidio anecdote lies in the fact that Bramante's plans described therein do not correspond to any of the extant drawings; such discussion must have taken place before the actual design work occurred. But also subsequently there exists no direct relationship between the numerous papal bulls and letters concerning St. Peter's and the course of planning as it can be reconstructed from Bramante's drawings. The idea of a "dialogue" between architect and patron is not confirmed. Most likely, the contact between them was less tight and less permanent than we are inclined to assume. Julius was a generous employer and precisely therein lay his strength. To what extent he was disposed to and capable of following the details of planning processes is difficult to say. If Julius and Bramante had visions of their new building, they belonged to two different worlds; likewise different were the points on which their interests concentrated.[55] Bramante was concerned with the realization of an architectural idea that only made sense as a whole; for Julius the choir chapel remained in the foreground. The liturgy, iconography, and theology continued to occupy him until, two days before his death, he gave definitive form to an endowment for his "Capella Julia." The model was the "Capella Sistina" of the old basilica, the choir and tomb chapel of his uncle, which Bramante also was not allowed to touch during the demolition of the old building;[56] here the motif of family succession retained the upper hand. However, pope and architect were united in their decision to establish a beginning. In this manner the building history started without really resolving the conflicts inherent in the plan. The result was a "pasticcio," the problems of which became apparent in the ground plan of the building left behind by Bramante (Fig. 71).

THE PLANNING

What did Bramante's St. Peter's look like? Until the middle of the nineteenth century historians of the building held onto Raphael's plan handed down by Serlio, which supposedly "followed Bramante's footsteps" (Fig. 70).[57]

72. Donato Bramante (attrib.), capital for St. Peter's, after 1506. Uffizi, Florence, Gabinetto dei Disegni, 6770A

The picture changed, however, when the Uffizi's collection of architectural drawings, which contained a rich depository of sheets concerning St. Peter's from the estate of Bramante's coworker Antonio da Sangallo the Younger, became known.[58] Here arose the opportunity to discover Bramante's drawings and to follow the evolution of his design. The question concerning "the" Bramante project thus split itself into one about the plan on which the building begun in 1506 was based, and one about the planning process that preceded it. Since then, art historians have been occupied with both questions without being able to agree on a single answer.[59] A certain consensus – albeit not unanimous – was reached only with respect to Bramante's own drawings. Sangallo himself had inscribed the so-called parchment plan, Uff. 1A (Fig. 63), as "Pianta di S. Pietro di mano di Bramante," and there is no reason to doubt the truth of this statement. In addition there are the red-chalk drawings on sheets Uff. 8A, 20A and 7945A (Figs. 59, 62, 66, 67, 69); the "pentimenti" documenting the author as the designing architect can serve, according to a proven principle of master-drawing analysis, as a criterion for attribution. These sheets do not depict finished projects but allow, for the first time in the history of architecture, insight

into its coming into being. They are snapshots of the design process and have to be interpreted as such.[60] Only in this limited sense is the term "project" used in the subsequent text. However, the material is incomplete. In order to bring these sheets into a meaningful sequence, it would be necessary to postulate drawings that no longer exist and to assume interventions in the planning process by the employer for which there is no documentary evidence.

Research from Geymuller to Metternich saw in the parchment plan Bramante's original project, the "ur-plan." But a presentation drawing like that on the parchment implies a longer planning process, and this process is documented in the large red-chalk plan, Uff. 20A.[61] The front of this fascinating sheet shows three superimposed layers: a ground plan of the old basilica and the Nicholas project (Fig. 60); a "project I" (as we call it), which started on the lower right but was not finished (Fig. 61); and the larger "project II" started on the lower left, which fills the rest of the sheet. On the reverse two small sketches are discernible that show the ground plan of the Nicholas project and its elevation from the west (Fig. 62). From this configuration emerges the following chronology.

Bramante began with suggestions for the modernization of Nicholas's project (sketches on the reverse): the dome was supposed to be expanded and to contain a drum, circular stairs were to ascend inside the four dome piers crowned with turrets, and the transept ends were to be equipped with apses similar to that of the western nave. Apparently the intention was to emphasize the centralizing character of the western part of the building. Following this as the next step (for which we have no sketches) was the expansion of this area through minor domes placed in the corners of the crossing arms and surrounding the main dome in a "quincunx" figure. This idea was worked out in project I on the large red-chalk sheet (Fig. 63). Bramante's interest was focused on the shape of the dome pier as the link between quincunx and nave. Thus, over the basic pattern of the basilica and the Nicholas foundation, the new architecture of St. Peter's began to emerge. The nave was intended to be preserved, but transformed into a basilica with piers. The result could be described as a combination of a central and a longitudinal plan; Francesco di Giorgio coined for this the term "figura composta."[62]

The western part of this first project is depicted on the parchment plan. Seen in isolation, the sheet seems to demand a mirrored addition; accordingly, Bramante would have had a pure centrally designed building in mind at that moment.[63] But in the context of the designs which, since the Nicholas plan, have the western part of the basilica as a theme throughout, this seems rather implausible. Also the foundation medal (Fig. 64),[64] which

73. Pieter Coecke van Aelst (attrib.), St. Peter's under construction. 1524/5. Biblioteca Apostolica Vaticana, Vatican City, coll. Ashby, n. 329

gives us an idea of the elevation of the project, depicts the western view: the pedestal area of the apse is intersected in the foreground by the rising "Vaticanus mons" (which had to be cleared off for the construction of the new apse). If one associates the parchment plan with project I of the work sheet Uff. 20 A (Fig. 65) then the identity of the project becomes apparent. In the parchment plan, single elements are developed further, the dome pier has found its final form, the difficult-to-comprehend internal structure of the plan shows itself to be determined by the axis system of the old nave.

"Non ebbe effetto," Antonio da Sangallo laconically remarked on the reverse of the sheet. The parchment plan was not executed. We are told nothing about the reasons. They could hardly have been due to a disagreement with the pope, who indeed had sanctioned the project in his medal. Possibly Bramante himself did not consider it in a form ready for execution. His thoughts were in flux; particularly the question of the transition from the domed quincunx to the nave required further clarification. Progress was introduced by project II of the red-chalk plan, in which Bramante liberated himself from his ties to the old basilica (Fig. 66). He remains with the "composto" scheme, but the elements are now more tightly integrated. Internal and external side aisles are now of the same width (namely, half as wide as the central nave), the internal ones circumnavigate the apses of the crossing arms as ambulatories and thereby connect quincunx and nave. The colossal columns in front of the dome piers were an additional

thought; Bramante explored them in a study sheet (Uff. 7945 A), but dropped them again later (Fig. 67).

Meanwhile it seems that the parchment plan had been seen by Bramante's old rival, Giuliano da Sangallo, who adopted it as his own and proposed to realize it as a centrally designed building symmetrical on all sides (Fig. 68). That this was a misunderstanding is shown by Bramante's correction on the reverse of the sheet (Fig. 69). The sketch is extremely summarily executed, but it shows that Bramante's own design had developed further since the large red-chalk plan; the disposition of piers and columns sketched into the right apse already corresponds with the definitive project. Nevertheless, the relationship between the central group and the nave still seems unresolved. Here an incisive change was required: the minor domes, which, since project I, had been half as large as the main dome, had to be reduced so that they could be repeated above the bays of the side aisles.

The consequence of this intervention is shown in Serlio's woodcut (Fig. 70).[65] Decisive is the step from a five-nave to a three-nave structure: the interior side aisles of the nave are blocked by transversely placed pillar bases, the external ones developed in alignment with the minor domes. The main innovation in the elevation is the "rhythmic travée," a triumphal arch motif which – after the model of Alberti's S. Andrea in Mantua – connects the domed crossing with the nave.[66] In this manner the "figura composta" was replaced by a longitudinal structure ("figura angulare," in the terminology

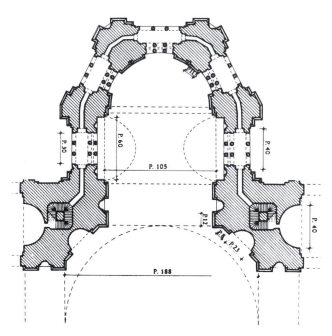

74. St. Peter's, Choir of Pope Julius II, plan (Bruschi 1987)

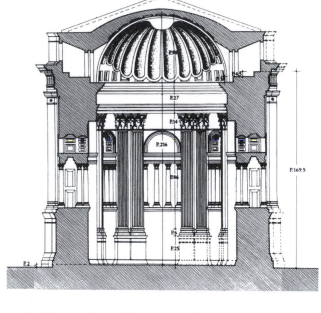

75. St. Peter's, Choir of Pope Julius II, section (Bruschi 1987)

of Francesco di Giorgio), which incorporated the quincunx motif. One could speak of a domed-cross basilica. This was Bramante's third and definitive project. It has not been handed down as a drawing but can be detected in the present-day building, whose pier and dome dimensions were established by Bramante in 1506. On April 18 of that year the foundation stone was laid. During the eight years before his death Bramante erected the four dome piers, the connecting arches, and the western transept arm. For this, however, he referred, surprisingly, to the ground plan of the Nicholas choir and thereby brought the ingeniously balanced system of the western part again into confusion (Fig. 71).

The events themselves remain in obscurity, but the most plausible hypothesis is that the pope, due to time or cost constraints, insisted on the use of the Nicholas foundation. But since Bramante did not want to abandon the main thought behind all his projects, that of the expansion of the dome space beyond the Nicholas crossing, the choir arm underwent a reduction to four-fifths of its original length. Its articulation had to be condensed appropriately and no space would remain for the western side domes. Bramante resolved this problem by furnishing the choir bay with arcade openings that in length and width corresponded to those of the transept arms and the nave. In this manner he left the possibility open for a later transformation of the western part into a full cupola quincunx. In fact, Bramante's apse was torn down in 1585 and replaced by a new one harmonizing with those of the transept. Bramante's building model remained "imperfetto," as Serlio writes;[67] the gaps

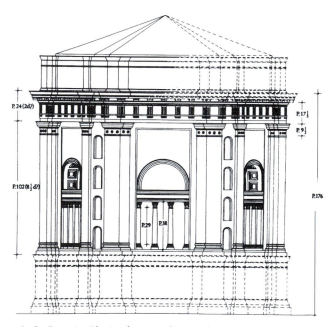

76. St. Peter's, Choir of Pope Julius II, elevation (Bruschi 1987)

must have concerned, on the one hand, the nave on the extension of which no agreement had been reached and, on the other hand, the attachment of the western part to the choir, possibly even the entire design of the exterior mantle. It seems that Bramante preferred to leave open the questions decisive for the continuation of construction. The contours of his plan as a whole remain elusive.[68]

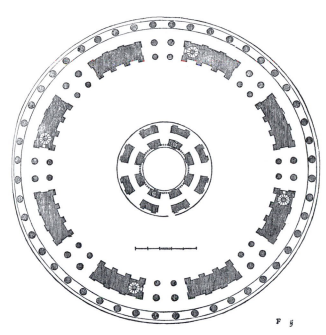

77. Bramante's project for the dome of St. Peter's, plan (Serlio 1540)

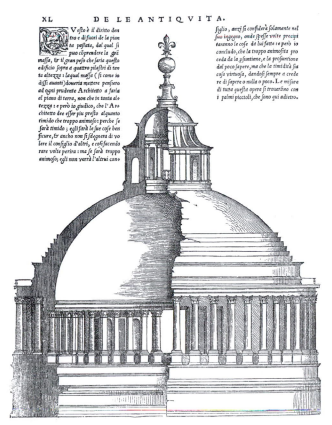

78. Bramante's project for the dome of St. Peter's, section and elevation (Serlio 1540)

THE CONSTRUCTION

Concerning the progress of the construction work, we have reports in different archives: first and foremost, the "Liber Mandatorum," a fairly complete collection of notary files regarding the financing of the building of St. Peter's from 1506 to 1513 in the archive of the chapter of the basilica; the archive of the Fabbrica, with its rather fragmentary documents; and the files of the Camera Apostolica, with several payment receipts.[69] Moreover, three drawings from the time of the actual construction found their way into the Uffizi collection: one working drawing for the design of one of the pilaster capitals of the dome piers, possibly by Bramante himself (Fig. 72);[70] a view of the scaffolding for the large coffered arches, most likely by the same hand;[71] and a study for the construction of the dome pendentives by Bramante's assistant, Antonio di Pellegrino.[72] The views of St. Peter's drawn mostly by Netherlandish artists constitute a third source, indispensable for the understanding of the documents.[73] These drawings, however, do not start until the middle of the 1520s (Fig. 73)[74] and develop into a more coherent series only after 1532 with the work of Maerten van Heemskerck and his circle. But since the construction progressed only slowly in these years, the later views nevertheless provide a good impression of the state of the building around the time of Bramante's death.

The evidence of the views is particularly important for Bramante's choir arm, which no longer exists but can be reliably reconstructed also with the help of the building surveys by Peruzzi and Antonio da Sangallo (Figs. 74, 75, 76).[75] The ground plan follows the Nicholas foundations, with a square choir bay, and a semicircular, polygonally encased apse. The large pilaster order of the dome piers continues along the walls. Light entered the interior through five high and widely arched windows that were barred with grates of architraved columns. The vault was coffered, the semidome of the apse was filled with a huge shell. The exterior was articulated with colossal Doric pilasters. It was this choir building which later determined Michelangelo's idea of Bramante's St. Peter's project and ultimately was responsible for the exterior appearance of the present-day edifice.[76]

The project of 1506 had fixed the interior structure of the building up to the summit of the large coffered arches that were intended to carry the dome. As the building grew to this height, Bramante turned his attention to the dome itself. He would not see it completed, but it was to crown his St. Peter's, bringing it to conclusion and assuring the future of his plan as a whole. Thus he bequeathed as a legacy to posterity – "prima che ei morisse," as Serlio wrote – his dome project.[77] The parallel to the old Michelangelo is remarkable. The

79. St. Peter's, interior looking west

latter fixed his project in the form of a wooden model; Bramante, pressed for time, appears to have limited himself to two drawings, which, however, completely defined the three-dimensional structure and thus simultaneously presented an example of modern planning techniques.[78] Serlio represented them in woodcut (Figs. 77, 78). They show the definitive formation of a thought that already had begun to emerge in the sketch (Fig. 62) and in the Caradosso foundation medal (Fig. 64): the dome as a piece of representational architecture in its own right, which already from a distance signaled the papal basilica to the pilgrims to Rome. Over seventy years were to pass until its completion, but Bramante's main idea, to place the semicircular dome of the Pantheon above a tholos surrounded by columns, which allowed streams of light to penetrate the interior, remained in spite of all later metamorphoses, from Sangallo to Michelangelo and Giacomo della Porta. Whether it could have been realized in the form Bramante imagined remains debatable.[79]

BRAMANTE'S ARCHITECTURE

Bramante's St. Peter's changed the standards of Renaissance architecture. Never before since antiquity had "size" been made such a theme in architecture as was the case with the colossal pilasters of Bramante's dome piers.[80] This was not simply a question of the absolute dimensions of the building; these had been largely determined by the imperial predecessor and would already have made Nicholas V's project the largest church in Christendom. But one would have experienced the Nicholas building as a gigantic cavity, not unlike that of the Cathedral in Florence or the Basilica of Loreto. What Bramante brought into play was size as a quality, and thereby those specific emotions which could be evoked by a building like the Pantheon. He formulated his aesthetic concept in a surprisingly determined way in dialogue with the della Rovere pope, if one follows Egido da Viterbo: the visitor to St. Peter will be shaken and overwhelmed by the sight of this huge building ("templum ingressurus . . . commotus attonitusque novae molis aspectu ingrediatur"), and thus made receptive to the truth of the Christian faith. It is easy to recognize herein the beginning of a tradition of architectural magniloquence of the type that is familiar to us from Western architecture of the next two hundred years; moreover, we see Bramante's piers today in the context of a Baroque decoration into which they fit seamlessly (Fig. 79). This has dulled our senses to the effect they must have originally provoked. To re-evoke it, one has to call to mind more purely preserved buildings of Bramante's Roman years, such as the Tempietto, the cloister of S. Maria della Pace, or the choir of S. Maria del Popolo: materially unpretentious, frugal, even dry in sculptural decoration, they stand out through their wealth of ideas, sharpness of articulation, compositional daring, and formal wit. Their effectiveness is of an intellectual, nonsensual nature.

"Invenzione nuova" is the key phrase in Vasari's assessment of Bramante: he should be placed alongside the Greeks rather than the Romans, as the former had invented architecture, while the latter had only imitated it.[81] Thus the gigantism of Bramante's St. Peter's must have impressed his contemporaries primarily as a new tour de force of its inventor, a bewildering idea like the round temple on the Janiculum, the spiral staircase of the Vatican with the four types of column orders, or the mock choir of S. Maria presso S. Satiro in Milan. It is true that Bramante did not shy away from adopting the expressive formulas offered by tradition, as in the case of the Corinthian order he took directly from the pronaos of the Pantheon; the capitals of the dome piers, according to the contract, were to be shaped after those "di Santa Maria Ritonda nel portico di fora . . . cusi bene cavati."[82] But the pier itself, as it first saw the light in the parchment plan, was an invention sui generis, without precedent in antique or post-antique architecture. The same holds true for Bramante's overall concept. Roman antique monumental buildings such as the imperial baths or the Basilica of Maxentius have been considered as precedents, but in none of them is the mass of the wall organized in a comparable fashion or the total structure as geometrically pre-formed as in Bramante's St. Peter's. On the other hand, the structural model of a tetrastyle building, to which Bramante's quincunx can be attributed,[83] seems nearly lost in the plan itself, dissolved in the configuration of domes, niches, and side rooms that determine the overall impression. In addition, Bramante also managed to make disappear the basic pattern of the old basilica, on which his design was developed. As an architectural work of art, Bramante's St. Peter's is the complete antithesis of the Constantinian building; only in the architraved colonnades in the apses, isolated as a quotation, was an estranged reminder of

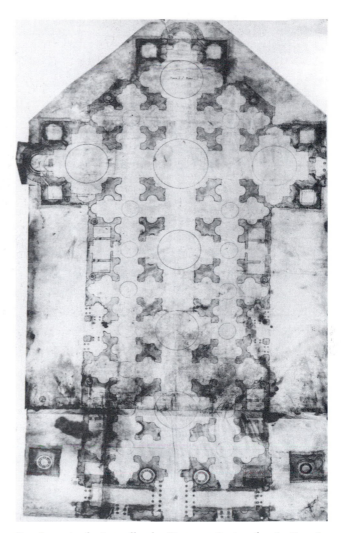

80. Antonio da Sangallo the Younger, Project for St. Peter's. 1516/17. Uffizi, Florence, Gabinetto dei Disegni, 254A

the old building to survive.[84] "Instauracio," renewal, not restoration of the old, was Bramante's and Julius's declared goal.[85]

Already Vasari treated the parchment plan as a paradigm of the new style. He took possession of the "mirabile disegno" in order to include it in his collection of original drawings.[86] Even today, after having been reproduced a thousand and one times, the effect of this sheet is surprising if not unsettling when seen in the original; in this it resembles the painting of "Christ at the Column" in the Brera in Milan, or the Prevedari etching. Indeed, the new does not simply reside in the architecture that it presents. Even more surprising is the pretension of a ground plan acting like a work of art. This is no building plan about which to have a discussion, but a message of things to come, hermetic and unalterable. It is not disturbing that the building itself appears only as a fragment: it actually activates the fantasy of

81. Antonio da Sangallo the Younger, projects for the elevation of the southern tribuna of St. Peter's, 1519. Uffizi, Florence, Gabinetto dei Disegni, 122A

82. Domenico Aymo da Varignana, elevation and section of Raphael's second project for St. Peter's, ca. 1518. Pierpont Morgan Library, New York, Codex Mellon, 1878.44

the beholder (primarily the employer) and involves him in the planning process. The project presentation takes on the character of a challenge.

No employer, and most certainly not Pope Julius II, could resist the temptation of such designs. Bramante seemed to be able to conjure up things that were deemed impossible. This corresponds to the impetus with which he attacked the challenge of St. Peter's as well as other Julian buildings. During the eight years under his leadership, St. Peter's grew more than over the span of the next few decades. Vasari writes that Bramante wanted to see his buildings "not constructed but born";[87] this phrase accurately describes the anticipatory character of his drawings as well as his architectural practice. Already the first beginnings were intended to bring the whole to life. The downside of such impatience consisted in a series of technical defects, which quickly became apparent and formed the basis for Bramante's "bad reputation" as an engineer.[88] The four great piers had insufficient foundations and, before they could carry the weight of the dome, had to be repaired several times at an enormous expenditure of time and money.[89] Bramante's choir, which, were it still standing today, would have been the most glorious testimony to his genius showed cracks already during its construction. By the time of its demolition the apse, according to the archive documents, was "tutta crepata."[90] It was the conception, not the material substance, which guaranteed the future of Bramante's work.

From Leo X to Paul III: Raphael, Sangallo, Peruzzi

THE MEDICI POPES

Julius II died in February 1513; Bramante, one year later. They left St. Peter's basilica a ruin opposite which the fragments of the new building soared into the sky. It was a situation that filled Julius himself, after the euphoria of the early years had dissipated, with trepidation and self-accusations.[91] Now critical voices began to be heard.[92] Already in the time of Nicholas V, contemporaries of the pope such as Maffeo Vegio and Poggio Bracciolini had warned of the destruction of the old basilica; Manetti had countered them with his enthusiastic description of the planned new building. The Bramante building, as it now grew, raised the problem of ecclesiastical luxury buildings, whose critics were able to refer to Early Christian and medieval tradition (Jerome; Bernard of Clairvaux). Most of them came from northern countries, such as Erasmus of Rotterdam or Ulrich von Hutten, while Italian theologians such as Egidio da Viterbo, but also humanists of the Curia such as Francesco Albertini, Andrea Fulvio, and Cornelio de Fine, argued the papal point. The controversy grew even wider when financial considerations came into play. In order to secure finances for the building, Julius extended the business in indulgences to the church provinces outside of Italy.[93] Martin Luther objected, thereby facilitating the outbreak of an indignation against the Roman Church that had been smoldering in Germany for generations. In this manner the building, intended to be the architectural symbol of the unity of the Church, became the trigger of the Reformation, which destroyed this very unity.

Giovanni de' Medici, who succeeded Julius II as Leo X (1513–21), hardly took notice of these events. While Luther formulated his Wittenberg theses Rome was wallowing in artistic visions. Raphael, who in accordance with Bramante's wish had been hired by Leo as the new builder of St. Peter's, wrote home that the church was the largest construction site in the world. It would cost more than a million gold ducats, and the pope was thinking of nothing else; daily he called on him to discuss the building.[94] Therefore, it is no surprise that the plan with which Raphael began his job (Fig. 70) simply ignored the problem of the Julius choir. He restored Bramante's project to its original form with a long western arm, ambulatories, and a cupola quincunx, and gave the nave a length of five bays.[95] Thus he initiated a development that was to become characteristic for the subsequent decades until Michelangelo intervened. Giuliano da Sangallo, Antonio da Sangallo, and Baldassare Peruzzi put lots of overall plans on paper, in which they toyed with every imaginable combination of the elements of Bramante's design, considered new

83. Baldassare Peruzzi's first project for St. Peter's (Serlio 1540)

details, tested new ground-plan varieties and expanded the whole to fantastic dimensions (Fig. 80).[96] Relieved of the concrete necessity of actual construction, the financing problems of which blocked any large-scale progress, the planning of St. Peter's developed into an academy of High Renaissance architecture.[97]

Not much happened on the building site in the interim. Bramante, in his last year, completed the vaulting of the Julius choir and began the construction of the "tegurio," a huge protective housing covering the basilica's apse and main altar that had been saved from demolition, and thus made it possible to resume the papal services above the tomb of St. Peter.[98] This was the new pope's most important construction undertaking. For the time being, no decisions regarding the future of Bramante's building were made. Raphael was fully occupied with his work in the Vatican *stanze* and with the tapestry series for Leo X, and hardly found time to concern himself with St. Peter's. Toward the end of 1516, Bramante's former assistant, Antonio da Sangallo the Younger, was called in as "architetto coadiutore."[99] He took on the task of planning (Fig. 81). Contemporary surveys show the appearance of a model for the whole building completed approximately two years later, which detailed the exterior of the structure and, with its nave, facade, dome, and campanili, must have represented a magnificent dream castle (Fig. 82).[100] In 1519 construction was resumed on the hemicycle of the southern transept, whose richly articulated architecture was handed down in the design sketches of Sangallo as well as in Heemskerck's

84. Maerten van Heemskerck, St. Peter's, exterior from the north, 1532/6. Stiftung preussischer Kulturbesitz, Kupferstichkabinett, Berlin, Heemskerck-Album, vol. 1, fol. 13^r

85. Giorgio Vasari, *Pope Paul III orders the continuation of the construction of St. Peter's.* Fresco, 1546. Rome, Sala dei Cento Giorni, Palazzo della Cancelleria

and Vasari's views, and which was later demolished by Michelangelo.

The sudden death of Raphael on Good Friday of 1520 caused a new break in the building history. Antonio da Sangallo moved up to the position of first architect of the Fabbrica. In a memo, a draft of which has been preserved, he criticized a number of details of the Bramante-Raphael project, particularly the nave, which he compared to a "long, narrow, and high alley."[101] Thus in the year 1521 he presented a new model, again known from survey drawings, in which the bay sequence of the

nave was brought into rhythm by a second large dome over the central nave.[102] Peruzzi received the vacant position of second architect; he came forward with the proposal to do without the nave and finish St. Peter's as a pure centrally planned building (Fig. 83).[103] According to Vasari, he hoped in this way to satisfy the pope, who had criticized the Julius project as "too large and too disjointed."[104] But Leo, only seven years older than Raphael, died unexpectedly in December 1521. His successor, Adrian VI from Utrecht (1522–23), mentor of Erasmus of Rotterdam, stood apart from the Roman

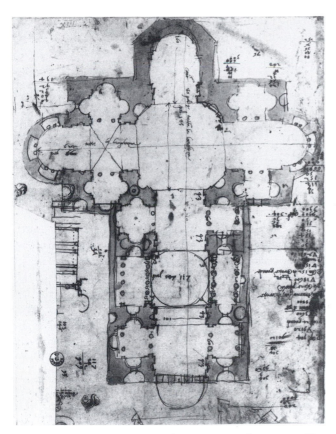

86. Baldassare Peruzzi, Project for St. Peter's, after 1527. Uffizi, Florence, Gabinetto dei Disegni, 16A

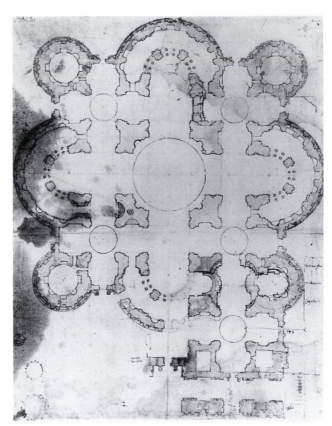

87. Antonio da Sangallo the Younger, Project for St. Peter's, 1534/7. Uffizi, Florence, Gabinetto dei Disegni, 39A

art scene and was more interested in a long overdue reform of the Curia than in St. Peter's. He was followed by the architecture-loving Clement VII (1523–34), again from the house of Medici. Under him the construction on the southern transept made significant progress.[105] But it came to an abrupt end when, in 1527, as a consequence of a chain of bad foreign-policy decisions, the troops of Charles V devastated the city and the high mood of the Renaissance plunged into deep pessimism.[106] After the "Sacco di Roma" the construction site of St. Peter's remained as deserted as the antique ruins of the city, and in this manner it was depicted by Heemskerck (Fig. 84). No one believed that construction would resume.[107]

PAUL III

If one looks back from the period of the Medici papacy to the founding years of the building, one notices a difference in the behavior of the popes. Julius was the man who wanted a new St. Peter's and took responsibility for the consequences. Leo and Clement fell into the role of successors, and what happened to the building under their papacies is associated more with the names of the planning architects than with their employers. Now, in

order to start the construction up again, a new type of initiator was needed. He presented himself in the person of Alessandro Farnese, who ascended the papal throne as Paul III (1534–49). Born in 1468 and raised to the position of cardinal already at the age of twenty-five, he had followed the fate of St. Peter's since its beginning and was aware of his significance for the future of the Church. He saw himself, like Julius II, as the restorer of the temple of Solomon with the declared intention, however, of finishing it (Fig. 85).[108] Curiously enough, Paul also followed Julius in the fact that, after he first assumed office, he turned his initial attention to the Vatican Palace and commissioned Sangallo with the erection of the Capella Paolina (in a sense, his "Sistine"), which he had painted by Michelangelo.[109] Only then was the question of St. Peter's addressed.

After the catastrophe of the sack of Rome it was firmly established that the future of the new building depended on the containment of its size. To that end Sangallo as well as Peruzzi produced a series of "reduction plans," which in part may have originated under Clement VII, in part already under Paul III (Fig. 86).[110] In the year of his election, Paul promoted Peruzzi to architect with full salary, equal to Sangallo, possibly to incite both of them to maximum performance, but it may also

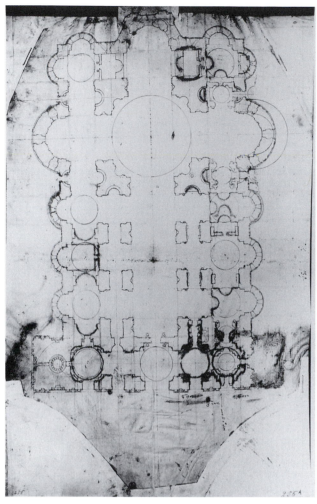

88. Antonio da Sangallo the Younger, Project for St. Peter's, 1538. Uffizi, Florence, Gabinetto dei Disegni, 256A

building back to the dimensions of the large nave projects and thus made the savings of time and expense desired by the pope illusory (Fig. 90).

Nevertheless, in 1539 Sangallo was asked to present his project in a wooden model (Fig. 91). Under the guidance of his assistant, Antonio da Labacco, a monstrosity measuring nearly 8 meters in length and 5 meters in height that reproduced the complete building in a scale of 1 to 30 came into existence after seven years of work (Fig. 92).[114] Sangallo summoned all of his skill to find rational answers to all the questions of this gigantic building. A great number of preliminary sketches, all done by his own hand, allow us to study his design techniques. They culminate in the project for the large dome, for which Sangallo found a completely innovative solution after intensively studying the dome of the Florence cathedral. For the exterior shell he kept Bramante's hemisphere, but the load-carrying inner shell was supposed to be constructed as a rotation ellipsoid.[115] The sequence of the "orders" was carried through uniformly in the entire building; half-columns (outside) and pilasters (inside) articulated pillars and walls. The Vitruvian correctness in detail contrasted with the fantastic overall appearance of the building; critics such as Michelangelo and Vasari were reminded more of medieval Gothic

have been because he favored Peruzzi's idea of a centrally planned building. Peruzzi died before building recommenced. Sangallo, now again solely in charge, proved by means of a comparative study that a plan for a nave was the only one which could do justice to the reality of the building site (Fig. 87).[111] However, the design he worked out on this basis and which he characterized in a sketch as "bella e breve," "beautiful and quick to execute," did not achieve realization (Fig. 88).[112] Instead, in the following months (between 1538 and 1539) a vast number of studies and sketches came into being in which Sangallo once again tried out all possible variations of ground plans and elevations (Fig. 89).[113] The precept of preserving the Julius choir was now finally abandoned; instead, the idea of a centrally planned building asserted itself. This provided Sangallo with the opportunity, once again, to return to his ideal of a richly articulated, rhythmically ordered overall composition. The result was a combination of a centralized quincunx structure with an absurdly lavish vestibule and facade, which brought the

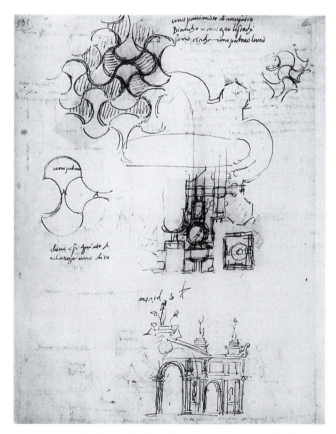

89. Antonio da Sangallo the Younger, Project for St. Peter's, 1538/9. Uffizi, Florence, Gabinetto dei Disegni, 110A

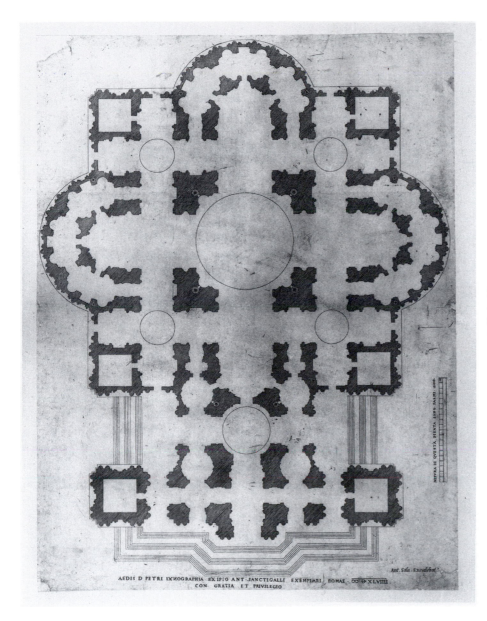

90. Antonio Salamanca, *Plan of Antonio da Sangallo's wooden model for St. Peter's*, engraving, 1549

cathedrals ("opera tedesca") than of Sangallo's classical models.[116] Nevertheless, Michelangelo was wrong when he demanded a return to the "clarity" and "truth" of Bramante, referring to the Julius choir.[117] He did not know, or had forgotten, that the ambulatories around the apses, which were the focus of his ire, were Bramante's own invention, whereas Sangallo, after the sack, had tried only to save the St. Peter's of the Renaissance, reformed and purged of its "mistakes."

Sangallo's first construction efforts were also of a conservative type.[118] The masonry of the new building, exposed to the elements, had to be repaired and covered up; the still standing eastern part of the old nave had to be secured statically and restored for use in ecclesiastical services. Sangallo closed it off against the building site with a transverse wall ("muro divisorio") (Fig. 93);

then he erected the eastern arm of the new building and connected it by a short intermediate tract with the old nave. From that point on the old and new buildings formed a spatial unity (Fig. 94); they communicated via an arched opening in the wall which, however, was soon closed with a door. None of this had anything to do with Sangallo's own project. But whereas this project disappeared from the building history with the death of Sangallo, the provisorium he had established remained until the seventeenth century; only in 1614, when Maderno's nave was under construction, was the "muro" dismantled. The new construction pushed Sangallo energetically forward; significant parts of the present building came into existence under his management.[119] But either they do not bear his handwriting, like the walls and vaults of the transept wings, which

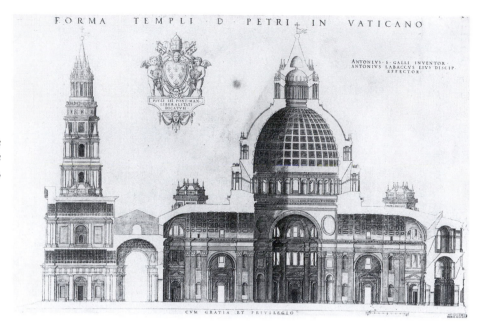

91. Antonio Salamanca, *Section of Antonio da Sangallo's wooden model for St. Peter's*, engraving, 1546

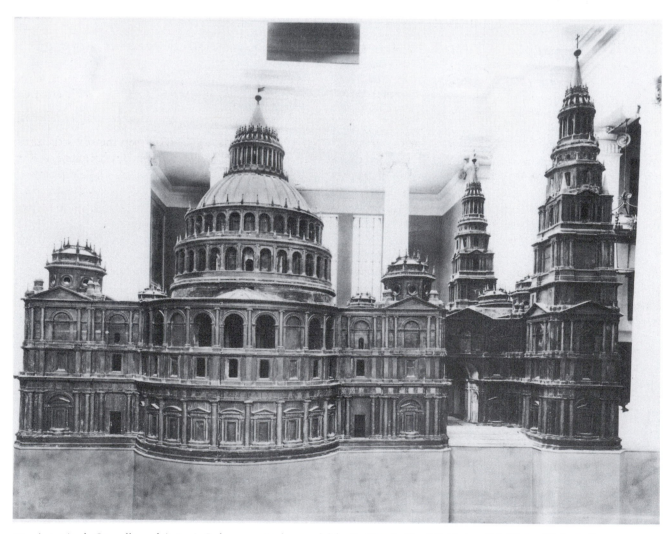

92. Antonio da Sangallo and Antonio Labacco, wooden model for St. Peter's. Rev.ᵃ Fabbrica di S. Pietro, Vatican, Rome

93. Collaborator of Maerten van Heemskerck (Anonymous A), St. Peter's from the north, 1538/42. Stiftung preussischer Kulturbesitz, Kupferstichkabinett, Berlin, Heemskerck-Alben, vol. 1, fol. 15ʳ

still belonged to the Bramante-Raphael project, or they remain hidden from the eyes of visitors, like the eight large octagonal domed spaces between the vault and the roof in which the museum of the Fabbrica is now being installed. In the interior of the building, only the altar aediculae of the dome- and counter-piers date back to Sangallo. Nothing remains of his exterior architecture.

With the death of Sangallo in August 1546, the aging Farnese pope, once again, was given the opportunity to shape the fate of the building. At first, negotiations were begun with Giulio Romano, the last heir of the Bramante school, who died in the same year.[120] The choice then fell upon Michelangelo who, after some hesitation, was ready to assume the job of chief architect of St. Peter's. Only a few years younger than Pope Paul and older than any of the other potential contestants, even older than his predecessor Sangallo, he had stayed away from the building ever since his Julius tomb project had foundered. Now he took over, determined to liquidate the utopias of the Bramante-Raphael era. The Sangallo clique did not concede defeat; its obstructions in the Fabbrica were to embitter Michelangelo's last years.[121] Labacco in 1546–8 came out with a series of engravings after the large model, "so that everyone could admire Sangallo's creativity and learn his thoughts, after Michelangelo Buonarotti had opposed them" (Vasari).[122] The model appeared for the last time on the reverse of a papal medal that Paul II had struck in 1546/7 and that was reissued in the jubilee year of 1550 under Julius III.[123] But this was without relevance to the subsequent history of the building.

EPILOGUE

Whereas Nicholas V had foundered with his new building project, Julius II had success, not because he thought more realistically, but because he dismissed reality in a more determined fashion and broke more ruthlessly with what existed. Yet Bramante's design remained "imperfetto," and after his death construction soon halted. Under Julius's successors the architects' plans grew to perfection on the design boards, but over them hovered a mist of unreality, as if the planners themselves no longer believed in the transformatory power of their designs. Instead, the basilica as a historic reality came back into consciousness. The "tegurio" of Leo X was the first in a series of provisions designed to keep the old structures practicable in the chaos of construction and sufficient for the liturgical needs of the papal church. They resulted from the consideration of time in the overall course of events: the new building would not come into being in one go, the old would not disappear immediately; the design for the future had to coexist with the demands of the present.

These contradictions culminated in the pontificate of Paul III, the Renaissance humanist who turned from "Saulus" to "Paulus" as the pope who launched the reform of the Church. Simultaneously Sangallo, while having the last of the great architectural dreams of the Renaissance executed in wood, occupied himself as a pragmatist on the building site by restoring the rest of the nave and connecting it with the fragments of the new building. He was hardly aware that this was a first step in the direction of the planning goal of the second half of the century: the restitution of the spiritual identity of the basilica Sancti Petri.

Thus our view turns to the real story of the building. It is not that of the overall projects replacing one another in succession, but a slow (though logical) process of growth from west to east, from the choir of Nicholas V and Bramante's domed crossing to Maderno's nave and Bernini's colonnade. It was the logic of successive

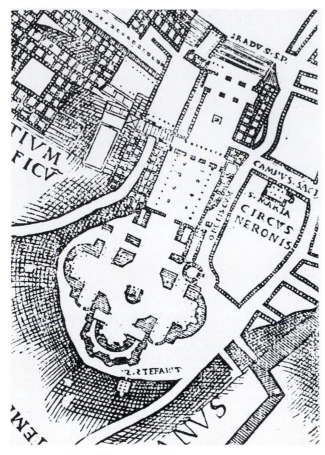

94. Leonardo Bufalini, *Map of Rome*, woodcut, detail, 1551

construction that inevitably asserted itself in a complex of this size, ignoring or superseding all individual efforts. Thus, none of the popes and none of the architects who pushed construction forward during the first half of the Cinquecento really achieved what they had planned, and what was achieved, after all, none of them had wanted. The future of the building remained beyond the horizon of its founders.

NOTES

I would like to thank Manfred Luchterhand for a thorough and critical reading of my manuscript. The text was translated from the German by Thomas Bayer.

1 Krautheimer 1980 and 1985.
2 Prodi 1982, especially 13ff., "La nuova monarchia: Dalle terre di san Pietro al Principato"; Pastor 1925–33, vol. 1.
3 Manfredo Tafuri, "Cives esse non licere, Niccolò V e Leon Battista Alberti," in Tafuri 1992, 33–88.
4 Urban 1963, 133. Pastor, 1925–33, 1:527, cites an unpublished manuscript, which mentions that a pilgrim to Rome reported already in 1450 on work done on a new building of St. Peter's.
5 Urban 1963, 133.
6 Frommel 1976, 87f.

7 *Acta Sanctorum, Junii*, VII, appendix, 71 (Lib. Quartus, 1st paragraph).
8 The extensive recent literature on the St. Peter project of Nicolas V is treated by Curti 1995 and 1997; Frommel 1997 and 1998, and Burns 1998.
9 Pastor 1925–33, 1:417.
10 Ibid.
11 Text by Magnuson 1958, 351–62.
12 For this see especially Urban 1963 and Curti 1995.
13 Compare below, n. 59.
14 Ferabosco/Grimaldi, Jovanovits, Magnuson, Urban, Frommel, Curti; best overview is by Curti 1997.
15 Pastor 1925–33, 1:428n2.
16 Alberti I, 10 = Alberti 1966, 1:75.
17 Drawing in Florence, Uffizi, 121 A; compare Thoenes 2000, 107f.
18 Pastor 1925–33, 1:428n1.
19 Lastly, Schütze 1994, with a discussion on preceding literature.
20 Frommel 1994, 399.
21 Magnuson 1958, 206, with a reference to Alberti VIII, 1 = Alberti 1966, 2:669f.; Frommel, 1977 21.
22 Pastor 1925–53, 1:148f.
23 Magnuson 1958, 206–10.
24 Ibid., 208.
25 First so described by Dehio 1880.
26 See above, n. 5.
27 See above n. 21.
28 See above n. 16.
29 Alberti X, 17 = Alberti 1966, 2:999.
30 Alberti I, 18 = Alberti 1966, 1:63.
31 Alberti VII, 3 = Alberti 1966, 2:547; cf. Krautheimer 1961; Thoenes 1988, 94f.
32 Alberti II, 1 = Alberti 1966, 1:101.
33 Ibid., 103.
34 Alberti IX, 11 = Alberti 1966, 2:865f.
35 Thoenes 1999.
36 This was suggested by Tafuri 1992, 62–7.
37 Vasari, 1878–85, 3:98–102. Also Manetti mentions Rossellino ("Bernardum nostrum Florentinum"), Magnuson 1958, 360.
38 Cf. Burroughs 1990, 243f.
39 Frommel 1983.
40 Urban 1963, 134; Cantatore 1997.
41 Frommel 1977, 30–3.
42 Pastor, 1925–33, vol. 3; Machiavelli 1965, 1:91f. (*Il principe*, chap. 25).
43 Frommel 1977, 413; Contardi 1998, 18f.
44 Frommel, 1977; Bredekamp 2000.
45 Frommel 1976, 97f., and 1977, 28–31.
46 Frommel 1976, 103.
47 Frommel 1976, 126ff. and 1977, 33–5.
48 Frommel 1976, 87f.
49 Lotz 1977, 130.
50 Bredekamp, 2000.
51 Frommel 1976, 59ff.
52 Ackerman 1974, 347; Thoenes, "S. Pietro. Storia e ricerca," 28n10.
53 For Panvinio, see De Maio 1978, 326. The opposite evaluation is in Vasari 1878–85, 4:145: Bramante had the good fortune to find in Julius a sovereign on whose account he could prove his genius.
54 Frommel 1976, 89f.
55 Cf. also Kempers 1996.
56 The demolition of the nave stopped at this line.
57 Serlio 1540, 36.
58 Thoenes, "S. Pietro. Storia e ricerca," 30n69.

59 This debate cannot be summarized briefly, nor documented bibliographically here. For the current state of the question, compare the diverse contributions by C. L. Frommel, A. Bruschi, and Ch. Thoenes in Tessari 1996 and Thoenes 1998, and the literature cited there. Arnaldo Bruschi has recently summarized his contributions in Bruschi 1997. Analyses of the drawings are provided by Wolff Metternich/Thoenes 1987, and Frommel 1994.

60 For methodology compare Thoenes, "Neue Beobachtungen," 110.

61 The following is the opinion of the author; it is substantiated in Thoenes, "Neue Beobachtungen." Another interpretation, different in many respects, is provided by Frommel 1994, and Frommel and Adams 2000.

62 Francesco di Giorgio Martini, 2:372 and plate 236; Thoenes, "Neue Beobachtungen," 112.

63 This is the dominating view, with the exception of Metternich (Wolf Metternich and Thoenes 1987, 17–23). In the source literature the question of a centrally designed building is not addressed.

64 Most recently, Frommel 1994, 603f. (interpreted as view from the east). For the inscriptions of the diverse medals, see Frommel 1976, 94f. and 100.

65 For Serlio's woodcut as a source for Bramante's "third project," see Thoenes 1990–2, 442f.

66 The term "rhythmic travee" was coined by Geymuller 1875–80, 71; compare Wolff Metternich and Thoenes 1987, 98, 112, and 142. For S. Andrea in Mantua, Burns 1998, 150.

67 See above, n. 57.

68 According to Frommel 1976 and passim, Bramante had reduced his project according to the wishes of Julius II and only in 1513 designed his monumental project for Leo X. The sources, however, do not contain any references for these events.

69 All written sources are reproduced by Frommel 1976. The most concise account of the entire building history still is Ackerman 1966, 2:85–115. Of only limited use is Francia 1977; compare for this also Thoenes 1978. For the archive of the Fabbrica, cf. Basso, 1987–8.

70 Together with the associated document from the "Liber Mandatorum," analyzed by Denker-Nesselrath 1990, 79–84; Frommel 1994, 609.

71 Frommel 1994, 610.

72 Ibid.; cf. Wolff Metternich and Thoenes 1987, 165–9.

73 Wolff Metternich and Thoenes 1987, 193–201; Thoenes 1986; Carpiceci 1987; Frommel 1994, 623 and 630–2.

74 *Vedute of the Biblioteca Vaticana*, Coll. Ash by, n. 329, 1424/5: Wolff Metternich/Thoenes 1987, 194; for attribution, Thoenes, "S. Pietro. Storia e ricerca," 28n21.

75 Most recently Bruschi, in Tessari 1996, 121–32.

76 Thoenes, "S. Pietro. Storia e ricerca," 30n69; see also below, n. 117.

77 Serlio 1540, 39; Wolff Metternich and Thoenes 1987, 164–74; Kraus and Thoenes 1991–2; Hubert 1992; Frommel 1994, 613f.

78 Thoenes 1993, 567.

79 Krauss and Thoenes 1991–2.

80 To visualize their original aspect, one has to add pedestals nearly 4 meters high, which have disappeared under the floor raised by Antonio da Sangallo. Wolf Metternich and Thoenes 1987, 175.

81 Vasari 1878–85, 4:146.

82 See above, n. 70.

83 Günther 1995.

84 The negative evaluation of the Constantinian architecture is documented by Sigismondo dei Conti in Frommel 1976, 124.

85 Inscription on the foundation medal of 1506, see above, n. 64.

86 Vasari 1878–85, 4:159; cf. Wolff Metternich and Thoenes 1987, 13–17.

87 Vasari 1878–85, 4:157; cf. Thoenes 1974, 395.

88 Ackerman 1974.

89 Krauss and Thoenes 1991–2.

90 Wolff Metternich and Thoenes 1987, 127; cf. also Thoenes 1998, 159.

91 Frommel 1976, 82 and 109: "... principis apostolorum basilica in magna esset ruina, quod nobis pudori dicimus" (*Breve*, 26 September 1508).

92 De Maio 1978, 310–18, 327, and most recently Günther 1997 and Miarelli Mariani 1997, who have compiled extensive material.

93 Frommel 1976, 81f., 101f., and passim; Thoenes, "S. Pietro. Storia e ricerca," 28n36.

94 Letter to Simone Ciarla, 1 July 1514; Camesasca 1994, 175f. cf. Thoenes, "'Il primo tempio del mondo.' Raffael, St. Peter und das Geld."

95 See above, n. 65.

96 Antonio da Sangallo, Uffizi 254 A, with a total length of ca. 450 meters, more than twice as long as the present-day building. Thoenes, "S. Pietro. Storia e ricerca," 20.

97 Frommel 1984, 1986, and 1994; Bruschi, in Tessari 1996.

98 Most recently, Tronzo 1997, proposing to see the *tegurio* as a permanent structure. Concerning questions of long-term provisions in the Peter building, compare Wolff Metternich and Thoenes 1987, 131f.; Thoenes 1992, 60; Kempers 1996.

99 Golzio 1936, 50f. The history of planning in the following three decades is amply documented in Sangallo's drawings, preserved in the Uffizi; cf. now the catalogue entries by A. Bruschi and Ch. Thoenes in Frommel and Adams 2000.

100 New York, Pierpont Morgan Library, Codex Mellon, attributed to Domenico Aimo da Varignana. Frommel 1984, 270–3, and 1994, 617f.

101 Uffizi, 33 A; Frommel 1984, 296f., and 1994, 621f.

102 Munich, Bayrische Staatsbibliothek, Cod. icon. mon. 195, Jean de Chenevières; Frommel 1984, 299–302, and 1994, 622.

103 Bruschi, in Tessari 1996, 197–248.

104 Vasari 1878–85, 4:599; cf. Thoenes 1995, 96.

105 Frommel 1994, 421; Frey 1910, 71–90. The material from the archives published by Karl Frey in the supplements to the *Jahrbuch der preussischen Kunstsammlungen* (1909–16) remain fundamental for the history of the building after Julius II. For the *Vedute*, see above, n. 74.

106 Wolff Metternich and Thoenes 1987, 196; Thoenes, "S. Pietro. Storia e ricerca," 20. For the Sack of Rome cf. Tafuri 1992, 223–53.

107 Thoenes 1986, 489f.

108 Saalman 1978, 491 doc. 9; cf. also Thoenes, "S. Pietro. Storia e ricerca," 22 f.

109 Frommel 1964.

110 Frommel 1994, 421 and 625–30; Thoenes, "S. Pietro 1534–46," 635; Thoenes 2000; for Peruzzi, cf. A. Bruschi in Tessari 1996, 222ff. No one of these drawings can be dated with certainty before 1534.

111 Uffizi, 39 A. Frommel 1994, 629f.; Thoenes, "S. Pietro 1534–46," 638; Thoenes 2000, 37, 73f.

112 Uffizi, 256 A and 40 A (sketch with notation); Frommel 1994, 628–30; Thoenes 2000, 37, 74f., 139f.

113 Thoenes 2000.

114 Benedetti, "Il modello per il San Pietro"; Thoenes, "S. Pietro 1534–46"; Thoenes 1997.

115 Thoenes 1996 and Thoenes, "Il modello digneo per San Pietro." For a different interpretation of the sphere profile, see Benedetti,

"Il profilo della cupola vaticana di Antonio da Sangallo il Giovane."

116 For Michelangelo's critique of the model: Vasari 1878–85, 5:467f. and 8:218f.; cf. Thoenes, "S. Pietro 1534–46," 637, and Bredekamp 1995.

117 Letter by Michelangelo to Bartolomeo Ferratino, in *Michelangelo. Il carteggio* 1965–83, 4:251f.

118 To the following, Thoenes 1992; Rice 1997.

119 Giovannoni 1959, 146–50; Millon and Smyth 1976.

120 Vasari 1878–85, 5:554.

121 Bardeschi Ciulich 1977; Saalman 1978.

122 Vasari 1878–85, 5:467; Thoenes, "S. Pietro 1534–46," 646f.

123 Thoenes, "S. Pietro 1534–46," 646.

6

MICHELANGELO TO MARCHIONNI, 1546–1784

HENRY A. MILLON

AT THE DEATH OF ANTONIO DA SANGALLO IN August 1546, the deputies charged with oversight of St. Peter's consulted Paul III about a successor. According to Vasari, the position was first offered to Giulio Romano, then in service to the Gonzaga in Mantua (Vasari-Milanesi 1878–85, 5:554–5). The Gonzaga were reluctant to have Giulio Romano leave, but his death early in November, less than three months after that of Sangallo, ended any negotiations that might have begun. It appears that Paul III may then have acted independently and in November or early December asked Michelangelo to become the new architect of St. Peter's. According to Vasari's account, to "escape the burden," Michelangelo refused the invitation, saying that architecture was not his vocation. The pope dismissed this protest and commanded Michelangelo's acceptance (Vasari-Milanesi 1878–85, 7:218). The appointment officially began only on 1 January 1547, but already by 10 December 1546 Michelangelo was at work on a large wood model that would thereafter guide construction of the main body of St. Peter's (Frey 1911, 29, 93).

To judge by the text of a famous letter written by Michelangelo early in 1547, which contains a scathing account of Sangallo's model, he saw his task at St. Peter's as restoring the "clear, simple, luminous" design laid down by Bramante in his first plan (Barocchi and Ristori, eds. 1965–83, 4:MLXXI, 251). In studying the models of both Bramante and Sangallo, Michelangelo found that the outer ambulatory of Sangallo's design blocked light from the interior resulting in many dark spaces at two levels within the basilica (Fig. 91). Furthermore, Michelangelo felt that the enlargement proposed by Sangallo's design would necessitate the destruction of the Pauline Chapel, the offices of the Piombo, of the Ruota, and perhaps the Sistine Chapel itself. He penned these thoughts in a letter to an unidentified friend who may have been one of the deputies, and asks that he help to explain Michelangelo's proposal to the pope.

A number of the deputies protested against Michelangelo's intentions, which included not only abandonment of Sangallo's model but reduction in the size of the planned basilica, the dismantling of walls and foundations of the south ambulatory, as well as the personal administrative coup of dismissing the staff they had appointed to coordinate and supervise construction under Antonio da Sangallo (Saalman 1978, 483–93; Bardeschi Ciulich 1977, 235–75).

In December 1546, Michelangelo was asked by Paul III to make a second, small model to reveal his intentions for St. Peter's. Vasari reports that the model was completed in two weeks (Vasari-Milanesi 1878–85, 7:219). It was likely made in clay. The larger model in wood, begun earlier, would not be completed until September 1547 (Frey 1913, 94). Even so, by March 1547, the two models seem to have been sufficiently developed for Paul III to tell the deputies that he approved of the drawings and models that Michelangelo had shown him (Bardeschi Ciulich 1977, 240). The pope instructed the deputies to support Michelangelo in all he wished, including the dismissal of Sangallo's staff. In the fall of 1549 Paul III issued a *motuproprio* enjoining deputies and ministers then and in the future to follow Michelangelo's instructions and models for St. Peter's. The *motuproprio* was later reaffirmed by Julius III in January 1552 (Vasari-Milanesi 1878–85, 7:220, 228).

While reducing the size of Sangallo's plan for the basilica, Michelangelo kept most of what had been built up to 1546, including the four great piers, arches, and pendentives of the crossing, the four secondary piers that form the two transepts to the north and south, the two secondary piers of the nave to the east, the main vaults of the south transept and of the nave to the east (Fig. 90). Sangallo also had completed the pairs of barrel vaults between the crossing and secondary piers (*navi piccole*) of the south transept, the pair flanking the nave to the east, and four of the "octagons," the domed spaces above the barrel vaults that join the crossing and secondary piers. One barrel vault to the east of the north transept was completed shortly after his death. Michelangelo built the barrel vault to the west of the north transept, and the two octagons to the east and west of the north transept, as well as the main vault of the transept. The octagons and choir vault to the west of the crossing were not built until Bramante's apse was replaced in 1581–8 under Giacomo Della Porta.

Michelangelo retained the south transept inner apse of Sangallo's design but removed the semicircular ambulatory around that apse which, together with the inner apse, had been built to two-thirds of the height of the first story. At the crossing, he retained the pendentives and the pendentive blocks placed by Sangallo that were awaiting the cornice ring and base of the principal drum and dome.

Although the four smaller domed satellite chapels of Sangallo's proposed plan were retained, their outer arms were eliminated. Four *lumache* (spiral ramps) for donkeys and mules to carry materials to the upper levels were placed within the secondary piers flanking the north and south transepts. Diagonal exterior walls sheathing the spiral ramps joined the transept apses and secondary piers to the satellite chapels. The exterior walls of Sangallo's transept apses and satellite chapels were thickened and became as massive as the crossing piers. For the elevation of the exterior, Michelangelo replaced the two levels and intermediate mezzanine of the Sangallo model design with a giant order of paired Corinthian pilasters. Once the peripheral spaces and walls were eliminated, the dimly lit transepts and satellite chapels were filled with direct exterior light.

In Michelangelo's reduced plan, satellite chapels and the vaulted spaces between the chapels and apses are subsidiary, dominated by the central domed area (Fig. 95). This plan is simpler and more focused than any preceding scheme, including the initial one of Bramante. By designing a majestic central dome and possibly eliminating secondary domes above the satellite chapels, Michelangelo may have wished to realize both a monumental reliquary tomb for the apostle Peter as well as the largest, most imposing building of the Christian West.

In adopting a giant order of paired pilasters set against pilaster strips for the exterior elevation of St. Peter's, Michelangelo perhaps wished to echo the pilaster pairs of Bramante's choir of 1514, where pairs of pilasters also flank the central window of the apse. (Bramante's choir also had large windows at the attic level, vaulted, with a segmental arch.) For the nearly thirty years while the completed south apse of Michelangelo and the west choir of Bramante coexisted, the relationship between the two apses would have been manifest to any observer.

Michelangelo's exterior elevation of the south flank of St. Peter's presents alternating bays of structural piers and stretches of wall with large openings at the second level (Fig. 96). The piers are defined by pairs of giant Corinthian pilasters placed against pilaster strips

and linked in the entablature by a single double salient ressaut. The wall is distinguished by niches at the first level and large openings to the interior at the second level. The recessed wall surface behind the opening at the second level appears malleable and to have a limited structural role.

Carrying through to the interior, a giant Corinthian pilaster-pier corresponds to the pilaster pair on the exterior and is similarly set against pilaster strips that together continue through the entablature with a double salient ressaut (Fig. 97). The interior wall at the second level is also recessed, but with yet more depth than on the exterior, as though to underline with its huge windows its nonstructural nature.

On the exterior, the reduced wall area between the pilaster pairs continues through the entablature to the attic. In the first design, tall arches encompass the full width of the area between the pairs of pilasters where vaults descend to the interior attic window. The first design for the attic seems to have intentionally revealed the interior vaulted structure at this level.

The second design for the attic, first realized on the north transept apse, places pilaster bunches above each of the pilasters below, but without their ressauts joined to unite them as a pair (Fig. 98). Between the pilaster bunches a shallow niche, crowned by papal tiara and keys, holds a candelabrum. In this second design for the attic, the wall area between the pilaster pairs always remains at the same level. The walls and piers below the attic demonstrate increasing differentiation between a massive structural pier and a wall that, as it rises, is progressively thinned and opened on both interior and exterior. The articulation of the second attic design blurs that distinction.

On the interior, from the pavement to the half-medallion of the apse vault, pedestals and ribs continue the verticals of the pilaster-pilaster strip-pier through the double ressauts. Between the ribs the billowing, doubly curved vaults recall the vaults of the exterior of the attic in its first design.

These undulating vaults of double curvature, sustained by ribs that emphasize the near-skeletal nature of the piers and pilaster strips on both interior and exterior, exhibit a fusion of ancient Roman scale and grandeur with medieval Christian vaulted cathedrals. Michelangelo's bold move toward a skeletal structure and fluid vaulting opened a path for the later works of Giacomo Della Porta, Carlo Maderno, Gian Lorenzo Bernini, and Francesco Borromini.

Michelangelo's choice of paired columns for the sixteen buttresses of the drum and dome was, most likely, to assure consonance with the paired pilasters of the main order below (Fig. 99). In the drum and dome, as in the body of the basilica, Michelangelo sought to emphasize the vertical continuity of the structural elements: paired

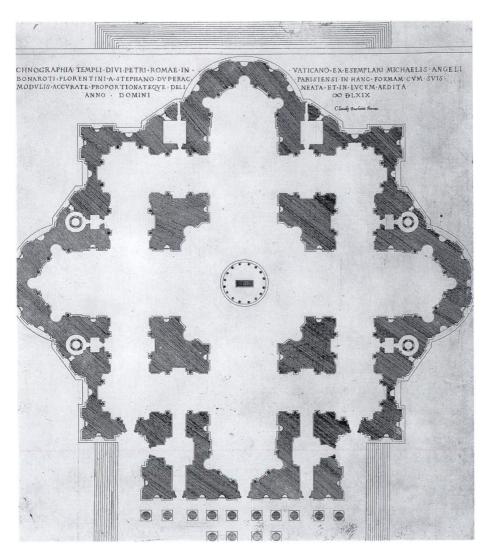

95. Étienne Dupérac, *Plan for St. Peter's*, engraving, 1569. The Metropolitan Museum of Art, New York, Harris Brisbane Dick Fund, 1941

columns of the buttresses, wide ribs in the dome, paired columns in the lantern with volutes at the level of the lantern's vault. In the drum and dome and lantern, Michelangelo differentiated between wall-pier sections and areas of vaulting. He also differentiated within each section the structural continuities and the wall or vault surfaces where openings for light were located. The articulation of wall and vault in the drum and dome and again in the lantern is consonant with the design of the main body of the basilica during the period of the first attic design. Had Michelangelo's drum and dome been built as intended in the model of 1558–61, and the first attic extended to the entire structure, all three layers of the basilica would have been consistent.

Drawings, prints, and paintings from the archive of St. Peter's enable a synopsis of the building's progress during Michelangelo's eighteen-year tenure and that of his successors throughout the sixteenth century. Whether or not to demolish the remainder of Old St. Peter's, a charged controversial issue, and propose a consequent

facade for New St. Peter's, was resolved only under the reign of Paul V (Borghese) and his architect, Carlo Maderno, early in the seventeenth century.

To judge by the documents, Michelangelo initially pursued the building program of Sangallo by erecting centering and then vaulting the north transept in 1549, the only arm that remained incomplete. He also continued the preparation of the crossing to receive the central drum and dome. On the other hand, he began eliminating the partially constructed ambulatory encircling the south apse. Within a year of his appointment, contracts had been signed for travertine capitals for the main interior pilasters of the north transept. As work went ahead on new foundations for the spiral ramps and transept apses, Michelangelo matured his thoughts about the crossing. He continued adding to the structure that would support the base of the drum. In December 1548 he began a detailed wood model of the principal cornice at the crossing, most likely full size for a section of the cornice, which was finished and painted before the end of the year

96. Unknown draftsman, *Elevation of a hemicycle for St. Peter's*, engraving published by Vincenzo Luchino, 1564. The Metropolitan Museum of Art, New York, Harris Brisbane Dick Fund, 1941

(Frey 1916, 67, 597a–d). At the same time, he directed the erection of centering (form work) for the great barrel vault of the north transept, completed in November 1549. A year later, in December 1550, the work of consolidating and leveling of the masonry bed at the crossing was completed and construction of the interior cornice, base of the drum, and exterior cornice began. By late February 1552 the base was ready to receive the drum (Frey 1916, 71, 616a).

While work continued but at a slower pace on the base of the drum in 1552–3, Michelangelo seems to have directed attention to construction of the apses of the south and north transepts together with their angled walls. Early in 1553, account records for liftings to the south apse by the windlass and mast system, used to raise cut stone above the level of the first story of the south apse, include substantial increases in numbers through 1556. In the summer of 1556, work was advanced sufficiently for liftings to the third level of the capitals of the main pilasters. The north apse lagged behind, with liftings to the second level beginning only in January 1556. Centering for the apse or hemicycle vault on the south apse was erected in the spring of 1557. Construction of the vault was interrupted upon the discovery of an error made by the supervising architect in laying the doubly curved stone vaults, an error which led to the rebuilding of the entire vault. The three vaulted windows of the attic level above the entablature of the south apse were completed in June 1557, and the rebuilt vault finished in May 1558 (Millon and Smyth 1976, 137–206).

Michelangelo's design for both the interior and exterior of the drum at the crossing was sufficiently fixed

in his mind by early 1554 for contracts to be written for the travertine columns for the exterior of the drum. These were followed in the spring of 1555 by contracts for Corinthian capitals for the pilasters on the interior of the drum.

While the vault of the south apse was being built and rebuilt, Michelangelo was persuaded by friends that he should construct a detailed model of the great central drum and dome (Figs. 100, 101). Once completed, it would assure that his design would be followed whether or not he was present. In the summer of 1557 he completed a small model of the drum and dome in clay, which was fired in July. That design seems to have been studied for almost sixteen months before he began building in November 1558 a large model in wood of a half-section through the drum and dome. The several drawings by Michelangelo for the drum and dome now in Lille, Haarlem, Oxford, and Florence appear to predate construction of the model (Millon and Smyth, *Michelangelo Architetto*, 139–57). Built at a scale of 1:15, it may be three times the uncertain scale of the large wood model built eight years earlier, which showed a sizable portion of the body of the building. The drum and dome model took three years to construct. On 14 November 1561 there are final payments for balusters for the lantern railing, columns for the lantern, and the wood sphere crowning the lantern (Frey 1916, 87, 668.41).

While the wood model was being constructed, travertine for the columns of the drum continued to be excavated and transported to the site. Carving of the interior pilaster capitals was interrupted in 1557, perhaps due to a deviation of thoughts to the model. Carving

97. St. Peter's, interior view of crossing and south transept (Photo: Millon)

resumed in September 1561 when the model was virtually complete. Contracts were let for carving the complex paired column and pilaster capitals above the paired columns of the buttresses on the exterior of the drum in the summer of 1561 and spring of 1562. Most of the capitals were completed, but some not yet in place on the drum at the time of Michelangelo's death on 18 February 1564. Contracts for the entablature of the drum above the paired columns were executed under the tenure of Michelangelo's successors, Pirro Ligorio and Giacomo Vignola. Before his death, Michelangelo had not only built the north apse and flanking angled walls up to the level of the entablature on the exterior, but he had also begun the foundations for both of the satellite chapels to the east and west of the north transept and apse (AFP, I, Armadi, vols. 65–6).

This synopsis indicates that, with the foundations for the satellite chapels in place, with the completed apse and attic on the south, with the north apse lacking only the corresponding apse vault and attic, with a model for the body of the building that included an elevation of a satellite chapel (1547), and a model for the drum and dome (1561), Michelangelo's intentions for the transepts, satellite chapels, and crossing of St. Peter's must have been reasonably well known to his contemporaries.

However, awareness today of Michelangelo's intentions for St. Peter's may be less clear than it was in 1564. There have been losses of drawings and models, lacunae among the documents, changes that may have been made to the design after the models were constructed, changes in design made by Michelangelo's successors, and conflicting information among the extant prints, drawings, and paintings.

Nonetheless, scholars accept as certain several aspects of Michelangelo's design for St. Peter's. These include: (a) the plan for the transepts, apses, and satellite chapels; (b) the interior elevations of the apses and apse vaults; (c) the exterior elevations of the apses, angled walls, and satellite chapels through the level of the entablature (the design of the attic is subject to differing interpretations); (d) the design of the drum and dome model, including the inner and outer dome (though parts of the design of the lantern are uncertain). The design of the drum and dome model as completed in 1561 can be reconstructed with confidence even though the outer dome has been lost. Measured drawings in the Metropolitan Museum in New York, made by architects associated with Etienne Dupérac around 1565 (before the hemispherical outer dome and lantern of the model were replaced in the 1580s by a taller, ovoid dome and

98. St. Peter's, attic of the north and west transept apses (Photo: Gallerie e Musei Vaticani)

lantern designed by Giacomo Della Porta), contain dimensions that indicate that both inner and outer domes were hemispherical (Wittkower 1978, 73–89; Millon and Smyth, *Michelangelo Architetto*, 103–9). Some scholars contend, nonetheless, that after the model was completed Michelangelo changed the profile of the dome. In this context, the Dupérac engravings follow the model of 1561 with respect to the dome and lantern, although the remainder of the print is a collage of designs for St. Peter's assembled from examination of the building as constructed, Michelangelo's models of 1547 and 1561, Sangallo's model of 1546, and drawings by Pirro Ligorio and Giacomo Vignola.

Still other sections of the building with associated documents and visual records that permit differing readings have led to imaginative and conflicting interpretations. In this category is the design of the exterior of the attic. By one interpretation, Michelangelo established the design for the attic of the south apse in 1557 and did not change his mind. In this reading, the attic that first appeared on the north apse after 1564 and eventually

on the entire building, replacing the earlier apse on the south apse, was put there by Ligorio and Vignola (Millon and Smyth 1969, 484–91; Millon and Smyth, "Pirro Ligorio," 216–86). An alternative view maintains that Michelangelo altered the design of the attic when contemplating the subsequent attic on the north apse, and that a drawing by Michelangelo can be associated with the new design (Hirst 1974, 662–5; Saalman 1975, 397n10, 401, 405; Elam 1981–2: 68–76; Joannides 1981, 621).

Additional areas of the structure that have invited differing inferences and interpretations include: (*a*) the axial alignment of the inner and outer windows of the transept apses; (*b*) the nature of the screenlike structure placed in the oculus of the drum and dome model of 1561; (*c*) the extent and size of the model of 1547; (*d*) the possibility of entrances planned for the satellite chapels from the east and west; (*e*) the reliability of the plan, elevation, and section published by Dupérac in 1569/70; and (*f*) the credibility of the state of construction of the building as shown in prints that include a date of execution.

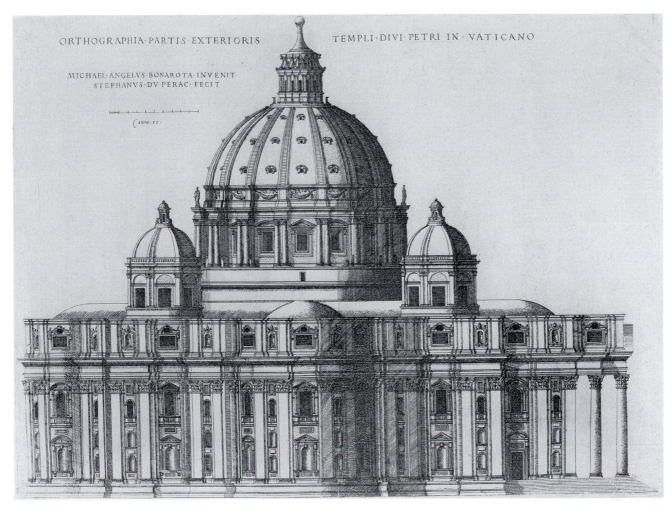

ORTHOGRAPHIA·PARTIS·EXTERIORIS   TEMPLI·DIVI·PETRI·IN·VATICANO

MICHAEL·ANGELVS·BONAROTA·INVENIT
STEPHANVS·DV·PERAC·FECIT

99. Étienne Dupérac, *Elevation of St. Peter's from the south*, engraving, 1569–70. The Metropolitan Museum of Art, New York, Harris Brisbane Dick Fund, 1941

Areas with insufficient evidence to ascertain what Michelangelo may have intended at St. Peter's include; (*a*) a facade to the east (an early sketch plan in the Vatican Library by Michelangelo indicates the location of a stairway to the Vatican palace in relation to the nave of New St. Peter's and includes an incomplete columnar portico); (*b*) the little domes above the satellite chapels. Current scholarship assumes that Michelangelo at his death left no record of a design for a facade nor for the little domes and assigns early proposals for these to Giacomo Vignola, who joined Pirro Ligorio as second architect in October 1564.

Given the loss of the model of 1549, perhaps partially represented in a print of 1564 by Vincenzo Luchinus (Fig. 96) and in a painting by Passignano of 1620 (Millon and Smyth, *Michelangelo Architetto*, no. 25, 137), it remains an open question whether Michelangelo ever considered a junction with the remains of Old St. Peter's to the east, or even whether he pondered what a facade design might have been and where it might have been located. We lack evidence of whether he intended to erect smaller domes above the inner domes of the satellite chapels or have the roof remain as it is today above the satellite chapels to the west of the crossing. Did Michelangelo intend to construct entrances to the two eastern satellite chapels from the east toward Old St. Peter's? When they were completed in the 1580s and 1590s, entrances that were later eliminated were built for these two chapels, as well as entrances on the west side of the satellite chapels to the west of the crossing. Did Michelangelo intend to replace Bramante's apse to the west as generally assumed on the basis of the plan published by Dupérac in 1569? With the loss of the outer dome and lantern of the model of 1558–61, can we be sure that Michelangelo intended the outer dome to be hemispherical, as shown by Dupérac in the prints of the south elevation and section of St. Peter's that accompany the print of the plan of 1569? Questions such as these have provided ample scope for scholarly debate, sometimes along nationalistic lines, for the past hundred years.

100. Michelangelo, Giacomo Della Porta, and Luigi Vanvitelli, *Model of the interior of one half of the drum and dome of St. Peter's*, limewood, tempera paint. Museo Petriano, Vatican City. (Photo: Gallerie e Musei Vaticani)

The windows on the exterior and interior of the apses are not in alignment. Students of Michelangelo's St. Peter's seem not to have made reference to this displacement. While in both the north and south hemicycles the interior openings of the central windows are on the axis of the transept, the exterior openings of both windows are displaced several feet to the east. In fact, all the windows of the exterior of the north and south apses are similarly shifted in relation to the interior, as if the outside walls of both had been rotated slightly toward the east with respect to the inner walls.

The nonalignment of interior and exterior windows had to be planned for early on in construction, and clearly must have been of much importance to Michelangelo. The reason becomes clear to one who stands where the pope stands as celebrant at the high altar, more than ten feet west of the center of the crossing, just above the Tomb of the Apostle. (Michelangelo is reported by Cardinal Barberini to have wished to add to the eastern face of the main altar, enlarging it so that the altar would be under the center of the cupola – but that did not happen [Pastor 1923–53, 26:476].) From this place at the altar, and this place alone, the central windows of

both levels on exterior and interior are aligned. In this place, moreover, no direct light is visible from any of the four great side windows at the second-story level of the two apses. The same is true of the side windows above, at the level of the apse vault. (Although the present exterior openings of these upper windows belong to the revised design of the attic, they are placed directly above the windows below.) At any location other than that of the celebrant, the central windows of the second and third stories are *not* aligned and direct light may be seen from one or more of the side windows.

The pope, celebrating mass at an altar sited over St. Peter's tomb, is the one person who can realize himself (and the tomb) to be at the "center" of the church framed by the placement of the windows and their light. Bramante had not been free to place the four piers of the main dome so that the altar of Old St. Peter's would be centered below and, consequently, the tomb of the Apostle glorified at the center of a cosmic analogue. Although there may be no explanation other than that suggested by Cardinal Barberini, it appears to be an inescapable conclusion that Michelangelo was able to so

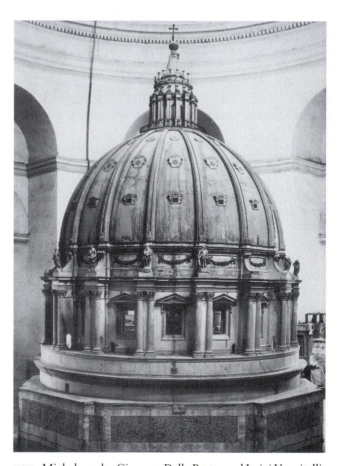

101. Michelangelo, Giacomo Della Porta, and Luigi Vanvitelli, *Model of the exterior of one half of the drum and dome of St. Peter's*, limewood, tempera paint. Museo Petriano, Vatican City. (Photo: Alinari)

manipulate those portions of the building as to reestablish the essential centrality of this most sacred site in St. Peter's. The concern to bring direct light from all the central windows to a point of focus at the altar suggests that, for Michelangelo, light in religious architecture was more than illumination and an element of form.

In his design for New St. Peter's, Bramante had placed a dome above the Tomb of the Apostle, both reviving and continuing a tradition, particularly strong in the East, for commemorating the site of a martyr's tomb. From ancient times domes have represented the heavens. Karl Lehmann chronicled the development and use of representations of the hemisphere of heaven in domical structures in which a representation of the highest heaven is included at the center (Lehmann 1945, 1–27). This center of heaven was represented as a circular ribbed canopy, or awning, from which the light of heaven radiated. In ancient times it was sometimes the light of Apollo the sun god; in Christian times, the light of Christ. The oculus of domed structures became, according to Lehmann, the site of the canopy, the highest heaven. The apse vault of Old St. Peter's contained a representation of the highest heaven with its canopy suspended above an image of Christ (Grimaldi 1972, 196–7 [fols. 158ᵛ,159ʳ]). Giulio Romano at the Palazzo del Te, Mantua, represented mighty Jupiter, enthroned as an eagle, under a golden canopy beneath the drum and dome of heaven. Sometimes the heavenly canopy includes a small circular opening in its center. Michelangelo's screen across the oculus of his drum and dome model – it, too, with a small central opening, as we know from a detailed drawing of the model in the Metropolitan Museum of Art – may have been intended to be a representation of that canopy. Given the Metropolitan drawings of the screen, it is reasonable to assume that Michelangelo's canopy was open, admitting light from between its radial members, and intended to function as the symbolic center of heaven, the source of divine light, recalling the heaven in the apse vault of Old St. Peter's (Millon and Smyth, *Michelangelo Architetto*, 102).

Pirro Ligorio became Michelangelo's successor at St. Peter's under Pius IV (Medici). According to Vasari's account in the *Lives*, and to letters Vasari wrote from Rome to Francesco de' Medici and Vincenzo Borghini in March 1567, Ligorio began to alter Michelangelo's order at St. Peter's and was dismissed by Pius V (Ghislieri) for doing so. Giacomo Vignola was then appointed to the position.

From the records of the *fabbrica* we can tell where construction was carried on during Ligorio's tenure. In addition to building at the Cappella del Imperatore (the north apse), work included continuation of the drum of the main dome, where Ligorio was responsible for much of the entablature and excavations for new foundations. Some work may also have been carried on at the Cappella

Gregoriana (the northeast satellite chapel), but, if so, very likely not above the first order of exterior niches of the chapel and probably not during most of the year before Ligorio was dismissed. At that time his attention was probably given chiefly to completion of the north apse and its vault. The attic of the north apse, not yet under construction when Ligorio took charge, offered an immediate opportunity to effect a significant change. There is, however, no evidence to suggest that Ligorio attempted to make a change in Michelangelo's order anywhere except here.

In all likelihood Ligorio was dismissed by Pius V in the winter of 1566–7 (Millon and Smyth, "Pirro Ligorio," appendix 4, 268–71). If altering the attic from Michelangelo's design was the reason for Ligorio's dismissal, he may have wanted to ensure that the elevation throughout its height would be consonant with ancient practice as seen, for example, in the articulated attics of ancient Roman triumphal arches and in the attic with pilasters and ashlar sheathing that Ligorio proposed in his reconstruction of the Pantheon published in his print of 1561 *Anteiqvae Vrbis Imago*. . . .

After the departure of Pirro Ligorio, Vignola continued work at the Cappella del Imperatore (the north transept apse), the Cappella di San Michele (the northwest satellite chapel), and, most likely, at the Cappella Gregoriana. There is no record of a workers' celebration upon the completion of the apse vault of the north transept, but in June 1567 formwork for the vault was taken down. Vignola may have supervised the closing of the vault. Also by June, the walls of the Cappella di San Michele were sufficiently above ground to necessitate liftings to the first level of the cut-stone sheathing. Though there are no recorded payments for similar liftings of cut stone for the Cappella Gregoriana, work may have continued there as well. The slope of the Vatican hill facilitated the use of ramps for construction at the lower level. In any case, it was not until after Vignola's death that payments for lifting cut stone to the second level are recorded, a height just above the pediments of the niches of the first story.

Vignola continued work on the attic above the vault of the apse of the north transept for the remainder of 1567, extending the attic to its full height and adding sections of a cornice along its northeast portion, perhaps placing stone that had already been prepared by masons in the masons' shed. Work on the attic seems then to have been interrupted, leaving it inexplicably incomplete. Several years later, in 1569, payments record the purchase of wood and nails for a roof to cover the exposed upper surface of the masonry vault over the north transept (AFP, ser. 1, filze 31, 407).

In the same year, Vignola seems to have begun excavations for a third satellite chapel to the southwest, the Cappella della Colonna. By September 1572 the walls of

102. St. Peter's, drum and dome, completed 1590. (Photo: Fototeca Unione)

that chapel extended above the height of the entrance from the west where, on the interior, a column and capital flanking the entrance were erected. Three of the four satellite chapels were well under way during Vignola's tenure, but the fourth, the Cappella Clementina, would not be begun for another six years.

Although Vignola died in September 1573, there is no record of a successor until July of the next year, when Giacomo Della Porta received his first payment as architect of St. Peter's. Nonetheless, liftings of cut stone to the Cappella Gregoriana had begun in November 1573, perhaps under the oversight of Giacinto Vignola, Giacomo's son and assistant architect, and work continued elsewhere at St. Peter's as well.

When Giacomo Della Porta took over as architect in 1574, work was under way on both the interior and exterior of the Cappella Gregoriana. A granite threshold for the entrance had been in place from 1572, and two marble capitals for one of the tabernacles had been erected on columns, perhaps the pair flanking the entrance. By April 1575 Della Porta had ordered wood for the centering for the two vaults of arches on the north and east sides of the chapel to match those of the barrel vaults between the crossing and secondary piers. In September 1576, carpenters were paid for making a template for the dome profile while capitals for the pilasters of the interior of the drum were already being carved. The dome was complete in January 1578. Stucco, gilding, and mosaic decoration of the arches, drum, and dome, as well as colored marble sheathing (revetment) of the walls of the chapel below was initiated shortly thereafter.

Travertine columns for the drum above the attic level of the chapel were ordered in 1578 as a wood roof was placed over the lower interior dome. Construction of the drum was under way in 1580. Early in 1584, a wood model was made for the lantern. When the lantern was built in 1584 it was topped by a copper sphere. By May 1585 the sphere was judged to be too small and was replaced by a larger one weighing three times as much (Bellini 2002, 333–46).

As we have seen, Ligorio and Vignola continued work on the Cappella di San Michele that had been begun by Michelangelo. They also began construction of the third chapel, the Cappella della Colonna. The inner dome of the Cappella di San Michele was structurally complete by June 1578, and the interior finished a decade later. Neither of the satellite chapels to the west of the crossing have upper-level domes. The Cappella della Colonna seems to have been substantially finished by 1584, though both it and the Cappella di San Michele had work done at the roof level after the completion of the west arm and apse that lies between them. Decoration of the interiors extended into the next century.

Foundations for the Cappella Clementina, on the other hand, were not begun until 1578 when the other three chapels were well along. A granite threshold for the entry from the east was in place by May 1579, and the marble door frame was finished in 1581. The inner dome was closed in July 1590, just as the main dome was nearing completion. The drum and dome at the attic level above the interior dome were built and finished in 1595–6 while the interior marble sheathing was in progress (Millon and Smyth 1980, 36). The drum and dome of the Cappella Clementina were built after the great central dome (1588–90) and were designed to conform to its elevated profile.

The new central dome, compared with Michelangelo's model of 1558–61, had increased height, thinner ribs, narrower pilaster bunches in the attic, and a more complex cornice (Fig. 102). The drum and dome above the Cappella Gregoriana, apparently first constructed with the earlier design in mind, was dismantled in 1590–1. In 1596–7 it was rebuilt to match the drum and dome over the Cappella Clementina.

While work on the four chapels and their decoration continued, in 1581 Giacomo Della Porta also began the foundations for the fourth arm of the basilica to the west. The final arm was to replace the choir and apse built by Bramante earlier in the century. The walls of the new choir (or tribune) were above ground by 1585, at which time cut-stone sheathing began to be applied. The structure was well along by early 1587, and it was possible to begin the task of demolition of the earlier choir and apse. The entablature on exterior and interior was placed early in 1588, and work could begin on the stucco, gilding, and marble decoration.

In 1585, Della Porta was joined by Domenico Fontana, Pope Sixtus V's preferred architect. Fontana, the head of a large architectural firm, had been given that year the task of moving the Vatican obelisk from a site southeast of the Cappella Clementina to the piazza in front of St. Peter's, where it was dedicated in 1586. Early in 1587, the pope requested that preparations be started for building the main dome of St. Peter's. Work seems not to have begun until the summer of 1588 – perhaps to allow the design to mature, perhaps to build a new outer dome to place on Michelangelo's model of 1558–61, perhaps to complete the structure of the fourth arm and the four satellite chapels to provide equal support and buttressing for such a massive, crowning addition to the building – or perhaps an amalgam of all these reasons. In any case, before construction of the dome could begin, the entablature had to be completed on the northwest. Among the first payments for the new dome are those to the *scarpellini* (stone carvers) for preparing new sections of the entablature in conformity with those already erected under Ligorio and Vignola. Once done, construction of the dome proceeded rapidly. Closing of the dome was achieved in May 1590 (Orbaan 1917, 189–207). Sixtus V died without blessing the dome he sought to complete. It would be Clement VIII (Aldobrandini), three years later, who would close this phase of construction and bless the cross that was to be raised on high to crown the lantern and basilica.

With the new basilica enclosed for the first time, it was possible for Clement VIII and Della Porta to focus attention on completing all of the interior, including the demolition in 1592 of the altar house built by Bramante to protect the altar and apse of the Constantinian basilica (Apollonj Ghetti 1951, 270). The new marble pavement of the crossing, the four arms, and the satellite chapels was laid in the late 1590s at an elevated level that provided headroom for the grottoes below belonging to the level of the Constantinian basilica. St. Peter's at this date, with its extensive marble sheathing, mosaics, gilded stucco, and marble pavements, was an exemplary manifestation of the new decorative program that accompanied the post-Tridentine reform of architecture and religion (Ostrow 1996; Benedetti, "Sintetismo e magnificenza," 27–56). In 1602, when Giacomo Della Porta died, the building was finished on interior and exterior up to the junction with Old St. Peter's. The lantern crowned the dome and the interior surfaces of the dome were resplendent with the new mosaics of the Cavaliere d'Arpino.

Carlo Maderno succeeded Della Porta as architect of St. Peter's. Maderno had replaced his uncle, Domenico Fontana, as head of the Fontana workshop at the time Domenico left for Naples. The successes of Domenico Fontana and his office in the relocation of the Vatican obelisk, the erecting of other obelisks to fulfill Sixtus's plan for Rome, and the rapid completion of the central dome of St. Peter's in 1588–90, weighed for the appointment of Carlo Maderno and his uncle, Giovanni Fontana (Domenico's elder brother) to succeed Della Porta as architects of St. Peter's. The appointments were made in 1603. As head of the Fontana office, Maderno had recently completed the facade of S. Susanna for Cardinal Rusticucci and a new palace for Asdrubale Mattei. Shortly after the death of Clement VIII in 1605, earnest discussions about the completion of New St. Peter's focused on the remaining portions of Old St. Peter's (Thoenes 1992, 171–81; Wazbinski 1992, 147–64). Cardinal Baronio and others opposed touching the venerated structure (Pastor 1923–53, 26:380–1, 385–8). Within the year, on the basis of reports of a dangerous inclination of the south wall of the nave in spite of buttresses erected to resist lateral movement, an avviso of 17 September 1605 reports that the congregation responsible for the oversight of St. Peter's had taken the decision to tear down the decrepit structure. On September 26 another avviso notes that Paul V had ordered the removal of the

earlier church and the recording of its remains (Hibbard 1971, 168).

According to Giacomo Grimaldi, appointed to record the ancient monuments inside Old St. Peter's (Rice 1997, 36), projects for the completion of New St. Peter's were received from, among others, several architects in Rome, from Domenico Fontana and Giovanni Antonio Dosio in Naples, and from Ludovico Cigoli in Florence (Grimaldi 1972, 243–4, [fol. 208ʳ⁻ᵛ]). It seems that the principal requirements of the new design were, in addition to the nave, a sacristy, a choir for the canons, and a benediction loggia. A number of drawings, including several by Maderno and Cigoli, and descriptions of others have survived.

The next year, an avviso of October 1606 reports that the congregation had decided on a centralized plan, but the following September, the pope had approved a scheme by Maderno that included a facade extending well into the atrium of the earlier structure (Hibbard 1971, 169, 170–1). A wood model of Maderno's design was constructed between April and November 1607 but was apparently sufficiently complete for the pope to approve it in September. Ever eager for work to begin, the pope had already ordered excavations to begin in March 1607 near the east facades of the Gregoriana and Clementina. The plan was, most likely, for a narrower nave than exists today without choir or sacristy, perhaps to save as much as possible of the east facades of the two satellite chapels. This initial excavation was abruptly halted in September 1607 when the Maderno model design was officially approved and new excavations begun for the foundations of the facade and narthex. Debate over the nature and extent of the nave continued until June 1608 when an avviso reports that the pope decided to follow another design of Maderno that required a wider nave than the previous plan (Hibbard 1971, 169).

Maderno added three bays, slightly less wide than the bays between the crossing and secondary piers of the Bramante–Michelangelo portion (Fig. 103). The nave occupied all of the sacred ground of Old St. Peter's and extended into the area of the portico of the atrium in front of the facade. The narthex extended farther, almost halfway to the site of the ancient Roman bronze pinecone. The entrance to the atrium, the benediction loggia, and the various palaces around the atrium were all demolished to enable preparation of an appropriate piazza in front of the new facade.

Late in 1611 or early 1612, the pope seems to have decided to add flanking bell towers to the facade, which was nearing completion. The single pilasters at each flank of the seven-bay facade were enlarged to pilaster clusters to effect a transition to the new towers. Foundations for the north tower were under way in the fall of 1612, and the base for the tower was completed by June 1617.

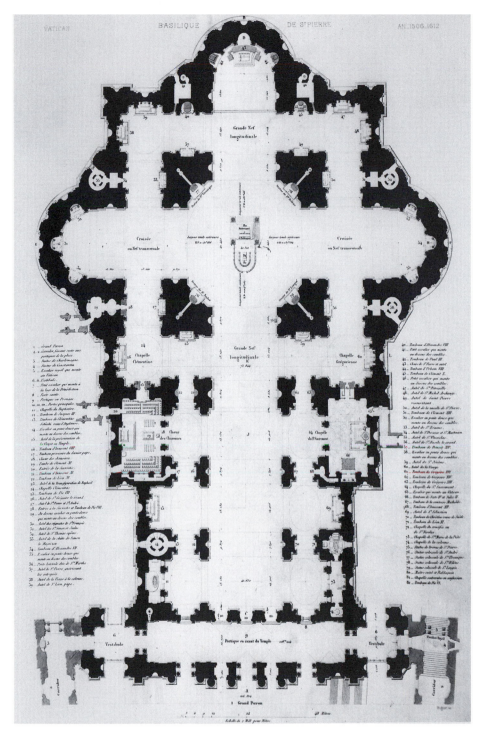

103. St. Peter's, plan. From P. Letarouilly and A. Simil, *Le Vatican et la Basilique de Saint-Pierre de Rome* (Paris, 1882), 1

Maderno had been aware of the unstable condition of the soil under the foundations beneath the base of the south bell tower. His design for the bell towers to rise above the attic level of the facade was limited to a single story with an open octagonal lantern above. The bell cage and lantern together roughly equaled the height of the main order below. Maderno's design is known from an engraving of the facade by Matteus Greuter executed in 1613. The base for the bell tower to the south, where difficult

subterranean conditions hindered the placing of secure foundations, was not finished until 1621. Maderno died in 1629 without realizing his tower design (Fig. 104). Bell towers were finally begun in 1636, but on designs of Gian Lorenzo Bernini, and will be discussed later.

Work on foundations for the new, wider nave of Maderno was begun in 1609. Stonework on the flanks was under way in late 1610/early 1611. Removal of the travertine east facades of the Gregoriana and Clementina

104. Carlo Maderno, St. Peter's, facade, 1607–21. (Photo: Alinari)

to facilitate the juncture of the new nave with the sixteenth-century structure was complete in May 1613. Centering for the vaults of the side aisles and main nave was erected in 1613/14 and the vaults themselves finished by December 1614.

The wall that had been erected in 1538 to separate New St. Peter's from the remainder of the earlier building was removed in March 1615, uniting the sixteenth- and seventeenth-century sections (Fig. 105). Maderno sought to preserve the spatial and structural integrity and identity of the Bramante/Sangallo/Michelangelo structure, even while adding three additional bays to the nave. Maderno's nave is wider and taller; it rests on slimmer piers; it contains windows in the vault above each of its three bays. The Bramante/Sangallo/Michelangelo structure, in contrast, has a lower, thicker, more massive vault without windows. The progression is from a darker area to a larger, lighted central space. Maderno also set the brick pavement of the nave at a lower level to differentiate yet further the new addition. The side aisles of the

new nave also rise higher, with windows in the exterior chapel walls and in the lanterns of the oval domes of each bay. The transverse walls between bays have been eliminated in Maderno's design. Only a segmental pediment, stressing openness by eliminating both the architrave and the frieze, separates the chapels. Openness, light, and fluidity of movement characterize the Maderno additions.

The project for bell towers to flank the facade, first requested by Paul V, was undertaken by Bernini in 1636 for Paul V's successor, Urban VIII (Barberini). In the fall of 1636, Bernini asked Giambattisti Soria to build a wood model of his design for the bell towers. Preparatory construction on the first tower began shortly thereafter, and by June 1639 the first story was finished. Scaffolding for the second story was already dismantled in January 1641, and by June the third story and crowning pyramid was in place. The third story, however, did not please the pope and congregation. To their eyes, it may have seemed the tower was not tall enough. It was dismantled shortly thereafter, leaving the two lower stories intact.

105. St. Peter's, interior of the nave from the east. (Photo: Alinari)

Not many months later, vertical cracks began to open in the central section of Maderno's facade. Nonetheless, work on the north tower proceeded and continued until construction at St. Peter's slowed and halted in the spring of 1643, no doubt due to the invasion of papal territory in September 1642 by Odoardo Farnese, the duke of Parma. Prosecution of the war and preparations for the defense of Rome seem to have occupied much of Urban VIII's time. In March 1644 the war ended, only three months before Urban's death (Pastor 1923–53, 29:398).

His successor, Innocent X (Pamphili), requested a report on the bell tower and fissures in the facade, and initiated an investigation that took almost a year. Though the investigation seems to have concluded that the Bernini bell towers might be saved, Innocent X, on 23 February 1646, ordered both towers to be dismantled to the level of the attic and the stone preserved (for future bell towers that were never to be realized). One large bell, cast by Luigi Valadier, now hangs inside the attic level of the base of the south bell tower. The bases of Maderno's

bell towers now are crowned by clock faces flanked by angels as supporters and surmounted by the papal tiara and keys of Pius VI (Braschi). Giuseppe Valadier, son of the bell caster, appointed architect of St. Peter's at age twenty-seven in 1789, erected the clock ensembles in the 1790s.

A recent publication (McPhee 2002) examines in detail the history of Bernini's aborted bell towers and considers the program for them. In a final chapter, McPhee demonstrates that the projects of Paul V, Urban VIII, and Innocent X to build the twin bell towers flanking the facade of St. Peter's resulted from a desire to retain in New St. Peter's essential portions of the Constantinian and later medieval building – portions that played an important role in the coronation ceremonies of the Holy Roman Emperor.

Church historians in the sixteenth and early seventeenth centuries argued that from the time of the coronation of Charlemagne in 800 the entrance to the atrium of St. Peter's included a church dedicated to Saint Mary.

106. Carlo Marchionni, St. Peter's, exterior of the Sacristy, 1776–84. (Photo: Anderson)

Standing at the top of the stairs at the entrance to the atrium, the pope welcomed the ascending emperor elect, who knelt before him. Then both pope and emperor entered S. Maria, where the emperor vowed to uphold the Catholic faith in the lands over which he reigned. Further stages in the coronation ritual took place within the basilica itself, where the emperor was crowned. Historians have argued that the church of S. Maria was originally located between two towers of the facade, although only a single tower, on the north, existed in the fifteenth century. The last coronation of a Holy Roman Emperor at St. Peter's was held in 1452 when Nicholas V crowned Frederick III.

An appropriate location for the pope to greet the emperor elect at the top of the steps before the new facade, flanked by the bell towers, would be required if further coronations were to take place at St. Peter's. When, in the reign of Innocent X, the emperor Ferdinand III ratified the Peace of Westphalia in 1648, he ceded control of religion to the ruler of the territory or region.

Provisions for coronation rituals became obsolete and were eventually abandoned. The memory, an attempt to embody the ancient tradition in New St. Peter's, remains visible today in the incomplete towers that flank the facade.

The existence of lesions inside the drum and dome of St. Peter's, which had been observed as early as the 1680s, led in 1742 to the convening of groups of architects, engineers, and mathematicians to inspect them. Luigi Vanvitelli, assistant architect of St. Peter's, prepared drawings that noted locations of the lesions and had them drawn on the drum and dome model of 1561 to assist the committees. He also submitted his proposal for stabilizing the structure (Di Pasquale 1997, 381–8; Di Pasquale 1994, 273–8; Di Stefano 1980). The several committees met in the fall of 1742. Benedict XIV (Lambertini) asked the noted professor of mathematics at the University of Padua, Giovanni Poleni, to review the reports and give his opinion as to an appropriate remedy.

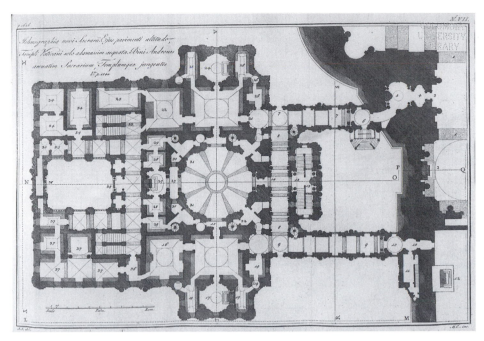

107. Carlo Marchionni, St. Peter's, plan of the Sacristy, 1776–84. From F. Cancellieri, *De Secretarriis Novae Basilicae Vaticanae* (Rome, 1786), vol. 4, pl. VII. (Photo: Avery Architectural and Fine Arts Library, Columbia University)

In March 1743, Poleni sent his "Reflections" on the issue and, after a visit to Rome to study the drum and dome firsthand with Vanvitelli in June, Poleni wrote his "Additional Observations," which included specific recommendations for additional encircling chains at several levels. Poleni was told that his recommendations were to be implemented and was asked to prepare a written record of the events surrounding the stabilizing of the drum and dome. Poleni's published account includes entire texts, summaries of many others, and illustrations of a number of the proposals, including his own (Poleni 1748). In the final event, five new iron chains were recommended to secure the dome. In opening channels for the new chains, one of the earlier chains was found to be broken and was repaired. A second original chain deep within the fabric was supplemented by a sixth new chain. By November 1748 the new additions and repairs were completed (Mainstone 1999, 21–39). Preparations for the Holy Year of 1750 could go ahead now that the drum and dome of St. Peter's were secured.

The final major addition to St. Peter's was the new sacristy on the south side of the basilica, built together with an accompanying residence for the canons of St. Peter's (Fig. 106). The new sacristy was to replace the late antique rotunda (S. Maria della Febbre) just to the south of the Cappella Clementina, which had been designated as a sacristy by Nicholas V in 1450 as plans were being developed for a new choir and transept for Old St. Peter's. (A second rotunda, dedicated to Saint Petronilla, to the west of S. Maria della Febbre had already been demolished when the foundations for the south apse were begun by Bramante.)

With the completion of the Cappella Clementina under Clement VIII, a passageway was opened from the new satellite chapel to the rotunda of S. Maria della Febbre. With this connection it served as the sacristy for over a hundred and eighty years. A number of popes commissioned designs, sponsored competitions, and sought proposals for a new sacristy, but it was not until Pius VI (Braschi) was elected in 1775 that the new sacristy was realized.

Replacement of the ailing nave of Old St. Peter's had been contemplated after the fourth arm to the west and the central dome were completed in 1590. A new sacristy and a canon's choir were even then felt to have high priority. Several proposed plans of the period included rectangular spaces flanking the nave that are likely to have been intended for these uses. It seems that a sacristy was indeed begun on 8 March 1607, following Maderno's plan, on the north flank of St. Peter's in front of the Cappella Gregoriana. That sacristy, however, had a short life, for in 1626 there was already talk of its conversion into the Sacrament Chapel, though the transformation was not official until 1638 (Rice 1997, 207–8). With the canon's choir in the matching space along the south flank, the rotunda of S. Maria della Febbre became once again the principal sacristy, and remained so until it was demolished to make room for the new sacristy.

In the interim, Alexander VII (Chigi) requested designs for a sacristy from both Bernini and Borromini. Innocent X solicited a second plan from Bernini. Innocent XII commissioned a design from Carlo Fontana, but refused to consider it when it included the demolition of S. Maria della Febbre. Early in the eighteenth century, in 1708, Clement XI (Albani) asked Fontana for new plans that also came to naught. In 1711 Fontana proposed that the project for the first class in architecture for the Concorso Clementino at the Accademia di San Luca be a design for a sacristy for St. Peter's. A few years later, in 1715, Clement XI sponsored an invitational competition for the sacristy that included the architect Filippo Juvarra, who the year before had proposed a plan. Among other architects invited to submit designs were Nicola Michetti, Domenico Paradisi, Antonio Canevari, and Antonio Valeri. Large wood models for a number of these designs are preserved today in the new Museo Petriano (Hager 1970). Clement XI died before any work of construction was begun.

Further initiatives were undertaken by successive popes, but only with the election of Pius VI (Braschi) was the problem of the new sacristy resolved. New drawings and models by Cosimo Morelli, Giuseppe Subleyras, and Carlo Marchionni were placed on view together with earlier models. The model by Juvarra was praised, and Carlo Marchionni, then architect of St. Peter's, successor to Vanvitelli from 1757, was directed to prepare drawings for the sacristy that would consider laudable aspects of Juvarra's design (Benedetti, "La Sagrestia," 246–57; Ceccarelli 1988, 57–133).

Marchionni's plan was to occupy an area south of the basilica and to demolish S. Maria della Febbre, the church of S. Stefano, and the German seminary (Fig. 107). The cornerstone was laid in September 1776 and was followed the next year by the several demolitions. Foundations were completed in 1778, and by February 1784 the new sacristy was ready to be occupied.

The sacristy is large, occupying an area about half that of Maderno's nave. The structure increases in height as it steps back from the basilica: two stories at its closest, four stories to either side of the tall drum, dome, and lantern, ultimately reaching six stories at the canon's residence. Marchionni placed the sacristy to the east of Michelangelo's south apse at a distance that allows an unencumbered view of the entire apse. Corridors on two levels connect the sacristy with the basilica. One corridor joins the southeast angled wall, the other leads to the canon's choir. The small open area between the corridors, Piazza Braschi, contains the main entry to the sacristy, with a grand double stair rising to the main level of both the sacristy and the basilica.

At this level, the great octagonal domed central space of the sacristy rises to the full height of the complex. With its lantern, the sacristy almost challenges the height of the adjacent flank of St. Peter's. The sacristy, which includes four levels to either side of the central octagon, is partially embraced from behind by the six-story canon's residence. A balustrade crowning the two corridors extends along the wider two-story portion of the sacristy and continues thereafter around the canon's residence, uniting all three sections of the building. Another higher balustrade crowns the four-story level of the sacristy. The cornice level under this balustrade is also continued around the canon's residence, further linking these portions of the complex.

The sacristy and connecting corridors are of travertine, matching the flank of the basilica. The canon's residence, more distant, is constructed in utilitarian brick, with travertine restricted to architectural membering. A giant order of pilasters and columns with ressauts extends through the two levels of the corridor and sacristy, and is repeated at all three entrances to the canon's residence on the east, west, and south. Doric columns set within deep pilaster niches flank and enhance significant entrances and passageways. The upper two levels of the sacristy are marked by a giant Ionic order with balustrade that also appears above the east and west entrances of the residence. Marchionni's vast knowledge of architecture in Rome is everywhere apparent in his deft inclusion of references to the works of Michelangelo, Vignola, Della Porta, Maderno, Borromini, Cortona, and Bernini.

In the domed central octagon, the folded Composite pilasters that mark the corners of the octagon are continued upward by ressauts in the entablature, and then through pedestal-piers into the double-layered ribs that end in the ring of the oculus below the lantern. On the cardinal axes, paired, fluted Ionic columns of a second subsidiary order frame openings to smaller sacristies to the east and west. The capitals and pediments, the coffered and ribbed dome quote Michelangelo, Borromini, and Cortona. The paired Ionic columns on the cardinal axes were brought from Hadrian's Villa. The Ionic capitals were taken from Bernini's bell towers. This display of judicious quotations is masterfully juxtaposed and integrated.

The octagonal space of the main sacristy, though possessing the double dome of St. Peter's, is similar in dimension to the domed space of S. Maria della Febbre, which served as the sacristy for nearly two centuries. It seems likely to have been intended to recall that venerable chamber with its layers of associations extending from Old St. Peter's through the eighteenth century.

7

BERNINI AT ST. PETER'S

Singularis in Singulis, in Omnibus Unicus

IRVING LAVIN

PREAMBLE

PERHAPS THE MOST PROFOUND INSIGHT INTO Bernini's conception of his work at St. Peter's is provided by a passage about the juvenile artist in Filippo Baldinucci's biography, published two years after Bernini's death at age eighty-two in 1680:

> It happened one day that he found himself in the company of Annibale Carracci [Carracci died in 1609; Bernini was born in 1598] and other masters in the basilica of St. Peter's. They had finished their devotions and were leaving the church when that great master, turning toward the tribune, said, "Believe me, the day will come, when no one knows, that a prodigious genius will make two great monuments in the middle and at the end of this temple on a scale in keeping with the vastness of the building." That was enough to set Bernini afire with desire to execute them himself and, not being able to restrain his inner impulse, he said in heartfelt words, "Oh, if only I could be the one." Thus, unconsciously, he interpreted Annibale's prophecy and later brought it to pass, as we will relate in due course when we tell of the wonderful works he executed for those places.[1]

The source of the anecdote can only have been Bernini himself, and although it implies a kind of providential intervention in the completion of St. Peter's on the artist's behalf, its art-historical significance lies in what it suggests about Bernini's underlying motivation in the work. It seems that, stimulated by the insight of one of the artists he admired most, Bernini from the beginning had in mind a vision, however vague and inchoate, of the church as a whole. In fact, drawings made half a century later show him realizing exactly this dream. As if in fulfillment of Carracci's prognosis, Bernini studies the visual relationship between two of the most magnificent art works of modern history, the view through the Baldacchino to the Cathedra Petri in the apse (Fig. 108).

This is not to say that Bernini had a preconceived scheme for the projects he would carry out at St. Peter's. But Carracci's remark, which applied to the specific problem of relating the high altar to the apse, represents a way of thinking that Bernini would develop into a comprehensive worldview, unified by certain threads of form and meaning common to everything he designed. Bernini was of course an employee of the papacy, and nothing happened without the initiative and/or approval of the authorities, including a supervising committee of the College of Cardinals, and often the pope himself. But Bernini was an employee of a unique and exalted sort. That he was able to realize his vision was due to the not less providential longevity of his responsibility for St. Peter's. His hegemony began informally soon after Urban VIII became pope and became official in 1629 when, on the death of Carlo Maderno, Urban appointed him architect of St. Peter's. Over the remaining half-century of his life Bernini was responsible for everything done at St. Peter's, serving no less than six popes (see Appendixes 1 and 2). Perhaps even more remarkably, and owing as much to his brilliant if volatile personality as to his talent, he maintained almost without interruption close personal relations with all of them. There is probably no example in history of such continuous (and continuously innovative) creativity, on such a scale, on a single project, over such a long period, by a single artist (Figs. 109, 110).

Four important caveats are in order before we consider this unexampled spectacle of creativity. First, the discussion that follows is woefully incomplete, if only because it deals exclusively with the monumental works that are still to be seen in St. Peter's. Bernini designed many works, small and large, that are left out of account, from church furnishings and liturgical vestments, to vast temporary decorations for canonizations; even huge bell towers, one of which was actually built but soon dismantled because it was deemed unstable. Second, although discussion will proceed in roughly chronological order, it is to a degree misleading, since many projects overlapped and others were planned and carried out in fits and starts over many years, even decades. Third, a veritable army of artists and artisans carried out these works, some of them gigantic, and although under Bernini's supervision they achieved a remarkable harmony of style, his personal participation in the execution varied greatly. Individual artistic personalities are often discernible. I have not attempted to disentangle these problems of authorship, but I am convinced that at least in some instances – notably the statues in the crossing piers and the angels of the Ponte Sant'Angelo – Bernini condoned, or deliberately encouraged, these individual differences, both for concerted expressive effects and in order to manifest the human comprehensiveness of the concepts and beliefs the works embody. Finally, although certain elements required for the outfitting of a church, even such a special one as St. Peter's, were predictable, Bernini obviously could not have premeditated some eventualities and projects; these had to be integrated into the overall scheme after the fact, as it were. Partly in response to such contingencies, and partly of his own volition, Bernini's vision evolved in detail; but it remained constant in essence. Through all the manifold vagaries of time, persons, places, and things, one and only one mind was at work at St. Peter's during the long period in which the building was brought to completion. Despite the vicissitudes of unforeseen developments and a situation fraught with conflicting interests, Bernini was able to impress his conceptual and visual stamp on the greatest building in Christendom and create the salient image of an entire epoch:[2] "singularis in singulis, in omnibus unicus" (Fig. 111).[3]

St. Peter's as *Summa Ecclesiarum*

Two major decisions, taken at an interval of a century, established the fabric of the mother church of Western Christendom as we know it today. The first, made early in the sixteenth century, was to bring down the venerable but tottering and by then inadequate Early Christian basilica. The old building had been erected in the early fourth century by Constantine, the Roman emperor who first recognized Christianity. The aim was to replace Old St. Peter's by a centrally planned structure built over the tombs of the apostles Peter and Paul.[4] The new design expressed above all the commemorative nature of the church, its concentric and symmetrical geometry evoking an ancient sepulchral tradition that had come to express the ideal, eternal perfection of the Christian martyr and of Christ's church, here manifested in the person of Saint Peter and in his office as the Vicar of Christ on earth. The second decision, made in the early seventeenth century, was to add a longitudinal nave, which thus restored to

the building a semblance of its original basilical form. The determination to add the nave was not so much owing to the failure of the Bramante/Michelangelo plan to fulfill its intended purpose (the reason given by the later generation) as the reflection of a profound change in values that radically altered the relative importance attached to the building's primary functions. In the wake of the Reformation the attitude of the Church had taken an extroverted and aggressive turn, which entailed a shift of emphasis in the liturgy from commemoration toward the practical aspects of performance and involvement of the faithful. In this new spiritual culture the earlier building made inadequate provision for the sacristy and for the canon's choir, and was wholly unsuited to the ceremonial processions that played an ever-increasing role in ecclesiastical devotions and celebrations. The same underlying spirit also reaffirmed the venerable traditions of the church, not only by returning to the basilical form of the original building, but also by recognizing the value and importance of its physical remains. A meticulous record of the Early Christian building was made before it was demolished, not merely as a historical record, but to ensure that many of its features might be translated into the new church. The problem of furnishing this hybrid structure, combining two complementary but contradictory ideological and functional traditions, confronted the newly elected Urban VIII – who had strongly opposed the demolition of the old building – and his chosen impresario. Reconciling the merger of centralized and longitudinal building types in New St. Peter's, and the corresponding merger of commemorative and liturgical values, became a fundamental, driving principle of the church's conceptualization and design.

The same merging and the problems attendant upon it were inherent in the Cathedral of Florence, the illustrious predecessor of St. Peter's as the largest church in Christendom and, as I believe, the prime model for both phases of its construction. At Florence the identical designs of the transept arms and choir created a centrally planned core around the high altar at the center, which in turn was the focus of the nave (Fig. 112). The Duomo was the single most important example to be emulated, and surpassed, not only with respect to its unexampled size and blending of central and longitudinal building types, but also in its devotion to Christ. Despite, or rather in a sense owing to its dedication, S. Maria *del Fiore*, its two main interior furnishings were Christological: the high altar, where Bandinelli's marble choir commemorated the sacrifice (1547–72, Fig. 113); and Brunelleschi's famous cupola, where Zuccari and Vasari had painted a vast fresco of the Last Judgment (1571–9, Fig. 114).[5] At St. Peter's this principle had already been adopted in part with Cesare d'Arpino's mosaic decoration of the cupola (Fig. 115): a Deesis composition including

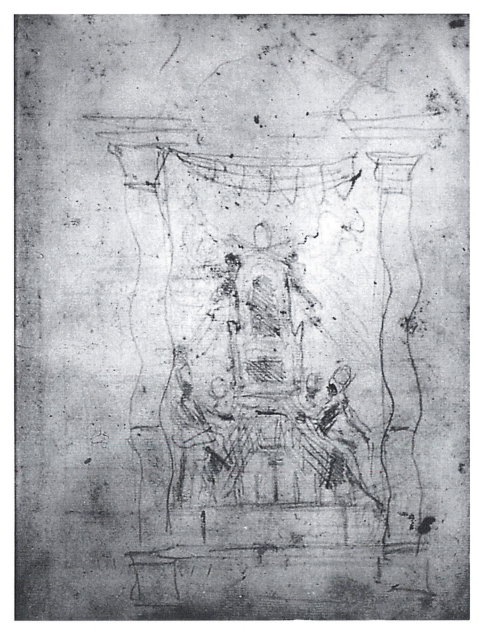

108. Bernini, view of the Cathedra Petri seen through the Baldacchino, drawing, ca. 1657. Biblioteca Vaticana, Rome

the apostles and angels holding the instruments of the Passion, which also alludes to the Last Judgment (1603–12).

THE APSE AND CROSSING
(Figs. 116, 117)

THE HIGH ALTAR

Although adding the nave solved some problems, it created others that came to the fore when the new structure was completed and ready to receive the requisite furnishings. The most essential components and the first to be attended to were the high altar and the choir. In the traditional basilica the high altar was placed at the entrance to the apse, and the choir for the attendant clergy was installed around its perimeter. In a central plan structure, with the high altar placed at a distance from the apse, such a solution was possible only by including a choir with the high altar at the center of the crossing, thus substantially blocking the view down the nave. This was the solution adopted at Florence when Brunelleschi surrounded the high altar with a low polygonal choir, after an earlier version had been rejected as too obstructive. The difficulty can be recognized in the fact that Brunelleschi's choir, which was built of wood and intended to be only temporary, in fact remained in place for more than a century, with no final decision being taken. Then, under very different circumstances, the Grand Duke Cosimo de' Medici

109. View of St. Peter's including Ponte and Castel Sant' Angelo

replaced Brunelleschi's choir with a much more elaborate and monumental marble enclosure. His intervention was counter-current. Contemporaries remarked on
the irony of Cosimo's act of high-handed, aristocratic
class-consciousness, in sharp contrast to the new open
policies of the mendicant orders, which were then sys-
tematically updating their churches by demolishing the
old choir screens that excluded the faithful from religious
functions and blocked the view down the nave to the high
altar.[6]

The difficulty was precisely the same at St. Peter's,
and the dilemma must have been intensely relevant for
Bernini as well as for Urban VIII, who came from
Tuscany and was thoroughly familiar with the situation in Florence. Early in Urban's reign the elements of
a coherent plan emerged that sought to reconcile the
centrality of the crossing as the commemorative location of the tomb of the apostles, with the longitudinal focus inspired by the new nave. Although analogous proposals were made, the kind of encumbrance imposed by the choir at Florence was ruled out, in favor
of a solution involving two altars, the isolated high altar dedicated to Peter and Paul over their "confessio,"

or subterranean burial place, and a second altar placed
toward the apse for papal functions involving the cardinals and associated with a choir. The dilemma inherent in the size, form, and function of St. Peter's was
such that no solution for a permanent choir was ever
achieved: to this day, when required for special occasions, temporary structures of wood are installed in
the apse with seating for the College of Cardinals. But
the idea for two major altars, one in the crossing and the
other in the apse, remained a permanent feature of the
church.

BALDACHINS AND CIBORIA

The solution in favor of two altars at St. Peter's was
adopted early in the reign of Paul V, when the drastic decision was taken to move the high altar to the
apse.[7] Thereafter, and continuing under Gregory XIV,
the two altars were given contrasting forms of covering,
reflecting their different functions. The high altar in the
apse was covered by a traditional architectural ciborium
surmounted by a cupola, distinguished in this case by
wings consisting of the precious twisted marble columns

110. Interior of St. Peter's

reputedly brought from Solomon's Temple of Jerusalem by Constantine the Great and installed at the high altar in the apse of the original basilica (Fig. 118, cf. Fig. 127). With the removal of the high altar to the apse the altar over the tomb became largely celebratory; it was marked by a series of what appeared to be, and actually were, temporary installations conceived as portable baldachins supported on four staves carried by standing or kneeling angels (Fig. 119). The idea of imitating a processional baldachin on a monumental scale served two purposes. The slender, open design permitted maximum visibility of the proceedings at the altar and beyond, toward the apse. But the disposition must also be understood in reference to the grand ceremonial papal procession of the Corpus Domini, which in some respects culminated the progressive magnification of the Sacrament during the Counter-Reformation as the theological heart of church doctrine (cf. Fig. 160). It had long since been decreed that the Sacrament be displayed at the high altar of every church, and Paul's baldachin was surely meant to evoke the honorific and celebratory message of the Corpus Domini procession, in which the pope paraded the sacramental Host from the basilica through the streets of Old Rome and back again, under a tasseled baldachin carried by acolytes. By the end of the sixteenth century, altars devoted to the Sacrament had multiplied and grown to huge proportions. At S. Maria Maggiore the centerpiece of the mortuary chapel built by Sixtus V is a bronze sacrament altar with four over-life-size angels carrying the tabernacle (Fig. 120). Around 1600, Paul V's predecessor, Clement VIII, erected a huge bronze sacrament altar in the transept of the pope's episcopal seat and the cathedral of Rome, S. Giovanni in Laterano (Fig. 121); these columns, too, were supposed to have come from the Temple of Jerusalem, brought back filled with earth from Mount Calvary by Empress Helen, mother of Constantine the Great. Emulating these illustrious precedents, Paul V planned to cast the processional baldachin at St. Peter's in bronze, creating a majestic, permanent "temporary" display, a kind of angelic celebration of the three distinctive features of the St. Peter's altar – the commemoration of the apostles, the celebration of the Sacrament, and the sanctity of the papacy. At opposite ends of the typological and topographical scale, the isolated baldachin served as a light, open structure to mark the tomb altar without blocking

111. Antoine Cheron, honorific medal of Bernini, with allegories of Sculpture, Architecture, Painting, and Mathematics, 1674

the vista toward the apse, where the ciborium appeared as an architectural monument in conjunction with an architectural setting.

THE BALDACCHINO (1624–35)

Urban VIII and Bernini approached the dilemma of St. Peter's in a fundamentally new spirit of consolidation and unification, seeking to encompass and subordinate under a dominant theme the disparate legacies of tradition and the contributions of their predecessors. This powerful new inspiration motivated two epoch-making decisions: the preeminence and centrality of the crossing was reaffirmed by returning the high altar to the tomb; and the altar was to be marked by a structure that would meld the heretofore distinct types of celebratory baldachin and commemorative architectural ciborium. (For Bernini's conception the term "baldachin," which normally refers to a nonarchitectural covering, is literally a half-truth. Wanting a better name, I have retained the Italian for Bernini's monumental version.) Visually, the effect was to reconcile, in permanent form on a colossal scale, the conflicting values of minimal structure and open visibility with architectural permanence and monumentality (Figs. 122, 123, 124).

Bernini's initial design consisted of four spiral columns supporting semicircular ribs that intersected diagonally; from the apex, crowning the whole structure, rose a figure of the Resurrected Christ holding the bannered cross (Fig. 125). Standing on the columns are angels who seem to carry a tasseled canopy by means of ribbons strung through loops on its top and secured to the ribs. The columns replace the staves of the earlier baldachins, their spiral form alluding to the Solomonic marble columns. The angels suspend the canopy of the baldachin from above, divine replacements for the ropes on which "floating" but stationary baldachins were hung from the vault above the pope in ceremonies when he was seated enthroned (Fig. 126); and the crossed ribs recall

those which had conjoined the marble columns in the Constantinian shrine (Fig. 127).

This astonishing amalgam of ephemerality and monumentality fused the processional character of the Sistine with the architectural character of the Lateran sacrament altars. The powerful, spiraling movement of the columns has its animate continuation in the angels, who perform the celebratory work of covering the altar, and culminates in the figure of Christ, who rises to take his place in heaven, as depicted in the dome above. One "material" key to the solution was the use of bronze, not normally associated with either the baldachin or the ciborium types, which permitted the vast scale and the daring structural engineering the project demanded. Bernini's Baldacchino was certainly the greatest enterprise of bronze casting since antiquity, and in this sense,

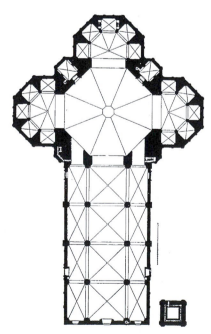

112. Plan of Florence Cathedral. From Paatz and Paatz 1952–5, 3:345

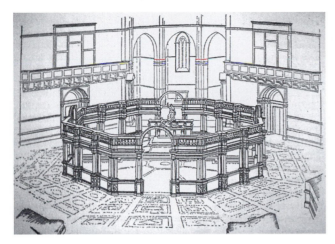

113. Baccio Bandinelli, choir of Florence Cathedral, reconstruction. From Heikamp 1964, 40

114. Federico Zuccari and Giorgio Vasari, cupola of Florence Cathedral, detail

as well as in its sacramental content, the project took up Paul V's homage and challenge to the Lateran sacrament altar – the greatest legacy of antiquity in this respect, and a particular model to surpass because of its provenance from the fabled Jewish Temple of Jerusalem. Beside emulating these predecessors, Bernini's use of bronze was a practical necessity, to achieve the Baldacchino's unexampled fusion of forms. But the amalgam also had particular significance as a material because of its continuity, fluidity, and transformability in the crucible of fire.[8] Associated with this quasi-alchemical process was an almost mystical sense of the spirit that animates all creativity: the matrix of a bronze cast was actually called the "anima."

After further deliberation, Bernini's initial idea had to be modified because it was feared that the weight and lateral thrusts of the superstructure might cause the columns to give way. In the final solution three major changes were made that resulted in an even more egregiously "impossible" design. The load was lightened by substituting for the complex, drapery-swathed figure of Christ, the simple, regular configuration of the globe-surmounted cross. The semicircular ribs were transformed into spring-like, curving volutes that served to raise the center of gravity and make the thrusts upon the columns more vertical. Finally, the canopy was lowered to coincide with the tops of the columns so that a continuous band could serve to tie the columns together (Figs. 128, 129).

Each of these changes entailed a shift of meaning. The resurrected Christ was replaced by the traditional symbol of Christianity's promise of universal salvation. Palm fronds, symbols of victory, grow from the crossed ribs, which take the form of a crown – the crown of martyrdom in memory of Christ's sacrifice and those of Peter and Paul whose relics sanctify the high altar. Each of the ribs consists of three volutes, which

115. Mosaic of cupola, St. Peter's, Rome

116. View of Baldacchino and choir, St. Peter's, Rome

differ in design and function. The larger, central volute rests directly on the inner corner of the column's impost entablature, whereas the two lesser, flanking scrolls curl up at the corners of the baldachin and seem to bear no weight – on the contrary, their spring-like coils suggest buoyancy. Wreaths of laurel held delicately by the angels with the tips of their fingers disappear beneath these spiral volutes and serve the ambivalent function of sustaining both the volutes and the canopy; conversely, the central, larger volutes disappear between their neighbors as they rise to the top. The superstructure of the Baldacchino is thus quite literally a mystery-bound affair, in which a triune summa of honorific markers – processional-carried and stabile-suspended baldachins, and architectural ciborium – is achieved by the angels who have alighted to conjoin – mysteriously, imperceptibly – heaven and earth. Considered thus, it is easy to see why, according to a critic of the project, Bernini insisted that "in any case, he wanted it to be sustained by angels."9

The same commentator also perceived and railed against the device that is the key to Bernini's solution in "architectural" terms, insisting that "baldachins are not sustained on columns but on staves," and that "the baldachin does not run together with the cornice of the columns." Bernini's entire design was created in order to make precisely those impermissible things happen: the cornice continues uninterrupted around the structure, while the frieze between the columns consists not of metopes and triglyphs proper to architecture but of lappets and tassels proper to a cloth canopy. This deliberate elision of the conventional grammar of design – a sort of visual "ain't" – makes a virtue of necessity, since only thus could baldachin and ciborium truly merge while retaining the essential integrity of both. No wonder Bernini referred to himself as a "bad Catholic" (preferable to Borromini, a good heretic) and believed that the great challenge of the architect was to make disadvantages appear to have been invented on purpose, and to "surpass the rules without breaking them." In the final analysis

117. View of choir, St. Peter's, Rome

Bernini's Baldacchino is exactly what the same detractor called it in derogation, a "chimera," a perfect, inextricable, and indissoluble fusion of three heretofore distinct categories of visually significant thought: the immediacy of the processional baldachin, the animated suspense of the hanging canopy, and the monumental stability of the ciborium. The task of accomplishing this unreasonable fusion is assigned, quite properly, to the angels, whose garland swags disappear from view to work their magic in privacy, as it were, at the crucial juncture of all three elements.

The change in the design and symbolism of the crown entailed a shift in emphasis from the sacrament itself to the universal dominion of Christianity as an institution, and in turn to the role of the papacy in the administration of that legacy. At the same time, insignia of the papacy in general and of Urban VIII in particular were introduced all over the Baldacchino, which is literally strewn with Barberini emblems: the sun, laurel, and the famous bees. What is important about this phenomenon is not its testimony to the personal egotism and ambition of Urban VIII – the usual cliché – but to the pope's view of the nature of his office and its role in the mission of the Church. A literally wondrous instance of the coincidence of the human and divine upon which the faith rested was the bee – a traditional symbol of Divine Wisdom – three

118. Borromini, ciborium for the choir of St. Peter's, drawing. Albertina, Vienna

Finally, it is important to realize that the revolutionary design of the Baldacchino was accompanied by a no less significant procedural revolution in the execution of the work. The idea of erecting a monumental architectural, or quasi-architectural, baldachin-ciborium over the high altar in the vast reaches of the new basilica posed quite unprecedented problems of scale and proportions, which were confronted in quite unprecedented ways. Under Bernini's direction Borromini produced detailed perspectival drawings – unlike any seen before – specifically intended to visualize the relationship between the proposed structure and the building itself (Fig. 130). And an equally unheralded procedure was followed in three dimensions: detailed models of various sizes up to the final, full scale were created and installed in situ so the effect could be judged.[11] No work of this kind and at this scale had ever been premeditated to this degree and in this way. Implicit in this method is a new, "wholistic" conceptual mode – the Baldacchino was not an independent piece of church furniture, as it were, but an integral part of the building itself. This attitude was adumbrated by the scale of Maderno's temporary baldachins, but now fully articulated in fully monumental form. Yet, the elaborate planning procedure notwithstanding, the biographers report that Bernini himself, speaking precisely of the matter of scale and proportional relationships, said that the Baldacchino had succeeded "per caso," by chance. The explanation of the paradox is implicit in the biographers' observations that because the scale of

of which formed the Barberini coat of arms. The vicariate of Christ was not only bestowed on Saint Peter by the Lord himself; its succession was also determined by an act of divine will, which inspired every papal election by the college of cardinals. In one way or another, all of Urban's emblems alluded to the intervention of divine will on earth. But this intervention had become direct and visible at his election when, upon his winning by a single vote (in a second ballot upon which he had himself insisted to confirm the previous count), the Sistine Chapel was invaded by a swarm of bees![10]

These considerations of material and design in turn help to illuminate the relationship between the bronze "anima" of the Baldacchino, its triune composition of celebratory and commemorative markers, and the Trinitarian theme that has often been noted in the spiritual ascent from the sacrament at the altar: the resplendent dove of the Holy Spirit on the underside of the canopy, the resurrected Christ seated in judgment in the cupola, God the Father in the lantern above (cf. Figs. 115, 124). The consonance of material, form, and meaning coincides with the great visual drama of the Baldacchino itself: massive in scale and ponderous in proportions, it fairly writhes in a powerful paroxysm of movement and energy to its own climax, and beyond toward the vault on high.

119. Temporary baldachin in St. Peter's under Paul V, 1617. Buonanni 1696, pl. 48

120. Cappella Sistina, S. Maria Maggiore, Rome

the undertaking was unprecedented there were no established standards, and ultimately no rule to guide the eye other than the mind and genius of the artist, whose judgment "happened" to be right.[12]

EXCURSUS A: BORROMINI AND THE BALDACCHINO

The legendary rivalry between Bernini and Borromini has been revived in recent decades by a veritable cabal of scholars bent upon "deflating" Bernini's "arrogant" artistic hegemony in seventeenth-century Rome and demonstrating that Bernini was "really" "only" a sculptor (although he designed many buildings and called himself "architetto"), whereas Borromini was the "real" architect (although he was also a competent sculptor). The ur-texts on the subject as it concerns the baldachin are a biography of Borromini written by his nephew Bernardo Castelli-Borromini and an appreciation by his erstwhile admiring friend and patron Virgilio Spada, which convey what can only have been Borromini's own bitter laments about how Bernini, architecturally inexperienced and

insecure, unscrupulously exploited his subordinate's professional expertise.[13] (In fact, both were then very young, and neither had produced any significant buildings.) Neither Bernardo Castelli-Borromini nor Virgilio Spada actually laid claim to a role for their hero in the design of the Baldacchino. But, taking up the cause, the modern protagonists seek, by tortuous and sometimes obfuscating means, to circumvent the plain facts of the case and arrogate to Borromini credit which even Borromini himself did not claim. (Among other things, it is astonishing how reluctant these writers are to quote the relevant statements by Borromini in their entirety and in their context.) Bernini, ambitious and exasperatingly self-confident, was, after all, specifically charged by Urban VIII with the creation of the Baldacchino and, as the documents show, Borromini was employed at St. Peter's in a secondary capacity. The reprise of tendentiousness began with the otherwise exemplary work on the early drawings of Borromini by Heinrich Thelen, and has reached a sort of reductio ad absurdum in a recent work devoted to the rivalry, which reaches the fantastic conclusion, baldly stated, that Borromini

121. Altar of the Sacrament, S. Giovanni in Laterano, Rome

was reponsible for the architecture of the Baldacchino, Bernini for the sculpture: "Im Entwurfsprozess für das definitive Baldachinprojekt erscheint Borromini massgeblich für die architektonische Durchbildung des monuments verantwortlich, wohingegen Bernini sich auf die plastische Dekoration konzentriert zu haben scheint."[14]

The plain fact is that there is not a shred of evidence – not a shred, visual or documentary – that Borromini played any role whatever in the design of the Baldacchino. The payment records show that he was employed at St. Peter's in two capacities, as a carver of minor works in marble and wood, and to make large, detailed drawings as templates for other artisans to follow, including some beautiful metal gratings that are certainly his own creations; Borromini's obsessively precise

draftsmanship and brilliant grasp of perspective and spatial relationships were ideally suited for the purpose of making detailed "demonstration" renderings. Bernardo Castelli repeatedly observed that Borromini's mentor, Carlo Maderno, appreciated his protégé's ability to make drawings "con grandissima diligenza e polizia" and employed him in his old age for this purpose. This in fact is exactly what the visual evidence confirms. All the known drawings by Borromini related to the Baldacchino are of this sort – not preliminary sketches or studies, but fully developed working or presentation drawings that served to visualize, not to work out, ideas. They are finely wrought "models" of decorative elements, obviously intended for approval and/or to serve as models for executing artisans, or elaborately rendered, spatially situated

122. View of Baldacchino and Cathedra Petri, St. Peter's, Rome

illustrations of projects for the Baldacchino itself, obviously intended to aid in judging the projected work in situ (Fig. 130).[15] Such drawings, along with trial models progressively larger in size up to full-scale and actually built and mounted in place, formed part of the revolutionary creative process that we have seen Bernini developed for carrying out the staggering enterprises at St. Peter's. The detailed drawings and models were of course especially helpful in aiding nonprofessionals, the pope and cardi-

nals who governed the Fabbrica, to visualize the final work; but they also reflect Bernini's own obsession with proportional relationships in the immense environment of the church. On the other hand, all known drawings by Bernini are precisely of the experimental sort – rapid sketches of ideas in which, in the heat of creativity, he tries out various solutions to all the crucial problems to which, as we know from the sources, the baldachin project gave rise (Figs. 128, 129). Bernini never made

123. Crown of the Baldacchino, St. Peter's, Rome

detailed drawings for architecture; he left that work to assistants.

But by far the most eloquent, and authoritative, testimony to the fact that Bernini, not Borromini, was responsible for the design of the Baldacchino, is Borromini himself. In 1660–3 his good friend Fioravante Martinelli wrote an excellent guide to the artistic monuments of Rome, which he submitted to Borromini for comment. The margins of the manuscript are in fact filled with corrections, additions, and suggestions in Borromini's own hand. Throughout the manuscript, at every opportunity, Borromini took care to insert his own name whenever Martinelli had omitted or obscured his contribution to the work in question.[16] On several oc-

casions he also took care to downplay, sometimes quite subtly, Bernini's role. Crucial to my point is that Borromini added by far his most circumstantial and elaborate comment to Martinelli's remarks about the Baldacchino, which the author had attributed to Bernini. Borromini is at pains to qualify Bernini's role: he gives his master Maderno due credit for the idea of combining a baldachin with twisted columns but stresses that the columns did not support the baldachin (baldachins were frequently suspended from above); he notes that some attributed the inspiration to the pope (a conceit that Bernini himself promulgated); he makes the absolutely decisive point that the crucial design invention in the baldachin-ciborium merger – the oxymoronic

124. View of the Baldacchino and dome, St. Peter's, Rome

entablature with an architectural cornice and frieze of canopy lappets – was specifically *ridiculed* as a chimera; and he reports also the criticisms that baldachins are not to be supported on columns but on staves, that the baldachin should not accompany the cornice of the columns, and that Bernini insisted in any case on retaining the supporting angels.[17] These are, after all, the essential, boldly unorthodox and innovative features of the design of the Baldacchino. It is simply unimaginable that Borromini would have reported these inventions as criticisms and failed to report his role, had he been responsible: here, of all places, where the subject is one of the most conspicuous and famous monuments of Rome; here, of all places, in a venue where he had the opportunity to make a public statement (since the guide was intended for publication) through the voice of another, respected authority. At best, Borromini's silence on these points bespeaks his honesty and strict sense of fairness, as well as the mutual respect these two giants had for one another, despite the rancor and resentment that spoiled their originally friendly relationship. In any case, here,

of all places, Borromini's failure to speak on his own behalf, as he did throughout the rest of the manuscript, speaks volumes. No wonder that none of the promoters of Borromini's authorship addresses this simple, obvious fact.

EXCURSUS B. A NEGLECTED PROTOTYPE OF BERNINI'S BALDACCHINO

In 1952, J. B. Ward Perkins collected the remains and evidence concerning a considerable group of post-classical marble, spiral-form columns dispersed in and around Rome and in Naples that are clearly related to and imitative of the Solomonic columns in St. Peter's. Two pairs of these columns concern us here – one at Cave, an ancient fief of the Colonna family in the periphery of Rome, the other at Naples – because of the particular ways in which they relate to each other and to St. Peter's. The relationship is explicit in the case of the pair that now flank the high altar of the church of San Carlo at Cave, which Ward Perkins determined to be medieval (post-eighth-century) copies of the columns in St. Peter's (Fig. 131).[18] The columns rest on plinths bearing inscriptions that refer the pair to the same Jerusalem provenance as their models: respectively,

MARMOREAE

COLUMNAE

and

SALOMONICI

TEMPLI

The importance of the Cave columns in our context lies in their history. They were transferred to San Carlo when they were willed to the new Jesuit church by

126. Giulio Romano, *Donation of Constantine*, detail showing suspended baldachin and reconstruction of the Constantinian presbytery. Sala di Costantino, Vatican Palace, Rome

Marchese Filippo Colonna in 1639.[19] They stood previously in the early medieval church of S. Lorenzo at Cave, to which they had been given by Marcantonio Colonna, who received them from Pius V after the great general's victory at the battle of Lepanto.[20] The treatment of the columns as Solomonic relics triumphantly converted to Christianity, as it were, was clearly a reference to Constantine and St. Peter's. The reference fulfilled the promise invoked at the outset of the campaign by the Holy League against the Turks, which Pius V had promoted. On 11 June 1570, in the Sistine Chapel, Pius had commissioned Colonna commander of the papal forces, personally handing him the standard of the Holy League bearing the inscription "In hoc signo vinces," the angelic message that appeared to Constantine himself on the eve of his battle with Maxentius.[21] Marcantonio's gift to S. Lorenzo may have a further bearing on our understanding of the high altar at St. Peter's. In its original form the altar was surely reflected in one of the earliest known depictions of the structure with spiral columns, an Early Christian medal with the martyrdom of Saint Lawrence on the reverse.[22] S. Lorenzo fuori le mura in Rome, be it recalled, was also a foundation of Constantine. Marcantonio's gift may have been inspired by these associations, which add considerable weight to those that underlay Bernini's reclamation of the primitive type.

The connection of the Naples pair is indirect, but nonetheless compelling (Fig. 132). These flanked the high

125. Bernini, first project for the Baldacchino, 1626. Buonanni 1696, pl. 50

altar of the church of S. Chiara in Naples, until they were destroyed by fire in 1943. Small fragments remain, as does a cast of one of the columns that had been made earlier. The relevance of these columns to Bernini's Baldacchino begins with their origin. They are first recorded in an order of the ruler of Naples, Robert of Anjou, who together with his wife, Sancia di Maiorca, a devoted patron of the Franciscan order of the Poor Clares, was then patronizing the construction of the new basilica, dedicated, it must be emphasized, to the Corpus Christi, also called the Sacred Host, and the adjoining convent of the Clarisse (whence the commonly used denomination of the church as S. Chiara). On 24 October 1317, Robert donated two marble columns not attached to any edifice, but formerly lying on the grounds of S. Maria del Monte, to the Monastery of the Holy Body of Christ that he and his consort, Sancia queen of Jerusalem and Sicily, were building in Naples, and ordered that they be transported by ship from Barletta.[23] Robert's and Sancia's interest in the columns, spurred by their own passionate devotion to the cause of Jerusalem, which included negotiating (and paying for) a permanent access to the Holy Sepulcher for the Franciscans, undoubtedly stemmed from several factors. The spi-

ral design and sculptural decoration patently related them to the Constantinian columns at St. Peter's; and these columns, too, were supposed to have come from the temple at Jerusalem, as reported by a Franciscan historian at the end of the sixteenth century.[24] This association may have accompanied the columns from their resting place at S. Maria del Monte, a Benedictine abbey near which the emperor Frederick II built his awesome fortress, Castel del Monte, in the 1240s. Frederick had conducted a crusade to the Holy Land, and in Jerusalem in 1229 assumed the royal crown of the city in the church of the Holy Sepulcher. It is perfectly possible, indeed probable, that, in emulation of Constantine the Great, Frederick on his return to Italy brought the columns back with him as souvenirs of the Jewish Temple.[25] Frederick had concluded a ten-year truce with the Sultan of Egypt, which provided access to the holy sites for Christian pilgrims. The truce ended in 1239, and the following year he announced his intention to build Castel del Monte, the design of which incorporates many features reminiscent of the fabled Temple of Jerusalem. In this very document Frederick fixes the prospective location of the castle with reference to S. Maria del Monte.[26] The capitals of the columns, which are of separate blocks of marble, are carved with eagles, one of Frederick's primary symbols of imperial authority.[27] Frederick must have known that the columns in St. Peter's were associated with Constantine, with the Temple, as well as with the Sacrament. And he must have understood that Constantine's appropriation of the columns for reuse in the apostolic altar at St. Peter's was a symbolically charged, Christian reenactment of the emperor Titus's victory over the Jews and removal of the Temple furnishings to the Temple of Peace in Rome, which his father Vespasian had erected to celebrate the suppression of the Jewish revolt.[28] Frederick must have conceived his own act of transferal in this grand tradition of imperial cooptation, and following him so also Robert of Anjou and Sancia.

It is not clear where the columns were first installed at S. Chiara or how they were used.[29] But shortly after the middle of the sixteenth century, following the decree that the Sacrament was to be displayed on the high altar of every church, two copies by the Roman wood carver Bartolomeo Chiarini (documented in Naples 1560–79) were added to create a ciborium over the tabernacle of the Sacrament.[30] Presumably, at that time the columns were placed on marble plinths with reliefs that illustrated their relationship with the Jerusalem Temple and the supercession of the Hebrew sacrifices by the Sacrament, bearing inscriptions borrowed from the liturgy for the Feast of Corpus Domini: Melchizedek's offering of bread and wine (inscribed PANEM ET VINVM OBTVLIT), and the sacrifice of Isaac (IN ISAAC IMMOLATVR), Old Testament prefigurations of the Last Supper and the Crucifixion.[31] The Solomonic origin of the columns was repeated by the

127. Modern reconstruction of the Constantinian Shrine at St. Peter's

128. Bernini, sketches for the
crown of the Baldacchino. Arch.
HDz. Rom XXX, VIII, 769,
Albertina, Vienna

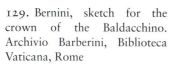

129. Bernini, sketch for the
crown of the Baldacchino.
Archivio Barberini, Biblioteca
Vaticana, Rome

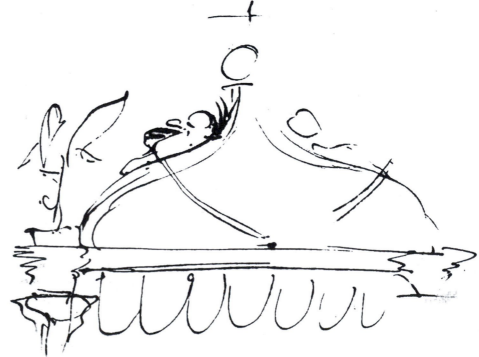

Franciscan historian Luke Wadding in his description of the four-columned high altar.[32]

The new arrangement is recorded in a medal commemorating an event of world-historical importance that took place in S. Chiara on 14 August 1571. In a solemn ceremony Don Juan of Austria received from the hands of Cardinal Antoine Perrenot Granvelle, Viceroy of Naples and papal legate to the city, the standard of the Holy League, blessed by Pius V. Don Juan was commander-in-chief of the Christian fleet in the victory at Lepanto on 7 October 1571. The cardinal is depicted seated on a faldstool consigning the standard to the kneeling Don Juan (Fig. 133).[33] Given the known dates of activity of Bartolomeo Chiarini, it seems likely that the installation shown on the medal was actually occasioned by the investiture ceremony. The action takes place before the altar on which the Sacrament tabernacle (Luke Wadding's "tholos") rests; four spiral columns at the corners support a horizontal entablature, without any superstructure. Apart from the superstructure, the disposition approximated the original Early Christian covering of the high altar at St. Peter's that had been dismantled around A.D. 600. By the same token, the arrangement and symbolism of the high altar at Naples strikingly anticipated the basic concept of Bernini's Baldacchino, with its reprisal of the Early Christian disposition of the high altar of old St. Peter's.[34]

The relationship in form and content is too close to be coincidental, and opens new perspectives on the ideological content of the work at St. Peter's.[35] The Naples monument commemorated one of the most providential events in the entire history of the Church, and its imagery as recorded in the medal must have seemed providentially relevant when it came to reinstall the prototypical spiral-columned altar tabernacle at St. Peter's. The circumstances of the epochal dedication at Naples of the European powers of the Holy League to the preservation and propagation of the Church under Pius V, served as a model and inspiration to their successors under Urban VIII in the Church's struggles with unbelieving enemies both in the East and in the North. The pertinence in Rome of the Naples monument and the event it celebrated was conveyed explicitly in the medal by the Constantinian accent of the text inscribed on the architrave of the structure in the background: IN HOC VINCES. Both the Cave pair and the Naples pair were associated with Lepanto, and it seems that the Solomonic columns were seen, not only as relics of Constantine and the Temple of Jerusalem, but as insignia of Christianity's great recent triumph over the infidel. The propitious events that took place in St. Peter's and in the Neapolitan church of the Corpus Christi, or Sacred Host, were thus seen in a world-historical context directly relevant in myriad ways in Rome, the Vatican, and St. Peter's.[36] In particular, the Naples monument dedicated to the Holy Sacrament

130. Francesco Borromini, perspective view of the Baldacchino in relation to its setting, drawing

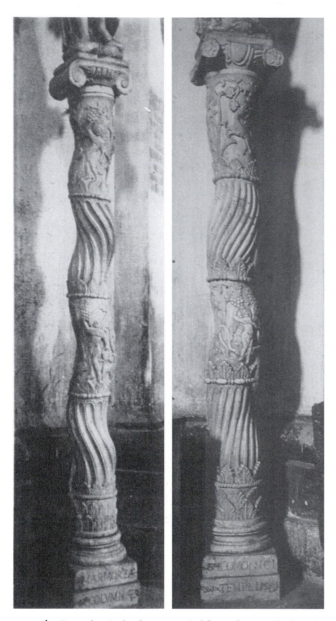

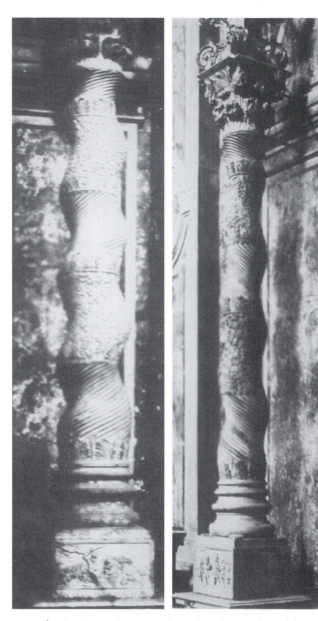

131a, b. Post-classical columns copied from those at St. Peter's. S. Carlo, Cave

132a, b. Ancient columns with medieval capitals and bases, now destroyed. S. Chiara, Naples

suggests that the Constantinian and Sacramental ideology we have found in Bernini's Baldacchino may have had heretofore unsuspected contemporary religious and political resonance.

PAIRED TOMBS

While under Urban VIII and Bernini the sacrifice of Christ occupied the center of the ideology of the crossing, the subject of papal succession was the focus of the building's longitudinal axis. These two complementary and mutually interdependent themes, which reflected the combination of building types engendered by the addition of the nave, were developed in tandem: the first was

embodied in the decision to treat the four crossing piers uniformly; the second in the decision to move the tomb of Paul III, which had occupied one of the piers, and pair it with that of Urban VIII in the niches flanking the altar in the apse.[37]

The tomb of Paul III, by Guglielmo della Porta, was originally a freestanding monument in a side aisle with four reclining allegories, two at the front and two at the back. Later, the tomb was moved to a niche in one of the crossing piers, and the figures of Justice and Prudence were placed at the base, while the other two, Abundance and Peace, were set on the pediment above. Retaining only the figures of Justice and Prudence, Bernini reinstalled the tomb on the south side of the apse, and conceived the monument to Urban as its matching partner in the corresponding niche on the opposite side (Fig. 134). The paired tombs evoke the basic typology established by Michelangelo in the Medici monuments in the New Sacristy at S. Lorenzo, Florence, with the deceased enthroned and pairs of allegorical figures below (Fig. 135). Following della Porta, Bernini made the effigy of bronze, the allegories of marble, and he complemented Paul's Justice and Prudence with Justice and Charity for Urban. Placed in the lateral niches of the apse, the twin monuments were thus coordinated in content as well as design. With the tomb of Saint Peter himself at the center of the crossing, they formed a coherent group of memorials that embodied the millennial papal succession initiated under Saint Peter, established under Constantine, and continuing ad infinitum.[38]

The particular choice of virtues for the two tombs, in part seemingly redundant, must be understood in the light of two medieval traditions of rulership and jurisprudence. As cardinal or moral virtues, Justice and Prudence were the chief attributes of earthly dominion – they characterized the good and wise ruler. Paul III was in fact the great militant pope of the Counter-Reformation, as his palm-down gesture of pacification suggests (Fig. 134). On the other hand, Justice and Charity, as attributes of Divine Wisdom, were proper to the spiritual magistrate, the Just Judge of biblical tradition.[39] Although the tomb of Urban VIII was the first time Justice and Charity had been paired in isolation on a papal monument, they appeared often in relation to papal portraits; from the Middle Ages on, these virtues played funda-

mental roles in defining the extent and limitations of papal rule – the so-called *plenitudo potestatis*.[40] The point here, in the context of St. Peter's as the seat of Christ's vicars, is twofold. The particular combinations of virtues, while perhaps appropriate to a specific individual, were primarily emblematic of the vicarious role inherited by all the successors of Peter as magistrates of the church. And, taken together, the paired tombs created a complementary contrapposto in meaning emblematic of the temporal and spiritual hegemony of the papacy.[41] With these changes of location and focus, Bernini transformed the Farnese tomb from an unwelcome obstacle to the unified program then emerging for the crossing piers into a providential blessing in the apse.

THE TOMB OF URBAN VIII (1627–47)
(Figs. 136, 137, 138, 139)

An important model for Bernini's treatment of the tombs was provided by the series of magniloquent papal portraits in the Sala di Costantino of the Vatican, the ceremonial hall frescoed a century before by Giulio Romano; the purpose of the series was to display the continuity of the Church in the papacy from its inception under Peter. Urban's pose, including his glance downward to the left and the posture of his uplifted right arm, specifically refer to Giulio's image of Saint Peter himself (Fig. 140). The seated allegories that accompany Peter in the fresco suggest the motivation for Bernini's reference: they represent Eccelesia at the left and Eternitas at the right. Peter, enthroned in heaven, seems to create the church by fiat with the expletive gesture of his raised right hand, while with his glance he regards its future on earth. Bernini has thus assimilated Urban to Saint Peter, except that the emphasis has shifted from simple chronology to an exposition of the underlying foundation for the eternal rule of the church in its earthly and heavenly domains – the exercise of Divine Wisdom.

Integral to their role as embodiments of the action of divine will is the fact that, without precedent in the traditions of papal portraits and tombs, Bernini's allegories do not sit or recline, but stand "on their own two feet" beside the sarcophagus, with whose spring-like lid segments they establish dynamic interrelationships. Lowered to the supporting plinth, they cease to appear simply as "attributes" and become intermediaries between the realm of the tomb and that of the spectator. Through their actions and emotional expressiveness the tomb becomes the focus of an interplay that relates the underlying abstract thought to human experience. Seen in this light, it is evident that Bernini's allegories are not mourners, as is often claimed. On the contrary, they illustrate the roles played by these divine virtues, acting through this pope and the papacy, in the process of salvation. Charity incorporates a binary complementary moral and

133. Giovanni V. Melone, Reverse of medal of Cardinal Granvelle showing installation of Don Juan of Austria, 1571. Museo di Capodimonte, Naples

he is the repentant sinner reaching desperately for redemption, so utterly consumed by self-recrimination as to be unaware of Charity's benign and compassionate response to his excruciating Jeremiad. Charity is a vigorously dynamic and earthly figure who contacts the papal tomb primarily by resting her sleeping charge against the sarcophagus – an image that insistently recalls the themes of the Pietà and the entombment of Christ, whose sacrificial death, which promised resurrection and salvation, was the prototype of all acts of charity.[43]

In sharp contrast, Justice stands, or more accurately leans, against the tomb in a pose redolent of languor and passivity (Fig. 137). Whereas Charity has fewer accouterments than usual (two babies rather than three), Justice has more: the book and fasces in addition to the canonical sword and balance. While the balance illustrates the impartiality of Justice, the other attributes relate to the three quintessential forms of justice derived ultimately from Aristotle, developed by the Scholastics, and formulated definitively at the Council of Trent. Cumulative justice, individual to individual, is symbolized by the sword; distributive justice, society to the individual, by the fasces; legal justice, the individual to society, by the book. Three points are of particular concern here. The cross-legged pose of the figure and the inclusion of the fasces have a common theme as compared with the balance and sword, which evoke the impartial and retributive nature of justice.[44] Crossed legs were a frequent attribute of figures representative of unhurried meditation and contemplation, and in this case the motif expresses one of the fundamental attributes of God's

134. Guglielmo della Porta, Tomb of Paul III. St. Peter's, Rome

psychological contrast – "contrapposto," Bernini would have called it – between the extremes of the soul's route to salvation.[42] One child, having absorbed the milk of God's forgiving goodness, sleeps blissfully until the end of time. The other soul bawls at the top of his lungs:

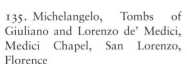

135. Michelangelo, Tombs of Giuliano and Lorenzo de' Medici, Medici Chapel, San Lorenzo, Florence

136. Bernini, Tomb of Urban VIII. St. Peter's, Rome

justice, that it is slow and deliberate. "Divine Goodness does not run quickly or noisily to castigate error, but belatedly and slowly, so that the sinner is unaware before he feels the pain."[45] With respect to divine justice, "the fasces with the ax, carried by the ancient Roman lictors before the consuls and the Tribune of the People, signifies that in the execution of justice overzealous castigation is unwarranted, and that justice should never be precipitous but have time to mature judgment while unbinding the rods that cover the ax."[46] The third point concerns the most commonly misunderstood feature of the allegory, that is, what might be called her mood: her head resting on her hand, her head and eyes turned upward, her lips parted as if in response to some message received from on high. There is nothing tearful or morbid about her expression, which is rather one of dreamy absorption tinged with a kind of melancholic lethargy. The very fact

that her right elbow rests on the book of law – Urban was first and foremost a jurist, and his rise within the church hierarchy rested on that basis – indicates that her action has to do with justice, not mourning. To be sure, all writers emphasize that divine chastisement is inflicted only reluctantly, and with dismay, and hints of fearsomeness and withdrawal are expressed by the putti, one of whom hides anxiously with the scales, while the other turns away with the fasces. The allegory herself, however, has a quite different attitude. The head-on-hand motif is one of the most consistent postures of the thinker, the contemplator, the mediator, and the turn of her head and glance makes it clear, not only that she is slow to act, but that what she is contemplating is the heavenly source of divine justice. Together the two groups offer a veritable counterpoint of psychological and moral states, active and passive, that illustrate the divine origin and

137. Bernini, Tomb of Urban VIII, Allegory of Justice, detail. St. Peter's, Rome

earthward dispensation of God's grace in the form of Charity and Justice.

The basic key to the significance of the allegories is that Bernini did not choose to accompany the pope with the cardinal moral virtues normally associated with the earthly ruler, whose loss they would properly mourn. Instead, he combined one of the cardinal virtues, Justice, with the chief theological virtue, Charity. This com-

bination was common enough, but in the context of papal portraiture it specifically denoted the role of the papacy in the execution of God's wish that man be justified – that is, made just – and so redeemed from original sin. God achieves this result through the sacrifice of his only son and the exercise of the chief attributes of his Divine Wisdom, the divine virtues of Charity and Justice. The two virtues are equal and interdependent, operating

138. Bernini, Tomb of Urban VIII,
Allegory of Death. St. Peter's, Rome

together in the interest of mankind. Far from lamenting the pope's demise, the allegories enact the roles of God's virtues in achieving the beneficent result implicit in the pope's salvific gesture.

A final correlation and contrast are evident in the treatment of what is, literally and figuratively, the central theme of Urban's tomb as well as that of Paul III, death. In both cases the caducity of earthly existence is conveyed by wing-borne inscriptions with the names of the deceased, except that Bernini assimilated this motif to the figure of *Historia* writing on a shield of victory, represented on the front of Paul III's cope, and to the traditional winged Angel of Death – which now becomes also the fateful, victorious recorder of life.[47]

The hyperbolic flattery usually taken as Bernini's exclusive concern in the tomb is belied not only by the universal significance of the allegories but also by the inordinate importance attributed to death itself: witness the prominent disposition of the Michelangelesque sarcophagus in front of the pedestal, and especially the central role played by the figure of the Reaper in the drama of the tomb (Fig. 138).[48] Death seems to rise up out of the sarcophagus itself, a conceit derived, I think, from the tomb of a great Flemish cardinal of the sixteenth century; well known through contemporary engravings of monu-

ments of famous persons, the tomb of Cardinal Érard de la Marck was an important progenitor of Bernini's ideology of death (Fig. 141).[49] In the Flemish monument, however, Death performs his role as memento mori in a traditional way, brandishing an hourglass and beckoning to the effigy, whereas Bernini's figure writes, or rather finishes writing, the name and title of Urban VIII in the black book of death. The bookish Death seems to recall that along with his literary interests the pope was an avid historian and bibliophile. A more specific reference is suggested by a rarely noted, and to my mind never properly understood peculiarity of the motif, that is, the name of Urban's predecessor partially visible on a preceding page. Often assumed to refer to Gregory XV, the letters are clearly legible as CL above and AL below, that is, Clement VIII Aldobrandini. And, as if to avoid any possibility of misunderstanding, exactly three pages, corresponding to the number of intervening popes, are shown between that with Urban's name and that with Clement's.[50] It is not hard to understand why the reference to Gregory was avoided: that pope's nephew, Cardinal Ludovisi, had been a bitter enemy of Urban's since the time of the conclave in which he had been elected. On the other hand, Urban had been a great favorite of Clement VIII, who had furthered his early career

139. Bernini, Tomb of Urban VIII,
escutcheon. St. Peter's, Rome

in many ways, and whose very name corresponds to the ideology of the tomb.[51] However, the motif of the funereal scribe and record book had another, more universal implication. Recording in reverse the sequence of Peter's successors, Death displays not only the ephemerality of earthly things, including Urban VIII, but also the permanence of heavenly things, notably the Church as embodied in the persons of its temporary heads. Therein lies the ultimate, and supremely paradoxical, significance of Bernini's tomb of Urban VIII. The very figure that represents the triumph of transience, winged Death, is at the same time scribe of the Book of Life, guarantor of immortality through the divine virtues vested in the institution of the Church and the papacy.

This same quality informs the notorious bees that have alighted here and there on Urban's tomb. Having passed through a window of the basilica, they now participate in the commemoration of Saint Peter's departed successor, just as they had done twenty years before on the occasion of Urban's election. Transforming the papal coat of arms into a trio of monumental insects bumbling over the papal tomb was, surely, an act of unparalleled imagination and wit, which also served to transform the mood of melancholy and despair usually associated with funeral iconography into a moment of surprise, and even of joy. Urban was an accomplished poet, and the bees certainly allude to his mellifluous verse. But in fact the three large bees that have escaped from the coat of arms are really the leaders – king-size bees, one

might say – of a swarm that populates the monument; the others are much smaller, worker bees – indeed, they are "life-size." This ingenious display conflates two distinct emblematic themes evoked by the pope's device. Bees swarmed over the tomb of the ancient Greek poet Archilochus, who was vilified for his pungent tongue but celebrated as the progenitor of the Pindaric tradition that Urban emulated in his own poetry (Fig. 142). And in an emblem of ideal social hierarchy and adhesion, the apian chorus is attracted to its beneficent ruler, Princely Clemency (Fig. 143). The bees thus celebrate the triumph of Christian virtue realized, poetically, in Urban's verses on religious themes, and institutionally, in the divine charity and justice of the rule of Christ vested in every pope.

Considered in this light, the seemingly casual, "bumbling" placement of the big Barberini bees becomes charged with meaning. All three are facing upward and seem to rise in an ascending march past the skeletal figure of death, as if in response to the resurrecting command of the pope, enthroned on his seat of wisdom, itself ornamented with bees. The lowermost bee, perched on the rim of the sarcophagus basin, has no stinger – "O death, where is thy sting? O grave, where is thy victory?"! (1 Cor. 15:55). The other two, as if already resurrected – bees literally embodied resurrection: ancient writers consistently reported that they were generated spontaneously from the putrefying corpses of animals, notably lions – are whole again and proceed in their journey up

140. Giulio Romano, *St. Peter*. Sala di Costantino, Vatican Palace, Rome

to the very border between death, commemoration, and life.

The startling confluence of past, present, and future in the tomb of Urban VIII is the very theme of the coat of arms of the Barberini pope attached to the face of the arch at the apex of the niche (Fig. 139). Here an extraordinary operation is performed by two divine messengers, who detach the Barberini escutcheon from the papal tiara and keys and carry it aloft. The image is a living demonstration of the fleeting earthly presence and spiritual sublimation of one mortal who briefly occupied the center of an eternally abiding creation of God's will.[52]

THE CROSSING PIERS (1627–41)

The treatment of the tombs in the apse can only be understood in relation to the larger project of which they were part: to integrate the choir and crossing, and ultimately the nave, in one comprehensive program. At the center, the tomb of Saint Peter was crowned with a new Baldacchino that expressed Christ's sacramental sacrifice and triumph in its very design. In turn, the papal altar was surrounded in the crossing piers with relics and images of saints evoking Christ's passion. Altogether, the program encompassed the entire process of salvation as envisioned by the Church.

When it was decided to replace the Resurrected Christ atop the Baldacchino by a cross and globe, traditional symbols of the universal dominion of Christianity, Bernini dealt with the new situation, typically, by exploiting it.[53] He found a new solution that expressed his underlying point of view even more vividly than before, in the context of the crossing as a whole, by interpreting the cross not simply as an emblem of the Church but as an allusion to the Crucifixion itself, the "real event." The result was a comprehensive, unified program, developed between June 1627, when it was decided to treat all four crossing piers in the same way, and April 1629, when the subjects and the basic form of the decorations were determined. This drastic, epoch-making decision inaugurated a new way of conceiving the relationship between a work of art and its environment, which might best be described as psychological. The principle of the scheme was to devote each of the niches to a saint whose relic was preserved in the basilica, thus also stressing the continuity between the old and the new. Simple, except that in the old basilica the relics, accumulated over centuries, and their reliquary altars were scattered throughout, whereas now the idea was to make a meaningful selection for a thematic union. The idea had various roots. There had been a proposal, presumably during the month-long reign of Leo XI, Paul V's predecessor, to place in the niches of the four crossing piers the tombs of four sainted popes who bore the same name.[54] The common denominator with the high altar dedicated to Saint Peter was the continuity and sacrality of the papacy, often expressed in the choice of papal names. Another precedent for the unified planning at St. Peter's was again the Cathedral of Florence, where the crossing was surrounded by chapels dedicated to the Twelve Apostles. The underlying theme was Christological, with historical reference to the church of the Holy Apostles at Constantinople, which Constantine had built as the eastern counterpart (rival) of St. Peter's. Finally, an important tradition of unified and coherent programming in central-plan churches was the scheme involving the major feasts of the Orthodox Church that developed during the Middle Ages in the Greek East. This Byzantine formula had a particular relevance because it functioned in the vertical as well as the horizontal plane, rising to a crescendo of sacrality with the image of the Pantocrator in the apex of the cupola.

What distinguished the arrangement at St. Peter's was, first, the use of the relics that had existed, dispersed, in the former building, and taking their exposition as the guiding theme of the design. The display, rather than simply the conservation of the relics, became the overriding concern. Second, the relics themselves were perceived not simply as precious remnants of an individual saint, but as integral parts of a coherent process, that of salvation through Christ's Passion. Two of the relics lent

141. Tomb of Érard de la Marck, engraving. Formerly in Liège Cathedral. From Boissard 1597–1602, part IV, vol. II, title page

themselves directly to this theme: the kerchief of Veronica, imprinted with the face of Christ on the road to Calvary, and the lance of the Roman centurion Longinus who, blinded by disease, pierced the side of the crucified Christ, "saw the light," and was cured by a touch of the blood. A third relic, the head of Saint Andrew, was indirectly related by virtue of the particular form of his martyrdom on a diagonal cross, which he requested of his oppressors in order to imitate but not presume to repeat Christ's own death. In other words, the three major relics of St. Peter's were perceived, for the first time together, as having a common denominator in Christ's sacrifice and its promise of salvation, precisely the theme that dominated in the conception of the Baldacchino at the same time. A fourth suitable relic was required to complete the scheme, the importance of which may be measured by the fact that in April 1629 the pope made bold to appropriate a portion of one of the most important relics, the True Cross, from one of the most important churches in Rome, S. Croce in Gerusalemme, also a Constantinian foundation and one of the city's venerable patriarchal basilicas.

The unprecedented ideology of the crossing of St. Peter's lay in its being conceived as a unified sa-

cred place devoted to the Christian process of salvation achieved through the sacrifice of Christ and the establishment of his church through Saint Peter and his successors. The key to the visual realization of this program was the idea of personifying the relics by representations of their respective saints. There was nothing inherently new about this idea: Veronica had often been shown displaying her kerchief, Longinus his lance, Andrew his cross, Helen the Cross. What was new was the combination of this mode of representation with the idea of a coherent theme, to be expressed by portraying the figures in such a way as to convey the significance of the relics, that is, the events that lent them their meaning and role in the process of salvation. Conceived in this way, the crossing of St. Peter's became a sacred space in which the very foundation of church ideology – the perpetual reenactment of Christ's sacrifice – took place. The whole project may have been generated by the idea of surrounding the tomb of Saint Peter with a sort of Greek chorus of colossal statues of the relic saints who would themselves, through their poses and expressions, reenact the portentous events in which they had participated. Veronica rushes in desperation to display the miraculous imprint of Christ's face on the way to the Cross (Fig. 144); Andrew and Longinus exult in their imitations of the Crucifixion (Figs. 145, 146); and the empress Helen seems to convey to her subjects the precious relics she had retrieved of Christ's sacrifice (Fig. 147). The figures

248   Andreæ Alciati

Maledicentia.
EMBLEMA LI.

ARCHILOCHI tumulo insculptas de marmore vespas
   Esse ferunt, linguæ certa sigilla malæ.

142. *Malediction*, Tomb of Archilochus, engraving. Alciati 1621, Emblema LI

thus perform dual roles. They are isolated and independent images, embodiments of the attributes they hold; at the same time, they are actors in a narrative, participants in a sacred mystery play, at once historical and imagined, taking place in the crossing of St. Peter's. The viewer who enters the crossing is inevitably caught up in the action that surrounds him – as never before on this scale and with this intensity – as if he himself, through the Eucharist, were the protagonist.

The drama is by no means "pure theater," however: it is modulated and controlled by an underlying principle that might best be called psycholiturgical, for in accordance with liturgical principle the figures are paired by their sexes and by their psychological states. In the traditional hierarchy of the Church, men precede women, and in the traditional psychology of the sexes, men are more intellectual and spiritually inclined, while women are more compassionate and earthbound. So the figures' locations were determined, and so their emotions were portrayed at St. Peter's. Together they enact a four-part, contrapuntal dialogue with the spectator, who thus participates in the sacrifice of Christ and the process of salvation as in no other church in Christendom. The women lament the earthly sacrifice – Veronica frantically, Helen majestically; the men exult in its eternal triumph – Andrew worshipfully, Longinus electrically. The sculptures display the respective stylistic propensities of the artists who made them, but Bernini provided the basic designs and remained very much in charge. This fact in itself testifies to an extraordinary achievement, precisely because of the variety of psychological states the figures portray. Never before had such a range of human emotions been magnified to such heroic grandeur. The psychological states of the figures match their superhuman scale, yet in form, expression, and action they are carefully modulated and orchestrated so as to transform the mute relics of the past into a veritable chorus of eloquent witnesses to Christ's sacrifice in the present. Most important is that together the statues create an environment, a space charged with powerful emotions into which the spectator is ineluctably drawn. The traditional veil between real and fictive space has been removed, and the spectator's experience of this world is uplifted to the level of a participant in the process of salvation to the next.

Architecturally, the plan entailed repeating the structures used for the relics in Old St. Peter's, free-standing reliquary tabernacles on three levels (Fig. 148): lowermost an altar, surmounted by an altarpiece with a representation related to the saint and/or the relic itself, and an uppermost compartment from which the relic was displayed on special occasions. In the new arrangement the lowermost level became fully developed chapels in the grotto beneath the piers, with depictions on the walls of the lives of the saints and altarpieces showing or referring to their martyrdoms. The wall frescoes in-

143. *Principis Clementia*. Alciati 1567, Emblema IX

troduce the equivalent of verb tenses in language; representing events from the past, portrayed in the technique and subterranean location of the first Christian paintings in the catacombs, they serve as preludes to the three-dimensional present represented by the sculptured figures in the church above.[55] The past included the genesis of the crossing project itself, recorded in a scene in the Veronica chapel in which Bernini is shown presenting to the pope his initial design for the upper reliquary niche – a remarkable testimony to the importance and self-consciousness of the entire undertaking (Fig. 149). The scene includes prominently a portrait of Bernini's brilliant younger brother, Luigi (1612–81), who served as his assistant (Fig. 150).[56] The function of the uppermost level of the old tabernacles was transferred to the balconied niches in Michelangelo's piers above the statuary. Bernini also transformed the upper niches into miraculous locales, introducing tabernacles that echo those of the original reliquary structures. These architectural frames themselves became reliquaries by virtue of incorporating the spiral marble columns that Constantine had taken from the Temple of Jerusalem to adorn the original choir and altar of Old St. Peter's. In their new location the antique supports give physical testimony to the idea of the fulfillment of the Old Dispensation of the Jews in the New Dispensation of Christ, the transferral from the earthly to the heavenly Jerusalem. The celestial nature of the "event" is conveyed by the treatment of the niche interiors, where angels and putti carry aloft the relics – partly rendered in three dimensions, as if there were no surface behind – against a polychrome "space." In the conches of the niches stucco clouds and putti bearing banderoles inscribed with texts referring to

144. Francesco Mochi, St. Veronica. St. Peter's, Rome

145. Francesco Duquesnoy, St. Andrew. St. Peter's, Rome

146. Bernini, St. Longinus. St. Peter's, Rome

147. Andrea Bolgi, St. Helen. St. Peter's, Rome

the relics, merge into the unfathomable gilded space of heaven, as in the golden backgrounds of medieval religious art.[57] In this way, the upper level also participates in and contributes to the perception through the crossing of a real, living space on high. The shift from painting in the subterranean chapels to sculpture in the church itself comprised not only a temporal shift from past to present, but also an existential shift from illusion to reality. Following a long tradition concerning the respective natures of the arts of representation, Bernini adhered to the view that painting, as false illusion, was indeed "inferior" to sculpture, which shares the three-dimensionality of God's own creation. Bernini here maintained the principle even in the celestial apparitions in the reliquary niches, since the space is defined "naturally" by veins in the carefully chosen colored marble; hence the surface is nowhere penetrated by "artificial" illusion.

THE NAVE: CONTINUITY

Two contemporaneous projects envisioned by Bernini under Urban VIII began the gigantic task of articulating the longitudinal axis defined by the apse and nave. In doing so, Bernini treated the crossing and the nave as the intersection of two complementary functions, not only of church architecture but of the house of God itself, as a locus of memory and as a place of action. The papal tombs in the apse represent the "sequel" to the crossing's commemoration of Christ's sacrifice and the building of his church on the cornerstone of St. Peter. The nave takes up the theme announced in the apse: history in action.

"FEED MY SHEEP" (1633–46)

The story begins, literally as well as figuratively, in the atrium above the main portal to the basilica, with a grandiose relief depicting the venerable theme of *Pasce oves meas*, "Feed My Sheep" (Fig. 151). The Gospel of John records that in a postmortem appearance to his disciples as the Good Shepherd, Christ assigned to Peter the task of nurturing his mystical flock. The episode was universally interpreted as the institution of the Church with Peter and his successors at its head.[58] The work thus illustrates the historical and divine sanction for Christianity and the authority of the popes. Bernini perceived the underlying paradox of this epochal theme, an august condescension of absolute power, in a context of a pastoral meekness and gentility. Both these qualities are conveyed by the "historicizing" style that recalls the venerable antiquity of the event and endows it with the visual authority of classical art. The subject is cast in a lyrical, idealizing mode that suggests the Augustan pastoral poetry of Christ's own time, notably the Georgics of Virgil. This classical tradition, to which Urban's own "Pindaric" po-

etry on sacred themes belonged, was deeply imbued with the idea of the perennially returning Golden Age. Church history thus begins and is perpetuated here, in the verdant landscape of an idyllic time and place – past, present and future – at the entrance to St. Peter's.

Bernini's presentation imparts a twofold message concerning the import of the scene. On the one hand, Christ displays his august authority in the ideal perfection of his human form and the noble grace of his dual action; he faces Peter to establish his primacy among the apostles as Christ's chosen spiritual heir, while gesturing behind to convey his authority over – and responsibility for – his flock. On the other hand, the composition also emphasizes the humility and obedience of Peter, who kneels in an attitude of devoted self-abnegation. In the gospel account, Peter affirms three times his love for Christ – who thrice affirms his charge, "Feed my sheep" – in penitential atonement for Peter's threefold denial of the Lord at the time of the Passion. Peter's supreme office is thus linked to his humble devotion, and to Christ's forgiveness of the first penitent.

MATILDA OF TUSCANY (1633–44)

The supreme, divinely ordained hegemony of the church and the papacy in the terrestrial realm is the theme of another "historical" work commissioned by Urban VIII at the same time, in the nave of the basilica. Following the initial foundations by Constantine the Great and his mother, there was another heroic instance in which secular rulers acknowledged the superior authority of the

148. Tabernacle reliquary of the Volto Santo, Old St. Peter's drawing. From Grimaldi 1972, fol. 92 recto

papacy and greatly augmented the church's earthly pat-rimony. Urban's eleventh-century compatriot, Countess Matilda of Tuscany, had been a staunch supporter of the papacy in its manifold and prolonged power strug-gle with the Holy Roman Emperor and donated to the Church her vast territories in south Italy. As he had ap-propriated for the crossing pier the relics of the pas-sion from S. Croce in Gerusalemme, Urban removed Matilda's body from its original resting place in Lom-bardy for reburial in a tomb in a niche in the north side aisle (Fig. 152). History is here portrayed metaphori-cally, for there is nothing medieval about the figure of the countess. Bernini represented her instead as a grandly re-gal Roman matron in a purely white environment clearly intended to suggest an ancient commemorative monu-ment. In form as well as content, the figure establishes a link between the empress Helen, with her attributes changed from the instruments of the Passion to Matilda's military command baton and the tiara and keys of the papacy, and the commanding Christ of the "Feed My Sheep."[59] Matilda is thus presented as the ideal com-panion of the original secular founders of the church.

The simple trapezoidal coffin (Fig. 153) suggests an-cient frieze sarcophagi, especially, and appropriately, the Etruscan sarcophagi of Tuscany. The relief celebrates Matilda's role in a signal victory of the papacy in the contest with the emperors over investiture, the right to nominate abbots and bishops. Henry IV is shown in ab-ject prostration receiving the forgiveness of Gregory VII at Matilda's castle at Canossa, thus acknowledging the superior authority of the papacy in the matter of investi-ture. The emperor's claim was in direct contradiction to the meaning of *Pasce oves meas* as understood by the papacy. The composition of the relief scene strikes an in-escapable analogy with the penitential obeisance of Peter and the pontifical forgiveness by Christ as depicted over the entrance. The conflict between secular and ecclesi-astical authority persisted in Urban VIII's time, and the work was surely intended to set an example to the cur-rent rulers of Christian Europe. This contemporary sig-nificance is made evident by the features of Gregory VII, which are those of Urban himself. Bernini declared vi-sually that this is a commemorative monument as well as a tomb, by placing on the lid of the sarcophagus an inscribed cartouche held up like a billboard by two kneel-ing putti. The inscription describes Matilda not simply as a donor but as a woman of male spirit, protector (*pro-pugnatix*) of the Holy See; she wears an armored breast-plate and carries a military commander's baton in allu-sion to the fact that she actually led her troops in defense of the papacy.

Most extraordinary, Bernini inserted the sculpture in a double niche, the outer shell of which consists of pan-els that diminish in perspective toward a vanishing point at the center of the figure. Physically, the double niche

allowed Bernini to include the whole monument in the narrow, shallow space available. The outer shell func-tions visually in two ways. The perspectivized coffering acts as a visual loudspeaker, magnifying the figure as it thrusts forward from the inner niche into the space of the spectator. At the same time, the expanded outer shell gives a wider "arc of visibility" within the restricted con-fines of the aisle. This ideal, antiquarian commemoration of a distant past is cast into an immediate, celebratory present by a pair of airborne putti who complete the monument by assembling the countess's coat of arms at the apex of the arch.

THE NAVE DECORATION (1647–8)

Early in the reign of Urban's successor, the Pamphili pope Innocent X, the concept of devoting the longitu-dinal axis of the basilica to the history of the Church came to fruition. The importance attached to the theme is indeed evidenced by the fact that it was retained and developed despite the new pope's bitter hatred for his pre-decessor and his equally hostile attitude, at least initially, toward Bernini. To illustrate this history, an extraordi-nary coincidence of form and content was worked out for decorating the nave piers that gave the church a new sense of direction. For the elaborate but mute abstract designs of flat, multicolored marble incrustation with which the surfaces had been reveted before the nave was built, Bernini substituted a simple, articulate, sculptured voice (Fig. 154; earlier revetment visible at far right).

The point of departure was one of the most important of all documents concerning the history of St. Peter's and its decoration, a letter composed at the end of the thir-teenth century by one of the church's greatest patrons, Nicholas III (1277–80). What has been called the Magna Carta for the canons of St. Peter's is a letter Nicholas wrote urging them, among other reforms, to look to the condition of their church to assure that its physi-cal state was worthy of its exalted spiritual status: "The Church Militant can be visualized as the holy city of the New Jerusalem, descending from heaven and prepared by God as a bride adorned for her spouse." Conceived as the Heavenly Jerusalem, the church was to be appro-priately arrayed. Under Nicholas, the adornment took the form of a series of medallions of the popes aligned along the clerestory wall. Representing the popes in this manner was, in fact, a cooptation of a much earlier sys-tem of church decoration in which medallion portraits of saints populated the celestial hierarchy represented by the building itself, except that earlier the medallions were generally confined to subsidiary locations in borderline friezes. Under Nicholas the papal portraits occupied a conspicuous part of the basilica's main field of decora-tion. And in the papal series the idea of a temporal se-quence provided the sense of continuity and perdurance

149. Bernini Presenting His Design for the Reliquary Niches to Urban VIII. Grotto Chapel of St. Veronica, St. Peter's, Rome

150. Bernini, Portrait of Luigi Bernini, drawing. Windsor Castle

the portraits are not arranged in a line, but in zigzag fashion back and forth across the nave. The disposition was clearly adopted from that of the series of standing papal portraits in the Sistine Chapel, where this serpentine organization serves to interlace and bind together the Old and New Testament narrative cycles running parallel along the chapel walls.[61] The Sistine Chapel is where the popes are elected, where the divinely ordained succession is perpetually renewed. Moreover, the medallions were not shown in isolation but as if born aloft, along with the papal tiara and keys, by pairs of winged putti. The "imago clipeata," as this motif was called, was the ancient method of illustrating the triumph of the soul and apotheosis, in this case clearly the saintliness of those portrayed.[62] And finally, Bernini's medallions are sculpted, not painted, so that they partake of a different level of reality. With gilded backgrounds and set against the polychrome marble pilaster surfaces, the white marble reliefs appear as real objects suspended in space, where they serve as animated memory messages miraculously transported from the past to the present. The nave fairly pulsates with the persistent rhythm and energy of their reminders.

In the spandrels of the arches huge female personifications of the virtues recline on the arches of the nave arcade (Fig. 155). They, too, make clear reference to antiquity, assimilating the analogous figures of Victory that were commonly placed in the spandrels of Roman triumphal arches. Through their reference to pagan triumphal imagery, the allegories emphasize that the victory of the Church was theological and moral, not military. Pervaded with the emblem of Innocent X, a dove with an olive branch in its beak, the traditional symbol of peace, the entire decorative system calls on the language

that was essential to the meaning of the frescoes. Recreating the program in the new nave was, it might be said, a double confirmation of the idea of continuity, in the sequence of popes and between the old basilica and the new.

The new version comprised several fundamental changes, in content as well as form. Most significant, perhaps, is that not all the popes were included, only those who were sainted.[60] There was thus a reversion to and convergence with the early tradition of medallion saints, as if to populate the Heavenly Jerusalem with its principal denizens from the church hierarchy. Second,

151. Bernini, "'Feed my Sheep.'" Portico, St. Peter's, Rome

of classical antiquity to express historically the divinely ordained, pacific triumph of Christianity.

The organization also suggests a progression reciprocal to our ordinary perception of the relationship between the nave and the crossing, from the entrance to the high altar. This transition from the mundane to the spiritual world is indeed the practical experience of the visitor; but for the believer, the direction of spiritual movement is exactly the opposite. As the dove of the Holy Spirit under the canopy of Bernini's Baldacchino sheds its light down upon the sacrament at the high altar, so its grace radiates outward from that epicenter to illuminate the world. Thus, once again, and most important, the Early Christian basilica is recalled: from earliest Christian times the movement, in theological and in decorative terms, was always from the altar outward to the entrance of the church.[63]

INGRESS AND EGRESS

THE PIAZZA AND COLONNADES (1656–67)
(Figs. 156, 157, 158, 159)

The same outward orientation drove the designs of the piazza and colonnades in front of the church and the Cathedra Petri in the extremity of the apse. These mighty

projects commissioned by Bernini's friend and multifarious Maecenas, Alexander VII, brought to completion and closure the longitudinal extension of the basilica. One of the fundamental concepts of Christianity, derived from the mystery religions of antiquity, was that of initiation, the process whereby neophytes, or catechumens, would "prepare" to enter the church proper. From the very beginning of church architecture this idea of a preliminary "foreclosure" was translated into an atrium or forecourt preceding the entrance to the building. At St. Peter's, the forecourt as a reception and gathering place for devotees was combined with another function that had developed relatively recently in the history of the church. From the beginning of the thirteenth century, there had been a phenomenal increase in devotion to the central mystery of the Eucharist. The devotion was greatly augmented in response to the attacks of Protestants on what they perceived as the theological

152. Bernini, Tomb of Countess Matilda of Tuscany. St. Peter's, Rome

and institutional trappings with which the Church had encumbered the simple facts of belief and grace. Such factors had led at St. Peter's to the development of the greatest annual "urban" devotion of the church calendar, the procession of Corpus Domini: the pope, displaying a monstrance containing the Host of the Sacrament and covered by a baldachin carried by acolytes, paraded with a vast entourage from the Vatican palace through the nearby streets of the Borgo, as the area was called, and back to the church. On these occasions two great long canopies supported by staves were extended far out, one from the entrance to the Vatican palace flanking the facade on the north, the other from the central portal of the church (Fig. 160). The canopies served two intimately related purposes, one practical, the other symbolic. The procession was a grueling exercise, especially for the popes, who were often relatively advanced in age, and the canopies served to shield both the participants and Holy Sacrament from the sun or inclement weather. The canopies also had an equally exigent ceremonial sense, doing honor to the importance of the event and its participants, and especially to the sanctity of the Sacrament itself.

The space before the church thus served a dual function, as an open area to contain the crowds assembled on special occasions, circumscribed by passageways specifically designed for the Eucharistic procession. Considered in this way, the piazza posed the same problem as had the church building itself, namely that of reconciling centrally and longitudinally organized forms and

functions. Earlier projects to create a unified and worthy overture to the church had tended to treat the space as a city square, creating an enclosure consisting of covered arcades with offices and apartments on top, recalling portico-lined city streets such as the one projected much earlier for the Borgo by Nicholas V and those common in many northern Italian cities. Bernini's totally different solution may best be understood in relation to the great public act, clearly intended to sound the thematic keynote of his reign, taken by Alexander VII almost immediately after his election on 7 April 1655. On 27 May the new pope introduced a radical innovation in the conduct of the Corpus Domini procession. Instead of walking or riding seated in the traditional *sedia gestatoria*, in origin a Roman symbol of imperial authority, Alexander was carried on a litter, kneeling and holding the Host before him. The austerity and self-control exhibited in this long, uncomfortable, and intensely concentrated devotion by the agonized (he had a painful infirmity) and perspiring pope, who remained absolutely immobile throughout, is movingly described by eyewitnesses.[64] This simple but stunning demonstration of humble adoration inaugurated a new era, defining the entire future development of St. Peter's and, with it, the public face of the Catholic Church itself.

Eloquent testimony to this awesome new attitude is the fact that, in planning a suitable frame for the forecourt of St. Peter's, Alexander would have nothing to do with the common idea of functionality. He rejected a project that included a usable second story, with the

153. Stefano Speranza, *Capitulation of Henry IV before Gregory VIII*. St. Peter's, Rome (after Bacchi 1998)

absolute requirement that the porticoes serve no other purpose than as passageways, effectively silencing those who argued that the structures should also have "practical" value. For Alexander, only self-sufficient porticoes could express without adulteration the spiritual values, celebratory and sacramental, he intended them to represent. We shall see that their public utility, which was indeed very great, lay in the work the huge undertaking would provide for the indigent unemployed of Rome, especially after the plague of 1656.

Division of the area into two parts was inherent in the project (Fig. 161a, b). The sizes and shapes of these contiguous spaces were also determined by interdependent features of the situation – features that must have seemed providentially "given" and susceptible, in Bernini's imagination, to incorporation into one coherent, unifying thought. The flanking sides of the area immediately in front of the church were fixed by a portion of the Vatican palace to the north, situated diagonally with respect to the facade. This corner of the palace was also a determining factor in the vertical sense, as the pope often made appearances from the balcony of his apartment overlooking the square, for which maximum visibility was required. Matching the palace front symmetrically to the south created the so-called *piazza retta* (i.e., aligned with the axis of the church), a trapezoid diverging toward the facade, clearly – and inevitably – evocative of Michelangelo's piazza of the Campidoglio. The space thus became the ecclesiastical counterpart to the secular capitol of Rome and the ancient empire.

The lateral, northern extension of the expanded space east of the *piazza retta* was delimited by the Leonine wall of the city, inviolable because it contained the famous corridor connecting the Vatican with the papal stronghold of the Castel Sant'Angelo. The configuration of this space and its relation to the *piazza retta* depended from the intersection of two axes, one running longitudinally with respect to the basilica, from the center of the facade of the church to the obelisk that Sixtus V had erected toward the middle of the piazza. The obelisk, in turn, was the point of intersection with an oblique axis, hence the name *piazza obliqua*, parallel with the church facade. A point on this transverse axis became the center of a circle whose perimeter happened to coincide both with the corner of the Vatican palace and the Leonine wall. When the corresponding circle was drawn on the opposite side of the piazza, the points of intersection between these two circles in turn became the centers for larger circles whose perimeters complete the oval on its long axis. A third axis was a line projected from the north end of the church facade, along the palace facade, through the Borgo Nuovo – the main thoroughfare from the center of Rome – to the front of Castel Sant'Angelo. The intersections of the north lateral circle with this axis

determined endpoints of the arc of the colonnade, so as to provide the approach from the Borgo Nuovo with the maximum view of the church facade.

These manifold "coincidences" must have confirmed Bernini's adherence to the quasi-mystical tradition of Pythagorean geometry in which the circle was the most perfect of divinely given forms. These factors, symbolic as well as practical, must also have recommended the oval shape, defined by intersecting circles, rather than the true ellipse, for the *piazza obliqua*. Although he attributed the conception to the pope himself, Bernini had had much prior experience with this shape, most notably in a chapel he had designed for Urban VIII's Palazzo di Propaganda Fide, the church's office dedicated to the worldwide dissemination of the faith (Fig. 162); this was, in fact, the first use of the transverse oval in Rome. The chapel was dedicated to the Three Magi and was therefore replete with astrocosmological symbolism; hence, the plan may also have anticipated the *piazza obliqua*'s reference to the ideal of a universal, all-embracing church, the first witnesses to which were indeed the Magi. At St. Peter's the obelisk is flanked by two fountains that give special prominence to the oval's transverse axis, which in turn calls attention to a particular feature of Bernini's design: the columns are aligned in concentric circles behind one another so that the centers of the lateral circles become, literally, vanishing points from which the welter of columns disappears. When seen at an angle, the columns seem multitudinous, disoriented, and dynamic; when seen from the center points, they look simple, regular, and stable. The moving visitor inexorably seeks out these "perfect" vistas, which are in fact marked in the pavement on the axis, perceiving the transitory and yearning for the permanent. Bernini had only recently employed a very different but fundamentally analogous "double perspective" system in the lateral walls of the Cornaro chapel in S. Maria della Vittoria. There the members of the deceased's family are shown in diagonally foreshortened architectural settings (Fig. 163a, b), so constructed that when the visitor approaching along the axis of the nave reaches the central vanishing point under the center of the dome, the perspectives "make sense" as a sort of triptych whose lateral wings form one coherent space (Fig. 164). In the Cornaro chapel the context was also a gathering of souls, deceased members of the donor's family, united in a kind of disputation of the sacramental event depicted in the central altarpiece, the Ecstasy of St. Teresa, and enacted at the altar. Viewed thus, the perspective "resolution" of the space of the piazza at St. Peter's stands in a long tradition, especially of sacrament tabernacles and altars, in which the satisfying sense of "truth" mysteriously evinced by perspective had become a metaphor for the mystical coincidence of opposites embodied in the Eucharist itself.[65]

154. Bernini, nave decorations, St. Peter's, Rome

155. Bernini, nave spandrels, Niccolò Menghini, allegories of Virginity and Obedience. St. Peter's, Rome

156. Bernini, Piazza S. Pietro.
Rome

157. Bernini, Colonnade, north
arm. St. Peter's, Rome

One of the most impressive, and unexpected, features of the piazza is the simple sobriety of the colonnades' Doric order, which has surprised observers who expect a more "Baroque," that is, more elaborate treatment, especially from Bernini. The Doric is of course the Greek order par excellence, and one of the most perspicacious students of Bernini, Rudolph Wittkower, made the trenchant observation that "No other Italian structure of the post-Renaissance period shows an equally deep affinity with Greece."[66] Part of the motivation for the relatively low and understated design of the colonnades was to magnify by contrast (*contrapposto*) the height and magnificence of the facade, bereft of the intended bell towers. With respect to the Corinthian order of the facade, the juxtaposition conformed to the traditional increase in elaboration with the superimposition of orders, most famously exemplified in the Colosseum (Fig. 165). The juxtaposition made social and ideological sense in that the gravity of the Doric resonated with the piazza's solemn function at Corpus Domini, whose ritual discipline Alexander had greatly augmented at the outset of his reign, and for the common masses of the faithful gathered there to receive the pope's public ministrations. No less important, however, was the resonance Bernini's Doric order created with what was in fact the most

158. Bernini, Colonnade, north arm. St. Peter's, Rome

159. Bernini, Colonnade, north arm. St. Peter's, Rome

160. Anonymous, Corpus Domini procession, ca. 1640. Museo di Palazzo Venezia, Rome

important Petrine building in Rome besides the papal basilica, the famous circular and domed *tempietto*, ringed by antique columns, designed in the early sixteenth century by Bramante to mark the actual spot of Peter's martyrdom (see Fig. 264). Bernini had paid specific homage to this martyrial tradition in certain sketches for the Baldacchino, where the upside-down cross of St. Peter appears atop the crown, along with the cross of Golgotha. The relationship between the two buildings had already been articulated by Bramante in the cupola of his project for New St. Peter's, and the analogy was retained in the basic configuration of the dome as built. As we shall see, Bernini conceived of the semicircular arms of the colonnade as the arms of St. Peter embracing the faithful, his head surmounted by the tiara crown as dome.

Bernini's colonnades are extraordinary – more Greek than the Greeks, one might say – in that they eschew an important decorative element, the frieze of triglyphs, of the traditional Doric order. In this form the porticoes clearly coopt the similarly bare first-story order of the Colosseum, the ancient structure whose oval shape the piazza most clearly echoes. The adoption was singularly appropriate as a solemn, even melancholic, reference to the ancient building's service as the "theater" of death for the early Christians who were martyred there – to be resurrected in the cordon of saints whose statues ring the piazza as a triumphal legion of honor guarding the entrance to St. Peter's. The association was given a personal reference in a medal designed by Bernini likening

the pope's salvific efforts during the plague to the victory of Androcles over the obeisant lion in the amphitheater (Fig. 232).

Wittkower's recollection of Greece, however, may have had more substance than he imagined. The allusion suggests an added dimension to the imperious or bucolic "classicisms" Bernini adopted in other contexts at St. Peter's. The Doric here becomes a kind of common- or everyman's visual *modus orandi* whose pristine simplicity and moral rectitude evoke the early Attic style that many ancient rhetoricians sought to retrieve.[67] An analogous association was imbued in the design of the colonnades themselves, with three aisles that provided the sacramental papal procession with a central, covered passageway also protected at the sides. This structure was sanctioned by an elaborate study of the literary evidence concerning ancient colonnades carried out by one of the leading scholars of the day, Lucas Holstein.[68] The study concluded that triple porticoes, called chalcidicae from Chalcis in Euboea, were common in the ancient cities of the Greek world, a happy coincidence in view of the fact that Alexander VII, through his namesake, had many associations with the Hellenic tradition. The sources are unclear as to what form the "triple portico" took, but neither they nor the preserved examples suggest that the central passage of the ancient avenues, which were flanked by covered porticoes, was itself covered;[69] Bernini's smooth annular vault here is again adapted from the Colosseum (Fig. 166). No less important than this invocation of an *imagined* classical

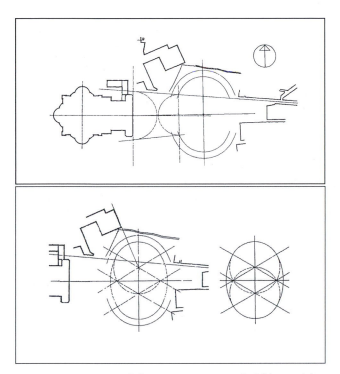

161. Determination of the *Piazze Retta* and *Obliqua*. After Birindelli 1981, 80, 82

precedent is the occurrence of the same term in the Old Testament, in no less significant a place than the prophet Ezekiel's account of the courtyard of the Temple of God, where he says there was a "porticus iuncta porticui triplici" (Ezek. 42:3).[70] In one of the most compendious and popular postmedieval allegorizations of scripture, Hieronymus Lauretus's *Silva allegoriarum*, first published at Barcelona in 1570 and reissued many times thereafter, the triple portico might designate the mystery of the Trinity: "Porticus atriorum templi, & praecipuè porticus triplex, mysterium sanctae Trinitatis designare possunt."[71] So far as I can discover, Bernini's quadruple colonnades comprising three covered passages were without precedent in antiquity. The motif constitutes a brilliant architectural neologism that melds classical and biblical references, and so embodies the fundamental concept of Christianity's historical role, proclaimed from the outset by the Fathers of the Church, as the *Ecclesia ex circumcisione* and *ex gentibus*, incorporating and superseding its predecessors.

Two species of appropriation and supersession are represented by the architecture of the facades and cross section of the porticoes (Fig. 167). The stepped, pedimented entrances with horizontal entablatures appropriately recall in simplified form the temple front design of the Lateran sacrament altar (Fig. 121). Within the colonnades, the raised semi-circular vault with flat wings refers to one of the most conspicuous of Renaissance architectural motifs, the so-called Serliana (derived from anti-

quity and popularized by the sixteenth-century architect Sebastiano Serlio). At St. Peter's the adaptation consisted essentially in the convergence of two important traditional contexts with which the motif was closely associated. One of these was the ancient triumphal *fastigium* in which the Serliana, covered by a pediment, served as a kind of proscenium or frame for the appearance or passage of the emperor. The most famous *fastigium* of antiquity had already been baptized, as it were, by the emperor Constantine himself, who erected a huge structure of this kind in the Lateran.[72] Conceived as a frame in depth, as it were, the Serliana had an "extended" life in the form of a vaulted, three-aisled passageway. Bernini used the motif in the lateral reliefs of the Cornaro chapel and, as a continuation of the piazza porticoes through the entrance to the Vatican itself, in the Scala Regia (Figs. 163, 178). In this form the design might be described as at once celebratory and transitional – a triumphal corridor for the procession that also defines the piazza, in which the perspective resolution from the vanishing points of the two arms of the colonnade comprises the universal embrace of the Corpus Domini.

Another feature that distinguishes the porticoes at St. Peter's are the statues of saints that surmount the balustrades. The image they create provides a celestial counterpart to the army of secular heroes who celebrate the Roman imperium on the balustrades of the palaces of the Campidoglio, site of the ancient Temple of Jove and seat of the modern city government.[73] Although there was no classical precedent for this arrangement in a portico, colonnades surmounted by statues were shown in a reconstruction of the ancient Capitoline published in 1648, surely an important model for Bernini (Fig. 168). Such figures seen atop a colonnade conveyed an additional sense that may have been a factor in the pope's extravagant insistence that the colonnades stand alone with no structure above them. In this way, the statues appear not simply to crown the balustrades but to stand directly on the columns, and so they are described in the contemporary sources. The sculptures were seen not only as a horizontal ring but as an alignment of triumphal columns, the most common form of imperial Roman honorific commemoration. The arrangement created a veritable legion of Christian heroes, joined together by faith, to replace the military heroes celebrated by statues placed on isolated columns in antiquity. A contemporary writer actually described the Corpus Domini procession at St. Peter's as the successor to the triumphal processions of the ancient imperators to the temple of the Capitoline Jove. Bernini gave form to this idea.

In a powerful explanation of the project Bernini gave his own definition of the basic theme that animated his conception of the colonnades, which he described as the arms of the mother church embracing all the world, including nonbelievers: "The church of St. Peter, being

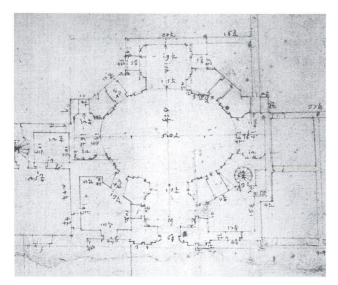

162. Francesco Borromini, plan of Palazzo di Propaganda Fide showing Bernini's chapel of the Re Magi, drawing, detail. Albertina, Vienna

virtually the mother of all the others, had to have a portico that would in fact appear to maternally receive with open arms Catholics to be confirmed in faith, heretics to be reunited with the Church, and unbelievers to be enlightened by the true faith."[74] He even drew a sketch in which this "open-arms" metaphor is transferred to St. Peter's represented as pope wearing the tiara (Fig. 169). The idea in fact had ancient roots, referring in the first instance to a classical anthropology of architecture – vigorously revived in the humanistic tradition of the Renaissance – in which the harmonious relationships among the parts of the central-plan building were correlated with the ideal proportions of the human body, the so-called

Vitruvian Man, whose extended arms and legs touched the perimeter of a circle centered at the navel. In the Christian tradition the metaphor's most familiar application was in the definition of the cruciform basilica as the image of Christ on the cross. Like the architectural forms themselves, the concepts were complementary – one man-focused, the other God-focused – but reconcilable only with difficulty; and both were based on essentially static, symbolic images. Bernini's conception of the relationship between the church of St. Peter's and the colonnaded piazza fused these themes, the ecclesiology of the basilica and the universality of the central plan, with a third: the institutional image of the church as Mater Ecclesia. Through this combination he created a new, dynamic metaphor for Christianity's universal embrace. Bernini's sketch of this idea – in itself a startling fusion of concept, elevation, ground plan, and bird's-eye view – concerned the preferred placement of a projected but never executed pavilion, appropriately called the Terzo Braccio, the third arm, at the entrance to the piazza. The purpose of the structure was at once conceptual and visual: it provided the optimum viewpoint from which to grasp the shape and space of the entire square, and hence its universal meaning. The difference from the preceding traditions is that Bernini's metaphor involves not only the static ground plan but the elevation as well, and conceives of the church and the piazza together as a unified whole, not a passive receptacle but a living organism acting on behalf of mankind.

A further unexpected but sharply illuminating insight into the kind of thinking that underlay the project is provided by the four explicative inscriptions, composed by the pope himself. They were placed at the outer and inner extremities of the arms of the colonnades, the latter pair

163. Bernini, Chapel of St. Teresa, lateral walls, members of the Cornaro family. S. Maria della Vittoria, Rome

164. Bernini, Chapel of St. Teresa, view of altar with "converging" perspectives. S. Maria della Vittoria, Rome

at the junctures between the colonnades and the corners of the *piazza retta*. Except for the one at the southeast entrance, which records the completion of the work in 1661, the texts combine passages from scripture in such a way as to define the nature and meaning of the structure, and address the viewer, exhorting him, in effect, to follow the pope's example. The texts are all from the Old Testament, as if to demonstrate the fulfillment of their auguries in the New. The inscription at the northeast entrance states the practical function of the colonnades, but in terms that express their higher import through the prophet Isaiah's description of the tabernacle/umbrella in the Kingdom of God: IN UMBRACULUM DIEI AB AESTU IN SECURITATEM A TURBINE ET A PLUVIA (Isa. 4:6: "et tabernaculum erit in umbraculum diei ab aestu et in securitatem et absconsionem a turbine et a pluvia." [And there shall be a tabernacle for a shade in the daytime from the heat, and for a security and for a covert from the whirlwind, and from rain; Douay-Rheims]). At the southeast entrance is the dedication: ALEXANDER VII PONTIFEX MAXIMUS A FUNDAMENTIS EXTRUX[IT] ANNO SALVAT[ION]IS MDCLXI. The inscriptions at the corners conflate Old Testament phrases in praise of God into prescriptions that evoke the Corpus Domini procession and

the Eucharistic worship it celebrated. That on the northwest invokes the procession and worship in the church: VENITE ASCENDAMUS IN MONTEM DOMINI ADOREMUS IN TEMPLO SANCTO EIUS (Come, let us ascend the mount of God, let us worship in his holy temple). The text combines Isaiah 2:3, "et ibunt populi multi et dicent venite et ascendamus ad montem Domini" (And many people shall go, and say, Come, and let us go up to the mountain of the LORD), with Psalm 137:2, "adorabo ad templum sanctum tuum et confitebor nomini tuo super misericordia tua et veritate tua quoniam magnificasti super omne nomen sanctum tuum" (I will worship toward thy holy temple, and I will give glory to thy name. For thy mercy, and for thy truth: for thou hast magnified thy holy name above all). The mountain alludes to the Temple on the Mount in Jerusalem, to the Mons Vaticanus where St. Peter's and the Vatican are located, and to the mountains that form part of the arms of the Chigi family. At the southwest: VENITE PROCIDAMUS ANTE DEUM/IN TEMPLO SANCTO EIUS ET NOMEN DOMINI INVOCEMUS (Come, let us bow down before God in his holy temple, and let us invoke his name), combining Psalm 94:6, "venite adoremus et procidamus et ploremus ante Dominum qui fecit nos" (Come let us adore and fall down: and weep before

165. Colosseum, Rome

the Lord that makes us) with Psalm 114:4, "et nomen Domini invocavi o Domine libera animam meam" (and I called upon the name of the Lord. O Lord, deliver my soul).

The genesis and meaning of the entire project were subsequently distilled into a medal issued in 1664 in commemoration of that extraordinary innovation, to celebrate the decennalia, or decadal anniversary of the pope's election (Fig. 170).[75] The image chosen for the occasion, Alexander kneeling in the Corpus Domini procession, is a measure of the importance attached to the event and the pope's extraordinary innovation. The motto, "Prodicamus et adoremus in spiritu et veritate" (Let us kneel and adore in spirit and in truth), is again an in-

genious amalgam of two scriptural passages, one from the Old Testament, the other from the New, which encapsulate the essence of the Corpus Domini devotion. The first part comprises David's exhortation to praise God in Psalm 94:6, the same text used in the southwest colonnade inscription. The second part repeats John's prescription for the inward disposition required of those who worship God, "God is a Spirit; and they who adore him, must adore him in spirit and in truth" ("Spiritus est Deus, et eos, qui adorant eum, in spiritu et veritate oportet adorare"; John 4:24). Together the passages describe the inward and outward expression of devotion proper to the Eucharist. The kneeling, immobile attitude of prayer had long been the canonical mode of devotion to the Eucharist – perpetual adoration was, as we shall see, the highest calling of the angels in heaven – but introducing it into the Corpus Domini celebration served to transform both traditions: the Eucharistic devotion was given a dynamic movement and an all-embracing scope, and the traditional procession of exultant triumph was enshrined, as it were, in a powerful sign of humble public worship, specifically associated with the Eucharist. The medal and its inscription have another sense as well. The Catholic understanding of the Eucharist, or rather the nature of the Eucharistic sacrifice in the mass, was one of the major targets of the Protestant reformers and had been emphatically reaffirmed at the Council of Trent. The council specifically imposed the Corpus Domini procession as a public demonstration of belief in the truth of the Eucharist, which would overcome and, it was hoped, convert the enemies of the church.[76] Alexan-

der's innovative inaugural procession and Bernini's welcoming piazza and colonnades gave new form to the new spirit that inspired the quintessential tenet of the church and its claim to universality.

COMMEMORATION

CATHEDRA PETRI (1657–66) (Figs. 171, 172, 173)

Contemporary and planned in concert with the piazza was the decision finally to resolve the problem of the choir of St. Peter's – foreseen "providentially" by Annibale Carracci at the beginning of Bernini's career. The solution was found in an idea that would celebrate, liturgically and visually, the legitimacy and authority of the Church as a divinely ordained institution. This claim was

166. Jean Grandjean, Annular vault of the Colosseum, 1781, watercolor (after Luciani 1993, 24)

167. Giovanni Battista Bonacina, plan of Piazza S. Pietro with facade and cross section of portico arms, engraving, detail. Archivio Chigi 25.27.4, Vatican Library, Rome

directions – between the enfolding arms, both revealing and screening the space of the piazza. As Bernini's project evolved, he shifted the structure to the east, beyond the perimeter of the arc of the colonnades; here it provided a kind of vestibule, or viewing space from which the "teatro" (the contemporary term for the piazza, better translated in this case as "totality" than as "theater") could be grasped and contemplated. During his visit to Paris in 1665, while work on the piazza was in progress, Bernini recommended just such a viewing area in a critique of purely round buildings, where the visitor tends to move inward without perceiving the whole: "…it would be a good thing to create a small space projecting from a completely round church, for on entering one usually takes six or seven steps and so is prevented from appreciating the circular form."[77] This imperative sense of perceiving the whole had a truly numinous quality for Bernini, which he expressed in describing his own feeling about viewing the interior of his transverse oval church of S. Andrea al Quirinale, designed at precisely this period. His son recalled his response upon finding him withdrawn in a corner of the church and asking him what he was doing there, so alone and quiet: "Son, this is my only work in architecture that gives me some particular pleasure at the bottom of my heart, and I often come here to find consolation with my work."[78] In the context of St. Peter's it is important to realize that the force of movement is inward from both extremities: the visitor entering from the city feels the piazza's embrace and is then drawn forward into the building to meet, in the frame of the high altar, the light of the Holy Spirit pouring toward him from the apsidal window above the throne of Christ's vicar.[79]

The relationship was articulated in the inscriptions on the medals (Figs. 174, 175) issued by the pope to commemorate the twin projects, piazza and cathedra, both of which texts include the same metaphor relating Saint Peter the man to St. Peter's the building, and to the church which Christ built on that rock. The 1657 foundation medal of the colonnade quoted Psalm 86:1, FUNDAMENTA EIUS IN MONTIBUS SANCTIS ("the foundations thereof are in the holy mountains"), anticipating the allusions that would appear in the portico inscriptions.[80] A 1662 medal of the cathedra is inscribed PRIMA SEDES, FIDEI REGULA, ECCLESIAE FUNDAMENTUM ("first seat, the rule of faith, foundation of the Church"). The words epitomize the major headings under which the papacy laid claim to the leadership of the Christian world: as the successor to the person first designated by Christ himself in his charge to Peter; as the arbiter of Christian belief, to whom Christ conveyed the power to bind and to loosen; and as the foundation on which the institutional Church was based. Whereas the Corpus Domini was a relatively modern feast of the Church, that of the Cathedra Petri (22 February), known from the mid-fourth

vested in the form and concept of the cathedra, the chair or throne of office, from ancient times the symbol of legitimate supreme authority, conveyed to Peter by Christ along with the responsibility to "feed my sheep." Understanding the piazza colonnades and the Cathedra Petri as simultaneous and interrelated projects provides a fundamental insight into the overall planning for St. Peter's under Alexander VII, most specifically the correspondence and reciprocity between the projected entrance pavilion, the Terzo Braccio, and the cathedra at opposite ends of the axis. Although never executed, the Terzo Braccio was a critical element in the design because it provided a sort of triumphal arch – an *arcus quadrifrons* in classical terms, since one passed through it in four

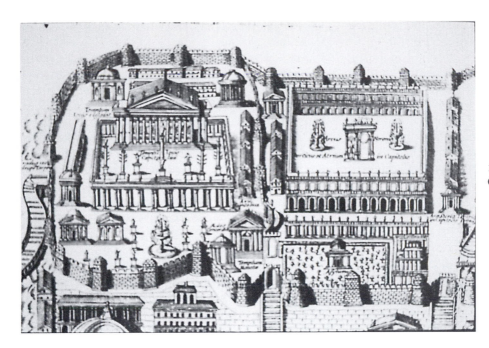

168. Reconstruction of ancient Capitol. Donato 1648, 108

century, was one of the oldest. Originally celebrating the concession by the emperor to the pope of the power to rule, the feast had from the beginning the imprint of imperial – that is, universal – authority. The long neglected commemoration was revived in 1588 by Paul IV with a bull that specifically stated the motivation: to confute the heretical Protestants who, following the schismatic eastern church, challenged the authority of the papacy, even denying that Peter had ever visited Rome.[81] The quasi-Trinitarian formulation of the medal was derived from the definition of the feast of St. Peter's chair in the Golden Legend, the great, omnipresent compilation of church tradition concerning the liturgical calendar composed in the thirteenth century by Jacobus of Voragine. For the Feast of the Chair of St. Peter, Jacobus gives a threefold significance: the chair of regal dignity, the chair of priestly dignity, and the chair of the teacher. These same domains are defined in the medallic inscription: Peter as the Prince of the Apostles (*prima sedes*), to whom Christ conveyed the keys to heaven and power to loose and bind (*fidei ragula*) and on whom He would build his church (*fundamentum ecclesiae*). And the three functions are illustrated in the reliefs that decorate the front and sides of Bernini's Cathedra Petri: "Feed my Sheep," Christ's charge to Peter Prince of the Apostles, as his earthly vicar; "Christ Giving the Keys to Heaven to Peter" as arbiter of the faith by which the gates will be opened or closed; and "Christ Washing the Feet of His Disciples," in the first instance Peter's, as Jesus' own example of the love and humility that would be expected of Peter in attending his flock.

The artifact symbol was preserved at St. Peter's in the form of the very chair Peter was supposed to have

used. Although on an unprecedented scale, the throne Bernini designed to contain the relic belongs in a long tradition of reliquaries that take the shape of the objects they contain. In the ninth century, the original plain oak chair had been decorated with antique ivory tablets, and by adding rings through which staves could be passed, it was altered into a *sedia gestatoria* on which the pope could be carried in procession.[82] Honorific levitation, so to speak, was thus an integral part of the significance as well as the very fabric of the chair. Bernini substituted the Fathers of the Church for the traditional "sediari" who

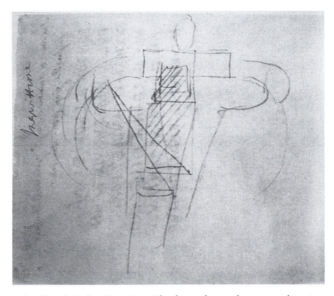

169. Bernini, St. Peter's with the colonnades as embracing arms, drawing. Biblioteca Vaticana, Rome

carried it in procession, and his colossal monument thus became an embodiment and perpetuation of the motivating power of the Holy Spirit. Apart from its punning reference to Peter's chair, Bernini's spectacular conception deliberately calls to mind one particular instance in which a reliquary-like, shaped container served as a monumental, sculptured altarpiece. This unmistakable precedent is the tabernacle of the Sacrament that forms the centerpiece of the mortuary chapel built by Sixtus V in S. Maria Maggiore at the end of the sixteenth century, to house his tomb and that of his predecessor, Pius V (see Fig. 120). Here four over-life-size angels are shown carrying a domed, centrally planned structure symbolic of the Holy Sepulcher as the locus of the Eucharist. The angels bear their burden effortlessly, on a single, delicately raised hand – as if in response to Christ's own exhortation to the faithful to "Take up my yoke upon you. . . . For my yoke is sweet and my burden light" (Matt. 11:29–30, "Tollite iugum meum super vos . . . iugum enim meum suave est et onus meum leve est"). Bernini's cathedra makes essentially the same point, transmitting Christ's mystical injunction to the faithful through his successor.

Bernini also imbued the ritual of the feast with new meaning by giving form to the words of Psalm 106:32, in which the church as an institution and the chair as an emblem of the transfer of power were linked in a prophetic act of exaltation: "Let them exalt him in the church of the people and praise him in the chair of the ancients" ("Exaltent eum in ecclesia plebis: et in cathedra seniorum laudent eum"). Those who exalt the chair are the Fathers of the eastern and western churches, who thus express the all-embracing ecumenism that underlies Bernini's works for Alexander at St. Peter's. The importance of this verse may explain the pride of place given to Saint Augustine at the right side of the altar. Augustine's comment on the passage in his sermon on the feast of the Cathedra Petri is recited in the lessons of that day: "In this way the Lord names Peter as the foundation of the Church, and so the Church rightly celebrates this foundation on which the whole lofty structure rises up. And it is fitting that the Psalm verse read today says, 'Let them exalt him in the church of the people and praise him in the chair of the elders.' Blessed be God, who commanded St. Peter the Apostle to be exalted in the Church; for it is right that in the Church this foundation should be honored by which she rises up to heaven."[83] There could hardly be a more apt commentary on Bernini's monument, which embodies the dual import of Augustine's understanding of the relationship between the chair and the church. The Fathers are shown as if they were supporting the chair ("Let them exalt him . . ."), but in fact it is carried aloft by some higher power ("God who commanded St. Peter . . . to be exalted . . ."), which animates them and their massive yet turbulent drapery through the intervening ribbons that seem to curl and writhe with the power they transmit.

The Cathedra Petri consists of four distinct yet interconnected elements: the altar proper; the "altarpiece" in the form of the chair; a concave platform on which stand four Doctors of the Church, two Latin in the front, Ambrose and Augustine, two Greek at the back, Athanasius and John Chrysostom; on the rear wall in gilded stucco a glory of the heavenly hierarchy that explodes into the space of the apse, clouds cascading down behind the chair; and, in the center, the window with the dove of the Holy Spirit, which was not originally stained glass but painted in oil on glass, surrounded by "molte teste di serafini." The curved platform, unprecedented for an altarpiece with free-standing sculptures, permitted Bernini to create an astonishingly subtle illusion that the two rear figures are some distance behind (as if the chair were square in plan), and that all four figures are complete and "in-the-round." In Bernini's vision the Holy Spirit passes through the rear wall and expands as it descends to fill the apse of the church, ultimately to include the high altar framed by the Baldacchino and the distant viewer in its exultant embrace (see Fig. 110). The essential point of the ideology of the Cathedra Petri is the singularity and unity of the Church under the papacy; reflecting this ecumenical theme, the gospel reading of the papal mass for the Feast of the Chair is recited in both Latin and Greek.[84] This is also the central point of Bernini's monument. The conceptual unity is conveyed by the Latin and Greek Doctors of the Church whose doctrines, under the divine inspiration of the Holy Spirit, are literally tied to Peter's throne. The unity is conveyed visually in the indissoluble fusion between two distinct apparitions, those of the miraculously suspended brazen chair to which its inspired acolytes are conjoined and the luminous infiltration of the Holy Spirit. The fusion is mediated by the implosion of the gilded stucco "Gloria" whose radiant beams shed the fiery light of the heavenly hierarchy from seraphs, to cherubs, to angels.[85] The spiritual progression from the divine will to its earthly manifestation has its visual and physical analogue in an imperceptible progression from two-dimensional, translucent polychromy, representing the pure spirit, through progressively "lower" and increasingly three-dimensional orders of reality, to reach, ultimately, our own. The conversion of the preexistent window into the luminescent Holy Spirit was a perfect instance of Bernini's definition of architectural merit: to make obstacles seem deliberately invented.[86]

Viewed in this light, the Cathedra Petri repeats in its own way the expansive, outward reach and all-encompassing unity that was the primary conceit of the Piazza S. Pietro, where in Bernini's mind the dome became the head, the facade the chest and shoulders, and the colonnades the embracing arms of the mother church

170. Decennial medal showing Alexander VII kneeling as in the Corpus Domini procession of 1655, 1664. Biblioteca Vaticana, Rome

(see Fig. 169). The viewer is enclosed in an arena of space in which the distinction between fiction and reality is almost imperceptibly bridged, and from which the ultimate focus is inward in a kind of existential self-reflection on the meaning of the experience.

THE CONSTANTINE AND SCALA REGIA
(1662–70) *(Figs. 176, 177, 178, 179)*

Innocent X had planned in 1654 to include in a side aisle of the new building a monument to the emperor Constantine the Great, as a counterpart to that installed by Urban VIII for the church's great medieval benefactress, Matilda of Tuscany (see Fig. 152). A completely new idea emerged when the project was taken up by Alexander VII as part of his ambitious plans for completing the new church inside and out. In this context Constantine would be commemorated for decreeing the recognition of the new faith as the state religion of the empire, and for building the original basilica dedicated to Christ's vicar. By these acts (and the fabled Donation of Constantine), the first Christian emperor established the Church's claim to terrestrial universality. It might be said, juridically speaking, that Constantine initiated the kingdom of God on earth. The intention from the outset was for an equestrian figure, in antiquity the imperial honorific portrait form par excellence, indeed the exclusive prerogative of the emperor. The intention must have been to create at St. Peter's a counterpart to the ancient equestrian statue of Marcus Aurelius that Michelangelo had erected at the secular center of the city

atop the Capitoline hill. Throughout the Middle Ages the famous sculpture had stood at the Lateran, mistakenly identified as Constantine. Ancient honorific equestrian portraits, apart from tombs, were almost by definition independent, free-standing monuments. Only during the Middle Ages did there develop what might be called a specifically architectural equestrian tradition in Italy, mostly in relief, and notably for placement on the facades of palaces (where they portrayed the noble owner) and churches (where they were often thought to represent Constantine).[87] By virtue of its design and location, the monument to Constantine comprises all these traditions. Alexander's and Bernini's new building scheme created a crucial juncture between the corridor from the north colonnade, the portico of the basilica extended by a vestibule, and a grandiose stairway built by Bernini, the Scala Regia, connecting with the Vatican palace. The location of the image here was not merely "strategic," to proffer an example to those passing between the church, the palace, and the city; the position at this topographical turning point also marked Constantine's historical role at the intersection between the public, the private, and the spiritual domains of Christianity.

The monument was equally unprecedented in the subject it represented. In the classical tradition, equestrian portraits depicted prototypical acts of imperial majesty, the emperor addressing his troops or spearing an enemy.[88] To portray a specific historical event was unheard of. Bernini's monument, by contrast, embodies the very turning point of Constantine's life, an instant when the emperor was himself subjected to a superior power. The origin of Constantine's devotion to Christianity was a famous vision of the Cross that inspired his great victory over his rival Maxentius and led him to adopt the new religion. In the Golden Legend, for the feast of the Invention of the Holy Cross, Jacobus da Voragine frankly, but with some embarrassment, gives two radically different accounts of the event. In one version, the vision occurs at night, on the eve of a crucial battle with barbarians on the bank of the Danube.

> At that time an innumerable horde of barbarians was massing on the bank of the Danube, making ready to cross the river, in order to subjugate the entire West. At these tidings, the Emperor Constantine marched forth with his army, and camped on the other bank of the Danube. But when the number of the barbarians continued to increase, and they began to make their way across the river, Constantine was filled with fear at the thought of the battle which he had to undertake. But in the night an angel awoke him, and told him to lift up his head. And Constantine saw in the heavens the image of a cross described in shining light; and above the image was written in letters of gold the legend: "In this sign shalt thou conquer!" Taking heart at the heavenly

171. Bernini, Cathedra Petri, St. Peter's, Rome

vision, he had a wooden cross made, and commended that it be carried in the van of his army; and then, falling upon the enemy, he cut them to pieces or put them to flight.

In the second version, for which Jacobus cites Constantine's biographer, Eusebius of Caesarea, the vision takes place on the day before the confrontation with Maxentius at the Milvian Bridge over the Tiber near Rome.

> The *Ecclesiastical History* [actually Eusebius's *Life of Constantine*] gives a different account of the victory of Constantine. It tells us that the battle took place near the Pontus Albinus, where Constantine encountered Maxentius, who was attempting to invade the Roman Empire. And when the care-laden emperor raised his eyes to Heaven to plead for succour, he saw in the eastern sky the gleaming sign of the cross, surrounded by angels who said to him: "Constantine, in this sign shalt thou conquer!" And as Constantine was wondering what this meant, Christ appeared to him during the night, with the same sign, and ordered him to have an image made of it, which would aid him in battle. The

emperor, now assured of victory, made the sign of the cross upon his forehead, and took a gold cross in his hand.... And Maxentius, when he was about to cross the river, forgot that he had caused the bridges to be undermined in order to draw Constantine to destruction; and he started to pass over a bridge which had been sapped, and was drowned in the river.[89]

Eusebius himself reports that the vision took place at noon and was repeated to Constantine in a dream that night, before the encounter with Maxentius:

> [Constantine] said that about noon, when the day was already beginning to decline, he saw with his own eyes the trophy of a cross of light in the heavens above the sun, and bearing the inscription, CONQUER BY THIS. At this sight he himself was struck with amazement, and his whole army also, which followed him on this expedition, and witnessed the miracle. He said, moreover, that he doubted within himself what the import of this apparition could be. And while he continued to ponder and reason on its meaning, night suddenly came on; then in his sleep the Christ of God appeared to him with the same sign which he had seen in the heavens, and commanded him to make a likeness of that sign which he had seen in the heavens, and to use it as a safeguard in all engagements with his enemies.[90]

The common denominator among these accounts, the sign of the Cross and the words that appeared with it, became the talismans of Constantine's victory and conversion. The sources, however, elicited two different ways of illustrating the vision. It might be depicted as a solitary event, experienced at night, with the emperor in bed. More frequently, the vision was depicted taking place in daylight, with the emperor peering at the luminous apparition in the sky and sometimes standing and haranguing his troops to carry the sign of the Cross, the first official, public declaration of the new faith (Fig. 180). Alternatively, Constantine might appear on horseback amid his army preparing to do battle in the first Christian military victory (Fig. 181). When mounted, his steed was portrayed in the walking gait proper to the imperial *adventus*, or triumphal entry. Another mode of representing the event developed in Byzantium, especially in psalter illustration, which was of great importance for Bernini: there he found the miracle isolated and distilled into a sort of icon. The vision (a disk inscribed with the Cross) and the military encounter were conflated and reduced to a single, composite action, with the victory conceived as a personal triumph of the emperor in combat – although the essential point of the story according to Eusebius was that, confronted by the Cross displayed by Constantine, Maxentius was defeated by his own guile, and no battle took place. The emperor was shown

172. Bernini, Cathedra Petri, detail. St. Peter's, Rome

charging forward on a rearing horse to dispatch the enemy with his spear, beneath the emblematic vision appearing in the sky (Fig. 182, where, significantly, the vision is represented as a shield). The motive for this deliberately ahistorical presentation was clearly its use in the Psalter, where it invoked the divine auspices for the military exploits of the Byzantine emperors, who considered themselves Constantine's successors. The subject illustrates a passage in Psalm 59:6–7, in which God's intervention is sought against the enemies of Israel: "Thou hast given a sign for those who fear thee, that they may flee from before the bow. Save me with thy right hand, and hear me" ("Dedisti metuentibus te significationem ut fugiant a facie arcus ut liberentur dilecti tui. Salvum fac dextera tua et exaudi me").[91] Because the church established under Constantine, who founded the Greek Orthodox capital, was universal, reference at St. Peter's and the Vatican to such an authentically Greek visual-

ization of the critical event implicitly suggested the essential unity of Eastern and Western Christianity. It is symptomatic of Bernini's thought, I believe, that even closer to his concept are certain related illustrations in the Greek psalters, not of the emperor but of military saints, notably Eustathius and Procopius, in which a vision is itself the subject: they are shown, alone and similarly mounted on charging horses, leaping up and gesturing toward heavenly apparitions. These visions were not related to battles, and the saints are represented without weapons and without adversaries (Fig. 183). The Byzantine formulations were readily available in a famous early Greek psalter in the Barberini collection at the Vatican.[92] Moreover, Bernini could find impeccable historical precedent for transposing this isolated type into sculpture in one of the most venerable and uncannily affective works of early Christian art, which formed part of the prehistory of the Byzantine Psalter miniatures of

173. Bernini, Cathedra Petri, Saints Ambrose and Athanasius. St. Peter's, Rome

Constantine. This is a leaf of an ivory diptych, the centerpiece of which is an armored imperial figure, mounted at the attack on a rearing horse, in the act of impaling with his lance an imaginary enemy below (Fig. 184).[93] Here, too, the group seems to thrust itself off the surface into the viewer's space. The artist manages to elide the distinction between front and side views, so that while the horseman is imbedded in the complex visual and thematic context provided by the "setting," he also takes a turn toward the spectator and his victory leaps out of the frame into the present. In Bernini's time the ivory was also part of the Barberini collection in Rome and was thought to represent Constantine himself, partly no doubt because the medallion image of Christ holding the Cross in the panel above suggested the emperor's vision. The subject matter would have been no less relevant to Bernini's enterprise than the virtuoso technique and subtle illusion. In fact, he seems to have had the Barberini plaque in mind, especially the movement of the horse, when he designed the unexecuted first version of the Constantine monument for Innocent X (Fig. 185).

Although the event was often depicted with the mounted Constantine in the field of battle or dispatching enemies, there is nothing in the literary accounts to suggest a violent response to the vision. Indeed, never before Bernini had the emperor been shown alone, in no other act than absorbing the apparition and mounted on a rearing horse which, unlike any of its ancestors, seems to be no less astounded by the miracle than he. In this respect, Bernini's invention may be understood in part as a conflation of Constantine's vision with the one equally portentous instance of precisely the same

phenomenon – that is, the conversion of Saint Paul, to which the Church devotes a feast in the liturgical calendar.[94] A non-Christian, in this case Jewish, equestrian military leader is suddenly confronted by a miraculous intervention from on high on behalf of the new faith. Through the power of his preaching and writing Paul established the spiritual hegemony of the Church, as Constantine was to establish its earthly dominion through his military power. Paul's vision also included a light in the sky and a verbal message, not written but spoken by the invisible Christ. The conversion of Saul of Tarsus was a violent event: he was toppled from his

174. Foundation medal Piazza S. Pietro, 1657. Biblioteca Vaticana, Rome

175. Commemorative medal of the Cathedra Petri, 1662. Biblioteca Vaticana, Rome

horse and relinquished his military life to become the apostle Paul, "a true warrior for Christ," in Augustine's words.[95] In the visual tradition of the conversion of Saint Paul, the man and animal might be shown alone, without accompanying figures. And, unlike the horse of the equestrian Constantine in the West, Paul's mount was often shown rearing up, as startled by the miracle as the rider. In one notable example, a medal of Pope Julius II, Paul is still on his rearing horse, reeling from the vision in the sky (Fig. 186).[96] In assimilating Constantine's vision of Christianity to that of Paul's conversion, Bernini created a concerted response of both rider and animal – man and nature, as it were – to the heavenly apparition.

In one of the most famous and important portrayals of Paul's conversion, that by Raphael in the tapestry series for the Sistine Chapel in the Vatican, Paul's reaction is particularly appropriate (Fig. 187). The open-armed gesture, suggestive of both surprise and receptivity, which Bernini had attributed to Saint Longinus, was understood as a reference to the Crucifixion, and was the authentic mode of prayer among the early Christians. Eusebius specifically ascribed this gesture to the full-length portraits of himself that Constantine erected at the entrances to his palaces:

> How deeply his soul was impressed by the power of divine faith may be understood from the circumstance that he directed his likeness to be stamped on the golden coins of the empire with the eyes uplifted as in the posture of prayer to God: and this money became current throughout the Roman world. His portrait also at full length was placed over the entrance gates of the palaces in some cities, the eyes upraised to heaven, and the hands outspread as if in prayer.[97]

Heinrich Valesius, who published what became the standard modern Latin translation of Eusebius in 1659, explained the history and symbolism of the gesture as follows:

> Whoever was the Translatour[*sic*] of this Book, he has rendered this place with little of attention, thus, *Et precantes forma manus sursum tollens, and lifting up his hands in the form of one praying;* whereas he ought to have rendered it, *manibus expansis, ut precantes solent, with expanded hands as persons praying are wont to do.* For the *Christians* were wont, when at prayers, to stretch forth their hands, that by this means they might represent the likeness of a Cross. Indeed, the *Christians* lifted up their hands, whilst they were praying. But this was not peculiar to the *Christians*, in this regard the Heathens did the same; as *Virgil* attests in these words,

> – *Et geminas tellens ad sidera palmas.*

> But, that was peculiar to the *Christians*, to expand their hands in the form of a Cross. *Tertullian*'s words, in

his *Book de Oratione* Chap. ii, are these: *Nos vero non attollimus tantum, Sed etiam expandimus, & dominica passione modulamur; We do not only lift up [our hands,] but do spread them also, and we put our selves into a form agreeable to Our Lord's passion.* He says the same in *his Apologetick*, chap. 30.[98]

The relationship between these two crucial divine interventions in the defense and dissemination of Christianity, one by the power of faith, the other by the power of empire, was not Bernini's invention. The comparison of Constantine to Paul was made explicitly by Rufinus of Aquileia, whose Latin translation of Eusebius's Greek was the source of all Western knowledge of this fundamental history of early Christianity. Rufinus's version, much criticized because of the many liberties it takes with the text, might better be understood as an interpretive commentary, and he made clear the sense in which he understood Constantine's vision by adding that Constantine's "heavenly invitation to faith" did not seem to him inferior to that of Paul, to whom heaven also spoke – except that "the invitation was no longer not to persecute, but to prosecute."[99] Conflation of the two events produced an image of immediate, unadulterated, and devastating awareness not inherent in either of its precedents. The reference to Saint Paul and the idea of conversion was explicit in the liturgy for May third, the feast of the Invention of the Cross: the first three lessons were taken from Paul's perorations on the Crucifixion in the epistles, and the fourth began the story of the True Cross with Constantine's vision and victory.[100] Constantine's rapturous expression and gesture epitomize a tradition, which included Bernini's *St. Longinus* in the crossing pier, specifically motivated by imitation of the Crucifixion and impassioned devotion to the Cross.

Allusion to the visionary conversion of Saint Paul was eloquent testimony to the history of divine intervention on behalf of the Church. However, the full import of Bernini's interpretation of Constantine's role cannot be comprehended without reference to a superficially quite different but profoundly related episode involving another pagan emperor – at least, as the story was interpreted by the one artist who above all others, as Bernini frequently acknowledged during his visit to Paris, struck him with admiration, even awe – Poussin.[101] Bernini's fundamental innovation of depicting Constantine's vision with rider and steed reacting together in response to the apparition on high is an explicit, undisguised "quotation" of the image of Titus, son of the emperor Vespasian and later also emperor, in Poussin's monumental *Destruction of Jerusalem*, which he painted for Cardinal Francesco Barberini in 1638 (Fig. 188).[102] As must have been intended from the outset, on 1 January 1639, the cardinal presented the picture as a diplomatic gift to the ambassador to the Holy See from the Hapsburg ruler

Ferdinand III, Constantine's successor as "Holy Roman Emperor." What Bernini admired in Poussin's art, apart from its sheer beauty and intelligence, was its narrative sagacity and power – *grande favelleggiatore* (great fabulator) was the phrase he repeated in response to Poussin. He certainly grasped the affective power of Poussin's majestic equestrian group, in the context of the heroic action performed on a stagelike piazza before a noble cityscape that is in itself a deliberate evocation of the tragic theater set, evolved since the early sixteenth century from Vitruvius's famous account of ancient scenography.[103] However, it is essential to understand, as Bernini certainly did, that Poussin's theme, and Titus's role in particular, were in themselves extraordinary, and charged with potent, immediate significance.

Poussin generally and in many details follows the primary description by the Jewish historian Flavius Josephus, who was a member of Titus's entourage, of the terrible mayhem wrought by the Roman army that fateful day in A.D. 70.[104] Indeed, Poussin seems to have depicted a specific moment: the city is in ruins and burning, but the Temple is still intact, except for the fire that has erupted in the inner sanctum sanctorum, as the looters make off with the precious ritual vessels and furnish-

176. Bernini, *Constantine the Great*. St. Peter's, Rome

ings. All this Josephus describes, while also emphasizing that Titus himself was opposed to the destruction of such a sacred and magnificent structure, and even tried, in vain, to restrain his impetuous followers. Poussin had illustrated this very theme in an earlier picture of the same subject, also painted for Francesco Barberini and presented to the representative of Louis XIII of France: Titus, on a walking horse, gestures toward his men to desist, while looking heavenward in an anguished appeal for clemency (Fig. 189).[105] In the second version, Titus and his rearing horse are shown as if awestruck by a sudden message from on high. Titus now acts as intercessor, with one hand lifted toward the vision he sees in the sky, the other lowered toward the carnage on the ground below. In this salient display of sudden awareness and compassion in the midst of fury, Poussin seems to reconcile Josephus's account with a diametrically opposed interpretation developed by the first writers to treat world history in Christian terms. In this view, the destruction of the Temple became a divinely providential act of vengeance upon the Jews – which Titus favored – for their martyrdom of Christ.[106] Clearly, it is this supernal, proleptic intimation of the Christological import of the event and his own role in it that is being revealed to Titus in Poussin's dramatization. In effect, Titus was inspired by Divine Wisdom, whose intervention on behalf of the Church was the very leitmotif of Urban's reign.

Poussin made this Christological meaning explicit through Titus's pose, calling on the Early Christian tradition in which the open-armed gesture patently evokes the Crucifixion.[107] Sulpicius Severus reports that Titus favored the destruction in order to eradicate both the Jews and their Christian heirs, but calls the destruction of the Temple and subsequent dispersion of the Jews an act of God.

> Titus is said, after calling a council, to have first deliberated whether he should destroy the temple, a structure of such extraordinary work. For it seemed good to some that a sacred edifice, distinguished above all human achievement, ought not to be destroyed, inasmuch as, if preserved, it would furnish an evidence of Roman moderation, but if destroyed, would serve for a perpetual proof of Roman cruelty. But on the opposite side, others and Titus himself thought that the temple ought especially to be overthrown, in order that the religion of the Jews and of the Christians might more thoroughly be subverted; for that these religions, although contrary to each other, had nevertheless proceeded from the same authors; that the Christians had sprung up from among the Jews; and that, if the root were extirpated, the offshoot would speedily perish. Thus, according to the divine will, the minds all being inflamed, the temple was destroyed....[108]

177. Bernini, *Constantine the Great*. St. Peter's, Rome

Two other texts must also have inspired Poussin's visualization of the tradition. Orosius, perhaps the most important early Christianizer of ancient historical texts, relates the destruction of the Temple to Titus's triumph in Rome (Poussin also alludes to the exhibition of the Temple spoils in the triumphal entry depicted on the Arch of Titus), to the decree of God, and to the avenging of Christ's blood and Passion:

> After the capture and overthrow of Jerusalem . . . and after the total destruction of the Jewish nation, Titus, who had been appointed by the decree of God to avenge the blood of the Lord Jesus Christ, celebrated with his

father Vespasian his victory by a triumph and closed the temple of Janus. . . . It was indeed right that the same honor should be paid to the avenging of the Lord's Passion as had been bestowed upon His Nativity.[109]

Perhaps the most explicit and lapidary formulation was that of Dante who, in the voice of his fellow poet Statius, speaks of the sudden, earthquake response to Divine Justice when it releases from Purgatory those pure spirits who lived "not yet with faith." Statius calls to witness "the good Titus," "In the time when the good Titus, with the help of the Highest King, avenged the wounds whence issued the blood sold by Judas, I was famous enough . . . but not yet with faith."[110]

The relevance of Poussin's painting to Francesco Barberini's mission to the Hapsburg emperor was above all in reference to the struggle with the Protestants, often likened to the Jews in their refusal to recognize the Church. Poussin was surely as familiar as Bernini with the equestrian Constantine tradition, and one might well suppose that Poussin's Christological interpretation of the destruction of the Jewish Temple already involved a proleptic reference to the revelation accorded to Titus's imperial successor, who adopted Christianity and protected the Church. The pose of Poussin's second Titus suggests that the "good" pagan is inspired by the same vision of Divine Wisdom acting through Christian charity and justice that informed the tomb of Urban VIII. For Bernini, the tradition was equally relevant at St. Peter's,

in a program specifically addressed to the same "political" problems. Titus and Constantine were links in a chain forged by Divine Wisdom that bound these early heroes to the current rulers of Europe and ordained the reigns of popes.

From a formal point of view, it might be said that Bernini abstracted Poussin's heroic group from its narrative context and infused it into the tradition of the independent equestrian monument. In this sense, Bernini alluded to a flourishing contemporary honorific mode: the equestrian monument with the rider mounted on a rearing horse, mostly cast in bronze, which in the course of the seventeenth century had become a veritable icon of sovereign display, both political and artistic (Fig. 190). The ruler was portrayed as a triumphant hero demonstrating his military prowess by defeating an enemy, shown prostrate beneath the animal's hooves; or

178. Bernini, *Constantine the Great* and the Scala Regia. St. Peter's, Rome

179. Bernini, Constantine's vision and the view beyond. St. Peter's, Rome

demonstrating his innate power of leadership through his consummate skill in the noble art of horsemanship, effortlessly commanding the huge beast, against its nature, to execute a veritable aerial levitation – the so-called *levade* of the high equestrian school then enormously in vogue.[111] Bernini's *Constantine* is also an emblem of victory, but of an entirely different, spiritual order – neither a military victory nor a triumph of the will, but a moral conquest of the self, a revolution of the soul in response to the revelatory power of divine grace. This emphasis on the spiritual nature of Constantine's historical role is completed by the events illustrated in the stucco medallions in the vault above – not the defeat of Maxentius as

in so many other narratives, but the emperor's baptism and his construction of St. Peter's.

In the traditional equestrian monument the sculptor's victory, his *virtù*, consisted in immortalizing the hero's victory over superior physical strength in the permanent but inherently amorphous form of bronze. In the case of Bernini's Constantine, where there are no reins or stirrups, and the hero's tour de force was his response to an act of divine will, the artist's achievement lay in "dominating" the inherently rigid material of stone. In fact, an important aspect of the significance of the work lies in its technical qualities, first among these being its colossal scale. In his biography of his father, Domenico

180. Giulio Romano, *Vision of Constantine*. Sala di Costantino, Vatican Palace, Rome

181. *Vision of Constantine*. Galleria delle Carte Geografiche, Vatican Palace, Rome

Bernini emphasized that the sheer size of the block, and by implication the skill required to carve such a large work from a single stone, were specifically intended to vie with antiquity itself: "a colossus . . . truly great for the subject it represents, for the place it was to be located, and for the material in which it was to be carved: in a thirty-wagon mass of stone (to use the proper terms) the likes of which had rarely been seen in Rome even in ancient times."[112] This agonistic attitude toward the past was not simply a matter of personal satisfaction or aggrandizement but carried specific meaning related to the

basic theme of the monument: Bernini's technical victory over the stone was an analogue of Constantine's moral victory over paganism. Domenico Bernini intimated this very point when he attributed the true greatness of the colossus to three factors: its subject, its location, and its material.[113] The significance of the technique in these terms was expressed directly and profoundly by Bernini's great friend and admirer Giovanni Paolo Oliva, who was general of the Jesuit order and apostolic preacher. In a sermon he delivered before the pope in the Vatican palace as the Constantine was reaching completion, Oliva used

182. *Vision of Constantine*, MS Barberini Gr. 372, fol. 75ʳ. Biblioteca Vaticana, Rome

183. *Vision of St. Procopius*, MS Barberini Gr. 372, fol. 85ᵛ. Biblioteca Vaticana, Rome

the feat of carving it as a metaphor for moral action in the achievement of a noble end.[114] The technique is also remarkable in that the work occupies a sort of intermediate realm of existence between the traditional domains of relief and freestanding sculpture. The equestrian is indeed carved from a single block of marble, which is, however, attached to the back wall of the niche. This device made it possible to create the rearing horse without artificial support, such as a defeated enemy underfoot, that would otherwise be required. Bernini was thus able to isolate the vision as a pure, unadulterated moment of revelation. At the same time, being carved virtually in the round, the sculpture appears completely independent, to all appearances a freestanding group. The figures seem to inhabit the spectator's space, and the horse's rear hooves actually do rest on the pedestal. A key to this effect is Bernini's virtuoso capacity, nurtured since his childhood training in his father's studio, for carving deeply undercut, perforated, and cantilevered forms.

The polyvalence of the subject and location of the Constantine monument has a counterpart in the design of the work. Bernini must have been well aware of the traditions in which equestrian sculptures were placed before palaces and churches, often in niches, parallel or perpendicular to the wall (Figs. 191, 192).[115] In its new location the Constantine might well have been intended to "reclaim" this hegemonic tradition for the papacy. The design certainly incorporates the seemingly incompatible alternatives of orientation, responding to the principal approaches in the Scala Regia. The horse, rider, and pedestal project sufficiently from the flat niche so

that from the corridor in front the sculpture suggests the freestanding equestrian ruler portraits that confront the visitor, sometimes quite aggressively. The "regal" entrance behind Constantine is marked by the huge coat of arms of the pope carried by trumpeting angels placed on the arched opening to the Scala Regia, whose triumphal

184. "Triumph of Constantine," Barberini plaque, ivory. Musée du Louvre, Paris

185. Bernini, study for the first version of the *Vision of Constantine*, drawing. Academia de San Fernando, Madrid

186. Conversion of St. Paul, medal of Julius II (after Hill 1930, pl. 139, no. 867)

fastigium design repeats the Serlian cross section of the colonnades. From the portico of the church the work appears as an equestrian monument placed laterally and framed by an arch, with the figures twisted outward by the force of the apparition above. Bernini fused the lateral and the frontal types in the way the figures are carved; at the rear, the animal's body, in high relief, is parallel to the spectator, while toward the front both horse and rider become fully three-dimensional, so the space into which they leap is to the side and forward. Some precedence for this sculptural ingenuity may be found in

a rare if not unique instance of an equestrian, as a deeply carved relief, shown frontally in a niche, at a corner of Arnolfo di Cambio's fourteenth-century altar tabernacle in S. Cecilia in Rome, which Bernini certainly knew (Fig. 193).[116] An analogous turn from the relief plane into space created the powerful thrust of the horseman of the Barberini plaque and its prototypes on Roman hunting and battle sarcophagi (Figs. 184, 194). Psychologically, this "bent" movement also helps to create the spatial elision and explosive power of Constantine and his horse, whose forward movement Bernini augmented by skewing the perspective of the coffered arch and the sweeping flow of the billowing drapery behind.[117]

When the huge marble block was acquired the sculpture would have more than filled the niche in the basilica

187. Raphael, *Conversion of St. Paul*, tapestry. Musei Vaticani, Rome

188. Poussin, *Destruction of Jerusalem*, 1638–9. Kunsthistorisches Museum, Vienna

189. Poussin, *Destruction of Jerusalem*, 1625–6. The Jewish Museum, Jerusalem

for which it was originally intended (Fig. 185).[118] The additional space available in the new location made it necessary – "possible" would be a more appropriate word, given Bernini's way of surmounting the challenges that confronted him – to provide the work with a context that would impart new meaning and expressive power. The horse and rider are now set up on a pedestal, so that the sculpture becomes a proper equestrian monument (Fig. 177). The monument is set within a framing arch

and given a background suggesting that the space continues behind to include accouterments in temporary materials as ephemeral as the fleeting moment represented by the sculpture itself: a circular baldachin over which is flung a huge, billowing cloth that sweeps forward behind the figures and loops down over the pedestal. At first glance, the setting suggests the military encampment where the emperor experienced the vision, including the commander's tent (Fig. 180), or the outdoor

190. Pietro Tacca, equestrian monument of Philip V, 1636–40. Plaza de Oriente, Madrid

draped audience chamber from which he made his *ad locutio* to inspire his troops before the battle (Fig. 195). In fact, these references are purely symbolic. The canopy, which recalls the baldachin suspended over the pope in Giulio Romano's *Donation of Constantine* (Fig. 126), has no visible means of support, but hovers above like the heavenly *umbralacum* of Isaiah cited in the inscription of the colonnade. The drapery is here an analogue of the *parapetasma*, or cloth of honor, against which in ancient funerary monuments portraits of the deceased were placed to signify apotheosis. In Bernini's memorial of Suor Maria Raggi in S. Maria sopra Minerva, the drapery became a kind of "magic carpet," suspended from her vision of the Cross above, on which the image is transported heavenward by two flying putti (Fig. 196).[119] The drapery behind Bernini's Constantine seems to respond to the blaring trumpets of the angels above who carry the papal coat of arms, echoing the description in the Acts of the Apostles (2:2) of the Descent of the Holy Spirit, when "suddenly there came a sound from heaven as of a mighty rushing wind," initiating the universal dominion of Christianity through the gift of tongues – the *ad locutio* – to the apostles.

It could well be argued that light is the true protagonist of the vision of Constantine as portrayed by Bernini. Taking advantage of the slope of the Vatican hill, he introduced a large window between the vault of the corridor from the colonnade and that of the landing. Light passes through the opening to illuminate the space, duplicating the radiance of the divine apparition described in the sources. A great effulgence descends mysteriously from the upper right, forming with the body of the horse one diagonal axis of a huge chiastic composition, of which the crossing diagonal is formed by the flowing

191. Entrance portal at Ecouen with equestrian statue of Anne de Montmorency, engraving by Jacques Androuet Ducerceau, 1579 (after Prinz and Kecks 1994, fig. 333)

drapery of the tent and the body of Constantine himself. The viewer is propelled forward in the direction of the light source by the displaced vanishing point of the perspectivized arch, and by the massive, billowing sweep of drapery. The view from the Scala Regia back toward the

192. Andrea Rivalta, equestrian monument of Vittorio Amadeo I of Savoy. Palazzo Reale, Turin

193. Arnolfo di Cambio, equestrian saint, ciborium of high altar, detail. S. Cecilia, Rome

a sculptured, floating banderole before which the cross is suspended. The text thus serves not only as an immaterial vision, but also as a sort of label, a physically substantive, heaven-sent message for the viewer as well as for Constantine, defining the meaning of the event and the monument as a work of art. Bernini had developed many of these devices long before. In his depiction of a vision of Saint Francesca Romana, a halo of light above the figures serves its historical function as a heavenly apparition (Fig. 197); and in his portrayal of the ecstasy of Saint Teresa light from a window above radiates down upon a sculptured relief that appears suspended in midair and is virtually carved in the round (Fig. 164). In both works real light had become an integral, active agent of the subject represented, which, in the case of Saint Teresa, is also "explained" by a message inscribed on a banderole fluttering at the apex of the entrance to the chapel (Fig. 198).[120] To re-present the "image" described by Eusebius, Bernini seems to have melded the cross-borne drapery inscription of the Maria Raggi monument with the heavenly inscribed banderole of the Teresa chapel. In the space of the Constantine memorial the spectator is not simply a witness but feels himself included in the event. The ultimate nature of this pervasive, mysterious illumination comes into focus when one faces in the opposite direction: from the top of the stairs leading up to the Sala Regia at the end of the long perspective of diminishing and receding ceremonial architecture that continues the colonnade, the light radiates exactly as it does in a splendid altar tabernacle in Bologna, which Bernini certainly knew, whose one-point perspective of the same design epitomized the Sacrament (Fig. 199).[121]

Here, as in no previous work, at the threshold of St. Peter's and the Vatican, real space and the space of the

entrance corridor portrays the vision itself: the window provides the bright light, while the cross and the words appear immediately below, conjoined in what might be called a literally miraculous way. Instead of appearing simply as a text in the sky, the motto is inscribed on

194. Roman hunting sarcophagus, detail. Palazzo Mattei, Rome

195. Giacinto Gimignani, *The Vision of Constantine*. Baptistery, S. Giovanni in Laterano, Rome

event re-created are one and the same. The crucial event of church history is isolated and distilled into a single, supreme moment of revelation. Constantine is at once the protagonist of a distant historical event and the subject of a commemoration in the present. And the viewer is inextricably conjoined with the architecture and the sculpture as participant in the visionary act taking place, then-now, there-here. The medium through which and in which this existential fusion transpires is the flood of light that accompanies the miraculous sign and message from on high. Having been embraced and urged forward by the arms of the colonnades, we enter a place charged with physical energy and optical radiance by a divine illumination revealed ultimately in the Sacrament, the ultimate goal of both patron and artist "at the end of the tunnel." Heaven and earth meet at the point where the spiritual pilgrim enters the sacred precinct.

THE TOMB OF ALEXANDER VII (1671–78) (Figs. 200, 201, 202)

On 8 April, the day following his election to the papal throne, it was reported that Alexander VII had given an urgent order to Bernini to have made a lead casket in which he would be buried; the coffin was to be brought to his room as a memento mori, a reminder of death. On 10 April the pope was said to have ordered a skull of marble, so that he might continuously meditate on the brevity of life.[122] Alexander's profound and humble devotion to the Sacrament was displayed in his unprecedented conduct of the Corpus Domini procession on 27 May. And his order to Bernini to

prepare a design for his tomb was reported on 28 August. All these actions not only reflected important aspects of the pope's character, they also sounded the keynote of his reign. Bernini's response to the personal impulse of what might be called Alexander's eschatological modus vivendi emerged ultimately in the tomb that was executed long after the pope's death. The situation chosen might seem to have been eminently inhospitable:

196. Bernini, Monument to Suor Maria Raggi. S. Maria sopra Minerva, Rome

197. Bernini, *S. Francesca Romana*. S. Francesca Romana, Rome

198. Bernini, Chapel of St. Teresa. S. Maria della Vittoria, Rome

199. Sacrament tabernacle. S. Paolo Maggiore, Bologna

200. Bernini, Tomb of Alexander VII. St. Peter's, Rome

a niche in the outer wall of the south aisle of the choir, containing the opening of a narrow service passageway for the basilica. The composition of the tomb takes up the theme of papal continuity in the nave by epitomizing the major commemorative types developed for Alexander's predecessors. The pyramidal form with the raised effigy flanked by pairs of allegories echoes the apsidal monuments of Paul III and Urban VIII, as does the inclusion of a skeletal allegory of death. As in the Urban VIII tomb, the allegories "participate," actively or passively, so as to animate rather than merely symbolize the concepts they represent. Harking back in part to the original form of the Paul III monument, the design suggests a freestanding tomb accompanied by four allegories of virtues, in this case Charity, Justice, Prudence, Truth. Finally, the deceased is shown kneeling in an attitude of prayer, fol-

lowing the late sixteenth-century tombs of Pius V and Sixtus V in S. Maria Maggiore, where the popes kneel in perpetual adoration toward the Eucharistic tabernacle at the altar in the center of their funerary chapel (see Fig. 120).

By virtue of synthesizing these elements of continuity, the work is kind of summa of papal tomb types: a "freestanding" monument with four "activated" allegories, surmounted by a kneeling effigy.[123] However, Alexander's tomb also comprises variations and innovations such that it becomes, as never before, a vehicle of concerted expressive power: the choice and treatment of the allegories, the great shroud enveloping the door at the rear of the niche, the figure of death emerging from beneath it wielding his hourglass, the pope's act of humble, intense devotion. The tomb is imbued with a sense of

201. Bernini, Tomb of Alexander VII, Allegory of Truth. St. Peter's, Rome

urgency that transforms the sepulchral monument from a record of passive commemoration to an expression of active protagonism. We have seen in considering the tombs of Paul III and Urban VIII that Charity, Justice, and Prudence were normal, and Charity and Justice together especially important, themes of papal ideology. Truth, however, was without precedent in this context. A clue to the significance of the choice of allegories may be traced to the very beginning of Alexander's papacy. In keeping with tradition, the pope had celebrated his election in 1655 by issuing a medal intended to define the guiding principle of his reign. The reverse (Fig. 203) shows Justice and Peace embracing one another, while the inscription – IVSTITIA ET PAX / OSCVLATAE SUNT – quotes a phrase from a famous passage in Psalms 85: 10–11, attesting faith in God's goodness: "Mercy and truth are met together; righteousness and peace have kissed each other. Truth shall spring out of the earth; and righteousness shall look down from heaven" ("Misericordia et veritas obviaverunt sibi, iustitia et pax osculatae sunt. Veritas de terra orta est, et iustitia de caelo prospexit"). Alexander's interest in the passage is subsequently recorded in an entry in his diary dated 26 January 1660, noting a visit from Bernini, in which it is cited (substituting, significantly if inadvertently, "modesty" for "mercy"), evidently with the tomb program in mind. Charity and Justice are proper virtues, the former theological, the latter moral, whereas Peace and Truth are rather the fruits of virtue, and Truth alone was never part of the traditional repertory of funerary allegory. The theme of Charity and Justice was retained on Alexander's tomb, while another cardinal virtue, Prudence, was substituted for

202. Bernini, Tomb of Alexander VII, escutcheon. St. Peter's, Rome

203. Justice and Peace, inaugural medal of Alexander VII, 1655 (after Buonanni 1699, 2:641, no. VI)

Peace. But Truth was also retained, and given pride of place with Charity in the forefront of the monument. This anomalous juxtaposition is a key to understanding the work. (Note: the draperies covering the body of Truth and the bosom of Charity are later additions.)

The unexampled pairing of the greatest of the theological virtues, Charity, with what Bernini in his testament called the most beautiful virtue, Truth, is based on a particular interpretation of the imagery of the virtues in the Eighty-fifth Psalm.[124] The passage entails two distinct aspects of truth: one (Ps. 85:10) focused on the quality itself as one of the special attributes of man before the Fall, which came to be known in allegorical tradition as the Four Daughters of God; the other aspect (Ps. 85:11) concerns truth alone as a cognitive, quasi-eschatological ideal, whose ultimate triumph the psalm declares as the promise of redemption that will emerge over the course of time.[125] Bernini had illustrated Truth before, in both aspects. She is one of the Four Daughters of God in a catafalque he designed for the death of Pope Paul V, and in a funerary chapel in S. Isidoro, where the four allegories – conjoined in pairs by drapery swathes that also anticipate the tomb – were assigned to two deceased couples of the family (Fig. 204). (Note: In the S. Isidoro tomb the figures of Mercy pressing milk from her breast, at the left, and Truth emerging from the shroud, at the right, were originally nude.) The promissory aspect of Truth was the subject of an independent monumental marble group, intended by the artist as a personal vindication of the calumnies of his enemies, showing Father Time revealing Truth and raising her from the earth to heaven by lifting her drapery (Fig. 205). On the Alexander tomb, Bernini combines both aspects of Truth, as a quality inherent from the beginning in God's plan for the salvation of mankind, and as a witness to salvation.

As in the tomb of Urban VIII, the attributes are not those of the pope individually, whose fleeting occupancy of the office is now evinced by the huge pair of wings that carry the coat of arms at the apex of the niche (Fig. 202), but of the papacy and the Church as institutions. Inspired by the pope's profound devotion, Charity rushes to offer up the fulsome charge reclining at her breast, while Truth, in a demure, expectant attitude, grasps the radiant sun, her exclusive charge, possessively to her bosom (Fig. 201). The emblematic nature of the allegory of Charity as a prelapsarian virtue is evident from the fact that, contrary to all tradition, here she has only one offspring. The single recipient of Charity's nurture may refer to the idea of a single, universal hospice for the poor in Rome to be housed in the papal palace of the Lateran, first bruited under Alexander VII and ultimately carried out by his successors, with Bernini's involvement. The sleeping infant's pose almost exactly duplicates that of his counterpart on the tomb of Urban VIII, again recalling the dead Christ held by his mother in depictions of the Pietà.[126] But here the isolated, unselfconscious, sleeping soul is also a kind of synecdoche for humanity, and can only refer to Adam in his original state of innocence. The original, unique, and quintessential act of charity

204. Bernini, tomb of Beatrix and Roderigo Lopez de Silva. (N.B.: The figures of Mercy pressing milk from her breast (*left*) and Truth emerging from the shroud (*right*) were originally nude.) S. Isidoro, Rome

was that of God in offering the sacrifice of his only son, the New Adam, in redemption for the sins of the Old Adam. The complementary, suprapersonal significance of Truth is apparent from the "geography" of the sphere of earth on which Truth's left foot rests: Italy with Rome at the center faces the spectator, while England, the unredeemed province of the Protestant heresy, remains downtrodden and benighted.[127] The unprecedented combination and prominence of Charity and Truth, and the high drama they enact, serve a coherent purpose: together they express the global reach of the Church's promise of redemption to those who follow the pope's example; perdition to those who do not.

The Eighty-fifth Psalm had a particularly important role in the liturgy, in the devotions that celebrate both the Birth of Christ and the special commemorations of All Souls (2 November) on behalf of the individual, all the faithful, and the pope. In the latter case, the recitation ends, significantly, with the refrain, *requiem eternam*, eternal rest.[128] The relevance of the psalm in those contexts is related to the most famous and influential of all interpretations of lines 10–11, that of the great Cistercian mystic Saint Bernard of Clairvaux, whose reading was determinant for the Four Daughters of God as a moral allegory. As interpreted by Bernard, the passage in Psalm 85 had long been understood as announcing the promise of salvation to those who died a "good death" in keeping with the teachings of the Church. And whether directly or indirectly, this reading determined the conceptual framework of the tomb. Bernard takes the passage as the theme of his sermon on the Feast of the Annunciation: "That glory may dwell in our land, Mercy and truth. . . . " The passage becomes a sort of allegorical mystery play celebrating the incarnation. The virtues, originally Adam's handmaidens, after the Fall become disputants over his fate, to be reconciled only by Christ's birth and sacrifice. The virtues represent the glory that inhabits the earth with the truth of Christ's salvation of those who love him. What makes Bernard's explication important here is that he relates this theme specifically to the redemptive power of truth to overcome death itself, and the terms in which he does so make a perfect commentary on the vision of Alexander's tomb.

The one [Truth] says: "I am undone if Adam does not die"; the other [Mercy]: "I am undone unless he obtains mercy. Therefore, let him die a blissful death and each will have her desire." . . . "But how shall this be done?" (Luke 1: 34) they asked. "Death is most cruel and bitter, death is terrible: its very name is enough to inspire one with horror. How then can there be such a thing as a blissful death?" To which the Judge replied: "It is indeed true that 'the death of the wicked is very evil' (Psalm 33: 22), but 'the death of the saints' can become 'precious in the sight of the Lord' (Psalm 115: 6). Will

205. Bernini, *Truth*, 1646–52. Galleria Borghese, Rome

death not appear precious if it become the portal of life, the gate of glory?"[129]

Bernard's reference to the portal of death that becomes the portal of life must have made the niche that contained a door at St. Peter's seem providential to Bernini: it coincided with what he considered to be the chief virtue of the architect, not to make beautiful and commodious buildings, but to make such use of a defect that if it did not exist one would have to create it.[130] The door to the underworld was a motif virtually endemic in Western funerary art: Roman sarcophagi often included scenes of Hermes Psychopompos, with a winged helmet and carrying his caduceus, exiting through the half-open door to the underworld, or leading by the hand a figure of the deceased from behind and beneath a curtain within (Figs. 206, 207).[131] Hermes in this case is the messenger who announces mortality, as does Bernini's skeletal personification of death, whose great shoulder wings and hourglass replace Hermes's winged helmet and caduceus. Bernini melded this classical motif of Hermes passing through the door to the underworld, with the representation on the tomb of Érard de la Marck of the skeleton emerging

206. Roman sarcophagus, detail. Museo Archeologico, Florence

from the coffin with an hourglass (Fig. 141), portrayed on the tomb of Urban VIII as the recording winged Angel of Death. Through this merging of motifs, Alexander's tomb becomes a literal enactment of Death's passage beneath the veil dividing this world from the next.

Drapery had a dual history in a mortuary context. In funeral ceremonies, which in the case of important personages might take place before the high altar of the church, the coffin of the deceased was often covered with a shroud expressive of respect and mourning.[132] Drapery also served as a cloth of honor on which an image of the deceased was carried aloft in a "miraculous" act of apotheosis (see Fig. 196).[133] The drapery curtain also played an important role in the seventeenth-century theater, where Bernini was an impassioned and innovative participant: it formed the transitory boundary between the domains of reality and the imagination.[134] The stage curtain did not at that period open and close in two parts, but rather was a single cloth that fell at the beginning and rose at the end of the performance. Bernini was acutely aware of the dramatic function, and indeed the metaphysical significance, of the curtain, as the plot of his comedy of Two Theaters amply demonstrates. When the curtain fell, the audience was confronted with a fictive realm of an altogether unexpected nature, at once nontheatrical and hypertheatrical: a duplicate audience in a duplicate theater, watching the beginning of a duplicate performance. For Bernini, evidently, the curtain did not reveal a one-way but a two-way opening, like the looking glass of Alice in Wonderland; he used a great swath of drapery in exactly

207. Hermes leading deceased from Hades, Roman sarcophagus, detail. Museo Civico, Velletri

208. Bernini, Sala Ducale, 1656–7. Vatican Palace, Rome

this way to frame the passage between two important ceremonial rooms in the Vatican palace, at the behest of Alexander at the very time he was planning the tomb (Fig. 208).

Bernini's conception of Alexander VII's tomb as a dramatic demonstration of the power of faith to overcome death recalls the de la Marck tomb in another sense. Here, on an architectural platform with niches containing figures of the theological and cardinal virtues, Érard kneels in prayer before his own sarcophagus, as if in response to the skeletal figure of Death who emerges from the opposite end, brandishing an hourglass in one hand and beckoning with the other. By contrast, Alexander takes no notice of Death, but turns his head toward the high altar, where Bernini had built the Eucharist into the very fabric of the design. It might be said that the Corpus Domini procession, at which Alexander provided an example of humble devotion by kneeling motionless and constantly in prayer before the Host, comes full circle at his tomb, where also the allegories seem to illustrate the exhortation to love in spirit and in truth inscribed on the pope's anniversary medal: "Prodicamus et adoremus in spiritu et veritate" (Fig. 170).

In sum, the strife between Mercy and Truth over the sin of Adam was resolved only by the truth of Christ's supreme act of charity. Bernard's explication provided the four main constituents of the tomb's message: the allegories from the Eighty-fifth Psalm, the theme of death, the door of death, and the sacramental sacrifice of Christ, with Alexander VII portrayed in the act of Eucharistic devotion. Alexander's prayerful attitude here was the culmination and perpetual repetition of his innovation in the Corpus Domini procession.[135] The tomb thus complemented the main theme of the program for the basilica, including the colonnades and the Cathedra, which became a monumental equivalent to the *splendore* of the Eucharistic monstrance the pope adored during the ritual. Visually, the monument is a "decompression" of that of Paul III, eliding the transition from a relief to a freestanding form – exactly what Bernini achieved in the Cathedra Petri. This special kind of illusionism, "optical refinement" might be a better term, also underlies the image of St. Peter's square, in which the arms reach forth from the church to envelop the spectator. Considered in this way, the illusion of the tomb also involves the spectator, now in a "living" memento mori that includes the

209. Ponte Sant'Angelo and Castel Sant'Angelo, Rome

menacing skeleton and the "door of death." The monument seems to emerge from the recess of the niche as Death seems to escape from the underworld. The pope, the door, and the skeleton confront the spectator, toward whom Death gestures just as menacingly as toward the pope. Comprising the door within the shroud effectively penetrates the invisible separation between fiction and reality.[136] Just as the colonnade in front of the church reaches outward to embrace the worshiper, so the tomb, with the example of Alexander VII, guarantees in all its amplitude the mercy and truth of faith.

PASSAGE TO THE HOLY CITY

THE PONTE SANT'ANGELO AND CASTEL SANT'ANGELO (1667–71)

PREHISTORY

Saint Michael and the City
Bernini's career at St. Peter's was a lifelong effort to convert the church and the Vatican into a vision of the Heavenly Jerusalem to which every believer aspires. The final work of this celestial urbanism focused on the bridge that led across the Tiber from the center of Rome to the Holy

City. The project consisted of clearing and reorganizing the areas at either end of the bridge, which was lengthened and refurbished with ten statues, five on either side, representing angels carrying the instruments of the Passion; the statues rest on pedestals placed at regular intervals in open, grilled balustrades that originally extended some distance on both sides along the river banks (see Fig. 235). Although evidently planned earlier, the work was begun soon after the election of Clement IX (June 1667) and completed in 1671 under Clement X.[137]

The Pons Aelius had been built in the second century A.D. by the emperor Hadrian, Publius Aelius Hadrianus, to give access from the city to the immense tomb that commemorated his power and that of the world domain he had ruled. In the course of the Middle Ages the area across the Tiber became the Holy City centered on the tomb of the apostles, the basilica of St. Peter's, and the Vatican, to which Hadrian's bridge and tomb became the monumental entranceway (Fig. 209). As the hegemony of the papacy was established, and challenged from many quarters, Hadrian's monuments had also taken on the aspect and function of a fortified bastion behind a moat crossed by a guarded bridge.

The transformation is implicit in the origin and meaning of the name applied to the bridge and the tomb in the Middle Ages, Ponte and Castel Sant'Angelo (Figs. 210, 211, 212, 213, 214, 215). This Christian reconceptualization of the site drew upon two distinct but convergent traditions involving the dual role of the Archangel Michael as patron saint of the city of Rome and Defender of the Church. The most obvious, literally, is the tradition that virtually identified Michael with Rome, celebrated by the towering figure of the saint that had replaced the bronze image of the emperor Hadrian atop his mausoleum after it was converted into the stronghold of the papacy. This substitution of angelic for imperial military rule was accomplished by a famous salvific apparition of the archangel to Pope Gregory the Great in 590. The story is told twice in the *Golden Legend*. On the feast of Saint Gregory, 12 March:

> The plague continued to rage, and the pope ordained that on Easter Day a procession should march around the city, bearing the picture of the Blessed Virgin which is in the possession of the church of Saint Mary Major. This picture, according to the common opinion, was painted by Saint Luke, who was as skilled in the art of painting as he was in medicine. And all at once the sacred image cleansed the air of infection, as if the pestilence could not withstand its presence; wherever it passed, the air became pure and refreshing. And it

211. Antonio Raggi, Angel with the Column. Ponte Sant'Angelo, Rome

210. Girolamo Lucenti, Angel with the Nails, detail. Ponte Sant'Angelo, Rome

is told that the voices of angels were heard around the picture, singing:

> *Regina coeli laetare, alleluja,*
> *quia quem meruisti portare, alleluja,*
> *resurrexit sicut dixit, alleluja!*

which means: "Queen of Heaven, rejoice, alleluia! For He Whom thou wert worthy to bear, alleluia! hath risen as He said, alleluia!" To this Saint Gregory promptly responded: "Ora pro nobis Deum rogamus, alleluja." – "Pray for us, we beg, alleluia!" Then, above the fortress of [Pope] Crescentius, he saw a mighty angel wiping a bloody sword and putting it back into its sheath. From this he understood that the plague was at an end, as indeed it was. And thenceforth this fortress was called the Fortress of the Holy Angel.

And on the feast of Saint Michael, 29 September:

> When Gregory had instituted the Greater Litany, and was praying devoutly that the people of Rome might be delivered of the plague, he saw an angel of the Lord standing upon the castle which was once called the

212. Bernini, Angel with the Crown of Thorns. Ponte Sant'Angelo, Rome

Tomb of Hadrian; the angel was drying a bloody sword, and putting it up into its sheath. From this sign Gregory understood that his prayers were heard, and erected a church at that same place in honor of the angel, whence the Castle has since been called the Fortress of the Holy Angel. This apparition is commemorated on 8 May.[138]

The conception of the plague as divine retribution, and specifically the theme of the plague angel wielding then scabbarding his sword, was appropriated from the Old Testament account of the retribution and forgiveness of David for his prideful act of numbering his people against the wishes of the Lord (1 Paralip. 21, Douay):

> 16 And David lifting up his eyes, saw the angel of the Lord standing between heaven and earth, with a drawn sword in his hand, turned against Jerusalem.

> 27 And the Lord commanded the angel: and he put up his sword again into the sheath.

This Old Testament prototype of crime, punishment, and reconciliation was central to the Roman Church's

213. Bernini, Angel with the Superscription. Ponte Sant'Angelo, Rome

understanding of its role in the entire process of salvation. To commemorate the miracle and the penitential procession by which the city celebrated it, Nicholas III (1277–80) erected a great marble sculpture of Michael atop the castle.[139] Seen high against the sky, the figure seemed to reenact the heavenly apparition of the angel with his sword in its scabbard, signaling the cessation of God's just ire at man's sins, as the apocalyptic rage of the plague was interpreted. The statue was succeeded by several replacements, including a figure with copper wings and sword commissioned by Nicholas V in 1453,[140] and a "gilded statue of the angel holding a sword outside

the scabbard," destroyed by an exploding powder keg in 1497.[141] Over the centuries the awesome image of the armored and winged protector looming watchfully from atop the fortress came to embody the very identity of the city.

Gregory's vision was often included in depictions of the life of the saint and the deeds of the archangel (Figs. 216, 228).[142] Saint Michael's miraculous "conquest" of the plague at the intervention of the pope, and their mutual dominion over the Castello and the bridge, came to symbolize the Church's dominion over the Vatican and Rome itself. Giulio Romano illustrated

214. Bernini, Angel with the Crown of Thorns. Sant'Andrea delle Fratte, Rome

215. Bernini, Angel with the Superscription. Sant'Andrea delle Fratte, Rome

this very point in the early 1520s in his portrayal of another, earlier visionary intervention on behalf of the Church, when Constantine saw an image of the Cross in the sky on the eve of his victory over Maxentius at the battle of the Milvian Bridge, which assured the establishment of the Church and the Christian empire (Fig. 217).[143] In the fresco, in the Sala di Costantino in the Vatican Palace, the triumphant inscription that appeared along with the Cross is placed directly over the bridge and the Mausoleum, shown surmounted by a statue holding a spear. The bridge is clearly copied from a bronze medal of Hadrian (Fig. 218), where it rests on seven arches, the four central piers of which were surmounted by tall columns carrying sculptures, doubtless conceived as Victories or trophies of arms and armor captured in war. The scene recaptures the original function of both monuments in antiquity as the triumphal approach to and commemoration of the divinized emperor; the "archaeologically" correct portrayal serves to celebrate both the Church's victory over the pagan empire and the individual Christian's victory over death.

Siege, Triumph, and Retribution

A further angelic intervention occurred shortly after the Constantine cycle was completed under Clement VII, when the ethos of the Sant'Angelo monuments was radically altered by one of the most disastrous and perilous events in the entire history of the Church. In 1527 Rome was sacked by the latter-day scourge of the troops of the emperor Charles V, and the pope was besieged in the Castel Sant'Angelo.[144] Clement managed to escape during the night of 6–7 December 1527 and flee to Orvieto. The bridge leading to and the piazza in front of the fortress were major focal points of the siege, and this ignominious defeat gave a new level of meaning to the relationship between the Vatican, the city of Rome, and the world at large. Clement regarded this tragic event, and his own "miraculous" salvation, as a providential liberation of the Church from the predations of secular power. The pope considered his escape a reiteration of what might be described as the original instance of angelic intervention on behalf of Christianity, that is, the liberation of Saint Peter from the Mamertine prison, which permitted Christ's first vicar to fulfill his mission of establishing the Church in Rome. The most familiar illustration of the liberation of Saint Peter was that by Raphael in the Stanza d'Eliodoro in the Vatican, where, behind the prison bars, the angel is shown breaking Peter's chains and leading him out of the darkness (Fig. 219). Clement's reference to this apostolic event in relation to his own liberation was made explicit in a medal attributed to Benvenuto Cellini in which the two episodes are melded into one image (Fig. 220); the medal was issued in two versions with different inscriptions, one referring to the pope himself, *Misit D(ominus) Ang(elum) suum et liberavit me*, the other to the city of Rome, *Misit Dominus angelum suum. Roma.*[145] The deliverance from pestilence was in fact twofold. The plague had also taken hold during the siege, and there was danger from this quarter as well as from the mercenary Lutheran *landsknechts* who made up the bulk of the imperial forces.[146] The great trauma thus also echoed the original Gregorian episode that occasioned the baptizing of Hadrian's tomb as the Castel "Sant'Angelo."

After returning to Rome in October 1528, Clement VII embarked on an aggressive campaign of commissioning images aimed at restoring the moral and by implication the temporal authority of the church. The entrance to the Holy City was to be given new importance with

a project designed around 1530 by Baccio Bandinelli – a huge bronze group representing Michael defeating the seven deadly sins, to be installed on the parapet of the military tower that had been placed in front of the Castello for added protection.[147] According to Vasari, Clement commissioned the sculpture in fulfillment of a vow, evidently to commemorate the intervention of the Almighty on behalf of the Church, and as a warning to its future enemies. A sketch by Bandinelli shows that, in this new context, the Archangel who earlier replaced his weapon in its scabbard in a particular act of benevolence was transformed into the prototypical champion of Christian virtue (Fig. 221). The project, never carried out, was evidently related to a plan, also never carried out, for Michelangelo to paint the same subject on the entrance wall to the Sistine Chapel, as the prelapsarian counterpart to the Last Judgment that he would depict on the altar wall. Facing each other at opposite ends of the Old and New Testament histories on the flanking walls, the two apocalyptic visions would have engulfed the visitor in the universal embrace of church doctrine. There is good reason to suppose that an awesomely incandescent altarpiece in Siena painted circa 1526–30 by Domenico Beccafumi and showing Michael defeating the rebellious angels (Fig. 222), which has much in common with Michelangelo's *Last Judgment*, is related to these unexecuted schemes.

Bandinelli's project would have given monumental form to the retributive association that had long been implicit in the relationship between the Archangel and the Castello. In his effort to reassert the power of the Church, Clement VII introduced this association explicitly in another way, extending its reach beyond the river to the city itself. He removed the decrepit structures from the area leading to the bridge and in 1534 had its entrance flanked by monumental statues of Peter with his keys and Paul with his sword, the principal apostles in the foundation of the Church, who are both commemorated in St. Peter's (Fig. 223). The saints had a particular significance in this context, however, to which voice was given in the inscriptions placed on the statue's pedestals: for Peter, as exemplum of humility and penitence, "here forgiveness to the humble" (*hinc humilibus venia*); for Paul, soldier in the battle for the faith, whom Augustine called a "true warrior for Christ," "here punishment to the prideful" (*hinc retributio superbis*).[148] Conceived in this way, the two apostles were surely meant to be seen in relation to the Archangel above. Taken together, the figures inevitably recall their traditional place in depictions of the Last Judgment. For the first time since antiquity, the bridge and the mausoleum were now linked as interdependent parts of a coherent whole, a monumental memento mori.

The quasi-antiquarian Christian theme implicit in the background of Giulio Romano's Constantine fresco

216. Vision of St. Gregory the Great. Trinità dei Monti, Rome

217. Giulio Romano, *Battle of the Milvian Bridge*. Sala di Costantino, Vatican Palace, Rome

was given an explicitly modern, political formulation by Clement VII's successor. As an act of reconciliation with Charles V, Paul III revived one of the glorious traditions of the ancient Romans. In 1536, following the emperor's victory over the Turks at Tunis, Charles was given a triumphal entry into Rome to be received by the pope. To celebrate his passage to St. Peter's and the Vatican, the bridge's parapets were provided temporarily with a new set of eight sculptures, presumably in recollection and emulation of the Victories or trophies shown on the Hadrianic medal (Fig. 224; see Fig. 218).[149] On the west side, behind the statue of St. Peter, who administers the New Law, were the four evangelists; on the east, behind St. Paul, apostle to the Hebrews, were the four Old Testament patriarchs Adam, Noah, Abraham, and Moses. In recalling and emulating the ancient parapet sculptures, both the choice and the disposition of the new figures endowed the bridge with a distinct and consistent liturgical dynamic. The arrangement was complementary bilaterally, with St. Peter and the evangelists on the dexter side, St. Paul and their Old Testament counterparts on the sinister; and the disposition was progressive longitudinally, with the evangelists presumably aligned in their canonical, the patriarchs in their chronological order.[150] The ancient theme of triumph thus acquired an entirely new content and purpose. The past became testimony to the present, history became a process of promise and fulfillment. The sculptures were only temporary, but the ideas they represented left an indelible mark on what now became the bridge to eternity.

The underlying eschatological theme was not motivated solely by the aftermath of the Sack of Rome. In the course of the sixteenth century, the papacy increased its hegemony over the city of Rome and demonstrated its jurisdiction by shifting the locus of criminal punishments, notably executions for capital offenses, from the center of Rome to the point of entry to the Holy City at the threshold of the Ponte Sant'Angelo. The ritual of execution was orchestrated by the Confraternity of John the Baptist Beheaded, whose mission it was to comfort and reconcile the prisoners to their fate, and which maintained a chapel adjoining the entrance to the bridge where they were prepared to meet their Maker.[151] Sentences were carried out after a procession through the streets deliberately suggestive of Christ's way to the Cross. Paintings depicting the Passion were held in front of the prisoners' faces. In an ironic evocation of the sculpted Victories or trophies that adorned the parapets in antiquity, the severed heads of the "giustiziati" were displayed on stakes placed along the flanks of the bridge – a kind of historical reminder to those crossing it of the

218. Pons Aelius, medal of Hadrian, reverse

ultimate judgment to which they, too, would be subject (Figs. 225, 226). The executions took place within sight of the Archangel atop the Castello, in an enclosure beside the sword-bearing figure of St. Paul (who was himself martyred by beheading), the sinister side traditionally reserved for the damned at the Last Judgment. The punishments themselves – hanging, decapitation, quartering et al. – were those traditionally meted out to the sinners in Hell and often depicted in scenes of the Last Judgment.

The Last Judgment

The contrasting themes of the beneficent Archangel scabbarding and vengeful Archangel brandishing his sword were replaced by a very different image under Paul III, who initiated the Council of Trent to defend, reform, and reaffirm the essential tenets of the Church. In 1544 the pope commissioned a new figure of marble with bronze accoutrements from Raffaello da Montelupo (Fig. 227).[152] Poised in a classical contrapposto pose midway between standing and striding, the Archangel seems inscrutably to contemplate the scene below, his naked sword held aloft, poised ambiguously between sheathing and unsheathing the weapon in the scabbard held at his side. This intermediate, "neutral" pose alludes to Michael's traditional role as weigher of souls at the Last Judgment, embodying both the promise and the threat, the salvific and punitive alternatives of the Archangel's invincible power. Montelupo's figure remained atop the Castello until it was replaced in 1752 by the historically minded Benedict XIV, who reverted to Gregory the Great's original vision with the heroic bronze monument by Peter Verschaffelt that now occupies the summit.

The comprehensive association of the Archangel, the Castello, and the bridge with the Last Judgment – particularly in relation to the plague and the inscrutability of divine justice – may indeed have originated with Gregory the Great. A seminal work in the creation of these eschatological themes was Gregory's Fourth Dialogue, in which he recounts visions of the underworld described by those who have returned from the dead, in particular a Roman soldier who

> died three years ago of the horrible plague which devastated Rome. During that time arrows could be seen hurled down from the sky, carrying death to many individuals. A soldier at Rome was struck down in this way. He did not remain dead very long, however, for, shortly after dying, he came back to life and told what had happened to him. The scene he described – one that became familiar to many others at this time – was as follows. He saw a river whose dark waters were covered by a mist of vapors that gave off an unbearable stench. Over the river was a bridge. It led to pleasant mead-

219. Raphael, *St. Michael Liberating St. Peter from the Mamertine Prison*, ca. 1514. Stanza d'Eliodoro, Vatican Palace, Rome

220. Attributed to Benvenuto Cellini, *St. Michael Liberating St. Peter from the Mamertine Prison*, 1527, medal of Clement VII (after Buonanni 1699, 184, 192, no. IX)

ows beyond, covered by green grass and dotted with richly scented flowers. These meadows seemed to be the gathering places for people dressed in white robes. The fragrant odors pervading the region were a delight for all who lived there. Everyone had his own dwelling, which gleamed with brilliant light. One house of magnificent proportions was still under construction and the bricks used were made of gold. But no one could tell for whom the house was meant. There were houses also along the banks of the river, some of which were infected by the vapors and stench rising from the river, while others remained untouched.

On this bridge saint and sinner underwent a final test. The unjust would slip off and fall into the dark, foul waters. The just, unhampered by sin, could walk over it, freely and without difficulty, to the beautiful

221. Baccio Bandinelli, *St. Michael Defeating the Seven Deadly Sins*, drawing Musée du Louvre, Paris

meadows on the other side. Below this bridge the soldier saw Peter, an overseer of the church who died four years ago, lying prone in the foul mire loaded down with heavy iron chains. When he asked why such terrible punishment was inflicted on him, the answer he received harmonizes well with what we of this household remember of Peter's life and actions. "He suffers these torments," he was told, "because whenever he was ordered to administer punishment, he would deal out the blows in a spirit of cruelty rather than of obedience." Everyone acquainted with Peter knows this is true.

According to the soldier's description, he also saw a priest of some foreign country stepping onto the bridge and walking over it with all the confidence that a life of sincerity had won for him. On the same bridge he saw and recognized the Stephen whom we mentioned above. In trying to cross the river, Stephen had slipped and fallen, leaving the lower half of his body dangling over the edge of the bridge. Some fiendish men from the river below seized him by the sides and tried to pull him down. At the same time, princely men dressed in white appeared on the bridge to draw him back to safety. While this struggle went on, with the good spirits drawing him up and the evil ones pulling him down, our spectator was called back to earth to be reunited with his body. *No one, therefore, knows what the final outcome of this struggle was* [italics mine].[153]

With the reference to the plague taking place in Rome, the bridge with the "heavenly mansion" at one end, the river, and the arrogant church official named Peter, the site can only be identified with the Ponte Sant'Angelo, the Tiber, and the tomb of Hadrian as the bastion of Saint Peter and the papacy. The Roman monuments thus become the locus of justice meted out at the Last Judgment and, through Gregory's seminal text, keys to the definition of the eschatology of the Church. The plague was seen as an act of divine retribution, an instrument of God's wrath, a presage of the Dies Irae and of Michael's role in the Last Judgment. The close association between the appearances of Saint Michael at the plague and at the Last Judgment is illustrated in a late fourteenth-century fresco by Spinello Aretino in the church of San Francesco at Arezzo (Figs. 228, 229).[154] The vision at Castel Sant'Angelo is shown in the upper two registers, while below Michael acts as the avenger of evildoers at the end of time.

The Bridge of Trial

The Bridge of Trial appears as an important feature of the fiery punishments described in many medieval apocalyptic texts, notably the Vision of St. Paul and the Revelation of Esdras.[155] But Gregory's specifically Roman vision in the Fourth Dialogue inspired what must have been one of the chief progenitors of Bernini's conception of the Ponte Sant'Angelo's place in the religio-topography of

222. Domenico Beccafumi, *St. Michael Defeating the Rebellious Angels*. Pinacoteca, Siena

223. Lorenzo Lotti and Paolo Romano, Sts. Peter and Paul. Ponte Sant'Angelo, Rome

the Church: its role as the eschatological bridge par excellence in Dante's *Divine Comedy*, which had also been Michelangelo's point of reference in imagining his *Last Judgment*. In the eighteenth canto of the *Inferno*, describing the place called Malebolge, Dante speaks of a fortress stronghold surrounded by deep pits spanned by a bridge. There he saw naked sinners passing in both directions, like crowds at the Jubilee year, and the tortures of the damned below:

> In this place we found ourselves dropped from the back of Geryon, and the poet held to the left, and I came on behind. On the right hand I saw new woe, new torments, and new scourgers, with which the first ditch was replete. At its bottom were the sinners, naked; on our side of the middle they came facing us, and, on the other side, along with us, but with greater strides: thus the Romans, because of the great throng, in the year of the Jubilee, have taken measures for the people to pass over the bridge, so that on one side all face toward the Castle and go to St. Peter's, and on the other they go toward the Mount. Along the dark rock, on this side and on that, I saw horned demons with large scourges, who smote them fiercely from behind.[156]

Dante thus associates the traditional Bridge of Trial with the bridge used by pilgrims to reach the Holy City to obtain the plenary indulgence, the first of its kind, during the first Holy Year of Jubilee, declared by Pope Boniface VIII in 1300.[157] With respect to these indulgences Dante gave the Tiber River a specific role in the divine scheme, for on its shore the chosen souls began their journey through Purgatory on their way to salvation.[158] Two themes that occur here, and frequently in such eschatological imagery, are particularly relevant to the ideological substructure of Bernini's project: the perilous bridge and the atrocious punishments of those who fail to make the crossing. A common feature in descriptions and illustrations of the Bridge of Trial was its perilousness – it was a hair's breadth wide and had no balustrades to hinder the wayward sinner's fall into the fiery flood below.

Purgatory and All Souls

Owing mainly to the nature and importance of this tract, Gregory became the intercessory saint par excellence for liberating souls from Purgatory.[159] His references to Rome, the plague, Saint Michael, the river, the bridge, the "mansiones" reached by the successful soul, were a congeries of allusions that ineluctably suggest the Tiber crossing, the mausoleum, and the angelic instrument of God's will. Apart from his contribution to the definition of Hell, Gregory's main purpose in the Dialogue is to demonstrate the efficacy of suffrage to alleviate the pains of those condemned to pay for their sins.[160] This compensatory capacity of the living to act on behalf of the dead became a fundamental ingredient of the theology and practice of the doctrine of purgatory. Liturgically, this relationship between offering and assuagement was embodied personally and particularly in the Mass for the Dead, but it was given universal status in the Feast of the Commemoration of All Souls, 2 November. In his discussion of the feast in the Golden Legend, Jacobus of Voragine gives elaborate explanations of all these points, based on Gregory's Dialogue and including the example of the Roman soldier at the Bridge of Trial.[161] The prayers offered in this context reach beyond the individual and gain in efficacy as acts of charity toward others who have died and therefore cannot help themselves. It is precisely in this sense that the offertory prayer used in both liturgies pleads that Christ liberate the faithful from the infernal torments, including the deep lake, and that Michael re-present them in the holy light:

> O Lord Jesus Christ, King of glory, deliver the souls of all the faithful departed from the pains of hell and from the deep lake; deliver them from the lion's mouth, that hell engulf them not, nor they fall into the darkness, but let Michael, the holy standard-bearer, bring them into the holy light which Thou once didst promise to Abraham and his seed.[162]

The Plague
A major impetus for refurbishing the entrance to the Holy City must have come from a recurrence of the plague, which, having devastated Naples, wracked

224. View of Ponte Sant'Angelo, drawing, ca. 1580. Kupferstichkabinett, Staatliche Museen, Berlin-Dahlem (after Weil 1974, fig. 17, p. 28)

Rome from May 1656 through the summer of 1657.[163] Alexander VII took drastic measures to confine the disease, and his efforts were credited with limiting the number of victims to some fifteen thousand, far fewer than usual in such outbreaks. To commemorate the event and pay tribute to the pope's succor, no fewer than three medals were struck, two in 1657, the third in 1659. In one, which seems to adumbrate the eschatological imagery of the bridge, an angel stands beside a cross holding the gentle yoke (Matt.11:29–30) and a book (doubtless the Gospels), treading underfoot a skeletal figure of Death; the legend reads POPVLVM RELIGIONE TVETVR (the people are protected by religion) (Fig. 230).[164] The intervention and ministrations of the pope were also celebrated in the second medal, designed by Bernini, who had lost one of his brothers in the plague while another, having fallen ill, "miraculously" recovered.[165] Issued in 1657 upon the cessation of the disease, the medal shows Saint Peter himself in the sky holding the keys and gesturing toward St. Peter's as the source and goal of healing faith (Fig. 231).[166] Dead, dying, and recovering figures are depicted below, partially immersed in the flowing river, while to the side a winged figure strides away carrying a skull and a flamboyant sword. The scene seems to be taking place in the area between St. Peter's and Castel Sant'Angelo, and the legend of the medal, VT VMBRA ILLIVS LIBERARENTVR, which derives from a passage in Acts that refers to Saint Peter as healer, also served to express in Petrine terms the continuity between the colonnade and the Castello: "5:15 (Douay Version) Insomuch that they brought forth the sick into the streets and laid them on beds and couches, that, when Peter came, his shadow at the least might overshadow any of them and they might be delivered from their infirmities."[167] The legend clearly anticipates the 1661 inscription of Isaiah 4:6 at the northeast entrance to the colonnade, the approach to St. Peter's and the Vatican from the bridge and Castello, where the portico is described as an *umbraculum*, a refuge from storm and rain. In effect, Peter and the pope are identified with the portico, as the angel is with the Castello and bridge. In fact, the plague was often conceived of as a rain of arrows cast down by an irate God upon sinners, who huddle beneath the ample, tentlike mantle of the Madonna della Misericordia, wherein the Virgin is seen as the sheltering church.[168]

In recognition of his actions, the Senate in 1658 decreed that a statue of the pope be erected on the Capitol; he refused the honor, and an inscription recording the city's gratitude was installed instead.[169] In 1659 a splendid third medal, again designed by Bernini, was issued by an official of the city (Fig. 232). The medal casts Alexander in the role of Androcles, the runaway Roman slave who healed a wounded lion. Recaptured and condemned to die in the amphitheater, Androcles was confronted by the same beast, which, instead of attacking fawned upon him, whereupon both were set free and Androcles became known as the Healer. Bernini shows Androcles, before whom the lion bows down in devotion, not as a slave but as a military hero wielding his sword as if he were the archangel Michael. The long inscription on the medal details many of the pope's benefactions to the city, but first and foremost its liberation from the plague.[170]

The pope's beneficent role in this horrendous event inevitably evoked the circumstances of the original vision of Gregory the Great, which had, in effect, converted the mausoleum of Hadrian into a Christian fortress under the aegis of Saint Michael, successor to the avenging angel of the Old Testament. Now, however, the stimulus of the past echoing in the present led to a comprehensive new program in which the bridge and the Castello would synthesize the traditions associated with the entrance to the Holy City.[171]

Preconception

Alexander VII died on 2 May 1667, Clement IX was elected on 20 June, and the first payments for work on the refurbishing of the bridge leading to the Vatican were made on 22 September. It is evident that at least the basic elements of the project, if not the actual plans, must have been conceived sometime during Alexander's papacy.[172] Indeed, thought must have been given from the outset to incorporating the entrance to the Holy City into the grand schemes the pope adopted and carried out in the basilica and the palace. The idea to create a major thoroughfare from the river to the basilica, carried out for the Jubilee of 1450, had been repeatedly broached since the

thirteenth century, and we have seen that the line of approach from Castel Sant'Angelo had been an important consideration in the design of the Piazza San Pietro and the Scala Regia with the equestrian statue of Constantine. A specific indication that Alexander was thinking about the relation between the Castel Sant'Angelo and the Vatican is an inscription of 1656 – that is, while the piazza in front of the basilica was first being planned – recording that the pope had installed the uppermost crown of the fortress so that for the dignity of the papacy the final decor would not be wanting.[173]

A hint as to the nature of Bernini's vision for the project emerges from a remarkable document of April 1659 concerning Montelupo's sculpture of the archangel Michael. A workman is paid for various repairs to the angel and for having disjoined the clamps that held it, "because Bernini wanted to raise it higher."[174] The point of the operation was surely to increase the visibility of the figure, obviously not from the city at large – the figure was already plain to see from a distance – but from below, so that it would continue to loom above as the visitor approached from the other side of the river. This concern indicates that Bernini had already invented a new conceptual and formal role for the angel bridge, and for the entire complex; perhaps he was already thinking of the Archangel as the commander of a celestial honor guard.[175]

One senses the germination of another aspect of Bernini's concept in two of the artist's apparent whimsies during his stay in Paris in the summer of 1665, recounted by Chantelou. On 31 July, Bernini made a point of visiting the Pont-Rouge, also known as the Pont Saint-Landry, which linked the Île Saint-Louis to the Île de la

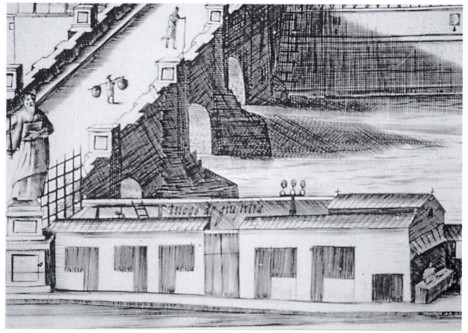

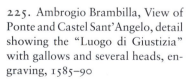

225. Ambrogio Brambilla, View of Ponte and Castel Sant'Angelo, detail showing the "Luogo di Giustizia" with gallows and several heads, engraving, 1585–90

226. Procession of Sixtus V showing severed heads of criminals displayed on stakes along the parapets of Ponte Sant'Angelo (after D'Onofrio 1981, fig. 47, p. 76)

Cité behind Notre-Dame: "Our evening drive was rather short; he wanted to go to the Pont-Rouge and stopped the coach on it for a good quarter of an hour looking first from one side of the bridge and then the other. After a while he turned to me and said, 'It is a beautiful view; I am a great lover of water, it calms my spirits.' Then we returned home." And the next day: "After we had gone towards the Cours-la-Reine he asked to go to the Pont-Rouge where we had been the night before; he remained there a good quarter of an hour; we came back by the Pont-Neuf and through the streets."[176] The bridge where Bernini lingered was carefully chosen and his interest far more than casual (Figs. 233, 234). Constructed in 1627, demolished in 1710, and now replaced by the Pont Saint-Louis, the Pont-Rouge was a narrow, fragile, wooden structure (painted red), often damaged and in need of repair; passage, only on foot, must have seemed perilous indeed, and the open railings provided a full view of the water below.[177] In a famous accident during a procession in 1634, the bridge gave way and many persons were killed or wounded; a similar and even more notorious disaster, accompanied by an outbreak of the plague, had befallen the pilgrims crossing the Ponte Sant'Angelo during the Jubilee of 1450.[178]

BERNINI'S WAY OF SALVATION

Bernini's project involved two fundamental innovations with respect to the prior history of the Ponte Sant'Angelo and of bridge design generally. The new features are

227. Raffaello da Montelupo, *St. Michael*. Castel Sant'Angelo, Rome

defined explicitly in the accounts given by Baldin-ucci and Domenico Bernini, doubtless echoing Bernini's own formulation of his concept: while taking great care to provide for the visibility of the river below, he incorporated the traditional Christian name of the bridge in a cohort of angels displaying the instruments of Christ's Passion.

> During the pontificate of Clement IX, Bernini finished the right wing of the portico of St. Peter's by the Holy Office and the ramp or, as we would say, the pavilion in front of the basilica of St. Peter's. He embellished the bridge of Sant'Angelo with statues of angels car-rying instruments of Christ's Passion and designed the balustrades. Bernini made with his own hand two of the angels that were to be placed with the others on the bridge. But it did not seem right to Pope Clement that such beautiful works should remain there exposed to damage from the weather. Therefore, he had copies of them made. The originals were placed elsewhere at the disposition of the cardinal-nephew. Nevertheless, Bernini carved another angel secretly, the one with the superscription, so that a work by a pope to whom he knew he owed so much would not be without some creation by his hand. When the pope learned of it, al-though he was very pleased, he said, 'In short, Cavalier,

228. Spinello Aretino, *Vision of St. Gregory*. Guasconi Chapel, S. Francesco, Arezzo

229. Spinello Aretino, *Last Judgment*. Guasconi Chapel, S. Francesco, Arezzo

230. Religion Protects the People, medal of Alexander VII (after Buonanni 1699, 649, n. X)

231. St. Peter Expelling the Plague, medal of Alexander VII. Biblioteca Vaticana, Rome

you wish to compel me to have yet another copy made.' And let my reader now consider that Bernini, though well on in years, carved three entire marble statues, larger than life-size, in the space of two years: a thing that to those most competent in art seemed to be an impossibility.

Baldinucci makes the following observation discussing Bernini's fountains:

Another of his precepts should be brought forth since we are speaking of fountains. It is that as fountains are made for the enjoyment of water, then the water should always be made to fall so that it can be seen. It was with such a precept in mind, I believe, that in his restoration of the bridge of Sant'Angelo by order of Clement IX, he had the side walls lowered so that the water could better be enjoyed. The eye may see with double pleasure from the banks of the river the flow of water as well as the bridge above, ornamented with angels that allude to its ancient name.[179]

Domenico Bernini introduces the idea while speaking of the bridge:

But Clement, desirous as his predecessors to increase the magnificence of the Temple of St. Peter's, the adornment of Rome, and the glory of his pontificate, ordered Bernini to adorn in the best way with some noble invention the bridge that takes its name from the nearby Castello, Ponte Sant'Angelo, deemed worthy of notable

232. Alexander VII as Androcles, medal of Alexander VII. Biblioteca Vaticana, Rome

embellishment both for the grandeur of the Mausoleum of Hadrian which presents itself to those who enter it, and because it is the most frequented way to the great Basilica of St. Peter. The idea that occurred to Bernini was most appropriate to the site and as majestic in appearance as can be said. He often observed that 'With respect to fountains or works involving water, the good architect will make sure that it will easily be seen, either in falling or in passing. Since the sight of water gives

233. Israël Silvestre, *View of Pont-Rouge from the North* (Paris), detail, engraving, before 1655

234. Israël Silvestre, *View of Pont-Rouge from the South* (Paris), detail, engraving, ca. 1657

great pleasure, to impede or block it removes from such works their most delightful value.' Toward this end, when ornamenting the bridge, the Cavaliere wished that the parapets, which are normally solid wall constructions, would include regular openings, protected by wrought-iron screens, so that the passerby might easily admire the flow of the water above which he happily moves.[180]

Open balustrades had never before been seen on the monumental stone bridges of Rome.[181] Bernini opened the parapets along the flanking banks of the Tiber as well, so that the river was visible even as one approached the crossing itself (Fig. 235; the flanking parapets were closed when the bridge was renovated after 1890). The biographers were justified in relating the innovation to Bernini's appreciation of the effect of moving water. In contrast to the thin, geometrically controlled jets of Mannerist tradition, he engineered for his fountain and theater designs spectacular aquatic displays, veritable cascades, abundant and potentially overwhelming. The innovation was exactly analogous to Bernini's transferal of other formal devices from the realm of the informal, rustic, and ephemeral to the context of urban "high art" – awesomely craggy rustication in palace architecture, aggressively crude draftsmanship in caricatures, menacingly failed scenic illusions in the theater.[182] These transformations of tradition were not merely formal but conveyed distinct and often disturbing meaning in their respective contexts. In one of his comedies, the river Tiber threatened to flood off the stage and inundate the audience![183] At the Ponte Sant'Angelo, as at the Pont-Rouge in Paris, the effect of the natural flow is quite different, inspiring, in Bernini's terms, a mood of meditative contemplation and tranquillity. His meaning in this case becomes evident only with an understanding of the Ponte Sant'Angelo project as a whole.

Beginning in May 1667, obstructive buildings at the entrance to the bridge (including the infamous executions precinct) were demolished to create the Piazza San Celso, and the open-grilled parapets were introduced flanking the bridge and along the river on either side.[184] The effect was to enlarge the vista from the Piazza San Celso and include the flood running under the bridge in the overall prospect. The bridge, the river, and the Castel Sant'Angelo behind it could now be comprehended as one vast, emblematic marker of the perilous transition from the secular to the sacred city, from this world to the next. The panorama is a "real"-world prolepsis of the otherworldly vision that awaits the faithful who, approaching the end of the pilgrimage inside the church, perceive the Cathedra Petri looming gloriously behind the angel-borne baldachin. On the other side of the bridge, the last remaining obstructions to the Borgo Nuovo were removed and the road was widened. The junction, formerly a focus of military defense, now provided an unobstructed view and passage to the hallowed precincts of the Vatican and St. Peter's.[185] This ultimate demilitarization and sacralization of the entrance to the Holy City might be thought of as the political counterpart of the spiritual embrace embodied in the open arms of the St. Peter's colonnades. With its thought-provoking view of the abyss, the Ponte Sant'Angelo evokes the perilously narrow, unguarded Bridge of Trial, now become a broad avenue protectively screened on either side by the perforated balustrades and guarded by troops of angels. In the horizontal axis the bridge becomes the intermediary between the secular and the holy city; in the vertical axis, it becomes the intermediary between the deep, dark river winding its way to the globe-encircling sea, and the infinite, angel-filled empyrean above. Bernini's transformation may be said to have given Ponte Sant'Angelo a cosmic expanse, fulfilling the destiny of Rome, center and capital of the world – *umbilicus mundi* in classical terms, in papal terms, *urbis et orbi*.

The Via Salvationis and the Arma Christi

Bernini's solution for transforming the ancient Pons Aelius into the modern Ponte Sant'Angelo consisted partly in assimilating to the classical tradition of triumph and apotheosis the vast accumulation of medieval eschatological associations. His essential contribution in doing so consisted in distinguishing, isolating, and integrating into this cumulative heritage the ultimate, salvific component that had been only implicit before: Christ's sacrifice. This innovation was perhaps inevitable, given the special emphasis upon and devotion to the Eucharist that had characterized church doctrine since the Council of Trent; we have seen that the Eucharist was the central theme of Alexander's pontificate from the outset, motivating in fundamental ways the unprecedented tasks he entrusted to Bernini at St. Peter's. Similarly, flanking the bridge with parallel sequences of monumental statues refurbished the idea of a triumphal honor guard inherent in the ancient, imperial heritage of the bridge, which had been revived in prophetic terms in the Old Testament–New Testament succession for the entry of Charles V, the Holy Roman Emperor. But representing the Eucharistic sacrifice as a sort of dramatization enacted by a procession of sculpted angels bearing the instruments of the Passion was a radically new conception that conflated two previously distinct but profoundly related traditions. The fusion of antecedents transformed the role of the bridge from that of an introductory "walk-on" to that of the prime protagonist in Bernini's Roman production of the divine mystery play of salvation. This reference to the mystery play tradition is by no means factitious.

The Passion of Christ was of course the original and ultimate Christian triumphal procession, toward victory over death through humility and self-sacrifice. Since the later Middle Ages, this eschatological dynamic of the Passion had been ritualized in an independent, penitential journey in the stages of which single episodes of Christ's immolation became the subjects of particular devotions; the faithful followed in Christ's footsteps, receiving at each step of the way indulgences of time released from Purgatory. The Stations or Way of the Cross was a penitential devotion developed originally by the Franciscans in the Holy Land, in which the worshiper retraced Christ's path to Golgotha, imitating his sufferings on behalf of humankind. Especially in the sixteenth century, the exercise became increasingly popular in the form of depictions of the events of the Passion distributed in chronological order along the nave of a church, or as sculpted tableaus placed along the ascending path of a "Holy Mountain." By re-creating the Passion in this way, the Stations of the Cross were permanent versions of the contemporaneous, ephemeral mystery plays produced in cathedral squares, where the sacred events were performed, not on a single stage as in the classical tradition, but on the platforms of individual, temporary "mansiones," with the populace following from one to the next.[186] Bernini's bridge combined both representational modes, in that the angels are arranged in succession yet are also perceived and meant to be understood as a unified whole.

A link between the Via Salvationis, as an expiatory meditation on the Passion, and the Last Judgment was grounded in the famous passage in the Gospel of Matthew (25:35–9) that was crucial to the Church's response to the Protestants' principle of justification by faith alone. Here Christ himself defined the Last Judgment and stipulated the good works – the acts of mercy – requisite to redemption.[187] Before reciting the six merciful obligations, Jesus says:

> 33 And he shall set the sheep on his right hand, but the goats on the left.
> 34 Then shall the King say unto them on his right hand, Come, ye blessed of my Father, inherit the kingdom prepared for you from the foundation of the world.

And, after reciting the failed opportunities for charity, he concludes:

> 41 Then shall he say also unto them on the left hand, Depart from me, ye cursed, into everlasting fire, prepared for the devil and his angels.
>
> 46 And these shall go away into everlasting punishment: but the righteous into life eternal.

The seventh work, Burial of the Dead, which integrated the series into the eschatological scheme, was added by the Church specifically in response to the ravages of the plague. In an elaborately illustrated treatise by Giulio Roscio on the acts of mercy published in Rome in 1586, the basic theme is illustrated in the frontispiece, where the seven are distributed in a frame surrounding the Last Judgment (Fig. 236).[188] And the physical good works named by Christ were supplemented by seven complementary spiritual acts of mercy. Meditation on the Passion conceived in the narrative sense of the Via Crucis was seen as an act of charity toward others, and therefore efficacious in the individual's search for salvation. Roscio included meditation on the Passion, as well as corresponding episodes from the Old Testament, as the fifth of these spiritual acts, that of bearing injury with patience, *ferre patienter iniurias* (Fig. 237).

Another theme in which episodes of Christ's sacrifice were singled out for inclusion in a comprehensive evocation of the Passion concerned not the sequence but the instruments used in his humiliation and martyrdom. The objects of torture and ridicule were isolated from their narrative contexts and reassembled as the "Arma Christi," an ironically ambivalent term referring to the instruments used to torment Christ both as weapons that served in the divine plan to conquer the Devil, and as the coat of arms of mankind's royal Champion in that

struggle.[189] In this context, the instruments are gathered together as *disjecta membra*, often in geometric rather than chronological order, and are displayed either in isolation or as accoutrements of an image of the suffering Christ, the Imago Pietatis (Fig. 238). The instruments of the Passion were displayed in one context that might be described as quasi-narrative – that is, the Last Judgment. The Arma Christi are here identified with the *signum Filii hominis in caelo* to which Matthew refers in his vision of the Second Coming (24:30): "And then shall appear the sign of the Son of man in heaven: and then shall all tribes of the earth mourn: and they shall see the Son of man coming in the clouds of heaven with much power and majesty."[190] The relics of the sacrifice appear in the heavens, not in chronological order, but as trophies of Christ's victory over death. As a heavenly vision the instruments are often carried by cloud-borne angels who serve as eschatological vexillaries displaying them as insignia of the Son's God-given authority to administer divine justice to humanity on the day of reckoning (cf. Fig. 115). In the context of the Last Judgment, moreover, there is an inherent link between the arms-bearing troops of angels and the Archangel Michael as the Lord's adjutant.

These essentially late-medieval forms of devotional piety were revived and brought together in the perfervid spiritual atmosphere of Rome around 1600. Inspired by and in collaboration with leaders of the newly founded Counter-Reformatory religious orders, some of the great papal and cardinalate families undertook to restore the neglected and decrepit early churches to a semblance of their pristine doctrinal purity. In two closely related instances, S. Prassede and S. Prisca, angels carrying the instruments of the Passion were aligned on the parallel walls of the nave, alternating with figures of saints in one case, flanking large scenes of the Passion in the other (Figs. 239, 240, 241, 242).[191] The cycle at S. Prassede is particularly noteworthy because the Passion scenes are accompanied by episodes from the history of Joseph the Patriarch, a prototype of Christ.[192] The sequence of angelic standard-bearers create a kind of heavenly honor guard for the Via Salvationis through which the worshiper passes recollecting Christ's progress, prefigured in the Old Testament, toward the salvation of mankind in the Eucharistic sacrifice at the altar. Standing on pedestals or surmounting the nave supports, the angels also emulate the ancient honorary mode of displaying statues on high pedestals or columns.

The Angels on the Bridge

Combining the Arma Christi with the Via Dolorosa traditions, these ecclesiastical mural decorations impart a sequential animation to the structures they occupy, anticipating Bernini's sacrificial activation of the Ponte

235. Giovanni Battista Falda, View of Ponte and Castel Sant'Angelo, engraving, 1671

236. *The Last Judgment with the Seven Acts of Mercy* (after Roscio 1586, frontispiece)

237. *Ferre patienter iniurias* (Suffer injuries patiently), Fifth Act of Spiritual Mercy, surrounded by six episodes of the Via Crucis and four Old Testament scenes (after Roscio 1586)

Sant'Angelo. His figures stand alone, however, and he found precedence elsewhere for a series of angels isolated from any represented narrative context but bearing the instruments of the Passion in chronological order. The idea was prefigured in a suite of ten half-length angels, numbered consecutively, engraved in 1631 by Crispijn de Passe, Senior and Junior (Figs. 243, 244, 245).[193]

Poetic invocations of Christ's sufferings are inscribed below the figures, whose dolorous expressions show their compassionate endurance of the same tribulations. The series also anticipates the theme of triumph that Bernini retained from the tradition of the bridge: the title page shows Christ "enthroned" as the Ecce Homo and wearing the Crown of Thorns, and in the final image an angel

238. Roberto Oderisi, *Imago Pietatis with Arma Christi*. Fogg Museum, Cambridge, Massachusetts

displays the banner carried by Christ at the resurrection, inscribed *Victoria Christi*. A similar suite was issued by Aegidius and Johan Sadeler, both *separatim* and as vignettes surrounding a central image of the Pietà (Fig. 246).[194] Bernini's angels are not arranged in a straight line, as would normally be the case with the Stations of the Cross in a church; instead, the sequence zigzags back and forth across the bridge as it proceeds from the secular to the Holy City (Fig. 247).[195] To be sure, this is the only bilateral arrangement that moves consistently forward, but it was also a reflection of the similar disposition of the papal portraits along the walls of the Sistine Chapel, and a prelude to Bernini's own distribution of the successors to Peter in the nave of the basilica. By this concatenation of associations the visitor is bound in the chain of spiritual teleology. At the same time, arranged at regular intervals in facing pairs along the bridge, the angels' rhythmic alignment creates a perspective focus on the Castello surmounted by the Archangel Michael, in his dual role as protector and avenger. In this sense, the bridge thus anticipates the perspective effects Bernini built into the colonnades in relation to the facade of the church and exploited in the nave of the basilica in relation to the high altar and the Cathedra Petri. Following the lead of the Peter and Paul monuments at the entrance to the bridge, as well as the Flemish engravings, the pedestals bear titulary inscriptions. The brief phrases, which are all quotations, offer a key to understanding the meaning of the images themselves and the significance of the bridge in the overall program for St. Peter's and the Vatican. The texts are taken not from the gospel accounts of the Passion, as might be expected, but from liturgical and Old Testament sources that emphasize the eschatological

239. Nave fresco. S. Prisca, Rome

240. Nave fresco. S. Prisca, Rome

241. Nave fresco. S. Prassede, Rome

destiny of Christ's sacrifice as the preordained fulfill-ment of Divine Providence.[196] In this view the inscribed words announce that the angels alighted on the bridge to complete the promise of the voices from the past.

Unlike their frescoed predecessors in the Roman basilicas, the angels of Bernini's bridge do not stand directly on their architectural supports but upon clouds.[197] The figures seem to have descended from the celestial realm of the Archangel Michael at the Last Judg-ment to escort those who undertake to follow in Christ's footsteps. Moreover, the frescoed angels are emblematic in spirit as well as in function: they convey their sym-bolic and celebratory status by their relative uniformity of type and action; and they "display" the relics by hold-ing them aloft like trophies won in battle. The bridge angels, in contrast, have individual personalities, in their appearance, their actions, and their relationships to the attributes they hold (Figs. 210–215). This chorus of an-gelic differentiation is due to the large measure of free-dom accorded, I believe knowingly, as in the crossing

242. Nave fresco. S. Prassede, Rome

243. Crispijn de Passe, *Ecce Homo*, engraving (after *Speculum* 1631, title page)

244. Crispijn de Passe, Jr., *Angel with Instruments of the Passion*, engraving (after *Speculum* 1631, no. 4)

245. Crispijn de Passe, *Angel vexillifer*, engraving (after *Speculum* 1631, no. 10)

of St. Peter's, to the sculptors who carried out the designs Bernini provided.[198] The gamut of expressions thus achieved was part of Bernini's intention, not simply to lend variety to the sequence, but also to suggest the singularity of each episode of the Passion and the meaning it held for the artists themselves. The artists become devotees, and through them the sculptures exemplify the individual souls of all for whom Christ suffered.

The Regal Couple

Within a few months after the projects began, Bernini made an important structural change at the north end of the bridge: he added buttresses to the piers footed at the river bank to strengthen them against the current and accumulation of silt and debris during high water.[199] The extension entailed adding two more angels, bringing the total number of statues on the bridge to twelve – perhaps not coincidentally equivalent to the number of apostles and the number of gates to the Heavenly Jerusalem. Bernini reserved two of the angels to execute

himself: the angel with the Crown of Thorns and that bearing the Title of the Cross (Figs. 214, 215). Why two, and why these two?

Among the Arma Christi the Title and the Crown were the royal insignia par excellence. They represented above all the *Maiestas Domini*, recalling the quintessential crime for which Christ was condemned by the Jews. These emblems encapsulate the paradox of the supreme lèse majesté: salvation attained through the immolation of the Savior, whose humiliating path to death became humanity's glorious route to salvation. This theme is expressed verbally in the inscriptions on the pedestals. The angel with the Crown of Thorns is accompanied by a passage from one of the penitential psalms (Ps. 31:4): "[I am turned in my anguish] whilst the thorn is fastened."[200] The use of the lament in the liturgy, as an antiphon in the feast celebrating the crowning of thorns, transforms Christ's ignominious, painful, mock-crown into a regal vestment.[201] The text for the angel with the Superscription, "regnavit a ligno deus," is of particular interest, as it is also taken from a psalm (95:10),[202] "Say ye among the Gentiles, the Lord hath reigned," but in a version different from the Vulgate. The citation comes from a hymn written by the sixth-century poet Venantius Fortunatus,

246. Johan Sadeler, *Pietà with Angels Bearing Instruments of the Passion*, engraving

247. Distribution of Angels on Ponte Sant'Angelo, with accompanying inscriptions (after Weil 1974, fig. 52)

CASTEL SANT'ANGELO

SPONGE
Antonio Giorgetti
POTAVERUNT ME ACETO
(Ps. LXVIII,22)

LANCE
Domenico Guidi
VULNERASTI COR MEUM
(Song of Solomon IV,9) .

SUPERSCRIPTION
Gian Lorenzo Bernini
REGNAVIT A LIGNO DEUS
("Vexilla regis prodeunt" ; a
hymn celebrating the Cross as the
instrument of salvation)

CROSS
Ercole Ferrata
CUIUS PRINCIPATUS SUPER
HUMERUM E IUS
(Is. IX,6)

ROBE AND DICE
Paolo Naldini
SUPER VESTEM MEAM MISERUNT
SORTEM
(Ps. XXI,19)

NAILS
Girolamo Lucenti
ASPICIANT AD ME
QUEM CONFIXERUNT
(Zach. XII,10)

CROWN OF THORNS
Paolo Naldini
IN AERUMNA MEA DUM
CONFIGITUR SPINA
(Ps. XXXI,4)

SUDARIUM
Cosimo Fancelli
RESPICE F ACIEM CHRISTI TUI
(Ps. LXXXIII,10)

SCOURGE
Lazzaro Morelli
IN FLAGELLA PARATUS SUM
(Ps. XXXVII,18)

COLUMN
Antonio Raggi
TRONUS MEUS IN COLUMNA
(Eccl. XXIV, 7)

ST. PETER
Lorenzetto, ca. 1534
HINC HUMILIBUS VENIA

ST. PAUL
Paolo Romano, 1464
HINC RETRIBUTIO SUPERBIS

PIAZZA DI PONTE SANT'ANGELO

where it is quoted in a passage identifying the Cross as the fulfillment of David's prophecy:[203]

Impleta sunt quae concinit
David fideli carmine,
Dicendo nationibus:
Regnavit a ligno Deus.

(The words of David's true prophetic song were fulfilled, in which he announced to the nations: "God has reigned from a tree.")

This famous poem celebrating the Cross, used in the liturgy for the Good Friday mass, begins: "The standards of the king appear. . . . " The phrase *vexilla regis prodeunt* specifies the regal nature of the insignia. Bernini's figures thus identify the angels as standard-bearers in a royal company. They bear the insignia that testify to the descent of Christ from King David and the majestic victory of his sacrifice. In this way, too, the angels reiterate the theme of the sculptures erected on the bridge to greet the emperor Charles V at his triumphal entry of 1536, except that here the progressive, zigzag dynamic of the arrangement serves to correlate the spiritual integration of the Old and New Testaments, inherent in the ideology of the Church, with the physical integration of the two sides of the bridge, as both move toward the goal of salvation.

Given the chronological sequence of the Passion and the zigzag placement of the instruments, Bernini's two figures cannot now be seen, and cannot have been intended to be seen, together on the bridge. Yet, everything about their design and the inordinately large series of preparatory studies made for the two figures indicates that they were conceived and meant to be comprehended as a complementary pair. Contemporary reports reveal that the pope thought of keeping them for himself, to be sent to his native Pistoia, where Bernini was then designing his family villa and a new high altar for the church of the Jesuits.[204] The first notice of the idea is recorded only after the sculptures had been begun, but the choice of themes, which precluded their being seen together on the bridge, and their contrapuntal, bilaterally symmetrical design, suggest that Bernini must have had something of the kind in mind from the outset, and their exquisitely nuanced surface finish was obviously meant for indoors.[205] The prospect of such a disposition would have been a powerful incentive for Bernini to have substitutes installed on the bridge, one by his own hand.[206] I suspect that Bernini intended his original pair for what they are, complementary pendants and supreme testimonials to the perfection, in the sense of consummate fulfillment, of his own witness to Christ's sacrificial triumph. These considerations may help to explain the otherwise mysterious fact that although Clement IX gave the sculptures to his nephew, Cardinal Giacomo, in December 1669, they remained in the possession of Bernini and his heirs until 1729, when the artist's grandson donated them to the church facing his house on the Via della Mercede, S. Andrea delle Fratte, where they were installed, appropriately, flanking the high altar.[207]

While the bridge angels display a greater variety of expression and action than their predecessors, they maintain a celebratory, essentially conventional mood. Bernini's figures (both on and off the bridge), on the contrary, have a special character quite apart from the intricate, profoundly musical counterpoint of their poses and the movements of their draperies. The intensity and depth of their responses reach far beyond the expressive range of their siblings, and even of their Flemish prototypes, to convey the objects they embrace not just as symbols but as actual relics of Christ's sacrifice. Bernini seems to have taken his cue for the poses and gestures of his two angels from the corresponding pair at S. Prassede (Fig. 242), but he imbued the figures with a wholly new, sinuous dynamic. Their lithe bodies and flamboyant movements seem to writhe in a crescendo to the open-lipped effusions of anguish on their faces. At the same time, Bernini makes a notable distinction between the two angels, who display distinct, gently gendered, characters.[208] The Angel with the Superscription, with its delicate features, curly locks, and downcast, watery eyes, stands passively and unfurls the scroll hesitantly, almost with reluctance: a distinctly interior, feminine sensibility. The Angel with the Crown, physique more robust, broad-faced with flowing locks, furrowed brow, and a distant, visionary stare, holds the precious emblem gingerly but thrusts it forward with heroic, masculine aggressiveness.

These qualities were inherent in Bernini's conception of the pair. He initially studied both angels as male nudes, and the proportions of both figures became taller and slimmer as they evolved. But from the outset the angel with the Crown was more robust and assertive while the angel with the Superscription was more delicate, hesitant, and withdrawn. The inordinate number of such preparatory studies for the angels testify that these effects of profound, unselfconscious, spontaneous feeling were the products of an equally feverish labor of experimentation and calculation.[209] The astonishing fact is that Bernini's creative process was no less innovative than the works themselves: on the one hand, no previous sculptor's preparatory studies are so numerous or show a comparable degree of rapidity and spontaneity in execution; on the other hand, the first known sculptural study marked for scaled enlargement is a model for the angel with the Crown (Fig. 248).[210] These twin innovations may seem paradoxical, but they are in fact mutually interdependent and offer an essential insight into the nature of Bernini's art. Bernini's choice of themes for his two angels and the complementary contrast he worked out for them were motivated by the significance of their respective instruments. Although both represent the pathetic irony of the mocked majesty of Christ, the degradation-exaltation of the Crown of Thorns was physical, that of the Superscription purely spiritual.

In sum, the features, expressions, coiffures, actions, and very physiques of Bernini's angels offer a profound psychophysical disquisition on participation in the Passion. Considered in this light the "individualization" of the figures serves a dual purpose. The differences seem to reflect the gendered nature of humankind and the basic distinctions between male and female spirituality long recognized by the Church. At the same time, the devotional passion that animates both figures recalls the passage in the Gospel of Matthew (22:30) in which Christ himself relates human gender to the divine status of angels: "For in the resurrection they shall neither marry nor be married; but shall be as the angels of God in heaven (22:30, Douay)" (*in resurrectione enim neque nubent neque nubentur sed sunt sicut angeli Dei in caelo*). Christ's words absorb gender into the communal state of angelic purity and, equally important, into the androgynous nature of divinity itself.[211]

Bernini's figures offer a preview of this state of angelic purity to which humankind aspires. Viewed from below against the blue Roman sky, the angels are epiphanic creatures, apparitions heaven-sent to convey to the present their bittersweet relics of the past. Delicately poised on white puffs, with graceful, lilting movements, they appear like momentarily congealed visions of the events they represent. Their wind-filled drapery floats, flutters, billows, and curls, and they hover weightlessly over the piers of the bridge. These are the angels of wind and clouds described by the Pseudo-Dionysius in the *Celestial Hierarchies,* the most famous of all Christian accounts of the angels, who are the motion and the light of the divine spirit.[212] With reference to John 3:8, "The wind bloweth where it listeth, and thou hearest the sound thereof, but canst not tell whence it cometh, and whither it goeth: so is every one that is born of the Spirit," the wind signifies the movement of life whose source is hidden, invisible, unknowable. Clouds evoke the mighty angel of the Apocalypse, 10:1, "come down from heaven, clothed with a cloud, and a rainbow was on his head, and his face was as the sun, and his feet as pillars of fire." But especially, the clouds signify light and the hidden, transcendent luminosity with which those divinely intelligent beings are filled.[213]

For Bernini these references were much more than metaphors. His figures complement each other not only in form but also in their very essence – they *are* wind, they *are* clouds, they *are* light. He said as much when he remarked that the greatest achievement of his chisel was to have rendered marble "malleable as wax," and to have had the heart to render stones obedient to his hand, "as if they were made of pasta."[214] In this quasi-material sense the angels may be said to evoke the transubstantial, sacramental nature of the majestic triumph they represent – the Corpus Domini, for the celebration of which Alexander had earlier built the colonnades, and for which Clement X, who completed the bridge decoration, would soon commission the Sacrament altar, where Bernini's pair of angels would fulfill their ultimate mission of perpetual adoration.

Blood and Water

The twin features of the Ponte Sant'Angelo noted by Baldinucci and Domenico Bernini, the view of the water and the parade of instrument-bearing angels, are related in a way that imparts to the bridge and its urban mission a specific sacramentary role. A devotional tradition closely linked to the Instruments of the Passion focused on the Crucifixion itself: the Five Wounds of Christ, of which the side wound opened by Longinus's lance was of central importance.[215] Water and Christ's sacrifice are conjoined in this crucial event, in which it has been said "the entire history of salvation is concentrated."[216] Bernini had long before celebrated the lance relic pre-

served at St. Peter's with his statue portraying Longinus's illumination in the crossing at the high altar of the basilica. On the bridge, the Way of the Cross ends with the lance, the instrument that signaled not only the ultimate desecration of the Son of Man, but also, and by the very same token, as it were, the salvation of mankind achieved by his sacrifice. This paradoxical, dual import of the lance wound was conveyed by the account of it given, uniquely, in the fourth Gospel (19:34–5), where John reports:

> 28 After this, Jesus knowing that all things were now accomplished, that the scripture might be fulfilled, saith, I thirst.
>
> 30 When Jesus therefore had received the vinegar, he said, It is finished: and he bowed his head, and gave up the ghost.
>
> 34 But one of the soldiers with a spear opened his side, and immediately there came out blood and water.
> 35 And he that saw it, hath given testimony, and his testimony is true. And he knoweth that he saith true; that you also may believe.
> 36 For these things were done, that the scripture should be fulfilled.[217]

In John's account, Christ had already given up the ghost; Christ was dead, and the lance wound was thus quite distinct from those inflicted by the Crucifixion. For such effusions to issue from a corpse was miraculous, and John reported his presence at the Crucifixion as his own eyewitness testimony of Jesus' true nature and proof of the realization of the divine plan.

The wound was also doubly miraculous, however, in that the effusion was of water as well as of blood, and from the earliest Christian times the lance wound became the prototype for the mixture of water and wine in the Eucharist. The dual constituents were also taken to signify the beginning and the end of the sacraments, the water being identified with baptism and the Church, the blood with the Eucharist and Christ. "Sts. Cyril and Chrysostom say that the water signifies baptism, which is the first beginning of the Church and the other sacraments, and the blood represents the Eucharist, which is the end and completion of the sacraments, to which they all refer as to their beginning and their end." Particularly important was the idea that, with the lance wound, the Old Law was succeeded by the New and God's entire plan for salvation was accomplished. According to John, just before giving up the ghost Christ knew that "all things were now accomplished that the Scripture might be fulfilled," and John himself reported them to show that they were accomplished in order that Scripture be fulfilled. And for the Fathers of the Church the effusion of blood and water signified that "from the death and side of Christ as a second Adam sleeping on the cross, the Church was formed as Eve the spouse of Christ."[218] A very suggestive association in relation to Bernini's eschatological conception of the Ponte Sant'Angelo is Rupert of Deutz's punning comparison of the mixture of blood and water in the Eucharist to the opening and closing of the Red Sea in the salvation of the Elect from their diabolic pursuer.[219]

The theme of sacramental and ecclesiological fulfillment in the lance wound at the end of the bridge is made explicit by the Old Testament text chosen for the inscription on the pedestal. Borrowed from the Song of Songs (4:9), the text invokes the theme in a special way: VULNERASTI COR MEUM (*soror mea sponsa vulnerasti cor meum in uno oculorum tuorum*) (Thou hast ravished [wounded] my heart, my sister, my spouse; thou hast ravished my heart with one of thine eyes). The Song of Songs was the pivotal text in the definition of Christ and his Church as the fulfillment of the messianic promise of the Old Testament synagogue; the Hebrew understanding of the passionate love lyric as an expression of God's love for his chosen people was converted, as it were, into a celebration of the marriage, consummated in the Passion, of Christ to the Virgin and through her to the universal community of the faithful.[220] The verse also announces the lance wound in its capacity to convert those who, like Longinus, are able to "see the light."[221] The Ponte Sant'Angelo thus offers safe passage over the Bridge of Trial. The Passion of Christ transforms the river Tiber into the river Jordan, conjoining the salutary water of baptism to the redeeming blood of the Sacrifice. We shall see presently that, in a contemporary image of the Crucifixion, Bernini actually commingled the blood and water into a veritable Eucharistic ocean. So, while Bernini's entrance to the Holy City promises the Last Judgment, it also offers the protection of the Church. The lance wound becomes the Wound of Love, and the Bridge of Trial becomes the road to redemption through the ministrations of Saint Peter and his successors.

We have seen that the idea of refurbishing and, as it were, reconverting the ancient bridge as a Christian triumphal entryway must have been converging in the minds of Alexander VII and Bernini well before the project came to fruition. Alexander's heroic actions during the plague and his prior planning of the bridge may explain the reluctance of his successor, Clement IX, under whom the project was actually carried out, to attach his name to it when it was finished. Clement IX's contribution was commemorated in an inscription added later by his successor, Clement X, who soon also brought to completion the daunting task and Bernini's lifework of furnishing and thereby giving voice to the new church.

248. Bernini, Study for the Angel with the Crown of Thorns. Hermitage, Saint Petersburg

CONSUMMATION

THE SACRAMENT ALTAR (1673–5)

Bernini's final work for St. Peter's was devoted explicitly to the theme that had been implicit in much of what he had done before, the Holy Eucharist. The Sacrament altar is in certain respects the most astonishing of all these creations, by virtue above all of its utter simplicity: it is a bronze tabernacle in the form of a peripteral tempietto, flanked by two kneeling angels (Figs. 249, 250, 251, 252, 253, 254). Bernini evidently felt compelled to distill to its quintessential elements the central mystery of his faith.

249. Bernini, Altar of the Holy Sacrament. St. Peter's, Rome

The project evolved in three phases. Begun under Urban VIII, it was taken up again under Alexander VII, and finally completed under Clement X. Important insights into the development and significance of this unexpected creation and the process that led to it is provided by a heretofore unpublished study by Bernini for the first altar of the Sacrament in New St. Peter's commissioned by Urban VIII (Fig. 255).[222] The drawing corresponds to the records of payment for the work Bernini designed in 1629. Figures of Peter and Paul stood on pedestals at the ends of the altar, while at the center small angels knelt around the base of the peripteral tabernacle covered by a cupola. Executed in temporary materials, the altar was initially erected in a chapel decorated by Gregory XIII with an altarpiece that incorporated a venerated image of the Madonna. In 1638 this provisional work was transferred to a large side chapel in the nave designated as the New Sacristy, where the niche behind the altar had been decorated with a great painting of

the Trinity by Pietro da Cortona, commissioned in 1628 and completed in 1632. Cortona's painting shows the Trinity at the top of the composition, with a large celestial globe below (Fig. 251). In the drawing, the composition sketched in the niche behind the altar shows no hint of the framed image of the Madonna in the center of the Gregoriana altarpiece in the Gregorian chapel, but is quite compatible with what became Cortona's design. The two works were executed in tandem, and the drawing indicates that Bernini's altar, though installed temporarily in the Gregoriana, was designed to be placed in front of Cortona's Trinity, with which it was intended to harmonize from the outset.[223] The main variations in the drawing concern the height of the altar: at first there is a low plinth on which the tabernacle alone rested; then a higher plinth is introduced, with the tabernacle flanked and perhaps lifted slightly off the surface by two or more kneeling angels (the documents speak first of two, then of four).[224] In this form the apostles would flank

Cortona's altarpiece, the angels remaining well below, and the level of the tabernacle would be calibrated so that only the semicircular cupola would appear just beneath the heavenly globe in the painting.

The temporary altar remained in situ for decades, and when the project was resumed under Alexander VII the attitude toward the Sacrament had changed and the altar underwent a significant development that is recorded in a series of drawn and terra-cotta sketches. the tabernacle grew in size and importance, and the figures of Peter and Paul were shifted to become the central pair in a ring of apostles standing on the entablature of the colonnade. The high plinth was retained and the sacramental presence was exalted by raising the tabernacle still higher, at

first by placing it in the hands of four, much-enlarged kneeling angels, who also held the candles that were important to the Eucharistic devotions (Fig. 256). In this form the altar struck a parallel between the Eucharist and the seat of its administration, the Cathedra Petri, sustained by the Fathers of the Church in the great reliquary altar in the apse, which Bernini was then executing for the same pope. In this elevated position the Sacrament tabernacle, rather than appearing as a subordinate altar furnishing, as in the drawing, would now appear to be equated with the celestial globe immediately behind, in Cortona's composition.

Bernini's final design was an amalgam of this second version with the original project. The tabernacle remains

250. Bernini, Altar of the Holy Sacrament. St. Peter's, Rome

251. Bernini, Altar of the Holy
Sacrament, with Pietro da Cortona's
Trinity. St. Peter's, Rome

elevated, while its central core is elongated by the introduction of a tall drum beneath the cupola. The kneeling angels, relieved of all ancillary duty, replace Peter
and Paul at the extremities of the altar. The supporting
role of the angels who bore the tabernacle in the second
version is now played by the angels in Cortona's *Trinity*,
who seem to embrace Bernini's tabernacle as well as the
globe behind (Figs. 249, 257). Taken together, the Sacrament altar and the Trinity now function effectively as a
coordinated whole. Divine grace descends from the Trinity through the universe, to be embodied in the Eucharist
on the altar. In the final version the angels become, exclusively, devotees. The decision to "defunctionalize" their
role recalls Alexander VII's insistence that the colonnades

of the piazza have no other purpose than to serve in celebration of the Corpus Domini. So also Bernini's angels
perform no other service than to kneel in perpetual adoration of the Holy Sacrament.

The angels, in fact, embody the celestial nature of
sacramental devotion.[225] The liturgy of the Church, especially regarding the Eucharist and especially in its original meaning of thanksgiving, is conceived as a mirror of
and participation in the liturgy celebrated in heaven by
the angels and the saints. The angels in heaven, to whose
status human nature aspires, are engaged in adoration of
the Eucharist – not occasionally but perpetually inton-
ing their joyous acclamations. Bernini's angels make this
vision visible and audible through their gracious smiles

252. Bernini, Altar of the Holy Sacrament, angel. St. Peter's, Rome

253. Bernini, Altar of the Holy Sacrament, angel. St. Peter's, Rome

and delicately parted lips. With their great wings and aureate glow the angels recall the golden cherubim who guarded the Old Testament Holy of Holies. According to some, the angelic hosts included the sublimated souls of just men made perfect, and Bernini's angels seem to reflect their human origin and inspire emulation of their devotion. The creature at the left has long, flowing hair and is fully clothed in the tunic of a subdeacon, with hands pressed together; the head, blank-eyed in ecstasy, inclines inward toward the tabernacle of the host (Fig. 250). The other, with short, radiant locks, one muscular arm and shoulder bare, and hands crossed at the breast, looks outward and down toward the altar with sharply focused pupils (Fig. 251).[226] This distinct, complementary contrast of spiritual natures – contemplative and active – seems to retrieve, in angelic terms, Bernini's demonstration at the beginning of his career of the psycho-physiognomic expression of extreme moral states in his "portrait busts" of the Blessed (female, wearing the tunic of subdeacon) and Damned (male, nude) Souls (Fig. 258a, b).[227] Through their inner- and outer-worldly-directed emotions and actions, the angels intone an acclamatory hymn: their contrapuntal voices reciprocate with impassioned serenity the two chief modes of Eucharistic devotion embodied in the allegories perched over the very entrance to the Sacrament. Corresponding to Faith, the joined hands of the contemplative angel

254. Bernini, Altar of the Holy Sacrament, Risen Christ. St. Peter's, Rome

255. Bernini, study for the Sacrament altar, drawing. Location unknown

were the expression par excellence of the act of adoration, prescribed in the rubrics of the Mass and serving even in a juridical sense in the solemn pledge of fealty. The crossed arms of the active angel, corresponding to the figure of Religion holding the Cross, were an expression of supplication, this attitude being adopted by the celebrant during the prayer *Supplices te rogamus* of the Canon of the Mass.[228] The benign response of the cross-armed angel to the sacrificial offering of the priest surely reflects the specific sense of that prayer, which is to implore the angels to carry the sacrifice from the altar on earth to the altar in heaven.[229]

By definition, angels are present and participate at the altar of the Eucharistic sacrifice. Indeed, the key to understanding Bernini's altar lies in the fact that the Mass is

above all the communal act of the church, where heaven and earth meet. Hence the altar and the Mass are the place and time when angels are present together with the faithful in the performance of this ritual offering and devotion. The Mass is, after all, a celebration, and what it celebrates is nothing less than the paradoxical redemption of mankind through Christ's death. In their form, Bernini's shimmering creatures display mankind's highest aspirations to perfection, and in their expression they evoke the joy that unites humanity and the angels at the Resurrection. Their effulgent and flamboyant drapery seems to consume their very essence in a pyrotechnical display of pure, coruscating energy. Both the fiery nature of these ethereal creatures and the ardor of their love are fused into the golden bronze of which they are made,

256. Bernini, study for the Sacrament altar, drawing. Hermitage, St. Petersburg

itself purified and formed in fire. Whereas the wind-blown angels of the Passion on the Ponte Sant'Angelo are epiphanic, the angels of the Sacrament are devotional, eternally fixed in the ecstatic bliss of their *visio dei*. In this sense they seem literally to reflect the Pseudo-Dionysius's description in the *Celestial Hierarchies* of the shining and enflamed garments that cover the nudity of the intelligent beings of heaven, as symbolizing the divine form.[230] The ardor of their devotion to the Sacrament is epitomized and announced by the emblematic flames and palm fronds of victorious martyrdom emblazoned on the gates to the sanctuary (Fig. 249).

As with the bridge angels, many autograph preliminary studies, drawn as well as sculpted, testify to the painstaking labor that lay behind these quite different, chiaroscuro effects (Figs. 259, 260).[231] In these sketches, Bernini sought deliberately not only to defunctionalize the figures, but also to "dematerialize" them. The continuous, predominantly linear definition of form in the bridge angels is here replaced by a flickering pattern that arises from the juxtaposition of discrete patches of light and dark. (It is no accident that the single preserved autograph drawing for the drapery of a bridge angel is in pen and ink, whereas all the drawings for the sacrament angels are brush and wash.) On the bridge the white marble reflects the spiritual movement and solar luminosity of those who bear witness to the salvific sacrifice. On the Sacrament altar the gilt bronze embodies the fiery substance and passionate bliss of Eucharistic devotion. In both cases the materials become as transcendent

as the images they represent. Evidently, Bernini's ultimate choice of medium in visualizing the Sacrament was
light: following a millennial tradition according to which
light was the visual manifestation of divinity, he imitated
God's own act of illumination at the end of the first day,
after creating the heaven, the earth and the sea (Gen.1:
1–3). Taken together, the altar, the figures, the tabernacle, and the Trinity fresco behind evoke, through a setting
for the earthly liturgy of the church, the heavenly liturgy
that celebrates all creation.

Since the early Renaissance there had been an ever-
expanding tradition to reserve the Eucharistic Host on
the altar. The Host was placed in an architectural container that might, in a sense, be described as a reliquary whose form reflects its ideal prototype, the Holy
Sepulcher. The decoration often also includes allusions
to Old Testament antecedents such as the Ark of the
Covenant, the Temple of Jerusalem, and the Heavenly
Jerusalem. Angels, in various acts of devotion or exaltation, were a standard part of the representational repertory. And Christ was commonly depicted in reference
to the Passion or the Resurrection, which might take the
form of a figure of the risen Christ placed atop a centrally

planned tabernacle. Bernini's altar refers to all these hallowed traditions but also breaks with them in nearly every respect. I have not encountered an earlier instance
in which, on a monumental scale, a free-standing tabernacle is flanked by two angels kneeling in attitudes of
prayer. In the nearest precedent, which Bernini certainly
knew, a sacrament altar of the early sixteenth century in
S. Croce in Gerusalemme in Rome, there are kneeling angels, but they serve as candelabra-bearers (Fig. 261).[232]
In plan, Bernini's altar is a subtle adaptation of his design
for the facade of the church of S. Andrea al Quirinale,
where the convex entrance "tabernacle" protrudes at the
center of two flanking, concave wings (Figs. 262, 263).
The curving wings of the altar end in diagonals, as do the
colonnades of the piazza, except that here the extremities serve as pedestals for the pair of angels kneeling in
adoration, who are placed diagonally with respect to the
altar itself. They thus appear in three-quarter view, in-
termediating by their postures and the directions of their
glances between the worshiper-celebrant before the altar
and the Sacrament itself. In this way, the angels initiate the spatial and conceptual continuum in which the
Sacrament proceeds from the divine grace of the Trinity
to the spectator.

Bernini's tabernacle follows that of S. Croce in referring to one of the most famous and widely imitated
buildings of the Renaissance, the so-called Tempietto designed by Bramante to mark the spot of Saint Peter's martyrdom not far from the Vatican, in the courtyard of the
Franciscan convent adjoining the church of S. Pietro in
Montorio (Fig. 264). Apart from its role as a paragon
of Renaissance architecture, Bramante's Tempietto entailed several associations appropriate for a sacrament
tabernacle. In its design it had assimilated the classical
peripteral temple to a centrally planned domical structure commonly associated with the Holy Sepulcher in
Jerusalem – hence its relevance at S. Croce – as well
as being used in temporary catafalques erected in the
churches as funeral commemorations.[233] At St. Peter's
the reference to the Tempietto served to relate Peter's
death to that of Christ himself, and had already been
cited by Bramante in his design for the cupola of the
church. The celebratory nature of the repository of the
Sacrament is expressed through the differences between
it and its monumental prototypes. The tabernacle is more
elaborate, its fluted Corinthian order and sumptuous materials – gilt bronze inlaid with azure lapis lazuli – recall
the lavishness of the biblical description of the Holy of
Holies and Saint John's vision of the celestial Jerusalem in
the Book of Revelations. On the pediment of the temple
door, the flanking allegorical figures of Faith and Religion convey the fundamental paradox of Catholic belief and doctrine, referring both to the tomb of Christ
and to his triumphant resurrection. Crowned with figures of the apostles, the tabernacle's colonnade recalls

257. Bernini, Altar of the Holy Sacrament; Pietro da Cortona,
Trinity, engraving. (after De'Rossi 1702–21, part III, pl. 22)

258. Bernini, *Blessed and Damned Souls*. Spanish Embassy to the Holy See, Rome

the semicircular colonnades of the piazza S. Pietro, so that the phalanxes of saints celebrating and guarding the processional way culminates here, in the apostolic guard of honor flanking Peter and Paul at the Holy of Holies. Bestrewn with the stars from the arms of Clement X, the cupola becomes a veritable Dome of Heaven. The sacramental theme of death and resurrection would have been the predominant image of the entire basilica in the crown of Bernini's first design for the Baldacchino over the high altar (Fig. 125). Now, half a century later, Bernini repeated in miniature essentially the same figure, for essentially the same reason, atop his sacrament tabernacle.

Although relatively small and difficult to discern in detail from below, the risen Christ is one of Bernini's most remarkable creations, unprecedented in its combination of four heretofore unrelated features (Fig. 254): the shroud of death is cast aside to reveal the nude body in its entirety along the right side; the Lord is shown without the wounds of the Crucifixion; the figure is carried aloft on a cloud; and while the right arm is raised heavenward, the face is inclined down to the right. The nude, perfect body is the glorified state of the New Adam to which he returned at the Resurrection – a clear recollection of Michelangelo's famous nude, *Risen Christ*, in S. Maria sopra Minerva in Rome.[234] With the apostles ranged about the tabernacle-tomb below, the cloud-borne Christ evokes the theme of the Ascension. The uplifting gesture of Christ's right hand – which echoes that of Christ in Michelangelo's Sistine Chapel fresco

(Fig. 265) – and the direction of his inclination suggest the Lord's salvific action on behalf of those whom he saves at the resurrection of all souls on the last day. With the force of a heaven-bent explosion the figure embodies, as does the Eucharist itself, the entire process of salvation from Christ's death to the Last Judgment. In this context, the relation between Bernini's tabernacle and Pietro da Cortona's composition becomes critically significant, because the Last Judgment, the ultimate act of the divine drama, is commonly represented as taking place under the aegis of the Trinity.[235] The relationship here recapitulates that which Bernini originally envisaged at the high altar, with Christ rising from the crown of the Baldacchino to take his seat at the Last Judgment in the dome, beneath the beneficent God the Father in the lantern (Figs. 125, 115). The lantern fresco, painted by Cesare d'Arpino following Michelangelo's image in the Sistine Chapel ceiling of God creating the sun and moon, shows the Eternal Father creating the "lights in the firmament of the heaven" (Gen.1:14,15; Fig. 266).[236] The providential coincidence of this religio-historical drama cannot have escaped the participants, least of all Bernini and Clement X himself: the pope under whom d'Arpino had begun the work of bringing the great dome over the tomb of the apostles to completion also bore the name Clement (VIII, Aldobrandini, 1592–1605), and was also identified by stars in his coat of arms. Inspired by divine clemency, the popes had vaulted the earthly image of the Heavenly Jerusalem with its celestial canopy.

259. Bernini, study for a kneeling angel, drawing. Windsor Castle

THE CHURCH, THE CITY, AND THE ARTIST

It would be a grave error to confine our perception of Bernini's work at St. Peter's in a narrow Petrine, or even ecclesiological, framework without considering its relation to the urban and social domain of the city as a whole, and to the inner, spiritual domain of the artist himself.

ROMA ALESSANDRINA: URBAN UNITY, PUBLIC WELFARE, AND UNIVERSAL CHRISTIAN CHARITY

The building was always the centerpiece of a worldview that was itself centered on the city of Rome, from which the pope spoke, as Christ's vicar, *urbi et orbi*. The conscious and explicit development of this programmatic relationship, initiated in the Renaissance, culminated in the seventeenth century, especially under Alexander VII, when Rome acquired three epithets – two contemporary, Roma moderna and Roma alessandrina, the third applied a posteriore in our own time, Roma barocca. The coincidence and significance of these new views of the city – chronological, papal, stylistic – were essentially the theme of one of the great books of recent urban history, Richard Krautheimer's *The Rome of Alexander VII, 1655–1667* (1985), consideration of which provides important insights into the nature of this epochal development of what can now with particular justification

260. Bernini, study for a kneeling angel, terra-cotta. Musée des Beaux-Arts, Besançon

261. Attributed to Jacopo Sansovino, Altar of the Sacrament. S. Croce in Gerusalemme, Rome

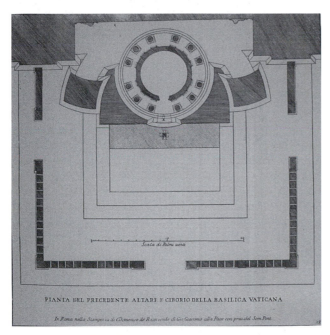

262. Bernini, Altar of the Sacrament, plan

properly be called "modern" history.[237] Contemporaries used the term "Modern" chiefly in the Petrarchan sense of postmedieval and in contrast to the ancient city, whereas for Krautheimer, Alexander's extravagant campaigns of building and embellishment epitomized the transformation of the chaotic and squalid medieval town that survived from antiquity into the splendid new capital of the Christian world.

Alexander was by no means the first pope with a passion for building, nor was he the first to regard Rome as a projection of himself and his office. But whereas Sixtus V, for example, still conceived of the city in largely symbolic terms – the avenues connecting the patriarchal

basilicas were seen as a star-shaped pattern reflecting his family emblem as well as the star of Bethlehem – Alexander's view was functional, in that he believed the city and its monuments served an urgent, contemporary ideological and strategic purpose. Indeed, perhaps Krautheimer's main contribution was to perceive a comprehensive significance underlying the building mania that has always been regarded as Alexander's chief strength – or weakness, depending on whether one gives greater importance to its effect on the city or its effect on the papal treasury. Krautheimer realized, first of all, that Alexander was not just a Maecenas in the popular sense of a vulgar Renaissance tyrant bent on a vulgar display of wealth and power, but a man of rare intelligence and refined taste who, moreover, followed the work personally, participating in the most minute details of planning with a passion that can only have been born of an innate gift and cultivated interest. In a sense, I suspect that this last may have been one of the mainsprings of Krautheimer's own interest, arising from his study and ultimate publication of the passages dealing with art and artists from Alexander's personal diary.[238] This document is in itself utterly extraordinary: I am not aware of a comparable personal record of any previous pope. (Fabio Chigi, from a great Sienese family, must have taken as his model the famous *Commentaries* of his compatriot predecessor, Pius II, Aeneas Silvius Piccolomini.) No less astonishing, however, is the amount of time and effort Alexander devoted to these matters. Bernini and Alexander were together constantly – consulting, discussing, planning, designing – often for long periods on a weekly basis, sometimes even more often. In this respect,

263. Bernini, S. Andrea al Quirinale. Rome

264. Bramante, Tempietto. S. Pietro in Montorio, Rome

too, Alexander was unprecedented, and Krautheimer perceived that, not only was the pope mad about architecture, but his madness encompassed the whole of the city. His improvements not only focused on the obvious, major places and monuments in the heart of Rome but also extended to the outskirts, the *disabitato*, to use the term Krautheimer preferred, although it was often populated by the poor, the dispossessed, and vagabond gypsies. I myself came to appreciate from the book that the Cathedra Petri was only the last stop on a physical and conceptual pilgrimage that began at the Porta del Popolo. The sharpness and comprehensiveness of Alexander's vision is attested in many subtle ways beyond, or underlying, the works themselves – for example, the new accuracy and comprehensiveness of the maps of Alexander's Rome, and the lists of his works compiled and portrayed in illustrated series of engravings. But perhaps there is no better indication of both the intimacy and the comprehensiveness of Alexander's vision than the fact that he kept in his private chambers a model of the city. (It is interesting to speculate where his miniature Rome fits in the history of city models;[239] it was, I suppose, as complete and accurate as the maps of Alexander's Rome, and it is the first model I can recall that was made for the purpose of urban planning. Evidently, the pope not only thought about the city in a modern, comprehensive way; he also had a modern, comprehensive way of representing it – a new kind of "three-dimensional" urban consciousness, one might say.)

Just as Alexander's vision was global, so is Krautheimer's, as he extends the normal purview of architectural history itself, and this in two senses. He is at pains not only to consider individual buildings but also to relate them to their contexts, their immediate surroundings as well as their interlocking connections with other works throughout the city, and even beyond. Moreover, architecture itself is no longer conceived of in terms of permanent structures, but includes city squares and public spaces of all sorts – marketplaces, theater sets and ephemeral spectacles, gardens, streets, and tree-lined allées – everything we tend to call, for want of a still more comprehensive term, the built environment. A vast panorama is deftly captured in what is, after all, a relatively brief text.

Considered thus, Krautheimer's book draws a thin line between the genres of building history and urban history. The ten chapters carry the reader through a sequence of ideas, beginning with the career and character of Alexander VII: his family, his education, his learning, his wit, his financial nonchalance, his love of architecture. The second chapter deals with what Krautheimer calls the urban substructure: the pope's efforts to widen and straighten the city's messy tangle of medieval "ways," partly to make them grand and beautiful, and partly to accommodate the growing traffic problems created by that monstrous newfangled conveyance, the horse-drawn coach; and his campaign to clean up the equally messy and unsightly markets that encumbered public spaces of high visibility, such as the Forum and the Pantheon, by confining the vendors to less conspicuous locations and/or providing new, more efficient accommodations. Chapter 3 deals with the pope's architects and some of their major projects. The central figure, of course, is Bernini, followed by Pietro da Cortona; Borromini, Krautheimer observes, was such a difficult character that Alexander wanted as little as possible to do with him! Chapter 4 explores the contemporary notion of "teatro," not in the narrow sense of a spectacle, but in the large sense of any global, encompassing idea, especially as the term applies to churches and the spaces before and around them. Cortona's S. Maria della Pace, Bernini's S. Andrea al Quirinale and St. Peter's, including both the square and the Cathedra, are cases in point. Chapter 5 concerns overall planning and opposition, primarily the careful control Alexander exercised, at vast expenditures of his own time and energy, over his projects and those of other patrons (who sometimes resisted) throughout the city. Chapter 6, entitled "Prospects," deals with unrealized projects that give us some idea of what Alexander might have achieved had he lived longer and had more money, but which also testify to the colossal scale of what he did manage to carry out. Chapter 7, called "Roma Antica and Moderna," deals with the treatment of classical remains, showing that, although ancient works could be treated cavalierly on occasion, the principal objective was to integrate them into the modern city so that they, too, could contribute *Ad Maiorem Gloriam Dei*. Chapter 8 is devoted to the Piazza del Popolo as a deliberately theatrical – that is, emulating contemporary stage designs – reformation of the principal entrance to Rome from the north. The piazza was the prelude to a whole series of works intended to embellish and aggrandize the processional way through the city to St. Peter's and the Vatican. Chapter 9, "The Reverse of the Medal," is devoted to the seamier side of Rome, the part that the kind of audience Alexander had in view was not supposed to see. Alexander's Rome may have been beautiful, but for many people it was not a very nice place in which to live.

Together, these chapters amount to a recitation of the main types of monumental urban and architectural projects undertaken under Alexander's direct or indirect control. Although richly informative, awash with stimulating observations, and written in Krautheimer's inimitably lively, informal style, they are essentially repetitions of the same theme: Alexander's passion for building and the grandeur of his ideas, as aided and abetted by his favorite artist-entrepreneur, Bernini. From a formal point of view, the accent is on the perspective vista, the dramatic focus, and majestic scale. Except for chapter 9, there is nothing about what we would today call the urban infrastructure – utilitarian projects (other than public markets) such as sewage and sanitation, ordinary housing, and the like. When Alexander said, "Let nothing built in honor of the Virgin be anything but great," it matched Bernini's statement when he reached Paris to redesign the Louvre for Louis XIV, "Let no one speak to me of anything small."[240] And Krautheimer gives a corresponding vision of grand ideas on a grand scale that defined Rome as a special place with a special role to play on the world stage. True to his subjects – Alexander VII, Bernini, and Rome – Krautheimer did not write microhistory!

If all this sounds very Baroque, the architecture of Krautheimer's book is itself rather Baroque. In fact, this sequence of contrapposto-like repetitions and variations on a dominant theme creates an increasing feeling of suspense, as one wonders what, in the end, is the point. The point appears dramatically in the last chapter, "City Planning and Politics: The Illustrious Foreigner," wherein Krautheimer presents what he considered to be the guiding principle – the "political" motivation – that lay behind Alexander's urban enterprises, which were concentrated primarily along the principal ceremonial route through the city and were intended primarily to impress the illustrious foreign visitor. Here it is important to bear in mind that, in a bibliographical note, Krautheimer explicitly disclaims competence as a historian, declaring his dependence in such matters upon von Pastor's *History*

of the Popes and other standard works on the period. And his political motivation turns out to be the standard one, familiar to all students of Italian Baroque: the victories of the Protestants and the rise in the industrial and mercantile power of the North; the establishment and hegemony over European affairs of the great national states, especially France, Spain, and the Hapsburgs – all these factors had led to a drastic diminution in the real power of the Church, in the face of which Pope Alexander adopted what might be described as a policy of "overcompensation," seeking to aggrandize and embellish the physical power of the city to make up for the loss of political power. He sought to convince the world that the papacy remained a factor to be reckoned with, by transforming Rome into a great modern city, or at least the appearance of one.[241] This perception of a "diplomatic" rationale underlying and motivating Alexander's architectural mania may be Krautheimer's most original contribution in the book.

Paradoxically, then, the modern city was created, not from any fundamental shift in attitude or values, but as an act of deception. At bottom, from a strictly art-historical point of view, the ultimate argument of Krautheimer's book is rather conventional. The effect is to "instrumentalize" the Baroque, which becomes an art of propaganda and representation rather than the expression of a new worldview, which the idea of modernity would suggest. This conception of the Baroque as an artificial, bombastic, overcompensatory reaction to the challenge of Protestantism, as an art of rhetoric, display, and theatricality, coincides with the equally conventional, absolutist conception of political consciousness in the seventeenth century.[242] Alexander's was preeminently an urban renewal program conceived as "of the elite, by the elite, and for the elite."

There was another side to this medal, however, no less important, in my view, than the obverse. Alexander's new urbanism had what I would call a subversive, underground aspect, of which Krautheimer caught glimpses but the implications of which he did not fully grasp. The point begins with the fact that the urban population of Rome was, after all, a very powerful force – moral, economic, and political. In this sense, Rome was like many other cities in Europe, where there was a growing consciousness of and concern for social problems that had no doubt long existed. Krautheimer is aware of this background to the extent that he devotes his next-to-last chapter, "The Reverse of the Medal," to a remarkable document written in 1656–9 by an absolutely minor and otherwise insignificant administrative employee, one Lorenzo Pizzati from Pontremoli, in which he details the execrable conditions of everyday life in the city and the pitiable state of its underprivileged population,

along with drastic and utopian suggestions for allevi-
ating them. For Krautheimer the report simply reveals
an underlying reality for which Alexander's urban program was a kind of cosmetic cover-up for the benefit
of visiting dignitaries. However, the improvements were
surely meant for the edification of the people of Rome
as well, and not only as embellishment. For example,
more than once it is reported that an important function
of the vast expenditures for the Piazza S. Pietro was as
a public work program to provide employment for the
indigent, especially the unskilled.[243] I think a good case
could be made that this attitude originated with Bernini
himself, who certainly promoted it. A primary source is a
remarkable document prepared circa 1657–8 by Bernini
in response to objections to his project, in which he eulo-
gizes Alexander's efforts to deal with precisely the problems of homelessness and unemployment described by
Lorenzo Pizzati. In response to criticisms of the "use-
lessness" of the piazza colonnades, Bernini replied – in
a wholly modern spirit of social welfare – that, on the
contrary, the work they provided for the poor and unemployed was the most efficacious charitable use of public
funds for the public good. Explaining the piazza project,
Bernini wrote:

> He [the pope] quickly applied opportune remedies to
> the evils, and, compassionate toward poverty – which
> not only wandered unemployed about the city but lan-
> guished under the oppression of a famine that increas-
> ingly elicited his pity the more it afflicted the people –
> he turned to distributing large quantities of gold, al-
> though the scarcer harvest limited the torrent of this de-
> vout munificence. Moved by wholehearted Charity, this
> most generous pope saw clearly that simply to open the
> Treasury for the common good was to promote idleness
> and nourish vice. Whence the very antidote one applied
> to restore health could be the potent toxin to poison
> it. He therefore repressed that flame of Charity, not to
> extinguish it, but so that it might be more greatly dis-
> persed to the benefit of his subjects, whence he thought
> to begin a great construction, through which to encour-
> age labor among the homeless, and by the expenditure
> of a large sum of money to alleviate the immediate
> need.[244]

When it is said, rightly, that Alexander's program nearly
ruined the papal finances, it was not merely a spendthrift
vanity, it was also the result of what today would be
called a program of public works for social welfare and
rehabilitation, the cost of which was ultimately beyond
the reach of the economic system on which it was based.
The proof of this point lies in the fact that Alexander
specifically opposed outright gifts to the poor, not only
because it engendered dependency on the dole, but also
because it was an indignity; instead, he favored helping

the poor by providing work for which they could be paid
and so retain their Christian pride.[245]

The great weight and import of the populace is also
evident from a fundamental source that is overlooked in
Krautheimer's Roma alessandrina: an official document,
deliberately compiled at the pope's behest. I refer to the
apostolic visitations commanded by Alexander VII to all
the churches and dioceses of Rome. Apostolic visits had
a long history, to be sure; and earlier in the century Urban VIII had ordered one that fills three very substantial
volumes. But none of these precedents even remotely approaches the scope, depth, and systematic coverage of
Alexander's effort to gather and organize information
about what ultimately mattered, the spiritual conditions
of the people of Rome. Alexander's apostolic visitation –
which continued throughout his reign – has been described as the most comprehensive in the modern history
of Rome.[246]

My reasons for emphasizing this reverse of the medal
are two. I am not concerned simply to reveal the existence of this social substructure of the city and its problems in Alexander's Rome; they had existed for a long
time. What is important to understanding Alexander's
modernity, and the scope and meaning of his vision for
the city, is the fact that he was aware of their existence; he
perceived the conditions in the city not only as a physical
but also as a social and moral whole; he sought to grasp
them by studying them carefully and in detail, and to do
something about them in a conscious and comprehensive
way. I do not want to overstate my case. Alexander was
a product of his age, not ours. He had his own defects,
he failed to realize many of his projects, and many of
the projects he did complete failed to achieve their purpose. But just as his urbanistic projects on the obverse
of the medal bore fruit in the subsequent history of architecture and urban planning, so did his ideas on the
reverse. Alexander was the first pope in modern times to
make a serious effort to end the tradition of nepotism,
and his effort was a direct inspiration for Innocent XI,
who actually did finally break the tradition.[247] A similar spirit underlay another great project of unification
and consolidation with which Bernini became involved,
effecting a new principle of what would come to be
thought of as state-sponsored social welfare. The myriad
private and selective charities of the city were subsumed
into a single, comprehensive institution devoted to all
the poor, under the aegis of the papacy. The entire indigent population was given shelter at the Lateran palace
of the popes, no less, which, it was reported in 1676,
Bernini was supposed to refurbish for this purpose. First
broached by Lorenzo Pizzati in his diatribe of 1656–9,
the idea was taken up under the succeeding popes by an
Oratorian priest, Mariano Sozzini (1612–80), and was
championed by Bernini's nephew, Francesco Marchese
(1623–97), who was also an Oratorian. The project was

266. Cesare d'Arpino, *God Creating the Stars*. Lantern of the cupola, St. Peter's Rome

265. Michelangelo, *Last Judgment*, detail. Sistine Chapel, Vatican Palace, Rome

actually carried out under the great reforming pope Innocent XII (1691–1700). Marchese was mainly responsible for the program, and he must have been instrumental in the institution' s decision to take Bernini's last work, the bust of the Savior (see Fig. 267), as the model for the sculpted insignias that were placed throughout the city on those buildings whose rents were devoted to the great cause (1694–5). For a variety of reasons, financial as well as social, the project was short-lived, but it engendered a sequence of institutions and programs of social welfare whose history can be traced thereafter down to our own time.[248] The obverse and reverse belong to the same medal, after all. Alexander's collective awareness of his distinguished aristocratic visitors from abroad was part and parcel of an equally collective awareness of his ordinary, often underprivileged, subjects at home. In this sense, too, he helped to transform Roma antica into Roma moderna, and Roma barocca.

THE BLOOD OF CHRIST (1669–70)

The spiritual pilgrimage at St. Peter's that Bernini envisaged from his earliest youth – "Oh, if only I could be the one" – reached its ultimate goal in the passage over the Ponte Sant'Angelo and the Sacrament altar. The feelings and ideas expressed in these works held deep personal significance for the now aged artist. Contemplating his own death during this same period, he created two works of what might be called devotional eschatology, with a view to achieving a "good death."[249] In his eightieth year he carved the recently rediscovered sculpted, half-length bust of Christ (Fig. 267), whose pose evokes

267. Bernini, bust of the Savior. S. Sebastiano fuori le mura, Rome

the Last Judgment and makes a particular point of alluding to the chest wound.[250] Nearly a decade earlier he had distilled in a spectacular, angel-filled apparition known as the *Sangue di Cristo* (Blood of Christ), an inner

268. Bernini, *Sangue di Cristo*, engraving by François Spierre, 473 × 290mm (after Marchese 1670). Vatican Library, Rome

vision that must have guided and inspired him through all the divagations of his life's work, including St. Peter's (Fig. 268). This famous composition, in which the Virgin intervenes between the Eucharist and the Trinity, was a veritable emblem of Bernini's sense of his personal raison d'être and his mission as a creative artist: he kept a large painted version of it before his bed until the end.[251] Often described as mystical – too often, in my view – the scene is a clear and impassioned articulation of Bernini's mode of preparing for death in accordance

with the precepts of a medieval tradition codified in a famous text, the *Ars moriendi*. The Art of Dying had been revived toward the end of the sixteenth century, notably by the Jesuits, who had institutionalized the tradition in the Confraternity of the Good Death (Bona Mors), of which Bernini was a long-standing and faithful member.

He undertook the design late in 1669, partly no doubt in commemoration of the great Florentine Carmelite mystic Maria Maddalena de' Pazzi, whom Clement IX

269. Michelangelo, *God Creating the Firmament*. Sistine Chapel, Vatican Palace, Rome

had recently canonized, and partly as a sort of votive expiation for the failure that year of a major project to refurbish the apse of S. Maria Maggiore, mother of all churches dedicated to the Virgin, including tombs for both Clement IX and his predecessor, Alexander VII.[252] With a view to both these causes, Bernini had the composition reproduced in a large, resplendent print by François Spierre, to be promulgated as an independent devotional image.[253] The print was carefully scaled so as also to fold neatly into the small octavo format of a devotional tract composed by the artist's beloved nephew and counselor in the "art of dying," the Oratorian father Francesco Marchese, which provides the work's full ideological context. Published in 1670 as work on Ponte Sant'Angelo was nearing completion, the theme of this volume, itself a modern version of the *Ars moriendi*, was epitomized in its title: *The Only Hope of the Sinner Consists in the Blood of Our Lord Jesus Christ*.[254] The theme of the engraving is epitomized by two inscriptions in which the blood of Christ's sacrifice is conceived as an offering on behalf of the sinner: one is from Paul's Epistle to the Hebrews, "The blood of Christ, who offered himself without spot to God, will purge our conscience";[255] the other quotes the new saint named after the Virgin and her first namesake, Mary Magdalene, both of whom had worshiped at the foot of the Cross, "I offer you, eternal Father, the blood of the incarnate word; and if anything is wanting in me I offer it to you, Mary, that you may present it to the eternal Trinity."[256] As if emergent from the whiteness of the paper, God the Father, with an expansive gesture that also echoes Michelangelo, dispels the threatening clouds and creates by fiat the exultant event that takes place between Himself and the world below. The gesture echoes that of God the Father in Michelangelo's *Separation of the Sky and Water* (the second day of Creation), where also only the sky and sea are visible (Fig. 269).[257] But Bernini introduces a significant change that suggests a reciprocal movement: God the

Father turns his left hand up, as if raising the Crucifixion heavenward, and his right hand down as if commanding the descent of the salvific blood. The reference to Creation may also allude to the commonly held view that the New Dispensation was foreordained. Christ sheds his blood in luminous streams that pour from the wounds in his hands and feet to form an infinite ocean inundating the earth. The Virgin receives the effusions from the chest wound and offers them to the Father on behalf of the sinner. This spectacular tour de force of aerial perspective and foreshortening revives and conflates a number of late medieval devotional traditions in a new synthesis.

Conceived as a cloud-borne vision with the Virgin kneeling as advocate before the Crucifixion, the composition follows the traditional mode of intercessory illustrations of the *Ars moriendi*, of which one of the primary injunctions was that the believer preparing for a "good death" should contemplate "holy images, especially the Crucified Christ and the Virgin." The prescription for divine intercession might be illustrated as a heavenly apparition above the deathbed: under the aegis of the Trinity, the virgin mother as Queen of Heaven offers her breast and pleads for the *moriens* on bended knee, while Christ on the cross points to his chest wound, for it is as sacrificial and sacramental son that he transmits her appeal to God the Father (Fig. 270).[258] None of these features is present in Bernini's composition, in which, moreover, the vision is conceived as appearing not *within* the picture to the moribund on his deathbed, but *through* the picture to the viewer. One cannot repress the suspicion that the whole image was conceived to be seen exactly as Bernini saw it at the foot of his own deathbed. Whereas the artists of the *Ars Moriendi* represented the death scene, Bernini isolated the vision and made the viewer of the engraving – imaginary *moriens*, disconcertingly suspended between the apparition above and the flood below – its witness. It is clear that while retaining essential elements of the *Ars moriendi* imagery, Bernini departed radically from the medieval tradition, which had focused on what might be called the external mechanism of intercession. He focuses instead on the inner, sacramental medium of salvation, that is, the Eucharist itself, corresponding to the mottoes inscribed below and to the title of Father Marchese's book in which they are explained.

The *Sangue di Cristo* incorporates three fundamental innovations – the ocean of blood, the chest wound of Christ, and the action of the Virgin – that together express the essential conception embedded in these texts: the Eucharist as a reciprocal offering to and by the sinner, and the only means by which universal redemption may be achieved. Metaphors expressing the generosity and ubiquity of the blood of Christ had frequently been cast in liquid terms, like the Fountain of Life, the flood of Noah, the sea, a river of blood. The idea was illustrated

270. *The Death of Moriens and the Intercession with the Trinity of Christ and the Virgin*, stained-glass votive window, Wettingen, Switzerland

272. Detail of Fig. 268, Virgin receiving Water and Blood in Her Hands

in Botticelli's Eucharistic depiction of the Crucifixion titled by Vasari "Triumph of the Faith," where the liquid descends from the Cross to form a cleansing river of baptism (Fig. 271).[259] This motif expressly illustrates the account of Christ's death given in the Gospel of John, discussed earlier.[260] Among the many interpretations of the miracle, the one associating the effusions from the chest wound with the Virgin Mary and the Church is most im-

portant here because it underlies the third innovation of Bernini's composition, the role of Christ's mother. The streams from the chest wound descend not to the ocean but to Mary's hands, where they disappear (Fig. 272). Mary kneels, arms and hands extended, palms turned up to receive the effusions, which, commingled within her body to become the Eucharist, she also offers up to the Trinity – exactly the process of receiving and offering

271. Sandro Botticelli, *Triumph of the Faith*, woodcut

273. Madonna avvocata ("Madonna di S. Sisto"). S. Maria del Rosario, Rome

274. Crucifixion, showing the Virgin as advocate and Ecclesia with the Chalice receiving the Water and Blood of the Sacrament, reliquary plaque, Musée de Cluny, Paris

275. Christ Crucified by the Virtues, Ecclesia with the Chalice receiving Water and Blood, Psalter, MS 54, fol. 15v. Musée Municipal, Besançon

that takes place at every Mass.[261] But the ocean of universal salvation in Bernini's engraving is unique, and specifically complementary to the hardly less extraordinary portrayal of the chest wound: instead of the usual single cascade of blood, two clearly distinguishable streams gush forth. This quite unprecedented act entailed the amalgamation of three related but heretofore distinct interpretations of the Virgin's role in the work of salvation. As Mother of Christ, Mary was the intercessor par excellence with her son, who could refuse her no request for mercy. In Rome this theme was associated above all with a particular class of images in which the Virgin lifts both hands upward in a gesture that suggests both an appeal

and an offering to heaven. The type was familiar from the classic Byzantine Crucifixion composition, in which the Virgin standing beneath the Cross gestures in this way, and had been isolated in Rome as a famous icon known as the Madonna Avvocata (Fig. 273).[262] Any Roman viewer would recognize the allusion in Bernini's figure. In response to Maria Maddalena de' Pazzi's invocation, the Virgin has become, not simply a mother and advocate, but the unique conduit for humanity's unique hope for salvation. This role she performs in her capacity as *Mater Ecclesia*, the Mother Church, a common epithet that alludes equally to the institutional church and to the Virgin as mother and spouse.[263] It was precisely in this capacity that the Virgin-Church participated in what might be called ecclesiological depictions of the Crucifixion collecting the blood from the side wound in an emblematic chalice.[264] In some cases, the institutional nature of the Sacrament is emphasized, as when Ecclesia, on the dexter side of the cross, is contrasted with Synagoga on the sinister side.[265] In some cases, the Virgin and Ecclesia might appear together, thus identifying Mary as compassionate intercessor with the Church as the administrator of the sacraments (Fig. 274). In one notable instance, Ecclesia gathers the water and blood in her chalice, while a personification of Charity inflicts the lance wound (Fig. 275).[266] While the blood and water were frequently shown as two adjacent streams, I have found no precedent for Bernini's absolutely distinct, gushing spouts, one to each hand of the Virgin – whose two breasts, it should be recalled, were traditionally understood as the Old and New Testaments, conjoined in her body.[267] The identification of the Eucharistic chest wound with the Church on the most popular level, as Ecclesia in the original, Greek sense of "community," was specifically relevant to the ecumenical ideal conveyed by the ocean metaphor in

276. *Mary as Priest offering the Chalice of the Sacrament to the Trinity*, engraving. Brussels, Jumpers Collection (after Missaglia et al. 1954, fig. 102, p. 111)

277. Caravaggio, *Madonna del Rosario*. Kunsthistorisches Museum, Vienna

Marchese's text and Bernini's composition. The formulation concerning the Eucharist given in the Catechism of the Council of Trent stressed that the water mentioned by John was identified with the word "used in the Apocalypse, to signify the people, and therefore, Water mixed with wine signifies the union of the faithful with Christ their head."[268]

The third manifestation of the Virgin associates her with the actual function of the Church in the administration of the sacraments, *Maria sacerdos*, the Virgin as Priest.[269] The concept of Mary-Ecclesia as equivalent to the consecrated male priest received its first explicit formulation by the eighth century from the Pseudo-Epiphanius: "equivalent to the priest and indeed the altar, she gives Christ our celestial bread in remission of our sins."[270] The principle is illustrated in a dramatic vision in a Flemish engraving of the early seventeenth century. Mary appears in this sacerdotal capacity, cloud-borne, kneeling before an altar and offering the chalice and wafer to God the Father and the Holy Spirit above (Fig. 276).[271] In this context it is significant that the closest antecedent I have found for the Virgin's gesture is that of the priest, Saint Dominic, in Caravaggio's *Madonna of the Rosary,* where it carries essentially the same meaning: Dominic receives the Rosary from the Virgin and offers her the devotion of the faithful (Fig. 277). Bernini's Virgin fuses all these characters in a single persona, and the symbolic chalice is replaced by Mary-Ecclesia's own hands, bathed in the humble and charitable sacrifice she shares as compassionate co-redemptress. The portrayal of the Madonna was a direct visualization of the most famous of all accounts of the Virgin's role as Eucharistic conduit in the process of salvation, Bernard of Clairvaux's sermon on the Nativity of the Virgin, called *De aquaeductu.* The title itself makes the point, which is defined explicitly in the final paragraph, to which Marchese himself alludes:

> But, my brother, whatsoever thou hast a mind to offer to the Lord be sure to entrust it to Mary, so that thy gift shall return to the Giver of all grace through the same channel by which thou didst obtain it. God of course had the power, if He so pleased, to communicate His grace without the interposition of this Aqueduct. But he wanted to provide us with a needful intermediary. For perhaps "thy hands are full of blood" (Is. 1:15) or dirtied with bribes: perhaps thou hast not like the Prophet "shaken them free from all gifts" (Is. 33:15). Consequently, unless thou wouldst have thy gift rejected, be careful to commit to Mary the little thou desirest to offer, that the Lord may receive it through her hands, so dear to Him and most "worthy of all acceptation" (1 Tim. 1:15). For Mary's hands are the very whitest of lilies; and assuredly the Divine Lover of lilies will never complain of anything presented by His Mother's hands that is not found among the lilies. Amen.[272]

The underlying principle was expressed in Saint Bonaventure's treatise on the Incarnate Word, in terms that seem perfectly illustrated in the *Sangue di Cristo:*

> one cannot reach the benefaction of this sacrament without the protection of the Virgin. And for this reason, as this holy body has been given to us through her, so it must also be offered by her hands and received by her hands as the Sacrament, which she procured for us and which was born from her breast.[273]

In the *Sangue di Cristo,* Maria Maddalena's first appeal is to the Father, then to the Virgin, and ultimately to the Trinity. Perhaps the most profound insight into the ultimate meaning of Bernini's image and Marchese's text is hidden, that is, to be found in the omission of the Holy Spirit from the Trinity evoked by the saint. The omission is certainly not inadvertent, since the Holy Spirit is a central step in the heavenly ladder of the saint's offering as

reported by her biographer, Vincenzo Puccini, referenced in the citation itself, by the saint herself in her *Colloqui* and by Marchese himself in the text of his book.[274] This is indeed the Hidden God secreted *in potentia* in every altar – many of which are actually inscribed with Isaiah's famous phrase, *Vere tu es Deus absconditus, Deus Israel salvator* ("Truly, thou art a God who hidest thyself, O God of Israel, the Savior"; Is. 45.15) – and whose presence is effected through the sacrament of the Eucharist offered through the Church.

The *Sangue di Cristo* thus incorporates into one comprehensive image of intercession an explicit and intensely personal expression of the human drama of the event described in the gospel, as well as its vast Eucharistic-ecclesiological legacy. The evangelist bore witness to the essential, complementary distinction inherent in the miracle of Redemption that took place on the Cross: the sacrificial blood of Christ's death, which brought the promise of salvation to all mankind; and the sin-cleansing fluids that poured from his chest after death as the sacraments bringing salvation to those who seek it through the mediation of his church. At St. Peter's, the same love wound completes the Passion sequence on the Ponte Sant'Angelo, fulfilling the Old Testament in the New. The way is thus opened to the ministrations the faithful will receive upon entering the embrace of the church dedicated to Christ's vicar, to receive at its altar the Sacrament administered by his successors.

The spiritual ideas and comprehensive mode of thought evident in the *Sangue di Cristo* composition extend their reach far beyond St. Peter's, especially through the reference in its powerful Mariological content to Bernini's project for the apse of S. Maria Maggiore. Having in mind the ancient temple associated with the Vestal Virgins, he envisaged a semicircular colonnade that would have resonated across the city with those of the Piazza San Pietro and the tempietto of the Sacrament altar. In this way, all Rome would have been enveloped in the universal embrace of the Church and the promise of salvation it offered. The thought was an urbanistic counterpart to the Corpus Domini procession emanating from St. Peter's, and to the greatest of the medieval processions, that of the Assumption of the Virgin, which Alexander VII sought to revive. Starting from S. Giovanni in Laterano, the cortege followed the miraculous icon of Christ as it was carried through the center of the ancient city to its "union" with the icon of the Virgin at S. Maria Maggiore, paying homage on the way to the Madonna Avvocata.

The idea of unity, artistic as well as spiritual, might be said to have preoccupied Bernini all his life – at St. Peter's since his childhood encounter with Annibale Carracci and the prospect of a future Baldacchino to provide the new building with a central focal point. In artistic terms his pursuit was epitomized in what he considered his greatest achievement: having surpassed the conventional boundaries between painting, sculpture, and architecture, and succeeded in merging all three in a new kind of unity – a kind of Trinity-in-art, as it were.[275] The conjunction of the visual arts as variants of one overarching principle had been part of the vocabulary of Italian art theory since Vasari described Disegno (meaning both drawing and conceptualization) as their "father." Federico Zuccari had spoken of God as "the true Design, and true author, and perfect and divine Painter, Sculptor and Architect," and had portrayed Disegno as a God the Father–like figure with a "halo" of three interlocking circles that replicated the personal emblem of the "divine" Michelangelo.[276] Bernini emulated Michelangelo in many ways, including his facility in all three visual modes and in regarding his genius as a humble and inadequate instrument of God's will.[277] In this sense, the conjunction of the arts of design was assimilated to the traditional theological metaphor that identified God as the original creative, multimedia artist of the world, *Deus Artifex*. Although Bernini was no theoretician, he was profoundly indebted to this ideological heritage, which attributed a profound spiritual significance to the visual arts. He changed – transmuted would be a better word – the essence of the relationship, however. His predecessors had conceived of the link between the arts as a common procedure that operated on the two levels implicit in the ambivalence of the word "design." For Bernini, the relationship among the arts was not procedural but substantive: painting, sculpture, and architecture were not simply linked but literally fused, melded into one another to create an unprecedented kind of unity, both material and visual, requiring a special name: a "bel composto."[278] God the Father's fiat in the *Sangue di Cristo* creates the spiritual equivalent of this infinitely adaptable and efficacious medium. Bernini's personal invocation of divine charity is confluent with his conception of the nature of his art and with his vision of universal redemption.

Appendix 1 – Bernini's Extant Monumental Works at St. Peter's
(Plans after Nolli 1748)

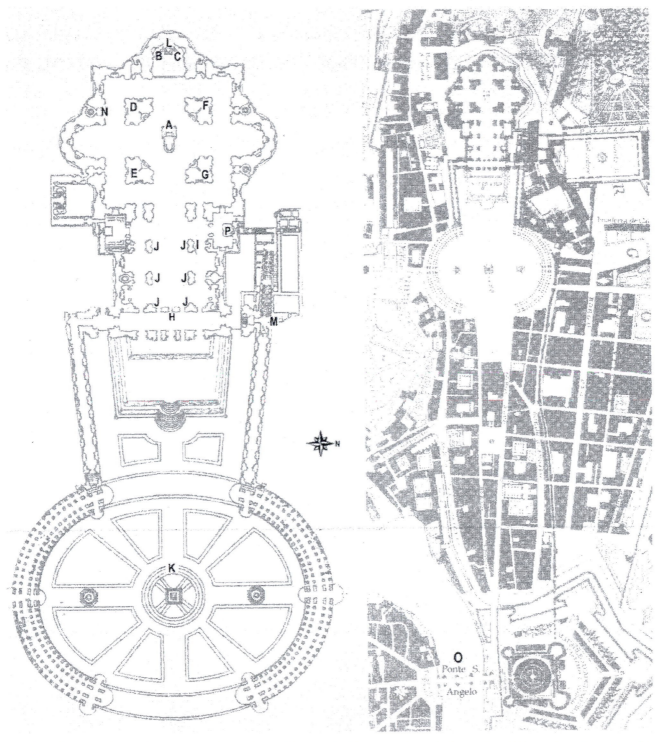

A. Baldacchino   B. Tomb of Paul III   C. Tomb of Urban VIII   D. St. Veronica   E. St. Andrew   F. St. Helen   G. St. Longinus   H. "Feed My Sheep"   I. Matilda of Tuscany   J. Nave Decoration   K. Piazza and Colonnades   L. Cathedra Petri   M. Constantine and Scala Regia   N. Tomb of Alexander VII   O. Ponte Sant'Angelo and Castel Sant'Angelo   P. Sacrament Altar

Appendix 2 – List of Popes during Bernini's Lifetime

Clement VIII	1592–1605	Ippolito Aldobrandini
Leo XI	1605	Alessandro Ottaviano de' Medici
Paul V	1605–21	Camillo Borghese
Gregory XV	1621–3	Alessandro Ludovisi
Urban VIII	1623–44	Maffeo Barberini
Innocent X	1644–55	Giovanni Battista Pamphilj
Alexander VII	1655–67	Fabio Chigi
Clement IX	1667–9	Giulio Rospigliosi
Clement X	1670–6	Emilio Altieri
Innocent XI	1676–89	Benedetto Odescalchi

Notes

This essay is a revised and expanded version of one published in Pinelli 2000, where full bibliography and a detailed catalogue by various authors will be found. The text of this version has benefited from the attentive editing of Mary Elizabeth Lewis and the exemplary research assistance of Uta Nitschke-Stumpf.

1   Baldinucci 1966, 10f. "*Avvenne un giorno, ch'e' si trovò col celebratissimo Anibal Caracci ed altri virtuosi nella basilica di S. Pietro e già avean tutti soddisfatto alla lor divozione, quando nell' uscir di chiesa quel gran maestro, voltatosi verso la tribuna, così parlò: 'Credete a me, che egli ha pure da venire, quando che sia, un qualche prodigioso ingegno, che in quel mezzo e in quel fondo ha da far due gran moli proporzionate alla vastità di questo tempio.' Tanto bastò e non più, per far sì che il Bernino tutto ardesse per desiderio di condursi egli a tanto; e non potendo raffrenare gl'interni impulsi, disse col più vivo del cuore: ≪ O fussi pure quello io! ≫ E così senza punto avvedersene interpretò il vaticinio di Annibale, che poi nella sua propria persona si avverò così appunto come noi a suo tempo diremo, parlando delle mirabili opere, che egli per quei luoghi condusse*" (Baldinucci 1948, 75f.).

2   The sometimes fractious and surprisingly arbitrary operations of the administrative authorities in the naming and decoration of the altars of the new basilica may now be savored in the careful study by Rice 1997. The fiasco of Bernini's bell towers has been exposed in detail by McPhee 2002.

3   Motto of a portrait medal of Bernini commissioned in 1674 in his honor by Louis XIV (Baldinucci 1948, 126f.; Bernini 1713, 147; see Tommaso Montanari in Bernardini and Fagiolo dell'Arco 1999, 302f.). I have taken the liberty of transposing to the multiplicity and unity of Bernini's work at St. Peter's the sense of the motto on the reverse of the medal, where it is accompanied by emblems of the three arts, painting, sculpture, and architecture (and mathematics). Bernini excelled in all three, but was considered the first to have merged them into a "bel composto" (for which see p. 230).

    After this preamble was written I (re)discovered the following passage in Rudolph Wittkower's fundamental monograph on Bernini's sculpture (1997, 120f.): "during the execution of this extraordinary amount of work, covering the span of almost two generations and for its physical extent alone, probably unmatched in the history of art.... Though undertaken without a premeditated comprehensive programme, Bernini's work in

and around St. Peter's embodies more fully the spirit of the Catholic Restoration and, implicitly, that of the Baroque age, than any other complex of works of art in Europe." An overview of Bernini's work at St. Peter's by Damian Dumbrowski (2003) appeared too late to be taken into account here.

4   A tradition universally accepted since the Middle Ages held that the bodies of both St. Peter and St. Paul had been divided; half of each had been deposited at Saint Peter's, the other two halves at Saint Paul's Outside the Walls (Lavin 1968, 1).

5   On this understanding of the Cathedral of Florence and its relevance for St. Peter's, see Lavin 1999b.

6   This phenomenon has been amply studied by Hall 1979.

7   Paul's solutions at St. Peter's – a "temporary" baldachin over the tomb altar and a ciborium toward the apse – took up proposals made under Clement VIII for the Lateran, where the matter of visibility, mainly of the new Sacrament tabernacle and altar in the transept, was also paramount. See Lavin 1984, 407ff., and Freiberg 1995, 52f., 181f., 310.

8   On this metaphorical sense of the material and process of bronze casting, see the illuminating paper by Cole 1999.

9   The passage is quoted and discussed in Lavin 1968, 11ff.

10 On Urban's election, see Lavin, "Bernini's Bumbling Barberini Bees" (1999), 63. The subject has been admirably explored in these connections by Scott 1991, 180–6, who scrupulously acknowledges (185n28) my calling his attention to the miracle of the bees and its relevance to the vault fresco by Pietro da Cortona.

11 The use of full-scale models, especially by Bernini, has been the subject of a series of excellent studies by Bauer, most recently, "Bernini and the Baldacchino" and "Arguing Authority in Late Renaissance Architecture" (both 1996).

12 Baldinucci 1966, 17: "Bernini used to say that it was by chance that his work came out so well, implying that under such a great dome and in such a vast space and among such massive piers, artistic skill alone could never arrive at suitable dimensions and proportions, although, on the contrary, the artist's genius and mind could envisage the appropriate dimensions without the help of any rules." (Baldinucci 1948, 83: "Soleva dire il cavaliere che quest'opera era riuscita bene a caso, volendo inferire che l'arte stessa non poteva mai sotto una sì gran cupola ed in ispazio sì vasto, e fra moli di eccedente grandezza dare una misura e proporzione che bene adeguasse, ove l'ingegno e la mente dell'artefice, tale quale essa misura doveva essere, senz'altra regola concepire non sapesse.")

    Bernini 1713, 39, repeats the same phrase about chance, and adds, p. 40: "Considerò, che in un tratto così smisurato di spazio, vana sarebbe stata la diligenza delle misure, che malamente potevano concordare col tutto di quel Tempio; onde facendo di mestiere uscir dalle Regole dell'Arte, difficilmente vi acconsentiva per timore di perdersi senza guida. Tuttavia accordò così bene quelle repugnanze, che nel dar loro la proporzione, seppe uscir dalle Regole senza violarle, anzi egli stesso da sè trovò quella misura, che invano si cerca nelle Regole."

13 Burbaum 1999, 279, 283.

14 Thelen, *Zur Entstehungsgeschichte* (1967) and *Borromini* (1967); Burbaum 1999, 71. It is indicative that in his monograph on the high altar of St. Peter's and the Baldacchino, Thelen nowhere cites the crucial statement by Borromini himself (see n. 17 below) in its entirety and in its context; and that the author of another recent monograph on the Baldacchino has taken the incredible step of dividing between the two artists a sheet of sketches showing an organic evolution of the design for the crown (our Fig. 128 is the recto), which has universally been regarded as Bernini's handiwork, by both Bernini and Borromini scholars (Kirwin 1997, 161). An important contribution to the whole subject of the conceptualization and realization of

the Baldacchino is that by Bauer, "Bernini and the Baldacchino" (1996).

15 One drawing by Borromini that might be described as a study but in no sense a sketch, confirms the principle, since it was made, as the inscriptions indicate, not for purposes of design but in preparation for the perspective renderings that are justly famous: at the left of the sheet is a perspective grid giving the distance from the projection point ("distanza dal centro della vista"), at the right a longitudinal section of the choir and crossing, with dimensions (Thelen, *Borromini*, 82–4).

16 D'Onofrio 1969, 13, 14, 15, 57, 67, 69, 80, 220, 282.

17 Fioravante Martinelli, *Roma ornata dall'architettura, pittura, e scoltura*, Rome, Bibl. Casanatense, MS 4984, 201 (D' Onofrio 1969, 158, incomplete; for identifications, corrections, and discussion of this passage, see Lavin 1968, 11f., 47):

It was the thought of Paul V to cover with a baldachin the high altar of St. Peter's, with a richness appropriate to the opening made to the confession and sepulcher of the saint. Whereupon Carlo Maderno presented a design with spiral columns; but the baldachin did not touch the columns or their cornice. After the death of Paul the project remained on paper until the pontificate of Urban VIII, who instructed Carlo to allow Bernini to execute the work. Celio, perhaps not fully informed, published that it was the invention of Divine judgment (that is, the Pope), carried out by Bernini. Vincenzo Berti, in a manuscript in the possession of Monsignor Landucci, Sacristan of Our Father Alexander VII, and one who for his eminent virtues is very worthy of a higher position, has written that the design was by Bernini's brother-in-law Ciampelli; I do not know if this is true; but he did not agree with Bernini about the decoration, etc., and said that baldachins are not supported on columns but on staves, and that the baldachin should not run together with the cornice of the columns, and in any case he wanted to show that it was held up by angels. And he added that it was a chimera.

The passage occurs as a marginal correction to the original text, canceled but decipherable, which attributes the design to Bernini: "The metal ciborium with twisted spiral columns is the design of the Cav. Bernini, and the casting by Gregorio de Rossi of Rome. But the Cav. Celio writes that it is the invention of Holy Judgment carried out by Bernini. Vincenzo Berti, in a manuscript in the possession of Monsignor Landucci, Sacristan of Our Father, wrote that it was the design of Bernini's brother-in-law Ciampelli." (Ciampelli was certainly not Bernini's bother-in-law.)

Fù pensiero di Paolo V coprire con baldacchino l'altar maggiore di S. Pietro con ricchezza proportionata all'apertura fatta alla confessione e sepolcro di d.o Onde Carlo Maderno gli presentò un disegno con colonne à vite; ma il baldacchino non toccava le colonne, ne il lor cornicione: sopragionse la morte di Pauolo, e restò l'op.a sul disegno sin al pontificato di Urbano VIII. il quale disse al d.o Carlo si contentasse, che il Bernino facesse d.a opera. Iɪ Cavalier Celio, forse non ben informato del tutto, stampò essere inventione di Santiss.o giuditio (cioè del Papa) messo in opera dal d.o Bernino. Vincenzo Berti manoscritto appresso Mons.r Landucci Sacrista di N'ro Sig.re Alessandro VII e p le sue eminenti virtudi dignissimo di grado superiore, ha scritto, esser disegno del Ciampelli cognato del d.o Bernino, il che non sò se sia vero; ma si bene non concorreva con d.o Bernino circa l'abbigliam.ti et altro; e diceva, che li Baldacchini non si sostengono con le colonne, ma con l'haste, et che il baldacchio non ricor(r)a assieme con la cornice dele colone, et in ogni modo voleva mostrare che lo reggono li Angeli: e soggiongeva che era una chimera.

Il Ciborio con colonne di metallo istorte a vite dell'altar maggiore è disegno del Cav. Bernino, et il getto è di Gregorio de Rossi Rom.o. Ma il Cav.re Celio scrive essere inventione di santissimo giuditio messo in opera dal d.o Cav.re. Vincenzo Berti manoscritto appresso monsig.re Landucci sacrista di N. S.re ha lasciato scritto esser disegno del Ciampelli cognato di d.o Bernino.

Here is a recent egregious example of tendentious obfuscation of Borromini's text, in this case by simply omitting the words that expressly interdict the author's interpretation: "Fioravante Martinelli (1660) sostiene, su indicazione del Borromini, che Carlo Maderno avrebbe suggerito la soluzione di un baldacchino sorretto da quattro colonne tortili già negli ultimi anni del pontificato di Paolo V: 'fu pensiero di Paolo V coprire con baldacchino l'altar maggiore (...) Onde Carlo Maderno gli presentò un disegno con colonne a vite (...)'" (Tuzi 2003, 186).

Bernini may have been returning the chimera barb years later when, discussing Borromini and architecture, he remarked that "a sculptor or painter took the human body as his standard of proportion; Borromini must take a chimaera for his" (Chantelou 1985, 326, 22 October).

18 Ward Perkins 1952, 32 ("The bases and Ionic capitals are carved separately, but may be contemporary"; no reference to the inscribed plinths).

19 The columns were in fact willed to the church of S. Carlo by Filippo Colonna in 1639 (Tomassetti 1975–7, III, 616na).

20 Mauceri 1898, 382n2. The earliest reference to the provenance of the columns is by Teoli 1648, 170f.: "Il Signor Conestabile Don Filippo Colonna hà donato à questa Chiesa [S. Carlo] due Colonne del famoso Tempio di Salomone, quali furono donate al Sig. Marc'Antonio Colonna, quando fù Generale dell'Armata Nauale per Santa Chiesa, al tempo di Pio Quinto Sommo Pontefice," followed by Piazza 1703, 228; and Tomassetti 1898, 216 (also 1975–7, III, 616), who adds that they came from San Lorenzo: "Da quest'antica ed importante chiesa provengono due nobili monumenti della scultura italica del sesto secolo, cioè due candelabri marmorei scolpiti in rilievo; e che ora si ammirano nella moderna chiesa di s. Carlo . . . ."

21 As described by Pastor 1923–53, XVIII, 380f. The visionary motto is quoted in the crossing pier above the figure of Saint Helen, who brought back a relic of the Cross from Jerusalem, and it was a crucial feature of Bernini's later portrayal of the equestrian Constantine.

22 This acute observation was made by Sartorio 1927–8, 600; on the medal, see Lavin 1968, 13f.

23 The document was first published by Minieri Riccio 1882, 260: "Cum velimus Columpnas duas mormoreas nulli edificio adherentes sed olim in solo terre Sancte Marie de Monte iacentes . . . per nos Monasterio Sancti Corporis Christi quod Neapoli cosituitur opus quidem nostrarum manuum et Sancie Regine Jerusalem et Sicilie consortis nostre carissime donates"; the order for shipment follows. The Naples columns have been discussed recently, although not in relation to Bernini's Baldacchino, by Leone de Castris (1986, 144–6; 1993) and Tuzi (2003, 94f.).

24 Gonzaga 1587, 144, describing the high altar: " . . . elegantissime exornatur: Praecipue vero duabus marmoreis columnis que ex amplissimo Salomonis templo allatae feruntur" (cited by Maresca 1888, 116). The Solomonic origin of the columns was repeated by the Franciscan historian Luke Wadding, describing the four-column high altar of S. Chiara.

25 Ward Perkins 1952, 26, concluded that the shafts of the Naples columns were ancient oriental imports and form a group with those at St. Peter's; he does not discuss the capitals or bases, except to note that they are medieval (26n26).

26 "Cum pro castro, quod aput s. Mariam de Monte fieri volumus
     . . ." (for the foregoing, see Huber 1997, esp. 49 and n. 31).

27 Minieri Riccio 1882, 260n4, and Mauceri 1898, 382, note the
     Swabian symbolism of the eagle capitals.

28 See Josephus, *The Jewish War* VII, 158–62. *Josephus* 1968, III,
     550–3.

29 Dell'Aja 1961, 105.

30 Ibid., 104; Gallino 1963, 340.

31 Reproduced in Carcano di Varese 1913, pls. 22, 23. The
     references to Corpus Domini were noted by Spila 1901,
     133 n. 1.

32 "Tholos quatuor innititur columnis quorum duae anteriores ex
     Salomonis Templo Hyerosolimitano extructae sunti" (Wadding
     1628–35, III, 124; cited by dell'Aja 1961, 104).

33 On the medal, signed by Giovanni V. Melone, see most recently
     Museo 1996, 296f. No. 8.143. The event is described by Pastor
     1923–53, XVIII, 415.

34 The design of the medal itself distinctly anticipates that of
     the 1629 medal commemorating the canonization of Andrea
     Corsini in St. Peter's, where Bernini's Baldacchino appears
     (Lavin 1968, fig. 32).

35 Maresca 1888, 116, suggested in passing that the Naples monu-
     ment might have inspired Bernini; the idea was summarily dis-
     missed by Fraschetti 1898, 391n1, and Mauceri 1898, 379fn3,
     on the grounds that such columns were also available in Rome.

36 The continuity of this world-historical, religio-imperial tradi-
     tion was expressed ceremonially, as it were, in Marcantonio's
     victory parade, which passed through the Arches of Constan-
     tine and Titus, and in the many attendant celebrations and
     monuments (see Pastor 1923–53, XVIII, 429–35). The subse-
     quent history of the Naples ciborium is uncertain, except that
     when the church was given a Baroque transformation in the
     mid-eighteenth century, the two marble columns were installed
     flanking the choir, where they remained until the fire of 1943
     (Dell'Aja 1961, 105f.).

37 For much of what follows concerning the tomb of Urban, see
     Lavin, "Bernini's Bumbling Barberini Bees" (1999), 50–71.

38 On this theme of papal succession in the arrangement of the
     tombs, see Borgolte 1989, 313–15, followed by Schütze 1994,
     265f., who notes that the reference would have been made ex-
     plicit by a depiction of Christ Giving the Keys to St. Peter (re-
     peating the subject of the medieval decoration in the apse of the
     old basilica) first planned for the altar in the center of the apse,
     between the two tombs.

39 Panofsky 1964, 94, noted the substitution in relation to the Paul
     III tomb of the theological virtue Charity for the moral virtue
     Prudence; but he failed to realize that this change implied a
     corresponding shift in meaning for Justice. Wilkinson 1971 rec-
     ognized that the allegories on the tomb of Urban were attributes
     of Divine Wisdom, followed by Lavin, "Bernini's Bumbling Bar-
     berini Bees" (1999).

40 This tradition was admirably outlined by Quednau 1979, 251–4;
     and, with respect to Bernini's monuments to Countess Matilda
     and Constantine, by Kaufmann 1970, 278f.

41 It has been suggested that Urban chose to pair his tomb with
     that of Paul III because the Farnese pope served as a model for
     his own nepotistic ambitions (Scott 1991, 6). My view is that the
     primary motive was the demonstration of papal continuity and
     the complementarity of papal terrestrial and spiritual dominion.

42 On Bernini's notion of contrapposto, see Lavin 1980, 9f., and
     compare his busts of the Damned and Blessed Souls (Fig. 258),
     Lavin 1993, 101–38.

43 Kauffmann 1970, 122, notes the analogy with the Pietà.

44 Ripa s.v. Giustitia: "Le bilancie significano, che la Giustizia div-
     ina dà regalia à tutte le attioni, & la spada le pene de' delin-
     quenti" (1603, 188). "Il mostrare la severità, il rigore della gius-

tizia per una spada ignuda . . . è stato trovato da moderni, i
quali per dar qualche cenno all'equità vi aggiunsero ancor la
bilancia" (Valeriano 1625, 565). It is tempting to think of the
damascene ornament on Justice's sword as alluding to the frequent metaphor for the Turkish menace, the "cruentes gladius
impiorum," as an instrument of God to test the Christian's faith
and will (O'Malley 1968, 177; Patrides 1963).

45 Cartari 1626, 30 " . . . la divina bontà non corre in fretta, nè
     con romore a castigare chi erra, ma và tarda, & lenta, & così
     tacitamente, che non prima se ne avede il peccatore, che senta la
     pena." An ancient representation of Justice as a figure leaning on
     a spear signified "la lentezza, per la quale le cause si mandano in
     lungo più del dovere: perche . . . significa tardanza" (Valeriano
     1625, 566).

46 Ripa 1603, 188, "Giustizia Divina": "Il fasco di verghe con
     la scure, era portato anticamente in Rome da littori inanzi a'
     Consoli, & al Tribuno della Plebe, per mostrar che nô si deve
     rimanere di castigare, ove richiede la Giustizia, ne di deve esser
     precipitoso: ma dar tempo à maturare il giuditio nel sciorre
     delle verghe." On the fasces as an attribute of Justice, see the
     discussion by Kissel 1984, 107f.

47 Ripa specifically identitifies the ancient image of victory as an
     "angel, with wings": "Gl'antichi dipinsero la vittoria in forma
     di Angelo, con l'ali . . ." (Ripa, 1603, 517). Paul III's winged
     personification of *Historia* is reproduced in Gramberg 1984,
     321, fig. 77.

48 Wittkower 1997, 123, also notes Bernini's emphasis on the
     sepulchral idea, in contrast to the commemorative and cere-
     monial monuments of his predecessors.

49 On the de la Marck tomb, see Lavin, "Bernini's Bumbling
     Barberini Bees" (1999), 34, and the references given there.
     Érard de la Marck (d. 1538) was an eminent cardinal prince-
     archbishop of that portion of the Netherlands that had remained
     in the Catholic faith. Until it was destroyed in the French Revo-
     lution, the gilt brass monument stood in the Cathedral of Liège.
     The tomb was illustrated as a frontispiece in one of the most
     popular and important handbooks of the antiquities of Rome
     by Jean-Jacques Boissard; the engraver, Theodore de Bry, was a
     native of Liège and must have intended to promulgate this local
     product in emulation of the monuments of ancient Rome.

50 Schiavo 1971 first noted that the reference was to Clement rather
     than Gregory; Schiavo recalled the disagreements with Gregory
     and Urban's debt to Clement, and also noted that Clement had
     dedicated the new high altar at St. Peter's, while Urban had
     consecrated the new basilica itself. For the correct identification,
     see also Fehl 1982, 354 (adding a letter in each line, however),
     and 1987, 194.

51 Pastor 1923–53, XXIII, passim; Fehl 1987, 194, who also calls
     attention to Urban's several poems honoring Clement.

52 On the tomb's escutcheon, see Lavin, "Bernini's Bumbling
     Barberini Bees" (1999), 69.

53 "Bernini had splendid precepts concerning architecture: first of
     all he said the highest merit lay not in making beautiful and
     commodious buildings, but in being able to make do with lit-
     tle, to make beautiful things out of the inadequate and ill-
     adapted, to make use of a defect in such a way that if it had
     not existed one would have had to invent it" (Baldinucci 1966,
     80). "Nell'architettura dava bellissimi precetti: primieramente
     diceva non essere il sommo pregio dell'artefice il far bellissimi
     e comodi edifici, ma il sapere inventar maniere per servirsi del
     poco, del cattivo e male adattato al bisogno per far cose belle e
     far sì, che sia utile quel che fu difetto e che, se non fusse, biso-
     gnerebbe farlo" (Baldinucci 1948, 146; cf. Lavin 1980, 11, 85).

54 Lavin 1968, 20n89.

55 On this theme of medium-illusion-temporality, see Lavin 1980,
     Index, s.v. "Illusionism."

56 The fresco, painted in 1630–3 under Bernini's supervision (Lavin 1968, 29), makes it possible to recognize and date the Windsor drawing reproduced here in Fig. 150. With remarkable perspicuity, Harris 1977, xv, no. 24, had rejected the previous identification as a juvenile self-portrait, suggesting a date "c. 1630." A closely related drawing in the British Museum attributed to Bernini also represents the brother; see Harris 1998, 640f., and Turner 1999, Catalogue, II, 640f., no. 14. On Luigi Bernini, who was named Supervisor of the Works at St. Peter's in 1634, see Hibbard in *Dizionario* 1960–, IX, 9:375f.

57 On the inscriptions, see Preimesberger 1984.

58 For a recent discussion of the relief as a document of papal primacy, see Bauer 2000.

59 The classicizing style of these and related works by Bernini has been the subject of much discussion. My view (Lavin 1956, 258; 1968, 33–5, 37; 1980, 23), that the classical references are not, as has been repeatedly suggested, a condescension to current fashion but a deliberate evocation of an antique ideal appropriate to the theme and context, has been taken up and developed in connection with the Matilda monument by Scott 1985.

60 The idea seems to recall the early project, mentioned above, to install in the four niches of the crossing piers the tombs of the sainted popes named Leo.

61 On the medieval and Renaissance systems of narrative church decoration, see Aronberg Lavin 1990, esp. 197.

62 On Bernini's use of the *imago clipeata*, see Lavin 1980, 69f.

63 See Aronberg Lavin 1990, chap. 1.

64 Alexander's suffering was graphically described in the biography by the pope's friend Sforza Pallavicino:

> Fu di singolare tenerezza al popolo il modo, col quale il Pontefice comparve nella celebrità del Corpo di Cristo; imperocchè non potendo egli far quella lunga funzione a piedi per la mala affezione, che ricordammo rimasagli dal taglio (per l'estrazione d'un calcolo dalla vescica, subito mentre era Nunzio a Colonia nel 1642), non volle portar l'Ostia sedendo, e coperto come avevano costumato gli antecessori, ma fè portarsi inginocchioni, ed a capo nudo, e gli si vedea grondar dalla fronte il sudore, al quale egli era dispostissimo per la rarità della sua carnagione, senza che per l'impedimento delle mani potesse tergerlo

(Pallavicino 1839–40, I, 269, cited by Incisa della Rocchetta 1932, 498). The diarist Giacinto Gigli recorded the powerful effect the pope's attitude and comportment had upon the eyewitnesses:

> "1655 A di 27. di Maggio fu la festa del Corpus Domini, et si fece la Processione solennissima, nella quale è solito, che il Papa è portato sopra le Spalle delli Scudieri in Sedia con maestà coronato tenendo nelle mani il SS.mo Sagramento. Ma il Papa Alessandro si fece portare, non in sedia, ma inginocchiato con la testa scoperta tenendo in mano il SS.mo Sagramento, essendo scalzo, et con tanta devozione senza movere gli occhi, ne la persona, che pareva più tosto una figura immobile, che un huomo, la qual cosa mosse tutti a gran devozione, et compuntione, che gli pareva vedere una visione in aria" (Gigli 1958, 468).

65 On the Cornaro chapel and this subject, see Lavin 1980, 95–8, 103.

66 Wittkower 1997, 129. On Bernini's use of the Doric here, see Roca de Amicis 2000, 294. Onians has discussed the ethos of the Doric order in relation to Bramante and the Dorian mode in music (1988, 235–9).

67 On this ancient theme in rhetoric and art, see expecially Gombrich 1966.

68 Del Pesco 1988.

69 Holstein thought the texts referred to three-sided piazzas, while Bernini evidently construed the term as referring to porticoes with three passages (see Roca de Amicis 1999 and 2000). In fact, taking into account the "third arm" Bernini intended, his project incorporates both interpretations.

Bernini later again "assimilated" Bramante's tempietto to the Colosseum, in a project for a commemorative Temple to the Martyrs to be constructed in the amphitheater, which he insisted on preserving intact, for the jubilee of 1675, just as he was adopting the tempietto model for the tabernacle of the Sacrament altar in St. Peter's; Di Macco 1971, 82–4, Hager 1973, 323–5. No doubt this project was in turn related to that for a hospice for the poor to be housed in the Lateran palace, which Bernini was commissioned to refurbish the following year (Fraschetti 1900, 398n1.; see Lavin 2000b).

70 The ambiguity of the phrase is evident from the English translations: Douay, "…there was a gallery joined to a triple gallery"; King James, "…gallery against gallery in three stories."

71 Lauretus 1971, 815, cited by Grunder 1985, 75.

72 For a reconstruction of the Lateran fastigium, see Nilgen 1977.

73 Haus 1983–4, 305–10.

74 "…essendo la Chiesa di S. Pietro quasi matrice di tutte le altre doveva haver'un portico che per l'appunto dimostrasse di ricevere à braccia aperte maternamente i Cattolici per confermarli nella credenza, gl'Heretici per riunirli alla Chiesa, e gl'Infedeli per illuminarli alla vera fede." Biblioteca Vaticana MS Chigi H II 22, fols. 105–9v, transcribed and dated 1659–60 by Brauer and Wittkower 1931, 70n1; dated 1657–8 by Krautheimer 1985, 174. See Kitao 1974, 14, and Index s.v. "arms of the church, image of."

75 See Buonanni 1699, II, 665ff. Bernini designed for the occasion a device, a sort of prayer stool called a *talamo*, that evidently braced the pope, so he could in fact kneel throughout the ceremony. The procession was recorded by Carlo Ceci in an engraving dated 1655 (reproduced by Incisa 1932, 498, and Grunder 1985, 71, fig. 1), whose central portion was in turn reproduced a decade later on the medal (concerning which see *Bernini in Vaticano* 1981, 301, where a document of 1656 recording Bernini's *talamo* is cited). It is sometimes said that Bernini's device allowed the pope to appear to be kneeling while actually being seated. Sforza Pallavicino's account, quoted in n. 64 above, belies this claim, which was also denied by Cancellieri (1790, 296f.), who noted that the *talamo* he knew, and described, could not have been used in a seated position. By contrast, the *talamo* used in the early nineteenth century by Pius VII (illustrated by Incisa 1932, 500) did include a seat.

76 The Protestant challenge is discussed in connection with Alexander's Corpus Domini medal by Buonanni 1699, II, 668. Council of Trent, Session XIII, chap. 5: "The Worship and Veneration to be Shown to the Most Holy Sacrament: There is, therefore, no room for doubt that all the faithful of Christ may, in accordance with a custom always received in the Catholic Church, give to this most holy sacrament in veneration the worship of latria, which is due to the true God. Neither is it to be less adored for the reason that it was instituted by Christ the Lord in order to be received. For we believe that in it the same God is present of whom the eternal Father, when introducing Him into the world, says: And let all the angels of God adore him; whom the Magi, falling down, adored; who, finally, as the Scriptures testify, was adored by the Apostles in Galilee. The holy council declares, moreover, that the custom that this sublime and venerable sacrament be celebrated with special veneration and solemnity every year on a fixed festival day, and that it be borne reverently and with honor in processions through the streets and public places, was very piously and religiously introduced into the Church of God. For it is most reasonable that some days be set aside as holy on which all Christians may with special and unusual demonstration testify

that their minds are grateful to and mindful of their common Lord and Redeemer for so ineffable and truly divine a favor whereby the victory and triumph of His death are shown forth. And thus indeed did it behoove the victorious truth to celebrate a triumph over falsehood and heresy, that in the sight of so much splendor and in the midst of so great joy of the universal Church, her enemies may either vanish weakened and broken, or, overcome with shame and confounded, may at length repent" (*Canons* 1978, 76). ["De cultu et veneratione huic sanctissimo sacramento exhibenda. Nullus itaque dubitandi locus relinquitur, quin omnes Christi fideles pro more in catholica ecclesia semper recepto latriae cultum, qui vero Deo debetur, huic sanctissimo sacramento in veneratione exhibeant. Neque enim ideo minus est adorandum, quod fuerit a Christo Domino, ut sumatur, institutum. Nam illum eundem Deum praesentem in eo adesse credimus, quem Pater aeternus introducens in orbem terrarum dicit: Et adorent eum omnes angeli Dei; quem magi procidentes adoraverunt; quem denique in Galilaea ab Apostolis adoratum fuisse, scriptura testatur. Declarat praeterea sancta synodus, pie et religiose admodum in Dei ecclesiam inductum fuisse hunc morem, ut singulis annis peculiari quodam et festo die praecelsum hoc et venerabile sacramentum singulari veneratione ac solemnitate celebraretur, utque in processionibus reverenter et honorifice illud per vias et loca publica circumferretur. Aequissimuni est enim sacros aliquos statutos esse dies, quum Christiani omnes singulari ac rara quadam significatione gratos et memores testentur animos erga communem Dominum et Redemptorem pro tam ineffabili et plane divino beneficio, quo mortis eius victoria et triumphus repraesentatur. Ac sic quidem oportuit victricem veritatem de mendacio et haeresi triumphum agere, ut eius adversarii in conspectu tanti splendoris, et in tanta universae ecclesiae laetitia positi vel debilitati et fracti tabescant, vel pudore afecti et confusi aliquando resipiscant" (Canones 1887, 61f.)].

77   Chantelou 1985, 34, 14 June. "Il leur a dit encore qu'il serait bon qu'on y eût quelque partie qui avançât sur le devant, parce que les églises qui sont rondes tout à fait, quand on y entre, on fait ordinairement sept à huit pas, ce qui empêche qu'on puisse pas bien voir la forme." (Chantelou 1885, 33f.).

78   "Quivi avvenne un giorno, che quel suo figlio, che presentemente scrive questo Libro, essendo per sua devozione entrato in quella Chiesa, e ritrovato havendo in un angolo di essa ritirato il Cavaliere suo Padre, che in atto di compiacenza vagheggiava con gli occhj tutte le parti di quel piccolo Tempio, ossequiosamente gli domandasse, Che facesse così solo, e cheto? e che gli rispondesse il Cavaliere, Figlio, di questa sola Opera di Archìtettura io sento qualche particular compiacenza nel fondo del mio cuore, e spesso per sollievo delle mie fatiche io quì mi porto a consolarmi col mio lavoro" (Bernini 1713, 109f.).

79   Domenico Bernini understood the complementarity of the two works: "Le due Opere e del Portico, e della Cathedra furono per così dire il principio, el fine della magnificenza di quella gran Basilica, rimanendo non men attonito l'occhio nell'ingresso per il Portico, che nel termine per la Cathedra" (Bernini 1713, 111).

80   Krautheimer 1985, 73.

81   Moroni 1840–61, X, 270.

82   Pastor 1923–53, XXXI, 299.

83   "Petrum itaque fundamentum Ecclesiae Dominus nominavit: et ideo digne fundamentumn hoc Ecclesia colit, supra quod ecclesiastici aedificii altitudo consurgit. Une convenienter psalmus, qui lectus est, dicit: Exaltent eum in ecclesia plebis: et in cathedra seniorum laudent eum. Benedictus Deus, qui beatum Petrum Apostolum in Ecclesia exaltari praecepit: quia dignum est, ut fundamentum hoc in Ecclesia honoretur, per quod ad caelum conscenditur" (*Hours* 1964, 1:1796).

84   Pastor 1923–53, XXXI, 303

85   The relationship of Bernini's "gloria" to the *Celestial Hierarchy* of the Pseudo-Dionysius was noted by Wittkower 1997, 58, and discussed by Minor 1989.

86   See pp. 118f.

87   Many antecedents are surveyed by Kauffmann 1970, 278–89, and Marder 1997, 180–8.

88   For the ancient equestrian monument types, see Brilliant 1963.

89   Voragine 1969, 271, 272.

90   Eusebius 1976, 490.

91   Der Nersessian 1966–70, II, 98. An exception is Ms. Paris Gr. 510, fol. 440, the earliest surviving representation of Constantine's vision (Walter 1997, 194); Brubaker (1999, 168f.) has shown that the miniature applies the imperial reference to a text in which Solomon speaks of "awakening and recovering my sight," and so leaving the pleasures of this world to pursue God's wisdom.

92   Delehaye 1975.

93   The importance of the ivory in the seventeenth century has been stressed by Fumaroli 1995, who also related it to Bernini's sculpture.

94   The relevance of the Conversion of St. Paul, though not Rufinus's text, was noted by Kauffmann 1970, 282, and Marder 1997, 188.

95   Augustine is cited by Voragine 1969, 127.

96   Cited by Kauffmann 1970, 282n34; Hill 1930, 225, no. 867.

97   *Life of Constantine*, Bk. IV, chap. xv, Eusebius 1976, 544. "Quanta porro divinae fidei vis ac virtus in ejus animo insederit, vel ex hoc uno conjici potest, quod in aureis nummis exprimi se jussit vultu in cœlum sublato, et manibus expansis instar precantis. Et hujus quidem formae nummi per universum orbem Romanum cucurrerunt. In ipsa vero regia juxta quasdam januas, in imaginibus ad ipsum vestibuli fastigium positis depictus est stans, difixis quidem in cœlum oculis, manibus autem expansis precantis in modum" (Migne 1857–1905, XX, col. 1163).

98   *The Life of Constantine* 1682, 611. Valesio's translation (quoted in the preceding note) and annotations were reprinted by Migne 1857–1905, XX: "*Quisquis fuit interpretes hujus* libri, parum attente hunc locum vertit, hoc modo, et precantis forma manus sursum tollens, cum vertere debuisset, manibus expansis, ut precantes solent. Christiani enim inter precandum manus expandere solebant, ut crucis similtudinem hoc modo adumbrarent. Allevabant quidem manus Christiani, dum preces funderent. Sed hoc non erat proprium Chritianorum, quippe cum gentiles idem facerent, ut testatur Virgilius, Aeneid., lib. I, vers. 97, dum ait: Et geminas [duplices] tollens ad sidera palmas. Illud vero peculiare fuit Christianis, manus in crucis formam expandere. Tertullianus in lib. De oratione, cap. 11: 'Nos vero non attollimus tantum, sed etiam expandimus, et Dominica passione modulamur.'" Idem in Apologetico, cap. 30 (Migne 1857–1905, XX, cols. 1163f.).

99   "... quod est: in hoc vince. Tum vero laetus redditus et de victoria iam securus, signum crucis, quod in caelo viderat, in sua front designat et ita caelitus invitatus ad fidem, non mihi illo videtur inferior, cui similiter de caelo dictum est: 'Saule, Saule, quid me persequeris? Ego sum Jesus Nazarenus,'" nisi quia hic non adhuc persequens, sed iam consequens invitatur" (Aufhauser 1912, 4f.).

100 *The Roman Breviary* 1879, I, 1056–61. After centuries of debate, the feast was suppressed in 1960 (*New Catholic Encyclopedia* 1967, IV, 482).

101 See the many passages cited in the indexes of Chantelou 1885 and 1985. The relationship discussed here is but one among many that give the lie to those who would regard Bernini's deference to Poussin in Paris as an insincere gesture of flattery to his French patrons. Nothing could be further from the truth, if for no other reason than that he unabashedly complained

about almost everything else in France. More important, the allegation betrays a baleful misunderstanding of Bernini's character and art. For another, important instance – among many that could be cited – of Bernini's profound understanding of the meaning and "authenticity" of Poussin's ideas, see his adoption and adaptation of the "non-penetrating" principle of Poussin's feigned stucco decoration of the vault of the Louvre; Lavin 1980, 5n4, 45n80. In the same vein, I want to express my solidarity with Tomaso Montanari's recent, resounding affirmation of the integrity and authenticity of Bernini's art in the face of current attempts to reduce it, notably his late style, to a sort of meretricious "self-representation" (Montanari, in Angelini 1998, 409).

102 On Poussin's picture, see Rosenberg 1994, 77, where the resemblance of Bernini's *Constantine* is noted.

103 See Bätschmann 1982.

104 *The Jewish War* VI, 241–66 (*Josephus* 1968, III, 444–55).

105 On the recently discovered early version, now in Jerusalem, see Mahon 1998. Rosenberg 1994, 77, suggests that the gifts were intended to balance the two great powers.

106 The Christian interpretation is alluded to by Stanic 1994, 94, and Rosenberg 1994, 77.

107 Poussin may well have been stimulated by the open-armed gesture of the standing figure of Titus in an engraving of the *Destruction* by Phillip Galle, designed by Maarteen van Heemskerck, as part of a series illustrating the disasters of the Jews (Veldman and Luijten 1993, 203, no. 258).

108 Sulpitius 1976, 111. "Fertur Titus adhibito consilio prius deliberasse, an templum tanti operis everteret. Etenim nonnullis videbatur, aedem sacratam ultra omnia mortalis illustrem non oportere deleri, quae servata modestiae Romanae testimonium, diruta perennem crudelitatis notam praeberet. At contra alii et Titus ipse evertendum in primis templum censebant, quo plenius Iudaeorum et Christianorum religio tolleretur: quippe has religiones, licet contrarias sibi, isdem tamen ab aouctoribus protectas: Christianos ex Iudaeis extitisse: radice sublata stirpem facile perituram" (Latin text cited after Thackeray, in Josephus 1968, I, xxv).

109 "Capta eversaque urbe Hierosolymorum . . . extinctisque Iudaei Titus, qui ad vindicandum Domini Iiesu Christi sanguinem iudicio Dei fuerat ordinatus, victor triumphans cum Vespasiano patre Ianum clausit . . . iure enim idem honos ultioni passionis Domini inpensus est, qui etiam navitati fuerat adtributus" *Hist.* VII, iii, 8 and ix, 9; quoted after Singleton in Dante 1970–5, *Purg.* 512f.

110 ". . . il talento che / divina giustizia, contra voglia, / come fu al peccar / pone al tormento . . . però sentisti il tremoto e li pii / spiriti . . . render lode . . . Nel tempo che'l buon Tito, con l'aiuto / del sommo rege, vendicò le fóra / ond'uscì 'l sangue per Giuda venduto, . . . era io di là, . . . ma non con fede ancora" (*Purg.* XXI, 62–4, 82–7; Dante 1970–5, *Purg.* 228, 229, 230, 231.) In Paradiso VI. 92–3, Dante speaks of Titus's vengeance as the effect of "living justice" (*viva giustizia*).

111 This development of the *art* of horsemanship as a distinction of nobility may be followed in Liedtke 1989.

112 ". . . Colosso condotto a fine dell'Imperador Costantino a Cavallo, Opera veramente grande per il Soggetto che rappresenta, per il luogo ov'era destinato a collocarsi, e per la materia, in cui doveva scolpirsi. In un Masso dunque di Sasso (per usare i termini proprij) di trenta Carrettate simile al quale rari ne hà veduti entro le sue mura anche negli antichi tempi la Città di Roma" (Bernini 1713, 106–7).

113 Interestingly, Bernini's comment on the manageability of marble was made in response to a criticism of the complex and perforated mane and tail of the horse of his equestrian monument of Louis XIV, commissioned after and in specific emulation of the

Constantine. In this work he actually accomplished the feat of carving a fully free-standing, rearing equestrian group in a still larger block (see Lavin 1993, 172–4). Bernini described the relation between the two works in a letter to Colbert: "Questa statua sarà del tutto diversa a quella di Costantino, perche Costantino stà in atto d'amirare la Croce che gl'apparve, e questo del Rè starà in atto di maestà, e di commando . . ." (30 December, 1669, Wittkower 1961, 521, doc. 24).

114 "Passo più oltra e manifestamente intimo, anche oue mancano intaccature di Passioni esercitate, oue abbondano fregi di virtù ottenute, bisognare tolleranza di chi ci lauori e sofferenze d'emende. Per non vscire dal Palazzo, oue discorriamo, l'ammirabile Colosso di Costantino, che si ripulisce per immortalare e la Basilica di S. Pietro e la reggia de'Pontefici; sarebbe non Simulacro d'vn Cesare tanto Benefico della Chiesa, mà vn informe sasso de'Monti Ligustici, quando la prodigiosa Mano di chi lo forma, con più ferite non lo scarnasse, e con durezza di scarpelli non ne perfettionasse le sembianze. Ne'quali prodigij d'amirata maestria, si osserui, non troncarsi dal Marmo, per farlo Statua d'infinito valore, ò selci rusticane, ò tegoli disprezati, ò neri carboni. Si tolgono al Masso parti totalmente omogenee e vniformi à quelle, che si lasciano, perche rappresentino vn'Augusto trionfante" (Oliva 1674, 278).

115 The example from Ecouen was cited by Marder 1997, 195.

116 On Arnolfo's horseman, see Carli 1993, 124, and the study by Pace 1991, esp. 349–51, who noted the relationship to Roman sarcophagus reliefs.

117 On the dual points of view and treatment of the relief, see Marder 1997, 165, 188–90.

118 There was a certain tradition for this idea: markedly similar is Parmigianino's fresco of St. Secundus in S. Giovanni Evangelista in Parma, where the hoof of the saint's rearing horse projects beyond the painted niche on a projection of molded, painted stucco (see Lavin 1980, 54f., Fig. 94; Rossi 1980, pl. VII).

119 Lavin 1980, 67–70.

120 NISI COELVM CREASSEM OB TE SOLAM CREAREM ("If I had not created heaven I would create it for you alone"). On this floating "label" see Lavin 1980, 139f.

121 The tabernacle was made in Rome when Bernini was working on the Theresa chapel. On this work and the metaphorical relationship between mathematical perspective and the Sacrament, see Lavin 1980, Index, s.v. Perspective.

122 Zollikofer 1994, 11; Schlegel 1996.

123 I have borrowed the term "activated" from the pioneering study of tomb sculpture by Panofsky 1964, 73, 76ff., who used it to describe "living" effigies.

124 On Bernini's view of the relationship between beauty and truth, see Lavin 1980, 70–6.

125 Traver 1907.

126 The theme of the sleeping infant in depictions of the Virgin and Christ Child as foreboding the Pietà has been familiar since the pioneering work of Firestone 1942. Adam was frequently shown reclining at the foot of the Cross (see Bagatti 1977).

127 Fehl 1966.

128 *Hours* 1964, I, 1164f., III, 1776f.; cf. Lasance and Walsh 1945, 1269.

129 St. Bernard's Sermons 1950, III, 134, 149. "Ut inhabitet gloria in terra nostra, misericordia et veritas obviaverunt sibi, justitia et pax osculatae sunt. . . . Haec dicit, Perii, si Adam non moriatur; et haec dicit: Perii, nisi misericordiam consequatur. Fiat mors bona, et habet utraque quod petit. . . . Sed id quomodo fiet, inquiunt? Mors crudelissima, et amarissima est, mors terribilis, et ipso horrenda auditu. Bona fieri quanam ratione poterit? At ille: Mors, inquit, peccatorum pessima, sed pretiosa fieri potest mors sanctorum. Annon pretiosa erit, si fuerit janua vitae, porta gloriae?" (Migne 1844–77, CLXXXIII, cols. 383, 389).

130 A signal instance of the principle of design Bernini enunciated as the true test of the architect:

Baldinucci 1948, 146f. "Nell'architettura dava bellissimi precetti: primieramente diceva non essere il sommo pregio dell'artefice il far bellissimi e comodi edifici, ma il sapere inventar maniere per servirsi del poco, del cattivo e male adattato al bisogno per far cose belle e far si, che sia utile quel quel che fu difetto e che, se non fusse, bisognerebbe farlo. Che poi il valor suo giugnesse a questo segno, conobbesi in molte sue opere, particolarmente nell'arme d'Urbano in Araceli che, per mancanza del luogo, ove situarla, che veniva occupato da una gran finestra, egli colorì di az-zurro il finestrone invetriato e in esso figurò le tre api, quasi volando per aria, e sopra collocò il regno. Similmente nel se-polcro di Alessandro; nella situazione della Cattedra, ove fece che il finestrone, che pure era d'impedimento le tor-nasse in aiuto, perché intorno a esso rappresentò la gloria del paradiso e nel bel mezzo del vetro, quasi in luogo di luce inaccessibile fece vedere lo Spirito Santo in sembianza di colomba, che dà compimento a tutta l'opera."

Baldinucci 1948, 131: "Mostrò in questo sepolcro il cav-alier Bernino la solita vivacità del suo ingegno, situandolo in una gran nicchia in luogo appunto, ove è una porta, per la quale continuamente si passa, servendosi di essa così bene al suo bisogno, che quello, che ad altri sarebbe po-tuto parere grande impedimento, a lui servì d'aiuto, anzi fu necessario requisito per effettuare un suo bel pensiero."

Bernini 1713, 57f.: "Hor se il Bernino in quel, che non era professione sua, si dimostrava tanto valente, quanto dobbiamo credere, che fosse in ciò, in cui consisteva il suo proprio talento raffinato dallo studio, e dall'arte? E come che soleva dire, che 'Il buon'Artefice era quello, che sapeva inventar maniere, per servirsi del poco, e del cattivo, per far cose belle, egli veramente fù maraviglioso a comprovarlo con gli effetti.'"

Bernini 1713, 166: "Ne intraprese dunque arditamente i principii, e colla solita vivacità del suo ingegno situòllo in una gran Nicchia sopra la Porta, che conduce dalla Sacres-tia alla Chiesa, con far servire il difetto a necessità della sua intenzione."

131 Andreae 1963.

132 Many examples will be found in Fagiolo dell'Arco 1997.

133 On this motif, see p. 172.

134 See the entry *"Sipario"* by Elena Povoledo in *Enciclopedia dello spettacolo* 1975, IX, cols. 1–8.

135 Grunder 1985, 71, citing Haus 1970, 161n375.

136 The effect recalls that of Bernini's famous comedy of the Inun-dation of the Tiber, in which the river on stage threatened to overflow its bank and inundate the audience.

137 There have been three monographic treatments of the bridge: Weil 1974, D'Onofrio 1981, Cardilli Alloisi and Tolomeo Sper-anza 1988; valuable essays have also appeared recently by An-gela Negro and Marina Minozzi, in Strinati and Bernardini 1999.

138 Voragine 1969, 180f., 580.

139 "...et ipse Angelus cum gladio in vagina sculptus in lapide mirae magnitudinis..." (*L'angelo e la città* 1987, I, 96–7).

140 "agniolo nuovo messo in chastello," with "l'ale e le penne e spada...tutti de rame" (D'Onofrio 1978, 168).

141 "una statua dorata dell'angelo tenente la spada fuori del fodera"; (Chastel 1983, 279n44; D'Onofrio 1978, 168–70).

142 A valuable survey will be found in *L'angelo e la città* 1987, I; see also Cavazzini 1989. On plague iconography generally: Crawfurd 1914; Ronen 1988, 1989; Ahl 1996, 141–6, 259f., and n. 171 below.

143 The Sala di Costantino fresco is admirably treated in Quednau 1979, 88–95, on the dating; on the vision, 330–45.

144 The history and art-historical repercussions of the Sack of Rome have been explored with magisterial scope and acumen by Chastel 1983.

145 On the two liberations and the medal, see Chastel 1983, 190–1.

146 On the plague during the siege, see D'Onofrio 1976, 233–58; Pastor 1923–53, IX, 427–31.

147 On the nature and significance of Bandinelli's project, see Lavin 2003a.

148 On the statues and their significance in this context, see D'Onofrio 1978, 74–8.

149 The drawing is of later date but evidently records the Charles V entry. Although made of temporary materials, the figures may have remained in place after the event.

150 I use the terms "dexter" and "sinister" in the hierarchic sense of the liturgy (as in the Last Judgment) and heraldry. On the tradition of paralleled Old and New Testament narrative cycles in nave decorations, see n. 61 above.

151 An excellent account of these punishments and the attendant rit-uals, noted by D'Onofrio 1981, 78n10, will be found in Ingersoll 1985, 408–40. For the Last Judgment hangings, see Blunt 1939–40, 59, 61.

152 For the payments to Montelupo, whose angel was later restored by Bernini, see D'Onofrio 1978, 280, 305, 314, 322.

153 Gregory 1959, 230–40; Gregory 1978–80, CCLXV, 128–32:

Qui ductus ad inferni loca uidit multa, quae prius audita non credidit. Sed cum praesidenti illic iudici praesentatus fuisset, ab eo receptus non est, ita ut diceret : "Non hunc deduci, sed Stephanum ferrarium iussi." Qui statim reduc-tus in corpore est, et Stephanus ferrarius, qui iuxta eum habitabat, eadem hora defunctus est. Sicque probatum est uera fuisse uerba quae audierat, dum haec effectus mor-tis Stephani demonstrauit. Ante triennium quoque in hac pestilentia quae hanc urbem clade uehementissima depop-ulauit, in qua etiam corporali uisu sagittae caelitus uenire et singulos quosque ferire uidebantur, sicut nosti, Stephanus isdem / defunctus est. Quidam uero miles in hac eadem nostra urbe percussus ad extrema peruenit. Qui eductus e corpore exanimis iacuit, sed citius rediit et quae cum eo fuerant gesta narrauit. Aiebat enim, sicut tunc res eadem etiam multis innotuit, quia pons erat, sub quo niger atque caligosus foetoris intolerabilis nebulam exhalans fluuius decurrebat. Transacto autem ponte amoena erant prata atque uirentia, odoriferis herbarum floribus exornata, in quibus albatorum hominum conuenticula esse uidebantur. Tantusque in loco eodem odor suauitatis inerat, ut ipsa suauitatis fragrantia illic deambulantes habitantesque sa-tiaret. Ibi mansiones diuersorum singulae magnitudine lu-cis plenae. Ibi quaedam mirae potentiae aedificabatur do-mus, quae aureis uidebatur laterculis construi, sed cuius esset non potuit agnosci. Erant uero super ripam praedicti fluminis nonnulla habitacula, sed alia exsurgentis foetoris nebula tangebantur, alia autem exsurgens foetor a flumine minime tangebat. Haec uero erat in praedicto ponte pro-batio, ut quisquis per eum iniustorum uellet transire, in tenebroso foetentique fluuio laberetur, iusti uero, quibus culpa non obsisteret, securo per eum gressu ac libero ad loca amoena peruenirent. Ibi se etiam Petrum, ecclesiasti-cae familiae maiorem, qui ante quadriennium defunctus est, deorsum positum in locis teterrimis, magno ferri pondere religatum ac depressum uidisse confessus est. Qui dum re-quireret cur ita esset, ea se dixit audisse quae nos, qui eum in hac ecclesiastica domo nouimus, scientes e ius acta recol-imus. Dictum namque est: "Haec idcirco patitur, quia si quid ei pro facienda ultione iubebatur, ad inferendas plagas plus ex crudelitatis desiderio quam oboedientia seruiebat." Quod sic fuisse nullus qui illum nouit ignorat. Ibi se etiam quemdam peregrinum presbiterum uidisse fatebatur, qui ad praedictum pontem ueniens, tanta per eum auctoritate transiit, quanta et hic sinceritate uixit. In eodem quoque ponte hunc quem praedixi Stephanum se recognouisse testatus est. Qui dum transire uoluisset, eius pes lapsus est, et ex medio corpore iam extra pontem deiectus, a quibusdam teterrimis uiris ex flumine surgentibus per coxas deorsum, atque a quibusdam albatis et speciosissimis uiris coepit per brachia sursum trahi. Cumque hoc luctamen esset, ut hunc boni spiritus sursum, mali deorsum traherent, ipse qui haec uidebat ad corpus reuersus est, et quid de eo plenius gestum sit minime cognouit.

154 Berenson 1963, 203, fig. 403.

155 Kauffmann 1970, 306, was the first to allude to these eschatological bridges in relation to the Ponte Sant'Angelo. They have been noted by Le Goff 1981, whose account of the "St. Patrick's Purgatory" (193–201) is particularly suggestive in our context. The Knight Owein succeeds in crossing the perilous bridge by invoking Christ's name as he goes:

> facing a very broad river of fire, traversed by what seems to be an impassable bridge, since it is so high as to induce vertigo, so narrow that it is impossible to set foot on it, and so slippery that it would be impossible in any case to maintain one's footing. In the river below, demons are waiting with iron hooks. Once again Owein invokes the name of Jesus and advances onto the bridge. The further he advances, the wider and more stable the bridge becomes, and half-way across he can no longer see the river to the right or the left. He escapes one last infuriated attempt by the demons and, climbing down from the bridge, finds himself facing a very splendid high wall whose gates, made of pure gold set off by precious gems, give off a delightful odor. He enters and finds himself in a city of marvels.

In my view, this is exactly the import of the Ponte Sant'Angelo.

156 Dante 1970–5, *Inf.* XVIII, 184f., vv. 19–36:

> In questo luogo, de la schiena scossi
> di Gerïon, trovammoci; e 'l poeta
> tenne a sinistra, e io dietro mi mossi.
> A la man destra vidi nova pieta,
> novo tormento e novi frustatori,
> di che la prima bolgia era repleta.
> Nel fondo erano ignudi i peccatori;
> dal mezzo in qua ci venien verso 'l volto,
> di là con noi, ma con passi maggiori,
> come i Roman per l'essercito molto,
> l'anno del giubileo, su per lo ponte
> hanno a passar la gente modo colto,
> che da l'un lato tutti hanno la fronte
> verso 'l castello e vanno a Santo Pietro;
> da l'altra sponda vanno verso 'l monte.
> Di qua, di là, su per lo sasso tetro
> vidi demon cornuti con gran ferze,
> che li battien crudelmente di retro.

157 Frugoni 1996, esp. 108.

158 *Enciclopedia dantesca* 1984, V, 601f.; cf. Dante 1970–5, *Purg.* II, 18, vv. 100–5; XXV, 274, v. 86.

159 Mâle 1972, 62–4.

160 This point was emphasized by Le Goff 1981, 90–5.

161 Voragine 1969, 653.

162 Lasance and Walsh 1945, 1272: "Domine Jesu Christe, Rex gloriae, libera animas omnium fidelium defunctorum de poenis inferni, et de profunda lacu: libera eas de ore leonis, ne absorbeat eas tartarus, ne cadant in obscurum; sed signifer sanctus Michael repraesentet eas in lucem sanctam: Quam olim Abrahae promisisti, et semini ejus."

163 See Pastor 1923–53, XXXI, 31–3, and D'Onofrio 1976, 221–60, with the vivid account in the diary of Carlo Cartari; Weil 1974, 93f., also regarded the plague of 1656–7 as a factor in the refurbishing of the bridge.

164 Bonannus 1699, II, 649, no. X.

165 D'Onofrio 1976, 252.

166 Bonannus 1699, II, 649–50, no. XI; *Bernini in Vaticano* 1981, 289.

167 "Ita ut in plateas eicerent infirmos et ponerent in lectulis et grabatis, ut, veniente Petro, saltem umbra illius obumbraret quemquam illorum, et liberarentur ab infirmitatibus suis et liberabantur ab infirmitate statim salvi fiebant."

168 Ronen 1988, 92ff.

169 Buonanni 1699, II, 650.

170 Ibid., 697f., no. XXXX. See especially Perlove 1982; Petrucci 1997, 190–5; Bernardini and Fagiolo dell'Arco 1999, 414f.

171 Perhaps relevant to the reaction in Rome was the commission by the governors of Naples to Mattia Preti for a series of intercessory frescoes for the city gates, concerning which see Clifton 1994, 479–501. The angel with sword and scabbard occupies the center of Preti's plague paintings, executed 1656–9, and Clifton shows that the location of the images at the entrances to the city had an apotropaic function; the same may be said of Castel Sant'Angelo. Depictions of the Naples plague itself, with an angel of Christ wielding the sword, are discussed by Roworth 1993, Marshall 1998, and Erben 1999.

172 The evidence for earlier ideas and planning for the bridge under Alexander VII is summarized by Weil 1974, 91–3.

173 D'Onofrio 1978, 82; for the inscription, Forcella 1869–84, XIII, 150, no. 282.

174 "…per haver schiodato li ferramenti dell'Angelo sudetto perche il Signor Bernini architetto ha voluto vadi più alto" (D'Onofrio 1978, 322; 1981, 81). Bernini also supervised substantial restorations necessitated by accidental damage in 1660 (D'Onofrio 1978, 322).

175 D'Onofrio 1981, 83, also perceived that the completion of the colonnade, the raising of the angel, and the plan for the bridge were related.

176 Chantelou 1985, 31 July, 1 August, 94n177, aptly referring the passage to the Ponte Sant'Angelo and its open-grille railings (96). Chantelou 1885, 78: "Le soir, la promenade fut assez courte; il a voulu aller sur le Pont-Rouge, et y a fait arrêter le carrosse un bon quart d'heure, regardant d'un côté et d'autre du pont, puis m'a dit: 'C'est là un bel aspect, je suis fort ami des eaux; elles font [du bien] à mon tempérament.' Après nous nous en sommes revenus"; "quand nous avons été vers le Cours, il m'a demandé d'aller sur le Pont-Rouge, comme le soir précédent; il y a demeuré un bon quart d'heure, puis nous nous en sommes revenus par le Pont-Neuf, par les rues." Lalanne identifies the bridge with the Pont-Rouge that linked Cité with the Île Notre Dame.

177 Babelon 1977, pls. 13, 14; Duplomb 1911–13, I, 291–7; Hillairet 1967, 39–42.

178 On the jubilee tragedy, see D'Onofrio 1980, 234f.

179 Baldinucci 1966, 63f., 81; Baldinucci 1948, 129f.:

> In questo pontificato finì il nostro artefice il braccia del portico verso il S. Ufizio, la cordonata alla scala, che noi diremmo padiglione, o scala a bastoni davanti alla basilica di S. Pietro; abbellì il ponte S. Angelo con statue d'angioli portanti gli strumenti della passione del Signore e fecevi le balaustre. Aveva egli condotto di sua mano due de'medesimi angioli per dar loro luogo fra gli altri sopra

di esso ponte; ma non parve bene a Clemente che opere sì belle rimanessero in quel luogo all'ingiurie del tempo; che però fecevene fare due copie e gli originali destinò ad esser posti altrove a disposizione del cardinal'nipote. Cionostante il Bernino ne scolpì un altro segretamente, che è quello, che sostiene il titolo della croce, non volendo per verun modo che un'opera d'un pontefice, a cui egli si conosceva tanto obbligato, rimanesse senza una qualche fattura della sua mano. Ciò risaputo il papa, ebbene contento, e disse: "Insomma cavaliere, voi mi volete necessitare a far fare un'altra copia." E qui consideri il mio lettore che il nostro artefice constituito in età decrepita in ispazio di due anni e non più condusse le tre statue di marmo intere assai maggiori del naturale, cosa che ai più intendenti dell'arte sembra avere dell'impossibile.

Baldinucci 1948, 147f.:

Ma giacché parliamo di fontane, è da sapersi un altro suo precetto; e fu, che essendo fatte le fontane per lo godimento dell'acque, doveansi quelle sempre far cadere in modo, che potessero esser vedute. Con tal concetto (cred'io) dovendo egli far restaurare per ordine di Clemente IX il ponte S. Angiolo sul Tevere, ne fece sfondare le sponde, acciò l'acque meglio si potessero godere, ond'è che con doppio piacere vede l'occhio dai lati del fiume il corso dell'aque e sopra quei del ponte l'ornato degli angioli, per alludere all'antico nome del ponte.

180 Bernini 1713, 158–60:

Màe Clemente desideroso ugualmente quanto i suoi Predecessori di accrescere magnificenza al Tempio di S. Pietro, ornamento a Roma, e Gloria al suo Pontificato, ordinò al Cavaliere, che con qualche nobile invenzione ornasse in miglior forma quel Ponte, che, prossimo al Castello, da lui prende il nome, di *Ponte S. Angelo*, giudicato degno di riguardevole abbellimento sì per la grandezza della Mole Hadriana, che, a chi v'imbocca, si offerisce avanti, come per essere la più frequentata via, che conduce alla gran Basilica di S. Pietro. E ne sovvenne al Bernino il pensiere proporzionatissimo al luogo, e maestoso quanto dir si possa all'apparenza. Fù suo detto assai familiare, che *Il buon'Architetto in materia di Fontane, ò di lavori sopr'acque, doveva sempre procurar con facilità la veduta di esse, ò nel cader che fanno, ò nel passare: Poiche essendo le acque di gran godimento alla vista, con impedirla, ò con difficoltarla, toglie à quelle opere il loro pregio più dilettevole.* Con questa intenzione, nell'adornamento dell'accennato Ponte, volle il Cavaliere ne'Poggi, che sogliono comporsi tutti di materia, e di muro si aprisse di tanto in tanto un proporzionato vano, assicurato da altrettante ferrate, per cui, commodo fosse al Passagiere rimirare il corso di quell'acque, sopra le quali esso felicemente camina.

181 D'Onofrio 1981, 94.

182 On this theme, see Lavin, "On the Unity of the Arts and the Early Baroque Opera House" (1990) and Lavin 1993, 147–55.

183 On Bernini and the theater, see Lavin 1980, 146–57.

184 Weil 1974, 32.

185 Ibid., 35; also D'Onofrio 1981, 48.

186 On these contrasting and normally incompatible traditions, see Lavin, "On the Unity of the Arts and the Early Baroque Opera House" (1990).

187 On the Works of Mercy and the Last Judgment, see Knipping 1974, II, 328–32; Harbison 1976, 106–16; Pacelli 1984, 31–48.

188 Roscio 1586, 82; part 1 of Roscio's treatise is devoted to the acts "quae ad corpus pertinent," i.e., those mentioned explicitly by Christ; part 2 (45ff.) considers those "quae ad animum pertinent," as defined by Thomas Aquinas. On Roscio, see Zuccari 1984, 118f., fig. 7; Pacelli 1984, 46f., figs. 30–2.

189 On the Arma Christi: Berliner 1955; Knipping 1974, II, 461–5; Suckale 1977.

190 Berliner 1955, 35f., cited by Preimesberger 1988, 207.

191 The seminal study of these works is that of Zuccari 1984, 92f., 109–37; followed by Macioce 1990, 126–8, 132f., 149f.; Caperna 1999, 97–101. In SS. Nereo e Achilleo, similar frescoed angels standing atop the nave columns carry the palm and crown of martyrdom. The relevance of these church decorations for the bridge sculptures was noted by Minozzi 1999, 81f., who also perceived the nature and novelty of Bernini's synthesis of the Via Crucis and the Arma Christi traditions in a progressive (and processional) series of independent angels bearing the instruments.

192 See Zuccari's excellent analysis of the significance of the Joseph story and its relevance to the conversion of Henry IV (1974, 115–19).

193 *Speculum passionis Christi salvatoris mundi*, Hollstein 1949–, XVI, 21–3, nos. 57–67ad.

194 De Passe: Bartsch 1978–, LXXII, part 1 (supplement), 107–19. Sadeler: Bartsch 1978, LXX, part 1 (supplement), 263f.; Knipping 1974, II, 462f. Other precedents are cited by Minozzi 1999, 81f.

195 For the order and disposition of the angels and the inscriptions on the pedestals, see Kruft and Larsson 1966, 157, Weil 1974, fig. 100, 52; our Fig. 247 is after Weil 1974, fig. 52, corrected.

196 The nature of the relationship between the instruments and the texts has been illustrated by Preimesberger 1988, 208–11; he does not consider the inscriptions discussed here.

197 In a number of drawings for the angels by studio hands the figures stand on oblong plinths, suggesting that the clouds may have been introduced at a later time in the development of the project. However, none of the autograph sketches, drawn or modeled, shows such a plinth instead of the clouds. The studies have been most recently surveyed by Tolomeo Speranza, in Cardilli Alloisi and Tolomeo Speranza 1988, 43–80.

198 Weil 1974, 139–51, outlines their careers and artistic personalities.

199 D'Onofrio 1981, 84, regards the buttresses as useless. Bernini's reconstruction remained in place until the modern embankment and street were installed after 1892. For Bernini's work and its replacement, compare Weil 1974, figs. 20–1, figs. 1–4, and see Stefano Funari and Giuseppe Biunno, in Cadrilli Alloisi and Tolomeo Speranza 1988, 224–38.

200 "[conversus sum] in aerumna mea dum configitur spina."

201 Gramatica 1951, 485.

202 "dicite in gentibus, quia Dominus regnavit."

203 "Vexilla Regis prodeunt . . ." Reydellet 1994, 57, 185.

204 See Angelo Negro, in Strinati and Bernardini 1999, 67–9.

205 Certain areas are left rough, and Negro 1999, 73, has suggested that the finish postdates Bernini; but the rough areas are invisible from the front and below, and indicate only that Bernini expected the huge figures mounted on pedestals to be viewed in that way – a frequent procedure in his work.

206 The replacements differ from their counterparts in varying degrees, but chiefly in the lower drapery of the angel with the superscription, executed by Bernini himself, which blows in the same, rather than the opposite, direction with respect to its companion; the change seems appropriate for figures meant to be seen in succession rather than as a pair.

207 I doubt that the angels were moved from Bernini's studio to the Palazzo Rospigliosi (D'Onofrio 1981, 87). They do not appear in the inventories of Bernini's possessions taken after his death, no doubt because they were not legally his property. The report that his grandson gave them to the church also suggests that they remained physically in Bernini's house.

208 Wittkower 1997 (1995), 57f., noted the gender difference and emphasized Bernini's debt to the Pseudo-Dionysius.

209 Following Weil 1974, the material is conveniently collected in Tolomeo Speranza 1988, but with a hopeless conflation of original and workshop studies. Valuable observations on Bernini's modeling technique have been offered by Sigel 1999.

210 On this subject and the history of the sculptural model generally, see Lavin 1967 (1964).

211 On these points, see Meeks 1974, Koole 1986, Mathews 1993, and Keck 1998.

212 Pseudo-Dionysius, XV, 6; 1987, 187f.:

They are also named "winds" 161 as a sign of the virtually instant speed with which they operate everywhere, their coming and going from above to below and again from below to above as they raise up their subordinates to the highest peak and as they prevail upon their own superiors to proceed down into fellowship with and concern for those beneath them. One could add that the word "wind" means a spirit of the air and shows how divine and intelligent beings live in conformity with God. The word is an image and a symbol of the activity of the Deity. It naturally moves and gives life, hurrying forward, direct and unrestrained, and this in virtue of what to us is unknowable and invisible, namely the hiddenness of the sources and the objectives of its movements. "You do not know," says scripture, "whence it comes and whither it goes." 162 This was all dealt with in more detail by me in *The Symbolic Theology* when I was explicating the four elements. 163 The word of God represents them also as clouds. 164 This is to show that the holy and intelligent beings are filled in a transcendent way with hidden light. Directly and without arrogance they have been first to receive this light, and as intermediaries, they have generously passed it on so far as possible to those next to them. They have a generative power, a life-giving power, a power to give increase and completion, for they rain understanding down and they summon the breast which receives them to give birth to a living tide.

213 On the mystical theology of clouds and light, see Puech 1938.

214 "...il pregio maggiore del suo Scalpello, con cui vinto haveva la difficultà di render' il Marmo pieghevole come la cera,...il cuore di rendere i sassi così ubbidienti alla mano, come se stati fossero di pasta" (Bernini 1713, 149); on this point, see Lavin 1980, 11f.

215 On the Wounds of Our Lord and the Spear Thrust, see *New Catholic Encyclopedia* 1967–89, XIV, 1036–7.

216 Malatesta 1977, 176.

217 28 postea sciens Iesus quia iam omnia consummata sunt ut consummaretur scriptura dicit sitio

30 cum ergo accepisset Iesus acetum dixit consummatum est et inclinato capite tradidit spiritum

34 sed unus militum lancea latus eius aperuit et continuo exivit sanguis et aqua

35 et qui vidit testimonium perhibuit et verum est eius testimonium et ille scit quia vera dicit ut et vos credatis

36 facta sunt enim haec ut scriptura impleatur os non comminuetis ex eo.

218 "...ut significaretur ex morte et latere Chrisiti, quasi secondi Adae dormientis in cruce, Ecclesiam quasi Evam Christi sponsam formatam esse... ut ait Cyrillus e Chrysostomus, acqua significet baptismum, qui est principium Ecclesiae et Sacramentorum caeterorum; sanguis vero repraesentet Eucharistiam, quae omnium Sacramentorum finis est et complementim, ad quae duo quasi ad principium et finem, caetera Sacramenta omnia deducuntur" (Lapide 1866–8, XVI, 621; Lapide 1876–1908, VI, 249, 248). The early interpretations are conveniently summarized by

Malatesta 1977 and Meehan 1985. See also the important work by Heer 1966, who relates the Johannine tradition to the devotion of the Sacred Heart of Jesus, followed by O'Donnell 1992. The first part of John 19:34 is quoted in the banderole in the upper part of the crossing pier niche with Bernini's sculpture of St. Longinus, in connection with which the text was discussed in a paper by Preimesberger 1989.

219 "Cur nec solus sanguinis nec sola aqua de latere eius exierit, vel cur aqua sanguini sociata sit.

. . .

Societate, inquam, vivifici pretiosi sanguinis hoc accepit, ut comparetur vera similitudine Rubro mari, per quod salvatus populus transivit Pharaone submerso cum currinbus et equitibus suis. Nam fugientes Aegyptum huius saeculi mundatos in veram repromissionis terram transmittit diabolumque persequentem penitus absorbet cum praeteritis actibus et pompis suis" (Rupert of Deutz 1999, III, 812–4).

220 Much material on the interpretation and art-historical ramifications of the Song of Songs is found in Aronberg Lavin and Lavin 2001.

221 The relationship between Song of Songs 4:9 and the lance wound has been explored by Hamburger 1990, 72–7, in connection with a diptych illustration in the Rothschild Canticles (Fig. 15): Sponsa, who gestures toward her eyes, thrusts her spear toward the figure of Christ with the instruments of the Passion, who points to the wound in his side. There is no allusion to John 19:34.

222 I received a photograph of the drawing in 1973 from a New York dealer, John A. Torson, who supplied no details. I have since been unable to trace the work.

223 The fact that the Trinity altar was widened when the temporary sacrament altar was moved, as the documents attest, is no proof that the transfer was not anticipated (Rice 1997, 208); the change indicates only that the original size of the Trinity altar may have been determined by other factors, or that it was installed before the dimensions of Bernini's work were determined. The documents concerning the early Sacrament altar were published by Pollak 1928–31, II, 36, Reg. 42, 301–5, Reg. 967–83.

224 The documents speak first of two, then of four angels.

225 For what follows concerning the angels I am much indebted to the inspired study by Eric Peterson 1964.

226 In her entry on Bernini's tabernacle in Pinelli 2000, Schede, 699, Evonne Levy also notes the gender distinction between the angels.

227 On these sculptures, see Lavin 1980, 101–29, and Schütze, in Coliva and Schütze 1998, 148–69.

228 Gougaud 1925, 19, 25f.

229 Keck 1998, 176.

230 XV, 4; Pseudo-Dionysius 1987, 186.

231 On the paradox of Bernini's "calculated spontaneity," see Lavin 1978a. On the *bozzetto* illustrated in Fig. 260, see Lavin 2001.

232 Cited by Hibbard 1965, 202.

233 See Fagiolo 1997, 129.

234 On the adult nude Christ, see Lavin 1977–8, Steinberg 1996, 19–22, 135–9, 146f., Hamburger 1990, 72f. It is important to note that the Minerva Christ has no chest wound and that the small holes representing the other wounds are certainly later "additions": they do not appear in the early copies (Tolnay 1943–60, III, figs. 236–42).

235 On the Last Judgment and the Trinity, see Harbison 1976, 159–68.

236 See Tolnay 1943–60, II, fig. 51.

237 This section was extracted from the writer's contribution to a symposium commemorating Richard Krautheimer; Lavin 1997.

238 Krautheimer and Jones 1975; supplemented by Morello 1981.

239 Aronberg Lavin 1994.

240 Chantelou 1885, 15; 1985, 12 (4 June 1665).

241 The notion of Alexander's Rome as Roma moderna, articulated in the publications of the period, stems from Pastor 1923–53, XXXI, 312.

242 See on this point my introduction to Panofsky's essay "What Is Baroque?" in Lavin 1995.

243 See Krautheimer 1985, 70, 80, 174; Pastor 1923–55, XXXI, 291.

244 "Applicò subito a i mali gl'opportuni remedii, e compassionando la povertà, che non solo priva d'impiego errava vagabonda per la Città, ma languiva oppressa da una carestia che quanto piu affligeva il Popolo, tanto maggiormente doveva far spiccare la sua pietà, si volse a distribuire grand.ma quantità d'oro, benche la scarsezza dell'erario fosse un'argine opposto al torrente di questa devota munificenza. Portato il nostro liberalissimo Prencipe dalla piena Carità ben providde, che l'aprire semplicemente a beneficio comune i Tesori era un fomentare otio, et un nudrire i vitii. Onde quell'istesso antidoto che s'applicava per la salute poteva essere un tossico piu potente per avvelenarla. Così dunque represse quella fiamma di Carità, non per estinguerla, ma acciò maggiormente à prò di suoi sudditi si dilatasse, quindi pensò dar principio ad una gran fabbrica, mediante la quale s'eccitasse l'impiego nei vagabondi, e si sovvenisse con il giro di grossa somma di denaro alle correnti necessità." Brauer and Wittkower 1931, 70n1. Brauer and Wittkower date the statement 1659–60, whereas Krautheimer 1985, 174, gives 1657–8; Pizzati's diatribe was composed 1656–9, as noted by Krautheimer 1985, 191.

245 This attitude is emphasized by Alexander's friend and biographer, the Jesuit Sforza Pallavicino 1839–40, II, 177f.

246 Fiorani 1980, 53–148, cf. 133.

247 Alexander's efforts, and ultimate failure, to break the tradition of nepotism are described by Pastor 1923–53, XXXI, 24ff.

248 On Bernini, charity, and the homeless, see Lavin 1997, 1998, and 2000b; for efforts to deal with the problem in the sixteenth century, especially a similar project under Sixtus V, see Delumeau 1957–9, I, 403–16. The immediate successor to the Lateran hospice, after the turn of the century, was the vast Apostolic Hospice of San Michele a Ripa (Sisinni, ed. 1990, Bevilacqua Melasecchi 2001).

249 On Bernini's death, the bust of the Savior, and the Sangue di Cristo, see Lavin 1972 and 1998.

250 The original of this long-lost work, known from an autograph drawing and several early copies and reflections, came to light at S. Sebastiano fuori le mura in Rome; see Cucco 2001, 119, where the connection with Bernini was overlooked; Fagiolo dell'Arco 2002, 71, where it is described as "attributed" to Bernini; and Lavin 2003b.

251 Among the many known copies, the one Bernini commissioned for himself has also recently been identified; see n. 260 below.

252 See Lavin 1998, 81–94; Lavin 2000; Anselmi 2001.

253 The print measures 473 × 290mm, the book 170 × 110mm; the thematic analogy between the composition and the Sacrament altar was noted and aptly discussed by Beck 1999.

254 Marchese 1670.

255 9:14 (Douay): How much more shall the blood of Christ, who by the Holy Ghost offered himself unspotted unto God, cleanse our conscience from dead works, to serve the living God?

256 "Vi offerisco il Sangue dell'umanato Verbo, o Padre Eterno: e se manca cosa alcuna, l'offerisco a voi, o Maria, accioche alla Trinità."

257 Cf. Tolnay 1943–60, II, 137.

258 On the stained-glass window at Wettingen, dated 1590, see Anderes and Hoegger 1989, 258f.

259 The composition is also interesting in our context because the Crucifixion–baptism juxtaposition alludes to the mixture of blood and water in the Eucharist, to be discussed below.

260 Without considering the significance of the motif, Francesco Petrucci has made the important observation that the painted version of the Sangue di Cristo in a private collection in Genoa actually shows the spouts as blood and water, unlike other painted replicas in which they are both red (Petrucci 2001, 81–4; Petrucci, in Tapié 2003, 272, with attribution to Borgognone; cf. the color illustrations in Bernardini and Fagiolo dell'Arco 1999, figs. 223, 226). Petrucci argues cogently that this detail favors the Genoa picture, which measures 99 × 70 cm, as the "large" original Bernini kept beside his bed, while the others are copies after the engraving. In the Eucharist itself, of course, the wine and water are mixed, and interesting in this context is a passage in Domenico's description of the composition, quoting the artist: "…(Bernini) said, 'in this Sea are drowned his sins, which cannot be found by Divine justice except amongst the Blood of Jesus Christ, in the tints of which they will either have changed color or by its merits obtained mercy.' [Et In questo Mare, egli diceva, ritrovarsi affogati i suoi peccati, che non altrimente dalla Divina Giustitia rinvenir si potevano, che frà il Sangue di Giesù Christo, di cui tinti ò haverebbono mutato colore, ò per merito di esso ottenuta mercede](Bernini 1713, 170).

261 All contemporary sources, including Bernini himself, identify the figure as the Virgin Mary or Queen of Heaven (as duly noted by Bindi in Bernardini and Fagiolo dell'Arco 1999, 445); indeed, only she can perform the task given to her by Maria Maddalena's invocation and in Bernini's composition. Mary is shown conspicuously barefoot as a sign of her humility, but the figure no doubt also alludes to the Virgin's two namesakes: Mary Magdalene, who is often shown as the penitent kneeling at the foot of the Cross (as noted by Brauer and Wittkower 1931, 168); and Maria Maddalena de' Pazzi herself, a member of the Discalzed Carmelites, the order dedicated to the Virgin. The saint was famed for her frequent ecstatic visions like the one from which the caption of the Sangue di Cristo was quoted. The relevance of Maria Maddalena is amply discussed by Beltramme 1994, who follows Blunt 1978 in actually identifying the figure as the Florentine mystic.

262 Marienlexikon (1988–94), I, 41; II, 549–59. The icon and the procession in which it had figured for centuries were part of the background for Bernini's projects for the tribune of S. Maria Maggiore and a hospice for the poor at the Lateran palace. As has been noted by Cardile 1984, 202, 208nn30, 50, the gesture is related to the manis expansis of the Offertory of the Mass.

263 Marienlexikon (1988–94), II, 312–14.

264 The relationship between these images and the blood and water was noted by Mâle 1984, 193f. (Tedaldi 1996, 90, and Bindi in Bernardini and Fagiolo dell'Arco 1999, 445, refer to the Ecclesia type but not its relevance to the Joannine theme.) Blood and water issue from the side wound in the Crucifixion in Duccio's triptych at Hampton Court (Shearman 1983, 96); the ecclesiological reference is here expressed through the extraordinary combination of the Crucifixion with Mariological scenes in the wings. The blood and water motif also refers to the institutional sacrament in Bellini's Blood of the Redeemer, National Gallery, London; the double stream from the chest wound, to which Christ gestures, is captured in a chalice by a kneeling angel (Goffen 1989, ill. 57).

265 See the examples illustrated in Seiferth 1970.

266 On the theme of the Virtues crucifying Christ, see Kraft 1976.

267 I have tried to show that this tradition underlay the particular relation between the Virgin and the Christ child in Michelangelo's Medici Madonna (Aronberg Lavin and Lavin 2001, 49–84).

268 "With the wine used in the sacred mysteries, the Church of God, however, has always mingled water, because, as we know on the authority of councils and the testimony of St. Cyprian, our Lord himself did so; and also because this admixture renews the recollection of the blood and water which issued from his sacred side. The word water we also find used in the Apocalypse, to signify the people, and, therefore, Water mixed with wine signifies the union of the faithful with Christ their head." (Apoc. xvii.15: "And he saith unto me, The waters which thou sawest, where the whore sitteth, are peoples, and multitudes, and nations, and tongues.") *Catechism* n.d., 151. ["Aquam vero Dei Ecclesia vino semper admiscuit; primum, quod id a Christo Domino factum esse et conciliorum auctoritate et sancti Cypriani testimonio comprobatur; deinde, quod sanguinis et aquae, quae ex eius latere exierunt, hac permistione memoria renovatur. Tum vero aquae, ut in Apocalypsi legimus, populum designant; quare aqua vino admixta fidelis populi cum Christo capite coniunctionem significat, atque hoc ex apostolica traditione perpetuo sancta Ecclesia servavit" (*Catechismus* 1989, 244).]

269 On this delicate and vexed subject, see *Marienlexikon* 1988–94, V, 314–18. In 1916 the Holy Office forbade the use of images of Mary portraying her as a priest, and in 1927 proscribed altogether the devotion to Mary Virgin Priest.

270 "sacerdos pariter et altar quidem ferens, dedit nobis coelestem panem Christum in remissionem peccatorem" (cited after Marracci 1710, 607).

271 Missaglia et al., 1954, fig. 102, p. 111. I have been unable to trace this Madonna–Priestess image. The inscription below (faintly legible in the bad reproduction from an unspecified source used for Missaglia's book, preserved in an album in SS. Andrea e Claudio dei Borgognoni in Rome) specifies that Mary offers to God her son's flesh and blood, consecrated by the priests: MARIA TANQUAM MEDIATRIX OFFERT DEO PATRI QUOD CONSECRATUM EST A SACERDOTIB' SCILICET [C]ARNEM VIRGINEAM ET SANGUINEM PRETIOSUM FILI EIUS DOMINI NOSTRI IESU CHRISTI.

272 Bernard of Clairvaux 1950, III, 305 (cf. Marchese 1670, 82): Caeterum quidquid illud est, quod offerre paras, Mariae commendare memento, ut eodem alveo ad largitorem gratiae gratia redeat quo influxit. Neque enim impotens erat Deus, et sine hoc aquaeductu infundere gratiam, prout vellet; sed tibi vehiculum voluit providere. Forte enim manus tuae, aut sanguine plenae, aut infectae muneribus, quod non eas ab omni munere excussisti. Ideoque [alias, itaque] modicum istud quod offerre desideras, gratissimis illis et omni acceptione dignissimis Mariae manibus offerendum tradere cura, si non vis sustinere repulsam. Nimirum candidissima quaedam lilia sunt: nec causabitur ille liliorum amator inter lilia non inventum, quidquid illud sit quod inter Mariae manus invenerit. Amen. (Migne 1844–47, CLXXXIII, col. 448)

273 Bonaventure 1934–64, V, 316: "...quia non nisi patrocinio beatae Mariae Virginis ad virtutem huius Sacramenti pervenitur. Et propeter hoc, sicut per eam hoc sacratissimum corpus nobis datum est, ita per manus eius debet offerri et per manus eius accipi sub Sacramento quod nobis praestitum est et natum ex eius utero" (*De verbo incarnato*, Sermo VI, par. 20, Bonaventure 1934–64, V, 316, cited by Crocetti 2001, 125).

274 T'offerisco adunque à te, ò Verbo; lo presento à te Spirito Santo, e se cosa alcuna ci manca, l'offerisco à te, o Maria, cho lo presenti all'eterna Trinità, per supplimêto di tutti i difetti, che fossero nell'anima mia, e ancora per sodisfazioi-jne di tutte la colpe, che fossero nel corop mio. (Puccini 1609, 241f.)

Io t'offero il Sangue del'tuo humanato Verbo, dico l'offero a te Padre, l'offero a te Verbo, e l'offero a te Spirito Santo. Et se nulla ci mancassi, l'offero a te Maria, che l'offerisca all'eterna Trinità per supplimento di tutti e' diffetti che fussino nell'anima mia, e ancora per soddisfatione di tutti e' difetto che fussino nelcorpo mio. (De' Pazzi 1960, 20)

Vi offerisco, ò Padre eterno, il Sangue dell'vmanità del vostro Verbo; l'offerisco à voi stesso, ò Diuin Verbo; l'offerisco anco à voi, ò Spirito Santo; e se manca à me cosa alcuna, l'offerisco à voi, ò Maria; acchioche, lo presentiate alla Santissima Trinità. (Marchese 1670, 83)

Bernini's *Sangue di Cristo* composition was by no means unprecedented in this respect. The Holy Spirit as such is not represented in Filippino Lippi's *Intercession of Christ and the Virgin* in Munich (Lavin 1972, 165, fig. 4), but is present by implication between the angel and Virgin of the Annunciation flanking the central presiding figure of God the Father; the Eucharist is alluded to in the body of Christ displayed in the predella below. Bernini also omitted the Holy Spirit in his drawing of Christ and the Virgin appealing to God the Father, in Leipzig (Lavin 1972, 165, fig. 3).

275 On Bernini's conception of the unity of the visual arts, see Lavin 1980, esp. 6–15, 143–5.

276 "Iddio adunque è il vero Disegno, e vero author, e perfetto, e divin Pittore, Scultore et Architetto"; for this and other citations, see Herrmann-Fiore 1979, 78–81, esp. 79 n. 192, fig. 31, p. 76. See also Merz 1999, 229.

277 For Michelangelo's self-deprecation with respect to his portrayal of God in the Sistine Chapel ceiling, see Lavin 1990b, 26f., and 1993, 36f.

278 On Bernini's "bel composto," see Lavin 1980, 6–15.

8

THEATERS FOR THE CANONIZATION OF SAINTS

ALESSANDRA ANSELMI

PREMISE

IN CONTRAST TO OTHER EPHEMERAL ARCHITEC-
ture, the temporary structures built in St. Peter's for
the canonization of saints had to meet precise and codified requirements.[1] This was especially true in the case
of the platform (Latin, *suggestum*) that was prepared
for the celebration of the actual ceremony.[2] This chapter
analyzes the manner in which seventeenth-century architects exploited the narrow margin of freedom allowed
by rigid ceremonial and liturgical protocols to modify
the platform-type inherited from sixteenth-century tradition. Their primary goal was to adapt these platforms
to increasing requirements of visibility and participation,
but above all to place greater emphasis on papal authority. The seventeenth century, in fact, proves to be the most
interesting in the history of such ephemeral structures, at
least from an architectural point of view, and later platforms only repeat the seventeenth-century model without any significant innovation.[3] Because the platforms
created for these occasions had to satisfy precise ceremonial requirements, it will be useful to summarize the
principal stages in the canonization ceremony before ex-
amining the platforms themselves.

THE CEREMONY

The images in an engraving by Antonio Tempesta allow
us to visualize the principal phases of the ceremony.[4] It
was engraved in 1608, evidently for didactic purposes,
to represent the canonization of Saint Francesca Romana
(Fig. 278).

A procession of the secular and regular clerics of
Rome, papal officials, and other dignitaries including
ambassadors and nobles accompanied the pope into
St. Peter's. Alighting from the gestorial chair, the pope
prayed before the altar and then processed to the papal
throne.

The first part of the ceremony was punctuated by
the triple request (the *petitio canonisationis*) of the con-
cistorial lawyer, who spoke on behalf of the Cardinal
Procurator in charge of the cause for the saint's canonization (Fig. 279). On the first two occasions (*instan-
ter* and *instantius*) the request was refused, since, in the
words of the Secretary of the Briefs who responded in the
pope's name, such an important decision required a great
deal of deliberation. Next the pope invited the people
to pray, going himself to the pontifical altar (Fig. 280).
At this juncture the third request of *petitio canonisationis* was made. This time (*instantissime*), the pope remained seated – in order to distinguish this act from every other judicial sentence – and pronounced the formula
proclaiming the sanctity of the beatified (Fig. 281).

This part of the ceremony concluded with the *Te
Deum laudamus* and a prayer in which the intercession
of the new saint was invoked for the first time. Then the
pope returned to the so-called seat of paraments, where
he was vested to celebrate the mass (Fig. 282). After the
celebration of the solemn mass (Fig. 283), the pontiff
returned to the throne and received the offertory
(Fig. 284). The ceremony in St. Peter's concluded with the
benediction and concession of a plenary indulgence to all
present (Fig. 285).[5] The pope then returned to his residence. After the ceremony, a solemn procession accompanied the canonization banner, bearing the image of the
new saint, to the church of his order or to another church
linked with his name, where it was received with great
fanfare. To enact the ceremony, as we learn from the di-
aries of the Magistri Cerimoniarum, a wooden platform
(*suggestum*) had to be erected in the nave of St. Peter's.[6]
In order to understand better the development of these
pivotal structures during the seventeenth century, we
shall first examine a canonization celebrated at the end
of the previous century.

278. Antonio Tempesta, *The Canonization of S. Francesca Romana*, engraving, 1608. Biblioteca Angelica, Rome

THE ANTECEDENTS: THE CANONIZATION OF 1588

During the course of the sixteenth century, five canonization ceremonies were celebrated.[7] Of these five, the structure that can be assessed with the greatest precision – as it is documented by four printed sources,[8] a fresco of the Vatican Library (Fig. 286), and a marble relief (Fig. 287)[9] – is the one created for the canonization of Diego of Alcalá, celebrated by Sixtus V on 2 July 1588 in the surviving fragment of Constantine's original basilica.

Since the scheme follows the prescriptions of the Magistri Cerimoniarum Johannes Burckard (1484), Patrizio Piccolomini (1488), and Paride de Grassi (1519) for much earlier canonizations,[10] the *suggestum* created in 1588 may be considered representative of those structures from the fifteenth and even sixteenth centuries for which we do not otherwise have visual records. The 1588 structure was created under the supervision of Cardinal

Gesualdo, Prefect of the Congregation of Sacred Ceremonies. A rectangular, wooden platform "not quite as tall as a man" (*alto poco manco della statura di un uomo*), twelve *canne* long and six and one-half wide, was constructed in the basilica's nave.[11]

As one can see in the fresco, at the shorter side of the platform facing the apse, there was a provisional altar for celebrating the mass, flanked by two little tables. On one table were the objects necessary *ad abluendum manus pontificis*, and on the other were the liturgical vessels. To the right of the altar, on the gospel side (our left), was the papal throne topped by a canopy, and it was here that the *petitio canonisationis* took place. Opposite this throne, *a latere epistolae*, was another one without a canopy, where the pope received the vestments for celebrating the final mass. The rest of the platform was surrounded by benches for the cardinals, arranged *ad modum quadraturam*; behind these benches were others reserved for the archbishops, bishops, and other prelates. In the fresco, this second row of benches is shown only

279. Antonio Tempesta, Detail of *The Canonization of S. Francesca Romana*, engraving, 1608. Biblioteca Angelica, Rome

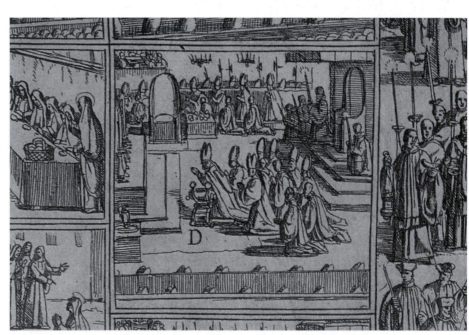

280. Antonio Tempesta, Detail of *The Canonization of S. Francesca Romana*, engraving, 1608. Biblioteca Angelica, Rome

on the right side. To the left, near the entrance to the *suggestum* flanked by Swiss Guards, one can see the table where the offertory gifts were placed. On the right, a small box for the musicians is visible outside the platform. The platform itself was covered with green cloth, except in the area bordering the papal throne, which was covered in red cloth.

As the above-cited sources indicate, the decorations consisted of tapestries and other wall hangings, suspended all around the platform (as it is visible in the fresco) as well as festooning the rest of the basilica. Four banners also hung at each corner of the platform, and

on these were painted the images of the saint, of King Philip II of Spain (as the saint was Spanish), and the papal coat of arms. After the clergy had processed into the church, a fifth banner with yet another image of Diego of Alcalá was suspended over the middle of the *suggestum*. Outside the *suggestum* was an enclosure for the Roman clergy, but no particular attempt seems to have been made to accommodate any other spectators. In his diary, Paride de Grassi affirms that he had tolerated the setting up of small makeshift boxes for the canonization of Saint Francis of Paola in 1519,[12] and perhaps something analogous was allowed in 1588.

281. Antonio Tempesta, Detail of *The Canonization of S. Francesca Romana*, engraving, 1608. Biblioteca Angelica, Rome

Whatever the case, given the rectangular form of the *suggestum*, its height and interior articulation, and the fact that the papal throne was placed *a latere evangelium*, the only participants who could have enjoyed a clear view of the whole ceremony were the cardinals and dignitaries hosted on the platform itself. Everyone else who had thronged to the basilica had to content themselves with admiring the banners and nave decoration, as well as the simple fact of being present in the place were the canonization was being celebrated, while the ceremony itself proceeded out of their sight. In part, this was due to the fact that the ceremonial arrangement on the platform derived from that used in the pontifical mass in the Sistine Chapel (Fig. 288), which was obviously a ceremony with relatively few participants.[13] Compared to canonization ceremonies prior to 1588, however, there is an important change. The reports of the canonization of Diego of Alcalá, published in 1588 in both Latin and Italian to explain the canonization "even to simple people" (*anco alle semplici persone*) – as well as our fresco and marble relief – demonstrate the Counter-Reform necessity to divulge the meaning of this important event to the greatest number of people possible. Indeed, the canonization of Diego of Alcalá, celebrated no less than sixty-five years after the last previous one, signaled the symbolic end of the defensive phase in the Catholic Church's reaction to Protestantism and the beginning of the *Ecclesia Militans*.[14] In fact, the veneration of saints, their canonization, and papal power in such matters were precisely those targets against which Protestants had originally launched their attacks on the Church of Rome.[15]

Nevertheless, it was only in the next century that the desire for a more direct and broader involvement of the general public in canonization ceremonies, and the

282. Antonio Tempesta, Detail of *The Canonization of S. Francesca Romana*, engraving, 1608. Biblioteca Angelica, Rome

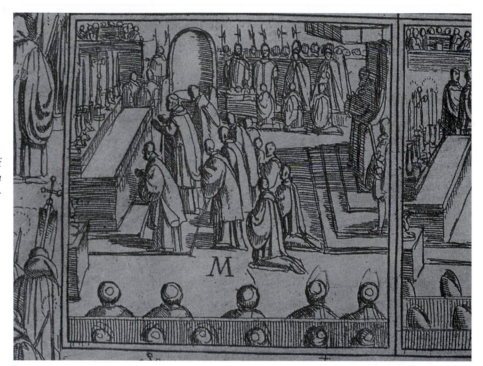

283. Antonio Tempesta, Detail of *The Canonization of S. Francesca Romana*, engraving, 1608. Biblioteca Angelica, Rome

collateral need to emphasize the figure of the pope, found clear expression in these ephemeral theaters. In the second half of the sixteenth century, as is well known, the Catholic Church's response to Protestant attacks came to privilege didactic overtones as weapons of defense and propaganda. The printed reports, the fresco, and the 1608 engraving (Fig. 278) here discussed are precise expressions of this didactic attitude, for they aim at defending tradition. As the fears of the Church receded during the course of the seventeenth century, further innovations became permissible. In time, the platforms for canonization ceremonies were also suitably transformed, becoming real theaters.

THE STRUCTURE OF 1601 AND THE ORGANIZATION OF THE *SUGGESTUM*

After the canonization of Diego of Alcalá followed that of Giacinto of Poland, celebrated on 17 April 1594 and also recorded by a fresco.[16] The canonization took place in St. Peter's, but this time in the Capella Gregoriana, because Clement VIII's refurbishment of the floor under the crossing and the new high altar were still unfinished.[17] There were, however, no particular innovations to the previous *apparato*. Instead, important changes for the future history of these structures first occurred at the canonization of Raimondo of Peñafort, the very first to be celebrated in the nave of the new St. Peter's, on 29 April 1601. A visual testimony is supplied by the marble relief that Giovanni Antonio Valsoldo

284. Antonio Tempesta, Detail of *The Canonization of S. Francesca Romana*, engraving, 1608. Biblioteca Angelica, Rome

285. Antonio Tempesta, Detail of *The Canonization of S. Francesca Romana*, 1608. engraving, Biblioteca Angelica, Rome

286. Cesare Nebbia and Giovanni Guerra, *The Canonization of Diego of Alcalá*, 1588–9, fresco. Gallery of Sixtus V, Vatican Library

carved for the tomb of Clement VIII (Fig. 289), but it is rather sparse in details and, moreover, was created eleven years after the actual ceremony took place.[18] Nevertheless, the detailed accounts of Francesco Peña and the Magister Cerimoniarum Mucanzio's diary give us sufficient information to understand how this structure was made.[19]

The most important modification – which necessitated the reorganization of the ceremonial platform – was the decision to use the permanent High Altar for the celebration of the mass rather than a temporary altar placed on the platform, as had occurred in previous canonizations. The High Altar had been consecrated by Clement VIII on 26 June 1594.[20] In 1601, this altar – located over the place where tradition holds that the remains of the apostles Peter and Paul are buried – was covered by a temporary canopy, which was later replaced by Gian Lorenzo Bernini's monumental bronze Baldacchino in 1624–35.

As Mucanzio's diary reports, in order to allow the pope to celebrate mass at this altar, it was necessary to make the *suggestum* slope. As a result, although the highest point of the platform was still about one meter in height, it sloped gently downward to a level of

287. Egidio della Riviera, The Canonization of Diego of Alcalá, detail of the Monument of Sixtus V, marble relief. Sistine Chapel, S. Maria Maggiore, Rome. (Photo: Private collection)

30 centimeters at the altar end, so the pope could comfortably celebrate mass.[21] A sketch by the architect Carlo Marchionni, even though made more than a hundred and fifty years later (in 1767), can help us to understand more clearly how the platform was arranged (Fig. 290).[22] But, not only did the High Altar require the creation of a sloping platform, it also entailed a different location for the papal throne. The throne was no longer located *a latere evangelium*, as it had been when the temporary altar was used, but rather behind the High Altar, on the chord of the apse and at the summit of the platform. The chairs for the cardinals and bishops were also necessarily arranged differently, and though they still maintained their placement *ad modum quadraturam*, they were now ranged between the papal throne and the altar. The proportions of the platform itself remained unchanged: 115 *palmi* long and 80 *palmi* wide.[23] Since no visual testimony of this canonization survives, to gain a clearer idea of all these changes introduced into the 1601 platform arrangement we must consult an engraving made for the canonization of 1610 (Fig. 294).

Another innovation of the 1601 canonization, however, is not recorded by this engraving, namely the creation of two boxes for distinguished spectators. These boxes stood against the piers that support the cupola.

Since the High Altar stands at the center of the area delimited by these four piers, those spectators who occupied these boxes must have enjoyed an excellent view of the ceremony.

By contrast, the decorations of the basilica in 1601 prove to have been quite similar to those adopted in 1588. In fact, Mucanzio's diary describes a frieze that ran the length of the aisles and was adorned with images of the saint and the insignia of the pope, King Philip III of Spain, and the religious order to which the saint belonged. Four images of the saint were placed in the large niches of the crossing piers and nine banners hung from the cupola.

In short, the most important innovations of 1601 were the use of the High Altar, resulting in a sloping platform; the siting of the papal throne behind the altar; and the creation of spectatorial boxes arranged "in the manner of a theater" (*a guisa di teatro*). As we shall see, all these features would prove decisive for the future history of the *suggestum*, especially the new emphasis on the figure of the pope. The prominence accorded to the pope is of considerable importance, if one remembers that Protestants questioned not only the

288. Etienne Dupérac and Lorenzo Vaccari, the Cappella Sistina, 1578. Private collection

necessity of canonizing saints but also papal authority to do so. In this regard it is instructive to compare the reliefs made to commemorate the canonizations of Diego of Alcalá (1588), Raimondo of Peñafort (1601),[24] Francesca Romana (1608), and Carlo Borromeo (1610) (Figs. 287, 289, 291).[25] In Egidio della Riviera's relief of the canonization of Diego of Alcalá (Fig. 287), based on the Vatican Library fresco (Fig. 286), Pope Sixtus V is represented twice (while preaching and while pronouncing the sanctity of the beatified) but otherwise has no particular prominence. He is an actor among many, including his assistants and the milling clergy, and the focal point, rather, is the crucifix above the temporary altar. In the next relief, recording the canonization of Raimondo of Peñafort (Fig. 289), the papal throne occupies the new pivotal position, and the pope, Clement VIII, who is the focus of the composition, can be clearly discerned while reading the proclamation of the sanctity of the beatified. Paul V is granted still greater prominence in the relief recording the canonizations that he celebrated (Fig. 291). The figures of the Swiss Guards and bishops have been eliminated from the foreground, and Paul V emerges with solemnity at the heart of the composition. The pontiff is ever more the protagonist of these reliefs, thus reflecting the progressive reinforcement of papal authority after the blow dealt by the Protestant attack.

Nevertheless, one must wait for a few more decades and the intervention of Gian Lorenzo Bernini before the Supreme Pontiff would acquire that true prominence in the ephemeral theater that Clement VIII and Paul V had tentatively assured themselves in these reliefs and in Giovanni Battista Ricci's frescoes in the gallery of the Vatican Library (Figs. 292, 293). Although Bernini's capacity for brilliant innovation in the theaters of canonization has already been emphasized,[26] his debt to the past has been previously ignored, and there are actually two important reasons to trace the progressive transformations of these structures *before* his intervention. First, because only in this way is it possible to gauge the extent of Bernini's departure from inherited models, and second, it is important to understand how much all transformations of the sacral stage reflect changes in the religious and political spheres.

Having treated the ceremony of 1601, it is now necessary to dwell upon the structures created for the 1610 and 1622 canonizations. Both were interesting experiments, whose complexity lifted them above the anonymity of preceding structures, which had been mainly the brainchildren of the Magistri Cerimoniarum.[27] These men would still exercise an important level of control, but in the seventeenth century much greater rein would be given to the creative intervention of the architects, who designed real "theaters," in both senses the word held in the seventeenth century.[28]

289. Giovanni Antonio Valsoldo, Jr., The Canonization of Raimondo of Peñafort, detail of the Monument of Clement VIII. Sistine Chapel, S. Maria Maggiore, Rome. (Photo: Private Collection)

THE CANONIZATIONS OF 1610 AND 1622: THE THEATERS OF GIROLAMO RAINALDI AND PAOLO GUIDOTTI BORGHESE – EPHEMERAL STRUCTURES AS PROPAGANDA FOR THE "SPONSOR"

Compared to the *apparato* of 1601, the structure built in 1608 for the canonization of Saint Francesca Romana under the supervision of Girolamo Rainaldi (Fig. 293) offers no substantial changes, except for its decorations.[29] In the case of the canonization of Saint Carlo Borromeo, celebrated two years later on 1 November 1610, Rainaldi's intervention was more extensive.[30] For this occasion, Rainaldi planned a theater in the true sense of the word, that is, a wooden structure with arcades backing the ranked seats of the spectators (Fig. 294). It is likely that the idea of this theater came to Rainaldi through practical necessity, as the new basilica was not yet finished and it was therefore preferable to create a closed structure that would hide the work in progress from view. A closed structure was also used by Paolo Guidotti Borghese for the canonization of five

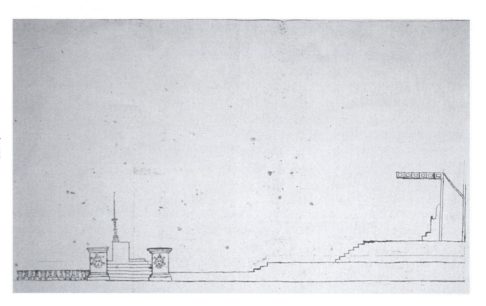

290. Carlo Marchionni, sketch for the *suggestum*, 1767. Archivio del Cerimoniere Pontificio, Vatican

saints – Isidore of Madrid, Ignatius of Loyola, Francis Xavier, Teresa d'Avila, and Filippo Neri – celebrated on 12 March 1622 (Fig. 295).[31]

The differences between the two theaters are limited to the greater decorative exuberance that Guidotti Borghese's structure vaunts over Rainaldi's more simple one. Rainaldi's theater is formed of arcades with attached columns, but Guidotti replaced this articulation with a system of arches alternating with trabeated apertures. The silvered and gilt candelabras above, accompanied by putti, cadenced this rhythmic articulation of arch and pier, while the trabeated openings were surmounted by papier-mâché figures painted in imitation of bronze. These figures, alternately seated and standing, portrayed the virtues of Isidore the Farmer, patron of Madrid.

Furthermore, between the ring cornice and the trabeated openings were set paintings of the miracles performed by Isidore. Below each painting hung a molded cartouche with an explanatory inscription. This feature was also resumed from the theater of 1610: Rainaldi had, in fact, hung a painted medallion surmounted by an inscription in every arch of his own theater. The tondos with the miracles of Saint Carlo Borromeo were eight *palmi* in diameter and the paintings of Saint Isidore were six; therefore these paintings were large enough to be seen easily even from quite a distance.

In addition to paintings of the saint, the insignia of the pope, the king of Spain, and that of the Spanish ambassador were hung on each of the piers and arches of the 1622 theater. There also hung the insignia of Diego de Barrionuevo y Peralta, who, as the representative of the city of Madrid, had supervised the various phases of the canonization process as well as the design of the structure.[32] Dominating the back wall of the theater, and therefore above the papal throne, was a painting of the deceased king of Spain, Philip III, who believed he had

been cured of an illness thanks to Isidore's intercession. Instead, the eight papier-mâché telamons fronting the theater's external circuit alluded to the vices put to flight by Isidore.

Consequently, it is obvious enough that in 1610 and 1622 the spectators were literally bombarded with images extolling the canonized saint; yet, once again, the ceremony itself remained as invisible to most onlookers as it was before. This was the case because Girolamo Rainaldi and Paolo Guidotti Borghese limited their interventions to simply surrounding the *suggestum* with an enclosure, without otherwise modifying it. Indeed, the internal arrangement of the *suggestum* as built in 1610 and 1622 remained the same as that inaugurated in 1601.[33] The enclosures to which both architects devoted their creative efforts skillfully accommodated the boxes for the spectators and supported the decorations relative to the saints, clearly visible on all sides; but neither architect concerned himself with (or succeeded in) establishing an organic visual rapport between the small spectatorial boxes and the place (i.e., the *suggestum*) where the ceremony occurred. Consequently, for many spectators, as is apparent from the engravings, the throne where the pope pronounced the judgment of canonization was almost completely obscured from view. The *suggestum* continued to host and define the area where the ceremony took place, but neither architect exploited its potential to become a real stage, and one that would give the pontiff more prominence. For this development we must await Bernini.

However, Rainaldi and Guidotti did satisfy the requirements of their patrons or, to use a modern term, their "sponsors." The real protagonists of the 1610 and 1622 ceremonies were, in fact, the canonized saints and the petitioners of the respective canonizations who, as was customary, paid for these theaters to be built.[34]

291. Giovanni Antonio Valsoldo, Jr., The Canonization of Santa Francesca Romana or Carlo Borromeo, detail of the Monument of Paul V. Pauline Chapel, S. Maria Maggiore, Rome. (Photo: Private collection)

The petitioners of 1610 and 1622 were, respectively, the representatives of Milan cathedral and the municipality of Madrid. A very particular case of exploiting the canonization structure for politically propagandistic ends is represented by the theater made for the 1622 canonization. One of the peculiarities of this theater was the fact that, although five saints were canonized, the structure only displayed images exalting Isidore the Farmer and the heraldic arms of Madrid, as well as those of the reigning Spanish king, Philip IV. The other four saints – Ignatius of Loyola, Francis Xavier, Teresa d'Avila, and Filippo Neri – all of whom were much better known and more acclaimed, were represented only by simple banners hanging in the middle of the theater; nor were there any insignia of their respective orders. This absence was also noticed by contemporaries, who justified the peculiarity by maintaining that Pope Gregory XV had made the decision to canonize the other four beatified when the theater planned only for Isidore of Madrid had already been finished.[35] As a matter of fact, archival documents establish that this official version disguised complex political maneuvers dating back to the papacy of Paul V. In fact, Paul V, as the cor-

respondence between Rome and Madrid testifies, had beatified Isidore on 14 June 1619 (Fig. 296) and had promised Philip III his canonization, expecting in recompense that the king "se sirviese de honrar la casa Burghesa mandando cubrir al Principe de Sulmona" – that is, that the king would nominate the pope's nephew Marcantonio Borghese to be a grandee of Spain.[36] Thus, the Borghese family gained one of the most important honorifics of the era, while the king of Spain obtained the canonization of the patron of Madrid, a city that had become the definitive capital of the Spanish crown at the beginning of the seventeenth century.[37]

Isidore the Farmer, in fact, had been considered the patron of Madrid since the thirteenth century and was venerated by the Spanish monarchs. Official recognition of his sanctity had become a necesssity, both because it was intolerable that the patron of the realm's capital was not officially canonized and because, for propagandistic motives in Spain, it was necessary to justify the choice of Madrid as capital over other Spanish cities. It was especially pressing because the court's transferral to Madrid had resulted in, among other things, the reorganization of the agricultural market to provision the new capital – to the detriment of other cities, like nearby Toledo.[38] Isidore's hagiography recounts that he was a humble peasant, who was born and died in Madrid in 1170 and confronted the same travails that afflicted the entire rural population.[39] Consequently, he was an auspicious choice as patron saint of all farmers, and this provided an ulterior justification for designating Madrid capital of the kingdom.[40]

Paul V died before he was able to canonize Isidore, but the propagandistic exigencies of the Spanish crown were satisfied by his successor. Gregory XV was also a Hispanophile, and even though he accepted the petitions that arrived from all over Europe requesting the canonization of the other four beati, he simultaneously facilitated the representative of Madrid, Diego de Barrionuevo, in obtaining a theater dedicated to Isidore alone.[41] Among the numerous documents that attest to this strategy, there is an amusing letter from Diego de Barrionuevo. He asserts that Gregory XV rushed him to realize the theater (mucha prisa . . . para hacer la fiesta).[42] Evidently, the pontiff had decided to satisfy the propagandistic needs of Madrid without compromising himself too much, by having the theater finished before the announcement of the canonization of the five beatified became official.[43] In this way it became easier to justify the fact that the theater's decorations concerned only Isidore. But the pope privileged Isidore even in the liturgy of the eventual ceremony. The proclamation of the saints took place, in fact, for the first and last time, "juxta ordinem antiquitatis" and not "juxta ordinem hierarchicum," a maneuver that favored Isidore, who by birth was the eldest. Had the ceremony

292. Giovan Battista Ricci, *The Canonization of S. Francesca Romana*, fresco. Gallery of Paul V, Vatican Library

293. Giovan Battista Ricci, *The Canonization of Carlo Borromeo*, fresco. Gallery of Paul V, Vatican Library

instead followed the "ordinem hierarchicum," Isidore, having been a humble peasant, would have been placed last, since the four other saints were hierarchically more important, being founders of religious orders. Such license was made possible by the fact that, up until then, multiple canonizations had been a rarity and a body of legislation on the matter did not exist, an oversight that was remedied some decades later.[44] In fact, Gregory XV's successors implemented a series of measures to rigorize the juridical process concerning can-

onizations, accentuating papal authority in the process. The liturgical corollary was that the freedom of petitioners for causes to articulate the theaters was progressively curtailed, and ever-increasing emphasis was focused on the *suggestum*, and in particular the papal throne. The decoration relating to the canonized saints continued to occupy a very important role, but no longer "overwhelmed" the pontiff.[45] Consequently, the platforms would become, above all else, stages for exalting the supreme authority of the Church Triumphant.

Nevertheless, the indirect influence of the two theaters of 1610 and 1622 cannot be discounted. First, because the sheer excess of licenses conceded by Gregory XV probably solicited the desire to establish more rigorous norms; and second, even though Rainaldi's and Guidotti's elaborated structures were abandoned as models, they had still heralded the idea that scenographic innovation was possible even for structures as rigidly traditional as the theaters for canonizing saints.

URBAN VIII AND GIAN LORENZO BERNINI: THE THEATERS OF 1625 AND 1629 AND THE AFFIRMATION OF PAPAL AUTHORITY

After the important reforms of Sixtus V, who in 1588 instituted the Congregation of Rites,[46] Urban VIII was responsible for the regulatory decrees of 1625 and 1634 that forbade any public veneration anticipating the official recognition of the sanctity of the beatified. Consequently, while images could be exhibited, particular attributes of sainthood, such as halos and rays, were forbidden and a more rigorous procedure was imposed on the entire canonization process.[47]

294. Theater for the canonization of Carlo Borromeo, engraving, 1610. Private collection

295. Theater for the canonization of the Five Saints, engraving, 1622. Private collection

These norms discouraged potential abuses, but they also reflected the will to affirm and assert the authority of the Apostolic See. This desire also found expression in the theaters created by Gian Lorenzo Bernini for the canonization of Elisabetta of Portugal (1625) and Andrea Corsini (1629). In fact, in the 1625 structure we see the most fundamental changes since 1601, namely, the drive to confer greater visual prominence on the papal throne and make the liturgical ceremony visible to all.[48] Bernini ingeniously exploited the modifications introduced in 1601 to construct a decidedly larger platform than any previous ones, but not a closed structure reserved for a restricted number of participants, as before, but rather a theater that opened out toward the nave (Fig. 297).[49] In addition, he eliminated the *ad quadraturam* scheme hitherto used to arrange the benches and seats for the cardinals and bishops, and instead arranged them fan-like on either side of the papal throne. This was a deceptively simple change that had the important consequence of removing the troublesome visual obstruction between spectators and papal throne. The throne's preeminence was accentuated in three ways: by the two wings of the Sacred College, seated on a slightly lower level and on simple benches; by the customary canopy that surmounted the throne; and, above that, by the broken pediment which housed the papal triregnum and the shield with the Barberini bees. A similar theater with a slightly different facade was created in 1629 for the canonization of Andrea Corsini, and contemporary descriptions emphasize that there was "facilis in area prospectus."[50]

Nevertheless, Bernini still knew how to gratify the sponsors – or rather the Portuguese representatives and the Corsini family who had financed the theaters in 1625 and 1629 – by placing statues and paintings of their saints and ancestors in the most opportune locations. The scale and arrangement of the *suggestum* devised by Bernini – whose full ingenuity can only be appreciated if we remember that its revolutionary effects were obtained with few essential changes and in full respect of the liturgical requirements – would become the standard for subsequent theaters. The elaborate and costly design of the elevations, on the other hand, was never repeated.

ALEXANDER VII, GIAN LORENZO BERNINI, GIOVANNI PAOLO SCHOR, AND THE CANONIZATIONS OF 1658 AND 1665: PERFECTING THE MODEL

Urban VIII's directives proved so severe that they arrested the causes for canonization then in progress. In fact, only in 1658 did it become possible to canonize

296. Luca Ciamberlano, The Beatification of Isidore of Madrid, engraving, 1619. Private collection

Tommaso of Villanova, because the new decrees had dictated that further verifications must be made to guarantee his process.[51] The decision of Alexander VII to oblige the petitioners of the cause to reduce the sum to be invested in a theater that was "ephemeral and almost temporary" (*nell'opera effimera e quasi che momentanea del teatro*) had a fundamental influence on the creation of future theaters. Indeed, the pope instituted a tax of 500 and 1,000 gold *scudi* per beatification and canonization respectively, which would be spent on acquiring chasubles, stoles, and other vestments for the daily use of St. Peter's sacristy, thereby guaranteeing it a rich supply. In order to facilitate the procedure for the petitioners, the following year (27 September 1659) the pope decreed that the funds should be paid directly to the Canons of the Sacristy of St. Peter's.[52]

Despite the new proscriptions, the *apparato* that the architect and decorator Giovanni Paolo Schor designed, probably with Bernini's help, for the canonization of Tommaso of Villanova under the direction of Servio Servi, archpriest (dean) of the basilica, was no less spectacular than preceding ones. The contemporary

297. Theater for the canonization of Elisabetta of Portugal, 1625. Private collection

report of Sigismondo Tamagnini does inform us that Schor adopted a decidedly original solution for the papal throne: this was set on a scaffold (about four and a half meters high, i.e., twenty *palmi*) covered with gold-colored mountains, while three stars of burnished gold adorned the back of the papal throne itself. The mountains and stars, which obviously alluded to the Chigi pope's heraldic arms,[53] "caught and pleased the eye in a marvellous manner."[54] This invention, exalting the pope, who "was seated in a more prominent and richly appointed chair than usual, surrounded by cardinals, bishops, and prelates of the court,"[55] nonetheless remained an episode without sequel. The same was not true for the decorations of the nave.

The regulations of Alexander VII so limited the expenses for the theater that any idea of making those monumental architectural elevations that had accommodated images of the saints in previous canonizations was now eliminated. Instead, adapting an idea first used by Rainaldi in the 1610 theater, the architect had fourteen medallions placed over each of the nave arches (Fig. 298). The miracles of Tommaso di Villanova were portrayed on these medallions, each 30 *palmi* in diameter, and below them hung placards bearing an explanatory legend.[56] This particular decoration served as a model for all subsequent canonizations (Fig. 299), right up until the end of the eighteenth century, if not further. The enduring success of these medallions can be attributed not only to their relative cheapness but also to the fact that the spectacle of these painted miracles ranged all along the nave was visually available to a far

larger number of people.[57] It is likely that Bernini dreamt up this solution, a rather simple solution resulting in a startlingly new effect, just as it had in the canonization of 1625.

With Alexander VII, the sumptuous damasks and velvet trappings that covered the piers and frieze of the nave would also become characteristic of all further festivities. In 1658 most of the damasks had to be borrowed from other churches and the wardrobes of Roman noble families, but Alexander VII soon took steps to have special damasks woven to enrich the Sacristy of St. Peter's, and paraments "suited to the expanse of these walls, so that in the future it will no longer be necessary to despoil all the wardrobes of Rome in order to adorn them."[58] Sixteen hangings of crimson damask, embroidered with gold lace, were used for the first time in the canonization of Francesco di Sales, celebrated by Alexander VII on 19 April 1665 (Fig. 300).[59]

This canonization again accorded with the pontiff's previous economic regulations, and consequently an ephemeral and monumental wooden facade was not erected. But another reason for this omission was that the pope had extorted still more taxes from the petitioners, 6,000 *scudi* in fact, which he obliged them to deposit with the "Fabbrica di San Pietro" to help pay off the debts incurred by such imposing papal initiatives as the Colonnade of St. Peter's, as well as an investment in the future maintenance of the basilica.[60] Nevertheless, the 1665 *apparato* turned out to be equally impressive thanks to yet another experimental *suggestum*. The designer was Gian Lorenzo Bernini, who built on his

298. Giovanni Paolo Schor, The decoration of St. Peter's nave for the canonization of Tommaso di Villanova, 1658. Royal Collection, Windsor Castle

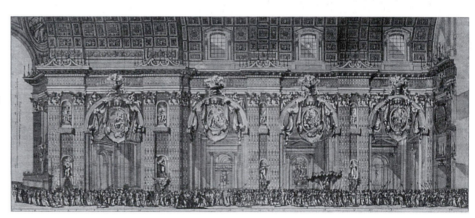

299. Decoration of the nave for the canonizations of 1726, engraving. Private collection.

previous innovations. In fact, the platform followed the model inaugurated in 1625 by opening out to the nave, and the seats for the cardinals once again fanned out along its walls.[61] The papal throne was placed on a stepped dais, and immediately to its sides stood the cardinals' seats, with the lower rows occupied by the archbishops, bishops, and penitentiaries of St. Peter's, the whole ensemble forming "a religious crown" around the pope. Other dignitaries, like the governor of Rome, the Auditor Camerae, and apostolic protonotaries were seated behind the bishops. Above the steps that bisected the *suggestum* and led to the papal throne were seated the Auditor Rotae, the Maestro dei Sacri Palazzi, the Clerici di Camera, and others. At the center of these steps, on a convex promontory, stood the *faldistorio* where the pope went to pray.[62] But the most striking aspects of the entire composition, and consequently the most impressive

innovations, were both the width of the *suggestum*, in the shape of a hemicycle, and its height. In fact, as the *suggestum* receded into the apse it became progressively taller until it reached a height of fourteen *palmi*: "molliter ascendebat amplissimum Theatrum ligneum,...totum viridi colore stratum tapetibus...at ubi altius elevabatur à pavimento, habebat palmos quatuor decim altitudinis."[63] Two of Raphael's tapestries formed the backdrop to this hemicycle, and a magnificent canopy of "capicciolo rosso tessuta d'api" hovered over the theater, although these details are either misrepresented or omitted in the engraving.[64] The canopy does, however, reappear in engravings of other canonizations (Figs. 301, 302, 303, 304). Given its breadth and height, this theater, which cost only 2,860 *scudi* and 60 *baiocchi*,[65] offered an even better view of the liturgical action than Bernini's previous creations. The design of this platform,

300. Theater for the canonization of Francis of Sales, 1665. Private collection

germinated in 1625 and perfected under Alexander VII, would become a model for subsequent structures, which repeated it without substantial innovations.

THE CANONIZATIONS OF 1669, 1671, AND 1690: THE STANDARDIZATION OF THE THEATERS

In 1669 a platform, similar to that realized in 1665, was created for Clement IX's canonization of Pietro d'Alcantara and Maria Maddalena de' Pazzi.[66] This pontiff also decided to continue the manufacture of damasks that had been initiated by Alexander VII.[67] Among the departures in the decorative scheme of the theater compared with that of the 1665 apparatus were four painted papier-mâché statues: two of them flanked the papal throne and represented Strength and Temperance, while the pair at the mouth of the hemicycle represented Tuscany and Spain. A medallion with images of the two saints hung above the papal throne (Fig. 305).[68] Statues and medallions of this sort would also adorn subsequent theaters. Similarly, the theater that Clement X made in 1671 to celebrate the canonization of five saints largely followed the architectural scheme of the 1669 one, except that the design of the *gelosie* (vanity screens) on the spectatorial boxes differed somewhat.[69]

During the austere pontificate of Innocent XI, no ceremonies of canonization were celebrated at all, although he did institute fresh regulations for canonizations. In 1680, Innocent formed a special congregation "pro moderatione expensarum" and introduced more reforms aimed at limiting still further the potential influence of petitioners for the causes. From now on, in fact, before any move to finance the theater, petitioners would have to present a complete list of expenses to be approved by the Congregation of Rites.[70]

The last canonization of the seventeenth century was celebrated by Alexander VIII on 16 October 1690 (Fig. 301). The architect in charge was Carlo Fontana, who based his scheme on the model that had matured up to that moment.[71] In Fontana's design, however, the *suggestum* and papal throne had now reached the impressive height of 26 *palmi* and become a true stage that handed down "to posterity," as Fontana himself wrote in the legend below the engraving, "the throne of Alexander VIII the Sanctifier" (*a posteri il trono d'Alessandro VIII santificante*). It is altogether significant that, in another version of this print, Fontana's inscription was erased and replaced by one in French that generally, without referring to any particular canonization, describes a theater "for the canonization of saints and other solemn ceremonies" (Fig. 302). The French inscription demonstrates that the solution Bernini had developed for specific canonizations had now become the

301. Theater for the canonization of five saints, 1690. Private collection

302. Theater for the canonization of saints. Private collection

standard model elaborated for ephemeral theaters with this function, a model that would be adopted for the entire course of the Settecento (Figs. 303, 304, 306, 307).[72]

THE STUDY OF EPHEMERAL *APPARATI* AND THE UNRELIABILITY OF THE ENGRAVINGS

In some entertaining and unpublished critical comments on the engraving made for the canonization of Saint Francis of Sales in 1665, Carlo Cartari calls attention to its inaccuracies and discrepancies with the real theater, which he himself had had the opportunity to see.[73] Cartari observes that the errors of the engraving result from its very marketability: in order to sell the image on the day of the canonization, the engraving had to be made before the theater was actually finished, and it was therefore impossible to illustrate the amendments made to the theater during construction.

The fact that such engravings are not always reliable is no novelty.[74] Yet, there has often been a tendency to forget their limitations in the study of ephemera,

303. Theater for the canonization of 1712, engraving. Private collection

304. Theater for the canonization of 1726, engraving. Private collection

because engravings often constitute the only testimony apart from printed descriptions, which are themselves fraught with the same problems. Among other things, it is precisely those engravings which illustrate temporary structures that betray the highest margin of discrepancy between representation and reality. The reasons are twofold. First, as Cartari observed, for commercial reasons engravings were made before the structures were complete. Second, engravers and printers knew that, due to the temporary nature of the subject matter represented, only the few attentive spectators who were present for the occasion would notice the discrepancies between the engraving and the actual structure. Moreover, the errors often involve design details. This is either because it was the details that were most easily modified in construction at the last minute, or because the engravings simply approximated them. Consequently, although the engravings at first sight seem so precise, their reliabil-

ity diminishes the more one studies the theater in detail. In short, even if descriptions and engravings are precious sources for the study of ephemera, they must always be considered alongside other documents, especially if any three-dimensional reconstructions of these structures are entertained.

In this essay, too, I have made wide use of engravings and reports, and the future discovery of new documents will certainly offer further clarifications and correctives. However, my objective has not been to reconstruct the canonization theater philologically so much as to trace the evolution of the *suggestum*. Indeed, I have tried to review the milestones in its gradual development as a response to precise ideological requirements, illustrating the process that led the essential structures of the Cinquecento to culminate in those of the Late Baroque – or, in other words, in the triumph of the self-representation of papal power.

305. Theater for the canonization of Pietro d'Alcantara and Maria Maddalena de' Pazzi, 1669. Private collection

306. Theater for the canonization of 1746, engraving. Private collection.

DOCUMENT I

From the diary of Cartari (ASR, *Cartari Febei*, vol. 80, fols. 149r–v). Comment for the engraving made for the canonization of Saint Francis of Sales.

Il fregio sotto il cornicione non fù altrimenti apparato, come fù apparato nella canonizatione di S. Tomasso, ma restò bianco.

Nel sito, dove tra li pilastri si vedono le armi di N. S.re e del Re di Francia, non vi erano altrimenti queste, ma bensì le coltri della basilica, in mezo alle quali erano riportati li miracoli di S. Francesco di Sales, dipinti a chiaro oscuro lumeggiati d'oro, quali per la troppa al-

tezza, poco si distinguevano: le dette armi stavano sopra le dette coltri, tra li capitelli delli detti pilastri.

La cornice tra un pilastro e l'altro, sopra li quali si vede posare l'arme detta, non era ornata con le calate, che qui si vedono, ma le coltri venivano uguali dall'altezza delli capitelli sino al pilastro; fu però osservato, che essendo li parati delli pilastri di damasco cremisino assai coloriti, e nuovi, con belle trine d'oro, e le dette coltri usate, questi facevano qualche scomparenza.

Alli archi delle cappelle pendevano ornamenti di taffettà rossi, e gialli, che qui non si vedono. Dalle ringhiere della Veronica, e di Santa Elena pendevano due stendardi, che qui non si vedono. La prospettiva del

307. Theater for the canonization of 1767, engraving. Private collection.

teatro era ornata con paramenti di velluto cremisino, e di broccati d'oro, cioè tramezzati di teli, e da una parte vi erano sopraposti dei grandi arazzi di Raffaelle, uno con la natività di Nostro Signore l'altro con l'andata al Limbo; ma in questa stampa vi si vedono delineate le coltri con li miracoli, quali, come ho detto si vedevano distribuiti tra i pilastri; mi dice però Monsignor Febei che il suo pensiero era stato di farle collocare nel teatro, come qui si vedono delineate.

Le gelosie delli palchi delle dame qui si vedono alzate; e pure è certo, che non potevano alzarsi, perché erano gelosie fisse, senza sportelli; avendo così ordinato il Papa.

L'istesso si osserva in quello de' cantori a S. Elena; anzi in questo si osserva di più, che vi si vede delineato l'organo; e pure della cappella pontificia si canta senza organo.

Le situazioni di molti della cappella sono poste malamente, poiché si sedette per appunto, conforme io ho descritto.

Gli errori sono nati perché l'intaglio seguì avanti si facesse la canonizazione, per haver pronto il foglio da venderlo immediatamente.

DOCUMENT II

Agreement (*capitolati*) between Filippo Corsini and the carpenter Giovanni Vulpeta for the theater for the canonization of Andrea Corsini.

Archivio Storico Capitolino, Archivio Urbano, Sezione Notarile I, J. Morer, 518, fols. 20–3, 23 January 1629: Filippo Corsini, Giovanni Vulpeta e compagni (n. 6): "capitula et conventiones" "super Theatro conficiendo in Basilica Principis Apostolorum de urbe pro futura canonizatione Beati Andreae Corsini ordinis Beatae Mariae de Monte Carmelo epi. Fesulan."

"Primo che detti Giovan Vulpeta et Compagni supranominati et ciaschedun di loro insolidum havendo ben visto et considerato il disegno, et pianta che il Sig.r Cavalier Giovan Lorenzo Bernini ha fatto per la detta canonizatione s'obligano fare il theatro, et compire l'opera dil detto disegno per prezzo di scudi quattromila moneta. . . . s'obligano . . . compirla per tutti li vintuno d'Aprile prossimo futuro . . . si obligano di mettere la tela, telari, tirature, bollette et chiodi et dar gli pezzi di tutti gli quadri che li pittori devono dipingere per detto teatro, à tempo, acciochè li pittori possino farli in tempo debito . . . ponghino in opera ad effetto tutta la detta opera di detto theatro . . . et doppo che serà levato il detto theatro debbiano a loro spesa turare tutti gli bugi fatti con occasione di detta opera. . . . ogni cosa s'intenda doversi fare à spesa de sopradetto Vulpeta et compagni . . . accetto però la scultura, pittura, et indoratura et carta pista quali doveranno farsi da chi ne haverà la cura. Che il sopradetto Vulpeta et Compagni insolidum si obligano far detta opera conforme le misure, et ordini che darà detto Sig.re Cavalier Bernini, et ordinando che si crescesse qualche cosa di suo gusto, o la altezza o grossezza di detto Theatro, o di alcuna cosa di esso, purché non passi un palmo, non possino pretendere altro prezzo ne pagamento ma si comprehenda il tutto nelli quattromila scudi promessi come di sopra quia sic. Et perché nel disegno, et pianta di detto Theatro non si vedono alcune particolarità, si dichiara et conviene che li sopranominati Vulpeta et compagni debbiano fare li piedistalle delle colonne tutti di tavole con sue cornici modinate di legname, le base delle colonne, et candelieri che vanno in detto theatro torniti e trecentocinquanta altri candelieri dipinti grandi à sua proportione da porsi sopra li cornicioni grandi della Basilica, et della cupola di San Pietro, balaustri torniti, capitelli di legno di ordine dorico, le cornici di legno modinate, et scorniciate tutte. Il tavolato dove va a posare la Santità sua con tutti li Sig.ri Cardinali assistenti, di quella altezza, et misura che ordinarà il d.o Sig.re Cavalier con suoi scalini, o scalinata, e sia di materia di olmo. Il palco dila musica, cancellati quanti bisognino, tutti steccati soliti, et tutti li palchi, et stanzini con le sue gelosie che bisognino dentro detto theatro, con le sue porte et serrature. Tutti gli altri contrapilastri, telari, membretti che vanno dietro le colonne ancorché siano di tela, vi sia et habbino la sua armatura acciò stiano dritti, et fatti, et fra le colonne ce ne habbino da essere duoi di albuccio le sue base et capitelli quia sic."

Notes

This essay is dedicated to the memory of my husband, Bruno Contardi. An earlier version of this essay was given as the paper entitled "L'apparato di canonizzazione di S. Isidoro di Madrid nella basilica di San Pietro, 1622" at the conference *Barocke Inszenierung: Das Ephemer in dauerhafter Erscheinung*, held at the Technische Universität in Berlin on 21–22 June 1996. I wish to thank Suor Maria Trinidad Ruiz, Padre B. Turec, and Antonio Schiavi for their kindness and competence, which remarkably facilitated my research in the Archivio del Cerimoniere Pontificio, the Archivio delle Cause per le Canonizzazioni dei Santi, and in the Biblioteca Apostolica Vaticana. In addition, very special thanks go to Irving Lavin and Fabio Barry and, for her kindness and essential help, to Beatrice Rehl. This paper was translated from the Italian by Fabio Barry.

1   We must remember that a canonization is the process through which the pope decrees that a person, already numbered among the beatified, is worthy to be declared a saint; G. Löw, "Canonizzazione," in *Enciclopedia Cattolica* (Rome, 1949), 3:570–607, and A. Vauchez, "Alle origini del processo di canonizzazione," in G. Morello, A. M. Piazzoni, and P. Vian, eds., *Diventare Santo. Itinerari e riconoscimenti della santità tra libri, documenti e immagini*, exh. cat., Biblioteca Apostolica Vaticana, 21 December 1998–16 March 1999 (Città del Vaticano-Cagliari, 1998), 53–8. Before the sixteenth century not all canonizations took place at St. Peter's, and in the eighteenth century the canonizations of 1729 and 1737 occurred at St. John Lateran; see G. Löw, "Canonizzazione," and the bibliography cited below in note 3. It was Benedict XIV who established that absolutely all canonization ceremonies had to be performed in St. Peter's; see V. Casale, "Benedetto XIV e le canonizzazioni," in *Benedetto XIV e le arti del disegno*, ed. D. Biagi Maino, Atti del Convegno, Bologna, 28–30 November 1994 (Rome, 1998), 15–27.

2   To my knowledge, Niels Krogh Rasmussen made the first study analyzing the relationship between the ephemeral *apparato* for a canonization and the ceremony that took place there; N. K. Rasmussen, "Iconography and Liturgy at the Canonization of Carlo Borromeo," in *Analecta Romana Instituti Danici* 15 (1986): 119–50. As far as the term "ephemeral" is concerned, see the interesting comments of V. Casale, "Quadri di Canonizzazione," in *La Pittura in Italia. Il Settecento*, ed. G. Briganti

(Milan, 1990), 554: "sarebbe erroneo ritenere che il contenitore effimero possa comprendere le feste di canonizzazione nella totalità dei loro aspetti. In effetti esse affacciano anche verso il permanente, almeno per quanto riguarda le immagini dei santi," because these occasions became the moment for fixing and disseminating the normative and canonical images of the newly canonized (see also V. Casale, "La canonizzazione di S. Filippo Benizi e l'opera di Baldi, Berrettoni, Garzi, Rioli, Maratti," in *Antologia di Belle Arti*, 1979, 126n2).

3   Obviously the *suggestum* was only a component of the canonization structures, whose decoration extended to include the whole basilica, and even its facade. The *suggestum*, however, is the *fil rouge* of the present analysis because its development from the sixteenth century to the High Baroque has never previously been analyzed. The manner in which various "sponsors" represented themselves and promoted their saint's image, in dialectical rapport and sometimes even in conflict with papal iconography, is also of enormous interest. Yet, to weigh such issues properly one must wait for in-depth studies of each canonization. As far as the decorations are concerned, see the previous note, and for banners and paintings with images of the saints and their relevant miracles, see the pioneering studies of V. Casale, "Gloria ai beati e ai santi. Le feste di beatificazione e di canonizzazione," in *La Festa a Roma dal Rinascimento al 1870*, ed. M. Fagiolo, exh. cat. (Rome, 23 May–15 September 1997), Rome, 1997, 124–41; see this article also for a previous bibliography by the same author. See also V. Casale, "Addobbi per beatificazioni e canonizzazioni. La rappresentazione della santità," in *La Festa a Roma dal Rinascimento al 1870. Atlante*, ed. M. Fagiolo (Rome, 1997), 56–65, and idem, "Santi, Beati e Servi di Dio in immagini," in Morello et al., *Diventare Santo*, 73–6. Fundamental departure points for the study of these structures are the repertories of M. Fagiolo dell'Arco, *Corpus delle feste a Roma / 1. La festa barocca* (Rome, 1997), and M. Fagiolo, ed., *Corpus delle feste a Roma / 2. Il Settecento e l'Ottocento* (Rome, 1997).

4   The engraving is found in the Biblioteca Angelica, $\overbrace{C}$ 2/11, int. 16. An engraving informed by similar didactic intentions was also printed for the subsequent canonization of Carlo Borromeo. The phases of the ceremony are explained, as well as the phases of the canonization process. The engraving is published in Casale, "Addobbi," 57, fig. 3.

5   For the ceremonies see P. Lambertini (Benedict XIV), *De servorum Dei beatificatione et beatorum canonizatione* (Bologna, 1734), vol. 1, b. 1, chap. 36, par. 6–14, pp. 287–308, and Rasmussen, *Iconography*. See also the contemporary printed reports cited here and those in the repertories cited above in note 3.

6   See M. Dykmans, "L'oeuvre de Patrizi Piccolomini ou le cérémonial papal de la première renaissance," in *Studi e testi* 293 (1980), 1: 129*–30*, 120–1, 238–44; P. Sposato, "Fonti per la storia di San Francesco di Paola. La sua canonizzazione attraverso il 'Diarium' di Paride de Grassi prefetto delle cerimonie pontificie sotto Leone X. Introduzione e Testo," in *Calabria nobilissima*, vol. 10 (1956), nn. 31–2, pp. 1–32 (esp. 22–31), and P. Sposato, "Testo del diario," in *Calabria nobilissima*, vol. 11 (1957), n. 33, pp. 1–29. According to M. Dykmans, the first canonization in St. Peter's to make use of a platform was the canonization of Santa Caterina of Siena (1461). Its use is prescribed as normal in the ceremonials of Johannes Burckard (1484) and of Patrizio Piccolomini (1488). See also F. A. Rocca, *De Canonizatione Sanctorum Commentarius* (Rome, 1601).

7   San Francesco di Paola (1 May 1519), San Casimiro (1521), Sant'Antonino Pieroni of Florence and San Bennone of Meissen (31 May 1523), San Diego of Alcalá (2 July 1588),

and San Giacinto of Poland (14 April 1594). Some references to the structures of 1523 and 1594 are contained in papal bulls: see J. Fontanino, *Codex constitutionum quas summi pontifices ediderunt in solemni canonizatione sanctorum a Johanne xv. ad Benedictum xiii sive ab A.D. 993 ad A.D. 1729* (Rome, 1729), 217, 256–7.

8 Cf. F. Peña, *De vita miraculis et actis canonizationis Sancti Didaci. Libri tres...* (Rome, 1589), 158–61; *Relatione della canonizatione di San Diego di Alcalà di Henares...* (Rome, 1588); P. Galesini, *Sancti Didaci Complutensis canonizatio* (Rome, 1588); *La vita, i miracoli, e la canonizatione di San Diego d'Alcalà d'Henares divisa in tre parti: et tradotta nella lingua italiana dal signor Francesco Avanzi Venetiano dalla latina di Monsig. Pietro Galesini...* (Rome, 1589). All are found in the Biblioteca Apostolica Vaticana (henceforth BAV). On the political meaning of this canonization, see T. Dandelet, "Celestiali eroi" e lo "splendor d'Iberia." "La canonizzazione dei santi spagnoli a Roma in età moderna," in G. Fiume, ed., *Il santo patrono e la città. San Benedetto il Moro: culti, devozioni, strategie in età moderna* (Venice, 2000), 183–92. See also T. J. Dandelet, *Spanish Rome 1500–1700* (New Haven and London, 2001), pp. 170–8 and M. A. Visceglia, *La città rituale. Roma e le sue cerimonie in età moderna* (Rome, 2002), 211–2.

9 For the Vatican Library frescoes, made between 1588 and 1589, see A. Böck, "Gli affreschi sistini della sala di lettura della Biblioteca Vaticana," in M. Fagiolo and M. L. Madonna, eds., *Sisto V. Roma e il Lazio* (Rome, 1992), 696, and A. Böck, "La Biblioteca Vaticana," in M. L. Madonna, ed., *Roma di Sisto V. Le arti e la cultura* (Rome, 1993), 79. For the relief, attributed to Egidio della Riviera, see A. Herz, "The Sixtine and Pauline Tombs. Documents of the Counter-Reformation," in *Storia dell'Arte* 43 (1981): 256. This list should not be considered exhaustive – for example, a small image of this canonization can also be found in a portrait of Sixtus V (cf. Ostrow, n. 15) – but only indicates the images deemed most useful to our study.

10 Cf. the bibliography cited above in note 6.

11 See *Relatione della canonizatione di San Diego di Alcalà di Henares* (n. 8). Instead, according to Galesini, *Sancti Didaci Complutensis canonizatio* (n. 8), 82, the platform was 86 *palmi* long, 47 wide, and rose five *palmi* above the floor. The measurements given above in the text, however, seem more reliable, both because they are similar to those given by Peña, *De vita miraculis et actis* (n. 8), 108 × 58 *palmi*, and because the platform created in 1519 had comparable measurements, eleven *canne* long and seven *canne* wide and eight *piedi* tall (cf. Sposato [n. 6], 19), as did the subsequent ones of 1601, 1608, 1610, and 1622 (see nn. 23 and 33).

12 "Multi fecerunt tabernacula in ecclesia quo ego permisi fieri sic alta ut non impedirent prospectum populi" (Sposato [n. 6], 20).

13 An explicit reference to the fact that the canonization platform had to be made "secundum mores capelle papalis" can be found in Burckard's diary (Dykmans [n. 6] 238–9). For the engraving in fig. 288, see N. K. Rasmussen, "Maiestas Pontificia. A Liturgical Reading of Etienne Dupérac's Engraving of the Capella Sistina from 1578," in *Analecta Romana Instituti Danici* 12, (1983): 109–48.

14 Cf. H. Hibbard, *Carlo Maderno and Roman Architecture, 1580–1630* (London, 1971), 16; T. Dandelet, "Celestiali eroi" (n. 8), 186; G. Sodano, "Il nuovo modello di santità nell'epoca post-tridentina," in C. Mozzarelli and D. Zardin, *I tempi del concilio. Religione, cultura e società nell'Europa tridentina* (Rome, 1997), 189–205, and R. Po-chia Hsia, *La Controriforma. Il mondo del rinnovamento cattolico (1540–*

1770) (Bologna, 2001), 161–80 (original title: *The World of Catholic Renewal (1540–1770)* [Cambridge, 1998]).

15 The bibliography on this topic is vast. Here I will limit myself to citing the recent in-depth study by S. F. Ostrow, *Art and Spirituality in Counter-Reformation Rome: The Sistine and Pauline Chapels in S. Maria Maggiore* (New York, 1996), esp. 140, 321–2. This book particularly analyzes the rapport between the Counter-Reformation and the figurative arts, especially the patronage of Sixtus V. In addition, see Dandelet "Celestiali eroi" (n. 8), 188.

16 For the painting by Federico Zuccari, "La canonizzazione di San Giacinto," in the church of Santa Sabina, see Rasmussen, *Iconography and Liturgy* (n. 2), 123.

17 Cf. F. Bellini, "La moderna Confessione di San Pietro: le proposte di Ferrabosco e Maderno," in A. M. Pergolizzi, ed., *La Confessione nella basilica di San Pietro in Vaticano* (Milan: Cinisello Balsamo, 1999), 43–55.

18 The reliefs on Clement VIII's tomb were placed there in May 1612. Cf. M. Herz, "The Sistine and Pauline tombs," 241.

19 Cf. *Relatione summaria della vita, de miracoli, et delli atti della canonizatione di S. Raimondo di Pegnafort scritta da Monsignor Francesco Pegna auditore di Rotta* (Rome, 1601 [BAV]) and Archivio del Cerimoniere Pontificio (henceforth ACP), *Diario di Paolo Mucanzio*, vol. 424, unpaginated. Mucanzio says that the description of the theater was given him by D. T. Latius. In addition, see BAV, *Urb.lat.1068*, fols. 73v, 127v–128, 135v, 153v–154, 175v, 193, 250v and *ibid.*, *Urb.lat.1069*, fols. 236 r–v, 244–5 r–v, 273: "La spesa fatta in questa canonizatione è stata in vero grandissima et vogliono passa 30 m. scudi.... In San Pietro poi fan conto che di acconcimi di legnami et altre cose fatte per li luminari, ci sia stata spesa di circa 3 mila scudi, restando detti legnami tutti alla Fabbrica di San Pietro." Moreover, 3,000 *scudi* were spent for tapestries (*paramenti*) and 2,000 *scudi* for the wax to illuminate the church. On this canonization, see also Dandelet, *Spanish Rome* (n. 8), 178–80.

20 Cf. F. Bellini, "La moderna Confessione," and V. Lanzani, 'Gloriosa confessio.' Lo splendore del sepolcro di Pietro da Costantino al Rinascimento," in A. M. Pergolizzi, ed., *La Confessione*, 39. See also A. Pinelli, ed., *La Basilica di San Pietro in Vaticano* (Modena, 2000), 2 (2): 797.

21 Cf. ACP, *Diario* (n. 18): "quale palco verso l'altare era basso et alto non più di palmi uno e mezzo, et veniva piacevolmente crescendo a poco a poco, talmente che dove stava il solio del papa veniva ad essere alto da terra circa palmi quattro et questo fu fatto con arte perché avendosi da celebrare sopra l'Altare maggiore se il palco fosse stato uguale non vi sarebbe stata proporzione conveniente ne vi si sarebbe potuto celebrare." A similar description is contained in the *Relatione summaria...* (above, n. 19).

22 The subsequent platforms, in fact, underwent further modifications in height, width, and decoration, but the scheme inaugurated in 1601, which was characterized by a platform sloping toward the main altar, remained unvaried, and we can therefore use the eighteenth-century design to illustrate the phenomenon. For the circumstances leading to the creation of this sketch and the difficulties that the creation of such platforms implied, see ACP, vol. 118, "*Memoriale particolare sopra il falegname e suoi lavori del teatro ed altro.*"

23 Cf. ACP, *Diario* (n. 19). By contrast, Paolo Alaleona's diary reports measurements of 120 by 66 *palmi* (ACP, vol. 444, fol. 94).

24 This relief records the canonization of 1601 and not the preceding one of Giacinto of Poland celebrated by the same pope. This can be deduced from the fact that the papal throne is positioned right in front of the altar.

25 In contrast to the relief on Clement VIII's tomb, in this case there are no elements to establish which canonization is portrayed. Probably no precise distinction was intended, and the purpose was only to register that Paul V had celebrated canonizations during his pontificate.

26 See the bibliography cited in note 48 below.

27 According to Paride de Grassi, he himself directed the creation of the 1510 structure: "feci suggestum...feci deputari unum festaiolum expertum et unum de meis capellanis presidentem deputavi super paratu festivo," etc. (Sposato, 1957 [n. 6], 19–20). The reports for the ceremony of 1588 record only Cardinal Gesualdo (cf. the reports cited above, n. 8). Still, it seems obvious that even in the sixteenth century there must have been an architect overseeing the creation of platforms, at least from a technical point of view. The accounts countersigned by Giacomo della Porta for the 1601 canonization (see A. Andrés, "Gastos de la canonización de San Raimundo de Peñafort," in *Hispania Sacra* 3 [1950]: 166) lead one to believe that it was the Architetto della Fabbrica di San Pietro who supervised the works, as was normally the case later on, with very few exceptions.

28 On this subject see R. Krautheimer, *The Rome of Alexander VII* (1655–1667) (Princeton, N. J., 1985), 3–7.

29 For this canonization and the others mentioned afterward, the reports, and all previous bibliography, see the *Corpus* of F. M. Fagiolo dell'Arco and M. Fagiolo cited above in note 3. Henceforth, printed reports, bibliography, and other documents will be cited only if they do not appear in this *Corpus*, or wherever it seems specifically expedient.

30 For this theater, see the important study of Rasmussen (n. 2). In addition, see the unpublished description of the theater in the Archivio Segreto Vaticano (henceforth ASV), *Archivio Congregazione SS. Rituum*, 1681, fols.196–209v.

31 For this theater refer to the sources and bibliography cited by M. Fagiolo dell'Arco, *Corpus* cit. It is necessary to add the detailed report of M. Ramirez, *Relatione sommaria della vita, santità, miracoli e atti della canonizatione di S. Isidoro Agricola...* (Rome, 1622; BAV and British Library), and G. Freiwald-Korth, *San Isidro Labrador und Santa Maria de la Cabeza Patrone Madrids–Patrone der bauern* (Hamburg, 1981). The author publishes the accounts for this theater found in the Archivo de la Villa de Madrid. A complete series of payments for this canonization, and the contracts with the various artisans and artists involved, which I have uncovered, is published in A. Anselmi, "Roma celebra la monarchia spagnola: il teatro per la canonizzazione di Isidoro Agricola, Ignazio di Loyola, Francesco Saverio, Teresa di Gesù e Filippo Neri (1622)," in J. L. Colomer, ed., *Arte y Diplomacia de la Monarquía Hispánica en el siglo XVII* (Actas del coloquio internacional de la Casa de Velázquez, Madrid 28–30 May 2001) (Madrid: Casa de Velázquez, 2003, pp. 221–46).

32 Isidore did not belong to any religious order, and therefore it was the town delegation (the Ayuntamiento) that assumed the burden of monitoring the cause and sustaining the expense of the process, although the Spanish sovereigns themselves petitioned the pope (see M. J. Del Río Barredo, "Literatura y ritual en la creación de una identidad urbana: Isidro, patrón de Madrid," *Edad de Oro* 17 [1998]: 149–68). Diego de Barrionuevo arrived in Rome in 1616 (see M. J. Del Río Barredo, "Literatura y ritual" 155).

33 The dimensions of these *suggesta*, which can be deduced from the steps and enclosure in the engravings, are similar to those of the previous structures. The *suggestum* of 1610 measured 120 × 70 *palmi* and sloped from five *palmi* in height to one (cf. ASV, *Archivio Congregatione SS. Rituum*, vol. 1681, f. 204) while the *suggestum* of 1622 was 100 × 66 *palmi* and also

sloped from five *palmi* in height to one (in Briccio's report it is written that the height was 50 *palmi*, but I think it is a mistake; cf. Fagiolo dell'Arco [n. 3] 242). The *suggestum* made in 1608 was 120 × 52 *palmi* and four *palmi* high at the point where the papal throne stood (M. Fagiolo dell'Arco, 210).

34 The term "petitioners" (or "postulators") refers to those men representing the bodies that promoted the cause for beatification or canonization, who paid for the creation of the structures as well as the expenses of the inquiry of canonization. The procedure required the presence of these representatives in Rome, who had to keep abreast of all phases of the inquiry, both to resolve any difficulties that might arise during the examination of the documentation gathered (during the remissorial and compulsory inquiries) and to solicit the cardinals of the congregation. Finally, it was their duty to finance the canonization structures and distribute the gifts that, on these occasions, were given to the pope, the representatives of the Sacred College, and other luminaries.

35 Cf. the reports and bibliography in M. Fagiolo dell'Arco, 241–3.

36 Archivo General de Simancas, *Estado*, 2994, *Consejo de Estado*, 5 November 1620. See also ibid., 20 February 1620. On 20 October 1620, Scipione Borghese communicated to the king of Spain that the pope, even though "havesse fermamente determinato di non venire più ad altre canonizzazioni...et avesse dato la negativa a diverse istanze grandissime per fondatori di religione, e per altri beati, fatte e reiterate particolarmente dai Padri Gesuiti," had resolved to canonize the Beatified of Madrid in order to please him in an affair "tanto desiderata." This promise had the designed effect, and two months later, on 29 December, Scipione was able to thank the king for the honor conceded to his cousin: "benigna dimostrazione stimata da noi infinitamente." Cf. ASV, *Fondo Borghese*, ser. II, vol. 422, fols.179r, 388v (I thank Michael Hill for mentioning these two letters to me). The reciprocity of the two "favors" is even clearer in the AGS documents cited above. In addition, see the Archivio della Congregazione per le Cause dei Santi (henceforth ACCS), *Decreta Con.Sac.Rit. Augustus 1610 usque annum 1621*, fols.159v–160, 192 r–v, 230 r–v, 232–3, where we find evidence of the pressure that Scipione Borghese brought to bear on the congregation that it proceed rapidly with Isidore's inquiry. Regarding the political reasons that could lead to canonizations, see also Dandelet, "Celestiali eroi" (n. 8), 190–1.

37 Philip II was the first sovereign to transfer the court to Madrid, in 1551, choosing it as the capital of the empire. In 1600 the court moved to Valladolid, and then in 1606 returned for good to Madrid. Apart from its geographic position in the middle of Spain, the seat of the monarchy could not boast other merits. Consequently, immediately after its designation as capital, studies proliferated tracing its origins to more or less legendary episodes that could furnish the city with the requisite patents of nobility. The decision to promote the beatification and canonization cause of Isidore the Farmer is closely associated with this phenomenon. See the bibliography in the following note.

38 For an analysis of the reasons that led to the canonization of Isidore, see M. J. Del Río Barredo, "Literatura y ritual," cit. and M. J. Del Río Barredo, "Agiografia e cronaca di una capitale incerta (Madrid e Isidro Labrador, 1590–1620)," in G. Fiume, ed., *Il santo patrono*, 45–67.

39 Cf. *San Isidro Labrador Patrono de la Villa y Corte* (Madrid, 1983); F. Moreno Chicharro, *San Isidro Labrador* (Madrid, 1982), 100–39; Freiwald-Korth (n. 31) and the following note.

40 Cf. J. Portús Pérez, "'Sono spagnolo per grazia di Dio': Caratteristiche di una religione nazionale," in *Immagini della Spagna barocca. Monarchia e religione*, exh. cat., Rome, 11 December 1991–31 January 1992 (Rome, 1991), 36–7, and J. Tazbir, "The

Cult of St. Isidore the Farmer in Europe," in *Poland at the 14th International Congress of Historical Sciences in San Francisco. Studies in Comparative History* (Warsaw, 1975), 99–111. These motives, in any case, are far from being the only reasons the Spanish monarchy and municipality of Madrid so strenuously fought for Isidore's canonization (see the essays of J. M. del Río, n. 38 above).

41 See note 43. As regards the Spanish sovereigns' support for the canonizations of the other four beatified, in particular Teresa d'Avila and Ignatius of Loyola, see ASV, *Armadio XLV*, vol.22, fols. 206–7v, 257 r-v and T. Dandelet, "Celestiali eroi" (n. 8), 192–8.

42 Cf. Archivo de la Villa de Madrid, 2/285/ *Copia de la ordenación de la cuenta dada por Don Diego de Barrionuebo…de los gastos que hizo en la ciudad de Rome…desde 20 de julio 1615 que salió de esta villa a la misma ciudad hasta 2 de junio de 1623 que bolbió a ella*, 15. The accounts have been published in part by Freiwald-Korth (n. 31).

43 The pope let it be known that he intended to canonize the four beatified ("Sacra Congregatione inclinavit porre inter istos connumerati etiam B. Philippu Nerium") *eodem diem* only on 21 December 1621 (cf. ACCS, *Decreta Con. Sac. Rit. Augus. 1610 usque ad an. . 1621*, fol. 259 v and, for the inclusion of Filippo Neri, ACCS, *Decreta Con. Sac. Rit. Ab an. 1622 usque ad an. . 1626*, fol. 1, 3 January 1622) when the theater made only for Isidore was almost finished, as is evident from the payments to the artisans (which I have discovered and publish in a study of this theater; see n. 31 above). But the documents (ACCS, *Decreta Con. Sac. Rit. Augus. 1610 usque ad an. . 1621*, fols. 241r-v, 243, 246–8, 256–7) clarify that the pope had already decided to arrive at the canonization of the other beatified between May and August 1621, at which time he began to urge Barrionuevo to finish the theater as soon as possible.

44 "né verun altro papa gli era andato innanzi, né di poi gli è andato dietro"; ACP, vol. 119. It was during the pontificate of Clement X that, on the advice of the famous G. B. De Luca, the Congregation of Rites issued a decree (26 December 1670) prescribing only canonizations "juxta ordinem hierarchicum." See ACP, vol. 119, and Lambertini (n. 5), b. 1, chap. 36, par. 4, pp. 284–6.

45 So one may gather from an analysis of the theaters, but this very complex theme requires further in-depth study. As Casale observes, with interesting examples, in "Gloria ai beati e ai santi," 129–33, the creation and decoration of the canonization structures were the fruit of complex negotiations among the various parties (i.e., the promoters of the cause, the pope, the master of ceremonies, the artists). Therefore, even if papal power was indubitably and progressively emphasized in the canonizations of saints (as I try to demonstrate), more exhaustive studies of each and every canonization are required to trace a more precise picture of this development. See the discussion in note 3 above.

46 See G. Papa, "La Sacra Congregazione dei Riti nel primo periodo di attività (1588–1634)," in *Congregatio pro Causis Sanctorum, Miscellanea in occasione del IV centenario della Congregazione per le cause dei Santi (1588–1988)* (Città del Vaticano, 1988), 13–52; G. Dalla Torre, "La nascita della Congregazione dei Santi," in Morello et al., 59–64, and M. Rosa, "Il Tribunale della Santità," in ibid., 65–72.

47 Cf. *Urbani VIII pontificis optimi maximi decreta servanda in canonizatione et beatificatione sanctorum* (Rome, 1642); P. Lambertini (n. 5), b. 1, chap 36, par. 4, pp. 284–6; G. Löw (n. 1); G. Della Torre, "Processo di beatificazione e canonizzazione," in *Enciclopedia del diritto* (Milan, 1987), 932ff.; G. della Torre, "Santità ed economia processuale. L'esperienza giuridica da Urbano VIII a Benedetto XIV," in *Archivio Giuridico "Filippo Serafini,"* 211, issue 1 (1991): 9–48; M. Gotor, "La fabbrica dei santi: La riforma urbaniana e il modello tridentino," in *Storia d'Italia. Annali 16. Roma, la città del papa. Vita civile e religiosa dal giubileo di Bonifacio VIII al giubileo di papa Wojtyla*, ed. L. Fiorani and A. Prosperi (Turin, 2000), 677–727. C. Renoux, "Canonizzazione e santità femminile in età moderna," in *Storia d'Italia. Annali 16. Roma, la città del papa. Vita civile e religiosa dal giubileo di Bonifacio VIII al giubileo di papa Wojtyla*, ed. L. Fiorani and A. Prosperi (Torino, 2000), 731–51; M. Gotor, *I beati del papa. Santità, Inquisizione e obbedienza in età modena* (Firenze, 2001).

48 Cf. M. Worsdale, "Arti decorative, apparati, scenografie," in *Bernini in Vaticano*, exh. cat., Braccio di Carlo Magno, May–July 1981 (Rome, 1981), 253; K. Noehles, "Apparati berniniani per canonizzazioni," in M. Fagiolo and M. Luisa Madonna, *Barocco Romano e barocco italiano* (Rome, 1985), 100–8.

49 Cf. previous note, G. Briccio, *Descrittione del ricco e sontuoso apparato…* (Rome, 1625), in M. Fagiolo dell'Arco (n. 3), 256, and also E. Gonzales, "Medaglia con la santificazione del Beato Andrea Corsini, 1629," in *Gian Lorenzo Bernini Regista del Barocco*, ed. M. G. Bernardini, M. Fagiolo dell'Arco, exh. cat. Rome, Palazzo Venezia 21 May–16 September 1999 (Milan, 1999), 421–2. Some documents for this theater are in Archivio Storico Capitolino, Sezione Notarile I, J. Morer, 515, fol. 41 (Miguel Suarez Pereyra, "Agente del Rey Nuestro S.r en esta corte por la Corona de Portugal," gives 12 March 1626, 236:2 scudi to Domingo de Rosis for "la hechura del friso del theatro…y por las armas de todos los señores cardenales…de papel molido y todo fue dorado"); fols. 41 v–42 (Miguel Suarez Pereira gives 700 scudi to Simone Lagi and Paolo Bassani "por pintar y endorar el theatro…y por endorar las candelas de leño…las tres coronas…y otras cosas"; fols. 42 r–v (Miguel Suarez Pereira gives 3000 scudi to Paolo Bassano "por endorar quatro stendarte…y los dos Baldaquinos o doseles…uno para el altar de San Pedro y el altro para encima la silla de Su Santidad"); fol. 76v (Miguel Suarez Pereira gives, 10 May 1626, to Gian Lorenzo Bernini, 450 scudi "por la architectura del theatro y por la statua del rey N.ro S.r que se hizo para ornado del dicho theatro" and 530 for the statues of 13 kings of Portugal "y dos Reyes" and 155 scudi for five paintings with the miracles). A complete series of payments, kept in Archivio di Stato di Roma, has been recently published by L. Lorizzo, "Bernini's 'apparato effimero' for the canonisation of St Elisabeth of Portugal in 1625," in *The Burlington Magazine*, CXLV, 2003, 1202, 354–60.

50 Cf. Archivio della Congregazione per le Cause dei Santi (henceforth ACCS), *Fondo dei processi antichi*, vol. 238 bis, S. Andrea Corsini, fols. 406–8. See also the reports and the drawing by Agostino Ciampelli published in Fagiolo dell'Arco (n. 3), 270–2. The description of the theater in ACCS constitutes a rather important document because it is attached to the official documentation produced for the canonization, and thus differs from the printed reports that almost always were written before the structure was finished. The wooden structure of this theater cost 4,000 *scudi*, see Document II.

51 Cf. ACCS, Q Thomas a Villanova, n. 206.

52 Cf. P. Lambertini (n. 5), vol. 1, b. 1, chap. 46, par. 5, pp. 432–4, and F. S. Tamagnini, *Relatione della canonizatione di S. Tomaso da Villanova…* (Rome, 1659), 25: "perché fu ordinato con somma providenza, che le spese degl'antichi teatri momentanei, e inutili si consagrassero à miglior uso, e beneficio della stessa Basilica, se gl'approntò per infinite mani una semplice vestitura, che ad ogni modo non lasciò d'abbagliare"; 46: "Et in queste tele più sacre…furon impiegate le spese solite consumarsi nell'opera effimera, e quasi che momentanea del Teatro." In

spite of all this, it has to be remembered that the expenses for a canonization turned out to be very high. The wooden structure for San Tommaso of Villanova's canonization was quite cheap, only 1,664 *scudi* and 57 *baiocchi* (while that for the canonization of Sant' Andrea Corsini in 1629 had cost 4,000 *scudi*, see Document II). But other 451:10 *scudi* were paid to gild the theater; 3,116 *scudi* and 90 *baiocchi* were given to the painters; and the liturgical vestments and other ceremonial cloth cost 12,813 *scudi* and 40 *baiocchi*, plus other expenses for a total of 38,870 *scudi* and 84 *baiocchi* (see BAV, *Vat. Lat. 11163*, vol. 3, f. 235, "Spese fatte per la canonizzazione di San. Tomaso di Villanova"). The fact that the rules of Alexander VII had only a partial result regarding the diminution of the expenses is demonstrated by the decision of Innocent XI to form a congregation "pro moderatione expensarum" (see below, n. 69).

53   Alexander VII also chose "Fundamenta eius in Montibus Sanctis" as the motto for the foundation medal of the colonnade around the Piazza di San Pietro; cf. M. Delbeke, "A Note on the Immaculist Patronage of Alexander VII: Chigi and the Pilgrimage Church of Scherpenheuvel in the Low Countries," *Bulletin de l'Institute Historique Belge de Rome* 71 (2001): 191.

54   Cf. F. S. Tamagnini (n. 52), 48: "Non fu senza il suo plauso [i.e., Giovanni Paolo Schor] la nova positura del Trono Pontificio, su di cui per occultarne il sostegno furono inalberati in più di 20 palmi i Monti Pontificii contorniti, e lumeggiati d'oro; e su la cima di questa una stella di tre imbrunita ad oro, e quasi che staccata, e da se stessa sostenuta su l'aria, come mostravano l'altre due, che terminavano le spalliere stesse del soglio, e per esser poste al primo incontro dell'occhio rapivano, et appagavano a meraviglia la vista." A drawing for this canonization (Christie's/London, Fine Old Master Drawings, 1 April 1987, lot. 19, p. 16) was identified by J. Montagu and J. Merz; see S. Schütze, "Urbano inalza Pietro, e Pietro Urbano. Beobachtungen zu Idee und Gestalt der Ausstattung von Neu-St. Peter unter Urban VIII," *Römisches Jahrbuch der Biblioteca Hertziana* 29 (1994): 269, n. 174 and 272, fig. 66. The drawing (perhaps made for an engraving) does not correspond exactly to Tamagnini's description. Indeed, even if the papal throne is set on a scaffold, the mountains and the stars are not represented. I thank Fabio Barry for mentioning this drawing to me. On the collaboration between Bernini and Schor for the theaters for *commedie*, see E. Tamburini, *Due teatri per il Principe. Studi sulla committenza teatrale di Lorenzo Onofrio Colonna (1659–89)* (Rome, 1997), 182–3, 282.

55   Cf. *La Breve relatione delle cerimonie, et apparato della Basilica di S. Tommaso da Villanova*...(Rome, 1658), in Archivio di Stato di Roma (henceforth ASR), *Cartari Febei*, vol. 78.

56   Cf. Tamagnini (n. 52), 28–44, and Fagiolo dell'Arco (n. 3), 394–9.

57   On this subject, see Lambertini (n. 5), b. 1, chap. 46, par. 7, p. 439, n. 41: "Porrò, ut alibi visum est, olim in canonizationibus alta voce legebantur Miracula Canonizandorum: sed, cum prae magna hominu moltitudine nemo profecto esset, qui legentem audire posset; ut hominum pietati nihilominus satisfieret, pictura, quae ab omnibus videri potest, in lectionis locum ideo est substituta."

58   Cf. B. Lupardi, *Relatione delle cerimonie, et apparato della Basilica di S. Pietro nella canonizatione del Glorioso Santo Francesco di Sales*...(Rome, 1665), and Tamagnini (n. 52), 26.

59   Cf. Worsdale (n. 48), 245, 255, and Archivio Capitolare della Basilica di San Pietro (henceforth ACSP), *Diario della Basilica Vaticana dal 1660 al 1669*, fol. 135v, 9 April 1665: "Giovedì si continuò ad apparare la chiesa mettendosi 16 calate de' damaschi nuovi fatti a questo effetto in 16 pilastri solamente nelli pilastri scannellati cominciando dalli pilastri dell'altar maggiore,

e seguiva sin al SS.mo Sagramento et ogni calata era di 5 teli, ogni telo erano palmi 84." On the day of the ceremony the diarist writes that the missing pieces of cloth were taken from the sacresties of other churches, as in the past (ibid., fols. 135v, 138).

60   Cf. P. Lambertini (n. 5), b. 1, chap. 46, par. 8, n. 48. In 1740, Benedict XIV reduced this sum to 3,000 *scudi* (see *Nuova tassa e riforma delle spese per le cause delle Beatificazioni e Canonizzazioni*...[Rome, 1741], 18–19). After Alexander VII's reforms, many other economic aspects of the canonizations remained unregulated, to the detriment of the postulators. It was Benedict XIV who subsequently tried to regulate all such aspects; V. Casale, *Benedetto XIV*, esp. 17–18.

61   An explicit reference to Gian Lorenzo Bernini as author of the structure is found in ACSP, *Diario della Basilica Vaticana dal 1660 al 1669*, fol. 138. The same document records that the theater had already been finished three years earlier (in addition, see ACSP, *Diario della Basilica Vaticana dal 1660 al 1669*, fol. 21v, 18 November 1662 and fol. 154v, 22 June 1655). For a description of the theater, see Lupardi (n. 58) and D. Cappello, *Contextus actorum omnium in beatificatione, et canonizatione S. Francisci de Sales episcopi geneuensis*... (Rome, 1665), 222–3. The platform was about 186 *palmi* in diameter, corresponding, as the engraving shows, to the span of the large arches supporting the cupola. The latter dimension is, in fact, 185 and 1/2 *palmi*. Cf. C. Fontana, *Il Tempio Vaticano e la sua origine* (Rome, 1694), 376.

62   Cf. Cappello, 223: "In media Theatri area, qua gradibus semicirculi formam referentibus distinguebatur, apparebat faldistorium, super quo Pontifex oraturus erat."

63   Ibid., 222; B. Lupardi.

64   Cf. ACSP, *Diario della Basilica Vaticana dal 1660 al 1669*, fol. 138v. As for the differences between the engraving and the real theater, see the last section of this essay and Document I. As regards the canopy, see ACSP, *Diario della Basilica Vaticana, 1668–1676*, fol. 57v, where it is written that "il teatro [i.e., for the canonization of 1671] era coperto con la solita coperta di broccatello fatta dalla S.ta memoria di Urbano VIII." Therefore, this curtain may have covered previous theaters, although it is represented for the first time only in the engraving made for the theater of 1669 (Fig. 305). Regarding the tapestries that form the backdrop of the hemicycle, this solution appears for the first time in the drawing made for the canonization of 1659 (quoted above, n. 54), and in one way repeats the solution adopted in the 1588 canonization.

65   The sum mentioned above refers to the cost of the wooden structure. Cf. D. Cappello (n. 61), 229. On the other expenses, see ibid., 224–32.

66   Cf. ASR, *Cartari Febei*, vol. 82, *Relatione delle cerimonie, et apparato della Basilica di S. Pietro*... (Rome, 1669): "si sollevava ampio, e spatioso Teatro, con quattro gradini che soavemente ascendendo venivano infine a formare un'altezza *godibile per tutte* le parti del Tempio."

67   Regarding the 1669 theater, Cartari writes that "la chiesa era tutta apparata né pilastri con damaschi cremesi, ornati con larghe trine d'oro, non solo nella nave di mezzo, ma anco nella tribuna e nella traversa, in modo tale, che più non nè restano à fare: e per compimento dell'apparato altro non vi resta che farvi il fregio sotto al cornicione, quale da N. S. è già stato ordinato à Monsig. Febei, che si faccia, uniforme all'apparato, essendo in essere certa quantità di denaro residuato da questo della presente canonizatione.... Merita lode non ordinaria Monsig. Febei, la cui diligenza, et applicatione indefessa hà fatto far questi lavori con molta celerità, e con vantaggi considerabili né prezzi tanto delli damaschi, quanto dell'oro." Cartari praises Clement IX's modesty because Clement wanted to use, also in

the damasks ordered by him, Alexander VII's heraldic arms (see ibid., vol. 82, fols. 49 r–v).

68   On this theater, cf. ACSP, *Diario della Basilica Vaticana, 1668–1676*, fols. 343–6, and D. Cappello, *Acta canonizationis sanctorum Petri de Alcantara et Maria Magdalenae de Pazzis* (Rome, 1669). Cappello's book has two engravings of this theater also published by P. Bjurström, *Feast and Theatre in Queen Christina's Rome* (Stockholm, 1966), 42, and Fagiolo dell'Arco (n. 3), 471, but it was unknown that the two engravings were originally published by Cappello, since both authors republished unbound copies.

69   Cf. ACSP, *Diario della Basilica Vaticana, 1668–1676*, fol. 57v: "un teatro fatto con bellissima architettura simile a quello che fu fabbricato al tempo della S.ta memoria di Clemente nono per la canonizazione di S. Pietro d'ordine d'Alcantara e S.ta Maria Maddalena de' Pazzi, solo vi era differenza che quello sopra le gelosie haveva un bellissimo fregio tutto di raccamo, con spalliere sotto di velluto e broccato d'oro e questo era tutto apparato di damasco cremisino con trine d'oro, e sopra il fregio delle gelosie vi erano alzate quattro grand'armi di N.S., della Maestà dell'Imperatore, Re di Spagna, e Repubblica di Venetia...." I did not find the name of the architect responsible for the theaters of 1669 and 1671, although it was probably Bernini. The similarity between the two theaters enabled the printer to reuse the engraving of the 1669 theater for the one built in 1671 (cf. *The Illustrated Bartsch*, ed. P. Bellini [New York: 1983], vol. 47, pt. 2, pp. 44–5).

70   Cf. ACP, vol. 119, fol. 876, and A. Lauro, *Il Cardinal Giovan Battista De Luca. Diritto e riforme nello stato della Chiesa (1676–1683)* (Naples, 1991), 528ff. It is a moot point how effective this decree was in regulating the creation of theaters, another aspect that requires further research.

71   For Fontana's role as Architetto della Fabbrica di San Pietro, see A. Anselmi, "Gli architetti della fabbrica di San Pietro," in B. Contardi and G. Curcio (eds.), *In urbe architectus*, exh. cat.,

Rome, Museo Nazionale di Castel Sant'Angelo, 12 December 1991–29 February 1992 (Rome, 1991), 273–6. For his experience in designing theaters, see B. Tavassi La Greca, "Carlo Fontana e il teatro di Tor di Nona," in *Il Teatro a Roma nel Settecento* (Rome, 1989), 1: 19–34, and G. Casale, "Il teatro delle Commedie di Carlo Fontana nel Palazzo Pamphilj al corso: Il cantiere (1684–1687)," in *Palladio*, n.s. 5 (1992): 69–116. It is interesting to note that such theaters were almost always realized by architects of the Fabbrica di San Pietro, but there are some exceptions to the rule. These exceptions sometimes arose from political reasons, for example, in 1608 when the theater was created by Girolamo Rainaldi, the architect of the "Popolo Romano" that promoted the canonization of Santa Francesca Romana, or in 1622 when the theater was built by Paolo Guidotti Borghese, architect of the Borghese family. In the eighteenth century the theaters were virtually always built by architects of the Fabbrica di San Pietro, except in 1729 when the theater for Giovanni Nepomuceno was realized by Ferdinando Reyff.

72   The structures for canonizations celebrated in the nineteenth century seem simply to have reinterpreted, in the taste of the epoch, the previous theaters, without any architectural innovation. But, for a more precise assessment of these theaters more extensive research is required. For the canonizations celebrated in the eighteenth and nineteenth centuries, see Fagiolo (n. 3), xii–xv, 28–30 (22 May 1712); 60–1 (10, 27, and 31 December 1726); 67 (16 May 1728); 71 (19 March 1729); 97–8 (16 June 1737); 132–3 (29 June 1746); 182–3 (16 July 1767); 274–5 (24 May 1807); 334–5 (26 May 1839); 383–5 (8 June 1862).

73   See Document I.

74   To the best of my knowledge, one of the most interesting and precise studies to analyze and point out the limitation of engravings is J. E. Moore, "Prints, Salami and Cheese: Savoring the Roman Festival of the Chinea," *Art Bulletin* 77, no. 4 (1995): 584–608.

9

ST. PETER'S IN THE MODERN ERA

The Paradoxical Colossus

RICHARD A. ETLIN

WITH THE CONSTRUCTION OF ST. PETER'S finished by the Baroque era, this grand church served as an object of reverence and a point of referene throughout the ensuing period that we are calling the modern era. Not until the mid-1930s would a new building program be undertaken, and this time not for the basilica itself but rather for its urban setting. Reaching across four centuries, this study can be likened to an ever-expanding spiral with St. Peter's at the center. For the seventeenth century, it circles closely around its subject to consider churches that took this basilica as its model. For the eighteenth century, it expands its focus to explore how St. Peter's became the pivot for a comprehensive reevaluation of architectural aesthetics. For the nineteenth century, the spiral enlarges still further to question the very basis of cultural activity. And for the twentieth century, this questioning extends to the very nature – and future – of Western civilization.

THE PARADOXICAL COLOSSUS

Even while it was being constructed, St. Peter's emerged as a colossus. This is clearly seen in the sketches from the 1530s (Figs. 8, 93), where the massive piers of the crossing and the barrel vaults that spring from these supports tower over the remains of the old Constantine basilica, which itself for more than a millennium had dwarfed the human beings who had come to worship there or to admire its architecture. Yet St. Peter's soon became a paradoxical colossus. The final shape of its floor plan retains the conflicting features of both the Greek cross and the Latin cross, whose champions had battled on behalf of either the new centralized or the traditional longitudinal layout. This ambiguity in form is apparent on the exterior, where the Greek cross reigns from the rear (Fig. 98) and the Latin cross at the front (Fig. 104). A hulking mass, the Renaissance basilica seems, through the stability of its giant body, to incarnate architecturally the pun on St. Peter's name as the stable rock upon which

the institution of the Catholic Church was erected; yet, through the skillful designs of Bernini in the Baroque era, the church's two points of visual and symbolic focus – the Baldacchino under the central dome and, behind it, St. Peter's Chair in the main apse (Figs. 116, 117, 122) – appear to defy the gravity that keeps all humans planted solidly on the ground, a weighty condition portrayed architecturally in the massive walls, piers, and vaults of the basilica. Finally, although the largest church in the world, St. Peter's paradoxically does not appear as big as it is.[1] This apparent contradiction has provoked widespread comment among architects, philosophers, connoisseurs, and even the ciceroni who for centuries have guided tourists through the famous sites of Rome and the Vatican. These three sources of paradox combined in various manners in the emulative building designs that used St. Peter's as a model.

THE GREEK-CROSS PLAN

The attraction of the Greek-cross plan that played a major role in the evolution of the design of St. Peter's was immediate and enduring. Even before the completion of the basilica, other architects emulated not simply the general configuration of the centralized cross plan but also the specific ways in which the various successive designers of St. Peter's had used this form. Historians today point to three churches in particular that re-create the Greek cross with five domes enveloped within a square after the manner of the early centralized plans for St. Peter's: Galeazzo Alessi's S. Maria di Carignano in Genoa (begun 1552; Fig. 308), a memorial church for the family of a Genoese banker; and then its two "purest" architectural descendants, Lorenzo Binago's S. Alessandro in Milan (begun 1602), his masterpiece, in the words of Nicholas Adams, and the Duomo Nuovo in Brescia.[2] Even Giuseppe Valeriano's Gesù Nuovo in Naples (designed 1584; Fig. 309), explains Christof Thoenes, "would not have been possible without Alessi's work."[3] Today, in the

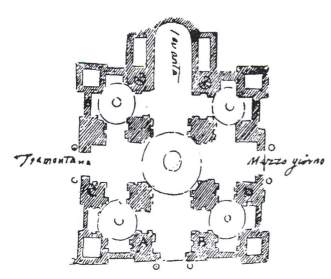

308. Galeazzo Alessi, plan of S. Maria di Carignano, Genoa, begun 1552

interior of this Neapolitan Jesuit church, one can experience the general effect of a unified and centralized Greek-cross design as envisaged by Michelangelo for St. Peter's.[4]

Any history of the importance of St. Peter's for later church architecture should pause momentarily at Pietro da Cortona's church of S. Luca e Martina in Rome (1635–69; Fig. 310). This church, explains Joseph Connors, was "Cortona's great commission of the Barberini period"; it was, affirms Christian Norberg-Schulz, the "most convincing High Baroque interpretation" of the "theme of the elongated Greek cross."[5] Just as Bramante's multipartite quincunx crossing (Fig. 63) was followed by Michelangelo's more unified Greek cross (Fig. 95), Cortona's church of S. Luca e Martina can be seen as the third stage of an evolution toward greater interior unification of the Greek-cross plan with the volumetric modeling of the interior. Here, in a building much smaller than St. Peter's, the architect has been able to fashion an interior volume for the Greek cross without the intermediary of the isolated piers at the crossing. Furthermore, as Norberg-Schulz has observed, in this church the "space has a singularly unified character determined by the rich plastic modelling of the bounding wall and the lack of colouristic differentiation."[6]

Like St. Peter's, Cortona's church was a martyrium, a building type that traditionally had been given a centralized form. S. Luca e Martina contains the relics of Saint Martina and three other saints martyred with her, who were newly discovered while Cortona's workmen were rebuilding the crypt of the earlier church then on the site, which had been constructed in the seventh and restored in the early thirteenth century.[7] Perhaps Cortona's use in this church of the "rib system of the half-domes over the

apses, which creates the effect of an umbrella billowing upward [and which] is based on Michelangelo's famous motif in the apses of St. Peter's,"[8] is still another signal, an act of homage to the master and his building, which was being emulated here.

St. Peter's also served as the model for two of the most important churches erected outside Italy in the late seventeenth century: the Dôme of the Invalides in Paris and St. Paul's Cathedral in London (Fig. 311). The Great Fire of September 1666 in London destroyed "more than thirteen thousand houses and eighty-seven churches...as well as the great [Gothic] Cathedral of St. Paul's."[9] Yet, in rebuilding St. Paul's, Christopher Wren turned to classical rather than Gothic architecture.

The architect's preferred scheme for the new St. Paul's presented a variant of St. Peter's Greek cross extended with a nave and entrance vestibule (Fig. 312). On the exterior of Wren's project a huge dome with lantern rises above a cylindrical drum to dominate a Greek-cross base that curves inward with concave walls along the diagonal axes. Both of these features appear as exaggerated simplifications of Michelangelo's design: Wren's proposed dome is relatively larger than its prototype and is placed atop the building without the same attentiveness to visual transitions, such that it dominates the composition more forcefully than the dome in Michelangelo's design, which enjoys a subtler rapport with the building below. Likewise, the modulated wall surfaces of Michelangelo's Greek cross (Fig. 95) offer a hint of concavity that Wren has asserted boldly and simply through his four, curved facades. This change in aesthetic sensitivity marks the stylistic transition from the late Italian Renaissance to the late English Baroque and alerts us to a trend that will become even starker in future years through the juxtaposition of simple volumetric prisms. Although Wren's preferred design was rejected by the clergy as not "enough of cathedral-fashion,"[10] the final building retained the dome, whose profile and impressive inner diameter (108 ft.) stood as a rival to St. Peter's (inner diameter 139 ft.), which it clearly emulated. Indeed, the Roman basilica was a repeated point of reference in the *Parentalia* (Fig. 311), the memoirs of the Wren family compiled by the architect's son, who relied heavily on conversations with his father.[11]

The Hôtel des Invalides (begun 1671; Fig. 313) was a home in the outskirts of Paris for invalid and indigent veterans whose functional program was subsumed within a more ambitious goal of glorifying the French monarchy. In many respects the complex of dormitories and related structures, organized around a church placed on the central axis, evokes the large ensemble of connected buildings that Philip II had created outside Madrid as the Escorial (begun 1563), which combined a Hapsburg mausoleum, a Jeronymite monastery and church, and a palace for the court.[12] It has been

309. Giuseppe Valeriano, interior view of Gesù Nuovo, Naples, designed 1584. (Photo: courtesy Giovanni Amato)

original. Here we turn to the assessment of Hardouin-Mansart's brother-in-law, the architect Robert de Cotte, who assisted in the design of the Invalides complex, and particularly in studies for the sweeping arms of the plaza. During his Italian voyage, de Cotte observed with consternation that the dome of St. Peter's was not satisfactorily visible from the square, which, in turn, although "grand" in aspect, presented an unfortunate "confusion, which resembles a forest," through its multiple rows of columns.[16]

The Invalides, with its references both to the Escorial and to St. Peter's, may have been the "Most Christian King's" response to the "Most Catholic King," thereby asserting French Bourbon over Spanish Hapsburg primacy as a defender of the faith.[17] It appears that the Dôme of the Invalides may have been intended alternately as a royal mausoleum either for Louis XIV or for the relics of Saint Louis,[18] thereby increasing the importance of the parallel with St. Peter's and its Hapsburg derivative. The unrealized 1677 program for the paintings of the interior of the dome, established in the aftermath of the Third Dutch War and determined over the course of an entire week in meetings between the artist and his two principal clients – the king

suggested that as the "Most Catholic King" Philip II may have intended the Escorial as an equivalent to St. Peter's and the Vatican, thereby asserting his role as combined temporal and spiritual leader for the Western Christian world in a time of relative papal weakness.[13] In fact, the contemporary historian of the Escorial, Fray Jose de Sigüenza, "characterized the design [of the Escorial's church] as a mere squared version of the plan of St. Peter's."[14]

From the early phases of the engagement of Jules Hardouin-Mansart as principal architect of the Invalides, this French ensemble of buildings was transformed to combine a reference not only to the Escorial but also to St. Peter's. With a longitudinal church embedded within the central fabric of the complex already envisaged, Hardouin-Mansart projected an additional centralized, domed church – a compact Greek cross within a square – as the head building and accompanied it with an unrealized project for a version of St. Peter's Square.[15]

Both the Dôme of the Invalides and its plaza can be understood as French attempts to improve upon the

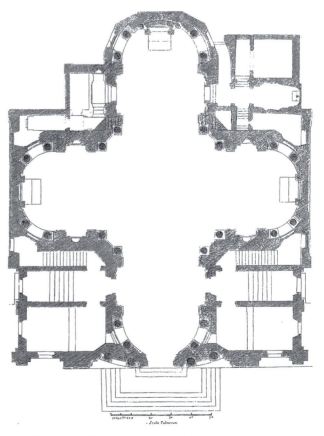

310. Pietro da Cortona, plan of S. Luca e Martina, Rome, 1635–69

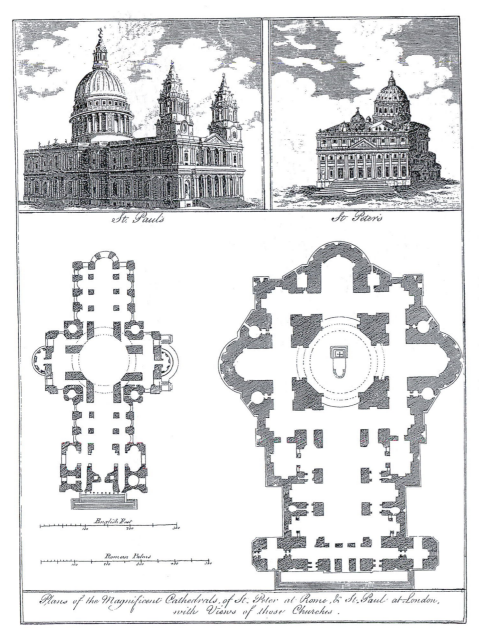

St. Pauls

St. Peter's

English Feet

Roman Palms

Plans of the Magnificent Cathedrals of St. Peter at Rome, & St. Paul at London, with Views of those Churches.

311. Comparison of St. Peter's (Rome) and St. Paul's (London). From Stephen Wren, *Parentalia. or Memoirs of the Family of the Wrens...but Chiefly of Sir Christopher Wren, Compiled by His Son Christopher: Now Published by His Grandson Stephen Wren* (London: T. Osborn and R. Dodsley, 1750)

and Louvois, the minister of war – would have made the imperial pretensions of this rival to St. Peter's and the Vatican explicit: "the Glory of Louis XIV," placed within a heaven that included the first Holy Roman Emperor, Charlemagne, Saint Louis the Crusader King, and other national saints, as well as "God the Father and Christ receiving and blessing the arms of the king," the Virgin, and finally the Archangel Michael "with the Defeated Netherlands as an old and wicked woman at his feet."[19] Like the Renaissance pope Julius II, Louis XIV was wont to veil his conquests with the mantle of religion.

In effect, the very history of the rebuilding of St. Peter's had combined pretenses of temporal power and spiritual authority. Bramante's project for a building that appears to elevate a new version of the Pantheon's dome (whose interior diameter measures 142 ft.) over a new version of the Basilica of Maxentius had imbued the new St. Peter's with imperial Roman imagery. Both the size and the scale of Bramante's St. Peter's – unprecedented for that time – and its specific architectural imagery made this Renaissance church into an evocation of ancient imperial Roman power and glory.

The analogy was not merely a metaphorical conceit. Alongside the idea that the Catholic Church had become the universal spiritual authority comparable to the universal political power of the ancient Roman Empire was the reality of the Church's military prowess, which "reestablish[ed] direct papal rule to Umbria and to Emilia-Romagna," with Pope Julius II at the head

312. Christopher Wren, unexecuted project for St. Paul's Cathedral, London

of his papal army. Julius's victories were feted on Palm Sunday of 1507 through the pope's triumphal "returning to Rome as a conqueror, celebrated [as] an entrance emulative of the triumphs of classical Rome." "[P]ersistently hailed...as 'Divis Iulius,' a second Julius Caesar," the pope engaged in a series of large-scale architectural projects in Rome and elsewhere to bestow upon the territories under papal control a visual aspect comparable to that of imperial Rome, with the rebuilding of St. Peter's being one of these grandiose projects.[20] Philip II, and then Louis XIV, continued this tradition.

In eighteenth-century France, St. Peter's pivotal position as the first church of the Catholic world received an ambiguous blessing. Major treatises written by Julien-David Leroy and Etienne-Louis Boullée, two French architects who played an important role in fashioning, through words or designs, the new Neoclassical style that replaced the Baroque, used St. Peter's as the central point of reference. Here the classical notion of emulation, in the dual sense of copying a revered model and of surpassing its virtues (and also correcting its faults) obtains.[21] Leroy's book, *History of the Different Forms that Christians Have Given to Their Temples from Constantine the Great to Our Times* (1764), was presented to the king that same year on the occasion of laying the cornerstone for the Parisian church of Sainte-Geneviève (1757–77; Fig. 314), designed by Jacques-

Germain Soufflot in the shape of a Greek cross with the five-dome sequence of St. Peter's. The main purpose of Leroy's study was to demonstrate the significance of the two new projected Parisian churches – Sufflot's Greek-cross Sainte-Geneviève and Contant d'Ivry's Latin-cross Madeleine – for the history of world architecture and for the glory of France. Yet at the figurative center of Leroy's study, and at the literal center of the engraving that presents scaled, comparative floor plans and sections of the greatest churches, stands St. Peter's (Fig. 315): an architectural section cut through the cross-axis of the church graces the middle position and is flanked by two floor plans, an elongated Greek-cross design attributed to Bramante to the left and the final plan to the right.[22]

Writing as a pantheist, Leroy observed that the grand "spectacle of the universe" has inspired humankind to raise "vast" religious structures to honor divinity such that the grandeur of their size conveys our awe of God and the Creation as well as giving testimony to the creative genius of the human spirit. After reviewing the immense dimensions of the great Egyptian and Roman temples, Leroy turned his attention to St. Peter's: "The basilica of St. Peter's and the circular colonnade that precedes it offer us an even more striking example of the grandeur of the enterprises which man is capable of executing."[23] In Leroy's pantheistic outlook, human genius and daring are mankind's equivalents to the marvels of nature, albeit with an important difference. Whereas nature has been constant over time, the creative human mind has been progressive. Consequently, Leroy proceeded to trace a course of successive refinements in the design of the most important building type, the religious edifice. This progress found its parallel in the spread of Christianity, which, though persecuted in its early days, "with time was to triumph over all the others."[24]

Imbued with the nascent Neoclassical aesthetic that favored simple prismatic forms and regular geometries, Leroy criticized the "imperfect cross" of the plan for Constantine's earlier basilica (Fig. 5). In contrast, the new Renaissance St. Peter's presented a praiseworthy regular Latin cross: "all people familiar with this building know that its four naves together form a very regular Latin cross, more perfect in form than all those constructed previously."[25] Unfortunately for the progress of the arts, Wren's subsequent St. Paul's Cathedral presented a defective Latin cross.[26]

Although never pronouncing explicitly in favor of the Greek cross over the Latin cross, Leroy seemed to favor those projects that transformed previous Latin-cross plans into Greek-cross plans[27] and agreed with what he termed the consensus that Michelangelo "contributed more to the perfection of St. Peter's" than any other architect. Yet Michelangelo had to share such honors with Bramante, for it was the latter architect's original idea to elevate a round dome the size of that of the Roman Pantheon over the Greek-cross component of the floor plan, whose vaults were deemed comparable to those of the grandiose Basilica of Maxentius. In this manner, Bramante had combined the general volumetric configuration and dimensions of two of the most impressive ancient Roman imperial buildings into a new architectural type.[28]

This image of the marriage of two perfect, stable, and centralized geometries – the Greek cross and the spherical dome – as envisaged at St. Peter's, guided Soufflot in his design of Sainte-Geneviève, as it would the architects and students of the French Académie royale d'architecture who followed his lead, especially after his death in 1780, honored the next year by the academy's prestigious, annual Grand Prix competition whose subject was declared to be "a cathedral for a capital like Paris."[29] The high significance of such a subject, which effectively asked the student competitors to design a hypothetical replacement for the Gothic cathedral of Notre-Dame, made St. Peter's the obvious point of reference in an age enamored of the classical style. Several decades previously, the French architect Pierre Patte had proposed for the tip of Île de la Cité a symbolic substitute for Notre-Dame in the form of a Latin-cross cathedral in a classical style.[30] Yet now the example of Soufflot's Greek-cross church prevailed.

In an apparent effort to continue the progressive development of church architecture beyond the accomplishments of Sainte-Geneviève, Louis Combes, in his prize-winning design (Figs. 316, 317), presented a Greek cross even more perfect in form that Soufflot's and with a quadripartite symmetry enhanced by four identical, pedimented porticoes, a legacy of Andrea Palladio's Villa Rotunda (Vicenza, 1565–9). Combes also placed his building within an urban setting (Fig. 318), clearly inspired by Bernini's St. Peter's Square, and possibly as well by the fresco in the Vatican Library that shows St. Peter's elevated on a platform and surrounded by a regular plaza. Here, then, was St. Peter's reinterpreted for Paris within the new Neoclassical aesthetic.

Just as Wren had designed with a more abrupt juxtaposition of volumetric elements than Michelangelo, so too did Soufflot and then Combes, as the Baroque style passed into the Neoclassical. Neither Soufflot nor Combes had any patience for the carefully modulated surfaces either of Michelangelo's Late Renaissance design, with its layering of engaged piers, or Hardouin-Mansart's Baroque aesthetic, with its clusters of columns and piers either engaged or placed close to the wall. The stylistic trend was toward unadorned prisms and

313. Jules-Hardouin Mansart, Hôtel des Invalides, Paris, with unexecuted curved forecourt, begun 1671

regular rows of free-standing columns. What little remained of Baroque modulation in Soufflot's church was
eliminated by Combes and then further transformed in
the direction of Neoclassical austerity by Etienne-Louis
Boullée. Each generation reinvented its own version of St.
Peter's according to its new standards of taste. In 1832,
to Victor Hugo, passionate champion of the medieval
Gothic styles, this change would be seen as a degenera-
tion, whereby the "beautiful lines of art gave way to the
cold and inexorable lines of geometry."[31] Yet Boullée
had a purpose as deeply impassioned as was Hugo's and
comparable in faith, albeit of a different nature, to the
designers of St. Peter's.

Boullée's unrealized design for a grand "metropolitan
church: (ca. 1781–2; Figs. 319, 320, 321) attempted to
improve not only upon Soufflot's and Combes's designs
but also upon the entire sequence of projects and buildings that had centered around St. Peter's since Bramante
had conceived of raising a dome equivalent to the Pantheon over a regular crossing.[32] Now the Renaissance
image of the perfect church, embodied in St. Peter's,
had been transformed into a Neoclassical vision of pure
geometries: the extended Greek cross with quadripartite symmetry created by four long and equal naves with
identical porticoes, and the entire building crowned by
a hemispherical dome elevated over two circular drums,
with each drum graced by its ring of regularly spaced
free-standing columns, and wall surfaces uninterrupted
by windows and free of sculpted adornments. Yet to understand the full significance of such changes, it will be
necessary to consider still another aspect of St. Peter's
legacy, namely the drama introduced there by Bernini's
Baroque additions.

FROM BAROQUE DRAMA TO THE
NEOCLASSICAL SUBLIME

Bernini's central Baldacchino and his St. Peter's Chair
(Figs. 116, 117, 122), both of bronze, added a visual element of the miraculous to the interior of the basilica of
St. Peter's in a manner that typifies Baroque architectural
and sculptural drama. The four spiral columns, propor-
tioned to the large space of the crossing and patterned
after actual columns found in the Old St. Peter's and
believed to have come from the revered Solomon's Temple in Jerusalem, which Christians saw as the Old Testament prototype that prefigured St. Peter's, are not simply
twisted in shape; rather they seem actively to spiral upward in defiance of the laws of gravity, with an energy
conveyed to the twisting scrolls that make up the central
canopy. The same abolition of gravity also obtains in St.
Peter's Chair, which, although nominally carried by the
four Fathers of the Church, appears to hover in the air,
as if sustained by a miraculous cloudburst at the center

314. Jacques-Germain Soufflot, Sainte-Geneviève, Paris, view,
1757–77

of which the symbol of the Holy Spirit sends forth rays
of sacred golden light.

Of course, such seeming miracles were not unique
to this church; through the work of Bernini and other
Baroque architects, they became common features in the
church architecture of the times. Yet within the context
of buildings that were modeled on St. Peter's, the allusion
to this prototype comes readily to mind. Hence we find a
"lighting, mysterious, even quasi-theatrical" in Lorenzo
Binago's church of S. Alessandro.[33] In the third quarter
of the eighteenth century, a large and dramatic organ
was suspended within each of the two bays that flank
the altar of the Neapolitan Gesù Nuovo (Fig. 322).[34]
The low rise and seemingly thin depth of the arch that
carries each organ, the massive size of the organ with its
pyramiding pipes and crowning broken pediment that
crowds the top of the open bay, and the bulging and billowing console whose smoke- or cloud-like swirls ten-
uously carry the projecting balcony as it hovers over
empty space, all these features combine to provide a
daring element of drama to either side of the main altar comparable to the miraculous features by Bernini at
St. Peter's.

Similarly, Hardouin-Mansart at the Dôme of the Invalides had introduced two magical features. One was
a *baldacchino* patterned after Bernini's at St. Peter's
and located so as to serve the two contiguous Parisian
churches. The drama of this double situation, whereby
the *baldacchino* appears simultaneously as the point
of focus in the visually stable field of the centralized
dome and as the endpoint in the directed, longitudinal

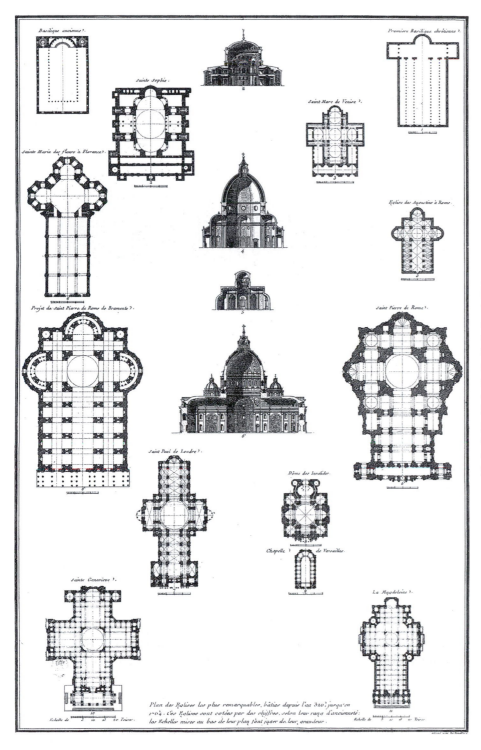

315. Julien-David Leroy, "Plans [and sections] of the most noteworthy churches built between AD 320–1764." Old St. Peter's is at upper right; new St. Peter's in the center; just below are St. Paul's (*left*) and the Invalides (*right*); on the bottom tier, Ste.-Geneviève (*left*) and the Madeleine (*right*). From his *Histoire de la disposition et des formes différentes que les Chrétiens ont données à leurs temples. depuis le règne de Constantin le Grand, jusqu'à nous* (Paris, 1764)

view of the adjoining church of Saint-Louis, is considerable.[35]

The second element of Baroque drama employed by Hardouin-Mansart at the Dôme of the Invalides was the introduction of a hidden source of natural illumination inside the dome, so that the painting on its surface appears lit miraculously by light that seems to issue from within the obscurity of the dome itself. Here was a fitting equivalent to Bernini's golden light that bursts forth from the center of St. Peter's Chair. To achieve this effect, Hardouin-Mansart built not one but rather two interior domes, one above the other, while opening the top of the lower dome to permit the viewer to look directly at the surface of the upper dome and furnishing the upper dome with windows that are hidden from view. Until this time, explained Leroy, architects had lit their domes through

316. Louis Combes, "Cathedral for a Capital like Paris," Grand Prix of 1781, section and elevation. (Photo: Inventaire générale des monuments et des richesses artistiques de la France)

windows opened in the drum situated below, windows that were visible to the viewer.[36]

Boullée, reviewing the merits and drawbacks of both St. Peter's and the Dôme of the Invalides, sought to improve upon both churches in his Metropolitan Church project (Figs. 319, 320, 321). Here the architect imagined other expedients not only to make the seemingly supernatural lighting of the dome more effective but even to transform the heavy weight of the vaults of the four naves into a source of gravity-defying wonder. As admirable as Hardouin-Mansart's clever invention of the pierced, double interior dome might have been, observed Boullée, the use of visible windows in the drum below

grievously detracted from the magic of the effect. Thus, in his Metropolitan Church project, Boullée also employed a pierced, double interior dome, but refrained from opening any windows in the drum below (Fig. 323). That way, the only light in the dome above the heads of the worshipers would be the seemingly supernatural illumination that appeared as if miraculously along the upper surface of the cupola.

To take full advantage of this arrangement, Boullée wanted to place in the drum a ring of free-standing columns to make what in the ancient classical world was a hypaethral temple, which now, instead of occupying its customary place on the ground, would seem to float among the luminous clouds painted on the surface of the drum and double dome, thereby appearing as the "aerial" "sanctuary of divinity." Just as Leroy had praised human creative genius as the earthly counterpart to God's creation of the splendors of the universe, so too in a similar pantheistic spirit Boullée sought to elevate the architect in a parallel with divinity by using the raw materials of the divine artist, most importantly light:

> From the three rows of windows, placed so that they cannot be seen, the brightest light would spread over the surface of the cupola. Hidden from the eyes of the spectators, mysterious in aspect and covering the entire vault, this source of light would produce the most striking and surprising effects... magical effects; and owing its sublimity only to means given by nature, this celestial tableau would bear witness that if there is one art through which one can put nature to work, it is without doubt the most precious of the arts.

"Master to dispense light as I wish," explained Boullée; then the architect could proudly announce, "you will have some claim to say *fiat lux*," let there be light. For the possible skeptic of such plans, Boullée had a ready reply: whether it was Bramante or Michelangelo who had imagined crowning the naves of St. Peter's with a dome the size of the Pantheon, the important point is that one of these two architects had an "idea so great, so daring, so astonishing that if it had been executed and if

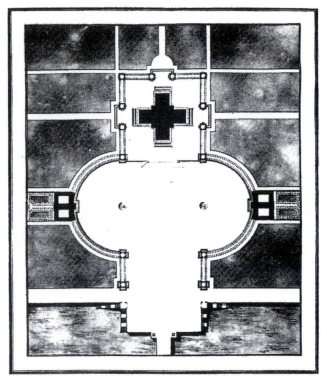

318. Louis Combes, "Cathedral for a Capital like Paris," site plan. (Photo: Inventaire générale des monuments et des richesses artistiques de la France)

today somebody had made such a proposal, it certainly would have been deemed impossible!"[37]

Spurred by a desire to rival the Creator to the degree that is permitted to mere mortals, and desirous of having all aspects of his Metropolitan Church commensurable with the magic of the dome, Boullée took the huge dimensions of St. Peter's and aggrandized them in his ideal building so that the people shown in his drawings are dwarfed within an impossibly huge edifice. These vaults, towering in height and seemingly endless in length, are not intended to be built as such but rather to present an idealized vision of the architectural equivalent to the universe: "This temple ought to offer the most striking and the grandest image of all existing things; it must, if it were possible, appear as the universe."[38]

Yet size alone was not sufficient for the naves of Boullée's Metropolitan Church project; their great mass had to seem suspended in air just as miraculously as the hypaethral temple that seems to float within the dome. The great height of the interiors of Gothic cathedrals and the seeming miracle of the vaults suspended on high over thin piers was greatly admired by the French Neoclassical architects. Soufflot had attempted to achieve these so-called Gothic qualities with classical architectural forms in Sainte-Geneviève;[39] Boullée would follow suit with the Metropolitan Church, where the massive vaults of

317. Louis Combes, "Cathedral for a Capital like Paris," plan. (Photo: Inventaire générale des monuments et des richesses artistiques de la France)

319. Étienne-Louis Boullée, view of "Metropolitan Church" project, ca. 1781–2. (Photo: Bibliothèque Nationale, Paris)

St. Peter's could be made to seem weightless. To this end, he employed deep rows of free-standing columns that hide the large piers which carry the huge barrel vaults. In this way, even the vaulted naves appear to float in midair, and are made to seem vaster than they truly are by hidden windows that wash the upper surfaces of the ceiling with light.[40]

At this point, Boullée passed beyond the Baroque world of wonder whereby isolated architectural features, such as the spiraling columns of Bernini's Baldacchino and the floating nature of St. Peter's Chair, appear as miraculous exceptions to the laws of gravity in order to enter into the Neoclassical world of the sublime. The sublime was an eighteenth-century aesthetic category that referred both to the experience of being transported beyond an earthly condition and to the scenes in nature that

could prompt an analogous response – such as erupting volcanoes, the vastness of the ocean, or the immensity of the sky, now available since 1783 through the new experience of floating high above the earth in a hot-air balloon. Boullée commented on all of these phenomena in an attempt to convey his purpose and to explore the ways in which he could impart such an experience, essentially an experience of religious transport, through his architecture.[41]

To this end, Boullée addressed the common eighteenth-century criticism of St. Peter's as paradoxically not appearing as big as it really is.[42] In some quarters and in other times, this unexpected contradiction has been made into a source of wonder. Balzac, for example, has a typical Italian cicerone, or guide, point out to the tourists visiting St. Peter's the astounding size of a

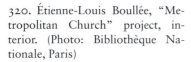

320. Étienne-Louis Boullée, "Metropolitan Church" project, interior. (Photo: Bibliothèque Nationale, Paris)

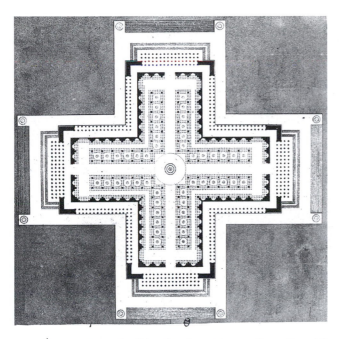

321. Étienne-Louis Boullée, plan for "Metropolitan Church" project. (Photo: Bibliothèque Nationale, Paris)

little finger on some statue high above.[43] Now apprised of the true measurement of the colossal human figure, the tourist can better ascertain the actual size of the architecture itself.

Yet to eighteenth-century observers, the failure of St. Peter's to impress the viewer with its true size was deemed a serious flaw. Kant, for example, philosophized about "the bewilderment or, as it were, perplexity which it is said seizes the spectator on his first entrance into St. Peter's in Rome."[44] Leroy, in his study of church architecture, attributed the problem largely to the massive size of the central piers, which blocked the view.[45] Wren fortunately had the "ingenious idea" of piercing the four central piers of St. Paul's to obviate this defect (Fig. 311), thereby allowing a free flow of space and view through these supports, but he unfortunately made the choir too narrow and the naves too small in proportion to the immense dome.[46] Leroy was more pleased with Hardouin-Mansart's openings in the four central piers of the Dôme of the Invalides (Fig. 315), which provide access to a chapel in each corner.[47]

Boullée also confronted the paradox of St. Peter's size and appearance and found the root of the problem not merely in the visually obstructive size of the piers but more generally in the small number of huge forms that constituted the interior (Fig. 105):

Why, then, does the basilica of St. Peter's appear so much smaller than it really is? This intolerable fault has resulted because far from offering the spectacle of space through the number of objects that a vast ex-

panse would naturally have, the architect has diminished the effect by giving each of the parts a colossal proportion; and, believing, as artists are wont to say, to have achieved something *grand*, only having achieved something *gigantic*.

The solution to this defect would be to create the effect of a multitude of successive images (Fig. 320):

When I pointed out that a temple ought to present the image of grandeur, I was not speaking only of its expanse; rather I wanted to direct the attention to that ingenious art by which one aggrandizes images by combining objects such that they appear in a way that augments their combined effect while enabling us to enjoy their multiplicity, such that they appear successively to us without end in a way that makes their number incalculable.[48]

Piranesi had addressed this issue in his idealized temple design (1743; Fig. 324). Apparently inspired by the succession of multiple domed and vaulted spaces in the

322. Gesù Nuovo, Naples, organ, ca. 1769. (Photo: courtesy Giovanni Amato)

323. Étienne-Louis Boullée, "Metropolitan Church" project, section. (Photo: Bibliothèque Nationale, Paris)

324. Giovanni Battista Piranesi, architectural fantasy entitled "Vestibule of an Ancient Temple." From *Prima parte di architettura e prospettive* (1743). (Photo: © Board of Trustees, National Gallery of Art, Washington. Andrew W. Mellon Fund)

fresco, *The School of Athens* (Vatican, 1510–11), where Raphael conveyed the sense of volumetric complexity of Bramante's project for St. Peter's, enhanced with a sense of infinite extension, Piranesi intensified these effects by adding more numerous components, including columnar screens.[49] Both Contant d'Ivry's design for the Madeleine and Soufflot's for Sainte-Geneviève applied the lessons of Piranesi's architectural fantasy with respect to the concatenation of volumes and the play of space, near and far, effected through free-standing columns.[50] Yet of all these ideal Neoclassical projects, only Soufflot's church was built, thereby rivaling the wonder of St. Peter's through a daring technical achievement of elevating vaults and domes over the attenuated piers at the crossing and over the relatively thin supports of free-standing stone columns.[51]

Free-standing columns and, more important, entire clusters of columns were favored architectural configurations of French Neoclassicism. If the interior of St. Peter's had been fashioned after the manner of Bernini's exterior colonnade, mused Abbé Cordemoy (Figs. 154, 155), then it would have been the most beautiful building in the world.[52] Such had been the merit and the promise of the designs under construction for Sainte-Geneviève and the Madeleine when Leroy wrote his book: "In effect, no prince is going to be able to build a church that would surpass in size St. Peter's of Rome; but perhaps it is not impossible to conceive buildings that will surpass it through design or decoration."[53] When the Académie royale d'architecture awarded Combes the Grand Prix for 1781 (Figs. 316, 317, 318), it was commending not only the advance in quadripartite symmetry made by this design but also the more numerous ensembles of free-standing columns utilized there.

From this perspective, one can gauge the significance of Boullée's even more extensive number of columns, which in addition to standing away from the wall were also free of any supporting function.[54] Leroy devoted an entire chapter to explaining the striking enchantment that results from the slightest motion inside a building filled with free-standing columns, which become "animated" and offer new scenes with every turn of the body and every step.[55] Boullée was more explicit in conveying the sense that we all relate through our bodily sense of

325. Andrei Voronikhin, view of Cathedral of the Kazan Mother of God, St. Petersburg, 1801–11. (Photo: courtesy William C. Brumfield)

self to the free-standing column. As we move through a field of columns, these forms appear to swirl around us: "It seems that they walk along with us and that we have given them life."[56] So profound is the pleasure that Leroy termed this the "metaphysical" aspect of architecture.[57] As Edmund Burke had explained in his pioneering and influential study of the sublime, the field of free-standing vertical objects – he had used the example of a planted woods – provides one way to create on earth the effect of the "artificial infinite."[58] The numerous free-standing columns in the churches of Sainte-Geneviève and the Madeleine, perhaps inspired, among various sources,[59] by Bernini's colonnade at St. Peter's Square and Piranesi's engraving, found their furthest development in Boullée's Metropolitan Church project, where the architect hoped to surpass the entire ascending line of progressively developing church buildings that had peaked in St. Peter's, whose defects nonetheless presented later architects with the possibility of re-creating that church so as to pass from the Baroque to the sublime.

ST. PETER'S IN THE AGE OF ECLECTICISM

Whereas it is possible to trace a sequential stylistic development from the origins of the Renaissance through the Neoclassical period, a development in which the history of St. Peter's has an integral place, after the Romantic revolution toward the 1820s, the culture of architecture took disparate paths with comparable results for the fate of St. Peter's as a prototype. From the fifteenth through the eighteenth centuries, classical architecture, what the French termed "la bonne architecture" (good architecture), was seen as an open-ended and living tradition ca-

pable of new stylistic adaptations. In the nineteenth century, the professional world of architecture devoted itself largely to the revival of historical styles, with eclecticism as the sign of the times. In this same period, though, the emerging engineering profession, working with the new, mass-produced iron and plate glass, challenged the tradition of masonry construction and its attendant historical styles to offer what reformers hailed as a revolutionary new architecture, characteristic of the age.[60] Any study of St. Peter's in this era has to look at each of these two cultural strands, beginning with eclecticism and then considering the responses of those two cultural giants, John Ruskin and Victor Hugo, to the confusion of the times.

Perhaps it is the combination of local context and historical moment that explains the ways in which the example of St. Peter's was used in three important churches of that period: the Cathedral of the Kazan Mother of God (1801–11) in Saint Petersburg; the church of S. Francesco di Paola (1817–44), with its antecedent piazza (begun in 1808, today Piazza del Plebiscito), in Naples; and the Cathedral of Saint-Jacques (1870–94) in Montreal. The first two of these buildings were designed at the transitional moment when the Neoclassical aesthetic that valued regular and simple prismatic forms intertwined with the new interest in historical revivals, whereby the specific features not only of past styles but also of specific buildings would be evoked. This was a universal phenomenon in Western architecture, shared by geographically distant examples such as Benjamin H. Latrobe's Bank of Pennsylvania (Philadelphia, 1798) and Karl Friedrich Schinkel's Altes Museum (Berlin, 1824–30).

Located on the major thoroughfare of Nevskii Prospekt, Andrei Voronikhin's Kazan Cathedral (Fig. 325) was built, as William Craft Brumfield explains,

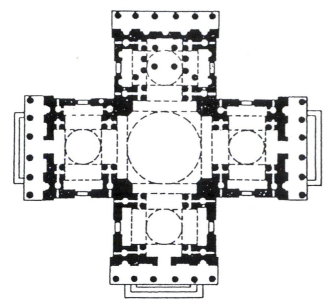

326. Vasilii Stasov, plan of Cathedral of the Trinity, St. Petersburg, 1828–35. From William C. Brumfield, *A History of Russian Architecture* (Cambridge: Cambridge University Press, 1993)

in what Russian aristocrats had been pursuing over the course of the eighteenth century as a "'civilized' architectural environment" achieved through a classical style. In particular, this cathedral was patterned after St. Peter's in order "to suggest [Emperor Paul's] desire to effect a reconciliation with Roman Catholicism, and implicitly, to establish his capital as a new Rome." "As a bastion of united Christianity," continues Brumfield, "Petersburg would have a cathedral to rival St. Peter's in Rome."[61]

The Kazan Cathedral combines the Neoclassical and eclectic approach to architecture common to Western architecture in this period. As a Neoclassical building, it participates in the progressive development of church architecture outlined by Leroy and continued by the architects of the French Académie royale d'architecture in the early 1780s, just before Voronikhin's own private architectural training in Paris where he appears to have learned of these new developments; they are evident in the use of free-standing columns throughout the interior, the diminution of the size of the piers at the central crossing, the regularity of the Latin-cross plan, the great height given the interior dome, the "weightless" aspect of the interior vaults, and the apparent

327. Auguste-Ricard de Montferrand, Cathedral of St. Isaac of Dalmatia, St. Petersburg, view, 1818–58. From James Fergusson, *History of the Modern Styles of Architecture* (London: John Murray, 1891)

to provide a new home for "the miraculous icon of the Kazan Mother of God, which had been brought to the city by Peter the Great, and was considered the palladium of the Romanovs." Yet this cathedral was not designed in a traditional Russian style but rather

328. De Montferrand, Cathedral of St. Isaac of Dalmatia, St. Petersburg, detail of the dome, 1818–58. (Photo: courtesy Sheppard Ferguson)

329. Leopoldo Laperuta and Antonio de Simone, then Pietro Bianchi, S. Francesco di Paola (1817–44) and Piazza del Plebiscito (begun 1808), Naples, view. (Photo: courtesy Leonardo Varone)

lightness of the exterior drum and dome.[62] As a historically eclectic building, the Kazan Cathedral used a free adaptation of Bernini's St. Peter's Square, which the architect applied to the north and south facades with mirrored images in the Palladian manner, thereby providing a majestic alignment for the cathedral along Nevskii Prospekt.[63]

The Kazan Cathedral was followed by two important five-domed Neoclassical churches in Saint Petersburg also inspired by St. Peter's, as viewed through the so-called progressive tradition that pivoted upon Soufflot's Sainte-Geneviève and its Palladian Neoclassical successors. One was the Greek-cross plan of Vasilii Stasov's Cathedral of the Trinity (1828–35; Fig. 326), "to this day one of the most prominent landmarks of the southern part of the old city."[64] The other was the Cathedral of St. Isaac of Dalmatia (1818–58; Figs. 327, 328) by the French architect Auguste-Ricard de Montferrand, which, James Fergusson explained, surpassed the Kazan Cathedral as the main church of Saint Petersburg. The site, which saw three previous churches, the first "nearly coeval with the city," appears "to have been destined to be occupied by the principal architectural monument" of Saint Petersburg.[65] Here rose a Neoclassical St. Peter's: Greek-cross plan with four seemingly identical porticoes and, above the center, a drum with dome in the manner of Sainte-Geneviève, these crowning features now constructed in iron, albeit presenting the aspect of a stone and wooden cupola.

The Church of S. Francesco di Paola (Fig. 329) combines with Piazza del Plebiscito to constitute a Neapolitan rendition of St. Peter's Square. The site, opposite the Royal Palace, had been given temporary decorations for festivities, the most recent involving the change in power between the Bourbons and Napoleon's conquering forces: in 1799 for the initial return of Ferdinando IV; in 1806 for the entry of Joseph Bonaparte; and in 1808 for Joachim Murat, the latter two men serving in succession as Emperor Napoleon's king of Naples. Joseph Bonaparte's unrealized project for a monument to Napoleon was succeeded by Murat's decision to create a forum (Foro Murat), whose design was selected through a competition won by Leopoldo Laperuta and Antonio de Simone with a Pantheon-inspired rotunda preceded by curved columnar arms reminiscent of St. Peter's Square.[66] Although recent historians have debated over the relative influence on the Foro Murat of St. Peter's Square and eighteenth-century French academic, Neoclassical designs it seems likely that the former provided the point of departure and that the latter offered a confirming aesthetic model, thereby conflating the Roman and French prototypes into an appropriately symbolic mixture. This forum had its own local Neapolitan precedents in Luigi Vanvitelli's curving Neoclassical facade for the Foro Carolino (1757–65, today Piazza Dante), erected by the citizenry to honor the enlightened Bourbon king Carlo III who, before leaving Naples in 1758 to govern Spain, had patronized the arts extensively, including the construction of a Neapolitan Versailles in the expansive palace, gardens, and new town of Caserta; the Carolino aqueduct; the Archaeology Museum; a new Royal Palace on the hill of Capodimonte to house a magnificent art collection (today the Museo Nazionale); and, next to the older Royal Palace, the Teatro San Carlo, conceived as Europe's largest theater.[67]

With the Bourbon restoration in 1815, the king, re-named Ferdinando I through the Treaty of Vienna, held a competition for the architecture of the unfinished forum, which now was to include a church of thanksgiving dedicated to San Francesco di Paola, patron of the long deserted and then dilapidated monastery that had existed on the site since the late fifteenth century.[68] First prize was awarded to the youngest contestant, twenty-one-year-old Pietro Valente, who designed a Greek-cross church preceded by a curved piazza, which, in effect, appears as a freely interpreted St. Peter's basilica and square, with alterations that reflect the Baroque and Neoclassical changes to the prototype. As Valente explained, he modeled his dome on Bramante's design for St. Peter's while adopting the perforated drum ringed by free-standing columns as found in St. Paul's Cathedral and the Eglise Sainte-Geneviève, this latter edifice also providing the inspiration for the deep columnar porch and the use of free-standing columns inside the church.[69] Yet the commission for church and square was actually given to Pietro Bianchi, who executed a plaza in honor of Ferdinando I with a variation of the Laperuta–de Simone project for the Foro Murat.[70]

The forum's allusion to St. Peter's was not lost on contemporaries; rather, it was an important point of reference. Gaetano Nobile, for example, in his 1863 guide to Naples, compared the size of S. Francesco di Paola's piazza, whose diameter is never less than 660 *palmi* (147 m), with St. Peter's, which never surpasses 750 *palmi* (168 m). Just as St. Peter's Square features a central obelisk topped with a cross, flanked in turn by giant fountains to either side in each of the two foci of its ellipse, so the foci of S. Francesco di Paola's square were given equestrian statues of the reigning Ferdinando I and his father, Carlo III. The sculptural program of ninety-six statues of saints and martyrs crowning St. Peter's Square was also mirrored here in Naples, albeit more modestly, with figures of the four theological and the four cardinal virtues placed on high. Finally, just as St. Peter's basilica was adjacent to the pope's living quarters in the Vatican, so S. Francesco di Paola was designed as the mortuary church of the kings of Naples, across the square from the Royal Palace.[71]

Thus, on the one hand, S. Francesco di Paola and its piazza satisfies the Neoclassical interest in pure form – the domed cylindrical building and the curved piazza. On the other hand, the reference to the Roman Pantheon inside the church is more direct than most Neoclassical architects of the preceding century would have permitted themselves to make; so, too, the allusion to Bernini's St. Peter's Square on the exterior. The ascendancy of historicism over Neoclassicism in the history of St. Peter's reached its climax with the Cathedral of Saint-Jacques in Montreal, which attempts to re-create St. Peter's in Rome at roughly half the scale (albeit with modifications

330. Giuseppe Mengoni, Galleria Vittorio Emanuele II, Milan, view, 1865–7. (Photo: Alinari/Art Resource, N.Y.)

to the exterior walls occasioned by the severe climate and a limited budget).[72]

Soon after the disastrous Montreal fire of 1852 that destroyed the previous cathedral (1825) and new episcopal palace (1851) as well as eleven hundred homes, Bishop Ignace Bourget decided to use this occasion to resituate the cathedral toward the west, near the new railroad station and in a Protestant neighborhood that he anticipated would soon become the new center not only of the expanding metropolis but also of the province. The presence of a magnificent cathedral on the elevated topography of Mont Saint-Joseph was intended both to impress wealthy Protestants and to encourage the Catholics of the denser sections of the lower city to move to this "well ventilated and more hygienic" site.[73] This location, near the cemetery, also reflected the current emphasis of the Romantic era on the importance of the neighboring city of the dead for that of the living.[74] Just as St. Peter's was widely considered in Catholic circles of the time to be the "basilica of the Christian world" and thus the embodiment of the "universal church,"[75] in Bishop Bourget's mind the scaled rendition of St. Peter's in Montreal would serve as the "Queen of basilicas in North America," thereby bringing an idea of the "seat of the Papacy and the center of Catholicism" to the New

World, where many of its denizens were physically so far removed from a Europe they would never be able to visit.[76] Over the course of the long gestation of this project, the bishop repeatedly sought to secure models and drawings of the basilica from abroad and sent successive architects to Rome to study St. Peter's firsthand.[77]

THE SYMBOL OF MODERN LIFE

Whereas the Montreal Cathedral of St. Jacques was the most literal nineteenth-century reincarnation of St. Peter's, the most freely interpreted rendition was the grand Milan Galleria, officially the Galleria Vittorio Emanuele II (1865–7; Figs. 330, 331). Perhaps here we encounter the greatest paradox that St. Peter's has engendered: not the ambiguity between the Greek- and Latin-cross plans, not the irony of the colossal proportions that do not reveal their full grandeur, and not the magic of Bernini's miraculous sculptural features inside that ponderous vessel. Rather, the greatest paradox resides in the capacity of St. Peter's at this time to serve as a point of reference for a total transformation to what contemporaries considered the "representative" architecture of the age.

It was a truism of nineteenth- and early twentieth-century Western thought that every age had its own character and spirit (hence the popular expression, the "spirit of the age").[78] Cultural figures argued over which domain best captured that spirit. For Ruskin, the answer was clear: "Great nations write their autobiographies in three manuscripts; – the book of their deeds, the book of their words, and the book of their art. No one of these books can be understood unless we read the two others; but of the three, the only quite trustworthy is the last."[79] Many observers agreed with the Reverend Thomas James, who affirmed that "nothing so expresses the character and genius of a nation" as its architecture: "Stern or frivolous, true or hollow-hearted, devoted to religion or to commerce, the ruling passion of a people is stamped on its architecture; and buildings will often give the true portrait of an age (unconsciously indeed, and therefore more faithfully), when historians flatter, and monuments lie, and records fail."[80]

Yet the realm of architecture itself was not vague and undifferentiated. Rather, it was widely held that in each era one particular building type best incarnated the highest or most typical values of the time: "The Greeks had their temples and propylaea; the Romans their amphitheaters and baths; the first Christians their catacombs and basilicas; the knights in armor their cathedrals and city halls, and so forth."[81] The nineteenth century was widely regarded as the age of the people, of the crowd, of liberty, of democracy.[82] Places of popular assembly were readily imbued with symbolic cultural significance as representative of the times. The new urban building type of the commercial arcade, that glass-covered shopping street with offices and sometimes residences above, stood out as exemplary.

In the aftermath of the 1861 unification of Italy, it was the new and most grandiose of all arcades, the Milan Galleria, that took on this symbolic function. When its

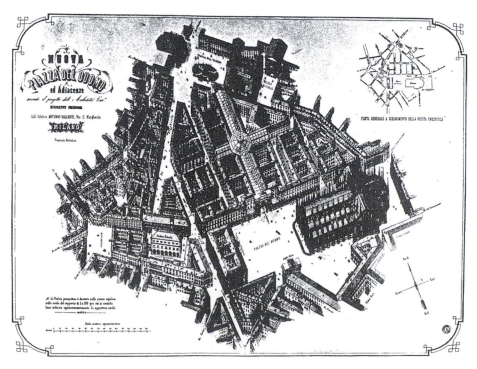

331. Giuseppe Mengoni, Galleria Vittorio Emanuele II, site plan: (*top*) Piazza del Duomo before 1850; (*bottom*) Galleria Vittorio Emanuele II connecting Piazza del Duomo with Piazza La Scala

architect, Giuseppe Mengoni, chose the size of the glass dome at its central crossing to equal that of St. Peter's, and when he literally traced the plan of both domes on top of each other on the same sheet of paper, he was affirming the importance of St. Peter's for the modern world.[83] As the glass and iron equivalent to St. Peter's, the Milan Galleria assumed its preeminent place within the contemporary debate about the cathedral of modern times.

Certainly Victor Hugo laid the cornerstone, so to speak, of the nineteenth-century cathedral with his novel *Notre-Dame de Paris, 1482* (1832), in which the medieval Parisian cathedral is as much the protagonist as any of the personnages who enter the scene. For Hugo, Notre-Dame was the embodiment of a people, the collective creation of generations of Frenchmen; it was, like other Gothic cathedrals, the expression of liberty and popular thought: "The cathedral itself, this building that had once been so dogmatic, henceforth invaded by the bourgeoisie, by the commune, by liberty, escapes from the priest and falls to the power of the artist." To Hugo, Notre-Dame belonged "to the imagination, to poetry, to the people." In short, it was "an architecture of the people."[84] Gigantic in size, Notre-Dame was a colossus: "we are piously going to admire the grave and powerful cathedral, which terrifies, according to its chroniclers: *quae mole sua terrorem incutit spectantibus* [which by its mass inspires terror in the spectators]."[85]

Yet Hugo was convinced that Gutenberg's printing press was killing the cathedral as the point of focus and hence the incarnation of the thought and creativity of an age. Thus, until the invention of the printing press in the fifteenth century, "architecture was the principal register of humanity; up until this time there did not appear in this world any thought of even minor complexity that was not transformed into building; [and] every thought whether popular or religious had its monuments."[86] And the greatest monument of all that captured those thoughts was the Gothic cathedral, whose day ended with the invention of the printing press. "Ceci tuera cela," this will kill that: "The book is going to kill the building." According to Hugo, the popular press – those twin worlds of literature and journalism – already had become a "giant machine that pumps without stop all the intellectual sap of society, that incessantly vomits new material for its work. The entire human race is on the scaffolding. Each mind is a mason. The most humble fills its hole or adds its stone.... Certainly here is also a construction that grows and piles itself up in spirals without end; there too is a confusion of languages, incessant activity, indefatigable labor, gripping competition among all of humanity.... It is the second Tower of Babel of the human race."[87] And what had happened to architecture since Gutenberg unleashed this "revolution," the "grandest occurrence of history"?[88] Hugo was convinced

that the printing press had slowly and progressively sapped the creative life out of architecture: "the printed book, this worm eating away at architecture, sucking away and devouring it."[89] Only the great Michelangelo, cognizant of this decline, in a desperate act of creative ingenuity, momentarily escaped the degenerative momentum in his brilliant but ill-fated design for St. Peter's, a building destined to be copied with fainter and fainter ingenuity and creativity over the course of time:

> Adieu to all sap, all originality, all life, all intelligence. [Architecture] drags itself from atelier to atelier, from copy to copy. Michelangelo, who since the sixteenth century no doubt felt it die, had one last thought, a thought of desperation. This titan of art had stacked the Pantheon on top of the Parthenon [*sic*] and made St. Peter's of Rome. Grand work that merited to remain unique, last originality of architecture, signature of a giant artist at the bottom of the colossal register of stone that was closing. Michelangelo dead, what did this miserable architecture do that outlived itself as a ghost and shadow? It took St. Peter's and traced it and parodied it. It has been a mania. It is a pity. Each century has its St. Peter's; in the seventeenth century the Church of Val-de-Grâce, in the eighteenth Sainte-Geneviève. Each country has its St. Peter's of Rome. London has its own. Saint Petersburg has its own. Paris has two or three. Insignificant testament, last death rattles of a great decrepit art that falls back into infancy before dying.[90]

Writing in the early 1830s, Hugo could not anticipate that architecture, in effect, was about to return to a productive infancy though the rise of the new iron-and-glass engineering structures. John Ruskin two decades later disdainfully dismissed the Crystal Palace of the Great Exhibition of 1851 (Hyde Park, London), along with its enlarged reincarnation in 1854 at Sydenham, with a memorable characterization that paradoxically captured the enchantment of this new architecture: "the first principles of architectural sublimity, so far sought, are found all the while to have consisted merely in sparkling and in space."[91]

Ruskin's derision could not dampen the groundswell of contemporary enthusiasm either for the new age – characterized in the catalogue of the 1853 Great Irish Industrial Exhibition as the "result of the extension of manufacturing and commercial industry," with a concomitantly "vast" increase in "the intercourse between different nations" – or for the international exposition buildings that followed in the wake of the Crystal Palace.[92] The universalist pretensions of the new World's Fairs were soon reflected in the giant, glass-covered domes that crowned the two expositions held in 1853 in New York (Fig. 332) and Dublin (Fig. 333), which were built on a scale comparable to St. Peter's: 103 feet in diameter at New York and 100 feet for the semicircular domed ends of the main hall at Dublin.[93] Indeed, at New York it repeatedly was remarked that the "dome ranks only after such as St. Peter's, at Rome."[94] Yet the difference between these new domes, along with their adjoining glass-vaulted halls, and the historical prototype was incommensurable. As one writer observed of the New York Crystal Palace: "The view of the dome can hardly fail to gratify and surprise the beholder, from the contrast of its vast size and its extreme airiness."[95]

As the symbol of the universal church, St. Peter's readily became a point of reference for a culture that idealized these fairs in terms of the divine spirit which presided over the world, symbolized and even made palpable by the dome. At the inaugural ceremonies in New York, while the "Hymn of Old Hundred" was sung, one journalist recorded that "the effect where we stood under the dome was mystically grand." And as the ceremony closed, the chorus of Handel's *Messiah* "came forth with the colossal effect of a multitude of singers, running through fugued, lyrical windings, typical of the circularities of the soul, boundless and sublime, and shouting the old church words and music – 'Hallelujah! Hallelujah!' as adapted by the genius of the composer, and turned into transcendental ecstatic declamations," for which "the arabesque aisles and the soaring dome" of glass and iron seemed superbly fitted.[96] At Dublin, a similar, albeit more traditional and less transcendental spirit prevailed, where the "Hundredth Psalm" – "With one consent let all the earth/To God their cheerful voices raise" – was read at the opening of the exposition.[97] An analogous spirit infused the organizers of the Industrial Exhibition of 1862 in South Kensington, London, where two "great domes, from their huge size, form one of the most prominent features in the building," especially since these two iron-and-glass dodecagonal domes "are the largest that ever have yet been executed, being one hundred and sixty feet in external diameter" each, as the catalogue emphasized, exceeding St. Peter's and also the local St. Paul's (Fig. 334). And, like that of St. Peter's (Fig. 105), the base of the dome was inscribed with capital letters (Fig. 335), combining Latin saying – "Tua est domine magnificentia, et potentia, et gloria, atqua Victoria" (1 Chronicles) – and English – "O Lord, both riches and honour come of thee, and thou reignest over all."[98]

Our acquaintance with late twentieth-century technology should not dampen our response to the ingenuity of these glass-and-iron domes. The official catalogue for the 1862 International Exhibition was justifiably proud in noting that the twin domes "have been the most difficult part of the works."[99] In an important study of domes published in 1855, the French engineer Charles-Edouard Isabelle reminded his readers that "the art of constructing spherical vaults in metal is, in many respects, still

a recent art."[100] The first grand glass-and-iron dome had been designed in 1808 and erected in 1811–13 to cover the circular, stone Neoclassical Halle au Blé (Grain Hall, Paris, 1762–5), modeled in circumference upon the Roman Pantheon, thereby providing the first exposed iron cupola "on the scale of the dome of St. Peter's."[101] In 1888, the engineer charged with converting the Halle au Blé into the Bourse de Commerce observed, "The elegant and slender ribs seen from forty meters below create an illusion of lightness surpassing that which is possible with traditional materials."[102] As Frances H. Steiner has reported, "The novelty of the use of iron and the thinner dimensions made the Halle au Blé a considerable attraction in Napoleon's day and throughout the nineteenth century."[103] In 1853–70, the Halle au Blé was made the head building of the new complex of glass-and-iron markets, the Halles Centrales, constructed to either side of a central, axial street that proceeded from the domed grain hall.

In his novel *Le Ventre de Paris* (1873), Emile Zola turned both Hugo and Ruskin on their metaphorical heads with an encomium to the new Halles Centrales that further sets the stage for our appreciation of Mengoni's conception of the Milan Galleria as the St. Peter's of the modern world. Early in Zola's novel it becomes apparent that the colossal Parisian complex of markets was the new Notre-Dame rendered in glass and iron. Here Zola found the same whirlwind of burgeoning human activity that Hugo had celebrated in the cathedral. This was the new building of and for the populace, the heart and lifeblood of new Paris. Now Zola refashioned Hugo's epigram, "Ceci tuera cela." Hugo had been premature in declaring the death of architecture through the agency of the printing press; it was the new glass-and-iron architecture, that evanescent glow of shimmering crystal derided by Ruskin, which was killing traditional masonry architecture. In the novel, Zola speaks through Claude, who directs Florent's attention to the Gothic church of Sainte-Eustache across the way from the new glass-and-iron markets:

> This will kill that, iron will kill stone, and the time is near.... Do you believe in chance, Florent? I suspect that the need for alignment was not the only reason that the rose window of Sainte-Eustache has been located in this way in the very middle of the Halles Centrales. You see, there is at that point an entire manifesto: it is modern art, realism, naturalism, as you like to call it, which has grown opposite ancient art.... Don't you agree?

In the face of Florent's silence, Claude continues with a speech that concludes:

> Since the beginning of the century there has been only one original monument, a monument that is not a copy in any aspect, a monument that has grown naturally in

332. George Carstensen and Charles Gildemeister, Crystal Palace, New York, view, 1853. From John Sproule, ed., *The Irish Industrial Exhibition of 1853: A Detailed Catalogue of Its Contents* (Dublin: James McGlashan, 1854)

the soil of the times, and this is the Halles Centrales. Do you understand, Florent, a bold work, and yet only a timid anticipation of the twentieth century.... That is why Sainte-Eustache is done for, buried! Sainte-Eustache is over there with its rose window, empty of devout people, whereas the Halles are growing beside it, fully burgeoning with life.[104]

Sainte-Eustache, as Claude had pointed out to Florent, was a building of mixed styles, part Gothic and part Renaissance. At another point in the novel, Claude views the church through the open pavilions of the market and sees the symbolic burial of the old world by the new:

Claude blinked his eyes, and saw, across the way toward the end of the covered [market] street, framed under this immense vessel of a modern hangar, the side facade of Sainte-Eustache, with its [Gothic] rose window and its two stories of [Renaissance] round-arched windows; he said, as a challenge, that the entire Middle Ages and the entire Renaissance would fit under the Halles Centrales.[105]

For Claude, the new boulevards with their wide sidewalks, the tall apartment buildings, and the "luxury" of the stores, those new glass-and-iron department stores that Zola would make the protagonist of still another novel, were images of "la vie nouvelle," the new life.[106] For numerous astute observers of contemporary life, the new glass-covered shopping street, known as the arcade, was a characteristic form of the modern age. Charles Fourier had made the arcade into the heart of his ideal community organized in a collective building called the Phalanstère; and in his study of Baudelaire and his times, Walter Benjamin observed, "Arcades where the flâneur would not be exposed to the sight of carriages that did not recognize pedestrians as rivals were enjoying undiminished popularity."[107]

In this cultural context, then, the Milan Galleria can readily be seen as the new St. Peter's for Italian society, just as the Halles Centrales were the new Notre-Dame for France. Created as a link between the city's "two major piazzas" – the cathedral square, whose Duomo was admired as a "sublime monument of architecture," and Piazza La Scala, with the famed opera house – the Milan Galleria occupied a central, symbolic place in the city

333. Sir John Benson, Irish Industrial Exhibition of 1853, view. From John Sproule, ed., *The Irish Industrial Exhibition of 1853: A Detailed Catalogue of Its Contents* (Dublin: James McGlashan, 1854)

334. Captain Francis Fowke, R. E., Exhibition of the Works of Industry of All Nations, London, 1862, view. From *The International Exhibition of 1862. The Illustrated Catalogue of the Industrial Department*, British Division, vol. 1 (London: Her Majesty's Commissioners, n.d.)

while assembling these major edifices, including itself, into a civic ensemble.[108] The evolution of its design, initiated by Mengoni as a single, covered shopping street conceived in the context of a public competition to link a refashioned cathedral square with Piazza La Scala, shows how the architect came to combine the arcade with the universalist vision of the World's Fair buildings, both existing under the metaphorical shadow of the domed Parisian market complex. Here the history of the Milan Galleria and its relationship to St. Peter's becomes inextricably intertwined with the story of Italian national unity and independence.

The need to enlarge and regularize the plaza in front of the Duomo and to link this space with Piazza La Scala, recognized by the municipal authorities in the 1840s and 1850s, acquired greater urgency after the liberation of Milan in 1859 and its union with Piedmont, thereby affording Milan further commercial development in an expanded hinterland without customs barriers. Throughout the subsequent deliberations of the various municipal bodies, both the economic and the patriotic aspects of this project fused together, since the Piazza del Duomo increasingly was seen as the "true and natural center" for commercial circulation across the city to and from the new train station and other points of entry: hence the need to rationalize the street system around Piazza del Duomo in order to organize this movement, by facilitating the flow of commercial traffic, especially in the north–south direction, just outside the confines of the square, while creating a link in the same direction between Piazza del Duomo and Piazza La Scala. Patriotic fervor both for the person of the king and for the newly created Italian state (1861), which commingled national pride with enthusiasm for the increasing commercial benefits of political union, prompted the desire not only to dedicate the new Galleria to Vittorio Emanuele II but also to conceive of the entire redesign of Piazza del Duomo as a national, "Italian plaza."[109]

The debate over the systematization of Piazza del Duomo, both in its own right and as part of a larger urban context, including the opening of a street in honor of

the king to connect with Piazza La Scala, pitted partisans of a pedestrian arcade against adherents of the more traditional vehicular thoroughfare bordered by porticoes for pedestrians.[110] Mengoni himself offered alternative solutions in response to a second and invited competition, in which he revised his earlier project for an arcade by adding an octagonal pavilion, approximately

335. Captain Fowke, Exhibition of the Works of Industry of All Nations, London, 1862, interior view. From *The International Exhibition of 1862. The Illustrated Catalogue of the Industrial Department*, British Division, vol. 1 (London: Her Majesty's Commissioners, n.d.)

the size of the dome of St. Peter's, to the center of the block. It is significant that Mengoni's site plan for this second project now shows the reflected ceiling plan of the neighboring Duomo, which itself has an octagonal cupola over its crossing.[111] In this way, Mengoni made the Milan Galleria into a multivalent symbol through reference to St. Peter's, to the Milan Duomo, and to the most grandiose arcades of recent years, Sillem's Bazar (Hamburg, 1842–5) and the Königen Augusta Halle (Cologne, 1845–63), each of which has an octagonal rotunda.[112] Mengoni subsequently added lateral arms to his Galleria to transform it into a cruciform, thereby fundamentally altering the visual weight and focus of this urban context. As Günther Bandmann has observed, "In this manner [the Galleria] was transformed from a connection between two plazas into a building with its own center."[113]

As the new St. Peter's for the nineteenth-century world of culture and commerce, the Milan Galleria recalled both the architecture and the cosmopolitan outlook of the recent, domed World's Fair buildings, which themselves had evoked St. Peter's as their forerunner. The intellectual distance between the new World's Fairs and the Milan Galleria was not as great at that time as it might seem today. Both building types were called by the same vocabulary, alternatively a "bazaar" or an "arcade."[114] Furthermore, after the surprise of the vastly expansive space of the first grand World's Fair building, the 1851 Crystal Palace for the Great Exhibition held at Hyde Park, London, numerous observers argued that improvements were needed. Architects were now intent to delimit the vast interior so that it could be grasped by the visitor: hence the need for scale and proportioning, and, more generally, for an intellectually and experientially recognizable form to best the London Exhibition with a "superior... architectural beauty."[115]

In the recent World's Fair buildings, the architects sometimes combined masonry walls with glass-and-iron vaulting or domes in ways that also paved the way for the design of the Milan Galleria. It was widely believed that a construction of glass and iron was not deemed suitable for a permanent structure and would not qualify as art, but rather remained in the lesser domain of mere engineering.[116] Masonry had been featured at both the domed International Exhibition of 1862 in London and the earlier 1855 Exposition Universelle in Paris, whose facade to the Palais de l'Industrie presented a central triumphal arch entrance that anticipated the analogous motif of the Milan Galleria. Yet in fashioning his broad facade with central triumphal arch, Mengoni made a virtue of the contemporary practice of eclectically mixing styles to present the Milan Galleria as a veritable encyclopedia of past Italian artistic history blended harmoniously together.[117] In this way, the facade of the Milan Galleria offered an image of Italian cultural

achievement through the ages, a fitting bearer of national identity.

Even the Duomo was considered part of this new patriotic ensemble, which, in Mengoni's plan, was to be completed with the never-to-be-realized Royal Loggia facing the Galleria and a Palazzo dell'Indipendenza opposite the cathedral. As the guests at the banquet that followed the ground-breaking ceremony were reminded, the first stone for the Milan Duomo had been laid by Gian Galeazzo Visconti, titled as both Duke of Milan and Duke of Lombardy and who, nearly five hundred years earlier, had hoped to become the first king of Italy. Thus, King Vittorio Emanuele II seemed predestined to initiate the Galleria, deemed a "worthy crown" to the Duomo.[118]

The grand size of the Milan Galleria, comparable to the interiors of the recent World's Fair buildings, transformed the scale of the "arcade" building type into heretofore unimaginable dimensions. As the preeminent historian of arcades has observed, "The effect of the Galleria Vittorio Emanuele was extraordinary and not to be compared with the response to any earlier arcade."[119] Or, in the words of the popular Italian magazine *Illustrazione Italiana* (1876), this was the "Leviathan... of the covered urban streets that are found in the principal cities of Europe."[120] In effect, the Milan Galleria's plan echoed the cruciform of the 1853 New York Crystal Palace, as well as width of its nave, along with the height of the 1853 Dublin exhibition building.

The Milan Galleria also adapted the iconographic program of these World's Fairs. Just as the statue of George Washington, celebrated as the father of the United States, stood under the dome in the New York Crystal Palace, so too were the coat of arms of King Vittorio Emanuele II's House of Savoy placed at the same position in the pavement of the Milan Galleria.[121] Just as the New York exhibition hall was conceived as a temple to inventive genius and artistic creativity,[122] so too was the Milan Galleria made into a symbolic pantheon of Italian creativity and accomplishment through the placement of twenty-four statues, "sixteen in the rotunda and two each inside the four entrances... of famous Italian artists, scientists, and politicians." As a culminating feature, on axis with the Galleria at Piazza La Scala, a monument was erected in honor of Leonardo da Vinci.[123]

In addition, the cosmopolitan allegories of the 1862 London International Exhibition were reiterated in the Milan Galleria. In both buildings the arches supporting the base of the dome were decorated with representations of the four continents to symbolize the entire world and were accompanied by neighboring figures depicting the entire range of secular human activity, such as art, agriculture, science, and industry.[124] These universalist

336. Thomas U. Walter, dome of the Capitol, Washington, D.C., view, designed ca. 1854–5. (Photo: courtesy Sheppard Ferguson)

pretensions were supplemented at the Milan Galleria with local geography through the coats of arms of major northern Italian cities – Monza, Venice, Treviso, Fiori, Padua, Bergamo, and Milan – placed on the inner faces of the entrance arches.[125] To enter into the spirit of Mengoni's iconographic program, it behooves us to recall the optimism of the times, perhaps best reflected in the observations made in 1891 by the British architect Robert Kerr about the World's Fairs:

> There are those, of course, who sneer at our Great Exhibitions, their puffs, and their prizes: but this is idle. More thoughtful people, and more practical, prefer to regard the celebrated concourse of 1851 as the successful commencement of a long and still continuing series of *International Industrial Convocations*, organised with enthusiasm in all the chief cities of the world in quick succession, with this magnanimous purpose – the universal expansion and improvement of the Arts of Industry, of every order equally, and alike in every land.[126]

The comprehensiveness of Mengoni's symbolic program, based on the cosmopolitan idealism of the World's Fairs, in conjunction with its corresponding architecture, leaves no doubt that the designer and his compatriots saw the newly united Italy as joining the international concourse whose aspirations Kerr and so many others expressed in words, such that the Milan Galleria became a political and cultural equivalent for the modern age, as St. Peter's basilica had been for previous times.

POLITICS AND POWER

St. Peter's basilica served as a model not only for churches but also for government buildings. The majesty of its dome was an apt symbol of authority and power that in the nineteenth and twentieth centuries was transferred to civic architecture. A significant example can be found in the rebuilding of the dome of the Capitol in Washington, D.C. (designed ca. 1854–55, Fig. 336).[127] The idea for a new dome emerged in the context of the remodeling of the Capitol building, long plagued by inadequate acoustics and now in need of larger chambers to accommodate the increased numbers of senators and representatives in response to the 1850 census.[128] Moreover, between 1846 and 1848, the United States had expanded westward to embrace the entire length of the North American continent through the addition of the Pacific Northwest, California, New Mexico, Nevada, and part of Arizona. An enlarged Capitol building would serve symbolic as well as functional needs in a country that was trumpeting the civilizing force of its "manifest destiny."[129] And the nation's capital had in the late 1830s given itself, in the appreciative words of the otherwise acerbic Charles Dickens, those "three handsome buildings in stone and marble"[130] – Treasury, Patent Office, and Post Office – on a monumental scale that reduced the uniqueness of the old Capitol's grandeur. On Independence Day, 4 July 1851, President Fillmore laid the cornerstone for the extension of the Capitol, which would add two new wings, to the north and south, thereby expanding the length of this building along its hilltop site from 352 feet to 680 feet.[131]

Although the authorship of the Capitol extension, along with its new dome, has a complex history that includes a public competition in 1850 and an amalgamation of projects from various hands, each of the two successive architects in charge, first Robert Mills and then Thomas Walter, attributed his respective design to the legacy of grand domes that St. Peter's had initiated and then inspired. To Mills, the genealogy included "St. Peter's Church in Rome, St. Paul's, London, the Church of Invalids, Paris, and other like buildings."[132] For Walter, the models were "St. Peter's, St. Paul's, St. Isaac's, the Dome of the Invalides, and the Pantheon of Paris."[133] With the construction of Walter's iron dome to replace Bulfinch's wooden cupola came the end of an era, not only with respect to materials, but also in a displacement of prototypes, with the taller profile of St. Peter's and its progeny replacing the lower profile modeled upon the Pantheon's dome.[134] Over the years, the new dome of the United States Capitol has come to stand for a world political power of the first order and – to those who believe in the ideals of this American democratic republic founded on Enlightenment principles grounded in human rights and liberty – for a moral order as well.

An uncanny and sinister reversal of values occurred in the other two most significant political uses of the design of St. Peter's: in Fascist Italy, Mussolini's creation of the wide, straight thoroughfare of Via della Conciliazione with St. Peter's as the focal point; and in Nazi Germany, Albert Speer's project for a comparable avenue leading to a projected Grosse Halle (Great Hall). In both cases these designs were part of a larger building program intended to imbue both countries with a grandiose

architecture and urbanism that bespoke power and empire.

Just as the Renaissance popes and their cultural milieu had portrayed the Church as the inheritor of the ancient Roman *imperium*, so too did later Italian patriots consider these two earlier eras as the glorious legacy that had to be equaled by contemporary Italy. Thus, we find the nineteenth-century republican champion of Italian unification, Giuseppe Mazzini, declaring, "After the Rome of the Emperors, after the Rome of the Popes, there will come the Rome of the People."[135] So, too, would Mussolini envision Fascist Italy as the inheritor of this dual imperial legacy, which he sought to express through the physical transformation of the city by fashioning wide avenues leading to major ancient monuments and by creating large plazas around important historical structures.

The two most symbolically important avenues created in Fascist Italy were Rome's Via dell'Impero and Via della Conciliazione. Inaugurated on 28 October 1932, Via dell'Impero extended from Piazza Venezia – with its grandiose late nineteenth-century Beaux-Arts monument to Italian national unification (Monument to Vittorio Emanuele II) – to the Colosseum, for centuries a symbol of Roman power and glory. The wide expanse of Via dell'Impero passed over the exposed ruins of the Imperial Fora and the Roman Forum, including the Basilica of Maxentius. Via della Conciliazione created a monumental axis from Hadrian's bridge and tomb (subsequently Castel Sant'Angelo, Fig. 203) to St. Peter's (Fig. 337).

As its name indicates, Via della Conciliazione celebrates the "rapprochement between Church and State" occasioned by the 1929 Lateran Accords, which had made Catholicism the state religion and had created an independent Vatican City for the papacy. After the possible connection from the two Hadrianic monuments to St. Peter's had been studied after the Lateran Accords, the decision to remove the central blocks of the Borgo – the neighborhood between these endpoints – was taken in 1935 in the context of the Italian invasion of Ethiopia.[136] Amid multicolor confetti-like paper extolling the "Founder of the Empire and Fascist Italy" fluttering down from the sky, Mussolini initiated the demolition in 1936 as part of the festivities celebrating the fourteenth anniversary of the October 28 Fascist March on Rome, ceremonies that included placing a plaque commemorating the founding of the empire on the Basilica of Maxentius.[137]

Thus, in this new political environment, Via della Conciliazione served still another propagandistic purpose: it became the pendant to Via dell'Impero. In a speech of 1934, Mussolini transformed Mazzini's famous dictum to say: "After the Rome of the Caesars, after that of the Popes, today there is a new Rome, Fascist

Rome."[138] Hence, each of these two major thoroughfares symbolically linked Fascist Italy with one of the two previous Italian empires. The imposing mass of St. Peter's, with its dual legacy of universal authority, spiritual and temporal, was now impressed into the scenography of Fascist imperial power.

The idea of opening a monumental axis from the bridge at the massive Castel Sant'Angelo to St. Peter's did not originate with Mussolini's regime. Rather, the project dates back at least to Carlo Fontana's design of 1694, which envisaged the destruction of the neighborhood in front of the basilica to an extent comparable to that actually undertaken during the Fascist regime. A similar scheme was proposed in 1776; then another in the early nineteenth century during the Napoleonic occupation of Rome; and subsequently in the first piano regolatore (official plan for urban development) for Rome of 1873, following upon the 1870 unification of the city to the new Italian nation and the transfer of the capital from Florence in 1871.[139]

Like Mussolini in Rome, Adolf Hitler had grandiose plans for his own capital city, Berlin, and, more generally, for the Nazi state that called itself the thousand-year Reich. The very word "grandiosity" does not begin to convey what might more aptly be termed the megalomaniacal vision of Hitler and his chief architect, Albert Speer.[140] At Nuremberg, for example, the major Nazi Party edifices were all conceived in multiples of size of the monuments of imperial Rome, which were the constant point of reference. The Zeppelin Field Stadium was, as Speer pointed out, "almost twice the length of the Baths of Caracalla,"[141] just as the German stadium could contain twice as many spectators as the Circus Maximus.[142] The same competitive spirit that gloried in surpassing "the other great buildings of history" marked Hitler's and Speer's plans for refashioning Berlin.[143] Here the point of reference was Rome as the imperial and papal city and St. Peter's as its preeminent building and square. Musing about the extraordinary size of his projected avenues and buildings, Hitler dreamt about "things to take your breath away!" "It's only thus that we shall succeed in eclipsing our only rival in the world, Rome. Let it be built, on such a scale that St. Peter's and its Square will seem like toys in comparison!"[144]

To achieve this goal, Hitler in January 1937 created for Speer the new post of Inspector General of Buildings for the Renovation of the Federal Capital and gave him the status of a state secretary of the Reich government.[145] This position provided Speer with the authority to develop a project for a never-to-be-realized monumental center for Berlin based on the three elements that, according to Speer, Hitler had envisaged toward 1925.[146] At the core was a grand axis wider than the Parisian Champs-Elysées. Taking as a prototype Napoleon's Arc de Triomphe, built in honor of his armies and crowning the hill at the far side of the Champs-Elysées, Hitler imagined an even larger triumphal arch as a World War I memorial inscribed with the names of the 1.8 million fallen German soldiers but placed as the entrance to the central axis, whose focal point would be the Grosse Halle, a gigantic domed building (Fig. 338), 825 feet in diameter, to accommodate 150–180 thousand standing people.[147] Once again, St. Peter's was the point of comparison: this "huge meeting hall," explains Speer, was to be "a domed structure into which St. Peter's Cathedral in Rome would have fitted several times over."[148]

Through Speer's hand, Hitler's initial sketch of circa 1925 for a Pantheon-like edifice[149] was suitably changed in an apparent response to current circumstances: Mussolini had begun to cut through the dense urban fabric of Rome to construct Via della Conciliazione as a wide avenue leading to St. Peter's, the symbol of papal power. Just as Hitler wished to outdo the grandiose combination of the Champs-Elysées and its Arc de Triomphe in Paris, now he would have to surpass the analogous urban combination of Via della Conciliazione and St. Peter's in the city that weighed more than any other as a point of comparison, Rome.[150]

Under Speer's pen, Hitler's domed hall now reemerged as an amalgamation of St. Peter's and the Pantheon, with an aggrandized version of the former's dome dominating the exterior and an aggrandized image of the latter's rotunda constituting the interior. Just as Bramante and Michelangelo had made plans to raise the dome of the Pantheon on top of a cross, and just as Mengoni had recapitulated the scale of the Pantheon's dome over the crossing of his glass-and-iron reinterpretation of the modern, secular equivalent to St. Peter's, now Albert Speer, in Hitler's service, eliminated the cross – reference to Christianity – to present a composite image of the Pantheon and St. Peter's, vastly enlarged, to symbolize Nazi values and to provide the space where the individual, as in the Nuremberg rally grounds, could lose him- or herself in the emotional transport of the chanting crowd.[151]

Hitler's Grosse Halle was to offer an alternative to the Catholic Church, persecuted by the Nazi regime not merely in the customary political sense but also through the promotion of an alternative outlook about life, what the Germans call Weltanschauung, in which through a mystical bond the Volk (the people) would find unity in its shared, so-called racial purity, symbolized and actualized through its "blood" and its "roots" in the native "soil." To this end, the Grosse Halle was to be the equivalent to the church, its substitute in the new Nazi world order. The Nazis, as Alex Scobie summarizes Hitler's speech of 6 September 1938, "had no rooms for worship, but only halls for the people (that is, no churches, but Volkshallen)."[152] Speer explained that the Grosse Halle,

337. Marcello Piacentini and Attilio Spaccarelli, Via della Conciliazione, Rome, 1936–50. (Photo: Alinari/Art Resource, N.Y.)

"over the course of centuries, by tradition and venerability, would acquire an importance similar to that of St. Peter's in Rome for Catholic Christianity." "Without such a religious context," continued Speer, the expenditure for this building "would have been pointless and incomprehensible."[153]

We should bear in mind the full extent of the ideology that underpinned this Nazi architectural vision, which would have made a travesty of the Christian values embodied in the dome of St. Peter's. This was a self-proclaimed "racial" state that since 1933 had practiced compulsory sterilization of the mentally ill, "asocial," and severely physically handicapped; compulsory abortions since 1935; and a so-called euthanasia program beginning in 1939 for those with so-called lives not worth living, who died through starvation, poisoning, and gassing, that is, by using methods and even personnel soon transferred to the Holocaust.[154] This was a society whose leaders derisively dismissed "muddleheaded humanitarianism" (*Humanitätsduselei*).[155] Both

the Christian values symbolized by the dome of St. Peter's and the Enlightenment values symbolized by the dome of the United States Capitol would have found their polar opposite in Speer's rendition of St. Peter's dome for the Berlin Grosse Halle.[156]

THE TRIUMPH OF ST. PETER'S

St. Peter's basilica has triumphed over the threat of the Nazi *Volkshalle*, has assimilated Via della Conciliazione into its modern scenography independently of associations with Italian Fascism,[157] and has seen the criticisms of the Neoclassical era turned into positive attributes. In *Rome. Ses monuments, ses souvenirs* (1890), Abbé Boulfroy reflected a new attitude toward St. Peter's that had been crystallizing over the course of the nineteenth century.[158] Once again, as in earlier times, St. Peter's was considered as nothing less than a "colossus," whose forms impress the viewer "with their powerful aspect."

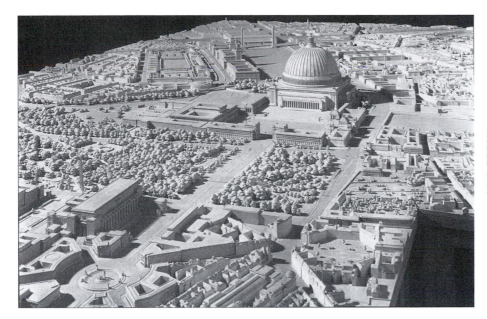

338. Albert Speer, after Adolf Hitler, central axis with Grosse Halle, project, Berlin, ca. 1937–41. (Photo: courtesy Barbara Miller Lane)

The large scale, which had troubled Kant and his contemporaries in their reflections on the sublime, was now considered a virtue for this "Mont-Blanc of buildings." Here Abbé Boulfroy offers a paraphrase of Byron, who in *Childe Harold's Pilgrimage* (canto 4, 1818) had expressed his admiration for St. Peter's:

Thou movest – but increasing with the advance,
Like climbing some great Alp, which still doth rise,
Deceived by its gigantic elegance;
Vastness which grows – but grows to harmonize –
All musical in its immensities.

Remarking how "the monument grows prodigiously through the examination of its details," Abbé Boulfroy marveled at the six-meter-high statues, as well as St. Luke's pen, longer than a meter, and the capital letters that ring the bottom of the interior dome, also over one meter, but appearing, like all the other colossal features, as if ordinary in size.[159] The result, inside and out, was "a serene majesty, full of gentleness." Here, then, we encounter a double paradox that operates in opposing ways: just as the details help to make St. Peter's seem more expansive, taking the building beyond a human's grasp, so too do these details humanize it by relating it to the size of the body, the focus of the eye, and the movement of the hand.

Where Hugo had celebrated first the Parisian Gothic cathedral of Notre-Dame and then its supposed replacement, that is, modern society characterized by the printing press, each as a type of Tower of Babel, now Abbé Boulfroy accorded the same accolade to St. Peter's: "Human beings, dispersed at the foot of the ancient Babel, seem to be reunited here, to get along with each other

and to chant the Credo under the dome of St. Peter's." Where Hugo had approvingly cited the ancient chroniclers who had spoken of the "terror" occasioned by the great size of Notre-Dame, now Boulfroy reminded his readers that this Gothic cathedral's towers "would not even reach" the base of St. Peter's dome. Here we find Boulfroy invoking Mme de Staël and Lord Byron, whose assessments of St. Peter's rival Hugo's enthusiasm for the dizzy heights of Notre-Dame and the spiraling fecundity of the age of print. Mme de Staël had found a comparable, breathtaking scene at St. Peter's itself (Fig. 124):

Stand near the altar under the middle of the dome and you will see, through the iron grillwork, the church of the dead, which is under your feet; and while lifting your eyes back upward, you will hardly reach the summit of the dome. This dome, by looking at it even from below, prompts a feeling of terror. You feel as if an abyss is suspended above your head.

Byron likewise had enthused about being suspended here between two endless voids:

– and haughty dome which vies
In air with Earth's chief structures, though their frame
Sits on the firm-set ground – and this the clouds must claim.

From the abyss below to the heavens above, St. Peter's, to those Romantics, was miraculously perched above the unfathomable depths while it reached toward an infinity above.[160] Yet we should return to a more stable footing and accord the last word to the eighteenth-century magistrate and man of letters Charles de Brosses, speaking with classically French rhetorical balance about this paradoxical colossus:

> Upon seeing the most beautiful thing in the universe, nothing surprised me more than my not being surprised. If, upon first impression St. Peter's does not startle, this is because it has that superior singularity of not being marked by any. It is more astonishing the thousandth time than the first; everything is in its place, with admirable proportion. Here, you can look, and then look again; you will always be content.

Notes

For an essay that spans four centuries and that radiates from Rome to Montreal, New York, Naples, Paris, and Saint Petersburg, I have turned to numerous colleagues and friends for assistance. I am particularly indebted to Christof Thoenes, who provided me with several crucial documents and who responded to numerous queries both about Renaissance Rome and Neoclassical Naples. Maria Ann Conelli has generously shared with me sections of her doctoral dissertation and her entire unpublished book manuscript on the Gesù Nuovo of Naples, and also has offered several suggestive interpretations about the intertwined relationship of the Escorial, the Invalides, and St. Peter's, all of which appear in my text, along with appropriate acknowledgments. For bibliographic assistance or documents, the following people have generously responded to my queries. The mere listing of their names does not begin to convey the extent either of their help or my gratitude; but their number precludes a more detailed account of their services. For Montreal, Isabelle Gournay and Anne Troise; for Naples and Milan, Leonardo Varone and Fabio Varone; for Yamoussoukro, Christopher Steiner; for Mengoni, Nicholas Perkins; for the Renaissance, Antonio Zagaroli and Henry Millon; for Lord Byron, J. Drummond Bone and Josie Dixon, who also assisted in a variety of ways; for Nazi Germany, Barbara Miller Lane and W. Richard Rehl; for illustrations, Sheppard Ferguson, William Brumfield, and Leonardo Varone. The Office for Inter-Library Loans at the University of Maryland provided invaluable assistance. In addition, I am grateful to William Tronzo for inviting me to participate in this anthology and to Beatrice Rehl, Fine Arts Editor of Cambridge University Press and initiator of this project, who has provided helpful comments about my manuscript. Unless noted otherwise, all translations are my own and, along with all the interpretations found herein, my full responsibility.

1   Several years ago the dome of St. Peter's, albeit not the entire vessel of the church, was copied at over twice the size at Our Lady of Peace Cathedral (1985–90, architect Pierre Fakhoury) in the newly planned capital of the Ivory Coast, Yamoussoukro, the hometown of the first president of the independent country, Félix Houphouët-Boigny, who is credited with having moved the capital to this location, to having penned the new city plan, and to having sponsored the construction of this church and plaza, with its ninety-meter diameter steel dome rising above reinforced-concrete walls, richly decorated with marble, and provided with a forecourt inspired by Bernini's St. Peter's Square. The Yamoussoukro basilica was consecrated by Pope John Paul II in September 1990. See "La Foi des grandeurs" and "Notre-Dame de la Brousse," *Architecture d'Aujourd'hui* (February 1989), 55, and (December 1989), 44–7; Roy Richard Grinker and Christopher B. Steiner, eds., "Introduction," in

Perspectives on Africa: A Reader in Culture, History, and Representations (Oxford: Blackwell, 1997), xxii.

2   Christof Thoenes, "S. Maria di Carignano e la tradizione della chiesa centrale a cinque cupole," in C. Maltese, ed., *Galeazzo Alessi e l'architettura del Cinquecento* (Genoa: Maltese, 1975), 322 ("gli esempi più puri"); Gary M. Radke, "Alessandro Alessi," in *Macmillan Encyclopedia of Architects* [henceforth *MEA*] 1:63; Christian Norberg-Schulz, *Baroque Architecture* (New York: Harry N. Abrams, 1971), 129; and Nicholas Adams, "Lorenzo Binago," *MEA* 1:211: "Binago combined elements from Donato Bramante's St. Peter's in Rome (the freestanding piers supporting the cupola) with a delicate clarity and elegance that recalls Alessi's Santa Maria di Carignano, Genoa." For an extensive account of the influence of St. Peter's from the Renaissance through the Neoclassical period, see Luciano Patetta, "La fortuna del modello di S. Pietro," *Storia e tipologia: Cinque saggi sull'architettura del passato* (Milan: CLUP, 1989), 75–117.

3   Thoenes, "S. Maria di Carignano," 322.

4   In her unpublished book manuscript, "*The Gesù Nuovo in Naples,*" Maria Ann Conelli stresses the difference between the more unified feeling of Giuseppe Valeriano's interior and the more compartmentalized nature of Alessi's S. Maria di Carignano, which presents "a series of separate spatial units." Conelli also notes that the "right-angled placement of the four crossing piers" in the Gesù Nuovo corresponds to an analogous arrangement in the church of San Lorenzo el Real (1573–84) at the Escorial in Madrid and hence differs from the "canted piers of Saint Peter's and Santa Maria di Carignano."

Conelli explains that the rich marble decor of the Gesù Nuovo dates from the early seventeenth century. Valeriano's "simple interior" of white painted walls follows in the tradition of restraint and simplicity of Juan Bautista de Toledo and, in the words of Pietro Pirri, of de Toledo's artistic "right arm," Juan de Herrara, an orientation directed by Valeriano's Jesuit Superior at the Gesù Nuovo, Padre Claudio Acquaviva, who instructed the architect to reserve *piperno* stone for necessary use only, such as in cornices, bases of pilasters, and frames for doors and windows, thereby bringing, in Conelli's words, the "current *herrerianismo,*" i.e., the "Spanish austere style," to Naples. See also Pietro Pirri, S.I., *Giuseppe Valeriano, S.I., architetto e pittore, 1542–1596*, Biblioteca Instituti Historici S.I., vol. 31 (Rome: Institutum Historicum S.I., 1970), 115, 217.

5   Joseph Connors, "Pietro Berrettini da Cortona," *MEA*, 1:458; Norberg-Schulz, *Baroque Architecture*, 142.

6   Norberg-Schulz, *Baroque Architecture*, 148.

7   In *La Chiesa dei SS. Luca e Martina nell'opera di Pietro da Cortona*, trans. Chiara Passanti (Rome: Ugo Bozzi Editore/ The Rome University Press, 1970), 108, 163, 165, Karl Noehles emphasizes that Cortona reiterated the Greek-cross plan of the upper church twice in the crypt: in the commemorative chapel for Santa Martina and her three fellow martyrs, which sits under the main altar, and in what Cortona called the "octagonal temple" of the vestibule, situated under the crossing, also serving as a martyrium.

8   Connors, "Pietro Berrettini da Cortona," *MEA* 1:459.

9   Norberg-Schulz, *Baroque Architecture*, 336.

10 Ibid.

11 Stephen Wren, *Parentalia, or Memoirs of the Family of the Wrens...., but Chiefly of Sir Christopher Wren, Compiled, by His Son Christopher; Now Published by His Grandson Stephen Wren* (London: T. Osborn and R. Dodsley, 1750), pt. II, sec. IV ("Of the New Cathedral Church of St. Pauls"), 280–95, including the chart, "The Difference between the Dimensions of St. Peter's Church at Rome, and St. Paul's in London" (294).

The inner diameter of St. Peter's dome given in *Parentalia* is comparable to the dimension later published by P. E. Visconti, *Metrologia vaticana* (Rome, 1828), tavola III: 139.72 feet.

12 On the relationship of the early planning of the Invalides under the architect Libéral Bruand to the Escorial, see Patrik Reutersvärd, *The Two Churches of the Hôtel des Invalides: A History of Their Design*, Nationalmusei skriftserie 11 (Stockholm: Kungl. Boktryckeriet P. A. Norstedt and Söner, 1965), 76–8.

13 Maria Ann Conelli in conversation with the author.

14 Maria Ann Conelli, "The Gesù Nuovo in Naples: Politics, Property, and Religion" (Ph.D. diss., Columbia University, 1992), 18–19. See also Catherine Wilkinson-Zerner, *Juan de Herrara: Architect to Philip II of Spain* (New Haven, Conn.: Yale University Press, 1993), 101: "Philip seems to have wanted his basilica to rival the greatest modern churches, most particularly St Peter's in Rome...." Wilkinson-Zerner explains that Juan Bautista de Toledo, the initial architect for the Escorial and the master who trained his successor, Juan de Herrara, "had been Michelangelo's chief assistant at St. Peter's in Rome for a number of years until he left for Naples, where he supervised a number of building projects for the Spanish viceroy" (7–10).

15 Reutersvärd, *The Two Churches*, 15–23, 28, 101. The project for the Dome appears to date from 1676, which is when the idea of an oval forecourt is mentioned. Reutersvärd publishes two sketches that he dates to ca. 1698 (figs. 4, 27) and attributes to Robert de Cotte. Pierre Bullet also developed a project for a plaza for the Invalides inspired by St. Peter's Square, which would have featured a replica of Trajan's column crowned by a statue of Louis XIV to portray the French king as emperor of the world (Runar Stranberg, "Libéral Bruand et les problèmes que soulèvent l'Eglise des soldats et le Dôme des Invalides," *Konsthistorisk Tidskrift* 35 [1966]: 20). In *Soufflots Sainte-Geneviève und der Französische Kirchenbau des 18. Jahrhunderts*, Neue Münchner Beiträge zur Kunstsgeschicte, vol. 2 (Berlin: Walter de Gruyter, 1961), 116, Michael Petzet observes, "The answer to St. Peter's by the contemporaries of Louis XIV was Saint-Louis-des-Invalides," by which Petzet means the Dome. Furthermore, as Strandberg has pointed out, "This is the time of Gallicanism, the doctrine that proclaims the independence of the sovereign in temporal matters, a principle recognized by the *Mémoires du clergé* in 1682" (8).

16 Bertrand Jestaz, ed., *Le "Voyage d'Italie" de Robert de Cotte. étude, édition et catalogue des dessins*. École française de Rome. Mélanges d'archéologie et d'histoire, no. 5 (Paris: E. de Boccard, 1966), 174.

17 Once again, Maria Ann Conelli in conversation with the author.

18 Reutersvärd, *The Two Churches*, 97–105.

19 Ibid., 103–4. Louvois's active role in the gestation of the design of the Invalides complex is amply established in Reutersvärd's book.

20 See Charles L. Stinger, *The Renaissance in Rome* (Bloomington: Indiana University Press, 1985), 238–81 ("The *Renovatio Imperii* and the *Renovatio Romae*"), which is the source for these quotations.

21 On emulation, see Richard A. Etlin, *In Defense of Humanism: Value in the Arts and Letters* (New York and Cambridge: Cambridge University Press, 1996), 45.

22 As Soufflot explained, during the seven years that he had lived in Rome (1731–8), he "measured the vast Church of St. Peter's down to the smallest parts." In May 1739, shortly after being inducted as a member of the Académie de Lyon, Soufflot used his plans of St. Peter's to illustrate his lecture on the basilica and its square. See Petzet, *Soufflots Sainte-Geneviève*, 111; Jean

Mondain-Monval, *Soufflot. Sa vie, son oeuvre, son esthéthique (1715–1780)* (Paris: Alphonse Lemerre, 1918), 19; and *Soufflot et son temps*, exh. cat. (Paris: Caisse Nationale des Monuments Historiques et des Sites, 1980), 19, 22.

23 Julien-David Leroy, *Histoire de la disposition et des formes différentes que les Chrétiens ont données à leurs temples, depuis le règne de Constantin le Grand, jusqu'à nous* (Paris, 1764), 1–2.

24 Ibid., 8.

25 Ibid., 11, 39.

26 Ibid., 42.

27 Note that Leroy was in the delicate position of not wanting to favor either of the two contemporary churches under construction by his fellow members of the Académie royale d'architecture, Soufflot's Greek-cross Sainte-Geneviève and Contant d'Ivry's Latin-cross Sainte-Madeleine: "I will not permit myself to offer a judgment in favor of one or the other of these churches before they are finished. It is for the public to decide between two artists who have won their respect . . . This propitious moment, when the King has singularly favored the realm of architecture, is not the only motive that has prompted me to write about Sainte-Geneviève and the Madeleine; . . . I have not been able to resist the desire to offer my colleagues a public testimonial of the reasons that lead me to conceive the greatest hopes for the success of these two churches" (ibid., 88–9).

28 Ibid., 31, 36–8.

29 Consider also the project for Sainte-Geneviève by the French architect Laurent Destouches, published in 1770, with its combination of Greek-cross plan and freestanding columns and its more literal copying of the profile of St. Peter's dome with flanking towers, the latter owing much to St. Paul's Cathedral. Destouches and his supporters claimed that his project dated from 1753 and that Marigny, the Directeur général des Bâtiments, having seen the drawings, conveyed the ideas orally to Soufflot, who then used them to fashion his own design for this church (Petzet, *Soufflots Sainte-Geneviève*, 60, figs. 43–4).

30 Pierre Patte, *Monumens érigés en France à la gloire de Louis XV* (Paris, 1765), or more recently, Richard A. Etlin, *The Architecture of Death: The Transformation of the Cemetery in Eighteenth-Century Paris* (Cambridge, Mass.: MIT Press, 1984), 28 (fig. 14).

31 Victor Hugo, *Notre-Dame de Paris, 1482* (1832; Paris: Garnier Frères, 1961), 221.

32 As Jean-Marie Pérouse de Montclos has observed, Boullée clearly saw himself as participating in a progressive development of church design. In his manuscript treatise "Architecture. Essai sur l'art," Boullée explained: "From these [preceding] observations about modern temples, it is evident that they are still far from the state of perfection of which they are capable. For this reason I thought it incumbent upon me to enter the lists." Etienne-Louis Boullée, *Architecture. Essai sur l'art*, ed. Jean-Marie Pérouse de Montclos (Paris: Hermann, 1968), 88n51, 89 (fol. 93).

33 Adams, "Lorenzo Binago," *MEA*, 1:211. Adams relates this lighting to the "contemporary work in Rome by Francesco Borromini.

34 Christof Thoenes with Thuri Lorenz, *Neapel und Umgebung* (Stuttgart: Philipp Reclam Jun., 1971), 139–40.

35 Hardouin-Mansart's use of the Bernini baldacchino follows upon the example of his great-uncle François Mansart, who also employed it in his domed Parisian church design at Val-de-Grâce. For Victor Hugo's understanding of Val-de-Grâce as having been inspired by St. Peter's, see below.

36 Leroy, *Histoire*, 44.

37 Boullée, *Architecture*, fols. 92v, 94–94v, 95v–96v, in Boullée, ed. Pérouse de Montclos, 88, 90–91, 93–5.

38 Ibid., 82 (fol. 89). Whenever Boullée thought that he might have an opportunity to construct one of his hypothetical designs, he drastically reduced the scale to an appropriate size.

39 Petzet, *Soufflots Sainte-Geneviève*, 89–90, 135–42 (Soufflot's memoir on Gothic architecture), 147 (Brebion); Richard A. Etlin, *Symbolic Space: French Enlightenment Architecture and Its Legacy* (Chicago: University of Chicago Press, 1994), 116–17; and Mondain-Monval, *Soufflot*, 423ff. (Part III is repeatedly concerned with Soufflot's interest in Gothic architecture.)

40 Boullée, *Architecture*, 93 (fols. 95–95v).

41 Ibid., 84–5 (fols. 90–91).

42 See Petzet, *Soufflots Sainte-Geneviève*, 111–12, including Soufflot (141).

43 Honoré de Balzac, *Splendeurs et misères des courtisanes* (Paris: Gallimard, 1973), 259.

44 Immanuel Kant, *Critique of Judgment*, trans. J. H. Bernard (1790; New York: Hafner Press/Macmillan Publishing Co., 1951), 26 (p. 91).

45 Leroy, *Histoire*, 39–41, 69. Soufflot repeatedly offered a similar criticism of the system of piers and arches, as had two important theorists who paved the way for the creation of the Neoclassical style, Abbé Cordemoy and Abbé Laugier. See Mondain-Monval, *Soufflot*, 424, 446–7; Jean-Louis de Cordemoy, *Nouveau Traité de toute l'architecture ou l'art de bastir* (1714 rev. ed.; Farnsborough: Gregg Press, 1966), 109; Marc-Antoine Laugier, *Essai sur l'architecture* (1755 2d ed.), 31–2, 175–6.

46 Leroy, *Histoire*, 41.

47 Ibid., 43.

48 Boullée, *Architecture*, 82–3 (fol. 89v).

49 Piranesi developed his spatial complexity by studying the dual lessons of the stage designs by members of the Galli Bibiena family, which often featured freestanding columns clustered together or in connection with wall fragments and engaged or coupled piers, and which often presented a series of successive volumes. For the former, see Mario Monteverdi, ed., *I Bibiena: Disegni e incisioni nelle collezioni del Museo Teatrale alla Scala*, exh. cat. (Milan: Electa, 1975), passim (especially fig. 7); on the latter, see Andrew Robison, *Giovanni Battista Piranesi: The Early Architectural Fantasies* (Washington, D.C.: National Gallery of Art, 1978), 14.

50 On Soufflot's debt to this print by Piranesi, see the ill-tempered remarks made by his rival, Desboeufs, who accused Soufflot of failing to understand the lessons of Piranesi's design while misunderstanding the virtues of Soufflot's adaption of Piranesi's vision. Desboeufs's text of 1765 is summarized with extracts by Petzet, *Soufflots Sainte-Geneviève*, 64–7.

51 The structural mastery of Sainte-Geneviève is stressed in Werner Oechslin, "Jacques-Gabriel Soufflot," *MEA* 4:112, and Joseph Rykwert, *The First Moderns: The Architects of the Eighteenth Century* (Cambridge, Mass., 1980; 1983 ed.), 437–8, 459, 462, 464, where the author places it within the contemporary French context.

52 Cordemoy, *Nouveau Traité*, 110, and Petzet, *Soufflots Sainte-Geneviève*, 112.

53 Leroy, *Histoire*, 88. Abbé Marc-Antoine Laugier had welcomed Sainte-Geneviève in 1760 as a church "that will present the first model of a perfect architecture!" (as quoted in Mondain-Monval, *Soufflot*, 449).

54 The new Neoclassical aesthetic rejected pilasters as deformities and engaged columns as inadequate. See Etlin, *Symbolic Space*, 91.

55 Leroy, *Histoire*, 46–64 ("De la Beauté qui résulte en général des péristyles dans les églises . . ."). Leroy returns to this subject on pp. 83–5.

56 Boullée, *Architecture*, 83 (fol. 90). This experimental aspect of architecture whereby it engages our personal or existential space, so to speak, became an important object of study in the late nineteenth century by the *Einfühlung* philosophers, who were able to explain the phenomenon more clearly. On this subject, see Richard A. Etlin, "Aesthetics and the Spatial Sense of Self," *Journal of Aesthetics and Art Criticism* 56 (Winter 1998): 1, 6–8, 11.

57 Leroy, *Histoire*, 71.

58 Edmund Burke, *A Philosophical Enquiry into the Origins of Our Ideas of the Sublime and Beautiful*, ed. J. T. Boulton (1958; Notre Dame: University of Notre Dame Press, 1968), 74–6, 139–40.

59 Also of importance are Christopher Wren's earlier London parish church of St. Stephen's Walbrook (1672–1717); a project by Pezzoni and Fayvi for the reconstruction of Saint-Jean l'Evangéliste in Liège, commended by Soufflot in 1753 for the intention to support the dome on columns rather than piers with arches to achieve greater "lightness" and more openings ("percés"); and Sant'Agostino in Piacenza (1569–87) by Abbé Dom Marc Antoine Bagarotti, admired by the Académie royale d'architecture in 1762 for the lightness obtained by the use of the Doric order. Soufflot volunteered to look into this last church more closely (Monval-Mondain, *Soufflot*, 435, 445–6).

60 On this subject, see Richard A. Etlin, *Modernism in Italian Architecture, 1890–1940* (Cambridge, Mass.: MIT Press, 1991), 4–19, and *Frank Lloyd Wright and Le Corbusier: The Romantic Legacy* (Manchester: Manchester University Press, 1994), 180–2.

61 William Craft Brumfield, *A History of Russian Architecture* (New York and Cambridge: Cambridge University Press, 1993; 1997 ed.), 349.

62 Brumfield reports that Voronikhin traveled through Europe between 1786 and 1790 and took private lessons in Paris at that time. On the vaults, this author writes, "Even the barrel vaults seem weightless with their network of hexagonal coffering and inset rosettes" (ibid., 349).

63 The southern exterior colonnade was never built. For the curved arms to either side of the building, see Palladio's final project for the Villa of Leonardo Mocenigo, river Brenta, Dolo (1561–4), conveniently reproduced in *MEA*, 3:355.

64 Brumfield, *A History of Russian Architecture*, 369. For an illustration, see 371 (fig. 496).

65 James Fergusson, *History of the Modern Styles of Architecture*, revised by Robert Kerr, 3d rev. ed. (London: John Murray, 1891), 2:257, 260.

66 Thoenes, *Neapel und Umgebung*, 110. For an illustration, see Arnaldo Venditti, *Architettura neoclassica a Napoli* (Naples: Edizioni Scientifiche Italiane, 1961), fig. 48.

67 Luigi Catalani, *I palazzi di Napoli* (1845; reprint, Naples: Colonnese, 1993), 22–3; *Guida d'Italia del Touring Club Italiana: Nápoli e dintorni*, 4th ed. (Milan, 1960), 174; Carroll L. V. Meeks, *Italian Architecture, 1750–1914* (New Haven, Conn.: Yale University Press, 1966), 181; Thoenes, *Neapel und Umgebung*, 360, 363, 371, 399; and George Hersey, "Luigi Vanvitelli," *MEA* 4:288–90.

68 Thoenes, *Neapel und Umgebung*, 111; Gaetano Nobile, *Un mese a Napoli. Descrizione della città di Napoli e delle sue vicinanze divisa in XXX giornate*, 3 vols. (Naples: Gaetano Nobile, 1863), 1:128–9; *Guida d'Italia del Touring Club Italiana: Nápoli e dintorni*, 39.

69 Venditti, *Architettura neoclassica a Napoli*, 165 (fig. 47), 168, 170–1.

70 Ibid., 168–72; Thoenes, *Neapel und Umgebung*, 110–11.

71 In addition, the colonnades of the piazza dedicated to Ferdinando I (today, Piazza del Plebiscito) extend to two facing palaces that completed the urban space: the late eighteenth-century Palazzo del Principe di Salerno to the south and the Palazzo della Foresteria (ca. 1815, today Palazzo della Prefettura) to the north. Nobile, *Un mese a Napoli*, 1:128–9; Thoenes, *Neapel und Umgebung*, 111, who believes that Laperuta was probably the architect for both buildings.

72 Frédéric Langevin, S. J., *Monseigneur Ignace Bourget. Deuxième évêque de Montréal. Précis biographique* (Montreal: Imprimerie du Messager, 1931), 253, 258, and Léon Pouliot, S. J., "Monseigneur Bourget et la reconstruction de la cathédrale de Montréal," *Revue Historique de l'Amérique Française* 17 [henceforth *RHAF*] (March 4, 1964): 488.

73 Langevin, *Monseigneur Ignace Bourget*, 184, 252–3 (for the quotation); Pouliot, "Monseigneur Bourget et la reconstruction de la cathédrale de Montréal," *RHAF* 17 (December 3, 1963): 341, 349–50; 17 (March 4, 1964): 484; 18 (June 5, 1964): 32, and *Les Dernières Années (1876–1885) et la survie de Mgr Bourget* (Montreal: Editions Beauchemin, 1960), 58, where the author points out that the railroad station was the only one for the period in Montreal. The land for the cathedral was purchased in 1854 and a cross erected on the site of the future main altar in 1857.

74 Pouliot, "Monseigneur Bourget," *RHAF* 17 (March 4, 1964): 484, 485n34. On the importance of the cemetery to the city in this period, see Etlin, *The Architecture of Death*, 367–8.

75 H. Lemaire, as quoted in Abbé A. Boulfroy, *Rome. Ses monuments, ses souvenirs* (Lille: Société Saint-Augustin/Desclée. De Brouwer et Cie, 1890), 68–9. See also 49, where Boulfroy calls St. Peter's the "cathedral of Catholicism."

76 Pouliot, "Monseigneur Bourget," *RHAF* 18 (June 5, 1964): 31–2. The quotation is from the local newspaper, *Le Minerve* (July 28, 1857), which is reporting on Bishop Bourget's speech on the occasion of the planting of the cross on the spot destined for the principal altar of the new cathedral. See also Bourget's words as reported in Langevin, *Monseigneur Ignace Bourget*, 254, who also relates that the citizens of Montreal considered their city to be the "Rome de l'Amérique" (253).

77 Pouliot, "Monseigneur Bourget," *RHAF* 18 (June 5, 1964): 32; Alan Gowans, "The Baroque Revival," *Journal of the Society of Architectural Historians* 14 (October 1955): 11, 14; and Raymonde Laundry-Gauthier, "Victor Bourgeau et l'architecture religieuse et conventuelle dans la diocèse de Montréal (1821–1892)," doctoral dissertation, Université Laval (1983), 177–81, which also explores the relative contributions of Bourgeau as the principal architect for Saint-Jacques and of his successor, Père Joseph Michaud. According to Pouliot, in spring 1856 Bourget was joined in Paris by his secretary, Joseph-Octave Paré, where he assigned Paré the task of visiting the great cathedrals of Europe to decide which should serve as the model for Montreal. Bourget accepted Paré's proposal to use St. Peter's (Pouliot, "Monseigneur Bourget," *RHAF* 17 [March 4, 1964]: 488).

78 See Etlin, *Frank Lloyd Wright and Le Corbusier: The Romantic Legacy*, chap. 4 ("The Spirit of the Age").

79 John Ruskin, *Saint Mark's Rest. The History of Venice . . .* (1884), in *The Works of John Ruskin*, ed. E. T. Cook and Alexander Wedderburn (London: George Allen, 1906), 24:203.

80 In a report of 1851 to the Architectural Society of the Archdeaconry of Northampton, quoted in George L. Hersey, *High Victorian Gothic: A Study in Associationism* (Baltimore: Johns Hopkins University Press, 1972), 44–5.

81 Camillo Boito, *Architettura del medio evo in Italia con una introduzione sullo stile futuro dell'architettura italiana* (1880),

viii–ix. Cf. also Richard Popplewell Pullan, *Elementary Lectures on Christian Architecture* (London, 1879), v–vi: "the mighty pyramids of Egypt and her vast temples . . . the thermae, circi, and amphitheatres of the Romans . . . the cathedrals of the Middle Ages."

82 On the crowd, see Walter Benjamin: "The crowd – no subject was more entitled to the attention of nineteenth-century writers" ("On Some Motifs in Baudelaire," in Walter Benjamin, *Illuminations*, ed. Hannah Arendt, trans. Harry Zohn [New York: Schocken, 1968], 166, passim). On all three of these themes, see Etlin, *Modernism in Italian Architecture, 1890–1940*, xviii–xx.

83 Johann Friedrich Geist, *Arcades: The History of a Building Type*, trans. Jane O. Newman and John H. Smith (1979; Cambridge, Mass., 1983), 378 (fig. 307), 384. The drawing is dated September 1865. Geist (394) lists the diameter of Mengoni's dome as 119 feet, which obviously differs from the measurement of the 139-foot inner diameter of St. Peter's. Recall that the Pantheon's diameter is 142 feet.

84 Hugo, *Notre-Dame de Paris*, 1482, 213–14, 216.

85 Ibid., 126.

86 Ibid., 217.

87 Ibid., 224.

88 Ibid., 220, 218.

89 Ibid., 220.

90 Ibid.

91 John Ruskin, "The Opening of the Crystal Palace" (1854), in Christopher Harvie et al., eds., *Industrialization and Culture, 1830–1914* (London: Open University Press/Macmillan, 1975), 298.

92 John Sproule, ed., *The Irish Industrial Exhibition of 1853: A Detailed Catalogue of Its Contents* (Dublin: James McGlashan, 1854), 1.

93 Ibid., 27, and *Art and Industry Represented in the Exhibition at the Crystal Palace, New York, 1853–4. Showing the Progress and State of the Various Useful and Esthetic Pursuits, from the "New York Tribune,"* rev. and ed. Horace Greeley (New York: Redfield, 1853), 14.

94 Greeley, ed., *Art and Industry*, xxiii. See also p. 15: "But the lofty, magnificent Dome of the American Palace has no parallel in the British [Crystal Palace], and probably has none in the world, unless it be that of St. Peter's at Rome."

95 William C. Richards, *A Day in the New York Crystal Palace* (New York: G. P. Putnam and Co., 1853), 9. Richards also was the editor of the official catalogue for this World's Fair. Consider also the description of the dome by George William Curtis: "It seems to have been borne in upon a zephyr. . . . [I]t floats over the whole, imparting an aerial grace, not be to comprehended without being seen." *Harper's Magazine* (November 1853), 844, cited by James Ford Rhodes, who devoted two pages to this Industrial Exhibition in his *History of the United States from the Compromise of 1850 to the Final Resolution of Home Rule at the South in 1877*, vol. 1 (1850–4) (New York: Macmillan, 1907), 414.

96 Greeley, ed., *Art and Industry*, 22–3, 25–6.

97 Originally scheduled to open on Ascension Day, the 1853 Irish exposition began with these lines and proceeded to Beethoven's "Hallelujah Chorus" and Haydn's "The Heavens Are Telling" as well as his "Hallelujah Chorus," among other stirring music (Sproule, ed., *The Irish Industrial Exhibition of 1853*, 13–15).

98 *The International Exhibition of 1862. The Illustrated Catalogue of the Industrial Department*, British Division, vol. 1 (London: Her Majesty's Commissioners, n.d.), 143, 146, 152–3.

99 Ibid., 146.

100 Charles-Edouard Isabelle, *Les Edifices circulaires et les dômes, classés par ordre chronologique sous le rapport de leur disposition, de leur construction et de leur décoration* (Paris: Firmin Didot Frères, 1855), 142.

101 This assessment is by Auguste Choisy, *Histoire de l'architecture* (Paris: Edouard Rouveyre, [1899]) 2:763. Designed by Nicolas Le Camus de Mézières with an open courtyard, the Hall au Blé soon needed more space, which had to be enclosed by a central dome, constructed in wood (1782–3) according to the design of the architects Jacques-Guillaume Legrand and Jacques Molinos, but destroyed by fire in 1802. François-Joseph Belanger, the architect of the new iron dome of 1808, had proposed a covering for the grain market in this material back in 1782, in a project developed in conjunction with a certain Deumier, who had considerable experience in large-scale iron construction. See Allan Braham, *The Architecture of the French Enlightenment* (Berkeley: University of California Press, 1980), 110, and Jean Stern, *À l'Ombre de Sophie Arnould: François-Joseph Belanger, Architecte des Menus-Plaisirs, Premier Architecte du Comte d'Artois* (Paris: Plon, 1930), 2:202.

102 Cosmo Canovetti, as summarized in Frances H. Steiner, *French Iron Architecture* (Ann Arbor: UMI Research Press, 1984), 31.

103 Ibid.

104 Emile Zola, *Le Ventre de Paris* (n.p.: Fasquelle, n.d.), 338–9. His ellipses throughout.

105 Ibid., 300–1.

106 Ibid., 301. This other novel would be *Au bonheur des dames* (1883).

107 Benjamin, "On Some Motifs in Baudelaire," *Illuminations*, 172.

108 Antonio Rondello, *La Galleria Vittorio Emanuele II, Milano* (Milan: Itala Are, 1967), 116 (quotation from Mayor Antonio Beretta), 56 (quotation from Giuseppe Mongoni), and Laura Gioeni, *L'Affaire Mengoni: La piazza Duomo e la Galleria Vittorio Emanuele di Milano* (N.p.: Guerini, 1995), 24–6, 32, who stresses that the dedication of the new street to honor the king would facilitate the expropriation of the land.

109 Rondello, *La Galleria Vittorio Emanuele II*, 27–32, 37–41, 80. The municipal bodies to which I refer are the Congregazione Municipale, Consiglio Comunale, and the successive arts commissions established by the former to assess the various projects submitted for the Galleria, Piazzo del Duomo, and their connection to an improved urban street network extending from major highway entrances to Milan and to the main train station. The quotation – "il centro vero e naturale" – is from the report of 10 December 1860, by the municipal commission established to review the 176 projects submitted to the public competition, announced the previous April 3; the phrase "piazza italian" comes from the Consiglio Comunale, *Atti del Municipio di Milano* (vol. 1864).

110 Ibid., passim, and Gioeni, *L'Affaire Megnoni*, 38, 43–4, for detailed arguments.

111 For illustrations of Mengoni's first project (1862) and his second project (1863), see Rondello, *La Galleria Vittorio Emanuele II*, plates II, IV, the latter erroneously labeled as "first design" in Geist, *Arcades*, 377 (fig. 305). For Mengoni's paired projects of 1863 for either a street with porticoes or an arcade, see Vincenzo Fontana and Nullo Pirazzoli, *Giuseppe Mengoni, 1829–1877: Un architetto di successo* (N.p.: Edizioni Essegi, [1987]), figs. 14–15, the latter offering a variation of Rondello's plate IV.

112 For the other arcades: Geist, *Arcades*, 244–7, 269–80. Like the Galeries St. Hubert (Brussels, 1846–7), Mengoni's Galleria at this point was to incorporate theater design into the project (ibid., 198–213, 377).

113 Günther Bandmann, "Die Galleria Vittorio Emanuele II. zu Mailand," *Zeitschrift für Kunstgeschichte* 29, no. 2 (1966): 86. In *Arcades*, 384, Geist concurs. Bandmann (86–7) also points out that the cruciform is Mengoni's own original contribution to the urbanistic development of the plaza, whose other main features had all appeared in the project of 10 November 1860, by the Commissione Municipale. It should also be added that Mengoni appears to have conceived the cruciform as a way to facilitate the rational and profitable division of the land to the west side of the Galleria into city blocks. In *L'Affaire Mengoni*, 60, Gioeni mentions a related point: that the addition of the "transverse arm" was the "result of the transformation of the side streets for service, previously suggested by the Commission responsible for the competition."

114 The new urban type of the "arcade" was often termed a "bazaar," a word apparently used in connection with Count Luigi Belgioioso's proposal of 28 June 1859 for a shopping street between Piazza del Duomo and Piazza La Scala (Bandmann, "Die Galleria," 85, and Geist, *Arcades*, 373). On the other hand, the official catalogue for the Great Irish Industrial Exhibition of 1853 termed the building "a gigantic bazaar," just as the editor of the official guide to the New York Crystal Palace referred to one section of the exhibition as "the Machine Arcade." (See Sproule, ed., *The Irish Industrial Exhibition of 1853*, 41, and Richards, *A Day in the New York Crystal Palace*, 9.) In *Arcades*, 5, Geist explains that in the nineteenth century, the word "bazaar" was "commonly used for retail marketplaces, department stores, and world exhibitions. The word [also] appears in connection with arcades...."

115 The two World's Fairs of 1853 in New York and Dublin addressed these concerns in ways that would prove to be fundamental for Mengoni's new idea for the Milan Galleria. The architect of the Dublin building, Sir John Benson, provided rounded glass apses to terminate the three parallel halls so as to keep the space within a person's visual and experiential ken: "The circular termination of the Hall at both ends also greatly adds to this effect, and diminishes the consciousness of extreme length, by making the vaulted semi-domes, with their ribs converging to a common centre a good deal within the extreme points of the length of the roof, seem very much nearer to the spectator than they really are" (Sproule, ed., *The Irish Industrial Exhibition of 1853*, 38). In New York, the designers created an octagonal building from which rose, on the second floor, a Greek cross of four vaulted wings. Whereas the main facade of the Dublin fair gave the appearance of a giant glass dome along the middle of its frontal expanse, the New York Crystal Palace, as it was called, featured a full glass-and-iron dome at the intersection of its four arms. Although immense by comparison with other edifices, the New York Crystal Palace was offered to the public as a well-proportioned work of art: "Within, at the entrance, the visitor sees an arched nave forty-one feet wide, sixty-seven feet high, and three hundred feet long. The dome is one hundred feet across. The building, though not nearly so large as its prototype of the London Exhibition, is superior in architectural beauty" (Greeley, ed., *Art and Industry*, 14).

116 Consider the judgment of James Fergusson, who enthusiastically welcomed the new iron structures as showing the way to an original architecture characteristic of the times: "Art, however, will not be generated by buildings so ephemeral as Crystal Palaces, or so prosaic as Manchester warehouses, nor by anything so essentially utilitarian as the works of our engineers" (*The Illustrated Handbook of Architecture, Being a Concise and Popular Account of the Different Styles of Architecture Prevailing in All Ages and All Countries*, 2d ed. [London, 1859], lvii).

117 *Atti del Municipio di Milano*, vol. 1864, as quoted in Rondello, *La Galleria Vittorio Emanuele II*, 80.

118 Rondello, *La Galleria Vittorio Emanuele II*, 129.

119 Geist, *Arcades*, 75.

120 *Illustrazione Italiana* (February 1876), as quoted in Bandmann, "Die Galleria," 104n9.

121 For New York: Greeley, ed., *Art and Industry*, 22, and Richards, *A Day in the New York Crystal Palace*, 11; for Milan: Geist, *Arcades*, 384. There was a strong Italian presence at the New York Crystal Palace: the statue of George Washington had been sculpted by Marochetti, then living in London, and contemporary Italian statuary was featured in alcoves around the perimeter of the central dome (Richards, *A Day*, 11, 14–15).

122 See the address by Theodore Sedgwick, president of the Association, at the ground breaking for the New York Crystal Palace, where he argues that "genius and ingenuity" should be put on display, not in the new Patent Office in Washington, D.C., but rather in the cosmopolitan setting of the World's Fairs, for which he hoped that the New York Crystal Palace would become "a permanent foundation" (xix–xx). See also xxiii, where after comparing the dome of the New York Crystal Palace to that of St. Peter's, Sedgwick then associates the "splendid innovation on stale precedent in the materials of the building – iron and glass," with the "skill, devotion, industry,... versatility, and genius" of the modern, especially labor-saving, inventions on display.

123 Geist, *Arcades*, 399, 384. See also Bandmann, "Die Galleria," 81.

124 For London: *The International Exhibition of 1862*, 153; for Milan: Geist, *Arcades*, 399.

125 Geist, *Arcades*, 399.

126 Kerr, "Preface," in Fergusson, *History of the Modern Styles of Architecture*, 1:vi.

127 Turpin C. Bannister, "The Genealogy of the Dome of the United States Capitol," *Journal of the Society of Architectural Historians* [hereafter *JSAH*] 7 (January–June 1948): 5.

128 William Sener Rusk, "Thomas U. Walter and His Works," *Americana* (April 1939): 171–5, and Rhodri Windsor Liscombe, *Altogether American; Robert Mills, Architect and Engineer, 1781–1855* (New York and Oxford: Oxford University Press, 1994), 156, 274–80 (with illustration on p. 277). On the problem of acoustics, see also Charles Dickens, *American Notes: A Journey* (1842; New York: Fromm International Publishing Corp., 1985), 118, and Robert Dale Owen, *Hints on Public Architecture* (1849; reprint, New York: Da Capo, 1978), 51–2, where the former senator complains of the lack of space in the Library (which would burn in 1851), of the "dark and damp basement" accommodations for the Supreme Court, of the exiguity of the Senate Chamber, and of the "sheer impossibility to hear" in the House of Representatives, where the spoken word is "swallowed up amid its vortex of sounds."

129 In *Out of Our Past: The Forces That Shaped Modern America*, rev. ed. (New York: Harper and Row, 1970), 108, Carl N. Degler reminds readers that the "irresistible territorial ambitions and sense of mission which gripped Americans in this era are only credible in the language of the time." Degler then quotes from a speaker at an 1844 Democratic state convention, who utilizes personification: "Make way, I say, for the young American Buffalo...." The term "manifest destiny" appears to have been penned in 1845 by a nationalist newspaperman, who "asserted that the American claim 'is by right of our manifest destiny to overspread and to possess the whole of the Continent which Providence has given us for the development of the great experiment of liberty and federated self-government entrusted to us.'" American continental expansion, stresses Degler, was not

"always a peaceful operation. There were constant wars against the Indians as well as a major war against neighboring Mexico" (424).

130 Dickens, *American Notes*, 115. Dickens is better known for his overall assessment of the American capital as "the headquarters of tobacco-tinctured saliva" (112), whose urbanism was marked by "spacious avenues that begin in nothing, and lead nowhere" (116).

131 H. P. Caemmerer, *Washington: The National Capital* (Washington, D.C.: Government Printing Office, 1932), 315, and Fergusson, *History of the Modern Styles of Architecture*, 2:330. On Mills's objection to this lateral extension and his preference for a Greek-cross plan as both more economical and more beautiful, see his memorandum of 1850 in H. M. Pierce Gallagher, *Robert Mills, Architect of the Washington Monument, 1781–1855* (New York: Columbia University Press, 1935), 71–2.

132 Mills, as quoted in Windsor Liscombe, *Altogether American*, 276.

133 The quotation is from Walter's assistant, August Gottlieb Schoenborn, in Bannister, "Genealogy," *JSAH* 7 (January–June 1948): 5, and appendix B: 24.

134 In "Genealogy," 3–4, Bannister stresses the deep impression that the 1851 burning of the wooden Library of Congress – then housed in the Capitol building – along with the destruction of half of the books, made upon Walter, who, although trained as a masonry architect, rebuilt the structure as one of the earliest rooms constructed of iron.

135 Quoted in Spiro Kostof, *The Third Rome, 1870–1950: Traffic and Glory*, exh. cat. (Berkeley: University Art Museum, 1973), 12.

136 The quotation is from Kostof, *The Third Rome*, 70. See also Antonio Cederna, *Mussolini urbanista: Lo sventramento di Roma negli anni del consenso*, 5th ed. (Rome: Laterza, 1981), 65; Valter Vannelli, *Economia dell'architettura in Roma fascista: Il centro urbano* (Rome: Edizioni Kappa, 1981), 341; and Reinhold Schumann, *Italy in the Last Fifteen Hundred Years: A Concise History* (Lanham, Md.: University Press of America, 1986), 296–7, 300–1, 341.

137 "Il Duce col primo colpo di piccone, inizia la demolizione della 'spina' dei Borghi," *Il Giornale d'Italia* (30 October 1936). For the plaque at the Basilica of Maxentius, see Cederna, *Mussolini*, 235. At this time, the name "Via della Conciliazione" was already under consideration. See Brigante Colona, "La risoluzione di un secolare problema. Il primo colpo di piccone alla 'Spina,'" *Il Giornale d'Italia* (30 October 1936).

138 Quoted in Cederna, *Mussolini*, 65.

139 Vannelli, *Economia*, 329–37. As Kostof (*The Third Rome*, 70), Cederna (*Mussolini*, 233), and others have observed, the *piano regolatore* of 1931 had rejected the demolition of the so-called *spina* of the Borgo.

140 In his postwar memoirs, even Speer entitled the chapter on the Nuremberg buildings "Gebaute Megalomanie" (*Erinnerungen* [Berlin: Propyläen Verlag, 1969], chap. 5; "Architectural Megalomania" (*Inside the Third Reich*, trans. Richard and Clara Winston [New York: Macmillan, 1970]).

141 Speer, *Inside the Third Reich*, 55.

142 Wolfgang Lotz in 1937, as summarized in Alex Scobie, *Hitler's State Architecture: The Impact of Classical Antiquity*. CAA Monograph 45 (University Park: Pennsylvania State University Press, 1990), 79.

143 The quotation comes from Speer's memoirs, where he recounts, "I found Hitler's excitement rising whenever I could show him that at least in size we had 'beaten' the other great buildings of history" (*Inside the Third Reich*, 69).

144 *Hitler's Secret Conversations, 1941–1944*, trans. Norman Cameron and R. H. Stevens, intro. H. R. Trevor-Roper (1953; New York: Signet, 1961), 103 (21–2 October 1941).

145 Speer, *Inside the Third Reich*, 76.

146 Speer recounts that Hitler had entrusted him unofficially with this project in the summer of 1936 (ibid., 73–4).

147 Ibid., 152–3.

148 Ibid., 74. Consider also: "The interior would contain sixteen times the volume of St. Peter's" (153).

149 For an illustration of Hitler's building project, see Scobie, *Hitler's State Architecture*, 110 (fig. 52).

150 Hitler's intense interest in architectural developments in the capital cities of rival regimes is manifest in his anxiety about the announced construction of the Palace of the Soviets in Moscow, which threatened to eclipse the height of his projected Grosse Halle for Berlin (Speer, *Inside the Third Reich*, 155; *Erinnerungen*, 170).

151 An important corollary in Nazi ideology to the importance of the assembled *Volk* was the self-image of the new Germany as the master of modern technology. Here, too, St. Peter's figured as a prototype that had to be bested in size through the construction of the new train station for Munich, dubbed Haupstadt der Bewegung (Main City of the [Nazi] Movement). Hermann Reinhard Alker's design of 1937–8 was inspired by St. Peter's and its square (Hans-Peter Rasp, *Eine Stadt für tausend Jahre: München – Bauten und Projekte für die Haupstadt der Bewegung* [Munich: Süddeutscher Verlag, 1981], fig. 59). This was followed the next year by Hermann Giesler's project, whose foundation was actually built, for "the largest steel-frame structure in the world, covering an area six times greater than St. Peter's," even exceeding in size Speer's Grosse Halle, and intended to be placed in the middle of a 6.6 kilometer-long avenue, 120 meters wide (Jochen Thies, *Architekt der Weltherrschaft: Die "Endziele" Hitlers* [Düsseldorf: Droste, 1976], 93, and "Nazi Architecture – A Blueprint for World Domination: The Last Aims of Adolf Hitler," in David Welch, ed., *Nazi Propaganda* [London: Croom Helm; Totowa, N.J., Barnes and Noble, 1983], 52). Engineering solutions to transform Giesler's domed hall into reality were solicited from various German steel companies; and toward 1940 a comparative drawing was prepared that showed the projected Munich railroad station reaching the height of St. Peter's while overwhelming it in actual breadth and volume (Rasp, *Eine Stadt*, 130–41, 201 [fig. 174]). For the Nazi fascination with technology, see Jeffrey Herf, *Reactionary Modernism: Technology, Culture, and Politics in Weimar and the Third Reich* (Cambridge and New York: Cambridge University Press, 1984), chap. 8.

152 Scobie also points out, "No Nazi forum planned for any German city was to incorporate a new church" (*Hitler's State Architecture*, 64–5).

153 Speer, *Inside the Third Reich*, 153 (translation modified); *Erinnerungen*, 167. Speer explains that in the course of planning the Grosse Halle, he traveled to Rome to visit St. Peter's. There he encountered the same problem of scale that had disturbed eighteenth-century observers: "I was disappointed that its size has no relationship to the impression on the observer. Already with this order of magnitude, I now recognized, the impression is no longer proportional to the size of the building. I then feared that the effect of our large Hall would not correspond to Hitler's expectations" (*Erinnerungen*, 169 [my translation]).

154 Robert N. Proctor, *Racial Hygiene: Medicine under the Nazis* (Cambridge, Mass.: Harvard University Press, 1988), 177–222 (chap. 7: "The Destruction of 'Lives Not Worth Living'"), and Michael Burleigh and Wolfgang Wippermann, *The Racial State: Germany, 1933–1945* (Cambridge: Cambridge University Press, 1991), 136–97 (chap. 6: "The Persecution of the 'Hereditarily Ill,' the 'Asocial,' and Homosexuals").

155 Proctor, *Racial Hygiene*, 89.

156 Speer, perhaps Hitler too, may have also had the dome of the American Capitol in mind. In his postwar memoirs, Speer observes about his Grosse Halle: "the Capitol in Washington would have been swallowed up many times in this volume" (*Erinnerungen*, 168).

157 Via della Conciliazione was finished in the Holy Jubilee Year 1950.

158 Boulfroy, *Rome*, 56–9, 68–9. The quotations that follow from Mme de Staël, Lord Byron, and Charles de Brosses can be found, respectively, in *Corinne ou l'Italie* (1807; Paris: Charpentier, 1839 new ed.), 71; Lord Byron, *The Complete Poetical Works*, ed. Jerome J. McGann (Oxford: Oxford University Press, 1980), 2:176–7; Charles de Brosses, *Lettres familières sur l'Italie* [1745–55], ed. Yvonne Bzard (Paris: Firmin-Didot, 1931), 2:3, 4, 22, 159. Abbé Boulfroy has made a collage of different lines from de Brosses. For Byron, I have used the English original rather than the Abbé's French translation.

159 For measurements, I have used Paul-Marie Letarouilly and Alphonse Simil, *Le Vatican et la basilique de Saint-Pierre de Rome* (Paris: A. Morel, 1882), and Visconti, *Metrologia vaticana*, rather than those related by Abbé Boulfroy.

160 These texts by Mme de Staël, Lord Byron, and Victor Hugo can be added to those assembled by Luzius Keller in *Piranèse et les romantiques français: Le mythe des escaliers en spirale* (Paris: José Corti, 1966), which studies the Romantic fascination with vertiginous heights and depths, either singly or paired together, as well as spiraling forms, all related by these poets and novelists to mind, spirit, and the human race. As we have seen from the mid-century musings in the United States about the "vortex of sounds" swallowed by the old House chamber at the U.S. Capitol, and about the "lyrical windings" of music and their analogy with the "circularities of the soul" experienced in the New York Crystal Palace, nineteenth-century architectural appreciation deserves its own literary history, centered on the leitmotif of the spiral, in which St. Peter's would occupy an important place.

SELECTED BIBLIOGRAPHY

Drawn from Sources Cited

Ackerman, James S. *The Architecture of Michelangelo*. Rev. ed. London, 1966.

——. "Notes on Bramante's Bad Reputation." In *Studi bramanteschi, Atti del congresso internazionale*, 1974, 339–49.

Agosti, Barbara. *Collezionismo e archeologia cristiana nel Seicento. Federico Borromeo e il medioevo artistico tra Roma e Milano*. Milan, 1996.

Ahl, Diane Cole. *Benozzo Gozzoli*. New Haven and London, 1996.

Alberti, Leon Battista. *L'architettura (De re aedificatoria)*. Ed. Giovanni Orlandi. Milan, 1966.

Alciati, Andreas. *Emblemata*. Frankfurt, 1567.

Alfarano, Tiberio. *De Basilicae Vaticanae antiquissima et nova structura*. Ed. Michele Cerrati. Rome, 1914.

Alföldy, Géza. *Der Obelisk auf dem Petersplatz in Rom. Ein historisches Monument der Antike*. Heidelberg, 1990.

Anderes, Bernhard, and Peter Hoegger. *Die Glasgemälde im Kloster Wettingen*. Baden-Schweiz, 1989.

Andreae, Bernard. *Studien zur römischen Grabkunst* (Mitteilungen des Deutsches Archäologisches Institut. Römische Abteilung, vol. 9, Ergänzungsheft). Heidelberg, 1963.

Angelini, Alessandro. *Gian Lorenzo Bernini e i Chigi tra Roma e Siena*. Milan, 1998.

L'angelo e la città. Exh. cat. 2 vols. Rome, 1987.

Anselmi, Alessandra. "I progetti di Bernini e Rainaldi per l'abside di Santa Maria Maggiore." *Bollettino d'Arte*, no. 117 (2001): 27–78.

Apollonj Ghetti, B. M., S. J. Antonio Ferrus, E. Josi, and K. Kirschbaum. *Esplorazioni sotto la confessione di San Pietro in Vaticano*. Città del Vaticano, 1951.

Arbeiter, Achim. *Alt-St. Peter in Geschichte und Wissenschaft. Abfolge der Bauten, Rekonstruktion, Architekturprogramm*. Berlin, 1988.

Archivio della Reverenda Fabbrica di San Pietro (AFP).

Aronberg Lavin, Marilyn. *The Place of Narrative: Mural Decoration in Italian Churches, 431–1600*. Chicago and London, 1990.

——. "Representations of Urban Models in the Renaissance." In Henry Millon and Vittorio Magnago Lampugnani, eds., *The Renaissance from Brunelleschi to Michelangelo. The Representation of Architecture*, 674–8. Exh. cat. Milan, 1994.

Aronberg Lavin, Marilyn, and Irving Lavin. *The Liturgy of Love: Images from the Song of Songs in the Art of Cimabue, Michelangelo, and Rembrandt*. Lawrence, Kans. 2001.

Aufhauser, Johannes B. *Konstantins Kreuzesvision in ausgewählten Texten*. Bonn, 1912.

Babelon, Jean-Pierre, ed. *Israël Silvestre. Vues de Paris*. [n.p.], 1977.

Bagatti, Bellarmino. "Note sull'iconografia di 'Adamo sotto il calvario.'" *Liber annuus. Studium biblicum franciscanum* 27 (1977): 5–32.

Baldinucci, Filippo. *Vita del cavaliere Gio. Lorenzo Bernino*. Ed. Sergio Samek Ludovici. Florence, 1682; Milan, 1948.

——. *The Life of Bernini*. Trans. Catherine Enggass. University Park, Pa., 1966.

Bardeschi Ciulich, Lucilla. "Documenti inediti su Michelangelo e l'incarico di San Pietro." *Rinascimento*, 2d ser., 17 (1977): 235–75.

Barocchi, Paola, and Renzo Ristori, eds. *Il Carteggio di Michelangelo*. 5 vols. Florence, 1965–83.

Bartsch, Adam von. *The Illustrated Bartsch*. New York, 1978–.

Basso, Michele. *I privilegi e le consuetudini della Reverenda Fabbrica di S. Pietro in Vaticano (secs. XVI–XX)*. 2 vols. Rome, 1987, 1988.

Bätschmann, Oskar. "Three Problems on the Relationship between Scenography, Theatre and Some Works by Nicolas Poussin." In *Atti del XXIV congresso internazionale di storia dell'arte (1979)*, 5: 169–76. Bologna, 1982.

Bauer, George C. "Bernini and the Baldacchino: On Becoming an Architect in the Seventeenth Century." *Architectura* (1996), 144–65.

——. "Arguing Authority in Late Renaissance Architecture." *Art History* 19 (1996): 418–33.

——. "Bernini's 'Pasce oves meas' and the Entrance Wall of St. Peter's." *Zeitschrift für Kunstgeschichte* 63 (2000): 15–25.

Beck, Melissa. "The Evolution of a Baroque Chapel: Pietro da Cortona's Divine Wisdom, Urban VIII, and Bernini's Adoration of the Sacrament." *Apollo Magazine* 150, no. 449, July 1999, 35–45.

Bellini, Frederico. "La moderna Confessione di San Pietro: Le proposte di Ferrabosco e Maderno." In *La Confessione nella basilica di San Pietro in Vaticano*, ed. A. M. Pergolizzi, 43–55. Milan, 1999.

——. "La costruzione della capella Gregoriana in San Pietro di Giacomo Della Porta: Cronologia, protagonisti e significato iconologico." In Maurizio Caperna and Gianfranco Spagnesi, eds., *Architettura: Processualità e trasformazione*, 333–46. Rome, 2002.

Beltramme, Marcello. "L'escatologismo ermetico del Mare di Sangue berniniano." *Storia dell'arte*, no. 81 (1994): 229–53.

Benedetti, Sandro. "La Sagrestia." In C. Pietrangeli, ed., *La Basilica di San Pietro*, 246–57. Florence, 1989.

——. "Sintetismo e magnificenza nella Roma post-tridentina." In Gianfranco Spagnesi, ed., *L'architettura a Roma e in Italia (1580–1621)*, 1: 27–56. Rome, 1989.

——. "L'officina architettonica di Antonio da Sangallo il Giovane per il San Pietro di Roma." *Quaderni dell'Istituto di storia dell'architettura*, n.s., 15–20 (1992): 15–20, 485–504.

——. "Il profilo della cupola vaticana di Antonio da Sangallo il Giovane." *Palladio*, n.s. 7 (1994): 157–66.

"The model of St. Peter's." In Henry A. Millon and Vittorio Magnago Lampugnani, eds., *The Renaissance from Brunelleschi to Michelangelo: The Representation of Architecture*, 631–3. Exh. cat. New York, 1994.

Berenson, Bernard. *Florentine Pictures of the Renaissance.* Vol. 1. London, 1963.

Berliner, Rudolph. "Arma Christi." *Münchner Jahrbuch der bildenden Kunst* 6 (1955): 35–152.

Bernardini, Maria Grazia, and Maurizio Fagiolo dell'Arco. *Gian Lorenzo Bernini. Regista del Barocco.* Exh. cat. Rome, 1999.

St. Bernard's Sermons for the Seasons and Principal Festivals of the Year. 3 vols. Westminster, Md., 1950.

Bernini, Domenico. *Vita del cavalier Gio. Lorenzo Bernino.* Rome, 1713.

Bernini in Vaticano, Exh. cat. Vatican City, 1981.

Bevilacqua Melasecchi, Olga, "Il complesso monumntale del San Michele. Dalle origini agli interventi di Clemente XI." In Giuseppe Cucco, ed., *Papa Albani e le arti a Urbino e Roma. 1700–1722,* 121–3. Venice, 2001.

Birch, Debra J. *Pilgrimage to Rome in the Middle Ages: Continuity and Change.* Woodbridge, Suffolk, 1998.

Birindelli, Massimo. *Piazza San Pietro.* Rome, 1981.

Blunt, Anthony. "El Greco's 'Dream of Philip II': An Allegory of the Holy League." *Journal of the Warburg and Courtauld Institutes* 3 (1939–40): 58–69.

"Gianlorenzo Bernini: Illusionism and Mysticism." *Art History* 1 (1978): 67–89.

Boissard, Jean-Jacques. *Romanae urbis topographiae et antiquitatum.* 2 vols. Frankfurt, 1597–1602.

Bonaventure, St. *Opera theologica selecta.* Ed. Augustin Sépinski. 5 vols. Florence, 1934–64.

Borgolte, Michael. *Petrusnachfolge und Kaiserimitation. Die Grabelegen der Päpste, ihre Genese und Traditionsbildung.* Göttingen, 1989.

Boulfroy, Abbé A. *Rome. Ses monuments, ses souvenirs.* Lille, 1890.

Brauer, Heinrich, and Rudolf Wittkower. *Die Zeichnungen des Gianlorenzo Bernini.* Berlin, 1931.

Bredekamp, Horst. "Michelangelos Modell-Kritik." In *Architekturmodelle der Renaissance. Die Harmonie des Bauens von Alberti bis Michelangelo,* 116–23. Munich and New York, 1995.

Sankt Peter in Rom und das Prinzip der produktiven Zerstörung. Bau und Abbau von Bramante bis Bernini. Berlin, 2000.

Brenk, Beat. "Spolien und ihre Wirkung auf die Asthetik der varietas. Zum Problem alternierender kapitelltypen." In *Antike Spolien in der Architektur des Mittelalters und der Renaissance,* ed. Joachim Poeschke, 49–92. Munich, 1996.

Brilliant, Richard. *Gesture and Rank in Roman Art: The Use of Gestures to Denote Status in Roman Sculpture and Coinage.* New Haven, Conn., 1963.

Brubaker, Leslie. *Vision and Meaning in Ninth-Century Byzantium. Image as Exegesis in the Homilies of Gregory Nazianzus.* Cambridge and New York, 1999.

Bruschi, Arnaldo. "L'idee del Peruzzi per il nuovo S. Pietro." In *Saggi in onore di Renato Bonelli,* vol. 1 (= *Quaderni dell'Istituto di Storia dell'Architettura,* n.s. 15–20 [1990–2]): 447–84.

"San Pietro. Spazi, strutture, ordini da Bramante ad Antonio da Sangallo il Giovane a Michelangelo." In Gianfranco Spagnesi, ed., *L'architettura della basilica di San Pietro. Storia e costruzione.* Atti de convegno internazionale di studi, Roma, Castel S. Angelo, 7–10 novembre 1995, 177–94. Rome, 1997.

Buonanni, Filippo. *Numismata summorum pontificum templi vaticani fabricam indicantia.* Rome, 1696.

Numismata pontificum romanorum quae a tempore Martini V. usque ad annum M.DC.XCIX. vel authoritate publica, vel privato genio in lucem prodiere. 2 vols. Rome, 1699.

Burbaum, Sabine. *Die Rivalität zwischen Borromini und Gianlorenzo Bernini.* Oberhausen, 1999.

Burns, Howard. "Leon Battista Alberti." In Francesco Paolo Fiore, ed., *Storia dell'architettura italiana. Il Quattrocento,* 114–65. Milan, 1998.

Burroughs, Charles. *From Signs to Design: Environmental Process and Reform in Early Renaissance Rome.* Cambridge, Mass. 1990.

Camesasca, Ettore. *Raffaello. Gli scritti.* Milan, 1994.

Cancellieri, Francesco. *Descrizione storico-critica delle sale regie e ducali e delle cappelle Paoline e Sistina del Vaticano e del Quirinale.* Rome, 1790.

Canones et decreta sacrosancti oecumenici concilii tridentini. Leipzig, 1887.

Canons and Decrees of the Council of Trent. Rockford, Ill., 1978.

Cantatore, Flavia. "Tre nuovi documenti sui lavori per San Pietro al tempo di Paolo II." In Gianfranco Spagnesi, ed., *L'architettura della basilica di San Pietro. Storia e costruzione.* Atti del convegno internazionale di studi, Roma, Castel S. Angelo, 7–10 novembre 1995, 119–22. Rome, 1997.

Caperna, Maurizio. *La basilica di Santa Prassede. Il significato della vicenda architettonica.* Genoa, 1999.

Carcano, Pietro Battista. *Guida della monumentale Chiesa di S. Chiara in Napoli.* Milan, 1913.

Cardile, Paul J. "Mary as Priest. Mary's Sacerdotal Position in the Visual Arts." *Arte cristiana* 72 (1984): 199–208.

Cardilli Alloisi, Luisa, and Maria Grazia Tolomeo Speranza. *La via degli angeli. Il restauro della decorazione scultorea di Ponte Sant'Angelo.* Rome, 1988.

Carli, Enzo. *Arnolfo.* Florence, 1993.

Carpiceci, Alberto Carlo. "La Basilica vaticana vista da Maerten van Heemskerck." *Bollettino d'arte* 44–45 (1987): 67–128.

Carpiceci, Alberto Carlo, and Richard Krautheimer. "Nuovi dati sull' antica basilica di San Pietro in Vaticano." *Bollettino d'Arte* 1, nos. 93–4 (1995): 1–70; 2, no. 95 (1996): 1–84.

Cartari, Vincenzo. *Imagini de gli dei.* Padua, 1626.

Casale, V. "Benedetto XIV e le canonizzazioni." In *Benedetto XIV e le arti del disegno,* ed. D. Biagi Maino, 15–27. Bologna, 1998.

The Catechism of the Council of Trent. Trans. J. Donovan. New York, n.d.

Catechismus Romanus, seu, Catechismus ex decreto Concilii Tridentini ad parochos Pii Quinti Pont. Max. iussu editus. Ed. Pedro Rodriguez, et al. Rome, 1989.

Cavazzini, Patrizia. "The Porta Virtutis and Federigo Zuccari's Expulsion from the Papal States: An Unjust Conviction?." *Römisches Jahrbuch der Bibliotheca Hertziana* 25 (1989): 167–77.

Ceccarelli, Simonetta. "Carlo Marchionni e la Sacrestia Vaticana." In Elisa Debenedetti, ed., *Carlo Marchionni: Architettura, decorazione e scenografia contemporanea,* 57–133. Rome, 1988.

Cederna, Antonio. *Mussolini urbanista: Lo sventramento di Roma negli anni del consenso.* 5th ed. Rome, 1981.

Celano, Carlo. *Delle notizie del bello, dell' antico, e del curioso della città di Napoli.* 4th ed. Naples, 1792.

Chantelou, Paul Fréart de. *Journal du voyage du Cavalier Bernin en France.* Ed. Ludovic Lalanne. Paris, 1885.

Diary of the Cavaliere Bernini's Visit to France. Ed. Anthony Blunt and George C. Bauer. Princeton, N.J., 1985.

Chastel, André. *The Sack of Rome, 1527.* Princeton, N.J., 1983.

Christern, Jurgen. "Der Aufriss von Alt-St.-Peter." *Römische Quartalschrift* 62 (1967): 133–83.

Clifton, James. "Mattia Preti's Frescoes for the City Gates of Naples." *The Art Bulletin* 76 (1994): 479–501.

Cole, Michael. "Cellini's Blood." *The Art Bulletin* 58 (1999): 215–35.

Colivia, Anna, and Sebastian Schütze, eds. *Bernini scultore. La nascità del barocco in casa Borghese*, exh. cat. Rome, 1998.

Contardi, Bruno, and Aurelio Amendola. *San Pietro*. Milan, 1998.

Corbo, Anna Maria, and Massimo Pomponi, eds. *Fonti per la storia artistica romana al tempo di Paolo V*. Rome, 1995.

Crawfurd, Raymond. *Plague and Pestilence in Literature and Art*. Oxford, 1914.

Crocetti, Giuseppe. *Maria e l'eucaristia nella chiesa*. Bologna, 2001.

Cucco, Giuseppe, ed. *Papa Albani e le arti a Urbino e a Roma, 1700–1721*. Venice, 2001.

Curti, Mario. "Indagini sul San Pietro di Niccolò V. La misura del 'cubitus' come chiave interpretativa." *Quaderni del Dipartimento, Patrimonio architettonico e urbanistico* 10 (1995): 55–72.

——— "'L'admirabile Templum' di Gianozzo Manetti alla luce di una ricognizione delle fonti documentarie." In Gianfranco Spagnesi, ed., *L'architettura della basilica di San Pietro. Storia e costruzione*. Atti del convegno internazionale di studi, Rome, Castel S. Angelo, 7–10 novembre 1995, 111–18. Rome, 1997.

Dante Alighieri. *The Divine Comedy*, ed. Charles S. Singleton, 3 vols. Princeton, 1970–5.

Debenedetti, Elisa, ed. *Carlo Marchionni: Architettura, decorazione e scenografia contemporanea*. Rome, 1988.

De Blaauw, Sible. *Cultus et décor. Liturgia e architettura nella Roma tardoantica e medievale*. Vatican City, 1994.

De Campos, Redig. "Les constructions d'Innocent III et de Nicolas III sur la colline Vaticane." *Mélanges d'archéologie et d'histoire* 71 (1959): 359–64.

Dehio, Georg. "Die Bauprojekte Nikolaus des fünften und L. B. Alberti." *Repertorium für Kunstwissenschaft* 3 (1880): 241–57.

Deichmann, Friedrich Wilhelm. "Saule und Ordnung in der frühchristlichen Architektur." *Römische Mitteilungen* 55 (1940): 121–9.

Delehaye, Hippolyte. *Les légendes grecques des saints militaires*. New York, 1975.

Dell'Aja, Gaudenzio. "Note sull'altare Maggiore della Basilica di S. Chiara in Napoli." *Asprenas* 8 (1961): 100–8.

Del Pesco, Daniela. *Colonnato di San Pietro. Dei Portici antichi e la loro diversità, con un'ipotesi di cronologia*. Rome, 1988.

Delumeau, Jean. *Vie économique et sociale de Rome dans la seconde moitié du xvi siècle*. 2 vols. Paris, 1957–9.

De Passe, Crispijin. *Speculum passionis Christi*. N.p., 1631.

De' Pazzi, Maria Maddalena. *I colloqui, parte seconda*. Ed. Claudio Maria Catena (*Tutte le opere di Santa Maria Maddalena de' Pazzi dai manoscritti*, vol. 3). Florence, 1960.

De Maio, Romeo. *Michelangelo e la controriforma*. Bari, 1978.

Denker Nesselrath, Christiane. *Die Säulenordnung bei Bramante*. Worms, 1990.

Der Nersessian, Sirarpie. "Two Images of the Virgin in the Dumbarton Oaks Collection." *Dumbarton Oaks Papers* 14 (1960): 69–86.

——— *L'Illustration des psautiers grecs du moyen-âge*. 2 vols. Paris, 1966–70.

De' Rossi, Domenico. *Studio d'architettura civile di Roma*. 3 vols. Rome, 1702–21.

di Giorgio Martini, Francesco. *Trattati di Architettura*. Ed. Corrado Maltese. Milan, 1967.

Di Macco, Michela. *Il colosseo. Funzione simbolica, storica, urbana*. Rome, 1971.

Di Pasquale, Salvatore. "Giovanni Poleni tra dubbi e certezze nell'analisi della cupola vaticana." *Palladio* 14 (1994): 273–8.

——— "La cupola, le fratture, le polemiche." In Gianfranco Spagnesi, ed., *L'architettura della basilica di San Pietro. Storia e costruzione*, Atti de convegno internazionale di studi, Roma, Castel S. Angelo, 7–10 novembre 1995, 381–8. Rome, 1997.

Di Stefano, Roberto. *La cupola di San Pietro. Storia della contruzione e dei restauri*. Naples, 1963. Rev. ed. Naples, 1980.

Dittscheid, Hans-Christoph. "St. Peter in Rom als Mausoleum der Papste. Bauprojekte der Renaissance und ihr Verhältnis zur Antike." *Blick in die Wissenschaft. Forchungsmagazin der Universität Regensburg* 1 (1992): 64–8.

Dizionario biografico degli italiani. Rome, 1960–.

Donato, Alessandro. *Roma vetus ac recens*. Rome, 1648.

D'Onofrio, Cesare. *Roma nel seicento. "Roma ornata dall' architettura, pittura e scoltura" di Fioravante Martinelli*. Florence, 1969.

——— *Roma val bene un'abiura*. Rome, 1976.

——— *Castel S. Angelo e Borgo tra Roma e Papato*. Rome, 1978.

——— *Il Tevere. L'isola tiberina, le inondazioni, i molini, i porti, le rive, i muraglioni, i ponti di Roma*. Rome, 1980.

——— *Gian Lorenzo Bernini e gli angeli di Ponte S. Angelo. Storia di un ponte*. Rome, 1981.

——— *Visitiamo Roma mille anni fa. La città dei Mirabilia*. Rome, 1988.

Dumbrowski, Damian. *Dal trionfo all'amore. Il mutevole pensiero artistico di Gianlorenzo Bernini nella decorazione del nuovo San Pietro*. Rome, 2003.

Duplomb, Charles. *Histoire generale des ponts de Paris*, 2 vol. Paris, 1911–13.

Dykmans, M. *Roma nel Seicento*. Florence, 1969.

——— "L'oeuvre de Patrizi Piccolomini ou le cérémonial papal de la première renaissance." *Studi e testi* 1, no. 293 (1980): 120–244.

Elam, Caroline. "Michelangelo: His Late Roman Architecture." *AA File* 1 (Winter 1981–2): 68–76.

Enciclopedia dantesca, 6 vols. Rome, 1984.

Enciclopedia dello spettacolo, 11 vols. Rome, 1975.

Erben, Dietrich. "Bildnis, Denkmal und Historie beim Masaniello-Aufstand 1647–1648 in Neapel." *Zeitschrift für Kunstgeschichte* 62 (1999): 231–63.

Esch, Arnold. "Spolien. Zur Wiederverwendung antiker Baustucke und Skulpturen im mittelalterlichen Italien." *Archiv für Kulturgeschichte* 51 (1969): 1–64.

Eusebius of Caesarea. *The Life of Constantine . . . done into English from that Edition set forth by Valesius and Printed at Paris in the Year 1659. Together with Valesius's Annotations. . . .* Cambridge, 1682.

——— *Church History, Life of Constantine the Great, and Oration in Praise of Constantine*. Ed. Philip Schaff and Henry Wace. Grand Rapids, Mich., 1976 (A Select Library of Nicene and Post-Nicene Fathers of the Christian Church, Second Series, vol. 1).

Fagiolo, M. *Sisto V Roma e il Lazio*. Rome, 1992.

——— ed. *La festa di Roma dal Rinascimento al 1870. Atlante*. Turin, 1997.

Fagiolo, M., and M. Luisa Madonna. *Barocco romano e barocco italiano*. Rome, 1985.

Fagiolo dell'Arco, Maurizio. *Berniniana. Novità sul regista del Barocco*. Venice, 2002.

Fehl, Phillip. "Bernini's 'Triumph of Truth over England.'" *The Art Bulletin* 48 (1966): 404–5.

——— "Christian Truth and the Illusion of Death." *Studies in Iconography* 7–8 (1981–2): 351–69.

——— "L'umiltà cristiana e il monumento sontuoso: La tomba di Urbano VIII del Bernini." In Marcello Fagiolo, ed., *Gian Lorenzo Bernini e le arti visive*, 185–208. Florence, 1987.

Finch, Margaret. "The Cantharus and Pigna at Old St. Peter's." *Gesta* 30 (1991): 16–26.

Fiorani, Luigi. "Le visite apostoliche del cinque-seicento e la società religiosa di Roma." *Ricerche per la storia religiosa di Roma* 4 (1980): 53–148.

Fiore, Francesco Paolo, ed. *Storia dell'architettura italiana. Il Quattrocento*. Milan, 1998.

Firestone, Gizella. "The Sleeping Christ-Child in Renaissance Representations of the Madonna." *Marsyas* 2 (1942): 43–62.

Forcella, Vincenzo. *Iscrizioni delle chiese e d'altri edificii di Roma dal secolo XI fino ai giorni nostri.* 14 vols. Rome, 1869–84.

Francia, Ennio. *1505–1605. Storia della costruzione del nuovo San Pietro.* Rome, 1977.

Fraschetti, Stanislao. "I sarcophagi dei reali angioini in Santa Chiara di Napoli." *L'Arte* 1 (1898): 385–438.

——. *Il Bernini. La sua vita, la sua opera, il suo tempo.* Milan, 1900.

Freiberg, Jack. *The Lateran in 1600. Christian Concord in Counter-Reformation Rome.* Cambridge and New York, 1995.

Frey, Carl. "Zur Baugeschichte des St Peter, Mitteilungen aus der Reverendissima Fabbrica di S. Pietro." *Jahrbuch der königlich preuszischen Kunstsammlungen,* Beiheft zum 31 (1910): 1–95; Beiheft zum 31 (1911): 55; Beiheft zum 33 (1912): 1–153; Beiheft zum 37 (1916): 22–136.

Frommel, Christoph Liutpold. "Antonio da Sangallos Cappella Paolina." *Zeitschrift für Kunstgeschichte* 27 (1964): 1–42.

——. "Die Peterskirche unter Papst Julius II. im Licht neuer Dokumente." *Römisches Jahrbuch für Kunstgeschichte* 16 (1976): 57–136.

——. "'Cappella Julia.' Die Grabkapelle Julius II. in Neu-St.-Peter." *Zeitschrift für Kunstgeschichte* 40 (1977): 26–62.

——. "Francesco del Borgo. Architekt Pius II. und Pauls II. Der Petersplatz und weitere römische Bauten." *Romisches Jahrbuch für Kunstgeschichte* 20 (1983): 107–54.

——. "Raffael und Antonio da Sangallo der Jüngere." In *Raffaello a Roma, Il convegno del 1983.* Rome, 1986.

——. "St. Peter's: The Early History." In Henry A. Millon and Vittorio Magnago Lampugnani, eds., *The Renaissance from Brunelleschi to Michelangelo: The Representation of Architecture,* 399–423 and 598–631. Exh. cat. New York, 1994.

——. "Il San Pietro di Niccolò V." In Gianfranco Spagnesi, ed., *L'architettura della basilica di San Pietro. Storia e costruzione.* Atti del convegno internazionale di studi, Roma, Castel S. Angelo, 7–10 novembre 1995, 103–10. Rome, 1997.

——. "Roma." In Francesco Paolo Fiore, ed., *Storia dell architettura italiana. Il Quattrocento,* 374–443. Milan, 1998.

Frommel, Christoph Liutpold, and Nicholas Adams, eds. *The Architectural Drawings of Antonio da Sangallo the Younger and His Circle,* vol. 2. Cambridge, Mass. and London, 2000.

Frommel, Christoph Liutpold, Stefano Ray, Manfredo Tafuri et al. *Rafaello architetto.* Milan, 1984.

Frothingham, Arthur L. "Une mosaïque constantinienne inconnue à Saint-Pierre de Rome." *Revue archéologique* 3 (1883): 68–72.

Frugoni, Arsenio. *Il giubileo di Bonifacio VIII.* Anagni, 1996.

Fumaroli, Marc. "Cross, Crown, and Tiara: The Constantinian Myth between Paris and Rome (1590–1690)." In *Piero della Francesca and His Legacy,* ed. M. A. Lavin, 89–102. Hanover and London, 1995.

Gallino, Tomaso M. *Il complesso monumentale di Santa Chiara in Napoli.* Naples, 1963.

Geymüller, Heinrich von. *Die ursprünglichen Entwurfe für Sanct Peter in Rom.* Vienna and Paris, 1875–80.

Gigli, Giacinto. *Diario Romano (1608–1670).* Ed. Giuseppe Ricciotti. Rome, 1958.

Giovannoni, Gustavo. *Antonio da Sangallo il Giovane.* Rome, 1959.

Goffen, Rona. *Giovanni Bellini.* New Haven and London, 1989.

Golzio, Vincenzo. *Raffaello nei documenti.* Vatican City, 1936.

Gombrich, Ernst. "The Debate on Primitivism in Ancient Rhetoric," *Journal of the Warburg and Courtauld Institutes,* XXIX (1966): 24–38.

Gonzaga, Francesco. *De origine seraphica religionis franciscana.* Rome, 1587.

Gougaud, Louis. *Dévotions et pratiques ascetiques du moyen-âge.* Paris, 1925.

Gramatica, Aloisius. *Bibliorum sacrorum iuxta Vulgatam Clementinam nova editio breviario perpetuo et concordantiis aucta adnotatis etiam locis qui in monumentis fidei sollemnioribus et in liturgia romana usurpari consueverunt.* Rome, 1951.

Gramberg, Werner. "Guglielmo della Portas Grabmal für Paul III. Farnese in St. Peter." *Römisches Jahrbuch der Bibliotheca Hertziana* 21 (1984): 253–324.

Gregory the Great. *Saint Gregory the Great. Dialogues.* Trans. Odo John Zimmerman. New York, 1959 (The Fathers of the Church, vol. 39).

——. *Grégoire le Grand. Dialogues.* Ed. Adalbert de Vogüé and Paul Antin. 3 vols. Paris, 1978–80 (Sources chrétiennes, vols. 251, 260, 265).

Grimaldi, Giacomo. *Descrizione della basilica antica di S. Pietro in Vaticano, Codice Barberini Latino 2733.* Ed. Reto Niggl. Rome, 1972.

Grunder, Karl. "Die Lünetteninschriften der Kolonnaden von Sankt Peter in Rom. Zum 'concetto' des 'Portico di S. Pietro.'" In Thomas Bolt et al., eds., *Grenzbereiche der Architektur,* 69–78. Basel, 1985.

Guarducci, M. *Cristo e San Pietro in un documento precostantiniano della Necropoli Vaticana.* Rome, 1953.

——. *I graffiti sotto la Confessione di San Pietro in Vaticano.* 3 vols. Vatican City, 1958.

——. *The Tradition of Peter in the Vatican in the Light of History and Archaeology.* Vatican City, 1963.

Gunther, Hubertus. "Leitende Bautypen in der Planung der Peterskirche." In *L'église dans l'architecture de la Renaissance, Actes du colloque tenu à Tours 1990,* 41–78. Paris, 1995.

——. "'Als ware die Peterskirche mutwillig in Flammen gesetzt.' Zeitgenössische Kommentare zum Neubau der Peterskirche und ihre Massstäbe." *Münchner Jahrbuch der bildenden Kunst* 48 (1997): 67–112.

——. "I progetti di ricostruzione della basilica di S. Pietro negli scritti contemporanei, giustificazioni e scrupoli." In Gianfranco Spagnesi, ed., *L'architettura della basilica di San Pietro. Storia e costruzione.* Atti del convegno internazionale di studi, Roma, Castel S. Angelo, 7–10 novembre 1995, 137–48. Rome, 1997.

Hager, Hellmut. *Filippo Juvarra e il concorso di modelli del 1715 bandito da Clemente XI per la nuova Sacrestia di San Pietro.* Rome, 1970.

——. "Carlo Fontana's Project for a Church in Honour of the 'Ecclesia Triumphans' in the Colosseum, Rome." Journal of the Warburg and Courtauld Institutes 26 (1973): 319–37.

Hall, Marcia B. *Renovation and Counter-Reformation: Vasari and Duke Cosimo in Sta. Maria Novella and Sta. Croce 1565–1577.* Oxford, 1979.

Hamburger, Jeffrey F. *The Rothschild Canticles: Art and Mysticism in Flanders and the Rhineland circa 1300.* New Haven, 1990.

Hammond, Frederick. "Bernini and Others in Venetian Ambassadorial Dispatches." *Source* 4 (1984): 30–5.

Harbison, Craig. *The Last Judgment in Sixteenth-Century Northern Europe: A Study of the Relation between Art and the Reformation.* New York, 1976.

Harris, Anne Sutherland. *Selected Drawings of Gian Lorenzo Bernini.* New York, 1977.

——. "Edinburgh. Bernini and His Roman Contemporaries." *Burlington Magazine* 140 (1998): 638–42.

Haus, Andreas. "Der Petersplatz in Rom und sein Statuenschmuck. Neue Beiträge." Dissertation, Albert-Ludwigs-Universität Freiburg, 1970.

——. "Piazza S. Pietro. Concetto e forma." In Gianfranco Spagnesi and Marcello Fagiolo, eds., *Gian Lorenzo Bernini architetto e l'architettura europea del sei–settecento,* 2:291–316. 2 vols. Rome, 1983–84.

Haussherr, Reiner, ed. *Die Zeit der Staufer. Geschichte. Kunst. Kultur.* 5 vols. Exh. cat. Stuttgart, 1977.

Heer, Josef. *Der Durchbohrte: Johanneische Begründung der Herz-Jesu-Verehrung.* Rome, 1966.

Heikamp, Detlef. "Baccio Bandinelli nel Duomo di Firenze." *Paragone* 15, no. 175 (1964): 32–42.

Herrmann-Fiore, Kristina. "Die Fresken Federico Zuccaris in seinem römischen Küstlerhaus." *Römisches Jahrbuch für Kunstgeschichte* 18 (1979): 35–112.

Hibbard, Howard. *Bernini.* Harmondsworth, 1965.
  Carlo Maderno and Roman Architecture 1580–1630. London, 1971.

Hill, George Frances. *A Corpus of Italian Medals of the Renaissance before Cellini.* London, 1930.

Hillairet, Jacques. *L'Île Saint-Louis. Rue par rue, maison par maison.* Paris, 1967.

Hirst, Michael. "A Note on Michelangelo and the Attic of St Peter's." *Burlington Magazine* 116 (1974): 662–5.

Hollstein, F. W. H. *Dutch and Flemish Etchings, Engravings and Woodcuts, ca. 1450–1700.* Amsterdam, 1949–.

The Hours of the Divine Office in English and Latin. 3 vols. Collegeville, Minn. 1964.

Huber, Florian. "Jesi und Bethlehem, Castel del Monte und Jerusalem. Struktur und Symbolik der 'Krone Apuliens.'" In Kai Kappel et al., eds., *Kunst im Reich Kaiser Friedrichs II. von Hohenstaufen*, 1:45–51. 2 vols. Munich, 1997.

Hubert, Hans. "Bramantes St.-Peter-Entwurfe und die Stellung des Apostelgrabes." *Zeitschrift für Kunstgeschichte* 51 (1988): 195–221.
  "Bramante, Peruzzi, Serlio und die Peterskuppel." *Zeitschrift für Kunstgeschichte* 55 (1992): 353–71.

Huchard, Viviane, et al. *Le Musée national du Moyen Age. Thermes de Cluny.* Paris, 1996.

Huelsen, Ch. "Der Cantharus von Alt-St-Peter und die antiken Pignen-Brunnen." *Römische Mitteilungen* 19 (1904): 88–102.

Incisa della Rocchetta, Giovanni. "La Processione Papale del Corpus Domini nel 1655." *L'illustrazione vaticana* 3 (1932): 498–500.

Ingersoll, Richard Joseph. "The Ritual Use of Public Space in Renaissance Rome." Ph.D. diss., University of California, Berkeley, 1985.

Iversen, Erik. *Obelisks in Exile, I, The Obelisks of Rome.* Copenhagen, 1968.

Joannides, Paul. *Burlington Magazine* 123 (1981): 621.

Josephus in Nine Volumes, vols. II and III: The Jewish War. Ed. H. St. Thackeray. Cambridge, Mass., and London, 1968.

Kaufmann, Hans. *Giovanni Lorenzo Bernini. Die figürliche Kompositionen.* Berlin, 1970.

Keck, David. *Angels and Angelology in the Middle Ages.* New York and Oxford, 1998.

Kempers, Bram. "Diverging Perspectives. New St. Peter's." *Mededelingen van het Nederlands Instituut te Rome*, Deel IV, 55 (1996): 213–51.

Kessler, Herbert L. "'Caput et speculum omnium ecclesiarum': Old St. Peter's and Church Decoration in Medieval Latium." In *Italian Church Decoration of the Middle Ages and Early Renaissance. Functions, Forms and Regional Traditions*, ed. William Tronzo, 119–24. Bologna, 1989.

Kinney, Dale. "The Apocalypse in Early Christian Monumental Decoration." In *The Apocalypse in the Middle Ages*, ed. Richard K. Emerson and Bernard McGinn, 200–16. Ithaca, N.Y., 1992.

Kirschbaum, Engelbert. *The Tombs of St. Peter & St. Paul.* London, 1959.

Kirwin, William Chandler. *Powers Matchless. The Pontificate of Urban VIII, the Baldachin, and Gian Lorenzo Bernini.* New York, 1997.

Kissel, Otto Rudolf. *Die Justitia. Reflexionen über ein Symbol und seine Darstellung in der bildenden Kunst.* Munich, 1984.

Kitao, Timothy K. *Circle and Oval in the Square of Saint Peter's: Bernini's Art of Planning.* New York, 1974.

Klauser, Th. *Die römische Petrustradition im Lichte der neuen Ausgrabungen unter der Peterskirche (= Arbeitsgemeinschaft für Forschung des Landes Nordrhein-Westfalen-Geisteswissenschaften*, Heft 24). Cologne, 1956.

Klodt, Olaf. "Bramantes Entwurfe für die Peterskirche in Rom. Die Metamorphose des Zentralbaus." *Festschrift für Fritz Jacobs*, 119–52. Münster, 1996.

Knipping, John B. *Iconography of the Counter Reformation in the Netherlands. Heaven on Earth.* 2 vols. Nieuwkoop-Leiden, 1974.

Koole, Boudewijn. *Man en vrouw zijn een. De androgynie in het Christendom, in het bijzonder bij Jacob Boehme.* Utrecht, 1986.

Kostof, Spiro. *The Third Rome, 1870–1950: Traffic and Glory*, Exh. cat. Berkeley, 1973.

Kraft, Heike. *Die Bildallegorie der Kreuzigung Christi durch die Tugenden*, Ph.D. diss. Frankfurt, 1976.

Krauss, Franz, and Christof Thoenes. "Bramantes Entwurfe für die Kuppel von St. Peter." *Römisches Jahrbuch der Bibliotheca Hertziana* 27/28 (1991/92): 183–200.

Krautheimer, Richard. "Alberti's Templum Etruscum." *Münchner Jahrbuch der bildenden Kunst*, 3d ser., 12 (1961): 65–72.
  Rome: Profile of a City. Princeton, N.J., 1980.
  The Rome of Alexander VII 1655–1667. Princeton, N.J., 1985.
  St. Peter's and Medieval Rome. Rome, 1985.
  "A Note on the Inscription in the Apse of Old St. Peter's." *Dumbarton Oaks Papers* 41 (1987): 317–20.
  "The Ecclesiastical Building Policy of Constantine." In *Constantine il Grande, dall'Antichità all'Umanesimo*, ed. G. Bonamente and F. Fusco, 2: 509–51. Macerata, 1993.

Krautheimer, Richard, A. F. Frazer, and Spencer Corbett. *Corpus Basilicarum Christianarum Romae.* vol. 5. Vatican City, 1977.

Krautheimer, Richard, and Roger B. S. Jones. "The Diary of Alexander VII: Notes on Art, Artists and Buildings." *Römisches Jahrbuch für Kunstgeschichte* 15 (1975): 199–233.

Kruft, Hanno-Walter, and Lars Olof Larsson. "Entwürfe Berninis für die Engelsbrücke in Rom." *Münchner Jahrbuch der Bildenden Kunst.* 17 (1966): 145–60.

Ladner, G. B. *Die Papstbildnisse des Altertums un des Mittelalters: II. Von Innozenz II. Su Benedikt XI.* Vatican City, 1970.

Lapide, Cornelius a. *Commentaria in scripturam sacram.* 21 vols. Paris, 1866–8.
  The Great Commentary of Cornelius a Lapide. 8 vols. London, 1876–1908.

Lasance, F. X., and Francis Augustine Walsh. *The New Roman Missal in Latin and English.* Boston, 1945.

Lauretus, Hieronymus. *Silva allegoriarum totius Sacrae Scripturae, Barcelona 1570. Fotomechanischer Nachdruck der zehnten Ausgabe Koln 1681.* Ed. Friedrich Ohly. Munich, 1971.

Lavin, Irving. Review of R. Wittkower, *Gian Lorenzo Bernini. The Sculptor of the Roman Baroque* (London, 1955). *The Art Bulletin* 38 (1956): 255–60.
  "Bozzetti and Modelli. Notes on Sculptural Procedure from the Early Renaissance through Bernini." *Stil und Überlieferung in der Kunst des Abendlandes. Akten des 21. internationalen Kongresses für Kunstgeschichte in Bonn 1964*, 3: 93–104. Berlin, 1967.
  Bernini and the Crossing of Saint Peter's. New York, 1968.
  "Bernini's Death." *The Art Bulletin* 54 (1972): 158–86.
  "Afterthoughts on 'Bernini's Death.'" *The Art Bulletin* 55 (1973): 429–36.
  "The Sculptor's 'Last Will and Testament'." *Bulletin of the Allen Memorial Art Museum, Oberlin College* 35 (1977–8):
  "Calculated Spontaneity. Bernini and the Terracotta Sketch." *Apollo* 107 (1978): 398–405.

"On the Pedestal of Bernini's Bust of the Savior." *The Art Bulletin* 60 (1978), 547.

Bernini and the Unity of the Visual Arts. 2 vols. New York and London, 1980.

"Bernini's Baldachin. Considering a Reconsideration." *Römisches Jahrbuch für Kunstgeschichte* 21 (1984): 405–14.

"High and Low before Their Time: Bernini and the Art of Social Satire." In K. Varnadoe and A. Gopnik, eds., *Modern Art and Popular Culture. Readings in High and Low*, 18–50. New York, 1990.

"On the Unity of the Arts and the Early Baroque Opera House." In Barbara Wisch and Susan C. Munshower, eds., *"All the world's a stage . . ."*: *Art and Pageantry in the Renaissance and Baroque*, part 2, 518–79. University Park, Pa., 1990.

Past–Present. Essays on Historicism in Art from Donatello to Picasso. Berkeley, 1993.

ed. Erwin Panofsky. *Three Essays on Style.* Cambridge, Mass., 1995.

"The Roma Alessandrina of Richard Krautheimer." In *In Memoriam Richard Krautheimer*, 107–17. Rome, 1997.

Bernini e il salvatore. La "buona morte" nella Roma del seicento. Rome, 1998.

"Bernini's Bumbling Barberini Bees." In Joseph Imorde et al., eds., *Barocke Inszenierung*, 50–71. Zurich, 1999.

Santa Maria del Fiore. Il duomo di Firenze e la Vergine incinta. Rome, 1999.

"Bernini in Saint Peter's: SINGULARIS IN SINGULIS, IN OMNIBUS UNICUS." In Antonio Pinelli, ed., *La basilica di San Pietro in Vaticano*, vol. 3: *Saggi*, 177–236. Modena, 2000.

"Bernini's Bust of the Savior and the Problem of the Homeless in Seventeenth-Century Rome." *Italian Quarterly* 37 (2000): 209–51.

"Bernini-Bozzetti: One More, One Less. A Berninesque Sculptor in Mid-Eighteenth Century France." In H. Baader et al., eds., *Ars et scriptura. Festschrift für Rudolf Preimesberger zum 65. Geburtstag*, 143–56. Berlin, 1999. Reprinted in *Accademia Nazionale dei Lincei. Atti dei convegni lincei 170. Convegno internazionale La cultura letteraria italiana e l'identità europea* (Roma, 6–8 aprile 2000), 245–84. Rome, 2001.

"The Angel and the City. Baccio Bandinelli's Project for the Castel Sant'Angelo in Rome." In Peta Motture, ed., *Large Bronzes in the Renaissance* (National Gallery of Art, Studies in the History of Art 64), 308–29. Washington, D.C., 2003.

Le Goff, Jacques. *The Birth of Purgatory.* Chicago, 1981.

Lehmann, Karl. "The Dome of Heaven." *Art Bulletin* 26 (1945): 1–27.

Leone de Castris, Pierluigi. *Arte di corte nella Napoli angioina.* Florence, 1986.

"Le colonne del tempio di Salomone nel meridione svevo ed angioino." In *Il classicismo medioevo rinascimento barocco. Atti del colloquio Cesare Gnudi*, 43–53. Bologna, 1993.

Letarouilly, Paul-Marie, and Alphonse Simil. *Le Vatican et la basilique de Saint-Pierre de Rome.* Paris, 1882.

Leti, Gregorio. *Vita di Sisto V. Pontefice romano*, 2 vols. Lausanne, 1669.

Liedtke, Walter. *The Royal Horse and Rider: Painting, Sculpture and Horsemanship 1500–1800.* N.p., 1989.

Liverani, Paolo. "La Pigna Vaticana. Note storiche." *Bollettino Monumenti, Musei e Gallerie Pontificie* 6 (1986): 51–63.

Lotz, Wolfgang. "The Piazza Ducale in Vigevano. A Princely Forum of the Late Fifteenth Century." In his *Studies in Italian Renaissance Architecture*, Cambridge, Mass., 1977. 117–39.

Luciani, Roberto. *Il Colosseo.* Milan and Novara, 1993.

Maccarone, M. "La 'Cathedra Sancti Petri' nel Medio Evo: Da simbolo a reliquia." *Rivista di Storia della Chiesa in Italia* 39 (1985): 349–477.

Machiavelli, Niccolò. *The Chief Works and Others.* Trans. Allen Gilbert. Durham, N.C., 1965.

Macioce, Stefania. *Undique splendent. Aspetti della pittura sacra nella Roma di Clemente VIII Aldobrandini (1592–1605).* Rome, 1990.

Madonna, M. L., ed. *Roma di Sisto V. Le arti e la cultura.* Rome, 1993.

Magnuson, Torgil. *Studies in Roman Quattrocento Architecture* (Figure 9). Stockholm, 1958.

Mahon, Denis. *Nicolas Poussin: Works from His First Years in Rome.* Exh. cat. Rome, 1998.

Mainstone, Rowland J. "The Dome of St Peter's: Structural Aspects of Its Design and Construction, and Inquiries into Its Stability." *AA files* 39 (1999): 21–39.

Malatesta, Edward. "Blood and Water from the Pierced Side of Christ (Jn 19,34)." In Pius-Ramon Tragan, ed., *Segni e sacramenti nel Vangelo di Giovanni*, 165–81. Rome, 1977.

Mâle, Émile. *L'art religieux après le Concile de Trente: Étude sur l'iconographie de la fin du XVIe siècle, du XVIIe, du XVIIIe siècle: Italie, France, Espagne, Flandres.* Paris, 1972.

Religious Art in France. The Thirteenth Century: A Study of Medieval Iconography and Its Sources. Princeton, N.J., 1984.

Marchese, Francesco. *Unica speranza del peccatore che consiste del sangue di N. S. Giesù Cristo.* Rome, 1670.

Marder, Tod A. *Bernini's Scala Regia at the Vatican Palace.* Cambridge, 1997.

Bernini and the Art of Architecture. New York, 1998.

Maresca, Antonio. "Su due colonne esistenti nella chiesa di Santa Chiara a Napoli." *Arte e storia* 7 (1888): 115–16.

Marienlexikon. 6 vols. St. Ottilien, 1988–94.

Marracci, Ippolito. *Polyanthea Mariana.* Cologne, 1710.

Marshall, Christopher R. "'Causa di stravaganze': Order and Anarchy in Domenico Gargiulo's Revolt of Masaniello." *The Art Bulletin* 80 (1998): 478–97.

Mathews, Thomas F. *The Clash of Gods: A Reinterpretation of Early Christian Art.* Princeton, N.J., 1993. Rev. ed. Princeton, N.J., 1999.

Matthiae, G. *Mosaici medievali delle chiese di Roma.* 2 vols. Rome, 1967.

Mauceri, Enrico. "Colonne tortili così dette del tempio di Salomone." *L'arte* 1 (1898): 377–84.

McPhee, S. C. *Bernini and the Bell Towers Architecture and Politics at the Vatican.* New Haven, 2002.

Meehan, Sister Thomas More. *John 19:32–35 and I John 5:6–8: A Study in the History of Interpretation*, Ph.D. diss. Drew Univ., 1985.

Meeks, Wayne A. "The Image of the Androgyne: Some of the Uses of a Symbol in Earliest Christianity." *History of Religions* 13 (1974): 165–208.

Merz, Gerhard. "Das Bildnis des Federico Zuccari aus der Accademia di San Luca in Rom." *Zeitschrift für Kunstgeschichte* 62 (1999): 209–30.

Miarelli Mariani, Gaetano. "L'antico San Pietro, demolirlo o conservarlo?" In Gianfranco Spagnesi, ed., *L'architettura della basilica di San Pietro. Storia e costruzione*. Atti del convegno internazionale di studi, Roma, Castel S. Angelo, 7–10 novembre 1995, 229–42. Rome, 1997.

Michelangelo. *Il carteggio.* Ed. Giovanni Poggi, Paola Barocchi, and Renzo Ristori. 5 vols. Florence, 1965–83.

Migne, Jacques-Paul, ed. *Patrologiae Cursus Completus: Series Latina*, 221 vols. Paris, 1844–77.

Patrologiae Cursus Completus. Series Graeca, 167 vols. Paris, 1857–1905.

Miniero Riccio, Camillo. "Genealogia di Carlo II d'Angiò." *Archivio storico per le provincie napoletane* 7 (1882): 68–261.

Millon, Henry A. "Pirro Ligorio, Michelangelo, and St Peter's." In *Pirro Ligorio Artist and Antiquarian*, ed. Robert W. Gaston, 216–86. Florence, 1988.

Millon, Henry A., and Vittorio Magnago Lampugnani, eds. *The Renaissance from Brunelleschi to Michelangelo: The Representation of Architecture*. Exh. cat. New York, 1994.

Millon, Henry A., and Craig Hugh Smith. "Michelangelo and St Peter's I: Notes on a Plan of the Attic as Originally Built on the South Hemicycle." *Burlington Magazine* 111 (1969): 484–500.

⸻ "Michelangelo and St Peter's. Observations on the Apse Vault, and Related Drawings." *Römisches Jahrbuch für Kunstgeschichte* 16 (1976): 137–206.

⸻ "Cappella Gregoriana." *Abstracts of Papers Delivered in Art History Sessions*, College Art Association, 68th Annual Meeting January 30–February 2, 1980, New Orleans, La., 35–6.

⸻ *Michelangelo architetto. La facciata di San Lorenzo e la cupola di San Pietro*. Milan, 1988a.

⸻ "Pirro Ligorio, Michelangelo, and St. Peter's." In Robert W. Gaston, ed., *Pirro Ligorio Artist and Antiquarian*, 216–86. Florence, 1988b.

Minor, Vernon Hyde, "Shapes of the Invisible: Bernini's Fiery Angels in Saint Peter's." *Artibus et Historiae* no. 19 (1989): 149–56.

Minozzi, Marina. "La decorazione di Ponte Sant'Angelo." In Claudio Strinati and Maria Grazia Bernardini, eds., *Gian Lorenzo Bernini. Regista del Barocco. I Restauri*, 77–84. Rome, 1999.

Missaglia, Giuseppe, et al. *La Madonna e l'eucharistia*. Rome, 1954.

Morello, Giovanni. "Bernini e i lavori a S. Pietro nel 'diario' di Alessandro VII." In idem, *Bernini in Vaticano*, 321–40. 1981.

Moroni, Gaetano. *Dizionario di erudizione storico-ecclesiastica da S. Pietro sino ai nostri giorni*. 103 vols. Venice, 1840–61.

Museo e gallerie nazionali di Capodimonte. La Collezione farnese. Le arti decorative. Naples, 1996.

Negro, Angela. "I due angeli di Sant'Andrea delle Fratte." In Claudio Strinati and Maria Grazia Bernardini, eds., *Gian Lorenzo Bernini. Regista del Barocci. I Restauri*, 67–75. Rome, 1999.

New Catholic Encyclopedia, 15 vols. New York, 1967.

Nilgen, Ursula. "Das Fastigium in der Basilica Constantiniana und vier Bronzesäulen des Lateran." *Römische Quartalschrift* 72 (1977): 1–31.

Nolli, Giovanni Battista. *Nuova pianta di Roma, 1748*. [Rome, 1751].

Nordhagen, Per Jonas. "A Carved Marble Pilaster in the Vatican Grottoes. Some Remarks on the Sculptural Techniques of the Early Middle Ages." *Acta ad Archaeologiam et Artium Historiam pertinentia* 4 (1969): 113–19.

O'Donnell, Timothy Terrance. *Heart of the Redeemer. An Apologia for the Contemporary and Perennial Value of the Devotion to the Sacred Heart of Jesus*. San Francisco, Calif., 1992.

Oliva, Giovanni Paolo. *Prediche dette nel palazzo apostolico*. 3 vols. Rome, 1639–74.

O'Malley, John W. *Giles of Viterbo on Church and Reform. A Study in Renaissance Thought*. Leiden, 1968.

Onians, John. *Bearers of Meaning. The Classical Orders in Antiquity, the Middle Ages, and the Renaissance*. Princeton, 1988.

Orbaan, Johannes A. F. "Zur Baugeschichte des Peterskuppel." *Jahrbuch der königlichen preuszischen Kunstsammlungen* 38 (1917): 189–207.

Ostrow, Steven. *Art and Sculpture in Counter-Reformation Rome: The Sistine and Pauline Chapels in S. Maria Maggiore*. Cambridge and New York, 1996.

Paatz, Walter, and Elizabeth Paatz. *Die Kirchen von Florenz. Ein kunstgeschichtliches Handbuch*. 6 vols. Frankfurt, 1952–5.

Pace, Valentino. "Questioni arnolfiane: L'antico e la Francia." *Zeitschrift für Kunstgeschichte* 54 (1991): 335–73.

Pacelli, Vincenzo. *Caravaggio. Le Sette Opere di Misericordia*. Salerno, 1984.

Pallavicino, Sforza. *Della vita di Alessandro VII*. 2 vols. Prato, 1839–40.

Panofsky, Erwin. *Tomb Sculpture: Four Lectures on Its Changing Aspects from Ancient Egypt to Bernini*. New York, 1964.

Panvinius, Onuphrius. *De praecipuis Vrbis Romae, sanctioribusque Basilicis, quas septem Ecclesias vulgò vocant liber*. Rome, 1570.

Pastor, Ludwig von. *The History of the Popes from the Close of the Middle Ages*. 40 vols. London, 1923–53.

Patrides, Constantinos Apostolos. "'The Bloody and Cruell Turke': The Background of a Renaissance Commonplace." *Studies in the Renaissance* X (1963): 126–35.

Pensabene, Patrizio. "Il reimpiego nell'età costantiana a Roma." In *Costantino il Grande dall'umanesimo. Colloquio sul cristianesimo nel mondo antico*, ed. Giorgio Bonamente and Franca Fusco, 749–68. Macerata, 1993.

Pensabene, Patrizio, and Clementina Panella. "Reimpiego e progettazione architettonica nei monumenti tardo-antichi di Roma." *Rendiconti della Pontificia Accademia Romana di Archeologia* 66 (1993–4): 111–283.

Perlove, Shelley. "Bernini's Androcles and the Lion: A Papal Emblem of Alexandrine Rome." *Zeitschrift für Kunstgeschichte* 45 (1982): 287–96.

Peterson, Eric. *The Angels and the Liturgy. The Statues and Significance of the Holy Angels in Worship*. London, 1964.

Petrucci, Francesco. "Gian Lorenzo Bernini per casa Chigi: Precisazioni e nuove attribuzioni." *Storia dell'arte*, no. 90 (1997): 176–200.

⸻ "L'opera pittorica di Bernini." In Maria Grazia Bernardini, ed., *Bernini a Montecitorio. Ciclo di conferenze nel quarto centenario della nascità di Gian Lorenzo Bernini in collaborazione con la Soprintendenza per i Beni Artistici e Storici di Roma (ottobre–dicembre 1999)*, 59–94. Rome, 2001.

Piazza, Carlo Bartolomeo. *La gerarchia cardinalizia*. Rome, 1703.

Picard, Jean-Charles. "Le Quadriportique de Saint-Pierre-du-Vatican." *Mélanges de l'École Française de Rome. Antiquité* 86 (1976): 851–90.

Pietri, C. *Roma Christiana. Recherches sur l'église de Rome, son organization, sa politique et son idéologie de Miltiade à Sixte III*. Rome, 1976.

Pinelli, Antonio, ed. *La basilica di San Pietro in Vaticano*, 4 vols. Modena, 2000.

Poleni, Giovanni. *Memorie historiche della gran cupola del Tempio Vaticano e de' danni di essa, e de' ristoramenti loro, divide in libri cinque*. Padua, 1748.

Pollak, Oskar. *Die Kunsttätigkeit unter Urban VIII*. Ed. Dagobert Frey et al. 2 vols. Vienna, 1928–31.

Prandi, Adriano. *La zona archeologica della Confessio Vaticana. I monumenti di II secolo*. Vatican City, 1957.

Preimesberger, Rudolf. "Die Ausstattung der Kuppelpfeiler von St. Peter, Rom, unter Papst Urban VIII." *Jahres-und Tagungsbericht der Görres-Gesellschaft* (1983, 1984), 36–55.

⸻ "Die Inschriften der Engelsbrucke." In Jörg Traeger, *Kunst in Hauptwerken. Von der Akropolis zu Goya. Vortragsreihe der Universität Regensburg*, 199–223. Regensburg, 1988.

⸻ "Berninis Statue des Longinus in St. Peter." In Herbert Beck and Sabine Schulze, eds., *Antikenrezeption im Hochbarock*, 143–54. Berlin, 1989.

Prinz, Wolfram, and Ronald G. Kecks. *Das französische Schloss der Renaissance. Form und Bedeutung der Architektur, ihre geschichtlichen und gesellschaftlichen Grundlagen*. Berlin, 1994.

Prodi, Paolo. *Il sovrano pontefice*. Bologna, 1982.

Pseudo-Dionysius. *The Complete Works*. New York, 1987.

Puccini, Vincenzo. *Vita della madre suor Maria Maddalena de' Pazzi*. Florence, 1609.

Puech, Henri-Charles. "La ténèbre mystique chez le Pseudo-Denys l'Aréopagite et dans la tradition patristique." *Études carmelitaines* 23 (1938): 33–53.

Quednau, Rolf. *Die Sala di Costantino im vatikanischen Palast. Zur Dekoration der beiden Medici-Päpste Leo X. und Clemens VII.* Hildesheim and New York, 1979.

Rasmussen, N. K. "Maiestas Pontificia. A Liturgical Reading of Etienne Duperac's Engraving of the Capella Sixtina from 1578." *Analecta Romana Instituti Danici* 12 (1983), 109–48.

Reydellet, Marc, ed. *Venance Fortunat. Poemes*, vol. 1. Paris, 1994.

Rice, Louise. *The Altars and Altarpieces of New St. Peter's. Outfitting the Basilica, 1621–1666.* Cambridge and New York, 1997.

——— "La coesistenza delle due basiliche." In Gianfranco Spagnesi, ed., *L'architettura della basilica di San Pietro. Storia e costruzione.* Atti del convegno internazionale di studi, Roma, Castel S. Angelo, 7–10 novembre 1995, 255–60. Rome, 1997.

Ripa, Cesare. *Iconologia ovvero descrittione di diverse imagini cavate dall'antichità, & di propria inventione.* Rome, 1603.

Roca De Amicis, Augusto. "Le prime idee di Bernini per Piazza S. Pietro: Lo stato degli studi e qualche precisazione." *Palladio*, no. 23 (1999), 43–50.

——— "La piazza e il colonnato." In Antonio Pinelli, ed., *La basilica di San Pietro in Vaticano*, vol. 3: *Saggi*, 283–301. Modena, 2000.

The Roman Breviary. 3 vols. Edinburgh and London, 1879.

Romanini, Angiola Maria, ed. *Roma anno 1300. Atti della IV Settimana di Storia dell'Arte Medievale dell'Università di Roma 'La Sapienza', 19–24 maggio 1980.* Rome, 1983.

Ronen, Avraham. "Gozzoli's St. Sebastian Altarpiece in San Gimignano." *Mitteilungen des Kunsthistorischen Institutes in Florenz* 32 (1988): 77–126.

——— "Divine Wrath and Intercession in Pietro da Cortona's Frescoes in the Chiesa Nuova." *Römisches Jahrbuch der Bibliotheca Hertziana* 25 (1989): 180–205.

Roscio, Giulio. *Icones operum misericordiae cum . . . sententiis et explicationibus.* Rome, 1586.

Rosenberg, Pierre. *Nicolas Poussin, 1594–1665.* Exh. cat., Paris, 1994.

Rossi, Paola. *L'opera completa del Parmigianino.* Milan, 1980.

Roworth, Wendy Wassyng. "The Evolution of History Painting: Masaniello's Revolt and Other Disasters in Seventeenth-Century Naples." *The Art Bulletin* 75 (1993): 219–34.

Rupert of Deutz. *Liber de divinis officiis.* Ed. Hrabanus Haacke, 3 vols. Freiburg, 1999.

Ruysschaert, J. "L'inscription absidale primitive de S. Pierre: Texte et contexts." *Atti della Pontificia Accademia Romana di Archeologia. Rendiconti* 40 (1967–8): 171–90.

Saalman, Howard. "Michelangelo: S. Maria del Fiore and St. Peter's." *The Art Bulletin* 57 (1975): 374–409.

——— "Michelangelo at St Peter's: The Arberino Correspondence." *The Art Bulletin* 60 (1978): 483–93.

Sartorio, Giulio Aristide. "Le colonne vitinee e le colonne tortili della chiesa romana." *Capitolium* 3 (1927–8): 595–607.

Satzinger, Georg. "Nikolaus V., Nikolaus Muffel und Bramante: Monumentale Triumphbogensäulen in Alt-St-Peter." *Römisches Jahrbuch der Bibliotheca Hertziana* 31 (1996): 91–105.

Schiavo, Armando. "Iscrizioni inedite del monumento di Urbano VIII." *Studi Romani* 19 (1971): 307–8.

Schlegel, Ursula. "'Das Leben' und 'der Tod' auf zwei Kissen." In Victoria V. Flemming and Sebastian Schütze, *Ars naturam diuvans. Festschrift für Matthias Winner zum 11 Marz 1996*, 524–8. Mainz, 1996.

Schütze, Sebastian. "'Urbano inalza Pietro, e Pietro Urbano.' Beobachtungen zu Idee und Gestalt der Ausstattung von Neu-St.-Peter unter Urban VIII." *Römisches Jahrbuch der Bibliotheca Hertziana* 29 (1994): 213–87.

Scott, John Beldon. "Papal Patronage in the Seventeenth Century: Urban VIII, Bernini, and the Countess Mathilde." In Roland Mousnier and Jean Mesnard, *L'Âge d'or du Mécénat (1598–1661)*, 119–27. Paris, 1985.

——— *Images of Nepotism: The Painted Ceilings of Palazzo Barberini.* Princeton, N.J., 1991.

Seiferth, Wolfgang S. *Synagogue and Church in the Middle Ages: Two Symbols in Art and Literature.* New York, 1970.

Serlio, Sebastiano. *Il terzo libro.* Venice, 1540.

Settis, Salvatore. "Von auctoritas zu vetustas: Die antike Kunst im mittelalterlicher Sicht." *Zeitschrift für Kunstgeschichte* 51 (1988): 177–8.

Shearman, John K. G. *The Early Italian Pictures in the Collection of Her Majesty the Queen.* Cambridge and New York, 1983.

Sigel, Anthony B. "The Clay Modeling Techniques of Gianlorenzo Bernini." In Ivan Gaskell and Henry Lie, *Sketches in Clay for Projects by Gian Lorenzo Bernini: Theoretical, Technical, and Case Studies*, 48–72. Cambridge, Mass., 1999.

Sisinni, Francesco, ed. *Il San Michele a Ripa Grande.* Rome, 1990.

Spagnesi, Gianfranco, ed. *L'architettura della basilica di San Pietro. Storia e costruzione.* Atti del convegno internazionale di studi, Roma, Castel S. Angelo, 7–10 novembre 1995. Rome, 1997.

Spila, Benedetto. *Un monumento di Sancia in Napoli* Naples, 1901.

Sposato, P. "Fonti per la storia di San Francesco di Paola. La sua canonizzazione attraverso il 'Diarum' di Paride de Grassi prefetto delle cerimonie pontificie sotto Leone X. Introduzione e Testo." *Calabria nobilissima* 10 (1956): 1–32.

Stanić, Milovan. "Le mode énigmatique dans l'art de Poussin." In Olivier Bonfait et al., eds., *Poussin et Rome*, 93–118. Paris, 1994.

Steinberg, Leo. *The Sexuality of Christ in Renaissance Art and in Modern Oblivion.* Chicago, 1996.

Steinke, K. B. *Die mittelalterlichen Vatikanpaläste und ihre Kapellen.* Vatican City, 1984.

Strinati, Claudio, and Maria Grazia Bernardini, eds. *Gian Lorenzo Bernini. Regista del Barocco. I Restauri.* Rome, 1999.

Suckale, Robert. "Arma Christi. Überlegungen zur Zeichenhaftigkeit mittelalterliche Andachtsbilder." *Städel-Jahrbuch* 6 (1977): 177–208.

Sulpitius Severus. *Vincent of Lerins. John Cassian.* Philip Schaff and Henry Wace, eds. Grand Rapids, Mich., 1976. (A Select Library of Nicene and Post-Nicene Fathers of the Christian Church, Second Series, vol. XI)

Tafuri, Manfredo. *Ricerca del Rinascimento.* Turin, 1992.

Tapié, Alain, ed. *Baroque, vision jésuite. De Tintoret à Rubens.* Exh. cat. Caen, 2003.

Tedaldi, Gianluca. "Il Baciccio e Bernini. Esame delle reciproche influenze sulla scorta della bibliografia critica. (Versione riveduta e corretta della tesi di specializzazione discussa nel 1996 presso la Facoltà di lettere dell'Università La Sapienza di Roma)." Unpub. thesis, 1996.

Teoli, Bonaventura. *Apparato minorico della provincia di Roma. . . .* Velletri, 1648.

Tessari, Cristiano, et al., eds. *San Pietro che non c'è.* Milan, 1996.

Thelen, Heinrich. *Borromini, Francesco, 1599–1667. Die Handzeichnungen.* Graz, 1967.

——— *Zur Entstehungsgeschichte der Hochaltar-Architektur von St. Peter in Rom.* Berlin, 1967.

Thoenes, Christof. "Bramante e la 'bella maniera degli antichi.'" In *Studi bramanteschi. Atti del congresso internazionale 1970*, 391–6. Rome, 1974.

——— Review of Francia 1977, in *Kunstchronik* 31 (1978): 474–89.

——— "St. Peter als Ruine. Zu einigen Veduten Heemskercks." *Zeitschrift für Kunstgeschichte* 49 (1986): 481–501.

——— "S. Lorenzo a Milano, S. Pietro a Roma: Ipotesi sul 'piano di pergamena.'" *Arte Lombarda*, n.s. 86/87 (1988): 94–100.

"I tre progetti di Bramante per San Pietro." *Quaderni dell'Istituto di storia dell'architettura*, n.s. 15–20 (1990–2): 439–46.

"Alt- und Neu-St.-Peter unter einem Dach, zu Antonio da Sangallos 'muro divisorio.'" In *Architektur und Kunst im Abendland. Festschrift für Gunter Urban*, 51–61. Rome, 1992.

"Madernos St.-Peter-Entwürfe." In *An Architectural Progress in the Renaissance and Baroque. Sojourns in and out of Italy. Essays in Architectural History Presented to Hellmut Hager on His Sixty-sixth Birthday*, ed. Henry A. Millon and Susan Scott Munshower, 171–94. University Park, Pa., 1992.

"Vitruv, Alberti, Sangallo. Zur Theorie der Architekturzeichnung in der Renaissance." In *Hülle und Fülle. Festschrift für Tilmann Buddensieg*, 565–84. Alfter, 1993.

"Neue Beobachtungen an Bramantes St.-Peter-Entwurfen." *Münchner Jahrbuch der bildenden Kunst*, 3d ser., 45 (1994): 109–32.

"S. Pietro 1534–46. I progetti di Antonio da Sangallo il Giovane per papa Paolo III." In Henry A. Millon and Vittorio Magnago Lampugnani, eds., *The Renaissance from Brunelleschi to Michelangelo: The Representation of Architecture*, exh. cat. (New York, 1994), 634–48.

"Pianta centrale e pianta longitudinale nel nuovo S. Pietro." In *L'église dans l'architecture de la Renaissance, Actes du colloque tenu à Tours 1990*, 91–106. Paris, 1995.

"Antonio da Sangallos Peterskuppel." In *Architectural Studies in Memory of Richard Krautheimer*, 163–7. Mainz, 1996.

"Il modello ligneo per San Pietro ed il metodo progettuale di Antonio da Sangallo il Giovane." *Annali di Architettura* 9 (1997): 186–99.

"S. Pietro. Storia e ricerca." In Spagnesi, ed., *L'architettura della basilica di San Pietro. Storia e costruzione*. Atti del convegno internazionale di studi, Roma, Castel S. Angelo, 7–10 novembre 1995, 17–30. Rome, 1997.

"'Il primo tempio del mondo,' Raffael, St. Peter und das Geld." In *Radical Art History, Internationale Anthologie*, 450–9. Zurich, 1997.

Sostegno e adornamento. Saggi sull'architettura del Rinascimento. Milan, 1998.

"Postille sull'architetto nel De re aedificatoria." In *Leon Battista Alberti. Architettura e cultura, Atti del convegno, Mantova 1994*, 27–32. Florence, 1999.

"St. Peter's 1534–46." In *The Architectural Drawings of Antonio da Sangallo the Younger and his Circle*, vol. 2: *Churches*, ed. Christoph Liutpold Frommel and Nicholas Adams, 2:33–43. Cambridge, Mass., and London, 2000.

"Bramante a San Pietro: I deambulatori.'" In Francesco Paolo di Teodoro, ed., *Donato Bramante, Ricerche, proposte, riletture*, 303–20. Urbino, 2001.

Tolnay, Charles de. *Michelangelo*. 5 vols. Princeton, N.J., 1943–60.

Tolomeo Speranza, Maria Grazia. "La decorazione del ponte." In Luisa Cardilli Alloisi and Maria Grazia Tolomeo Speranza, eds., *La via degli angeli. Il restauro della decorazione scultorea di Ponte Sant'Angelo*, 43–79. Rome, 1988.

Tomassetti, Giuseppe. "Cave (di Palestrina)." *Giornale arcadico di scienze, lettere ed arti*, Ser. 3, Anno I, no. 9 (Sept. 1898): 203–17.

La campagna romana antica, medioevale e moderna. Ed. Luisa Chiumenti and Fernando Bilancia. 6 vols. Florence and Rome, 1975–7 (1913).

Torrigio, Francesco Maria. *Le Sacre Grotte Vaticane*. Viterbo, 1618.

Toynbee, Jocelyn, and J. B. Ward Perkins. *The Shrine of St. Peter and the Vatican Excavations*. London, 1956.

Traver, Hope. *The Four Daughters of God; a Study of the Versions of this Allegory, with Special Reference to those in Latin, French, and English*. Bryn Mawr, Pa., 1907 (Bryn Mawr College Monographs, vol. 6).

Tronzo, William. "Setting and Structure in Two Roman Wall Decorations of the Early Middle Ages." *Dumbarton Oaks Papers* 41 (1987): 477–92.

"Il Tegurium di Bramante." In Gianfranco Spagnesi, ed., *L'architettura della basilica di San Pietro. Storia e costruzione*. Atti del convegno internazionale di studi, Roma, Castel S. Angelo, 7–10 novembre 1995, 161–6. Rome, 1997.

Turner, Nicholas. *Roman Baroque Drawings c. 1620 to c. 1700 (Italian Drawings in the Department of Prints and Drawings in the British Museum)*. 2 vols. London, 1999.

Tuzi, Stefania. *Le colonne e il Tempio di Salomone. La storia, la leggenda, la fortuna*. Rome, 2003.

Ugonio, Pompeo. *Historia delle stationi di Roma che si celebrano la Quadragesima*. Rome, 1588.

Urban, Gunter. "Zum Neubau-Projekt von St. Peter unter Papst Nikolaus V." In *Festschrift für Harald Keller*, 131–73. Darmstadt, 1963.

Valeriano, Giovanni Pierio. *I ieroglifici overo commentarii delle occulte significationi de gl'Egittij, & altre nationi*. Venice, 1625.

Vasari, Giorgio. *Le Vite de più eccellenti pittori, scultori ed architettori*. Ed. Gaetano Milanesi. Vols. 1–9. Florence, 1878–85.

Veldman, Ilja M., and Ger Luijten. *The New Hollstein. Dutch and Flemish Etchings, Engavings and Woodcuts. 1450–1700. Maarten van Heemskerck. Part I*. Roosendaal, 1993.

Visconti, P. E. *Metrologia vaticana*. Rome, 1828.

Voci, A. M. *Nord o sud? Note per la storia del medioevale palatium apostolicum apud Sanctum Petrum e della sue cappelle*. Vatican City, 1992.

Voragine, Jacobus da. *The Golden Legend*. New York, 1969.

Wadding, Luke. *Annales minorum*. 7 vols. Lyon, 1628–35.

Waetzoldt, S. *Die Kopien des 17. Jahrhunderts nach Mosaiken und Wandmalereien in Rom*. Vienna and Munich, 1964.

Walter, Christopher. "IC XC NI KA. The Apotropaic Function of the Victorious Cross." *Revue des Études Byzantines* 55 (1997): 193–220.

Ward Perkins, J. B. "The Shrine of St. Peter and Its Twelve Spiral Columns." *Journal of Roman Studies* 42 (1952): 21–33.

Waszbinski, Zygmunt. "Il cardinale Francesco Maria del Monte e la fortuna del progetto buonarrotiano per la basilica di San Pietro a Roma 1604–1613." In Henry A. Millon and Susan Scott Munshower, eds., *An Architectural Progress in the Renaissance and Baroque, Sojourns in and out of Italy. Essays in Architectural History Presented to Hellmut Hager on His Sixty-Sixth Birthday* Part I, 146–70. University Park, Pa., 1992.

Weil, Mark S. *The History and Decoration of the Ponte S. Angelo*. University Park and London, 1974.

Wilkinson, Catherine. "The Iconography of Bernini's Tomb of Urban VII." *L'arte* 14 (1971): 54–68.

Wittkower, Rudolf. "The Vicissitudes of a Dynastic Monument: Bernini's Equestrian Statue of Louis XIV." In Millard Meiss, ed., *De Artibus Opuscula XL. Essays in Honor of Erwin Panofsky*, 497–531. New York, 1961.

"Michelangelo's Dome of St. Peter." In *Idea and Image: Studies in the Italian Peninsula*, 73–89. London, 1978.

Bernini. The Sculptor of the Roman Baroque. London, 1997 (1955).

Art and Architecture in Italy, 1600–1750. Harmondsworth, 1965 (1958).

Wolff Metternich, Franz Graf, and Christof Thoenes. *Die frühen St.-Peter-Entwürfe 1505–1514 (= Römische Forschungen der Bibliotheca Hertziana 25)*. Tübingen, 1987.

Zollikofer, Kaspar. *Berninis Grabmal für Alexander VII. Fiktion und Repräsentation*. Worms, 1994.

Zuccari, Alessandro. *Arte e committenza nella Roma di Caravaggio*. Turin, 1984.

INDEX

∞